Principles and Types
of Speech Communication

Seventh Edition

For this edition,
RICHARD L. JOHANNESEN,
Department of Speech Communication,
Northern Illinois University,
contributed extensively to
the revision of Chapters 8 and 17
and also provided
substantial advice regarding
the revision of the text as a whole.

Principles and Types of Speech Communication

Seventh Edition

ALAN H. MONROE
Purdue University

DOUGLAS EHNINGER
The University of Iowa

Scott, Foresman and Company
Glenview, Illinois · Brighton, England

ISBN: 0-673-07830-2
Library of Congress Catalog Card Number: 73-90591
Copyright © 1974, 1967, 1962, 1955, 1949, 1939, 1935
   Scott, Foresman and Company, Glenview, Illinois.
Philippines Copyright 1974 Scott, Foresman and Company.
All Rights Reserved.
Printed in the United States of America.

Regional Offices of Scott, Foresman and Company are located in
Dallas, Texas; Glenview, Illinois; Oakland, New Jersey; Palo Alto,
California; Tucker, Georgia; and Brighton, England.

The authors and the publisher of this book would like to thank all
sources for the use of their material. The credit lines for
copyrighted materials appearing in this work are included in the
list of Illustrations, Pictures, and Credits, pages xii–xiii; at the ends
of respective chapters in the Footnotes; or, in certain instances,
on those pages where the credited materials actually occur—all
of which are an extension of this copyright page.

41,277

PREFACE

The Seventh Edition of *Principles and Types of Speech Communication* represents a judicious balance between what we deem the best and most enduring of traditional concerns in the field of speech communication with what we believe to be the most applicable and exciting of new interests and emphases. Although all of the features which have contributed to the wide use of the book in the past have been retained, the work as a whole has been significantly revised, and much fresh material reflecting recent developments in research and pedagogy has been added.

Following a description of the essentials of the oral transaction in all its forms, the student now first is introduced to the principles and methods of the person-to-person interchange as it occurs in informal conversations and in information-gathering and job-seeking interviews. Once a solid foundation in these more familiar forms of communication has been laid, the concerns and procedures of group discussion and public speaking are given systematic attention.

But while the book as a whole thus provides for a natural progression from informal to more formal types of oral communication, each major topic is treated as an independent and self-contained instructional unit. Hence the teacher who prefers to begin the course with the study and practice of public speaking or of group discussion is free to do so. The instructor may, for example, first assign the chapters in Part Two, "Modes of Speech Communication: Nonverbal and Verbal," and/or in Part Three, "Public Communication: Preparation and Adaptation to the Audience," saving for later the chapters on person-to-person and small group communication. Additional suggestions for using the book, including the organization of a course in terms of selected instructional objectives, are detailed in an accompanying *Guide to Using Principles and Types of Speech Communication, Seventh Edition*, available on request from the publisher.

Three chapters in the present revision are entirely new: "Speech Communication: Process and Forms," "Communicating with Another Person," and "Listening, Evaluation, and Ethical Judgment." In addition, the chapters on "Analyzing the Audience and Occasion," "Determining the Basic Appeals," and "Selecting Material That Will Hold Attention" have been carefully reworked to accord with recent trends in psychology, ethics, and the sociology of values. Treatments of organization and outlining, formerly independent, have been combined and streamlined, and the material on using the voice has been given sharper focus. The texts of fifteen sample speeches and an annotated transcript of a job-seeking interview involving a recent college graduate are included for analysis and evaluation.

Clearly, these and other improvements give *Principles and Types of Speech Communication* a new and contemporary character. At the same time, teachers acquainted with the book in its earlier editions will find many long-standing features—the motivated sequence, the classification of supporting materials, the discussion of speech types and purposes, and the advice on style—strengthened by the introduction of fresh illustrative material and reinforced by the citation of recent behavioral research. The special types of public address, previously treated separately, are integrated into a single chapter, with material on public discussion and debate added. The problems and projects provided for each of the twenty-three chapters have been thoroughly revised, and the Suggestions for Further Reading are almost entirely new.

Typographically, more generous spacing and larger type should make for greater ease of reading and comprehension. Color has been used to accent and enliven many of the central concepts, and numerous new illustrations contribute clarity and contemporaneity. As a result, we hope students will find that reading the book can be both a practical and pleasant experience, and instructors will find it more effective as a teaching instrument.

In preparing this Seventh Edition of *Principles and Types of Speech Communication*, the authors were fortunate to have the recommendations of a number of critics, among them: Professors Gerald Miller, Michigan State University; Malcolm Sillars, University of Massachusetts; Arthur Smith, State University of New York at Buffalo; and Richard L. Johannesen, Northern Illinois University—all of whom examined the entire manuscript and made useful suggestions for its improvement.

In the light of new research relevant to certain specific subjects, Chapter 6, "Using the Voice to Communicate," was examined by Professor J. Donald Ragsdale of Louisiana State University; Professor John Kline of the University of Missouri checked Chapter 9, "Determining the Basic Appeals," and Chapter 13, "Adapting the Speech Structure to the Audience: The Motivated Sequence"; and Professor Dennis Gouran of Indiana University made a number of recommendations concerning Chapter 3, "Communicating in Small Groups." The Suggestions for Further Reading were assembled by Mr. John Cortright of the University of Iowa; and Professor Bruce Gronbeck, also of the University of Iowa, prepared the *Guide to Using Principles and Types of Speech Communication, Seventh Edition.*

Finally, it should be observed that in addition to the critical and substantive contributions of the above-named individuals, the authors had the benefit of suggestions from more than eighty teachers who, having used the Sixth Edition of the book, helpfully responded to a detailed questionnaire regarding their ideas and preferences. We gratefully acknowledge their cooperation and are pleased to include their names on page 611.

If students using this latest edition learn more fully to appreciate the values of good speech and thereby become more effective communicators in the various kinds of informal and formal speaking situations they encounter, the purpose of this book will have been richly fulfilled.

A. H. M.
D. E.

CONTENTS

PART ONE
SPEECH COMMUNICATION: ORIENTATION, PROCESS, AND FORMS

"Communication and Change"   4

Chapter 1.   SPEECH COMMUNICATION: PROCESS AND FORMS   8

Factors Common to All Speech Communication, 8   The Speaker, 10   The Message, 15   The Listener, 16   The Channel, 18   The Communicative Situation, 19   Interaction of the Speech Communication Elements, 23   Basic Forms of Speech Communication: Person-to-Person, Small Group, and Public, 26

Chapter 2.   COMMUNICATING WITH ANOTHER PERSON   34

Interpersonal Speech Communication: Definition and Dimensions, 34   Some General Principles, 35   Establishing Rapport, 36   Maintaining Interaction, 41   Terminating the Transaction, 47   Interviews, 48   The Information-Seeking Interview, 49   The Job-Seeking Interview, 55   Sample Transcript of a Job-Seeking Interview, 76

Chapter 3.   COMMUNICATING IN SMALL GROUPS   88

Characteristics and Conditions, 88   Major Purposes, 90   Essentials for Effective Interaction, 91   General Preparation, 93   Participating, 95   Leadership and Leadership Functions, 100   The Effective Discussant, 105   The Discussion Plan, 106   Suggested Discussion Questions, 114

Chapter 4.   COMMUNICATING IN PUBLIC: SOME INITIAL CONCERNS   123

Definition and Dimensions, 123   Foundational Factors, 124   Characteristics of the Competent Communicator, 124   Understanding Basic Guidelines and Principles, 134   The Functions of Speech, 134   Practicing Communication Orally: First Classroom Speeches, 141   Presentational Methods, 142   Preparing the Formal Speech: Essential Steps, 146   Effective Speech Delivery, 152   A Speech Evaluator's Guidelist, 161

PART TWO
MODES OF SPEECH COMMUNICATION: NONVERBAL AND VERBAL

Chapter 5.   USING THE BODY TO COMMUNICATE   164

Message Delivery and the Communication Process, 164   Nonverbal Delivery: Components and Reinforcements, 165   Physical Appearance, 165   Physical Behavior, 166   Posture, 168   Bodily Movement and Gestures, 168   Nonverbal Behaviors in the "Manuscript Speech," 177   Practicing for Skills, 179

Chapter 6.   USING THE VOICE TO COMMUNICATE   185

Characteristics of a Good Speaking Voice, 185   Voice Quality, 186   Intelligibility, 186   Articulation, 189   Pronunciation, 196   Variety, 197   Rate, Force, and Pitch, 198   Exercises for Voice Practice, 203

PART THREE
PUBLIC COMMUNICATION: PREPARATION AND ADAPTATION
TO THE AUDIENCE

Chapter 7.   CHOOSING SPEECH SUBJECTS AND PURPOSES   226

The Subject, 227   The Title, 228   The General Ends of Speech, 230   The Specific Purpose, 233   Determining Factors, 234   Subject Categories: Aids to Choosing Speech Topics, 237

Chapter 8.   ANALYZING THE AUDIENCE AND OCCASION   242

The Audience, 242   General Analysis-Factors, 243   Factors in Message Acceptance: Audience Beliefs, Attitudes, and Values, 248   Predominant Value-Orientations, 254   Reading and Reacting to Audience Feedback, 257   The Speech Occasion: Basic Analytical Questions, 258   Sources of Direct Information About Audiences and Occasions, 259

Chapter 9.   DETERMINING THE BASIC APPEALS   264

Motivation and Attitude-Change, 264   Motives: Concepts and Classifications, 265   Motivational Appeals: Some Types and Implications, 270   Making Motivational Appeals to Listeners, 282

Chapter 10. LOCATING AND CLASSIFYING SPEECH INFORMATION   288

Useful Sources of Message Materials, 288   Recording the Speech Communication Materials, 294   Classifying the Collected Materials, 296

Chapter 11. SUPPORTING THE MAJOR IDEAS   300

Verbal Supporting Material: Types and Uses, 301   Explanation,
Analogy or Comparison, Illustration, Specific Instance, Statistics,
Testimony, Restatement, 302   Nonverbal Supporting Material:
Types and Uses, 315   Using Supporting Material: The Single-
Idea Speech, 317

Chapter 12. SELECTING MATERIAL THAT WILL HOLD ATTENTION   332

The Nature of Attention, 332   The Factors of Attention: Activity
and Movement, Reality, Proximity, Familiarity, Novelty, 336
Sustaining Attention: Problems and Materials, 342

Chapter 13. ADAPTING THE SPEECH STRUCTURE TO THE AUDIENCE:
THE MOTIVATED SEQUENCE   353

The Listener's Mental Processes: Some Psychological Bases, 353
The Motivated Sequence, 356   Applying the Sequence to Various Types of Speeches, 358   The Steps of the Sequence: Attention, Need, Satisfaction, Visualization, Action, 368

Chapter 14. ORGANIZING AND OUTLINING THE SPEECH   381

Selecting the Major Ideas for the Outline, 381   Phrasing the Major Ideas, 383   Arranging the Major Ideas: Sequential Patterns,
385   Arranging Subpoints and Supporting Material, 388
Preparing the Actual Outline, 391   Types of Outlines, 395
Steps in Preparing the Outline, 396

Chapter 15. BEGINNING AND ENDING THE SPEECH   409

The Importance of Planning and Preparation, 409   Beginning
the Speech, 410   Methods and Materials, 410   Ending the
Speech, 420   Methods and Materials, 421

Chapter 16. USING WORDS TO COMMUNICATE MEANING   428

Accuracy, 428   Simplicity, 430   Appropriateness, 431   Imagery, 431   Types of Imagery, 431   Using Imagery, 436
Loaded Words, 438   Triteness, 439   Slang, 440   Connective Phrases, 440   Building a Vocabulary, 441

Chapter 17. LISTENING, EVALUATION, AND ETHICAL JUDGMENT   447

Listening, 447   Inefficient Listening Habits, 448   Getting
Ready to Listen, 451   Listening for Appreciation, 451   Lis-
tening for Understanding, 452   Evaluation: Criterial Concerns,
453   Ethical Judgment, 457   Ethical Perspectives, 457
Judgmental Questions, 462   The Student as Classroom Speech
Critic, 464   Evaluation Forms, 465, 466

PART FOUR
PUBLIC COMMUNICATION: TYPES AND OCCASIONS

Chapter 18. THE SPEECH TO ENTERTAIN   472

Typical Situations, 472   Purpose, 473   Content and Delivery,
473   Some Uses and Forms of Humor, 474   Organization of
the Speech to Entertain, 481

Chapter 19. THE SPEECH TO INFORM   489

Types, 489   Purposes, 490   Manner of Speaking, 490
Treatment of Content, 490   Organization of the Informative
Speech, 492   Defining Terms, 497   Concluding the Speech,
499

Chapter 20. THE SPEECH TO PERSUADE   515

Situations Requiring Persuasion, 515   Purpose, 516   Analyzing the Claim, 516   Organization of the Speech to Persuade,
518   Manner of Speaking, 524   Content, 524   Special
Techniques, 527   Adapting the Speech Organization to the
Audience, 529

Chapter 21. THE SPEECH TO ACTUATE   547

Situations Requiring Speeches to Actuate, 547   Purpose, 547
Manner of Speaking, 548   Characteristics of Content, 548
Organization of the Speech to Actuate, 548

Chapter 22. SPECIAL TYPES OF SPEECHES AND PUBLIC DISCUSSION   561

Speeches of Introduction, 561   Speeches for Courtesy: Welcomes, Responses, Acceptances, 563   Speeches of Tribute: Me-
morials, Farewells, Presentations, 566   Speeches of Nomination,
579   Speeches to Create Good Will, 580   Public Discussion:
Four Types, 585   Planning the Public Discussion, 590   Broadcasting the Public Discussion, 591

Chapter 23. ADAPTING SPEECHES TO RADIO AND TELEVISION   597

The Purpose of a Broadcast Speech, 597   The Radio and Television Audience, 598   Types of Broadcast Speeches, 598   The
Manner of Speaking for Radio, 599   The Manner of Speaking
for Television, 604   Principles of Content and Organization,
607

INDEX   612

Sample Speech Communication Materials for Study and Analysis

Communicating with Another Person:
    A JOB-SEEKING INTERVIEW — SAMPLE TRANSCRIPT   Page 76

Communicating in Public: First Classroom Speeches:
    WHY ICE FLOATS, by Joyce Miller   155

Supporting Major Ideas:
    LOST: FOUR FRIENDS, by Clarence Yurk   326

Selecting Material That Will Hold Attention:
    CHOOSE ONE OF FIVE, by Edith S. Sampson   344

Adapting the Speech to the Audience:
    NICE PEOPLE, by Jan Bjorklund   358

Using Words to Communicate Meaning:
    YOU — A SPONGE? by Ann E. Bogaard   441

Speaking to Entertain:
    A CASE FOR OPTIMISM, by Douglas Martin   483
    A FUNNY THING HAPPENED TO ME ON THE WAY TO THE WHITE HOUSE, by Adlai Stevenson   485

Speaking to Inform:
    BACKACHES, by Dennis Owen Ragan   505
    THE INFLUENCE OF PUBLIC SPEAKING IN AMERICA, by Robert T. Oliver   506

Speaking to Persuade:
    THE PERPETUATION OF OUR POLITICAL INSTITUTIONS, by Abraham Lincoln   534
    MAN'S OTHER SOCIETY, by Richard Marvin   541

Speaking to Actuate:
    MEDICAL CARE, by Thomas J. Watson, Jr.   554

Special Types of Speeches:
    EULOGY FOR THE ASTRONAUTS, by Eric Sevareid   570
    THE TESTIMONY OF SCULPTURE (dedication), by Harold Haydon   572
    A FAREWELL TO THE AMERICAN PEOPLE, by Spiro T. Agnew   573

Illustrations, Pictures, and Credits

Drawings and paintings for *Cover* and *Part pages*, Franklin McMahon 2-3, 162-163, 224-225, 470-471

Figure 1, *A Speech Communication Transaction*, George Suyeoka 9

Student discussion at college of pharmacy, courtesy Herb Taylor/Editorial Photocolor Archives 20

Old men in park, courtesy Ellen Levine/Editorial Photocolor Archives 20

Sargent Shriver, courtesy Paul Sequeira 20

George Wallace, courtesy Don Getsug from Rapho Guillumette 21

Buckminster Fuller at Katonah Gallery, photograph by Rae Russel 21

Figure 2, *A Speech Communication Transaction: A More Detailed Model*, George Suyeoka 25

Figure 3, *Basic Forms of Speech Communication*, George Suyeoka 26

Figure 4, *Communicating with Another Person*, George Suyeoka 27

Figure 5, *Communicating in a Small Group*, George Suyeoka 27

Figure 6, *Communicating in Public*, George Suyeoka 28

Student counseling at Queens, courtesy Eugene Luttenberg/Editorial Photocolor Archives 42

Sensory awareness—young man and woman, courtesy David Glaubinger from Jeroboam 42

Old woman with boy on bus, © George W. Gardner, 1973 43

Woman with flag, talking to youth, courtesy Bruce Anspach/Editorial Photocolor Archives 43

Hardhat and manager, courtesy Herb Taylor/Editorial Photocolor Archives 43

Figure 1, *Process-Phases of the Job-Seeking Interview*, George Suyeoka 60

Class at Montreal University, courtesy Robert Karam/Editorial Photocolor Archives 98

Old women talking, courtesy Hanna Schreiber from Rapho Guillumette 98

Gordon Parks, Ossie Davis, courtesy Mark Chester/Editorial Photocolor Archives 99

University of Michigan students with administration, courtesy Andrew Sacks/Editorial Photocolor Archives 99

Figure 1, *A Six-Stage Agenda for Problem-Solving Groups*, George Suyeoka 112

Types of Small Group Discussants, George Suyeoka 119

Sketches of Public Speakers, George Suyeoka 132

The Speech Communication Chain, George Suyeoka 139

Edward Hanrahan, courtesy Paul Sequeira 144

Kate Millet at Columbia, courtesy Don Koblitz/Editorial Photocolor Archives 144

Think Indian, courtesy Bruce Anspach/Editorial Photocolor Archives 145

Student addressing audience, courtesy Michael Meadows/Editorial Photocolor Archives 145

Ralph Abernathy, courtesy Bruce Anspach/Editorial Photocolor Archives 145

Figure 2, *Seven Essential Steps in Speech Preparation*, George Suyeoka 147

Man gesturing with hands, courtesy Steve Eagle 174

Young girl, courtesy D. C. Johnson 174

Old woman, courtesy Geoffrey Gove 174

Man smiling, courtesy Andrew Sacks/Editorial Photocolor Archives 175

Young man with sunglasses, courtesy D. C. Johnson 175

Tattooed man in parade, © George W. Gardner, 1972 175

Positioning of Articulators in the Formation of Certain Sounds, Jim Ballard 190

Left, top right, courtesy Leonard McCombe; bottom photograph by Friedman-Abeles 192

Top, courtesy Leonard McCombe; bottom photograph by Friedman-Abeles 193

Figure 1, *Four General Ends of Speech*, George Suyeoka 230

VISTA volunteer reading, photograph by Ken Heyman 252

Bluegrass festival, courtesy Roy Ellis from Rapho Guillumette 252

Vietnam Veterans, 71, courtesy Steve Eagle 252
Senior citizens parade, courtesy Lawrence
    Frank from Rapho Guillumette 253
Nuns at rally, courtesy Paul Sequeira from
    Rapho Guillumette 253
Police line at parade, courtesy Paul Sequeira 253
Figure 1, *A Hierarchy of Prepotent Needs*
    (after Maslow), George Suyeoka 268
Halls Crown Center, courtesy Tina Grant,
    Sales Promotion Director, and Dan
    Proctor, Art Director 272
Courtesy of International Correspondence
    Schools 272
Courtesy Mobil Oil Corporation 272
Courtesy of Outdoor Life Conservation 273
Courtesy of Harrison Air Conditioning 273
Speech and Theatre journals and periodicals 291
Figures 1-2, *Source-Material Notecards* 295
Figure 1, *Forms of Verbal Support for an
    Idea*, George Suyeoka 301
Top, courtesy General Motors Corporation 316
Man explaining motor, courtesy Fred Leavitt 316
Children at Katonah Gallery, photograph by
    Rae Russel 317

Instructor with chalkboard, courtesy
    Pace Magazine 317
Bell telephone class, courtesy Illinois Bell
    Telephone Company 317
Nonverbal Support: A Diagram, *Types of
    Municipal Government* 322
The Motivated Sequence, George Suyeoka 355
Motivated Men Made America Great, courtesy
    of Maritz, Inc. 357
Figure 1, *Ethical Judgment: Four Perspectives* 458
Humorous Sketches, George Suyeoka 476-480
After-dinner speaker, courtesy Donald
    Patterson from Stock Boston 582
Academy Awards acceptance, courtesy
    Academy of Motion Picture Arts and
    Sciences 582
Dedication ceremony, courtesy of The
    Northbrook Public Library 583
Edmund Muskie at graduation, courtesy Clif
    Garboden from Stock Boston 583
Paris peace talks, courtesy Orville Schell from
    Jeroboam 583
TV director's signals, courtesy Leo Photos 600-601

Charts

Basic Forms of Speech Communication: Qualities and Interrelationships Page 72
A Six-Stage Agenda for Problem-Solving Groups 112
Basic Forms of Speech Communication: Qualities and Interrelationships (extended) 116
Seven Essential Steps in Speech Preparation 147
Basic Forms of Speech Communication: Qualities and Interrelationships (extended
    further) 154
The International Phonetic Alphabet 195
Generating, Shaping, and Influencing the Total Speechmaking Enterprise 227
Four General Ends of Speech 230
A Hierarchy of Prepotent Needs 268
Functional Relationship of Sequential Steps to Speech Purposes 361
The Motivated Sequence Applied to Speeches to Actuate 362
The Motivated Sequence Applied to Speeches to Inform 364
The Motivated Sequence Applied to Speeches to Entertain 365
Adaptation of the Motivated Sequence to the General Ends of Speaking 367
The Relationship Between the Steps of the Motivated Sequence and the Traditional
    Divisions of a Speech 377
Parliamentary Procedure for Handling Motions 588-589
Checklist and Index for Evaluation and Improvement of Student Speeches *Inside Back Cover*

Principles and Types
of Speech Communication

Seventh Edition

PART ONE
Speech Communication: Orientation, Process, and Forms

COMMUNICATION AND CHANGE

Let us begin with a story about the mythical metropolis of Center City and a college student named Claire Lumen.

Center City is a community of 15,000 persons and the home of Victor College, a four-year undergraduate institution with about 2800 students. For many decades, Center City had been governed by a five-member city council elected by the voters at large. That is, a candidate for a council post was not required to live in any particular part of the city, and—once elected—was regarded as representing all of the citizens rather than as the voice of only one ward or municipal area.

On the whole, this system worked well and had many advantages. Some years ago, however, as the students of Victor College became more active in local affairs, they realized that many of their legitimate interests as citizens of the community were being ignored by a council composed entirely of business and professional persons. The city council, for example, despite repeated requests and petitions, steadily refused to act against a local factory whose smoke and fumes polluted the campus. It also rejected, after only cursory examination, a tenant-landlord code drawn up by students to protect their rights as renters.

After studying the problem for several months, Claire Lumen, a senior majoring in political science, decided that the only practical remedy was to elect to the council some person whose special concern would be the protection and promotion of student interests. Yet, since the students could at most muster no more than 2800 votes in a city of 15,000, this task would be far from easy; and obviously something more than a simple get-out-the-vote campaign was called for.

The solution, Claire concluded, lay in a reorganization of the city council itself, a plan that would ensure that each council member, rather than being elected as a representative-at-large, would be elected by and primarily responsible to the voters of only one of Center City's five wards. In this way, since Victor College was located in Ward 5 and since most of the students lived there, they could be assured of electing someone who would speak for their special interests.

For a time Claire considered this plan without mentioning it to anyone. Would such a reorganization be possible? Was there an easier and less roundabout way to ensure students an effective voice in city affairs? Could the students be stirred into translating their grumblings into concrete actions? What were the advantages and disadvantages of the ward-representation system? Had other cities changed from the council-at-large to the ward plan and, if so, with what success? What did the experts and the textbooks on municipal government say about the matter? Claire used all of her spare time to question informed members of the college faculty and to read pertinent books and articles.

At last, Claire was ready to try out her proposal on others. So one evening after dinner, she broached the idea to her roommate, Joan Harmon. To Claire's surprise, she ran into a hornets' nest of objections. The students, Joan argued, despite their dissatisfaction with the present system, would never devote the time and energy required to push through so drastic a change. The Center City Chamber of Commerce and the Downtown Business Bureau would fight the proposal because it was to their benefit to have a council dominated by business and professional interests. The League of Women Voters and the Citizens' Committee for a Better Center City would no doubt argue strongly for the present arrangement.

Claire tried to meet each of these objections as it was raised, but only in about half of the cases was she successful. Arguments were tossed back and forth far into the night, each party advancing a new claim or developing a new line of reasoning as soon as an old one had been shot down. Finally, more out of weariness than because any basic agreements had been reached, Claire and Joan called it a night and went to bed.

Joan, however, was not the only individual Claire talked to in an effort to "sell" her idea. During the next few weeks she buttonholed friends on campus, at meals, in the union building—anywhere she could find someone who was willing to listen or argue back. Gradually a little knot of opinion favoring the plan began to emerge. The campus newspaper, *Victor Victorious*, carried several editorials favoring the idea, and the proposal was discussed tentatively at a meeting of the Student Senate.

As a result of these developments, Claire felt confident enough to proceed to the next step. She proposed that a special committee of the Student Senate be appointed to explore the possibility and to recommend to that body whether the idea should be dropped or pursued further. After a lengthy debate, such a committee was appointed, with Claire as chairperson.

This committee, consisting of five persons—four representing such major campus groups as the Women's Caucus, the Board of Student Publications, and the Athletic Council, and one representing the class presidents—engaged in a long series of informal discussions. In addition, each committee member studied the matter independently and laid before the group the results of this private research.

At the meetings, an attempt was made to consider the problem in an orderly fashion, but without a strong initial commitment to any one position and without resorting to set speeches or saddling the group with a rigid set of rules and procedures. Under Claire's impartial leadership, all facets of the subject were explored, witnesses were called in to testify, and alternative courses of action were weighed. Although initially opinion was sharply divided, eventually a consensus was reached; and the group as a whole decided to endorse the idea and to recommend the next logical step toward making it a reality.

This step consisted of holding a public meeting to which all citizens of Center City, students and nonstudents alike, were invited. At this meeting, the members of the committee reviewed their deliberations and reported and defended their conclusion that, in the interest of fairness to the students as voters residing in the city, the council should be reorganized on the ward system.

Needless to say, this recommendation elicited both opposition and support from those present. Working under the rules of parliamentary procedure, members of the audience made speeches *pro* and *con*, and for a time the issues were hotly debated. By the end of the evening, however, the recommendation of the committee appointed by the Student Senate was endorsed by a narrow margin, and the group voted to continue to explore the idea.

For this purpose, small discussion groups were formed in neighborhoods throughout the city to study the matter and to inform the citizens of the issues. But although the discussion process again took over, this time its purpose was not so much to bring forth recommendations for action as to inform the voters of the nature of the problem and to examine the alternatives offered. More citywide meetings also were held, and at these meetings more speeches were made and the proposal vigorously debated. Other speakers, favoring or opposing reorganization of the city council, appeared before service clubs, civic organizations, and campus groups. Opinion both in the city and at the college began to grow more strongly in favor of the change.

At this point, a petition favoring a public referendum on the ward system of council representation was circulated by Claire and her committee and was signed by some 6000 persons—enough to require that the question be brought to a vote at a special municipal election.

While the petition was being circulated and after its results were announced, conversations between individuals and among persons in small groups meeting on social and business occasions continued at an accelerated pace. So also did the speeches before clubs and organizations. The facilities of the local radio and television stations were utilized to make pertinent announcements, and talks and discussions on the subject were frequently broadcast.

In due time, the referendum was held; and of the 9300 votes cast, a majority favored representation by wards. Consequently, that form of government is now in effect in Center City, and the students as well as the townspeople are satisfied that a fair and equitable decision has been reached.

Although our story is fictional, it is nonetheless typical of the way in which social and political changes often are effected not only in a community, but also in any kind of organization or institution that is governed by democratic processes. Moreover, it illustrates the role that speech communication characteristically plays in promoting such changes, and the various forms that this speech communication takes: in some cases, that of *one individual talking to another;* in others, *a small number of persons thinking and conversing together in an informal discussion group or a more structured committee meeting;* in still others, of *one woman or man speaking to an audience of many* in an effort to inform or persuade them.

In the pages that follow, we will see what these various forms of speech communication—person-to-person, group, and public—have in common. Then in subsequent chapters, we shall explore the principles that must be observed and the practices that must be avoided if speech communication in all of these forms is to carry ideas clearly and effectively from speaker to listener.

1
SPEECH COMMUNICATION: PROCESS AND FORMS

As we traced the steps by which Claire Lumen and her fellow students brought about a change in the composition of the city council of Center City, we were able to observe the basic forms which speech communication most commonly assumes. In some cases, you will recall, Claire presented her ideas to a single individual in a two-party or *interpersonal* speaking situation. In other instances, the proposal was discussed by *small groups of persons* meeting socially or coming together for committee-work sessions. Finally, on still other occasions, advocates and critics of the change made *public speeches* and engaged in debates at mass meetings, presented prepared addresses to civic clubs and organizations, or gave talks over the local radio and television stations.

In succeeding chapters we shall look at each of these forms of speech communication more closely and survey the rules and principles which should guide us in their use. Here at the outset, however, let us take some time to consider the traits or properties which interpersonal, group, and public communication have in common.

FACTORS COMMON TO ALL SPEECH COMMUNICATION

If you will think back over "Communication and Change," the detailed hypothetical illustration with which we introduced this section, you will realize that although the three forms of speech communication we have distinguished differed in many ways, the same five basic elements or factors always were present. In each case, a *speaker*, operating within the constraints of a given physical and social *situation*, originated a *message* which was carried over a *channel* to one or more *listeners* who then, influenced by the constraints of the same situation, responded to this message in some way.

The speakers, we may be sure, exhibited quite different patterns of behavior as they moved from one situation to another, sometimes standing, sometimes sitting, sometimes talking in a formal manner, sometimes adopting the tones of casual conversation. The messages which the speakers framed varied also, ranging from organized speeches of some length to the briefest kinds of chance comments and questions. On some occasions, the listeners responded immediately and overtly by raising objections to the speaker's views, or perhaps by showing through applause, changes in facial expression, and the like that they agreed with him. In other instances, their reactions were delayed and expressed only weeks or months later when they cast their ballots in the citywide referendum. When the interchange took place face to face, light and sound waves carried the message directly from speaker to listener. When talks were given over the local radio and television stations, electronic channels of transmission were employed. In each case, however, the same five factors of speaker, situation, message, channel, and listener were involved in one way or another. Indeed, as a moment's reflection will show you, had any one of them been absent, no act of speech communication could have occurred. These factors and the way in which they interact in a unitary phase or "transaction" of the speech communication process is illustrated in the following diagram:

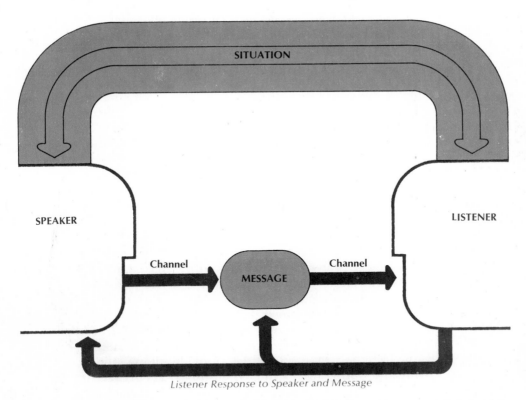

Figure 1. A SPEECH COMMUNICATION TRANSACTION: Basic Factors and Relationships

Keeping this diagram in mind, let us now examine each factor more fully, beginning where a speech communication transaction itself normally begins — with the speaker.

THE SPEAKER

Insofar as the speaker is concerned, all speech acts of whatever kind share four important, common characteristics: communicative purpose; knowledge of subject; command of speech skills; and attitudes toward self, listeners, and subject.

The Speaker's Purpose in Communicating

> *Whenever we speak — whether in the interpersonal,*
> *group, or public situation — we do so in order to*
> *achieve some purpose or satisfy some desire.*

Except in the rarest of instances, we do not speak to others out of accident or whimsy. We speak to achieve some purpose or attain some goal. Our purpose may be as simple as the wish to be sociable or to befriend a stranger. We may, at the other extreme, seek to alter our listeners' most cherished values or move them to a course of action fraught with uncertainties and dangers. Our purpose may be to reinforce an existing attitude, to reduce dissonance, or to increase the saliency of an issue. We may wish to provide entertainment, call attention to a problem, test an idea, refute an assertion, ward off a threat, establish or maintain status, or achieve any number of similar ends. Sometimes our communicative behaviors are primarily *defensive;* sometimes they are *aggressive* and *threatening.* In every case, however, we communicate with others because there is an end we seek to achieve or a desire we wish to fulfill.

To say that whenever we speak we have a purpose is not, of course, to assert that in all cases our audience is aware of what that purpose is. Sometimes what the listeners regard as an objective statement of fact is actually a subtle piece of propaganda or persuasion designed to influence their belief or direct their behavior. At other times, remarks we intend ironically or satirically are interpreted literally. Even we ourselves may not always be aware of the purpose our message is designed to serve, or we may be deceived concerning the motives that prompt it. What we honestly regard as an effort to provide information or clarify a problem may, in reality, spring from a hidden desire to gain prestige or erect a defense against criticism. Or, what seems to us to be an honest attempt to appraise another's argument objectively may actually be an attempt to needle or deride an opponent. In speech communication, no less than in other aspects of behavior, the human being is an exceedingly complex creature whose true motives often remain beneath the surface. If, however, we look deeply enough into the origins of any speech act, the desire to achieve some end or to fulfill some purpose always will be revealed.

The Speaker's Knowledge of the Subject and Command of Speech Skills

> *In every speaking situation—whether interpersonal, group, or public—our knowledge of the subject and our command of speech skills condition in a significant way the nature of our message and the effectiveness with which it is transmitted.**

Knowledge of Subject

In casual conversations, no less than in formal speeches and addresses, if we have only a surface knowledge of what we are talking about, our ideas are likely to be thin and ill-digested, and we will probably present them in ways that are cloudy and confusing. When, on the other hand, we have a broad and thorough knowledge of a subject, the chances are strong that we will present significant ideas in a clearer and more orderly fashion.

Skills in Vocal and Bodily Communication

Besides a knowledge of subject matter, our command of the fundamental skills of vocal and physical delivery likewise is important regardless of the situation in which the speech act occurs. Mumbled or inaudible words, a monotonous and unexpressive pitch pattern, a harsh or breathy voice detract from any message in a major way.

Whether we are speaking to one listener or to thousands, then, two things always are of first importance: (1) we must always have a thorough knowledge of what we are talking about; and (2) we must, through the skillful use of our voice and our body, be able to express ideas so that they can be easily understood.

**Because of the extensive coverage given to the importance of the speaker's knowledge of subject matter in Chapters 3, 8, and 11 and also because considerable emphasis is attached to the speaker's command of body and voice in Chapters 5 and 6, we shall not consider these matters in depth here. There are some things, however, that ought to be said at this point in order to accord them their proper role in the speech communication process and to place them into the broader perspective of the present analysis.*

The Speaker's Attitudes

In every speaking situation—whether interpersonal, group, or public—our attitude toward ourselves, our listeners, and our subject significantly affects what we say and how we say it.

Attitude Toward Self

All of us carry about with us a picture of ourselves as persons—a self-conception or image of the kind of individual we are and of how others supposedly perceive us. We think of ourselves as successful or unsuccessful, as liked or disliked, as someone whose opinions are respected or discounted, as effective or ineffective under various conditions, as competent or incompetent to discuss a given topic or make a given judgment.

The form our self-image takes influences how we are likely to behave in a given speaking situation. If we have a low estimate of our abilities or are unsure of ourself or our subject, we tend to advance ideas diffidently and often in a random or confused manner. Usually, our voices are weak and unsteady, our bodies stiff and restrained, and our gaze directed toward the floor or ceiling rather than toward the persons addressed. We may, because of timidity or fear, weaken or qualify the opinions we advance and, as a result, state them less strongly than the supporting facts or circumstances warrant.

In contrast, if we have an exaggerated idea of our knowledge or abilities, we are more likely to adopt a strong and overbearing manner, to disregard the need for facts and proofs, and to state our ideas without regard for the opinions and feelings of others. In both instances, our self-image exercises a major, negative influence on the content and the style of our message and, to a considerable extent, determines in advance how our ideas will be received.

A previously formed self-image is not, however, the only factor that affects our speaking behavior. What happens during the course of the communicative encounter also has a significant influence. If, despite an initial lack of confidence, we find that what we say is well received, that our listeners are interested and attentive, our fear and reluctance are gradually replaced by a growing sense of assurance. As a result, our words begin to flow more fluently, our ideas come through more cogently, and our conclusions are expressed with increased force and emphasis. When, on the other hand, we approach the communication situation with confidence and find the listeners uninterested, annoyed, or hostile, our initial confidence may well give way to anxiety, so that our thinking becomes confused and our delivery less poised and forthright. Because outward speech behavior is a faithful mirror of inner thoughts and feelings, our self-image, as challenged or confirmed by *feedback** from listeners, has quite correctly been called "the starting point or base line from which all communication proceeds."†

Attitude Toward Listeners

A second important influence on speaking behavior, irrespective of the situation in which it occurs, is our attitude toward our listeners.

Each time we speak we do so from a certain *status-* or *role-position* — that of seller or buyer, parent or child, teacher or student, boss or employee, creditor or debtor, doctor or patient, stranger or friend. And as our role-positions change, so also do our attitudes toward the persons we are addressing. As a result, we talk in one way to individuals we know well and in quite a different way to casual acquaintances or strangers. Similarly, our speaking manner changes as we communicate with those who stand above or below us in a social or professional hierarchy. The middle-management executive, for example, uses a deferential manner when talking to the "big bosses," an open and relaxed style when conferring with other middle-management persons, and an authoritative tone when addressing executives in a lower range or when instructing shop foremen. By the same token, most students contest the opinions of other students more vigorously and freely than they contest the opinions of a professor whose knowledge and attainments they admire.

In addition to social position and role-relationship, how we regard the person or persons we are talking to influences our speaking behavior in many subtle but unmistakable ways. Admiration or contempt, sympathy or indifference, love or hatred, patience or impatience, approval or annoyance are mirrored not only in the tone and inflectional patterns of the voice but also in facial expression, muscle tension, and bodily posture. Although for a time we may try to dissemble or conceal these states of mind, sooner or later such attempts usually break down, and listeners are able to read the telltale signs we are attempting to hide.

Attitude Toward Subject

Finally, our behavior as speakers inevitably is influenced to a greater or lesser degree by how we feel about the subject we are discussing. Whether we regard it as interesting or boring, pertinent or irrelevant, crucial or trivial, whether we believe or disbelieve what we are saying, our attitude not only conditions

---

*For a fuller discussion of feedback and its role in the speech communication process, see p. 257.

†*George A. Borden, Richard B. Gregg, and Theodore G. Grove,* Speech Behavior and Human Interaction *(Englewood Cliffs, N.J.: Prentice-Hall, Inc., 1969), p. 101.*

the ideas we present and the language in which we express them, but it is reflected also in the same subtle cues of voice and appearance that disclose our attitudes toward ourselves and toward our listeners.

The Speaker's Credibility

> *In every speaking situation—whether interpersonal, group, or public—our success in winning agreement, inspiring confidence, or promoting action depends in large measure upon the listeners' estimate of our worth and competence as a person.*

We have already observed that our command of the subject matter we are discussing determines to a significant extent both the message we transmit and the likelihood that this message will be accepted. Knowledge, though important, is not the only factor, however, on which personal effectiveness in speaking depends. If we wish to have our ideas believed or our proposals endorsed, we must possess other qualities as well. Prominent among these are *reputation, character, personality, intention, competence*, and *dynamism.*

Speakers who have acquired a reputation for unreliability or shady dealings, whose personalities are drab and colorless, who by nature are withdrawn and phlegmatic, or whose motives are suspect have little hope of winning adherents. On the other hand, speakers who are known to be of good character, who have warm and colorful personalities, who are alive and alert in manner, and seem to be genuinely interested in the well-being of their listeners always are more readily attended to and believed.

Traditionally, the persuasive forces residing in the reputation and personality of the speaker have been called "ethical proof," after the Greek work *ethos*, meaning "character." Today they are more generally referred to as *source-credibility.** Of all the means of persuasion, source-credibility is perhaps the strongest and—if appropriately reinforced—may, in fact, retain its potency for extended periods of time. For these reasons, it constitutes an indispensable component of any speech act.

**James McCroskey sees a communication source as having three possible process dimensions: (1) initial credibility, (2) produced credibility, and (3) terminal credibility. See, for example, James C. McCroskey, Carl E. Larson, and Mark L. Knapp, An Introduction to Interpersonal Communication (Englewood Cliffs, N.J.: Prentice-Hall, Inc., 1971), pp. 84–85.*

THE MESSAGE

In all speech communication—whether interpersonal, group, or public—the messages which speakers seek to transmit are made up of the same three variables of content, structure, and style.

Content

That the messages which we as speakers wish to transmit to our listeners have a *content*—are about something we want them to be aware of—is self-evident. What we say may take the form of an assertion, a question, or an exclamation; it may report an observation, express a feeling, or prescribe a course of action; it may or may not be accompanied by visual or auditory cues that enhance or detract from our meaning. In every case, however, the message has a thought-content or subject matter of some kind.

Structure

Any message we transmit, whether a single sentence or many, whether long or short, simple or complex, is of necessity structured or organized in some way. Its structure may be dictated by the nature of the ideas themselves or may, as in the case of the marriage ceremony or pledge of allegiance, be imposed upon the ideas by a socially or institutionally approved formula. The structure may be direct or circuitous, loose or compact, clear or confusing, progressive or redundant. It may, at one extreme, entail no more than the ordering of a few sentences, or—at the other—require the strategic structuring of large-scale units of thought. But because we can express only one idea at a time, we always must make a choice as to what to say first, second, or last; and in so doing, we inevitably give the message a certain organization or structure.

Style

The third variable in every spoken message is *style*. Although spoken language is not the only medium through which speech communication is effected, it is nevertheless, the principal one. When we communicate solely by gestures or other visual, nonvocal, or nonverbal means, we are said to be employing sign language, pantomime, or some communication system other than speech. But insofar as spoken language is involved, just as we must make choices in the selection and arrangement of units of thought, so also must we make choices in the selection and arrangement of words to express those thoughts. One word must be used rather than another, and must be placed in the sentence in one position rather than another.

Depending on the choices we make, our style may be plain or elevated, smooth or awkward, rhythmical or jumpy, pleasing or irritating. In comunicating ideas through the use of words, however, we always must try to choose and arrange them in a way that produces an appropriate style and one that is maximally contributive to the meaning we hope to communicate. This is a matter we shall explore at some depth in Chapter 16, "Using Words to Communicate Meaning."

THE LISTENER

In all instances of speech communication—whether person-to-person, group, or public—how the listener receives and responds to a message varies according to: (1) his knowledge of and interest in the subject; (2) the level of his listening skills; and (3) his attitude toward himself, the speaker, and the speaker's message.

The Listener's Purpose

> *Whenever we listen—whether in the interpersonal, group, or public situation—we do so in order to achieve some purpose or satisfy some desire.*

Listeners, no less than speakers, seek rewards of some kind. Otherwise, they wouldn't listen. They must have a purpose just as the speaker does. Since all communication must be *multidirectional*, unless listeners listen, there can be no transaction. In broad outline, the listener's purpose in listening often is congruent or consistent with the speaker's purpose in speaking. We may listen *to be entertained, to be informed, to be persuaded*—or to *refuse* to be persuaded, or *to be actuated*—or to *resist* actuation. When, in a subsequent chapter, we delve into the problem of human needs and motives, we will see that both listeners and speakers possess, employ, and are significantly influenced by the same hierarchy of human necessities and motivations. By all of this, we do not mean to imply that the purposes of listener and speaker are ever really identical; rather, we wish to emphasize that speaker purpose and listener purpose are inseparable concerns in the *functioning* of the speech communication process.

> *In every listening situation—whether interpersonal, group, or public—our knowledge of and interest in the speaker's subject and the level of our listening skills condition in a significant way our reception of that message and the effectiveness with which we respond to it.*

Whether a listener finds a speaker's ideas easy or difficult to understand depends in part upon how much he already knows about the subject under consideration. Whether he finds these ideas interesting and pertinent depends, in part, upon his personal needs and concerns at the time the speech encounter occurs. When a listener already has some knowledge of and interest in the subject matter of the transaction or when that subject touches upon matters that are of importance to the listener, the speaker's task is easier; in proportion as these elements are lacking, it becomes more difficult. Indeed, at times the listener's previous knowledge of a subject may be so deficient that the speaker is unable to communicate with him at all concerning it.

Listener knowledge and interest are not, however, the only relevant variables. As you yourself have no doubt frequently observed, and as research has substantiated, people differ considerably in their skill as listeners. Some are able to follow the speaker's ideas more easily than others; some are quicker to catch errors in inference or to note deficiencies in evidence. How much of this variation in listening skills is the result of differences in training and how much of it reflects differences in native ability is still an open question and one which we will attempt to weigh more critically in Chapter 17, "Listening, Evaluation, and Ethical Judgment." Listening skills do, however, obviously vary considerably from person to person and are, therefore, an important variable which helps to shape and condition all kinds of speech transactions.

The Listener's Attitudes

> *In every listening situation—whether interpersonal, group, or public—our attitude toward our self, the speaker, and the subject significantly affects what we hear, how we interpret it, and how we respond to it.*

We have said that a speaker's behavior in sending a message is influenced by his attitude toward himself, his subject, and the other person or persons involved in the communicative transaction. These *same* factors influence how a listener responds to the message that is transmitted. Listeners who have poor images of themselves and little confidence in their own judgments tend to be swayed more easily than those whose self-esteem is higher. Listeners also tend to be more readily influenced by views which confirm their own opinions and values than they do by views which run counter to their thinking. Further, listeners deliberately seek out speakers whose positions on issues they already agree with, and they retain longer those ideas of which they approve than those of which they disapprove. Finally, listeners change continuously throughout interaction, just as speakers do.

As a result, the relationship between speaker and listener is never static; it is always dynamic. It is never one-sided or one-dimensional; it is always *reciprocal* and *multidirectional*. For all of these reasons—irrespective of the particular form taken by the speech act—the knowledge level, listening capabilities, and attitudes of the transactors must always be reckoned with in the speech communication process.

THE CHANNEL

> *All speech communication—whether interpersonal, group, or public—is conditioned to a greater or lesser extent by the channel over which the message is transmitted.*

For our purposes, a channel may be defined as the pathway over which a message travels in reaching its destination. When the participants in a communication interchange meet face to face, two channels usually are employed, the speaker's message being communicated in part by what is said (the oral channel) and in part by gestures, facial expression, posture, etc. (the visual channel). When, as with messages transmitted by radio or telephone, the speaker cannot be seen, the vocal mechanism alone must do the work it normally shares with the rest of the body. Under such circumstances, the rate of speech may be reduced, words grouped into shorter phrases, more pronounced inflectional patterns employed, and sounds articulated with more than ordinary care. In addition, the structure and style of the message may be modified so as to compensate for the loss of visual contact.

Finally, the fact that the channel may be either "clear" or "noisy" will require that appropriate adjustments be made in the message. If the channel is free of interference in the form of physical or psychological distractions, the volume of the voice may remain at its usual level, and ideas may need to be stated only once. When, on the other hand, the channel is noisy, vocal volume must be raised, sounds articulated more sharply, and ideas repeated or given more than a customary amount of elaboration.

THE COMMUNICATIVE SITUATION

All speech communication—whether interpersonal, group, or public—is conditioned by the communicative situation: the physical setting and social context in which it occurs.

Physical Setting

Listeners' anticipations or expectancies, as well as their readiness to respond, are to a considerable extent determined by the physical setting in which a speech act occurs. Persons waiting in the quiet solemnity of a great cathedral for the service to begin have quite a different expectancy than do theatergoers gathered to witness the opening of a new Broadway play or musical revue. Similarly, listeners at an open-air political rally held in the midst of an exciting campaign have a different expectancy than they would have if they were about to hear a scholarly lecture on political theory presented in a college classroom.

The furniture and decor of the room in which speaker and listeners find themselves also make a difference. Words of love are best spoken in soft light or before an open fire. Comfortable chairs and pleasant surroundings tend to put the members of a discussion group at ease and to promote a more productive interchange. The executive who talks to an employee from behind a large desk set in the middle of an impressively furnished office with the title "President" on the door gains a natural advantage not only because of a superior position in the corporate hierarchy, but also because of the setting in which the conversation occurs.

Social Context

Even more important than physical setting in determining how a message will be received is the social context in which it is presented. Custom and good manners decree, to a considerable extent, the kind of message and the style of presentation that are appropriate under a given set of circumstances. At many social events, for example, to engage in "shop talk" or to dwell on a subject that is of interest to only a few of those present is considered poor taste. At business luncheons, serious discussion of the matter at hand often is delayed until the conferees have finished eating. Committee meetings frequently are opened with a few moments of general conversation of a personal or incidental nature. In the public situation, memorial services and award dinners are not considered proper places at which to launch attacks upon a political opponent or to engage in discussions of abstract philosophical questions.

Speech communication takes three basic forms: interpersonal communication or one-to-one interaction; small group communication or all-to-all interaction; and public communication or one-to-many interaction.

Moreover, there is a difference between what people consider appropriate to say to one another in private or in the company of a few close friends and what is acceptable when talking to strangers or addressing a large audience. All this, of course, is not to suggest that the rules of custom and good manners are never violated. What is important to note is the extent to which these socio-cultural constraints often influence the content of the messages which speakers send, the manner in which such messages are transmitted, and the feelings of uneasiness or disapproval which departures from them may arouse in listeners.

Besides influencing the structure and content of messages framed by speakers, social context also is influential in determining how these messages will be received by the persons to whom they are directed. Remarks that win the evident approval of respected individuals sitting or standing near a listener are more likely to win the approval of that listener also. When people are in the company of others—especially large numbers of others—they generally are more highly suggestible, and therefore more easily swayed, than when they are alone. Persons in the middle of an audience tend to respond more readily than those on the periphery. Persons crowded closely together or sitting elbow to elbow tend to react as a unit; a handful of listeners scattered at random throughout a large auditorium show less uniformity of response. Facts reported or opinions expressed at a party often are taken less seriously than the same facts or opinions stated at a congressional hearing or as part of a formal lecture. Advice offered in moments of crisis usually is endorsed more readily than the same advice offered under less pressing circumstances.

The overt responses that individuals make as they listen to a message likewise vary from situation to situation. Persons who listen patiently to a long speech or lecture with which they thoroughly disagree and then applaud politely at its close may, when participating in a business or social conversation, be among the first to register displeasure with an idea they disapprove of. At a political rally, vigorous applause or shouted approval of the speaker's ideas is expected; at a church service, such overt forms of response generally are avoided. In these and similar ways, the behavior of listeners, no less than that of speakers, is conditioned by the physical, psychological, and socio-cultural circumstances surrounding the speech act.

Speaker, message, listener, channel, and *situation*—these, then, are the five factors or elements basic to the speech communication transaction regardless of whether it occurs in an interpersonal, small group, or public form. In our examination of these factor-elements, certain indications of their *interaction* necessarily have emerged also. As you have no doubt noted, between and among them there is a continuous interplay, an influencing and counter-influencing, a shaping and a reshaping. To further an understanding of this *mutuality of influence,* let us now take a closer and more direct look at the concept of interaction.

INTERACTION OF THE SPEECH COMMUNICATION ELEMENTS

All speech communication—whether interpersonal, group, or public—entails a complex pattern of inter-action among the communication elements: speaker, message, listener, channel, and situation.

As our discussion in the preceding pages has more than once suggested, the nature of a given speech transaction is conditioned not only by forces playing upon it from without, but also by a complex pattern of interaction *among* and *within* the elements or variables of which it is composed. As a result, any speech act—irrespective of the subject treated, the number of persons involved, or the conditions under which it occurs—is an extremely complex phenomenon.

The personality, values, and aims of the speaker, together with the physical surroundings and social context in which the speech act occurs and the channel over which it is transmitted, influence the content, structure, and style of the message. The message as thus framed and communicated alters or fails to alter the listeners' beliefs or behavior, and changes or confirms their attitudes toward the speaker and the message. The listeners' responses, as fed back to the speaker during the course of the speech act, influence the way in which subsequent portions of the message are presented. The physical setting and social context, in addition to influencing the content of the message transmitted, influence the language or style in which the content is couched and how the speaker's ideas will be received by the listener. The oral and/or visual channels, in turn, limit the kind of message that can be transmitted, determine the range of auditory and visual stimuli which the speaker may utilize, and affect the listeners' expectations and patterns of response-behavior.

Numerous and intricate as they are in themselves, these patterns of interaction are rendered still more complex by the fact that an act of speech communication, while in itself a discrete unit of thought or action bounded by a definite beginning and ending, has antecedents that stretch into the indefinite past and consequents that reach into the indefinite future. What the speaker says and how he chooses to say it are influenced not only by the demands of the immediate speaking situation, but also by the accumulation of many years of personal growth and conditioning—years in which knowledge has been acquired, judgments formed, attitudes toward other persons shaped, and speech skills and habits learned. The background of knowledge, the attitudes, and the listening skills which listeners bring to the speech encounter likewise are the result of a long process of conditioning. Even the mold and structure that a message takes and the channel over which it may appropriately be transmitted have histories that influence both its content and the manner in which it is presented. Sermons, for example, have for centuries opened with a reference to a Biblical text and then proceeded to an explanation of the text's significance or a hortatory appeal based upon the ideas it contains. In social introductions younger persons are presented to older ones and men to women. News of the death or serious injury of a loved one is, when at all possible, always communicated to an individual in a face-to-face meeting rather than over the telephone.

In sum, no communication encounter is an isolated event. It is heavily conditioned (1) by outside forces operative at the time the speech act occurs, (2) by the past experiences of the communicators—experiences extending back into their life histories almost from the moment of birth, (3) by what follows the communicative interchange, (4) by the way other persons visible to the communicator and receiver are reacting during the communication, etc. In fact, a unitary phase of the speech communication process—a communication transaction—is merely a moment in an ongoing process, a single, discrete occurrence within a total universe of experience. It is embedded in a situation that affects the expectancies of those who hear it, and is in many instances governed by a convention or custom of long standing.

As an illustration, consider the speech, "Man's Other Society," presented by Mr. Richard Marvin and reprinted on pages 541–543. When, would you say, did this speech really begin? At the instant when Mr. Marvin stood up to speak? When, some days or weeks before, he first began to gather material and prepare his remarks? Or even in infancy, when his personality, cast of mind, and habits of oral expression began to develop? And what of the shape or structure of the message? Is it totally the result of decisions made during the actual preparation process, or may it not also have evolved over a period of time?

When, on the other hand, will Mr. Marvin's speech actually end? When the final word is spoken? When the last of the listeners who were affected by its ideas dies? When the changes in understanding or belief which it may have wrought in society as a whole finally wear away? Will it, in fact, ever end? Isn't assigning an end to a speech, no less than assigning a beginning, after all, a purely arbitrary decision? Clearly, all acts of speech communication, from the simplest greetings to the most complex public addresses, have origins that are lost in the past of the speaker and of the social group he represents and contain consequences that stretch into the indeterminate future.

A Communication Transaction: A Model of Interactions and Relationships

Near the beginning of this chapter we presented a simplified diagram showing the basic elements and relationships involved in a unitary phase of the speech communication process, which we call a transaction. Now that we have examined them more fully and considered some of their interactional and transactional features, we may find it helpful to review them in a reconstructed and somewhat more elaborate model, as follows:

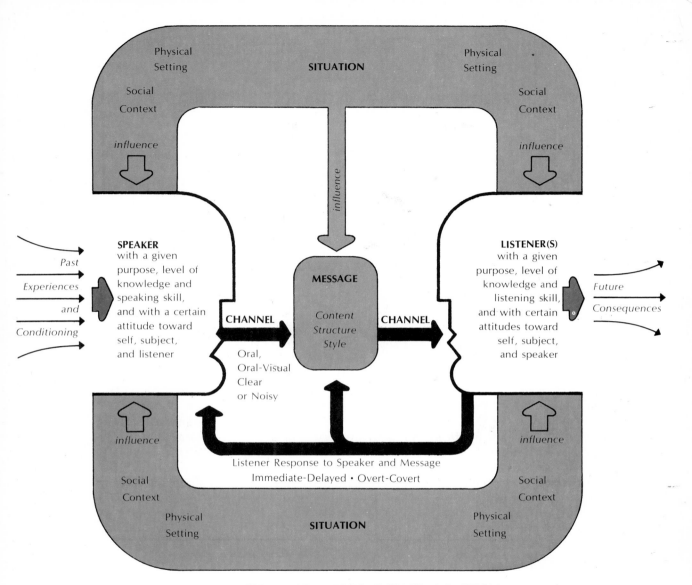

Figure 2. A SPEECH COMMUNICATION TRANSACTION

A SPEAKER, influenced by past conditioning, present SITUATION, communicative purpose, level of knowledge and speaking skill, and attitudes toward self, subject, and listener(s), transmits a MESSAGE which has content, structure, and style, over a CHANNEL which limits or shapes the message to one or more LISTENER(S) whose reception of the message is, in turn, influenced by conditioning, purpose, listening skill, situation, and attitudes toward self, subject, and speaker. The LISTENER(S) responds to the speaker and message with cues that cause the speaker to modify subsequent portions of the message or to alter his or her verbal or nonverbal behavior. Insofar as a communication transaction affects the beliefs or behaviors of speaker or listener(s), it has consequences for their future thought and action.

BASIC FORMS OF SPEECH COMMUNICATION

To be broadly inclusive, a typical classification of generally recognized communicative relationships as depicted on a continuum would include:

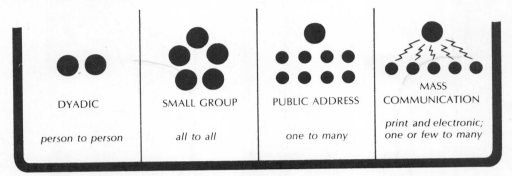

Figure 3. BASIC FORMS OF SPEECH COMMUNICATION

However, for reasons that must by now be evident, our focus in this book is necessarily more selective and more heavily centered on communicative *interaction between and among people.* We do, of course, take some cognizance of communication generated by the electronic media, but this form is largely unidirectional, at least in the sense that there is no immediate response or feedback. We also recognize that, in the *intra*personal sense, people frequently talk to themselves to think their way through a problem, screw up their courage, or relieve their loneliness. Speech communication, however, as we treat it in this volume is characteristically an activity of the human being's *social* or *communal* self — something the individual turns to not in moments of solitude or introspection, but when he or she wishes to *establish or maintain relationships with other persons.*

Thus we take the position that in using speech to initiate, establish, and maintain relationships with others, human beings tend generally to employ one of three distinguishable *relational forms:*

1. Interpersonal
2. Small Group
3. Public Communication

The essential speaker-listener relationship characteristic of each of these forms is contained in the following definitions and the diagrams accompanying them.

In the *interpersonal* relationship — or, as it is frequently called, the dyadic form — two persons, assuming alternately the role of speaker and listener, either exchange purposive information and ideas about a subject of mutual concern or engage in conversation simply because they enjoy each other's company.

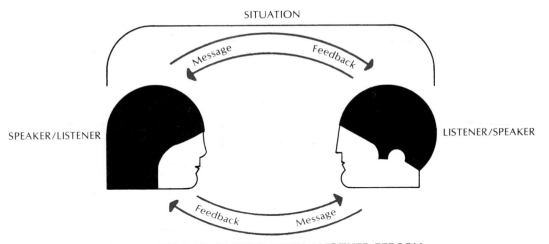

SITUATION

Message

Feedback

SPEAKER/LISTENER

LISTENER/SPEAKER

Feedback

Message

Figure 4. COMMUNICATING WITH ANOTHER PERSON

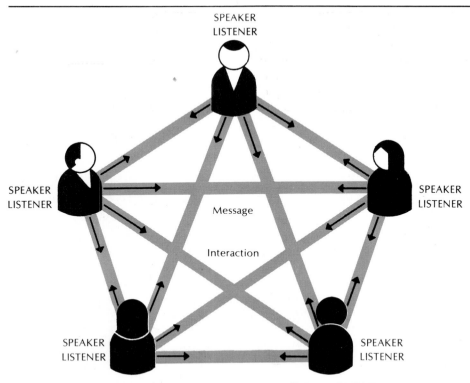

SPEAKER
LISTENER

SPEAKER
LISTENER

SPEAKER
LISTENER

Message

Interaction

SPEAKER
LISTENER

SPEAKER
LISTENER

Figure 5. COMMUNICATING IN A SMALL GROUP

As shown in Figure 5, page 27, in the *small group* relationship, a number of persons—from three to approximately fifteen, usually—variously engage in comparatively informal interaction to achieve a common purpose or objective, to identify a common problem or seek a solution, or to make a decision of some kind. This form of communicative engagement is often referred to as "group discussion."

In the *public communication* format, a single speaker, employing a relatively formal tone and manner, presents a continuous discourse on a subject of supposedly general interest to a sizeable number of other persons.

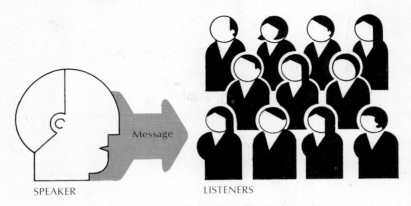

SPEAKER   LISTENERS

Figure 6. COMMUNICATING IN PUBLIC

Some Similarities and Differences in the Forms of Speech Communication

These three forms, of course, have certain similarities, but they also exhibit some very significant differences. Moreover, each has its unique advantages and disadvantages—depending upon the outcome it is supposed to achieve and the skills of the interactants; and no one form can be labeled superior or "better" than any other in the total communication picture.

In what kinds of *specific* situations, then, are these forms commonly employed? What traits or properties do the respective forms exhibit under these circumstances? *How do they differ as the speaker and listener move from one situation to another?* A consideration of such questions will supplement in a useful way what we have been and will be saying about speech as an instrument for communicating ideas and promoting constructive social relationships.

In the list that follows we have set down certain *qualities* and *conditions* discernible in the functioning of the three forms. These should not be looked upon as fixed or finite, but rather as base points from which to understand and evaluate the potentialities, as well as the inherent problems, likely to be encountered in each. They can probably best be viewed as *gradational* qualities having varying degrees of applicability in any given instance, and they include:

A. Number of persons involved.
B. Degree of intimacy between or among interactants.
C. Degree of formality typically observable.
D. Durational determinants or time limits imposed.
E. Need for prestructuring the message.
F. Evidence of communicator purpose.
G. Effort required for nonverbal projection of the message.
H. Degree of stability of speaker-listener roles.
I. Opportunities for perceiving listener feedback.
J. Opportunities for adjusting to listener feedback.
K. Opportunities to assess fulfillment of communicator purpose.
L. Opportunities for exploring ideas together.

In your thinking about these qualities or traits, note, for instance, that the *number of persons characteristically involved*—as indicated in the illustrative diagrams above—is a significant determinant for each of the respective forms. The *degree of intimacy* that might be experienced by speaker and listener ordinarily could be expected to be greater in the dyadic form than in the public form. Typically, we would anticipate a higher *degree of formality* in the public speech than in the person-to-person interchange. In a one-to-one conversation we would expect to find more and better *opportunities to assess the fulfillment of communicator purpose* than in, say, group communication, and so on.

In the remaining chapters of Part One, as we move to a closer, individual examination of the interpersonal, small group, and public forms of speech communication, observe and try to become increasingly aware of how these gradational qualities influence the interactive process and condition the outcomes of given communicative transactions.

Problems and Probes

1. Specify the different uses you have made of speech communication during the past week. Which of these uses did you find most gratifying? With which uses were you most successful? Least successful? Make a list of these uses and attempt to ascribe reasons for the varying degrees of success you experienced.

2. Using as a basis the speech encounters or transactions which you *observe* for a period of one day, for each instance jot down (*a*) the

speaker's purpose and (*b*) the listener's apparent purpose or reason(s) for being willing to listen.

3. Again using as a basis the observed encounters referred to above, attempt to evaluate (*a*) in one instance how the speaker's *knowledge of the subject* contributed positively to the accomplishment of his or her apparent purpose, and (*b*) in another instance how the speaker's *lack of skills in vocal and bodily communication* seemingly detracted from the achievement of his or her purpose.

4. In one instance that you observed, analyze to what extent the success or failure of the speech transaction appeared to be significantly influenced by the speaker's (*a*) attitude toward *self*, (*b*) attitude toward *other interactant(s)*, and (*c*) attitude toward *the subject* under consideration.

5. Calling on your recollection of speech communication transactions in which you have been involved personally, cite one instance in which you judged the speaker's credibility to be questionable. List the factors that led you to this feeling or impression. Cite an instance (it may or may not be the same one) in which you felt that the listener(s) may have had some justification for questioning *your* credibility. Did he, she, or they do so? If they did, how did you handle the situation?

6. After you have read Chapter 1, describe how—in your opinion—the obligations of speaker and listener differ in each of the three forms of speech communication: interpersonal, small group, and public.

7. Using as a point of reference your responses and observations connected with Problems 2 and 6, make a list of the *listening skills and abilities* which you consider essential to any kind of speech communication transaction. (*Note:* You will want to refer to this list from time to time in connection with subsequent chapters, especially Chapter 17.)

8. Identify and describe three speech transactions in which you personally participated during the past week or two. In at least two of these encounters you should have been the speaker initiating the interaction. Formulate answers to the following questions:

   a. In which of the three *forms*—dyadic, small group, or public communication—did these three transactions take place?
   b. What *purpose* did you have in each case?
   c. What *channel* or *channels* did you use?
   d. What was the extent of your *message-preparation* in each of the three instances? If that preparation was more extensive and mandatory for one than for the others, explain why.
   e. Show how, in one of these transactions, the *physical setting* probably influenced what went on. In another, explain how the *social context* tended to affect the outcome.

f. To what extent do you feel you accomplished your *communicative purpose* in each transaction?

9. Using the models developed in Chapter 1 to depict the interrelationships of the five basic factors in the speech communication process (pages 9 and 25), write a description of a recent speech transaction in which you were involved. Concentrate your analysis on the interactions among the five elements and show the parallel relationships in your own communicative experience. If you find it necessary to adapt the models shown in the text, do so. Explain the reasons for your modifications.

10. Here at the outset of the course, carefully consider the three prevalent forms of oral communication which were analyzed in this chapter: dyadic, small group, and public. Review your past encounters and experiences in each of these forms, and then try to arrive at some conclusions concerning which of them "works" best for you—the one in which you feel most comfortable, "at home," and generally effective. When you have determined this preference, carefully analyze for your present information and future use the reasons for that preference *at this time.* (*Note:* From time to time, as the course progresses, you should reevaluate your preference and make notes regarding any significant changes that may have taken place.)

11. Recall a person-to-person speech interaction in which there was a definite *failure to communicate.* This may be an encounter in which you were personally involved or one which you observed. Consider such problems as: (*a*) Were the speaker's purpose and the listener's purpose congruent? (*b*) Was there anything in the speaker's vocal mannerisms, bodily behaviors, style of dress, etc., that appeared to offend the listener? (*c*) Were the listener's knowledge and interest apparently "equal" to the speaker's ideas and presentation? (*d*) Did the communicative situation—physical setting and/or social context—have a negative effect? In other words, explore as fully as possible the reasons for the failure. Attempt to provide reasons for any emotional reactions you may have had to the situation. (Keep this description in your Personal Speech Journal which is described in Problem/Probe 12 below and to which you will be asked to return later.)

12. In a notebook set aside for the particular purpose, start a Personal Speech Journal. The contents are to be seen only by you and your instructor, who will call for the Journal several times during the term. During the first week of this course, write an inventory—after thoughtful analysis—of your personal speech needs and abilities. Include an evaluation of your past experience in individual and group speech situations, and also outline your goals and desires for the course.

Your instructor may ask you to include in this journal any of the written work you have done in regard to the Problems and Probes in the textbook, or he or she may make other or additional assignments of a written, evaluative nature. At your instructor's direction, in any case, along with any other written assignments include at least one page of written commentary per week bearing upon your own communicative behavior. Involved in this report also should be your perceptions of and reactions to the pertinent communicative behaviors of the members of the class; analyses of your feelings about your own communicative efforts and the consequences and difficulties growing out of these efforts; and, finally, the effectiveness of class activities in contributing to your personal improvement in speech communication.

Oral Activities and Speaking Assignments

1. To the extent that the physical facilities of the classroom permit, your instructor will arrange for the members of the class to be seated in a large circle or—as an alternative—in smaller groups around two or three separate tables. This setting should be as comfortable and relaxing as possible; informality should be the keynote in this particular activity. After the instructor has briefly introduced himself or herself to the others, the student at the instructor's right will orally provide a self-introduction more or less in terms of the following general pattern:

"My name is _____.
My major (or my major interest) is _____
_____. I am in college because
_____.

In addition to a grade credit, what I hope to get from this course in speech communication is _____
_____."

When the first speaker has concluded his or her self-introduction, the next one begins—and so on around the circle or table until everyone present has had a chance to make himself or herself known to all of the others.

2. Participate actively in a general class consideration of the subject "Things That I Like (or Dislike) in a Speaker." As you and the other members of the class mention your likes and dislikes, your instructor may want to list them in two columns on a chalkboard. At the conclusion of this oral consideration, help your instructor summarize by formulating a composite picture or list of those speaker traits or qualities to which the majori-

ty of the class members would respond *favorably* and of those traits or qualities to which the majority would respond *unfavorably*.

3. Participate actively in a class consideration of five or six areas of interest (other than childhood memories) which might enable the individual members of the group to discover some *common ground*. Using a list of five or six such areas of possible commonality (prepared in advance), informally discuss these lists with the class as a whole, compare them, and arrive at a consensus as to the two or three topics in which the majority of the class might be interested. And, finally, with everyone participating, select one of the topics by a majority vote—a topic which all members of the class are willing to discuss with some enthusiasm.

Suggestions for Further Reading

George A. Borden, *Human Communication Theory* (Dubuque, Iowa: Wm. C. Brown Company, Publishers, 1971).

Charles T. Brown and Charles Van Riper, *Communication in Human Relationships* (Skokie, Ill.: The National Textbook Company, 1973).

Theodore Clevenger, Jr., and Jack Matthews, *The Speech Communication Process* (Glenview, Ill.: Scott, Foresman and Company, 1971).

Robert J. Kibler and Larry L. Barker, *Speech Communication Behavior: Perspectives and Principles* (Englewood Cliffs, N. J.: Prentice-Hall, Inc., 1971).

Gerald R. Miller, *An Introduction to Speech Communication*, 2nd ed. (Indianapolis: The Bobbs-Merrill Company, Inc., 1972).

C. David Mortensen, *Communication: The Study of Human Interaction* (New York: McGraw-Hill Book Company, 1972).

Nan Lin, *The Study of Human Communication* (Indianapolis: The Bobbs-Merrill Company, Inc., 1973).

Wilbur Schramm, *Men, Messages, and Media* (New York: Harper & Row, Publishers, 1973).

2
COMMUNICATING WITH ANOTHER PERSON

Interpersonal or dyadic speech transactions are, without doubt, the most common form of oral communication, and also are among the most important.* Countless numbers of such encounters, ranging from chance street-corner meetings to carefully planned business interviews and formal diplomatic interchanges, take place every day. This is, moreover, the form of communication with which, by long habit, we are most familiar. It is the form we have used most frequently from the time when, as infants, we made our first efforts at coordinating speech to engage the attention of others and induce them to respond to our needs and wants. And, regardless of our station and vocation as adults, the dyadic interchange is doubtless the form we will continue to employ most often throughout our lifetime.

INTERPERSONAL SPEECH COMMUNICATION: A DEFINITION AND SOME DIMENSIONS

In Chapter 1, you will recall, we defined interpersonal communication as *a relationship in which two persons, alternating in the roles of speaker and listener, engage in face-to-face interaction because of their shared desire for social facilitation or fulfillment or because they feel a need to exchange ideas or information about a topic of mutual concern.* Sometimes these dyadic encounters are coincidental, unstructured, and only casually purposive; at other times, as in the case of formal interviews, they are scheduled, prestructured, and highly purposive.

---

*See, for example, Michael Argyle, Social Interaction (New York: Atherton, 1969); W. G. Bennis et al., Interpersonal Dynamics (Homewood, Ill.: Dorsey Press, 1964); Elihu Katz and Paul Lazarsfeld, Personal Influence (Glencoe, Ill.: The Free Press, 1955).

We may further delineate the interpersonal form by noting certain of its gradational qualities and characteristics, as follows: (*a*) It allows, typically, an extremely high degree of physical and — often — psychological closeness or intimacy. (*b*) In its conversational context at least, the atmosphere will probably be less formal than for any of the other forms of communication. (*c*) The time limits tend to fluctuate considerably, becoming less flexible probably in the more highly structured interview. (*d*) Messages are often impromptu, especially in casual, social-facilitation settings; but for the structured interchange, quite specific and definitive lines of inquiry often are spelled out and mutually agreed to in advance. (*e*) Nonverbal communication, particularly facial cues, abounds; and interactants tend to rely heavily on such cues to determine agreement as to the meanings and progress of the interaction. (*f*) Communicator purpose usually emerges quickly and — again in the instance of the formal interview particularly — may be spelled out in detail before the conversers come face to face. (*g*) Especially because of the physical closeness of the two persons in a dyad, and (*h*) the frequent alternation of speaker-listener roles, there are maximal opportunities for reading, reacting, and adjusting to speaker/listener feedback. (*i*) Finally, there is usually a strong and sincere desire on the part of both individuals *to explore ideas, experiences, and opinions together.*

Whatever the character of the dyadic encounter, however, if interpersonal speech transactions are to be productive, certain principles should be observed and certain guidelines followed by the transactors. In this chapter, we shall first discuss these guidelines and principles. Then we shall look more specifically at two important types of interpersonal communication that most persons at one time or another find it necessary to engage in: *the information-seeking interview* and *the job-seeking interview.*

SOME GENERAL PRINCIPLES OF INTERPERSONAL SPEECH COMMUNICATION

As a rule, interpersonal speech transactions fall of their own accord into three discernible steps or stages:*

1. An opening period of exploration or "fencing" in which the ice is broken, rapport built, and a working relationship established between the two persons involved.

---

*Compare these intervals or stages with the "succession of stages of activity" described in C. David Mortensen, Communication: The Study of Human Interaction (*New York: McGraw-Hill Book Company, 1972*), pp. 258–266.

2. A period in which, through the processes of interaction and mutual stimulation, the subject matter of the transaction is explored or its business is conducted.

3. A stage in which the encounter is terminated and closed off.

Let us examine these intervals or stages in order and in some detail.

Establishing Rapport

If two friends or associates who see each other several times a day come together to discuss a matter of common interest, they may turn to the topic at hand with few if any preliminaries. Usually, however, the interactants in a social conversation or a business conference first take a few moments to feel each other out and to build the rapport and good feeling upon which a healthy relationship depends. Long experience, as confirmed by recent research, has isolated a number of factors that are important in this regard.*

Respect Existing Conventions

In establishing rapport with another person—and especially with a stranger whose status or position is superior to your own—nothing is more important than adhering in a reasonable way to the conventions that normally govern behavior in interpersonal speaking situations.

As we saw in Chapter 1, in person-to-person interaction—no less than in other forms of speech communication—each party brings to the transaction or interchange certain anticipations and expectancies that are the result of long conditioning.** When either person violates these expectancies—and particularly when the violation seems deliberate—it is only natural that the other should tend to react negatively.

Many of the conventions governing our behavior in interpersonal speech transactions are culturally determined, and, therefore, vary widely from

---

*On establishing rapport and maintaining interaction in the interpersonal speech encounter, see among other works: David Berlo, The Process of Communication (New York: Holt, Rinehart & Winston, Inc., 1960), pp. 106–132; Michael Argyle, The Psychology of Interpersonal Behavior (Baltimore: Penguin Books, Inc., 1967), pp. 46–48; John W. Keltner, Interpersonal Speech Communication (Belmont, Calif.: Wadsworth Publishing Company, Inc., 1970), pp. 274–275 et passim; James C. McCroskey, Carl E. Larson, and Mark L. Knapp, An Introduction to Interpersonal Communication (Englewood Cliffs, N.J.: Prentice-Hall, Inc., 1971), pp. 37–53; R. Wayne Pace and Robert R. Boren, The Human Transaction (Glenview, Ill.: Scott, Foresman and Company, 1973), pp. 190–199, 309–316; Thomas Scheidel, Speech Communication and Human Interaction (Glenview, Ill.: Scott, Foresman and Company, 1972), pp. 238–263.

**See again pp. 10–14 and 16–18.

country to country. The kind of ritual or ceremony that must be observed, how close to the co-conversant one is expected to stand or sit, the degree of intimacy permissible in language and subject matter, whether one may touch his partner physically—all fall into this class.* In addition to these broad rules of a cultural nature, many of the business and social situations in which we daily find ourselves have a clearly established "etiquette" of their own. As a rule, a visitor to another person's home or office is expected to stand until he is invited to sit down. When smokers and nonsmokers are together in a closed room, smokers are expected to ask permission before lighting up. When making introductions, men are presented to women and younger persons to older ones.

No one, particularly in this age of freedom in language and behavior, is expected to be a slave to custom; and there are times when convention should be thrown to the wind and a person should speak or act as his convictions dictate. When one does depart from an accepted practice, however, he always should be aware that by such a departure he runs the risk of alienating the person he is talking with and, hence, of getting the relationship off to a strained or halting start. To build rapport with another individual most quickly and surely, therefore, adhere generally to the rules of accepted behavior as they commonly apply in the interpersonal speech encounter.

Find a Common Bond of Interest

If two persons find they have nothing in common, their relationship soon ends and each goes his own way. On the other hand, if they discover, for instance, that they both have a lively interest in baseball or art or politics, or if they find that they have had similar experiences in military service or foreign travel, they are likely to enter into a long and animated conversation. Take a few minutes to search out the interests of the person you are talking with; and when you find a topic of mutual concern or hit upon a common set of convictions or values, use this as a basis for building a congenial relationship. Remember that whereas people often are reluctant to walk out on a public speaker or to withdraw from a discussion group they find boring, they have much less compunction about breaking off a person-to-person conversation in which they are not interested. Remember, too, that while a public speaker or a discussion group usually can survive the loss of one or two listeners, when your partner in an interpersonal speech transaction departs from the scene, the encounter necessarily is terminated and you are left with your point unestablished or your purpose unfulfilled.

See, for example, Edward T. Hall, The Silent Language *(New York: Doubleday & Company, Inc., 1959).*

Show a Genuine Interest in the Other Person

Be interested in the ideas the other person is expressing, and indicate this by giving him signs of positive reinforcement. Show by your facial expressions, nods of the head, alertness of bodily posture, and other signs of attention and openness that you anticipate an interesting and enjoyable interchange. When we find ourselves trying to interact with a stolid and unresponsive listener, in most instances we tend to withdraw from the encounter as quickly as possible.

Put the Other Person at Ease

It has often been remarked that one of the traits shared by most great men and women is the ability to break down barriers of rank or position and put the other person completely at ease. Whenever you have reason to believe that the other party to an interchange will be uncomfortable or apprehensive, begin by getting him to talk about himself or discuss some subject with which you know he is familiar. Let your own manner show openness and warmth rather than distance and reserve. Call the person by name. Come out from behind a desk or table to take a chair next to his. Indicate by word and manner that you have plenty of time to hear him out or to consider his problem. Offer him coffee or a cigarette, or arrange to conduct your business over lunch. Above all, be at ease yourself. Ease and relaxation are highly contagious: if you yourself appear relaxed, the other person also will try to be less tense.

Build the Other Person's Confidence in You

Along with doing all you can to put the other person at ease and show interest in what he is saying, build up his confidence in your discretion and good judgment. If you are conversing about a confidential matter, assure him that you will not reveal to others anything he may tell you on a private basis. Give him reason to believe that you will keep any promises you make or carry out any tasks you agree to perform. Do not appear excitable or seem in any way sly or devious. In interpersonal interaction, as in all other forms of speech communication, the ability to inspire trust is an important asset. Cultivate it carefully.

Be Open-Minded—Don't Prejudge the Other Person

Sometimes, on the basis of information that has come to us prior to the encounter, we have a tendency to pigeonhole or stereotype the individual we are talking with. We may have read or heard that he is a flaming liberal or an arch conservative, or been told that he is a nuisance or a bore. We may know that he recently lost two jobs, and, therefore, mark him down as "hard to get along with." We may think that because he is a member of an ethnic minority, he has all of the characteristics which the popular imagination attributes to that group. Prior information about a person we are to talk with always is helpful, of course; and if the transaction is an important one, we obviously should try to learn as much about him as we can. We must not, however, make the serious mistake of closing our minds in advance and letting such prejudgments color our thinking during the course of the interchange.

Remember, too, that people may change greatly over a period of time, so that judgments based on the experiences you or someone else has had with an individual in the past may no longer be valid. In the interest of building good rapport with another individual, therefore, avoid preconceptions and approach him with an open mind. Discount rumors and gossip; don't be fooled by past impressions. When you meet a person on these grounds, you will be surprised to discover how many times your advance information about him turns out to be wrong.

Be Natural—Avoid Pretense and Artificiality

Because pretense undermines the genuineness and sincerity on which effective oral communication so largely rests, carefully avoid it in all forms of speech communication. In the interpersonal or dyadic situation, however, it is especially destructive of a warm and productive relationship. Ordinarily, in such encounters you stand or sit close to and in full view of your partner, so that artificial mannerisms of voice and body are easy to detect and are magnified to the point that even the slightest cues become important. Moreover, in most instances your partner has an opportunity to question you and to probe your views the moment they are expressed, thus exposing at once unguarded claims to knowledge or exaggerated statements of personal importance.

In the interest of building a sound relationship with another person, therefore, *simply be yourself.* Speak in a natural tone and without assuming "airs." Don't brag or exaggerate. Don't adopt a superior manner or pretend to be what you are not. Nothing causes an individual to lose face more readily than to have such pretenses exposed.

Be Subject- or Problem-Oriented

Sometimes people engage in interpersonal speech encounters not for the purpose of promoting sociality or exchanging ideas, but rather with the aim of confusing or belittling the other party. They view the transaction as an opportunity to conduct a personal vendetta, to degrade or embarrass the other person, and in this way to gratify their own egos and demonstrate their own superiority.

Not only are such tactics to be decried on moral grounds, but they also are to be avoided for quite practical reasons. No matter how subtle the techniques employed, sooner or later it nearly always becomes evident to the other person that your real aim is to attack him. As a result, he "puts up his guard" against you, thus destroying once and for all any possibilities of a harmonious and beneficial relationship.

If the person with whom you are talking is in error on some matter, point this fact out as tactfully and as objectively as you can. If it is your responsibility to reprimand another individual, do it in the way that least wounds his pride and self-confidence. In all cases, whatever the nature of the transaction in which you find yourself, focus to the fullest extent possible on the subject matter at hand rather than aiming your remarks at the person or self of the other individual. Good rapport is built on a background of common interests combined with mutual respect.

Ask "Open" Questions

A simple but effective way to break down another person's initial reserve and establish a productive relationship is to ask "open" rather than "closed" questions. A closed question is one that invites or compels a simple "yes" or "no" response. An open question, on the other hand, asks the respondent to supply information or to express and support an opinion. Instead of asking, "Did you by any chance read the editorial in this morning's paper?" ask "What did you think of the editorial in this morning's paper?" or "How well do the ideas in this morning's editorial agree with your own reactions to the election?" An open question not only requires the quiet or reluctant individual to begin talking, but it also may call forth ideas which will serve as springboards to an interesting conversational exchange.*

Try to Be an Interesting and Worthwhile Person

A final technique for building rapport in an interpersonal speaking situation is to make as certain as you can that you yourself are an interesting and worthwhile person to talk with. Express original and stimulating ideas, view old facts in a fresh light, link the trite and commonplace with the novel, inject an occasional bit of humor into your remarks. In short, be well informed, alert, and intellectually alive. We are all automatically drawn to persons who have interest-

---

*For a further discussion of the question-and-answer mode, see "Types of Questions Useful to the Interview Process," pp. 61–62.

ing ideas and stimulating insights, and we escape as soon as we can from those who are dull.

Maintaining Interaction

Good interpersonal communication depends not only on the removal of barriers and the establishment of an initial rapport, but also on a lively exchange of ideas throughout the course of the speech encounter. If one person dominates the conversation or intimidates the other, interaction is impaired, and the speech experience becomes both less satisfying and less productive than it might otherwise be. To generate continuing and productive interaction in a person-to-person speech transaction, observe the following guidelines.

Give Timely Signs of Reassurance

A productive interaction between two people is more likely to be achieved when each from time to time reassures the other that he is receiving a fair and sympathetic hearing. Avoid, even in the heat of argument, doing or saying anything that threatens your partner's ego or leads him to believe that you are impatient with him. When you agree with what he is saying, indicate this by your facial expression or a nod of the head. When you disagree, as previously urged, focus your rebuttal on the substance of his remarks rather than on the character or competence of the person himself. Say, "That is certainly an idea worth considering, but I wonder if you looked into the cost of putting such a plan into effect," *not* "If you had taken a minute to look into the cost of this thing, you never would have proposed it." People whose sensibilities are wounded or who feel threatened usually pull into their shells and are reluctant to express their ideas, no matter how sound and useful these may be. Signs of reassurance, on the other hand, often will draw out a shy individual and encourage him to express ins.ghts that he might otherwise refrain from advancing.

Share the Channel

For the most part, we talk with other individuals in order to exchange ideas or enjoy the warmth of their company. Neither of these objectives can be attained, however, if both persons in the interchange are not given easy access to the communication channel. Do not dominate the conversation to the point that the other person is shut out or merely becomes a sounding board against which your own convictions are tested. Interpersonal speech experiences are most satisfying to the participants and most likely to yield useful results when the interaction is constant and lively and when the parties share the communication channel just about equally.

Interpersonal communication is the most familiar form of speech communication for nearly all of us. From confidential whispers to noisy confrontation, from casual conversation to formal interview, we encounter this form of communication constantly throughout our lifetime.

Adapt to the Conversation as It Develops

In rare instances a conversation between two persons may be carefully planned in advance and perhaps even rehearsed for public presentation. Usually, however, you come to such an interchange not knowing exactly what the other person plans to say or how he will react to your ideas. For this reason, person-to-person speech encounters tend to take many unexpected turns and twists. Matters which you assumed would be understood immediately prove difficult to comprehend; points on which you anticipate no resistance are rejected out of hand or are refuted strongly. In addition, interpersonal interchanges have a way of wandering from the original topic and moving into areas that were not at all foreseen.

Some persons, seemingly blind to these possibilities, plow ahead minute after minute with comments or arguments they have prepared in advance. As a result, their remarks are often irrelevant and contribute little, if anything, to advancing the interaction or enriching its contents. When speaking with another individual, be flexible in your approach. Of course, if the conversation is to be an especially important one, settle in your own mind on the points you wish to make and even on a tentative order in which you might present them. But once the interchange has begun, be ready to adjust your plans to the situation *as it develops*. In this way, you will be able to keep the "ball" of conversation passing back and forth in a lively fashion, and you will be sure that what you say bears on the point under consideration.

Negotiate Differences

Healthy interpersonal relationships cannot be built on a foundation of submerged disagreements or smoldering resentments. When differences arise, instead of pretending they do not exist, usually you should bring them into the open and face them frankly. Often a difference can be settled readily and amicably if the issues are laid out and examined. Even if it cannot, however, it is still better to know where the other person stands and to agree to differ rather than to let buried misunderstandings or disagreements impair the future progress of the conversation.

Be a Good Listener

In order to speak to the point and carry the conversation toward a satisfying conclusion, you must listen carefully to what your co-communicator is saying.* Do not assume that when he speaks you can relax your attention or spend

---

*For a further discussion of listening, see pp. 447–453.

the time preparing a remark of your own. Concentrate on the ideas he is expressing, evaluate their substance and worth, and relate them to the matter under consideration. Then frame your own response accordingly. Two persons, no matter how profound each may be in his own right, cannot carry on a productive interchange unless each listens sharingly and attentively to the other.

Balance the Desire to Control with the Willingness to Be Controlled

As we have already emphasized in various ways, effective interpersonal communication is essentially a cooperative enterprise in which the interactants are more interested in maintaining a healthy and continuing relationship than in enhancing their own egos or asserting their own superiority.

Being cooperative does not mean giving in to one's co-communicator on every point or violating one's own convictions simply for the sake of being agreeable. It does, however, mean a willingness *to share* control of the direction the conversation takes and the conclusion that it reaches. You cannot be a dictator, determining the content and focus of the discussion down to the last detail. Be willing—even eager—to concede control of the interchange to your partner when considering matters on which he obviously is better informed than you are or when his suggestions seem more practical than yours. Admit frankly mistakes in your own facts or reasoning when they are pointed out to you. Remember that there is little use in attempting to exchange ideas with another person if you insist upon dominating every aspect of the conversation.

Maximize Rewards: Minimize Costs

Because a healthy interpersonal relationship is a transactional, give-and-take affair, it always involves some "costs" or sacrifices on the part of both transactors. Neither can always have his own way on every issue, point, or preference. Each must compromise and adjust—must accommodate his desires and objectives to the wishes of his partner. When, however, the "costs" of the relationship become greater than the rewards, when one must give up or concede more than he gains, his natural and understandable tendency is to break off the transaction, seek a new partner, or "go it alone."

The rewards growing out of interpersonal communication are many and varied. By talking with another individual, for example, you may acquire interesting information, be mentally stimulated, gain status, profit financially, or simply enjoy the pleasures of human companionship. In order to promote a mutually satisfying interaction and thus sustain the relationship, see to it that the other person is being similarly rewarded. Do what you can to maximize *his* gains and to reduce the costs he must bear to attain them. If you study to make yourself an interesting, well-informed, warm, and thoughtful person, this task should not be too difficult.

Search Out the Other Person's "Hidden Agenda"

In many instances, there will be a difference between your co-conversant's actions and his intentions, between what he says or does and what he thinks, between what appear to be and what actually are his motives. When you suspect this to be the case, take time to dig beneath surface appearances and try to find out what his actual feelings and intentions are. When he supplies detailed information on a point at issue, is his real aim to share useful knowledge or to display his own brilliance? When he concedes a point, is it because he really agrees or because he is merely trying to be congenial? Are his compliments genuine or feigned? Is he engaging in social conversation not for its own sake, but as a way of softening you up for a "sales pitch"? Fair and objective answers to such questions are important if you are to assess accurately the progress and/or outcome of a dyadic encounter.

Of course, you must not view everything your co-communicator says or does with skepticism or suspicion. Respect his integrity, but try always to *understand* the real motives prompting his behavior. Not all hidden motives are selfish ones, by any means. Sometimes a person who professes to come to you on a matter of business or who seeks your aid on an assignment is only trying to be friendly, and uses this device as a means of striking up a relationship. Or a person who persists in talking in a light and trivial way about a matter you regard as serious may actually be trying to get your mind off your troubles. Whether the other person is acting selfishly or altruistically, however, unless you divine his true motives you can hardly hope to carry on a productive conversation with him. Strive, therefore, to discover his real purposes and priorities—his "hidden agenda"—and to react accordingly. In this way, you will make your meeting with him both more honest and more useful.

Reduce Your Own Defensiveness

It is natural for all of us to protect our own ego and to resent unjustified attacks upon it. Such self-protectiveness is not, however, to be confused with the sort of excessive sensitivity or defensiveness which leads an individual to interpret every comment by a co-conversant as in some way a slur or personal put-down. When talking with another person, get your mind off yourself. Do not, as the old saying goes, "carry a chip on your shoulder." If you set out to look for slights and deprecations every time you converse with someone else, sooner or later you will almost certainly find them. Productive interaction in interpersonal communication depends in large part upon keeping an objective attitude not only toward the subject you are discussing and the person you are discussing it with, but also toward yourself.

Respect and Trust the Other Person

Any person who is worth talking with is deserving of trust and respect. Much of what we have just said, both about building rapport and maintaining interaction in an interpersonal situation, comes down to this simple rule: *Understand, respect, and trust your partner; treat him as you wish him to treat you.* Respect your partner's right to speak up in behalf of what he believes. Respect his feelings and sensibilities. Assume him to be a person of integrity and good will, and give him credit for high motives. Sometimes, of course, you will be deceived and your assumptions proved wrong. To start with suspicion and distrust, however, is to get the relationship off on the wrong foot—to condemn it to failure without giving it a fair chance to succeed.

An age-old principle governing speech communication is that people will "come back" to you in just about the same way you "go out" to them. Instead of approaching the other person with suspicion and distrust, approach him openly and with confidence. Be genuine yourself and expect him to be the same. You will be surprised how often your respect and trust are merited. When two people meet and converse on these grounds, the chances are strong that rapport will be established, that an active interchange of ideas and values will ensue, and that the interaction will prove helpful as well as pleasant.

Terminating the Transaction

The third stage in an interpersonal communication encounter is its termination or conclusion. Here, too, certain principles and guidelines should be observed: (1) know when to terminate the conversation; (2) observe the appropriate conventions; (3) summarize the progress and outcomes; and (4) arrange for the next encounter.

Know When to Terminate the Conversation

Even the most interesting interchange between two people can become tiresome if continued for too long. It is surprising how many persons who are fascinating conversationalists in every other respect never seem to know when to stop talking—when to break off the interaction, or to rise, thank their host or hostess, and depart. Develop a sense of *timing*. Sense when the business of an interpersonal interchange has been completed or when your partner begins to tire, and excuse yourself at this point. By continuing longer you may lose all you have gained in the direction of understanding, persuading, or building and maintaining good will.

Observe the Appropriate Conventions

Observing the appropriate conventions is important not only when opening a dyadic speech encounter, but also when closing it. You are expected, of course, to thank your host or hostess at the end of a social event or to thank the individual who has granted you a business or professional interview. Similarly, it is considered good form when breaking off a conversation to tell the other person you have enjoyed talking with him. To ignore these and similar conventions is to display poor manners and run the risk of undoing any progress you may have made or benefit you may have achieved earlier.

Summarize the Progress and Outcomes

If a conversation has for its purpose reaching an agreement or settling upon a course of action, generally you and your co-conversant should take a few moments at its close to summarize the points on which you have reached agreement or to review the unresolved differences. This helps to assure both of you that you understand matters in the same way; and if action is required, both of you will know exactly what to do in carrying it out.

Arrange for the Next Encounter

If two persons who meet to solve a problem or review a situation are unable to conclude their business at a single encounter, they should not separate before agreeing as to when and where they will meet again. They should also determine, at least in a general way, how they will proceed at their next meeting. By reaching an agreement on future proceedings, the two not only make the subsequent meeting potentially more efficient, but each one will also be able to plan his contributions to the next interaction in a more direct and purposeful manner.

INTERVIEWS

The term *interview* is commonly used to refer to a specific type of interpersonal speech communication in which two persons *pre-arrange* an encounter and in which at least one of the two has a certain serious and preconceived purpose and seeks to achieve that purpose by eliciting appropriate verbal responses from the other.[1] Because at least one of the two individuals (and, often, both) has this serious, preconceived, specific purpose, interviews differ from random, unstructured "social conversations" where, as a rule, congeniality and enjoyment are the primary ends.

Interviews serve a variety of purposes and are widely used in such interpersonally communicative activities as selling, counseling, problem solving, polling of public opinion, and providing medical diagnosis and psychiatric therapy. Here, as we indicated at the beginning of the chapter, we shall be concerned with only two of the most important and basic types: (1) the *information-seeking interview* and (2) the *job-seeking interview*. In the first, we shall assume that you are acting only as interviewer; and, in the second, we presuppose the desirability of your being familiar with the roles and requisites of *both* interviewer and applicant in order to attain a fuller understanding of the transactional nature of the interview process.

THE INFORMATION-SEEKING INTERVIEW

A well-managed information-seeking interview normally involves seven separate but related tasks:

1. Selecting the informant.
2. Obtaining the informant's cooperation.
3. Learning about the informant.
4. Developing a plan or procedure.
5. Formulating specific questions and tactics.
6. Conducting the interview.
7. Interpreting and evaluating the results.*

Selecting the Informant

Although selecting the informant—the person from whom information is to be sought—may at first appear to be a simple matter, this is not always the case. If, for example, your subject is a controversial one and you intend to interview only one informant, you must try to choose someone who will approach the subject with reasonable objectivity and be able to give you all relevant points of

---

*Compare these steps with those found in Raymond L. Gorden, Interviewing: Strategy, Techniques, and Tactics (Homewood, Ill.: Dorsey Press, 1969), pp. 42–48.

view concerning it. If you plan to gather the necessary information from a large number of individuals, you should select them at random or should choose those most likely to represent all prevailing shades of opinion. In every instance, pick your informant or informants with care. Remember that the data you gather will be no more reliable than the persons with whom you talk.

Obtaining the Informant's Cooperation

If you wish to interview a busy or important individual, usually you will get better results if you get in touch with him in advance. Write or telephone for an appointment, telling him your purpose and explaining why you think he can supply you with the information you desire. Promise to keep his identity confidential if he wants you to do so; and if you would like to tape all or a part of the conversation, be sure to get his permission. Promise also that, if he so desires, you will let him check over any written materials in which you quote him directly.

If the person or persons you wish to interview are employed by someone higher up or are subject to the authority of another person, be sure to take the steps necessary to obtain that individual's permission before proceeding. For instance, if you want to interview the clerks and checkout girls in a supermarket, don't begin until you have cleared your plan and procedure with the manager and have his authorization. Don't interview the members of a college class about their attitudes toward a given course and teacher unless that teacher has agreed to let you do so.

Learning About the Informant

Between the time you obtain permission to conduct an interview and the time the interview actually takes place, find out as much as you can about the person you will be talking with. What is his current position? What positions or jobs has he previously held? What books or articles has he written? Has he been interviewed on this same subject or similar ones before? What opinions has he expressed on the subject? Information gained from these questions will help you frame more pertinent and penetrating questions and will also help you interpret and evaluate the responses you receive. In addition, since most persons are gratified when others know of their views and accomplishments, the fact that you have such knowledge and that you let it surface during the course of the interview may cause your informant to take a greater interest in your project and to give your inquiries more than ordinary attention.

Developing a Plan or Procedure

An interview, like any other important speech transaction, requires planning and preparation. To enter upon it unprepared will in most instances waste the time of your informant and greatly reduce the profit that you yourself derive.

Clarifying and Focusing Your Purpose

Before you can make specific plans for an interview, you must get clearly in mind the precise purpose you wish to achieve as a result of the encounter. *What is it that you want to know?* Do you wish to learn more about the early history and development of the subject? About its economic or social aspects? Or about its moral and ethical implications? Are you interested in digging out new facts or do you want to learn your informant's interpretation of facts you already know? One of the least productive ways to approach an expert on any matter is with the vague request that he tell you what he knows or thinks about a subject. As a general rule, when you are asking for information, keep your questions simple, direct, and *very specific*. If the person is, indeed, an "expert," he will know so much and will have thought about it for so long that unless your questions are well-framed and centered directly on the point, he will not know where to begin. Only when a definite and focused purpose is clear in your own mind can you hope to elicit from your informant those facts and judgments which will be of maximum use to you.

Choosing the Format of the Interview

With your specific purpose clarified and information about your informant carefully gathered, you are ready to choose the format you will follow in conducting the interview itself.* Although many variations are possible, the formats from which you may select are basically these: (1) the structured interview, (2) the non-structured interview, and (3) the guided interview.

In the *structured interview*, each of the questions you wish to ask and the exact sequence in which you will ask them are determined in advance. Usually, the questions are written out word for word, and you read them to the informant, noting his responses in spaces provided for this purpose.

The *non-structured interview*, though also carefully planned and aimed at achieving a specific purpose, is more flexible, allowing you to word your questions as you go along and to determine the most productive order in which to ask them during the course of the interaction.

*In this connection, see Stephen A. Richardson, Barbara Snell Dohrenwend, and David Klein, Interviewing: Its Forms and Functions (New York: Basic Books, Inc., Publishers, 1965), pp. 32–55.

The *guided interview* strikes a balance between the structured and the non-structured formats. Although most or all of the questions may be worded and arranged in a preferred sequence, the communicative climate is somewhat less formal and more relaxed, and you feel free to depart from your plan in order to follow up on interesting points evolving unexpectedly out of the interaction, or to skip matters you had planned to bring up but on which your informant is reluctant to talk.

Because the structured interview, with its precisely worded and systematically arranged questions, provides a fixed and constant stimulus, it is generally regarded as most useful in those situations where you are attempting to measure differences in background or attitudes among a heterogeneous group of people. The non-structured and guided interviews, on the other hand, because of the flexibility they allow both to the questioner and the informant, provide excellent opportunities for drawing out an individual when you are seeking additional information or points of view on a given subject.

Choose the interview format you will follow by considering its suitability to the purpose you wish to achieve, the subject you are investigating, and the qualifications and preferences of the informant. The format preferred by the informant (if that information can be ascertained) should, of course, weigh heavily in the choice of the procedure to be followed. In any case, however, always have a definite format in mind before you begin an interview and stay with that arrangement until you have good reason to abandon it.

Formulating Specific Questions and Tactics

If you plan to conduct a structured interview, your questions—as we have already said—will probably be written out word for word and their sequence definitely fixed in advance. Even when using the more flexible non-structured and guided formats, however, you will find it important to settle on the principal questions you wish to raise and to determine at least tentatively the order in which they might best be introduced. In doing this, see to it that your questions are clear, specific, and to the point, and that the majority of them are of the "open" rather than the "closed" variety. Plan to begin the interview with questions that are likely to arouse the interest of the informant and stimulate him to start talking freely. Save for last the questions that probe into difficult or sensitive matters. Finally, think over your plan again to make certain that any question which logically grows out of a previous answer or which assumes a certain set of facts will not be asked until the proper groundwork has been laid.*

---

*For further discussions of the question-answer process in the interview situation, see Robert D. Brooks, Speech Communication (Dubuque, Iowa: Wm. C. Brown Company, Publishers, 1971), pp. 129–134; W. V. D. Bingham, B. V. Moore, and J. W. Gustad, How to Interview (New York: Harper & Row, Publishers, 1959), p. 74; and Stephen A. Richardson, Barbara Snell Dohrenwend, and David Klein, Interviewing: Its Forms and Functions (New York: Basic Books, Inc., Publishers, 1965), pp. 138–217.

Conducting the Interview

In conducting the interview itself, bear in mind the following "do's" and "don't's":*

DO

Be on Time. When a busy person does you the courtesy of agreeing to an interview, the least you can do is to appear at the appointed time. Remember that in supplying information you desire, he is helping you; you are not helping him.

Restate Your Purpose. Even though you already have told the informant your purpose in a prior letter or phone call, take a minute or two at the outset to remind him and also to make clear why you think he can be of help. This will strengthen the focus of the interview and direct the informant's attention to the areas you are most interested in exploring.

Observe Not Only "What" the Informant Says, but Also "How" He Says It. The tone of voice or inflectional pattern with which the informant makes a response may be highly revealing of his attitude on a given point—whether he regards it as important or unimportant, desirable or undesirable, etc. Changes in his facial expression and bodily posture provide similar cues. These kinds of *feedback*, as we emphasized in Chapter 1, are basic to all successful communicative interaction and must, therefore, be taken into careful account when you are trying to interpret an informant's comments and draw correct conclusions about him and the answers he is giving to your questions.

Move the Interview Ahead at a Lively Pace. Don't rush the informant, but—on the other hand—don't let the conversation drag or die. When one question has been answered to your satisfaction, move on to the next one without a long and awkward pause or undue shuffling of notes and papers. Preserve a businesslike manner at all times, avoiding side issues or wandering into matters totally unrelated to the topic you are exploring.

Respect Your Informant's Time. When you have concluded the last of the questions you wish to ask, terminate the interview and depart. To prolong the interaction unduly is to run the needless risk of sinking into trivial matters or treading ground you already have covered.

Compare the advice given here with that found in John W. Keltner, Interpersonal Speech Communication (Belmont, Calif.: Wadsworth Publishing Company, Inc., 1970), pp. 276–280; and Raymond L. Gorden, Interviewing: Strategy, Techniques, and Tactics (Homewood, Ill.: Dorsey Press, 1969), pp. 251–308.

Terminate the Interview with Thanks. Don't forget to thank your informant as you depart. Also assure him once again that you will not reveal anything he has told you in confidence and that, if he desires, you will give him an opportunity to approve of any passages in which you quote him directly.

Make a Record of What Transpired. Either during the course of the interview or immediately thereafter, when everything the informant said is still fresh in your mind, make a record of his remarks. Very probably, you will be surprised to discover how much and how easily you can forget after only a short period of time. The able interviewer cannot afford to forget.

DON'T

Don't Request an Interview Until You Already Know a Good Deal About the Subject. The more you know about a subject, the more intelligent and provocative your questions will be and the better you will be able to evaluate your informant's responses. As a rule, an interview should not be scheduled until you already are well along with your other research into a topic. It never should be used as a way of avoiding the thorough examination of printed sources or of the gathering of information by firsthand observation.

Don't Parade Your Own Knowledge of the Subject. Your purpose in requesting an interview is to get information from the respondent, not to give it. Demonstrate your knowledge of the subject by asking intelligent questions, but do not use the encounter as an excuse for "showing off" your own brilliance.

Don't Reveal Your Doubts or Disagreements in Point of View. If your informant says something with which you disagree or which you believe to be factually wrong, keep your feelings to yourself. Do not frown, shake your head, or look skeptical. Above all, do not argue with him about the matter. Remember that your purpose is to get your informant's view of the subject—not to expound or defend your own. You can discount a dubious opinion or check up on a doubted fact later. During the interview itself, maintain a courteous and attentive attitude.

Interpreting and Evaluating the Results

The final step in an information-seeking interview—and one which takes place after you have left your informant—consists of *interpreting* and *evaluating* what he has told you. To make the necessary interpretations and evaluations you may have to draw inferences and conclusions from data he has supplied. This may involve comparing his opinions with those expressed by other persons in order to discover similarities and differences. It may entail thinking back over the conversation to spot subtle evidences of bias or partisanship which went undetected during the interview itself. Sometimes it necessitates deciding how certain statements of fact are to be classified or categorized—the general heading or rubric under which they properly fall. In any event, do not consider your task complete until you have reviewed in your own mind all the informant has said and determined its meaning and worth as you understand them. To stop short of this final analysis often is to lose much of the value the interview might have for you or to carry away false and unfounded impressions of what you have been told.

THE JOB-SEEKING INTERVIEW

How well you acquit yourself in an interview with a prospective employer will, as a rule, be the key to success when you are applying for a job of any kind. Indeed, if the job under consideration is really important to you, in few situations in life will your communicative skills and interactional judgment be more significant or provide you with a more visible and immediate measure of their effectiveness. Few communicative encounters are likely to have a greater impact on your self-esteem and—oftentimes—on your working career.*

Frequently in the foregoing pages we have emphasized the *transactional* nature of the speech communication process, and in the job-getting interview we may witness the very essence of it. As Harry Walker Hepner points out in his *Psychology Applied to Life and Work:*

> The interview is an occasion where employer and applicant consider each other's mutual problems and interests. The applicant is not asking a favor nor is the employer granting a privilege. Each has something to give and each has needs which may or may not be of mutual advantage.[2]

Here, each party brings to the transaction something of value and urgency: the interviewer has a job-opening and is actively seeking a competent person to handle it; the applicant brings a belief that—by reason of his unique talents, training, competencies, and obvious desire—he is the person best qualified to take on that job. In the ensuing interchange, *job* and *desire for job* are carefully

---

See, for example, Harry Walker Hepner, Psychology Applied to Life and Work, 4th ed. (Englewood Cliffs, N.J.: Prentice-Hall, Inc., 1966), pp. 239–257, 301–321; Robert S. Goyer, W. Charles Redding, and John T. Rickey, Interviewing Principles and Techniques (Dubuque, Iowa: Wm. C. Brown Company, Publishers, 1968); Roger M. Bellows, Employment Psychology: The Interview (New York: Holt, Rinehart & Winston, Inc., 1954); and Walter Van Dyke Bingham and Bruce Victor Moore, How to Interview, 3rd rev. ed. (New York: Harper & Row, Publishers, 1941).

and strategically placed on the "bargaining table" in the hope that a true transaction will be achieved.

The likelihood of satisfactorily negotiating such a transaction can be appreciably enhanced, we believe, by looking analytically at the purposes and process phases of the employment interview and at the roles and tasks of the transactors — both applicant and interviewer. In so doing, we shall also be looking at the criteria by which the latter will judge the potentialities of the former, at some of the useful procedures and behaviors by which both may help to guide the course of the interaction.

Communicative Purposes of the Job-Seeking Interview

On relatively rare occasions, an employer will have determined in advance that a particular person is eminently well qualified to fill a position, and he will use the interview to try to persuade that person to accept his offer of employment. More commonly, however, the direction is reversed; and the applicant tries to induce the employer to hire him. From this we might conclude that the basic and pervasive purpose of the job-seeking interview is *to persuade.* We must be careful, however, that this assumption does not lead us into mistaken notions or limit our view. By some definitions of this type of interview, the applicant is considered to have little control over the direction the interaction takes, but must — for the most part — content himself with answering questions and supplying only the information called for. He must "score his points" only as the opportunity arises, and must make a favorable impression without being too aggressive or seeming to take the initiative away from the interviewer.

To view the employment interview only in this way, however, is not to look at it as *transaction*, as we have been defining it. If the interaction is to be truly transactive, there must be genuine give-and-take, a frequent alternation of speaker/listener roles, *a collaborative search for mutual benefit.* Much of this search must be something other than persuasive, and at no time should it be allowed to become one-sided or manipulative. In addition to the obvious persuasive intent, as the transaction process moves through successive stages both interviewer and applicant will want *to inform* and *to be informed, to appraise* each other as well as the unfolding circumstances that have drawn them together. They will try *to predict* the effect of a particular remark or the way in which a disclosure will affect the thinking and judgment of the other. Throughout they will be trying by means of interpersonal communication *to investigate, to explore, to probe, to negotiate,* and — finally — *to actuate.*

Process Phases of the Job Interview

Closely akin to the foregoing purposes and growing out of them are certain "process phases" which further help to mark the progression of the interaction. Earlier in this chapter we noted that all interpersonal communication develops through three steps or phases: (1) establishing rapport, (2) sustaining the interaction, and (3) terminating it. In the more structured job-seeking interview, some interviewers see only two: appraising and hiring-or-not hiring. For our considerations here, however, an understanding of what goes on in an employment interview can be made clearer if we view the process as having *five* phases or steps, namely:

1. Initiate   2. Investigate   3. Negotiate   4. Actuate   5. Terminate

Of course, we do not mean to imply that all interviews can be cleanly and neatly divided into these five phases. There will be some overlapping and, at times, even occasional repetition. In general, however, they can serve usefully to illuminate the process as a whole.

Initiation

In the first of these phases, of course, the interactants meet, exchange greetings, introduce themselves, and observe the courtesies characteristic of our culture. They try to "break the ice," to reduce the necessarily formal atmosphere somewhat, to "personalize" it, to put each other at ease. In a word, they *initiate* the interaction.

Investigation

As the interviewer and the applicant endeavor to sustain and advance the interaction, they move into an *investigative* phase. They begin to "feel each other out," to determine what the other is like. They attempt to find out what interests the other, how quickly or strongly he reacts to certain stimulus-statements. They ask and answer questions—tentatively at first, and then with increasing confidence and openness. They try to discover topics that may be pursued "safely" and profitably, to detect promising lines of inquiry on which the other is likely to converse freely. The applicant senses what the interviewer is after and tries to provide appropriate responses.

The spirit of inquiry and the question-and-answer mode will, of course, continue throughout the interview. In the investigative phase, however, more and more of the discourse becomes idea-oriented because ideas, after all, are a major commodity in this transaction. The relevant and potentially productive ideas and assets of the applicant emerge. Also emerging should be some information concerning the history, nature, and goals of the employer's enterprise. The applicant will be trying to investigate the dimensions of the available job and its potentialities and problems as these are known and disclosable by the interviewer (although the latter's strategy may be to deal later with such matters). Understandably, this phase is often the longest and most informative portion of the interview.

During the investigative phase of the process, both transactors should strive to the greatest extent possible for a *mutual understanding* as to meanings, goals, work objectives, points of view, preferences, etc. If pertinent disclosures have not yet been made, they should be asked for; if relevant points are not yet clear, clarification should be sought. Typical of this process phase are such questions as: "Tell me a little more about your idea of . . ." "Going back to your earlier point about initiative . . ." "I'm not quite sure what you mean by . . . ." In sum, both parties to the transaction should feel that each has "investigated" the other sufficiently and on a reasonably forthright basis. Note that as yet there is no offer or commitment by either person. If, as the investigative phase nears it evident conclusion, either party—on the basis of his inquiries—has reason to feel that the job should not be offered or, if offered, should be refused, the interview should be terminated here.

Negotiation

If, however, both interviewer and applicant feel that the employment goal is possible and mutually attractive and therefore desire to sustain the interaction, the process moves into the *negotiative* phase. Here the pace tends to quicken; the focus of the interaction sharpens noticeably.

If the job is an unusually important one or if the employment conditions and remunerations are more than ordinarily complex, the negotiation may have to be lengthy and detailed. Usually, however, the interviewer describes the more or less exact nature of the job and explains and interprets—within broad outlines at least—the employer's policies, procedures, pay schedules, fringe benefits, etc., pertinent to it. The interactants then proceed to negotiate a congruent understanding of the import and specific application of these matters. If more information is needed, it is requested. If either has any doubts or reservations about any item, these should be brought out, considered, and—if possible—resolved and cleared up. In brief, the transactive *appraisal* of applicant, job, and employer should be completed insofar as that is achievable within the interview setting.

At this point, the interviewer—if he has not done so earlier—usually gives some explicit indication to the applicant that his qualifications for the job seem more or less satisfactory (if that is indeed the case) and that the company quite possibly *may* be interested in him. The applicant, for his part, will give some indication to the interviewer that he has some interest in the job as outlined (but not yet offered), or that he really is not interested, or that he might be interested subject to certain conditions. Especially note, however, that the interviewer has as yet made no actual job-offer, nor has the applicant made a definite commitment one way or the other. This is the careful "dance of the tentative," the "might-or-might-not." The process of feeling out the other interactant, characteristic of the early investigative phase, comes back into play; but now its purposive thrust is narrower and more intensely focused.

Actuation

Clearly now the interaction stands at the climactic moment. A decision must be *made*, and it must be *actuated*. To hire or not to hire, to accept or not accept—this is the crux. Customarily, the interviewer makes the move. If he doesn't, however, and if the investigative phase is clearly at an end, the applicant may decide to venture a carefully phrased question, something like: "I've been wondering . . . if it turns out that you're interested in my possibilities for the job, when would you want me to start work?" This tactic involves an obvious risk, of course; but it is almost sure to evoke a response from the interviewer; and if it is a positive one, it may edge him toward a specific overture.

Usually, however, the applicant may expect the interviewer to take the initiative. If he intends to hire and has the power to do so, he may say something like: "Well, I think we've covered just about everything. The job is yours if you want it." The applicant may say, in effect, "Great! When do I start?"

Frequently, however, in actual practice, a flat offer and acceptance are not consummated in an interview of this kind. Typically, the outcome may take one of three turns: (1) *outright employment or rejection,* (2) *referral to another person* for a second or follow-up interview, or (3) *deferral or postponement* of a final offer or acceptance until a designated future date.

Quite often, for example, after a tentative offer has been extended and the applicant has tentatively indicated his satisfaction with it, the interviewer may say, in substance: "I like very much what I have seen and heard so far. But if we agree you're to have the job and if you agree to take it, you'll be working closely with the manager of Department X, Ms. Soandso. I'd like you to meet and talk with her before we make a final decision."

Or, again, he may say, "A number of applicants are interested in this job, of course, and I've promised to talk with them, too. I think, therefore, we'll have to defer making a final choice until Friday of next week." Regardless, however, of whether the decision at *this* time is acceptance, referral, deferral, or rejection, the actuative stage of the interview is finished, and the process now moves into its concluding phase.

Termination

In the terminating phase of the interaction, the pair observe the conventional courtesies of thanking each other, the applicant for the opportunity and consideration given by the interviewer, the interviewer for the interest, information, and time given by the applicant. If the ultimate decision has been referred to another, then there should be a clear and mutual understanding as to the time and place for the next interview, with whom it will be, etc. If the decision has been deferred, there should be an expressed understanding as to when it is likely to be forthcoming, where, and from what source. If the decision has been a definite "no hire," then the good-byes are of course truly terminative.

Remember, however, that although this terminating phase is typically brief and may sometimes appear to be anticlimactic, do not undervalue its importance. The effects of interview transactions, like the effects of other speech communications, have a way of lasting far beyond the moment of their immediate conclusion. If the interaction can be made to end on an air of friendliness, good will, and mutual respect, there is always a chance that there may in the future be other openings for which the applicant may be considered or for which he may wish to re-apply.

As you may have gathered from this brief overview of the process phases of the job-seeking interview, the lines dividing them cannot be sharply drawn. Nor are they mutually exclusive. Some of the phases, as we have noted, may *re-occur* at various points within the interaction as a whole. Moreover, in a given interview the interaction may be concentrated on only one or two of them; and there will also be interviews in which certain of the phases are not discernible at all. Essentially, however, we believe the process can usefully be viewed as we have outlined it and as it is summarized in the diagram below.

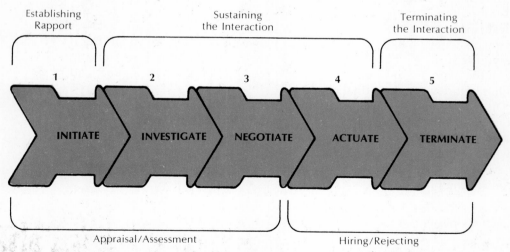

Figure 1. PROCESS PHASES OF THE JOB-SEEKING INTERVIEW

Regardless of how you as applicant or interviewer prefer to see the structure of the interview, what is really important is that you view it as a *process—a transactive* process. On pages 76–86 you will find a "Sample Transcript" of a job-seeking interview. Study it carefully, noting especially the five phases described above and the ways in which they tend to shape and influence the ongoing, transactional nature of the interview.

Types of Questions Useful to the Interview Process

The heavily investigative nature of the job-seeking interview means that much of it must be spent in asking and answering questions. Most authorities on this subject refer in one way or another to the following types: (1) closed questions, (2) open or open-end questions, (3) pin-it-down questions, (4) probe-and-prompt questions, (5) leading questions, and (6) trick-and-trap questions.

The *trick question* no doubt has its uses in courtroom interrogation; but within the transactive frame of the employment interview, it is obviously inappropriate and should be avoided. The *leading question*, since it answers itself and obviously "leads" the respondent to parrot information already known both to him and to the interrogator, merely *verifies*. It is not truly transactional and is little used in the employment interview. "You can drive a car, I assume?" "You are married and have three children, right?"

The *closed question*, as we mentioned earlier, calls for yes-or-no answers or short, succinct responses. "How old are you?" "Did you vote in the last election?" Information thus derived often is necessary to the interaction, but usually does little to move it forward. Indeed, such questions tend to be conversation-stoppers.

A much more useful and used type is the *open-end question* which, as we have also noted, typically calls for broadly inclusive statements, assertions, narrations, etc. Such responses are often thoughtful and detailed, and they are likely to give the applicant freest rein to get his own ideas, thinking, preferences, and self-assessment out into the open. These are the conversation-starters and are extremely useful in the investigative phase of the interview especially. "Tell me your ideas about employee responsibility to the employer, and vice versa."

The *pin-it-down question* calls for a more specific answer, one that is fairly detailed, but carefully focused. "You seem to have a good, overall picture of the process. Now describe the specific steps involved—in one-two-three order, please." Frequently, this type of inquiry may be used as a follow-up to an open-end question to which the response may have been somewhat *too* broad or general.

As a result of the information flowing from the response to an open-end or the pin-down query, the interviewer may find himself intrigued by the topic and want to pursue a particular facet of it or explore it further. The *probe-and-prompt type of question* will be useful in such circumstances. "A few moments ago you mentioned in passing that your supervisor on a former job was the most 'interesting' person you had ever worked with. Interesting in what way?" Or "I think you summed up pretty well the kind of supervisor you like. Now tell me about some supervisors you haven't liked." A variation is the "nudge" question which signals the speaker merely that the listener is interested and to keep on talking. "How's that?" "And so?" "Ummm . . . I see." "Yes?" "How do you mean?"

The Interviewer

Unless you are planning to become a professional interviewer, the chances are high that in your working lifetime, your role will almost always be that of applicant. And almost invariably, of course, you will be an applicant *before* you are an interviewer. These "priorities" notwithstanding, and because we prefer the position that all interpersonal communication must take into close consideration the *other* person's background, knowledge, purposes, sensitivities, biases, etc., we shall consider the roles and requisites of *both interviewer and applicant*. To begin, we will assume that you are the interviewer and that what we have to say about that role will, at the same time, provide information and insights useful to you as an applicant.

A Profile of the Effective Interviewer

Since the interviewer has the job-opening and seeks applicants for it, he assumes primary responsibility for the handling of the interview. In effect, he is the "host," and the initiative and authority are his unless or until he chooses to share or relinquish them. The good interviewer, therefore, tries to put the applicant at ease, takes the initiative in establishing and maintaining rapport, and sees to it that the interaction moves steadily in a mutually productive direction. He does not try to dominate or manipulate; he realizes that each interactant has something valuable to offer the other and that true transaction cannot be one-sided. He provides ample opportunities for the applicant to talk and to demonstrate that he knows how to *think* as well as how to *do*.

The effective interviewer understands quite fully the nature of the work the applicant will be doing if he is hired. He therefore centers his communicative efforts on (*a*) trying to ascertain the applicant's probable strengths and weaknesses in terms of that job and (*b*) trying to *predict* whether the applicant will fit in socially and emotionally with the job situation and the other workers in it. These considerations motivate most of the questions he will ask — questions that will be thoughtfully and considerately phrased and free of efforts to trick, upset, or embarrass the applicant. While he will be paying close attention to the applicant's voice, "body English," and physical appearance, he will read resultant clues to ability and adjustability with an objective eye and an awareness of his own biases.

Finally, the good interviewer gives sufficient information about the job to enable the applicant to make a sensible decision as to whether or not he *wants* it. He scrupulously avoids questions and comments that might mislead the applicant into thinking he is being hired when he is not. He keeps the transaction open until both he and the applicant sense that it's time to close it. Throughout, he tries to be honest and forthright with the applicant; and if from his investigation, he concludes that he isn't talking to the "right" person for the job, he tells the applicant so, as tactfully as possible, but with the necessary firmness and forthrightness.

Criteria by Which the Interviewer May Judge the Applicant

Some years ago, the psychologist Ralph Wagner examined a large number of standard forms used in employment interviews. Among the ninety-seven items he isolated as a result of this study, far and away the most frequent was the applicant's *appearance*. There followed in order *manner, intelligence*, and *judgment*. Grouped in fifth position—and equally weighted—were *alertness, ability to get along with others, language usage*, and *leadership*.[3]

An Employment Evaluation Form for Interviewers developed by The Psychological Corporation recommends judging the applicant on the seven points of *experience, training, manner and appearance, sociability or teamwork, emotional stability, maturity*, and *leadership*.* These criteria, clearly, must be of considerable concern to both interviewer *and* applicant; and while the interaction proceeds, the interviewer will be asking *himself* a number of "silent" questions in order to satisfy that concern.

In their standard work, *How to Interview*, Walter Van Dyke Bingham and Bruce Victor Moore put a specific list of judgmental criteria into interrogative form:

1. How does [the applicant's] appearance impress you, especially his facial expression, physique, carriage, and neatness?
2. How responsive is he toward the interviewer?
3. How intelligent and mentally alert do you think he is?
4. Does he appear to have good health?

---

*See Roger A. Fear and Byron Jordan, Employee Evaluation Manual for Interviewers (New York: The Psychological Corporation, 1943); C. Harold Stone and William E. Kendall, Effective Personnel Selection Procedures (Englewood Cliffs, N.J.: Prentice-Hall, Inc., 1956), pp. 216–219.

5. Has he an analytical mind? Does he get to the root of matters quickly?
6. Is he frank and straightforward? What impressions does he give you as to his character and integrity?
7. How well informed is he in his field of specialization?
8. Does he give evidence of initiative? Does he originate ideas?
9. Has he a good command of language? Does he speak good English?
10. Is he decisive? Does he know his own mind?
11. Does he understand the significance of our project and the social philosophy behind it?
12. Is he in sympathy with our objectives?[4]

The Bingham/Moore criteria may be usefully enlarged by adding such questions as the following:

Has this applicant obviously made some attempt to familiarize himself with our company?

Has he apparently made any study of our procedures in order to familiarize himself with what goes on in our business?

Do his remarks and responses reveal an awareness of the problems which typify our enterprise, and does he make any suggestions or advance any ideas that indicate that he might be able to help us to solve a problem?

Has he studied our service or product? Does he appear to have any ideas as to *why* it sells—or how it might be made to sell better?

Do this applicant's remarks, ideas, etc., suggest that he's taken the trouble to read relevant trade or professional journals, textbooks, manuals, and news stories?

Does he know clearly and specifically *what he wants to do* in terms of one job in particular and in his career as a whole?

Why does he *want* the job? The money—mainly? Because he thinks our field is somehow "glamorous"? Because he knows somebody else who works here? Or because, *primarily*, he sees it as a challenge and a chance to learn and advance in a field he really likes and enjoys?

How friendly is he—really? Does he appear to like people? To tolerate them? To ignore them if possible?

How well is this applicant likely to get along with the people he would be working with?

How well, probably, can this applicant get along with persons of the opposite sex? With members of various minority groups?

Do his words and actions reflect a genuine *sincerity?* Or is he "faking it" and giving me answers and attitudes he supposes I'm looking for?

Does he tend to make unsupported assertions, or does he back up his statements with facts, figures, etc.?

Are this person's reactions to problems and obstacles likely to be largely objective and analytical or mainly subjective and emotional?

What about his self-control? Does he tend to keep his feelings in check? Would he be likely to submerge his own preferences and judgments for the good of an idea, cause, or project even if it were not one that he had originated or was sponsoring?

Is there anything about this individual—anything at all—that sets him apart from others I've interviewed for this job? Or is he obviously just another run-of-the-mill job-hunter?

Obviously, certain qualities are more important in one line of work than in another, and we do not mean to imply that when you are interviewing an applicant for a particular job or position, you can expect him to rank at or near the top in each of criterial categories suggested by the foregoing "silent" questions. The traits, attitudes, and capabilities inherent in them do, however, *typify* those that many employers and their interviewers look for when evaluating an applicant and trying to predict his suitability for a job.

Specific Questions the Interviewer May Ask the Applicant

Some of the information you will need will be supplied on an application form or through correspondence with the applicant. Much of the necessary data, however, you will have to obtain in a face-to-face interview in which you ask the applicant a number of *direct, personal, probing questions* based largely on the criteria we have just considered. Some of your questions will, of course, deal with details of the applicant's background and training; others will be devised to remove doubts from your mind, and a few may be aimed at testing the applicant to see how he reacts in various kinds of stress situations. It is impossible, obviously, to list every question that, as an interviewer, you will want to ask or that, as an applicant, you might be called upon to answer. Frequently asked, however, during the interview are such questions as: *Why do you want the job for which you are applying? Why do you think you can help our company? Why did you leave your last job? (Or why do you want to change jobs?) What rank or salary would you expect? On what date could you begin work? How would you handle this situation or solve this problem?*[5]

In addition, you may want to inquire more closely into the applicant's education, family situation, early life, military service, hobbies, travel experiences, awareness of current issues, prior work experiences, and the like. For example:

Did you take any courses in high school or college that have any bearing on the job you want with us?

Did you ever have to write a report or a term paper? What was your subject? What grade did you get?

Did you take any "cinch" or "Mickey Mouse" courses? Why?

Did you ever try to sell anything? With what success?

Can you think of a person—parent, teacher, minister, or some other individual—whom you greatly admired? Why did you admire this person?

Have you talked with any of the people who work for us? Don't tell me who they are, but do tell me what you learned from them that might help you handle the job you're applying for here.

Do you personally use our product (or service)? Why or why not?

Do you have any ideas why other people do or do not use it?

Think for a moment, and then tell me what you believe to be the most successful thing you've ever done.

On the basis of what it contributed to you personally and to your success as a worker, what's the best job you ever had? Please tell me why— in detail.

All of us make mistakes from time to time. On your last job, did you make any mistakes that you think you can avoid making in future jobs?

Essentially, what we have tried to do here is to suggest the kinds of information the interviewer probably will be seeking. How ably, appropriately, and tactfully you are able to phrase your questions to the applicant will depend, naturally, upon the range of your experiences, the depth of your insights, and the extent of your interactive skills. In sum, as you can readily see, as an interviewer your task and required abilities include skillful questioning, a thorough knowledge of the job or position to be filled, a broad knowledge of your company's origins, policies, and employment practices, and an ability to interpret accurately both verbal and nonverbal messages given by the applicant.

The Applicant

Now that we've examined the concerns of the interviewer in the job-seeking situation, let's look next at the "other side of the table" and consider the *applicant* and some of *his* concerns.

In a study reported by Harry Walker Hepner in his *Psychology Applied to Life and Work,* one hundred college students and graduates who had applied for positions were asked to list pressing problems they had encountered before, during, and after their interviews.[6] The concerns of these applicants appeared to center around questions of *experience, truth-telling, self-presentation, salary, reasons for applying, job details, nervousness, judging the probable success of the interaction,* and its *results.* Some of these problems, of course, involved matters of *content,* but many of them had to do chiefly with strategic and presentational *timing* and *techniques.* Like the interviewer, the applicant will—as a result of the above concerns—doubtless have certain "silent," self-questions he will be asking himself, typical questions for which he should seek answers before, during, and after the interview.*

Typical Questions Which the Applicant Should Ask Himself

1. How can I best determine the type of approach to take with this interviewer?
2. How can I "sell" myself—my qualifications and capabilities?
3. Should I admit that I have no work experience and face the possibility of not being hired?
4. How do I answer, "What can you *do?*"
5. Without any experience, how can I convince a prospective employer of what I can do?
6. How can I answer, "Why did you choose this type of work?"
7. Should I talk freely and frankly about what I consider my abilities?
8. How can I best emphasize my scholastic achievements—since, at this time, that's really all I have?
9. How can I overcome the nervousness I'm almost sure I'll have before and during the interview?
10. What can I, as probably the younger and "lesser" party to the interview, do to help create a friendly, informal atmosphere?
11. While being interviewed, should I ask questions about the job until I thoroughly understand all that is involved?
12. Or should I wait until I get the job and am able to see for myself what's required of me?
13. Am I able to do, actually, what this job requires?

The twenty-five self-questions presented here are derived in part from the study reported by Hepner, but the list has been modified and expanded to include a number of questions based on the authors' own observations and experiences.

14. Will I find the work rewarding in other than a financial sense?
15. Will I fit in? Will I like the people I will be working with?
16. Am I sure—or making sure now—that I am aware of the difficulties and disadvantages of the job and am ready to cope with them?
17. How can I tell whether I'm making a good impression on the interviewer and giving him the "right" answers?
18. How can I tell that I'm getting accurate answers to the questions *I* am asking?
19. Should I try while being interviewed to determine what the job offers in terms of employee advancement and its probable rapidity?
20. What is the best way to answer, "What salary do you expect?"
21. How am I to know that I'm not asking too much or too little?
22. Or should I say, "Well, from my study of the pay rates in this field, the *range* for this type of job appears to be somewhere between $_____ and $_____. How well does that align with what you as an employer have in mind?"
23. During the interaction, should I attempt to introduce the names of persons who would recommend me?
24. At what point in the interview do I ask the interviewer, "Do I get the job?"
25. How can I judge the success of the interview?

Obviously there is no way to devise and standardize a complete and invariably appropriate list of such questions, and certainly there would be no way to provide full, firm, and individualized answers to such questions even if they could be devised. However, if you have considered carefully what we have said about the process phases of the job-seeking interview and have a clear understanding of the functions, aims, and expectations of an interviewer, then you have at least some notion of what the answers to certain of the foregoing questions should be and also, perhaps, how to generate useful answers to many of the others.

To gain further understanding of how you may best prepare for and present yourself in the employment interview, study the following well-established guidelines and carefully consider some of the traits and behaviors to be avoided.

Some Useful Guidelines for the Applicant

In general, your behavior before and during the job-seeking interview should be guided by the principles of productive interpersonal interaction described in the opening pages of this chapter. In addition, you should try to observe the following specific recommendations:

1. If you have not previously supplied a personal data sheet or filled out a job-application form, *bring a summary of your training and experience to the interview itself* so the prospective employer may study and use it for reference. Do not forget to include the names of three or four persons to whom he can write or telephone for recommendations.

2. If appropriate to the job-seeking circumstances, *also bring to the interview a sample of your work:* a drawing or design you have made, a report you have prepared, an article, term paper, or story you have written—something you have created. Leave these materials with the interviewer if he wishes to study them further.

3. In the initiatory and also in the early part of the investigative phase at least, *let the interviewer take the initiative, set the general tone and direction of the interaction, and draw you out in his own way.* He may be deciding not only whether to hire you, but also considering the department to which you might best be assigned, how well you compare with other employees in the same age-bracket, etc. For many good reasons unknown to you, he may lead the interaction into fields that seem to you remote from the business at hand and even prefer to do much of the talking himself.[7] Later, the balance of the interaction will undoubtedly shift and "equalize" in ways that will give you an opportunity to voice your questions and concerns.

4. Show a knowledge of the business or institution the employer represents. Be able to discuss its past history, its present condition, and its future prospects. Understand the philosophy by which it is guided and the policies to which it adheres.

5. Keep the interactive emphasis on what you can do for the employer, not what he can do for you. Inquire about working conditions, fringe benefits, vacations, and the like, but make it clear that you are more interested in doing a good job and in meriting the confidence he may place in you.

6. Don't oversell yourself by asserting that you are sure you can "do anything" the employer asks, or can solve any problem that arises. *Be confident, but modest.* In no way suggest that the job is beneath your abilities or that you are interested in it only because you can find nothing better.

7. Use good speech and correct grammar. *Be courteous.* Say "yes, sir" or "yes, ma'am." Look directly at the interviewer as you talk. Be poised and alert.

8. In those portions of the interview where the subject and context indicate that you should lead the conversation, tell the interviewer about yourself and point out those aspects of your training and experience that particularly qualify you for the job-opening. Then *ask intelligent questions about the nature of the work, compa-*

ny policy and procedures, and opportunities for advancement.[8] Many experienced interviewers believe they can tell more about a person by the questions he asks than from any other single source of information.

9. Do not become so interested in getting the job that you lose sight of your own best interests. During the course of the interaction, elicit from the interviewer the information and—to the greatest extent possible—the commitments you desire. Remember that any employment interview not only provides the employer with a chance to size you up, but it is also an opportunity for you to size up him and the institution he represents.[9]

Behaviors and Traits Tending to Negate Interaction

While the interviewer is trying to discover your suitability for the job-opening, he will be attempting to extract from your words and actions the maximum number of clues of both a positive and negative nature. A natural assumption he will make is that you will not *wittingly* say or do anything that will hinder or negate your chances. He will, therefore, be paying especially close attention to the nonverbal messages you send out, particularly those reflecting *carelessness, crudity, indifference, arrogance, belligerence, lack of awareness, evasiveness, self-pity*, and similarly unproductive and irritating demeanors.* Needless to say, you should avoid these pitfalls. In fact, avoid doing or saying anything that will irritate the interviewer and cause him to form a negative impression of you as a person.

A Profile of the Effective Applicant

In view of what we have been saying about the interviewing process, the interviewer, and the continuing concerns and objectives of the job-seeker, you should now have a fairly clear and well-enfleshed image of the ideal applicant and how you can function most effectively in that role. Indeed, it seems fitting to sum up our consideration of the job-seeking encounter by putting together a picture-profile. In brief, you are likely to be an effective applicant if:

You know the kind of work you want and can perform. You know *why* you want the job—what your short-range and long-range *goals* are. You know you cannot "sell" yourself and your qualifications unless you know what you have to offer.

For an analysis of these negative behaviors and traits and their effect on the job-interview, see Charles S. Goetzinger, "An Analysis of Irritating Factors in Initial Employment Interviews of Male College Graduates" (Ph.D. diss., Purdue University, 1959). Reported in William D. Brooks, Speech Communication (Dubuque, Iowa: Wm. C. Brown Company, Publishers, 1971), p. 139.

You are well informed. You have read books, papers, and trade or professional journals having to do with your vocation and career. You have studied your potential employer's organization, its scope and history. You are familiar with his product or service, his vital interests, and at least a few of his problems. You have talked with one or more of his sales representatives and with some of his customers.

You want to make a contribution to the organization you work for.

You know that ideas are a rare commodity, and so you have trained yourself to *think* and *analyze* as well as to *do.*

You are proud of your abilities and capabilities and eager to talk about them if invited to do so, but you are modest. You do not boast, overestimate yourself, or promise obviously impossible results.

You conceive of the interview as a transactional process, and you are alert and well prepared to work with the interviewer in moving it forward in positive, productive directions.

You are fully aware that the effective applicant must be able not only to give intelligent and knowledgeable answers, but must also ask sensible, information-gathering questions—about the job, company potential and policies, growth opportunities, pay scales, employee-evaluation frequency, fringe benefits, etc.

You have determined in advance of the interview some of the questions you will ask, and you have also planned two or three useful approaches you will take to your self-presentation when and as opportunities arise during the interaction.

You tell the truth about your background and qualifications even if your answers are disadvantageous to you and your cause.

You give careful attention to the clarity and intelligibility of your speech and language because so much of effective communication depends upon them.

You use good judgment about such matters as your personal appearance and appropriateness of dress, bodily cleanliness, neatness, and the conventional courtesies because you are aware that most people—including employers—give considerable weight to first impressions.

You know what the "going" wage and salary ranges are for the kind of work you will be doing. While you recognize that, at least until you have proved your worth, the employer is entitled to start you "low," you also recognize that you are entitled to have your performance and contribution re-evaluated on a reasonable and regular basis and to receive deserved remuneration accordingly.

You are open, sincere, honest, and friendly, conducting yourself always as you would in any polite and businesslike conversation.

Characterizing QUALITIES and CONDITIONS	DYADIC *person to person*	SMALL GROUP *all to all*	PUBLIC ADDRESS *one to many*	MASS COMMUNICATION *print and electronic; one or few to many*
Number of Persons	2			
Degree of Intimacy	High			
Degree of Formality	Minimal			
Time Limits	Flexible			
Need for Prestructuring of Message	Minimum to medium			
Role of Nonverbal Factors in Projection of Message	Minimal			
Evidence of Communicator Purpose	Emerges quickly — usually			
Alternation of Speaker-Listener Roles	Frequent			
Opportunities for Perceiving Listener Feedback	Maximal			
Opportunities for Adjusting to Listener Feedback	Maximal			
Opportunities to Assess Fulfillment of Communicative Purpose	Numerous			
Opportunities for Mutual Exploration of Ideas	Many			

Figure 2. BASIC FORMS OF SPEECH COMMUNICATION: SOME GRADATIONAL QUALITIES AND INTERRELATIONSHIPS

In this chapter we have viewed the processes, principles, and possibilities involved in one of life's most prevalent and important activities: trying to communicate with *one other human being*. Our approach has been primarily a practical one, stressing interpersonal relationships as they function—or at least probably ought to function—in an everyday, workaday world. Among the basic dyadic relationships we have identified are a respect for, understanding of, and a searching for mutuality in such things as aims, backgrounds, attitudes, feelings, etc. We have noted both the unstructured and structured contexts of person-to-person interchange in general, and have focused strongly on two specific situations: the information-getting interview and the job-seeking interview. The former should be of particular use as you endeavor to enrich your knowledge of a given subject; the latter may—if it has not already done so—bring you a measure of career satisfaction and financial security.

At the outset, you may recall, we cited some of the qualities which characterize and condition the interpersonal form. To review and summarize our considerations, let us look again at those characteristics—this time within the diagrammatic framework with which we closed Chapter 1, as shown in Figure 2, on the opposite page.

FOOTNOTES

[1] *Adapted from Robert S. Goyer, W. Charles Redding, and John T. Rickey,* Interviewing Principles and Techniques *(Dubuque, Iowa: Wm. C. Brown Company, Publishers, 1968), p. 6.*

[2] *Harry Walker Hepner,* Psychology Applied to Life and Work, *4th ed. (Englewood Cliffs, N.J.: Prentice-Hall, Inc., 1966), p. 244.*

[3] *Ralph Wagner, "The Employment Interview: A Critical Summary,"* Personnel Psychology II *(1949): 36–38. Reprinted in Roger M. Bellows,* Employment Psychology: The Interview *(New York: Holt, Rinehart & Winston, Inc., 1954), pp. 120–122.*

[4] *Abridged and adapted from pp. 80–85 in* How to Interview, *3rd Rev. Ed., by Walter Van Dyke Bingham and Bruce Victor Moore. Copyright, 1931, 1934, 1941 by Harper & Row, Publishers, Inc. By permission of the publishers.*

[5] *Ibid., pp. 80–85.*

[6] *Hepner, pp. 247–248.*

[7] *Frances E. Drake,* Manual for Employment Interviewing, *Research Report No. 9 (New York: American Management Association, n.d.), pp. 12–14.*

[8] *Bingham and Moore, p. 83.*

[9] *Ibid., p. 80.*

Problems and Probes

1. In your Personal Speech Journal, keep a log of all interpersonal or dyadic speech transactions in which you take part during an entire day.

For each encounter, note especially the following factors: (*a*) the relationship between you and the other person as that relationship is structured by the societal positions held by each of you; (*b*) your communicative goals and the goals of the other interactant; and (*c*) the extent to which you feel these goals were accomplished.

2. Review the ten principles for establishing rapport (pages 36–41) when communicating with another person. Use these principles to analyze a dyadic communication transaction in which you recently took part. Summarize your analysis with the description of the effect which the other person had on you, and—insofar as you can determine—the effect that you had on him or her. Keep in mind that a factor called *feedback* is significant in helping us to measure the effect created by communication, and attempt to identify instances of feedback in your analysis.

3. Observe a verbal disagreement between two people, either in person or on television. Using the concepts in this chapter, single out the factors that in your opinion contributed to the disagreement. Can you offer any psychological explanation for it?

4. Observe an information-seeking interview. (A televised interview or "talk show" may prove a fruitful source.) Describe and evaluate the overall performance of the interviewer, indicating as much as you can about his or her skill in handling the seven "Do's" on pages 53–54.

5. Choose a public personality whom you would like to interview, employing a *structured format*. Prepare a list of questions suitable for this individual, situation, and purpose. Your questions should reveal (*a*) your exact purpose in conducting the interview and (*b*) the adequacy of your preliminary research with reference to the basic subject and the qualifications of the informant to provide helpful information regarding it.

6. In Assignment 2 in the Oral Activities suggested below, you will be paired with another member of the class for purposes of demonstrating an information-seeking interview for the class as a whole. (*Note:* The pairing may be effected in advance of the activity if that seems desirable to the instructor.) In preparation for this interview, formulate *two sets of questions* that you might use. The questions, ten in each set, should be the kind that will elicit interesting information that you can subsequently employ to introduce the informant (your classmate) to the class as a whole. The questions you develop for "Set A" should be the *closed* type that require very brief answers or simple "yes" or "no" responses. To prepare "Set B," revise the questions in "Set A," converting them to the *open* type. These inquiries should cover, essentially, the same general areas; but the open questions should be such as to draw out the informant and lead to a lively, interesting interview.

Oral Activities and Speaking Assignments

1. Prepare an oral report on "The Problems of Maintaining Interaction in Dyadic Speech Encounters." To broaden the base and scope of this presentation, draw upon the sources suggested in the footnote on page 36, the Suggestions for Further Reading on page 87, and/or other sources suggested by your instructor. Conclude the report by describing some of the ways which you personally have used successfully to maintain interaction in person-to-person settings: conversations, structured and unstructured interviews, etc.

2. For this oral activity, draw upon the materials you were asked to prepare in Problem/Probe 6 above. If the pairing-off process was not effected at that time, it should be done now. Basically, your task is to interview your assigned partner, using first the set of closed questions, and following with the open questions. If possible, time should be allowed for the other members of the class (as observers) to comment on the comparative effectiveness of the two types of questions asked: the closed and the open.

3. Pair off with another member of the class and engage in a job-seeking interview in which you demonstrate the principles and guidelines set forth in this chapter. The remainder of the class will serve as critical observers.

With your partner, agree on (a) the assignment of the roles of interviewer and job applicant, (b) the name and nature of the company doing the hiring, (c) a description of the specific job or position to be sought by the applicant, and (d) the experiential and educational requirements for that job, as well as the personal qualifications required of the applicant.

Exchange no further information. Prepare *separately* for your in-class presentation which should simulate, insofar as possible, a "real-life" job interview in which both participants seek and supply information in accordance with the advice given in this chapter and the five basic "Process-Phases" described on pages 56–61.

As additional preparation for this oral activity, read the transcript of the "Sample Interview" on pages 76–86. Carefully consider (1) wherein the Sample appears to *fulfill* the form and requisites of a good job-seeking interview, and (2) wherein it *fails* to fulfill them. In the latter instances, *revise* the Sample Interview—including the "silent" commentary that has been offered from the perspective of the interviewer and of the applicant.

At the conclusion of these demonstration interviews, opportunity should be provided for the entire class to react orally as to their effectiveness and ineffectiveness and to suggest possible factors responsible for those results.

A JOB-SEEKING INTERVIEW—SAMPLE TRANSCRIPT

Name of Employing Company: Wilson-Petty Paper Products
Interviewer: Mr. Richard Scott
Job Applicant: Ms. Jane Foresman
Type of Position Available: Customer Service Representative (CSR)

From the Interviewer's Perspective	THE INTERVIEW	From the Applicant's Perspective
	1. THE INITIATIVE PHASE	
Taking the initiative; observing the amenities.	DICK SCOTT: *(Rising as Jane Foresman enters his office.)* How do you do, Miss Foresman? Please come in.	
	JANE FORESMAN: *(Pleasantly; with a smile.)* Ms. Foresman. But just call me Jane. I hope I haven't kept you waiting.	*Being agreeable, but wanting to set Scott straight at the outset.*
	SCOTT: Not at all . . . Jane. *(Also smiles.)* I appreciate your coming in on such a rainy day.	
	JANE: I was lucky enough to get a ride, so there was no problem.	*Also striving to put the interaction on a positive but informal plane.*
	SCOTT: Good. *(Indicating a chair.)* Won't you sit down? I'm Dick Scott.	
	JANE: *(Seating herself.)* Thank you, Mr. Scott.	
	(Scott picks up Jane's written application from his desktop and studies it for a few moments as he reseats himself.)	
	2. THE INVESTIGATIVE PHASE	
An "ice-breaker" question.	SCOTT: Well . . . how do you feel—now that you're out of school?	
	JANE: Well, I have mixed feelings about it. I really enjoyed school, and I'm almost sorry it's over. But at the same time, I'm really looking forward to starting a career.	*Wanting to appear serious, conscientious.*
	SCOTT: I know exactly how you feel. I felt the	

Establishing shared feelings, common ground. Encouraging applicant to talk about herself.

same way myself when I graduated. *(Scanning job application papers.)* I see that you went to State University at Brookville. What made you decide to go there?

JANE: Well, when I started college, I really didn't know what I wanted to do or be, and State had a wide range of fields of study. Plus, it was far enough away from home for me to be independent, but not so far as to be inconvenient. *Plus* — the state universities are considerably less expensive than private colleges.

Probably has anticipated this question and prepared an answer.

Suggesting that money, economics are important considerations.

SCOTT: Yes, I guess the financial aspect is pretty important to us all. Tell me . . . are you living away from home now?

Continuing to draw the applicant out.

JANE: No, I just can't afford to live by myself until after I've worked a while. So I'll be staying at home for the next few months at least — living with my parents.

SCOTT: What about your father . . . what does he do?

JANE: He manages the furniture division of Smith and Blake Department Store — near our home.

Wanting to know whether Jane has seen the woman of the family in a career situation.

SCOTT: How about your mother? Does she work, or is she a housewife?

JANE: *(Somewhat sharply, in spite of herself.)* Any woman who is "a housewife" *works*, Mr. Scott.

Choosing a risk-taking response.

SCOTT: *(With a small, apologetic laugh.)* You're right, Jane. What I meant was — does your mother work *outside* the home?

JANE: My mother has worked part time as a teacher's aide since I started to school. She has always enjoyed working.

Reflecting a positive attitude toward the working-woman role.

Returning to the open-ended type of question.

SCOTT: Tell me, what made you decide to come here to Wilson-Petty Products for a job?

JANE: Well, I saw your ad in the Sunday paper, saying that you have several positions open for college graduates. And since I've been familiar with Wilson-Petty products and have used them for some time, I felt

Showing a familiarity with the company.

that this might be an ideal place to start a career. Plus, it's easy to get here from Kingston, where I live.

SCOTT: Do you have a car, Jane?

JANE: No, I'll have to rely on public transportation or a car pool until I can save enough to buy a car. If I decide I really want and need one, that is. Ecology, you know.

SCOTT: I see. *(Thoughtfully.)* Jane, at the moment you're living with your parents . . . and I gather that you want a working career. I've been wondering . . . do you have any plans for marriage in the near future?

JANE: N-n-no . . . not at the moment. Of course, you realize *(with an emphasis she hopes Scott won't miss)*, *personal* plans like that can change, though.

SCOTT: I understand. But, well—there is no one special person you're planning to marry at this time?

JANE: No, not at present.

SCOTT: Incidentally, we have a lot of eligible bachelors here. *(Laughs, then resumes in a more serious tone.)* A moment ago you said that you liked Wilson-Petty products. Why?

JANE: Oh, I guess I think your things reflect good taste, mostly. I always try to use your stationery—when I can afford stationery, that is. I like nice writing paper and notecards and things like that. And yours just always stand out on the store shelves.

SCOTT: That's very nice of you to say that. We've always felt that way, of course. We've been very fortunate in having a lot of really good people working for us— both women and men. *(Starting a new tack.)* Tell me, Jane . . . outside of working, what are your plans for the near future?

JANE: I really don't know. But I've thought about that a lot. I think someday I might want to go back to school and get an advanced degree of some kind—depending on where my interests take me in the near future. And I may want to get married in the next few years—I don't know. I'd like to get involved in community activities: maybe do volunteer work of some kind when I can. But I really can't be too definite right now. I've got to get a job first.

SCOTT: I can understand that. *(Indicating the application papers again.)* I see here that you got your degree in psychology. What made you decide on that as a major?

JANE: Well, the study of people's *behavior*—the workings of their minds—has always fascinated me.

SCOTT: I have to agree with you there. What subject did you do best in at school?

JANE: Psychology, naturally. That's another reason I wanted to study it—I was good at it. I had a B average in Psych.

SCOTT: I see. When you were at State University, where did you live?

JANE: In a dorm my first two years. Then I moved into an apartment and shared it with several other girls.

Wanting to learn something about how Jane gets along with other people.

SCOTT: Why did you decide to move out of the dorm?

JANE: Mostly, I think, because I wanted to be more "on my own." The dorms are really a kind of artificial housing arrangement—everything is done for you, and you don't really learn much about living in a real world. In an apartment you have to be responsible for meals, cleaning, paying the bills—you just learn more about life that way. Plus, there's more personal freedom if you live in an apartment.

Using this opportunity to let the interviewer know that she wants—and is capable of handling—responsibility. And . . . she also wants "personal freedom."

Beginning to look for leadership qualities.

SCOTT: *(Turning a page of the application forms.)* I notice that you were involved in several extracurricular activities on the campus. What did you do for the Student Senate?

JANE: Well, the Student Senate was really like a student council, and I was my dorm representative during my sophomore year, and an off-campus representative in my junior year. I was too busy in my senior year to continue with the Senate.

Electing to give a fairly modest answer, not wanting to exaggerate her achievements in this regard.

SCOTT: Did you like that kind of work?

JANE: Oh, yes. I've always liked politics and community work, and this was a kind of combination of the two. We handled student grievances, and tried to make life on the campus a bit better for everyone. The Senate was a good introduction to the real workings of politics — on a very modest scale, of course.

Reflecting her prevailing interest in people.

Probing for experience and skill in handling money.

SCOTT: I notice also that you were treasurer of the campus Psychology Society. Just what did *that* involve?

JANE: The treasurer keeps the books — financial records.

SCOTT: Financial records?

JANE: Yes, but there really wasn't that much to it. We weren't trying to make a profit or anything. I just kept track of dues and any money we made from fund-raising activities. And I paid out money for social events and the occasional guest speakers we had. That sort of thing.

SCOTT: *(Jocularly.)* Did you end up in the black or the red?

JANE: *(Laughingly.)* Oh, we just barely stayed in the black, but that's all we wanted.

Again probing for leadership qualities.

SCOTT: I see that you were also chairman of the lecture committee for the Student Union. What did that entail?

JANE: Well, the Student Union at State sponsors once-a-month lectures by well-known or controversial people from all fields. The lecture committee "screened through" all the suggestions from the students, the faculty, and the community. Then — in essence — we decided upon the speakers. A faculty advisory committee did the final selecting from a list we would give them.

SCOTT: That sounds like a lot of responsibility.

JANE: It really wasn't a personal, individual responsibility. The group—the committee—worked together to find speakers. There was a lot of work for each committee member, I will admit that. But it was very interesting, and I enjoyed it immensely.

SCOTT: Interesting in what way in particular, Jane? Tell me a little more about it.

JANE: Well, for example . . . there were a great many requests for lectures by psychics or experts in the field of ESP. I always felt that this was quite a commentary—that we all want to be told about the future, the unknown. Then, one of my jobs as chairman was to contact the person who was selected to give the lecture and make final arrangements for his appearance on campus, agree on an exact topic, and so forth. I always enjoyed the personal contact with these well-known people.

SCOTT: That would be pretty satisfying, I can well imagine. In contacting these various people, I suppose you had to do a lot of telephoning and corresponding. Do you know how to type?

JANE: Just for my own personal use. Not very fast, but adequately for my own purposes.

SCOTT: Do you know how to operate any office machines—a calculator, an adding machine, perhaps even a computer?

JANE: *(With a laugh.)* Well, I make a great xerox, but that's about it.

(Scott laughs also, then refers to the application again and resumes more seriously.)

SCOTT: I see here that you worked for the last three summers at the Dalton Warehousing Company. How did you get the job?

JANE: The first year, a friend who worked there told me about an opening. I applied for a job and got it. And each summer after that, they asked me to come back.

SCOTT: Did you like the Dalton job?

JANE: Well, it was pretty routine. Mostly folding and stapling. Just processing orders. But I liked the people I worked with. And I was grateful for the job experience—and the money, of course. But I wouldn't want to make it my life's work.

Letting the interviewer know that she has been successful in "landing" and holding onto a job.

"What I'm 'wondering' is: Will I have to compete with others for this applicant?"

SCOTT: I've been wondering, Jane . . . have you had a number of job interviews since you graduated? Talked with other companies?

Trying to let the interviewer know that she is seeking something more than a "routine" job.

JANE: No, I honestly haven't. I did go back to Dalton's, sort of out of loyalty. But they really didn't have any positions for a college graduate. Not the type of job I'm looking for. However, I do have a few leads now, and I plan to pursue them until I find just the right position for me.

Telling him: "I'm looking around and will be very selective . . . won't take just any job that's offered."

Saying, in effect: "You define the job. If we have it, we may—just may—try to negotiate."

SCOTT: Do you know what you're looking for?

JANE: Yes. I've always wanted a job where I work with *people*—where I can help people solve their problems, where I can maybe make someone's day just a little better. That's another reason why I chose psychology as a major. I felt that if I had a little more information about how and why people act as they do, I would know better how I could help them. I don't mean I want to be a counselor, or anything like that. But I do want a job where I'm dealing with people, and where I can help them.

Wanting him to know that this is important to her and that she has given it serious consideration. Narrowing down the possibilities.

Using a "pin-it-down" question to get to the nitty-gritty of what she has in mind.

SCOTT: *(Thoughtfully.)* I can see, all right, in a *general* way, how your psychology background could help in a job like that. But—well, I'm not sure I see all of the specifics. Can you pin them down for me a bit?

JANE: Oh, I just think I would be able to understand people more because of my psych. I mean, I would be able to recognize—oh, say—stress situations, and be able to adjust my own behavior when I thought the situation required it.

SCOTT: I see.

JANE: May I ask a question here?

SCOTT: Certainly. Go right ahead.

JANE: Well, exactly what positions are open here at Wilson-Petty's—positions that I qualify for?

Wanting to take the initiative and direct the course of the interaction.

3. THE NEGOTIATIVE PHASE

Having completed the investigative phase of the interview and having a fairly clear picture of the applicant's background, training, and abilities, he is ready to begin "fitting" her into a specific job-situation.

SCOTT: That's a very good question—one that I was about to bring up. As you mentioned, in our advertisement we indicated that we had several positions open for college graduates. A few of these jobs are for specialized or technical people. For accounting or design majors, for example. But we do have some openings in our Customer Service Department. And—certainly as a beginning at least—I believe you might find that working in customer service is very close to what you have in mind. Especially with your background in psychology.

JANE: Just what is "customer service"?

SCOTT: What is *your* idea of a customer service job? What do you think it might involve?

JANE: Well, from the job title, I'd guess it involves working with customers in some way or other.

Not reluctant to ask a question when she is unsure of the meaning of a term.

Explaining the specific nature and scope of the job opening . . . being realistic, but also trying to emphasize its appeal.

SCOTT: You're pretty close. In some companies, it is referred to as *inside sales*. As you probably know, we have sales representatives who call on stationery and paper-specialty departments of large retail stores. The Customer Service Representatives—or CSR's, as they are often called—work as adjuncts to the sales force. The CSR han-

Suggesting the possibilities . . . selling, but not over-selling . . . the opportunities.

dles any problems that may arise in ordering, shipping, or billing. The CSR's also handle the sales for any smaller stores which don't do enough volume to justify having a sales representative call on them. And CSR's also prepare and send out sales promotions to stores—either on their own, or in conjunction with a sales representative.

JANE: What kind of opportunities for advancement are there in Customer Service?

Showing some interest, but mainly curious as yet.

Trying to make the job sound appealing.

SCOTT: Many. There are opportunities aplenty—depending partially on you, of course. Just where do you want to *be*—what would you like to be *doing*—five years from now?

JANE: Well, as yet I don't really know that much about business. But I think I'd like someday to be some sort of manager or supervisor—someone who not only still works with people on the job, but also supervises people under her. I never want to get away from direct contact with people. I don't want to be any ivory-tower executive or anything like that—but, well, I would like to move up the corporate ladder, so to speak.

Not afraid to reveal her ambition, will to succeed.

SCOTT: Then I think you'll find Customer Service a good position to start from. Several of our CSR's have become sales representatives, and sales managers can go on to become managers in our district and regional offices. And, of course, many go into management of some kind here and in the home office. Or, for those CSR's who prefer not to go out into the field into direct sales, there are many opportunities *inside*—either moving up within Customer Service or moving out into other departments: advertising, market research, or others. A job in sales or Customer Service is one of the best training grounds for advancement here at Wilson-Petty's.

JANE: I must say that sounds quite encouraging. Very appealing, really.

SCOTT: A CSR works hard. Let me emphasize that. But the long-range rewards can be good.

JANE: Can you—well, can you tell me something about the more immediate rewards?

SCOTT: *(Genially.)* You mean salary and benefits, I take it.

JANE: Yes—for the person you decide to hire. Money isn't the first consideration, by any means. But—well, it's important.

Showing, once again, that the salary, as well as the job, is important to her.

Unable to give a specific figure, but wanting her to know that salary will not be a problem.

SCOTT: I quite agree. Actually, at the moment, I'm afraid I won't be able to tell you exactly what the salary is for a CSR. That's decided by our Mr. Bedloe, head of the Customer Service Department, and is based on the applicant's experience, college background, and other factors. I can say, however, that our salary ranges are competitive.

JANE: I can understand that.

SCOTT: As for benefits, we have life, medical, and major medical insurance, paid vacations, and sick time. *(Picks up brochure from desk, rises, and hands it to Jane.)* Maybe you'd like to look this over. It spells out our company's employment policies, working conditions, fringe benefits, and all the rest.

JANE: *(Taking the brochure.)* Thank you very much.

SCOTT: If you find that you do have any questions after you've read that brochure, just ask.

JANE: *(With evident enthusiasm.)* I surely will because—well, because this CSR job sounds as if it could be just what I want— working with people—a chance to work my way up. I think I could really bring a lot to that job. And get a lot from it, too.

Showing enthusiasm for the job and confidence in her own abilities.

4. THE ACTUATIVE PHASE

Something close to a "meeting of the minds" has begun to form, and the interviewer takes the decisive step toward doing something about it: actuation.

SCOTT: You know, Jane *(smiles, also evidences enthusiasm)* . . . I quite agree. And I'm glad you feel that way. I don't have *all* the say-so on who's hired and who isn't, but—well, let's just say I have some *influence. (Laughs, and Jane joins in.)* In my opinion, you could do Wilson-Petty a lot of good—and yourself, too. I've liked what you've said and the way you've said it. Spunk—but good sense with it. So if you have the time now, I think you should talk with Mr. Bedloe.

JANE: *(Very pleased; rises.)* Oh, I've got the time, Mr. Scott—all the time in the world.

SCOTT: Fine. Fine. *(Crossing toward door to outer office.)* You might just take a chair out here in my outer office and look over that brochure while you're waiting. *(Opening door for her.)* I'll put a call through to Mr. Bedloe and see if I can arrange for you to speak with him right away.

5. THE TERMINATIVE PHASE

JANE: *(Walking toward door.)* That would be great. Thank you, Mr. Scott. Thank you *very* much.

Observance of social amenities.

SCOTT: And I thank *you.* After you've had a chat with Bedloe, I'll want to talk with you again—more specifically—Miss Foresman. *(Catching himself.)* Er—uh—I—mean—Ms. . . . Ms. . . . *(having trouble pronouncing it)* . . . how do you *say* that, anyway?

JANE: *(Turns in doorway.)* I think it will be easier, Mr. Scott, if you just call me Jane.

(She laughs; he joins in. She goes out and closes the door.)

Extending the conventional courtesies.

Suggestions for Further Reading

Michael Argyle, *Social Interaction* (New York: Aldine-Atherton, Inc., 1969).

Dean C. Barnlund, ed., *Interpersonal Communication: Survey and Studies* (Boston: Houghton Mifflin Company, 1968).

Warren G. Bennis, *et al*, eds., *Interpersonal Dynamics: Essays and Readings on Human Interaction* (Homewood, Ill.: Dorsey Press, 1968).

George A. Borden, Richard B. Gregg, and Theodore G. Grove, *Speech Behavior and Human Interaction* (Englewood Cliffs, N.J.: Prentice-Hall, Inc., 1969), Chapter II, "Interpersonal Communication," pp. 75–127.

Erving Goffman, *Relations in Public* (New York: Harper & Row, Publishers, 1971).

Robert S. Goyer, W. Charles Redding, and John T. Rickey, *Interviewing Principles and Techniques* (Dubuque, Iowa: Wm. C. Brown Company, Publishers, 1968).

Robert Sommer, *Personal Space: The Behavioral Basis of Design* (Englewood Cliffs, N.J.: Prentice-Hall, Inc., 1969).

John R. Wenburg and William W. Wilmot, *The Personal Communication Process* (New York: John Wiley & Sons, Inc., 1973).

3
COMMUNICATING IN SMALL GROUPS

Increasingly in our society more and more of the functions of government, business, industry, and education are being energized and guided by small groups of people meeting as committees, boards, or councils. Politicians, legislators, corporate executives, business managers, teachers, students, ministers, social workers, office workers, hardhats, community-action leaders—indeed, people from all corners and walks of life are utilizing small group communication as an effective means of discovering and sharing vital information and points of view. Through small group interaction they are identifying common problems, seeking viable solutions, and initiating purposeful action for personal, familial, vocational, and community betterment. Very probably, in our time the need and urgency to learn about communicative behavior in small groups is greater than in any earlier era of our history. Very often our success and satisfaction as a person, a parent, a citizen, a breadwinner depend on the insights and skills with which we can participate and lead in small group communication.

SMALL GROUP COMMUNICATION: CHARACTERISTICS AND CONDITIONS

Some Definitions

This form of human interaction is variously referred to as "group dynamics," "group process," "group-centered interaction," "small group communication," and "group discussion." Since in this book our primary concern is with the communicative aspects of the process, we shall use interchangeably the terms *small group communication* and *group discussion*.

Specifically, what do we mean by the term *discussion*? Although in daily interaction it is loosely used to cover almost any interchange of ideas or opinions, as we employ it here we mean a *cooperative and relatively systematic process in which a group of persons—typically, three to twelve or fifteen—exchange and eval-*

uate ideas and information in order to understand a subject or solve a problem.

We may further define the form by noting that it is characterized by (*a*) a fairly high degree of physical and psychological closeness; (*b*) an atmosphere that tends to become increasingly informal as the interaction proceeds; (*c*) time limits that are frequently pre-set, the durational determinants being the complexity of the subject to be learned or the problem to be solved; (*d*) messages that are typically extemporaneous and tend, therefore, to be only loosely prestructured — if at all; (*e*) nonverbal projection of messages that requires, usually, a somewhat greater effort than in one-to-one relationships; (*f*) communicator purposes that are frequently evident and an interaction that provides numerous opportunities to assess and reassess the degree of purpose-fulfillment; (*g*) frequent opportunities for perceiving and adjusting to speaker-listener feedback; (*h*) very frequent alternation of speaker-listener roles; and (*i*) a predominant and continuing concern for exploring ideas together — individually and collectively.

Group Effectiveness Versus Individual Effectiveness

From taking part in discussion in the classroom and in campus, social, or church activities, you have undoubtedly discovered that merely having a group of people talk together does not ensure that understanding will improve or that a wise and expedient solution will be reached. Sometimes a well-informed individual can think through a subject or solve a problem more rapidly and efficiently than a group can. Sometimes, when the resolution of a difficulty requires a single, concentrated insight or a uniquely innovative decision, a one-person or two-person approach may be superior.

A group, however, is more likely than an individual to be aware of and give attention to all aspects of a matter. This is because many of the problems we daily confront call for a wide variety of skills and knowledge, for a cross-check of data and ideas. Feedback, adjustment to feedback, and the open and lively interchange of ideas which should characterize good group interaction tend to stimulate a wealth of possibilities that cannot be generated by a one-person effort.

Furthermore, since people tend to support more strongly the decisions they themselves have helped to make, a group consensus is more likely to produce satisfying and permanent results.* A communicative transaction in which a

---

*For explorations of the relationship between group consensus and subsequent behavior of participants, as well as information on many other aspects of the group communication process, see especially Warren G. Bennis et al., Interpersonal Dynamics: Essays and Readings in Human Interaction, *rev. ed.* (Homewood, Ill.: Dorsey Press, 1968); Dorwin Cartwright and Alvin Zander, eds., Group Dynamics: Research and Theory, 2nd ed. (New York: Harper & Row, Publishers, 1960); Robert S. Cathcart and Larry A. Samovar, eds., Small Group Communication (Dubuque, Iowa: Wm. C. Brown Company, Publishers, 1970); Joseph Luft, Group Processes: An Introduction to Group Dynamics (Palo Alto, Calif.: National Press Books, 1970).

goal is shared inevitably calls for a cooperative effort to discuss, define, and achieve that goal. This means a greater need for *involvement* by all members of the group—an involvement which, in turn, tends to create a sense of *individual responsibility* for the decision of the group as a whole. Thus involvement leads to responsibility which leads to an *increased commitment* to the group goal and, probably, *loyalty* to the group as such.

Finally—and of considerable import—a group decision is more democratic than an individual one. As Joseph Luft points out:

> A society which places highest value on the worth and freedom of the individual also encourages the strongest independent thought, independent work, and independent responsibility. An inherent goal of a sound group in such a society is the reaffirmation of true independence while meeting group needs concerning tasks and morale.[1]

In contemporary society, certainly, there is a need to increase the openness with which we try to relate to one another; to recognize the inseparability of tolerance, responsibility to others, and freedom; and for these purposes to improve our understanding of self and others. Skill in small group communication cannot but contribute to these ends.

In view of these inherent complexities, successful small group communication obviously can never be instantaneous. Group discussions admittedly take *time*. Fortunately, however, there are methods by which their efficiency can be increased significantly and their outcomes made more effective. In brief, the group members should:

1. Set a reasonably well-defined goal.
2. Prepare themselves well on the subject to be learned or the questions to be explored.
3. Grasp the essentials for productive group interaction and leadership functions.
4. Follow a clear and mutually agreed-upon plan to guide—within flexible limits—the direction to be taken by the communicative transaction.

This chapter has been designed to help you understand and use these methods of group discussion effectively.

MAJOR PURPOSES OF GROUP DISCUSSION

Group discussions, as we have already suggested, usually have one of two major purposes: (1) *to exchange information or ideas*, or (2) *to reach an agreement or a decision*.

To Exchange Information or Ideas

Sometimes the purpose of a discussion is to explore a subject of common interest to the members of the group so that they may come to a fuller understanding of it. Thus a number of persons interested in improving their understanding of art or literature or foreign affairs may meet on a more or less regular basis as an *information-learning group* or *study group.*

To Reach an Agreement or Make a Decision

Distinguished from a learning group is a so-called *action group* or *decision-making group* — a number of persons who engage in a discussion for the specific purpose of reaching an agreement or deciding what the group as a whole should believe or do. In discussions of this kind, conflicting facts are examined and differences of opinion are evaluated in an effort to arrive at a common judgment or consensus. Where a consensus proves impossible, at least the range of disagreement may be narrowed and a clearer understanding of outstanding differences attained. Usually, in action-oriented discussions the procedure is relatively informal; but occasionally, when disagreements persist and a decision must be made, a vote is taken.

ESSENTIALS FOR EFFECTIVE INTERACTION

Whether the purpose of a discussion is to enhance understanding or decide upon a course of action, the individuals who take part in it must be capable of contributing worthwhile ideas, and the conduct of the group must be such that an objective and systematic examination of the subject is possible.

Essentials for the Group as a Whole

The first requisite for productive discussion is *orderliness*. This does not imply a high degree of formality. Indeed, formality usually is undesirable. Orderliness does require, however, that only one person talk at a time, that the discussants be consistently courteous, and that some fairly definite plan of procedure be followed.

Second, for discussion to be productive, every member of the group must have *a cooperative rather than a competitive attitude*. If each person insists on having his or her own way, the discussion will get nowhere. Individuals must be willing to consider points of view different from their own and, instead of criticizing other members for mistakes in analysis or reasoning, should try to understand and assist them. Moreover, there must be a willingness to compromise. Sometimes, of course, compromise is impossible, but reasonable compromises generally hurt no one and often are the only way of reaching an agreement or making a decision. If a desire to meet the other person halfway prevails, there is likely to be a better feeling among the members of the group and a more fruitful exchange of opinions.

Finally, a group needs *a sense of accomplishment.* Unless people feel they are getting somewhere, their interest and enthusiasm soon lag. Before the consideration of the subject or problem actually begins, a goal should be set and the field for discussion limited. This can best be done by putting the matter for consideration in the form of a simple and impartially phrased question. A group seeking information on the subject of higher education might, for example, focus on the question: "What philosophical assumptions underlie the modern college curriculum?" Or an action-oriented discussion on the problem of traffic deaths might ask: "What practical steps can we take to reduce fatal accidents on our highways?" *In general, it is wise to avoid questions which present the group with only two alternatives or choices,* for such questions tend to produce contending factions and to make an impartial exploration of a problem difficult. For instance, because the question "Should we raise the sales tax in this state from three to four percent?" invites a "yes" or "no" answer, it might well lead to a two-sided argument or dispute.

Essentials for the Individual Participant

If a discussion for whatever purpose is to be successful, each participant must have a *thorough knowledge of the subject being considered.* Unless this is the case, misinformation rather than solid facts will be exchanged, and a decision will be made on the basis of incomplete or incorrect data. A second essential is an *acquaintance with the other members of the group.* The more the participants know about one another, the better they will be able to understand why certain persons take the positions they do, and why at a particular point the discussion may cease to be productive. Third, the participants must pay *close attention to the discussion* as it proceeds. Unless they listen carefully to what is going on, they will lose track of where the discussion is, double back to repeat points already covered, or entertain mistaken ideas concerning the views of the other discussants. Finally, *meaningful contributions* to the discussion itself are imperative. A person who remains silent may learn much, but silence does not enhance the knowledge of others or help to solve the problems faced by the group. A good discussion participant has the ability to present ideas clearly and tactfully and knows how to interject them at the most strategic time.

These essentials, of course, have numerous ramifications and specific applications; and as we proceed with our examination of the discussion process, you should note them and use them to put together a more detailed "profile" of the effective discussant.

GENERAL PREPARATION FOR SMALL GROUP COMMUNICATION

How should you prepare to participate in a discussion? What should you do to ensure that you will be able to contribute to the best of your ability? As we have suggested, two fundamental steps are required. First, you must study and analyze the specific problem to be solved or subject to be considered. Second, you must find out all you can about the other members of the group. Let's now consider the procedures which can help us to ensure this very basic preparation.

Analysis of the Subject or Problem

The more you know about the subject under discussion, the better. Don't rely on obsolete information, however; make sure your facts are up-to-date. The broader and readier the knowledge at your command, the better able you will be to take part in the discussion no matter how it may develop or what course it may follow. Although many persons believe they do not need to prepare as carefully for a small group discussion as for a public speech, the truth of the matter is just the opposite. In group communication of this kind, you cannot arbitrarily narrow the subject or determine the specific purpose in advance; nor can you be sure of the exact direction the group will take. To be ready for any eventuality, therefore, you must have a flexibility born of broad knowledge. For each aspect of the subject or implication of the problem you think may possibly be discussed, make the following analysis.

First, review the facts you already know. Go over the information you have acquired through previous reading or personal experience and organize it in your mind. Prepare as if you were going to present a speech on every phase of the matter. You will then be better qualified to discuss any part of it almost spontaneously.

Second, bring your knowledge up-to-date. Find out if recent changes have affected the situation. Fit the newly acquired information into what you already know.

Third, determine a tentative point of view on each of the important issues. Make up your mind what your attitude will be. Do you think that Hemingway was a greater writer than Faulkner? If so, exactly how and why? What three or four steps might be taken to attract new members into your club? On what medical or health-related grounds should cigarette-smoking be declared illegal? Stake out a tentative position on each question or issue that is likely to come before the group and have clearly in mind the facts and reasons that support your view. Be ready to state and substantiate this opinion at whatever point in the discussion seems most appropriate, but also be willing to change your mind if information or points of view provided by other discussants show you to be wrong.

Fourth—and finally—to the best of your ability anticipate the effect of your ideas or proposals on other members of the group or the organization of which the group is a part. For instance, what you propose may possibly cause someone to lose money or to retract a promise that has been made. Forethought will enable you to understand opposition to your view if it arises and to make a valid and intelligent adjustment. The more thoroughly you organize your facts and relate them to the subject and to the people involved, the more effective and influential your contributions to the discussion will be.

Analysis of the Group's Authority and Constituency

Even though you are thoroughly familiar with the subject to be considered, you will be unable to interact with maximum effectiveness unless you clearly and fully understand the relationship between the subject or problem and the objectives of the group as a whole. Equally important is a clear recognition of the *range of authority*—the power to act on a decision—which the group may have. Find out whether the group has any official status or power. What resources are at its command? What channels of action are open to it? Consider the larger unit of which the group is a part. If, for example, you are a member of a student-government committee, you must know not only the function of that committee, but also the policies and traditions of your college or university.

In order to analyze pertinent aspects of the group's constituency, you will of course need to know as much as possible about each of the individuals who compose it—status, beliefs, attitudes, biases, background, personality, special knowledge, competencies, etc. In particular, seek answers to the following questions: What is the official position of each member of the group? What are the personal traits of each? What knowledge of the subject or problem does each one have? What attitude will each probably show toward the interpretations or proposals I plan to offer? What is each participant's special field of competence—something I will need to know so that when a certain type of information is being explored, I can immediately look to the person most likely to supply an authoritative opinion?

What about the *status* of the participants? How are individual members looked upon by others in the group? Are their knowledge and judgment highly regarded or generally discounted? Are they sought after as influential members of their community? Are any of my co-communicators extremists, and—if so—how can I help to limit or counterbalance their contributions when the interaction begins? Which members of the group are likely to talk too much or too little, and how can I go about preparing to adjust that imbalance? And, finally, who among them has administrative or actuative skills—in case committees have to be designated to follow through on a group decision?

Only by such thoughtful, careful probing can you hope to gain the information and special insights upon which genuinely productive small group interaction depends. For discussion participants, a thoroughgoing analysis of this kind is both necessary and useful; for discussion leaders—as we shall see in a subsequent section of this chapter—it is doubly so.

PARTICIPATING IN GROUP COMMUNICATION

Although thorough preparation by all concerned is an essential ingredient of productive group communication, it is not in itself a guarantee of success. If a group is to achieve its goals, all participants must observe certain principles and fulfill certain obligations *while the discussion is proceeding.*

The Participant's Responsibilities

In a typical discussion, each member of the group does some speaking, but much of the time necessarily is spent listening to the ideas and opinions of others. The participant must, therefore, be a good *listener*, able to understand what others are saying and skilled in judging the worth of their contributions. As the interaction progresses, you will better be able to evaluate the opinions of your co-communicators if you can provide for yourself definitive answers to the following questions:

1. *Is the speaker qualified by training and experience to express an opinion on the point at issue?*
2. *Are the speaker's remarks obviously the result of long and thoughtful study of the subject?*
3. *Are the speaker's opinions prejudiced by personal interest or the desire for selfish gain?*
4. *Is the speaker stating opinions frankly and with a full disclosure of the facts on which they are based?*

5. *Are the facts or opinions presented consistent with human experience?*
6. *Are the facts or opinions presented consistent with one another?*
7. *What weight are other members of the group likely to give to this person's opinions?*

If you can answer these questions about the contributions of each participant, you will be able to evaluate them more accurately, and also to arrive at a better understanding of the subject being considered.

When to Participate in Discussion

There is no dogmatic answer to the frequently asked question, "When should I talk and when should I keep quiet?" In general, the longer you have been a member of a group, the freer you may be with your comments. In most cases, the following suggestions apply:

Speak when you have a constructive comment or suggestion to offer. Frequently some aspect of the subject will be neglected, or an important idea will slip by unnoticed. Even when you have no tangible information on the matter at hand, you may stimulate others to contribute the needed facts if you comment briefly on the omission or raise a question concerning it.

Speak when you can clarify a point muddled by another participant. Someone else may try to make an important point, but express it so vaguely that the group fails to appreciate its significance. If you can tactfully clarify the point, you will perform a valuable service and facilitate the interaction.

Speak when you can correct an error. In correcting an error, you must of course exercise tact to avoid starting a fruitless argument. If the point is important, however, and you know the other discussant is mistaken, by all means make the correction. If you are courteous and modest, avoiding any suggestion of officiousness, you should be able to correct the error without giving offense.

Speak when you can offer useful information. No one person knows everything. By combining the information provided by the entire group, a sound judgment will more likely be formed. If, therefore, you can illuminate a matter by an apt illustration, if you can cite accurate figures bearing upon it, or if you can relay the testimony of someone outside the group, by all means do so. Be sure, however, that what you say has a direct bearing on the point at issue. For someone to inject irrelevant information can be disruptive and disconcerting.

Speak when you can ask an intelligent question. If you are in doubt about something and are fairly sure that others also are in doubt, inquire into the matter at once. Do not allow a decision to be made until your doubt is resolved. Obviously, you should not ask questions continually, but a question asked at the proper moment will often prevent a great deal of muddled thinking and needless talk. Moreover, when the discussion has wandered, often a well-directed question can be used to bring it back to the main issue. And, by no means of minor importance, ask questions to bring out the facts behind unsupported opinions.

Speak when you can inject humor to enliven or ameliorate interaction. This suggestion needs to be followed with extreme caution. Once in a while, however, a little humor will enliven a tired group and quicken the pace of the discussion. Moreover, if strong disagreement boils over into personal animosity, a light-hearted jest or good-natured comment often will serve to relieve the tension that has built up. Joseph Luft, noting that humor "may be related to group tension and the unknown," emphasizes its potential by noting:

> Group-relevant feelings, when brought into the open suddenly and in a manner that is not too threatening, may precipitate a discharge of feeling with an accompanying sense of relief. Groups often generate themes or processes of particular importance to the life of the group, and it is around these themes that indigenous humor may arise. . . . Because humor touches on vital matters, albeit in a special and limited way, it facilitates communication and decision making.[2]

Of course, if the joke falls flat or the humor backfires, it will retard rather than facilitate good interaction. Moreover, while humor may serve usefully as a *temporary* flight from the tensions at hand, it should not be prolonged unnecessarily or allowed to become disruptive and divert the discussion from its true course. Finally—and above all—avoid using humor to express antagonism or mask hostility toward other members of the group.

How to Participate in Discussion

In general, speak in a direct, friendly, conversational manner. Your style and vocal tone will, of course, vary according to the nature and purpose of the discussion as a whole, the degree of formality that is being observed, and your psychological frame of mind as you approach the task. As the interaction proceeds, differences of opinion will naturally arise, tensions will increase, and some conflict is almost certain to surface. You will need, therefore, to be sensitive to these changes and to make necessary and desirable adjustments in the way you voice your ideas and reactions. In general, however, your remarks should have the spontaneity, directness, and immediacy of good conversation, as described in Chapter 2.

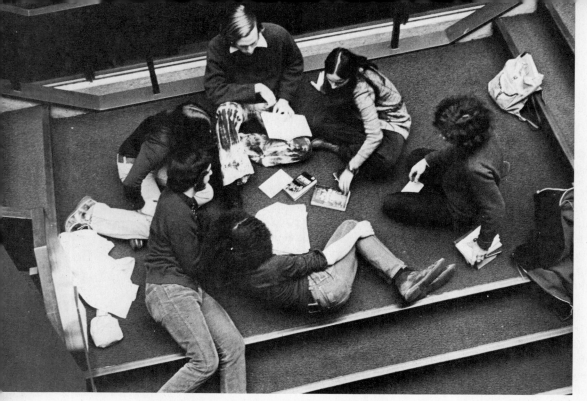

Like interpersonal communication, small group communication is a form of speech we encounter and employ often, in situations ranging from impromptu group conversations to formal problem-solving meetings.

Present your point of view clearly, succinctly, and fairly. Participation in discussion should always be guided by one underlying aim: to help the group think objectively and creatively in analyzing the subject or solving the problem at hand. To this end, it is generally desirable to organize your contribution not in the way best calculated to win other people to your point of view, but rather in the fashion that will best *stimulate them to think for themselves.* Therefore, instead of stating your conclusion first and then supplying the arguments in favor of it, let your contribution recount how and why you came to think as you do. Begin by stating the nature of the problem as you see it; outline the various hypotheses or solutions that occurred to you as you were thinking about it; tell why you rejected certain of them; and only after all this, state your own opinion and explain the reasons that support it. In this way, you give other members of the group a chance to check the accuracy and completeness of your thinking on the matter and to point out any deficiencies or fallacies that may not have occurred to you. At the same time, you will also be making your contribution in the most objective and rational manner possible.

Maintain attitudes of sincerity, open-mindedness, and objectivity. Above all, remember that a serious discussion is not a showplace for prima donnas or an arena for verbal combatants. When you have something to say, say it modestly and sincerely, and always maintain an open, objective attitude. Accept criticism with dignity and treat disagreement with an open mind. Your primary purpose is not to get your own view accepted, but to work out with the other members of the group the best possible choice or decision that all of you together can devise.

LEADERSHIP AND LEADERSHIP FUNCTIONS

All of the things we have thus far said about the need for well-defined goals and purposes, constructive attitudes, orderliness, thorough preparation, individual and group responsibilities, analytical abilities, listening and speaking skills, status-awareness, objectivity, tact, and the other requisites for productive group interaction—all apply with a very special force to the *discussion leader.**

The fruitfulness of a discussion depends to a noteworthy extent on the leader's *capacity for rapid analysis*—the ability to sense almost immediately the direction in which the group is going, to catch significant ideas even when they

---

*We are aware of the distinction sometimes drawn between the "appointed" or "nominal" group leader and the so-called "real" or "emergent" leader—the person who, because of his or her superior knowledge, prestige, or insight, is most influential in moving the discussion forward and determining the direction it will take. However, we still prefer the term leader rather than chairperson on the ground that it reflects more accurately the functions that the appointed or nominal group leader is usually expected to perform.

are ambiguously worded or buried in superfluous detail, to note points of agreement between two seemingly diverse opinions, and to strip controversial issues of unnecessary complexity so as to narrow the discussion to basic issues. In short, the leader needs to be alert, quick-witted, and clear-thinking, with the ability to draw distinctions, state insights lucidly, and make essential points stand out vividly.

Just as important for the leader is a sense of *impartiality* or *fairness*. Allowing minority views full expression, phrasing questions accurately, and summarizing contributions fairly are important means of ensuring cooperation among persons who may differ vigorously. At the same time, however, keen analysis and impartial leadership must be tempered with *tact* and *good will* both in words and in manner. There is no place in the good discussion for a leader who is easily irritated or who says things in a way that irritates others.

In addition to maintaining the attitudes of objectivity and helpfulness that should characterize the behavior of any person participating in group interaction, the discussion leader has certain *special functions* that must be performed well. These are:

1. Getting the discussion started.
2. Keeping it on the major objective.
3. Bringing out the essential facts.
4. Ensuring opportunities for all members to participate.
5. Helping to resolve conflicts.
6. Summarizing the progress of the group.

These functions, it should be emphasized, are not *solely* the responsibility of the leader. Each individual in the group must *share* these tasks. Sometimes — with or without guidance from the leader — the other group members will perform many or all of them satisfactorily. The leader, however, must stand ready to aid the discussants if needed and, by studying the interplay of opposing views or factions, keep in broad perspective the progress of the discussion as a whole.

Getting the Discussion Started

As a rule, the leader should begin the discussion by stating the subject, question, or problem to be considered and pointing out its importance, especially as it relates to the members of the group. This statement, while brief, should be made with vigor and earnestness, suggest the vital nature of the subject, and be expressed in concrete terms supported by specific facts and data. It should, moreover, lead into a series of provocative questions designed to pull members of the group into the discussion.

In a problem-solving discussion, for example, the leader might ask, "In what way have you, personally, met this problem recently?" Or better, "Bob told me that he ran into this problem in the following way. . . . [Briefly describe the circumstance.] Have any of you had a similar experience; or, if not, how did your experience differ?" If such questions fail to stimulate discussion, individuals may be asked to explain how they would like to approach the subject, or to tell how they analyze the problem initially. Or the leader may go to the board and start a list—of causes of the problem, of types of people or groups affected by it, of terms needing definition, of proposed courses of action—of anything which relates to the matter under study and calls for enumeration. Curiously enough, people who hesitate to speak up on their own initiative seldom hesitate to add to a list once it has been started.

Still another method of getting a discussion started is to bring out, at the beginning, one or more extreme points of view concerning the question. The leader can introduce these views very briefly or, better, call on members of the group who hold them. Nothing seems to stir people into active participation quite so readily as an extreme statement with which to disagree. The danger of this method, of course, is that it may start a verbal battle which can lead the discussion astray or stir up personal animosity. Judiciously used, however, it is an effective discussion-starter.

Keeping the Discussion on the Major Objective

The tendency of a group to stray from the central issue can be greatly diminished if the leader writes on a chalkboard a short, tentative outline of the points that need to be considered. If a board is not available, the leader may be prepared to supply each participant with a dittoed or mimeographed copy of the outline. When people can see what points need to be taken up and in what order, they are more likely to follow them systematically. Unless something important has been inadvertently omitted from the outline, the leader can—from time to time—direct attention to the various items in it, one after another, and thus keep the discussion progressing steadily.

Using the main points of the outline as a skeletal framework, often a leader also fills in the subpoints on the board as they are brought up and developed, thus providing the group with an ever-present visual summary of what has been said or decided. Then, if the discussion takes an irrelevant turn, all the leader usually needs to do is call attention to the irrelevancy and refer again to the outline. This kind of reference-check is also useful when someone doubles back to a point already covered or jumps ahead to a point the group is not yet ready to consider. Of course, the leader must be sensible and fair in trying to hold the group to an outline or plan that is, at best, tentative and untested. If it obviously will not serve the interests and inclinations of the discussants, the profitable course is to modify it or to depart from it. In general, however, unless flaws do emerge, the group will do well to hold to the outline as they develop or approve of it at the outset.

Bringing Out the Essential Facts

Normally, if one of the foregoing procedures is followed and if the participants are well informed and fair minded, the information needed to solve the problem or cover the subject will almost surely be brought out, and no special effort beyond that indicated will be required. Unfortunately, discussion groups do not always function so smoothly and efficiently, and then the leader must make sure that important data or views are introduced and that opinions are not mistaken for facts.

When something has been overlooked, the leader may tactfully inquire, "Has anyone noticed that . . . ?" or may say, "Mary called my attention yesterday to the fact that . . . . Has anyone else noticed this to be true?" It is even better, of course, to ask some individual in the group a question that will elicit the needed fact. Similarly, if there is a tendency to dwell on one point of view to the exclusion of an equally important one, the leader may call attention to the neglect by suggesting, "Perhaps we should ask John to express his view of this" or "I have heard this other point of view expressed, too . . . . What do you think of it?"

While a discussant should never directly be accused of twisting facts or making unsupported claims, such statements—if made—should not be allowed to pass unchallenged. The leader or any other member may handle them by asking the speaker for further details or for the evidence on which a statement is based. Thus the leader may say, "I wonder if you would tell us, Helen, what has led you to this conclusion?" or "Is that a statement of your own opinion, Henry, or have you observed it to be true in actual practice?"

In sum, by skillful questioning, all points of view can be brought out, crucial facts made available, misstatements corrected, and the group provided with the background on which thorough knowledge or wise judgment depends.

Ensuring Participation by All

At times, one or two persons in the group may begin to monopolize the interchange. Frequently such persons have a great deal to contribute, but there is also a strong possibility that they will repeat themselves or expand obvious points needlessly. When this occurs, the leader may avoid recognizing a talkative member by looking the other way. Or, calling on other members of the group—

by name if necessary—he may ask questions which will lead the discussion forward and away from the overworked point or the over-talkative person. In extreme cases, he may find it necessary to suggest in a tactful manner that if the discussion is to be profitable, all must have an opportunity to participate; or he may have to set a limit on the number of times any one member can speak. If the time for closing the discussion is drawing near, sometimes a statement of that fact will spur into action members who hitherto have remained silent. Remember that the duty of the leader is not to tell the group what to think, but to maintain an atmosphere in which all members can think most productively; and such an atmosphere will not be possible unless they have an equal chance to participate.

Resolving Conflict

Vigorous conflict among discussants' ideas is essential to productive, creative interaction; and in its positive manifestations, it can help to integrate contrasting ideas and contribute toward a better and more practical solution than might otherwise have been the case. Occasionally, however, on problems concerning which the members of the group have deep feelings or ingrained biases, the conflict becomes emotionalized and bitter. If the discussants themselves cannot resolve their differences, then the leader must act to ease the tensions.

Sometimes it is sufficient merely to restate the emotionalized comments in neutral or less conflictive language, and thus bring the discussion back to a more rational or objective level. Humor, as we have suggested, may prove a useful "escape valve" in situations of this kind. As we have mentioned earlier, a good-natured and well-intended jest or a light-hearted remark may break the tension, dissipate the animosity, and get the discussion back on the track. If this fails, the leader may suggest that unless comments are kept fact-centered and rational, a wise or workable decision cannot be reached. In cases where conflict persists and opposing factions seem unable or unwilling to compromise their views, a vote can be called for and the group asked to abide by a majority decision. Sometimes it is even advisable to adjourn the discussion for a period of hours or days and to tackle the problem again later when tempers have had a chance to cool. This kind of heat-reducing interim is frequently employed in labor-management negotiations and in other situations where divergence of goals or values makes the reaching of agreement difficult.

Summarizing Progress

Often a group becomes so concerned with the details of a problem or so engrossed in the consideration of one or two isolated points that it fails to realize how much ground it has already covered or how much yet remains to be done. For this reason the leader should, from time to time, summarize the progress which has been made, recalling those facets of the subject that have thus far been explored, recounting those points that have been agreed upon, and calling attention to the major differences that yet remain to be resolved. Such summing up, obviously, must reflect what the group has said or decided, and not what the leader thinks about the matter. Moreover, the members always should have an opportunity to correct or to add to the summary as given. Unless accurate and well-timed summations are injected into the discussions at appropriate points, it is almost impossible for a group to keep aware of its progress.

At the conclusion of the discussion as a whole, of course, the leader—either alone or with the aid of the other group members—should summarize the discussion in its entirety, making clear exactly what has been agreed upon and specifying any problems or disagreements that remain to be settled. This final summary, like the internal summaries made earlier, should reflect the conclusions of the group rather than those of the leader, and should give attention to all important points of view. In addition, in the closing summary the leader should remind the members of the methods they have chosen to put their decision into effect and single out such provisions—the appointing of committees, the scheduling of future meetings, if any, etc.—as are necessary to make sure that the decision is carried out.

PROFILE OF THE EFFECTIVE DISCUSSANT

Earlier, in our brief overview of the "Essentials for the Individual Participant" (pages 92–93), we suggested that as we proceeded with our analysis of the discussion process you should note the ramifications and specific applications of those essentials and put together a more complete profile of the competent discussant. This seems a fitting juncture, therefore, at which to review and enlarge that profile by noting that to be genuinely effective each individual's participation should reflect to a significant degree:

1. A thorough grasp of the subject.
2. Pertinent insights into backgrounds of other members of the group.
3. An ability to think clearly, alertly, and quickly.
4. Skills in listening and paying attention.
5. An ability to devise, introduce, clarify, and support new ideas.
6. A capacity for accepting criticism of one's own ideas.
7. An ability to analyze, evaluate, and relate others' views.
8. An ability to agree with good ideas at variance with one's own.
9. Skill in tactful disagreement when indicated or required.

10. Skill in phrasing and asking questions.
11. A willingness to move continuously toward the group's major goal.
12. An ability to summarize points or group progress.
13. A willingness to share leadership responsibilities when and as need arises.
14. An ability to differentiate significant information and superfluous details.
15. Patience.

THE DISCUSSION PLAN

Earlier we have noted that a sense of *orderliness* should characterize small group interaction, and we have emphasized from time to time that a discussion will proceed more systematically and be more likely to reach a satisfying conclusion if it follows a previously worked-out outline, plan, or agenda. Ideally, the entire group should participate in developing such a plan. If, however, circumstances make this impossible, the leader must take responsibility for originating it and submitting it to the group for its consideration, approval, or modification.

Groups having as their purpose the pooling and exchanging of ideas and information will, for obvious reasons, find it desirable to follow a plan that differs in a number of significant respects from the plan that works best for groups having as their purpose the reaching of an agreement, the making of a decision, or the solving of a problem. We shall, therefore, consider agendas for these two major types of discussions separately.

A Discussion Plan for Learning Groups

Often a study group discusses a book, or parts of it, and occasionally uses a study outline or syllabus prepared by an authority in a given field. When this is the case, the discussion should, as a rule, follow a sequence similar to the outline of the material studied. Usually, however, no prepared outline is available; or if it is, it is not suited to the needs of the particular group. In such situations, the discussion may be broken down into four major phases or stages: (1) introduction, (2) analysis, (3) investigation, and (4) summary.

Phase 1: Introduction of the Discussion Question

The introduction consists of a statement of the discussion question by the leader, together with one or two illustrative examples showing its general importance or its relationship to the individuals in the group.

Phase 2: Analysis of the Discussion Subject

After this introduction, the members of the group analyze the subject and then proceed to the discussion of those aspects or facets of the subject which seem most essential to their major purpose. They should explore such typical lines of inquiry as:

A. What importance does the subject have for this group? Why?
B. Into what major topical divisions may the subject conveniently be separated? (See p. 296 and pp. 385–388 for suggestions.)
C. To which of these topical divisions should the discussion be narrowed?
    (1). Which topics are of greatest importance to this group?
    (2). Upon which topics are the members of this group already informed so fully that further discussion would be fruitless?

Summary of the Analysis Phase. At the conclusion of the analysis phase, the leader or the group as a whole should summarize the list of topics to which the general subject has been narrowed, and suggest the order in which these may best be considered.

Phase 3: Investigation of Selected Topical Divisions of the Subject

In the investigative phase, the members should consider systematically and in order each topic chosen as a result of Question C above. The ensuing discussion of each topic usually may be centered in such exploratory inquiries as:

A. What terms need definition? Is there agreement as to their generally accepted meaning? What definition does the group prefer?
B. What background material needs to be considered: historical, social, geographic, etc.?
C. What personal experiences of members of the group might illuminate and clarify the topic?
D. What principles or causal relationships may be inferred from the information thus brought forth?

Phase 4: Final Summary of the Discussion as a Whole

In this concluding phase, the leader—with the aid of the other group members—should summarize briefly the most important matters covered in both the analytical and investigative phases of the discussion. This concluding summary need not be exhaustive. Its purpose is to bring together the more important points emerging from the interaction and to do so in such a way that they will be easily remembered, and their relationship to each other and to the general subject clearly recognized.

Adapting the Plan for Learning Groups. Obviously this plan for information-gathering and learning is only a general one. For any actual discussion, it will need to be adapted to the particular subject and to the purpose for its exploration; and it will also need to be developed in more detail. Whether you are a group leader or a participating member, by thinking through this general plan in the light of your own knowledge of the subject, you will, of course, be able to prepare specific questions that will bring out needed information from various members; and by properly analyzing the interests and knowledge of the other people in the group, you may predict with some accuracy the direction in which their interests will probably lead them during the discussion.

A good method is to prepare an outline of such a plan, phrased as a series of questions rather than as a series of statements. Above all, however, remember that the function of a discussion plan is to *guide* rather than to straitjacket the group. It must, therefore, be kept *flexible* and *changeable* in any way that seems advisable as the discussion proceeds. Nor should it be supposed that the plan outlined here is the only sensible way in which a learning discussion can be structured. If you are a novice in the discussion process and have no notion of how to proceed, it will provide you with something to start on. As your experience grows, however, you will be able to strike out for yourself and to devise approaches particularly suited to the subjects you deal with. In discussion, as in so many other activities, it is results rather than adherence to form or procedure that is important; means should serve ends rather than direct or stifle them. It is always important to have a plan of some kind, and it is important that this plan be reasonable and systematic. Beyond this, however, *adaptability to need and purpose should be your guide.*

A Discussion Plan for Decision-Making Groups

Decision-making groups, as we said earlier, are concerned with more than the exchange of opinions and information; they are faced with situations requiring agreement on beliefs or on courses of action to be pursued. If the group is one which meets regularly, such as an executive committee, the members may not be aware of the problem prior to the meeting at which it is to be discussed. More frequently, the problem will be known in advance, and at times a serious difficulty or conflict of interests may be the very reason for calling the group together. At any rate, *the principal function of a decision-making group is to solve a problem: to reach a consensus on what to do about it and how to do it.*

As in the case of the learning or study group, there is no one plan that should always be followed by groups concerned with decision and action. A procedure that has proved practical for such groups in a variety of situations, however, is based on John Dewey's analysis of how individuals think reflectively when confronted with a problem that requires solution.[3] As modified for a discussion agenda, this plan involves six stages:

1. Defining the problem.
2. Analyzing the problem.
3. Suggesting solutions to the problem.
4. Evaluating the suggested solutions.
5. Choosing the preferred solution.
6. Putting the preferred solution into effect.

Stage 1: Defining the Problem

This stage opens with:

A. Brief introductory remarks by the leader touching on the general purpose of the discussion and its importance to the group, followed by:
B. Consideration of the following questions:
    (1). How can the problem under consideration be phrased as a *question?* Usually, the question will have been phrased by the leader or the group before the actual discussion begins. If not, it should be phrased and agreed upon at this time.
    (2). What terms need defining?
        a. What do the terms in the question mean?
        b. What other terms or concepts likely to be encountered during the course of the discussion should be defined at this time?

Stage 2: Analyzing the Problem

The analysis of the problem confronting the group consists of evaluating its scope and importance, discovering its causes, determining the essential matters that need correction, and setting up the basic requirements for an effective solution. The following sequence of questions is suggested:

A. What is the evidence that an unsatisfactory situation exists?
    (1). Is the problem sufficiently serious to warrant discussion and action at this time? (If the answer to this question is negative, further discussion is obviously pointless.)

(2). Is the situation likely to improve by itself, or will it become worse if nothing is done about it?

B. What caused this difficulty?

   (1). Are its causes primarily economic, political, social, etc.?

C. What conditions in the present situation must be corrected? What demands must be met; what desires satisfied?

D. What satisfactory elements in the present situation must be retained?

E. In the light of the answers to Questions C and D above, what are the essential criteria by which any proposed plan is to be judged?

   (1). What must the plan do?

   (2). What must the plan avoid?

   (3). What limits of time, money, manpower, or other restrictive circumstances must be considered?

Summarizing the Analysis of the Problem. The leader, with the help of the group, should summarize the points agreed upon thus far. Particularly important is a clear statement of the agreements reached on Question E because these requirements will subsequently serve as the basic criteria for evaluating the proposed solutions. Moreover, a clear understanding regarding these requirements will tend to make further discussion more objective and will minimize the tendency to attack and defend proposals because of personal prejudices.

Stage 3: Suggesting Solutions to the Problem

In this step, the group should:

A. Bring forth all proposed solutions for the difficulty.

   (1). Be sure that each proposal is defined or explained briefly, but clearly.

   (2). If many solutions are suggested, group them according to type for initial consideration.

B. Be sure that all the proposals are listed, preferably on a chalkboard, so that the subsequent evaluations and comparisons will be complete.

Stage 4: Evaluating the Suggested Solutions

The various proposals suggested for meeting the problem now should be examined and compared in an attempt to determine the relative merits of each, to detect the advantages and disadvantages. In this stage, of course, the group's objective is to arrive at the most satisfactory solution and one which will be acceptable—ultimately—to most, if not all, of its members. The following procedure is suggested:

A. Note the elements that are common to all the proposals and reach agreement for their retention.
B. Examine the differences in the proposals in the light of the criteria set up in Question E of the analysis step.
C. On the basis of this examination, eliminate the less desirable proposals and narrow the discussion to those which remain.
D. Examine the remaining proposals to see (1) whether one of them can be revised to eliminate objectionable features or to add desirable ones, or (2) whether the better parts of two or more plans can be combined into a new and more satisfactory one.

Stage 5: Choosing the Preferred Solution

When the suggested solutions to the problem have been evaluated and weighed, the group—guided by the leader—will have to choose the best or most workable one. Sometimes the most desirable or practical solution will have emerged during the evaluation stage. If it has not, the members must now choose the one they prefer, either by consensus or by vote.

When an agreement has been reached, the leader—again with the aid of the other discussants—should sum up the principal features of the accepted solution. In a group having no power or authority to act, this summation will normally end the discussion. If the group is empowered to take the necessary action, the process moves into a sixth and final stage.

Stage 6: Putting the Preferred Solution into Effect

When a group is able to put its proposed solution into operation—to *actuate* it—the members should consider the following possible steps:

A. Selection of persons or committees to be responsible for taking the action agreed upon.
B. Determination of the time, place, and other circumstances which govern putting the proposal into effect.
C. Taking official action, such as appropriating money or providing legal authorization whenever such action is necessary.

Summarizing the Actuative Stage of the Discussion. The leader should briefly restate the action agreed upon to be sure that it is clear to the group and has its concurrence. This summarization normally ends the communicative transaction.

Adapting the Plan to the Proper Stage of the Discussion Question. The foregoing plan for decision-making groups covers, of course, the whole deliberative process from the first analysis of existing conditions to the taking of the final action. In concise, diagrammatic form, the stages of that process may be depicted thus:

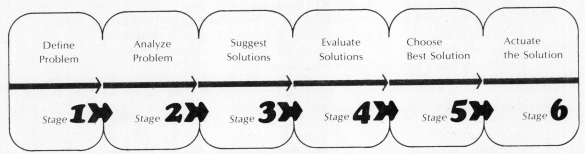

Figure 1. A SIX-STAGE AGENDA FOR PROBLEM-SOLVING GROUPS

In actual practice, however, this entire process may not be required. As Harrison Elliott points out in *The Process of Group Thinking*, when members of a group first face a problem, they may find it in any one of several conditions or stages.[4] For instance, when initially encountered, the problem may be (*a*) in a baffling or confusing condition with no clear outlines; or (*b*) at a stage where the difficulty already has been well defined; or (*c*) at a point where alternative solutions have been proposed; or (*d*) at a stage where a single definite proposal exists; or (*e*) where all that remains is to settle on ways and means of carrying the solution to a conclusion.

How much of the decision-making process will need to be included in the discussion plan will depend, then, upon the *stage* at which the question comes before the group. If a proposal has already been approved at a previous meeting, or if the group finds itself in immediate agreement on it, all that needs to be discussed is the method of putting the proposal into effect. Similarly, if the group meets to consider the merits of a single definite solution to a recognized problem, the analysis stage, as outlined above, can be condensed to a brief discussion of the essential requirements for a satisfactory plan; or, following a brief, concise summary of those criteria by the leader, the discussants may proceed immediately to an examination of the proposal in the light of requirements specified. *An essential part of preparing a discussion plan, therefore, is to determine at what stage the question is likely to come before the group.* You can then limit your outline so as to pick up the discussion at that stage without needless reconsideration of points already settled. The leader, however, should study the entire outline so that he will be able to adapt accordingly if something he thought was settled turns out still to be in dispute.

A Plan for the Discussion of a Series of Problems

Executive committees, governing boards, and similar groups often are faced with the necessity of discussing several problems during the course of a single meeting. Some of these problems may be related to one another, while others may have little or no connection. Obviously, related questions should be discussed together or in immediate sequence, but the order in which unrelated questions are to be considered requires some thought by the chairman. The following procedure, or a similar one, may be helpful in arranging the agenda for such a meeting:

Make a list of all the items to come up for consideration. Include both important and less important matters, those which need immediate attention and those which can be postponed.

Reduce this list to fit the time limit. Determine how much time is available for the discussion, and cross off enough of the less important items to bring the list within that limitation. The deleted items can be put on a supplementary list to be used in case the primary items are disposed of in less time than expected.

Arrange the items to be discussed in an orderly sequence. Some matters are dependent upon others. Suppose, for example, that the managing board of a college newspaper is meeting to decide upon the size of the editorial staff, but a proposal is also under consideration for issuing the paper daily instead of weekly. Obviously, the second item would have to be settled before the first. If you are to lead the discussion efficiently, you must arrange the items for consideration so that there will be no need to duplicate or double back on what has already been discussed.

Outline the subsidiary questions involved in each major problem to be discussed. In the proposal to issue the college paper on a daily basis, a number of subordinate and consequent questions will need to be considered: What will be the added cost of printing and distributing? Can enough advertising space be sold to meet this added expense? What will be done about existing advertising contracts based on the weekly plan? Is there enough local news to provide copy for a daily paper? Should an attempt be made to carry national as well as local news? The leader must have such points well in mind so that none of them will be overlooked. A mimeographed list or chalkboard outline of these points will often help keep the discussion centered on the problem and moving in an orderly fashion.

Finally, to the greatest extent possible, anticipate the questions that will arise from each decision that is made. If, for example, a decision has been made to publish the paper daily, a procedure must be agreed upon for getting the approval of the college authorities; a date must be set for instituting the change; and plans must be laid for putting the proposal into effect. As each decision is reached, the leader must be ready to lead the discussion on to problems growing out of that decision. Leadership of this kind will make the discussion orderly and productive.

SUGGESTED DISCUSSION QUESTIONS

The first list includes both questions of fact and questions of value, suitable for use in study groups. The second list contains questions of policy for decision-making groups.

For Study Groups:

1. How effective is our freshman-orientation program?
2. What benefits does the undergraduate gain from participating in extracurricular activities?
3. Why do students flunk out of college?
4. How does the government regulate the food and drug industries?
5. How do Russian and Chinese communism differ in philosophy and purpose?
6. What are we learning from the exploration of space?
7. How have expressways affected American cities?
8. In what ways does the federal government support research in science (or the humanities)?
9. How effective is our present foreign policy?
10. How does our court system work?

For Decision-Making Groups:

1. What can be done to increase the effectiveness of student government in our college?

2. How can colleges and universities meet the problem of increased costs?
3. What can be done to increase church attendance?
4. How can we control unethical practices in political campaigns?
5. How can we fight racial and sex discrimination in the United States?
6. How can labor and management increase their understanding of each other's problems?
7. How can the quality of television programs be improved?
8. How can we reduce the number of traffic deaths?
9. What policy should the United States pursue in Southeast Asia?
10. Should we have governmental censorship of the arts?

The small group communication process, its dimensions and dynamics, have been our central concerns in these pages. We have considered the purposes and procedural requirements for successful group discussion, emphasizing in particular the roles, responsibilities, and leadership functions of the group as a whole and of the individual participant. Using as a focus the learning or study group and the decision-making group, we have laid out a "working" plan for each and have stressed throughout the importance of careful preparation and the need for perception and skill in defining, analyzing, evaluating, and summarizing the factors in and progress of the interaction as it moves through successive phases or stages toward outcomes that are group-determined and group-rewarding.

Finally, we hope that as a result of your study of this chapter you have further clarified and expanded your understanding of the speech communication process as a whole, and that you have sharpened your perceptions of the similarities, differences, and interrelationships inherent in the *various* forms of communication. Again to review and summarize to this point, we have attempted to place the essential qualities and their interrelatedness within the diagrammatic framework, as shown in Figure 2, page 116.

FOOTNOTES

[1] *Excerpt from* Group Processes: An Introduction to Group Dynamics *by Joseph Luft. Copyright 1970, National Press Books. Reprinted by permission. Also note the entirety of Luft's excellent summary of "Group Versus Individual Productivity," pp. 30–31.*

[2] *Ibid., p. 42.*

[3] *John Dewey*, How We Think *(Boston: D. C. Heath & Company, 1910), p. 72.*

[4] *Harrison S. Elliott*, The Process of Group Thinking *(New York: Association Press, 1932), p. 89 ff.*

Characterizing QUALITIES and CONDITIONS	DYADIC *person to person*	SMALL GROUP *all to all*	PUBLIC ADDRESS *one to many*	MASS COMMUNICATION *print and electronic; one or few to many*
Number of Persons	2	3–15		
Degree of Intimacy	High	Fairly high		
Degree of Formality	Minimal	Minimal to medium		
Time Limits	Flexible	Pre-set—usually		
Need for Prestructuring of Message	Minimum to medium	Increased—but flexible		
Role of Nonverbal Factors in Projection of Message	Minimal	Moderate		
Evidence of Communicator Purpose	Emerges quickly—usually	Fairly clear and strong		
Alternation of Speaker-Listener Roles	Frequent	Frequent, but more restricted		
Opportunities for Perceiving Listener Feedback	Maximal	Numerous and frequent		
Opportunities for Adjusting to Listener Feedback	Maximal	Numerous		
Opportunities to Assess Fulfillment of Communicative Purpose	Numerous	Numerous and continuing		
Opportunities for Mutual Exploration of Ideas	Many	Extensive		

Figure 2. BASIC FORMS OF SPEECH COMMUNICATION: SOME GRADATIONAL QUALITIES AND INTERRELATIONSHIPS

Problems and Probes

1. Compare and contrast *small group discussion,* as defined in this chapter, with the following types of oral interchange: social conversation, interviews, ongoing communication in the classroom, and "rap sessions."

2. Listen to a four- or five-member group discussion involving a decision-making task, and—using as a basis what you hear and observe— evaluate the extent to which you feel that each of the discussants demonstrated the essentials of good participation. Review pages 105–106. *(Note:* For this evaluation you may use a discussion that takes place in any one of your classes, on the radio, or on television.) To help you pinpoint your evaluations, use the "Discussion Checklist" shown on the following page. Feel free to modify it to suit your purposes; it is offered only as a tentative guide.

3. What special problems or difficulties does a decision-making group face, which a study group does not need to deal with? Does the absence of these problems mean that it is easier to conduct a profitable study-group discussion than to conduct a productive decision-making discussion?

4. If you were planning a small group discussion on the first, fourth, or tenth question for decision-making groups, as listed on pages 114–115, what specific sub-questions or issues would you want to be sure to include? In what *order* do you think these issues might best be considered by the group? Why?

5. If you were planning a decision-making discussion on the third, fifth, or ninth subject in the list referred to above, what information in the nature of facts, figures, etc., would you want the group to have at its disposal? Why would each of these kinds of information be crucial to an intelligent decision?

6. Remembering that a good question for discussion should be stated briefly, clearly, and objectively, frame a question on each of the following subjects suitable (*a*) for a study group and (*b*) for a decision-making group:

School Dropouts	Safety Features in
The Military Budget	Automobiles
Space Travel	Intercollegiate Athletics
Governmental Support	Business and Government
of the Arts	Modern Architecture
Civil Defense	Mass Transportation

SMALL GROUP COMMUNICATION—A DISCUSSION CHECKLIST

Below, in the column at left is a list of preparative qualities and participative skills and abilities desirable in small group interaction. On the basis of what you hear and observe during the progression of a small group discussion, evaluate the extent to which you feel that the comments and contributions of each of the discussants demonstrate evidence of the specified skills, abilities, etc. In the spaces provided at the right of the items, write in either an "X" or an appropriate evaluative term such as "Little," "Some," "Much," "Few," "Many," "Several," etc. If you conclude that there is no basis for reaction or insufficient evidence to warrant a judgment, leave the space blank.

DISCUSSION QUESTION: _____   Date: _____

Skills, Abilities, and Qualities	Discussant A	Discussant B	Discussant C	Discussant D	Discussant E
1. In-depth knowledge of subject					
2. Insights into co-discussants					
3. Straight, orderly thinking					
4. Listening skills					
5. Ability to phrase and ask questions					
6. Analytical/evaluative skills					
7. Origination of new ideas					
8. Skill in interjecting ideas					
9. Ability to develop ideas					
10. Constructive acceptance of variant views					
11. Skill in disagreeing with others' views					
12. Skill in moving discussion forward					
13. Helping to keep discussion goal-oriented					
14. Willingness to share time with others					
15. Willingness to share leadership functions					
16. Skill in summarizing points					
17. Skill in summarizing group progress					
18. Tact					
19. Patience					

Names of Discussants: (A) _____   Name of Evaluator/Reactor:

(B) _____   _____

(C) _____

118   (D) _____

(E) _____

7. Formulate some of the significant criteria which you think a decision-making group should employ in evaluating proposals for:

A new superhighway between your town and the state capital.

A plan for having the students in your college grade the faculty members on the effectiveness of their teaching.

A law requiring periodic reexamination of each automobile driver's knowledge of traffic laws and driving skills.

Raising the sales tax in your state.

8. In considering "Leadership and Leadership Functions" (pages 100–105), we emphasized the importance of ensuring to all members of the group an opportunity to participate and also to help resolve conflict. Nearly every small group discussion will include people who—because of their backgrounds, training, and predispositions—are reluctant to participate, tend to dominate, etc. We might describe such members as:

"The Reticent Reactor"   "The Wandering Willie"
"The Garrulous Gabber"   "The Confirmed Conformist"
"The Defensive Detractor"   "The Constant Challenger"

"The Reticent Reactor"   "The Garrulous Gabber"   "The Defensive Detractor"

"The Wandering Willie"   "The Confirmed Conformist"   "The Constant Challenger"

Prepare a brief written description of the typical interactive behaviors of these six types and—assuming that you are serving as the group leader—describe how you would handle each one in order to keep the discussion balanced and moving steadily forward.

9. Listen to a small group discussion—in class or outside—and analyze what went on in terms of *leadership*. In particular, evaluate the extent to which the instructor or discussion leader exemplified the qualities outlined on pages 101–105.

10. Assume that you are to be the nominal leader of a small group discussion in which the participants will be considering one of the learning or study questions listed on pages 114–115, or a similar question of your own choosing. Work out a *plan* for this discussion, following the steps outlined on pages 106–114 of this chapter.

11. Assume that you are leading a discussion on some subject or problem of current interest. Frame several tactful questions or comments which you might use if some of the participants were (*a*) monopolizing the interaction, (*b*) remaining silent, (*c*) wandering from the point under consideration, (*d*) failing to back up an expression of opinion with solid facts, (e) making comments that threaten to create emotionalized conflict.

12. In small group communication, as we have repeatedly emphasized in this chapter, the interaction will be most genuine and productive only when each member *participates* frequently. Observe either a learning group discussion or one in which decision-making is a goal, and keep a record (*a*) of the *number of times* each discussant speaks and (*b*) the *persons to whom his or her comments are directed.* For this particular analysis, do not be concerned with the quality of the contributions—only with their frequency and direction. For this probe, use the "Participation Check-Chart" shown on page 121 for your record-keeping.

Oral Activities and Speaking Assignments

1. Your instructor will divide the class membership into small groups of approximately five or six students each. Each group should then select a nominal leader and—with the approval of your instructor—work out a plan for a decision-making discussion. Under the guidance of the leader, reduce this plan to a workable outline which all members of your particular group may keep before them during the discussion of the question.

SMALL GROUP COMMUNICATION: PARTICIPATION CHECK-CHART

Listen carefully to a group discussion, and—using the chart below—indicate (a) the number of times each discussant speaks and (b) the individuals to whom he or she addresses the comments. If the speaker appears to be addressing remarks to the entire group, so indicate. Remember, you are concerned here with the quantity or frequency of interaction—not with its quality.

DISCUSSION QUESTION: _____ Date: _____

Origin of Comment	Comment Directed to					
	Discussant A	Discussant B	Discussant C	Discussant D	Discussant E	Entire Group
DISCUSSANT A	■					
DISCUSSANT B		■				
DISCUSSANT C			■			
DISCUSSANT D				■		
DISCUSSANT E					■	

Name of Discussants: Observer's Name:

(A) _____   _____

(B) _____

(C) _____

(D) _____

(E) _____

When the plan is ready, proceed with the discussion as such. Allow at least one or, preferably, two class periods for this oral activity as a whole. While a given group is engaged in the actual presentation of its discussion, the rest of the class members will serve as critical observers and evaluators, using for purposes of their assessment the "Discussion Checklist" (page 118) or the "Participation Check-Chart" (page 121).

2. Drawing upon the sources listed in the Suggestions for Further Reading at the close of this chapter and upon your own personal experience with small group discussion, prepare and present to the class a brief, informal speech or oral report on "What I Think Group Discussion Can Do for Me Personally." The presentation should be approximately three minutes in length and may be presented from a standing or sitting position—as your instructor may indicate.

Suggestions for Further Reading

Ernest G. Bormann, *Discussion and Group Methods* (New York: Harper & Row, Publishers, 1969).

D. Cartwright and A. Zander, eds., *Group Dynamics: Research and Theory* (New York: Harper & Row, Publishers, 1968).

Halbert E. Gulley, *Discussion, Conference, and Group Processes*, 2nd ed. (New York: Holt, Rinehart & Winston, Inc., 1968).

Carl E. Larson, "Forms of Analysis and Small Group Problem-Solving," *Speech Monographs* XXXVI (November 1969): 452–455.

Joseph Luft, *Group Processes: An Introduction to Group Dynamics* (Palo Alto, Calif.: National Press Books, 1970).

James C. McCroskey and D. W. Wright, "The Development of an Instrument for Measuring Interaction Behavior in Small Groups," *Speech Monographs* XXXVIII (November 1971): 335–340.

Gerald M. Phillips, *Communication and the Small Group* (Indianapolis: The Bobbs-Merrill Company, Inc., 1966).

Lawrence B. Rosenfeld, *Human Interaction in the Small Group Setting* (Columbus, Ohio: Charles E. Merrill Publishing Company, 1973).

Marvin E. Shaw, *Group Dynamics: The Psychology of Small Group Behavior* (New York: McGraw-Hill Book Company, 1971).

4
COMMUNICATING IN PUBLIC: SOME INITIAL CONCERNS

SOME DEFINITIONS AND DIMENSIONS

Broadly interpreted, any utterance—whether heard by one, few, or many—may be said to be "public." As we have defined the term, however, *public communication involves a single speaker who, in relatively formal tone and manner, presents a continuous, uninterrupted, informative, persuasive, or entertaining discourse on a subject of supposedly general interest to a sizeable number of other persons.*

We may further describe the form by noting that public communication is characterized, usually, by (*a*) an appreciable physical and, sometimes, psychological distance that separates speaker from listeners (*b*) in a communicative climate that remains fairly formal throughout (*c*) more or less definite, prescribed time limits and (*d*) lacks the intimacy typical of person-to-person and small group interaction; (*e*) messages that most often are carefully preplanned and prestructured and "tailored" to the special circumstance, and that (*f*) require significantly more sustained verbal and nonverbal presentation/projection than do other forms; (*g*) an apparent, overriding communicator purpose that is necessarily specific, sharply and steadily focused, and—quite often—expressly announced, but for which there are (*h*) minimal opportunities for ongoing, on-the-scene assessment of purpose-fulfillment; (*i*) a continuous and constant role-stability in which speaker *remains* speaker and listener *remains* listener throughout the speech event; (*j*) comparatively few opportunities for speaker perception of and (*k*) adjustment to listener feedback—all of which, in turn, greatly reduce opportunities for speaker and individual listeners *to explore ideas together.*

The public communication form is variously referred to as "public speaking," "public address," and "one-to-many interaction." By some it has been described as a science, by others as an art, and by still others as a "practical art." It is, of course, practical in that it is *useful* and performs numerous *functions* for the speaker, the listeners, and society as a whole. It is an art in the sense that some speeches, certainly, possess harmony of form, grace in delivery, and aesthetic qualities having poetic dimensions. And, like other arts, it has *methods* and a *system of principles* which can be taught, mastered, and applied to the many decisions that must be made about the content, language, organization, and delivery of messages.

Those principles and methods are the central concern of many of the remaining chapters of this book. In the present chapter, however, our interest centers on introducing certain foundational and practical matters which underlie these principles and give them point and purpose. Our remarks, we hope, will help you understand many of the more specific rules and directions you will encounter later.

FOUNDATIONAL FACTORS IN EFFECTIVE PUBLIC COMMUNICATION

Here, in the beginning, a word of caution is in order. Note that we have said that principles and methods can be taught. Their individualized *application* cannot be. Effectiveness as a speaker is something *you must learn for yourself through long and persistent effort*. Books and manuals may explain the rationale upon which competent public speaking rests and suggest methods that may have proved useful to others; your instructor may counsel with you concerning problems and help you overcome weaknesses. *Ultimately, however, the responsibility rests with you.* Unless you yourself are impelled by a genuine desire to improve, your communicative output is likely to be random, routine, and lacklustre. Unless you are willing, even eager, to invest the requisite time and effort, you cannot hope to become a really competent communicator.

At the foundation of all successful speaking—whatever the form—are certain personal qualities or attributes. To these characteristics you must add a knowledge and understanding of basic principles and functions of public speech communication, reinforced by systematic observation of what other speakers do, and by guided oral practice.

Characteristics of the Competent Communicator

If at this point you were to review what we have said about the communicator's qualities and traits, you would probably conclude correctly that the personal characteristics essential to effective communication in any form are (1) *integrity*, (2) *knowledge*, (3) *self-confidence*, (4) *verbal and nonverbal skills*, and (5) *sensitivity to people and situations*. Let us now look at these qualities as they characterize the public speaker in particular.

Integrity

More than two thousand years ago, the Greek philosopher Aristotle emphasized a truth that was then already old and widely recognized: *An effective speaker must be an effective person.* Success as a public speaker, he declared in his treatise on *Rhetoric*,[1] involves more than a ready vocabulary, pleasing diction, and coordinated gestures. To succeed, he must be intelligent and well informed not only about his immediate subject, but also about human affairs in general; and he must possess a high degree of poise and self-control. But above all, if an individual is to win public acceptance for his ideas, he must be respected as a person of character and moral worth by those who hear him.

This emphasis upon character as an essential element in public speaking has been echoed by major writers on the subject from Aristotle's time to our own. People never merely listen to a speech; they always listen to a *person* speaking. And because a speaker's words and manners mirror what he is, the *self* and the *expression of the self* can never be divorced. The person who has a reputation for seeking the facts and speaking the truth will be listened to because people believe in his integrity. Conversely, the person who is not respected can seldom, even with the strongest arguments or most subtle appeals, win lasting adherence to his views. "What you *are*," as the old proverb points out, "speaks so loudly that I cannot hear what you *say*."

In Chapter 1, we introduced the concept of *ethos* or *source-credibility* as being that persuasive force which resides in the character or reputation of the speaker. Of all the modes of persuasion, it is perhaps the strongest and most permanent; for when actions contradict words, we lose faith rather quickly in what is said. A speaker of poor character may win a temporary success, but soon he becomes known as a person who seeks unfair personal advantage or who suppresses or warps evidence to prove his case, and his ability to convince an audience is lost. The currency of his speech has been recognized as counterfeit.*

Knowledge

When Daniel Webster was asked how he was able to prepare his famous reply to Senator Robert Y. Hayne on such short notice, he replied that the ideas came to him like thunderbolts which he had only to reach out and seize, white hot, as they went smoking by. Of course, this store of "thunderbolts" was by no means an accident. Webster's credibility was already well established, certainly. In addition, over many years his constant study of law, literature, politics, and

---

For a detailed discussion of speaking ethically as a part of responsible communication, see Chapter 17, "Listening, Evaluation, and Ethical Judgment," pp. 447–469. Also see Robert L. Scott, The Speaker's Reader: Concepts in Communication (Glenview, Ill.: Scott, Foresman and Company, 1969), Part II, pp. 222–264.

human nature had filled his mind with an abundant supply of facts, illustrations, insights, and arguments. When faced with a specific speaking situation, he had only to call these forth. Successful communicators in all ages have had a similar "arsenal" of knowledge upon which to draw.

If you wish to broaden your knowledge and enhance your understanding of the world and the ideas and values of people within it, you, too, must read widely and observe carefully. Through such study and observation, your utterances will grow in depth and maturity. Fortunately, you need not wait, however, until you have reached middle age before you dare to speak in public. *You can start immediately.* The background you already have, when carefully considered and supplemented by additional study, will provide at the very least sufficient material for your practice speeches; and the actual process of selecting and organizing that material for a speech will help you to marshall and clarify your thinking.

As you grow in skill and confidence, you will of course want to reach out beyond immediate and familiar topics—to learn and to speak about subjects in *new* fields. In particular, since many of your speeches in subsequent years will no doubt deal with ideas and developments pertinent to your chosen field, you may want to investigate topics related to the business, profession, or career you intend to enter. From your study of the job-seeking interview in Chapter 2 you probably have a clearer concept of what you want to be and do. The more you learn about such matters at this time, the better you will be able to communicate intelligently about your profession and work in years to come and the more effectively you will be able to interact with others engaged both inside and outside of it.

Even the most thorough knowledge of your own field, however, is not sufficient. If you wish to become a well-rounded and interesting speaker, you must know about more than this single subject. Develop interests *outside* your job or profession. Keep abreast of current events by reading at least one daily newspaper and listening frequently to news broadcasts. Do science and technology intrigue you? If so, make it a point to keep up with recent developments in biology, chemistry, physics, and computerization. Study the findings of current research in medicine, electronics, astronomy, aeronautics, ecology, and population control. Do you like good literature? Find out as much as you can about current books and authors, both classic and contemporary. Cultivate a hobby. Widen your horizons. In short, try to become well informed on current trends and developments and on at least two or three subjects outside your chosen vocation.

Remember, too, that in order to communicate your ideas to persons who do not have your specialized knowledge, you will need to draw upon a variety of illustrative material. You will need to broaden your awareness and sharpen your perceptions. For this you will need also to read widely, observe carefully, and listen discerningly. Perhaps you will want to build up a file of pertinent notes and clippings. In speaking, as in any other activity, there is no substitute for knowledge that is thorough and varied.

Self-Confidence

The self-confident speaker is characterized by certain physical behaviors and mental attitudes. Among other things, he has an erect but comfortable posture, easy movements free of fidgeting or jerkiness, direct eye-to-eye contact with his listeners, earnestness and energy in his voice, and an alertness of mind which enables him to adapt his remarks to the nature of his audience and the demands of the occasion.

If you lack self-confidence, not only will you find it difficult to communicate with your listeners, but you will also experience difficulty in convincing them that you and your ideas merit their attention and respect. Among the major enemies of self-confidence are, of course, *self-consciousness* and *excessive nervousness.* In subsequent pages, we shall examine this matter of nervous energy more closely and suggest some things you may do to control, channel, and utilize it to your positive advantage. First, however, let us consider some of the steps you may take to reduce an undue consciousness of self and strengthen your poise and self-control in the speaking situation.

Choose an Interesting Subject. Have you ever noticed how a shy youngster loses his bashfulness when you get him to talk about what really interests him: his new telescope, the rabbit his dog was chasing, or the model moon rocket he is building? The more a speaker thinks about his subject and the less he thinks about himself, the less self-conscious he tends to become. Choose, therefore, material in which you are vitally interested; avoid topics toward which you are indifferent. Don't talk about something merely because you think it might make a good subject for a speech. Select instead a topic that will make you *want* to speak out—an idea that you are *eager* to communicate to others. On such a subject you usually will be able to talk more freely and confidently. If you "lose yourself" in your subject, you are almost sure to be less self-conscious.

Know Your Subject Thoroughly. Compare your feelings if called on to recite (*a*) when you have studied an assignment and (*b*) when you are unprepared. If you are thoroughly familiar with your subject, you will almost invariably feel more confident than when you are inadequately prepared. One way to gain an adequate knowledge of a subject is to study it assiduously to find out more about it than anyone in your audience will know. Another way is to pick a subject from your own experience—a subject about which you already have broad, direct, and personal knowledge. This sense of subject-mastery will do much to increase your poise and feeling of self-control.

For these beneficial and practical reasons, we strongly recommend—for your first few speeches at least—that you choose subjects you already know a good deal about. For later speeches, as your self-confidence increases and as your interests broaden and you enrich your understanding of communicative interaction, you will naturally want to select subjects that require more research and lead to new perspectives and insights. In neither case, however, should you choose a subject that is too broad or inclusive. You will tend to feel more confident if you talk about problems, situations, and events that you *experience* or *observe* in your day-to-day campus life or in your hometown than if, for example, with a smattering of information obtained from hasty reading, you try to compare American lifestyles with those of other countries.

Learn Thoroughly the Sequence of Ideas You Intend to Present. The motorist who travels along a familiar highway is confident of reaching his destination; but if he gets off on a strange or unmarked road, he grows less certain of his direction, hesitates at every turn, becomes increasingly confused, and may eventually become lost and miss his intended destination entirely. Similarly, you and your listeners will feel more confident if you have the direction of your speech firmly in mind—if you have memorized completely for instant recall the *major ideas* and the *sequence* in which you intend to present them. Do not interpret this advice to mean that you should memorize your speech word for word. We are speaking here only of the memorization of your main ideas and their interrelationship. The so-called memorized speech is quite another matter and one which we shall consider on page 143.

Speak in Public as Often as You Can. If you have learned to swim or drive a car or fly an airplane, you will remember how—in your first attempts—you were tense and unsure of yourself. But with each subsequent, successful try, your self-confidence grew. In the same way, each speech you deliver will strengthen your self-assurance and increase your poise. Therefore, speak to an audience as often as you can. Repeated attempts to interact with others, repeated exposures to audiences of different sizes and types, will remove much of the fear or apprehension such groups may now generate in you.*

Focus Your Attention on Your Audience. As we have steadily emphasized, in any kind of speaking, one of your basic, underlying purposes is to communicate ideas and feelings to someone else. When you enter a neighborhood store to make a purchase, ordinarily you do not worry about how you look or how you

---

*See, in this connection, Stanley F. Paulson, "Changes in Confidence During a Period of Speech Training," Speech Monographs XVIII (November 1951): 260–265; Edward R. Robinson, "What Can the Speech Teacher Do About Students' Stage Fright?" Speech Teacher VII (January 1959): 10–11; Louis Lerea, "The Verbal Behavior of Speech Fright," Speech Monographs (August 1956): 233.

are standing or speaking. Initially at least, you are primarily concerned only that the clerk understands you correctly. This same goal—to be sure that you are understood fully and accurately—should dominate your efforts in all forms and contexts of communicative interaction. In public, one-to-many situations, to concentrate on the reactions of the individuals to whom you are speaking is, of course, at least as important as it is in person-to-person and small group interaction. Perhaps more so. Certainly it is more *difficult.* Among the complicating factors the public speaker must consider are the sheer numbers of listeners; the enlarged spatial and, often, psychological distances involved; the uninterrupted and typically unidirectional flow of the discourse; and—above all—the fact that almost all of the feedback will be nonverbal rather than verbal.

These complexities, needless to say, demand that to be a successful public communicator you must concentrate constantly on your *audience.* Obviously, in your first speeches you are not going to be able to see and interpret everything that is happening—everything your listeners are doing. You can, however, at least watch for general responses—for verbal and nonverbal feedback—that indicate that most of your hearers appear to be getting your point. If not, you must say it over again in a different way or explain it more completely. One of the obvious, solid advantages in all this is that if you are thinking always of your hearers and the impact that your message is having upon them, inevitably you will have less and less time to worry about yourself. To be more *audience*-conscious is to be less *self*-conscious.

Learn to Use Physical Activity Purposefully. Properly employed, bodily movement serves two important functions: (1) it helps you communicate ideas and reinforce their presentation, and (2) it tends to "drain off" the tension generated by excessive nervous energy. We shall examine these functions more fully in Chapter 5, but in this brief overview you should take note of them and think of the implications they hold for you—especially as a public speaker.

Many factors contribute to the degree of nervousness you may feel as a speaker—including the state of your indigestion and the evident friendliness or hostility of persons to whom you are speaking.* Do not labor under the misapprehension that because you are tense you are in some way different from other people. Surveys have shown that from 60 to 75 percent of college students experience nervousness when speaking to an audience, and more than 30 percent consider it their most serious problem.[2] In fact, it is normal for you to feel keyed up because measurable changes in pulse rate, blood pressure, and muscle tension probably are occurring within your body.[3] Even in deepest sleep your muscles are never completely relaxed; they invariably have a certain amount of tension

---

*See Theodore Clevenger, Jr., "A Synthesis of Experimental Research in Stage Fright," Quarterly Journal of Speech XLV (April 1959): 134–145.

which physiologists call "muscle tonus." When you are awake, this tonus is higher; and it increases when you are preparing to do something important.

Begin, then, by recognizing that *for all of us* the speechmaking event or the anticipation of communicating with others generates a certain amount of nervous energy. This is *normal.* This is *desirable.* So decide now to make this energy work *for* you. Experiment with it. Try to discover various ways to make it serve you and your speech purpose.

Just as the runner is tense before the gun is fired to start a race, so the speaker who confronts an audience of whatever size justifiably feels nervous strain. But the runner's nervousness disappears almost at the instant the race begins and his muscles "go into action." Very likely, as a public speaker you will enjoy a comparable experience: the moment you start to speak, that tense, "uptight" feeling will begin to drain away, and the built-up overcharge of nervous energy will begin to level off. Especially will this be the case if you begin immediately to harness that energy and channel it into constructive communicative behavior. This is one of several good reasons why we urge you to *speak often.* Even if you are unusually nervous or tense, when you have prepared well and know what you want to say, the more often you face an audience, the easier it will become.

One of the constructive ways in which you can use physical activity is, of course, in the expression and reinforcement of your ideas. When you are trying to communicate with others, especially in a public setting, move purposefully in relation to your audience, and experiment with bodily gestures to help you describe and present your ideas more clearly and appropriately. Very probably you will discover rather quickly that such physical activities, even if a bit awkward at first, can help stimulate energetic thought and expression. If you clarify and reinforce what you say with bodily movements and with gestures of your head, hands, and arms, you are almost sure to speak more vigorously and to feel greater self-assurance and confidence.

As you turn to a new idea, for instance, walk from one part of the room or rostrum to another. This serves usefully in effecting transitions. Go to the chalkboard and draw a diagram or write down the points you especially want your audience to remember. Use bodily movements to describe for your listeners the object you are talking about and/or to demonstrate how it works. Imagine that you are personally on the actual scene you are describing, and use your hands and arms to point out where each object is located. By learning to expend nervous energy in these and similarly positive ways, you can increase your self-confidence and—simultaneously—add meaning and vitality and vividness to what you say.*

Much of the sparkle and alertness that we admire in good speakers

---

*For a full discussion of bodily action and its role in effective speaking, see Chapter 5.

comes from this physical verve and energy. If, therefore, you experience some tension before you start to speak, regard this as a good sign. It means that there is little chance of your making a dull and listless speech. Instead of worrying because you feel keyed up, be happy that your nerves and muscles are alive enough to put vigor into your speaking.

Never Allow Yourself to Give Up. This applies not only to the intelligent use of physical energy, but to the preparation and presentation of the public communication as a whole. Each time you meet a situation and master it, the more poised and confident you will become. Each time you acknowledge yourself beaten or avoid an issue, the harder you will find it to face next time. For your first few practice speeches, of course, do not make your task unnecessarily difficult by selecting subjects that are abstract or complex. Once you have begun to work on a suitable topic, however, *go through with it.* Confidence, like muscles, develops by use and by overcoming resistance to obstacles.

Communicative Skill

Fluency, poise, control of the voice, and coordinated movements of the body mark the skillful speaker.* Combined with the qualities of integrity, knowledge, and self-confidence, such skills can significantly heighten your effectiveness by enabling you to communicate your ideas clearly and attractively.

Skill in speaking is gained principally through practice. In practicing, however, take care not to develop artificiality. Good speaking is distinct and lively; it is forceful, but it is also *natural* and *conversational.* It commands attention not through the use of tricks or techniques, but because of the speaker's earnest desire to communicate. By way of contrast, you will doubtless recognize the following types of speakers who are *ineffective* either because they have not mastered all of the requisite skills or because they have learned only one or two of them and thus created a distractive imbalance.

The Elocutionist—one who talks to display his skills rather than to communicate ideas. He permits himself to be carried away by the sound of his voice and the graceful manipulation of his body, and forgets that his purpose is to induce other people to understand, enjoy, or believe what he says.

The Jabberwacky—one who emits a continuous stream of words with little or no thought behind them. Speaking rapidly, inarticulately, and often foolishly, he is "skillful" chiefly in jumping from one point to another until his listeners are thoroughly confused. He usually concludes his speech with the abrupt remark, "Well, I guess that's all I have to say on the subject."

These skills are, of course, extremely important in all forms of communicative behavior; and we, therefore, give them considerable emphasis in Chapters 5 and 6.

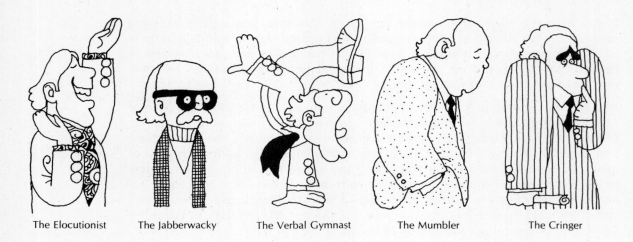

| The Elocutionist | The Jabberwacky | The Verbal Gymnast | The Mumbler | The Cringer |

The Verbal Gymnast—one whose skill is mainly in parading language for language's sake. Excessively proud of his large vocabulary, he never uses a familiar word if he can find an esoteric one. Often, too, he delights in complex sentences and mouth-filling phrases. Disraeli once described the verbal gymnast as a man "intoxicated with the exuberance of his own verbosity."

The Mumbler—one who mumbles to himself. He may have a wealth of ideas, well-organized and developed; but, unfortunately, he directs them to the ceiling or floor, talks in a weak or monotonous voice, and makes no effort to be heard or understood.

The Cringer—one who seems ashamed of what he is saying. Seemingly servile or fearful or both, he shrinks from his hearers both in voice and manner. Sometimes he apologizes verbally, sometimes bodily; always he appears self-conscious and tentative. Instead of being firm and forthright in his statements, he gives the impression that even he himself doesn't quite believe what he is saying.

How can you develop the natural, energetic, conversational delivery skills so lacking in the "Elocutionist" and the other ineffective types of speakers? The course of training you are beginning is designed to encourage and enlarge your communicative abilities steadily and naturally; Chapters 5 and 6, as we have pointed out, will suggest many specific ways in which you can improve your skill in using your body and voice to communicate ideas and feelings; and your instructor will work with you to overcome any special difficulties. For the present, however, it will help you speak in a lively, conversational way if you always: (1) *have something you want to say;* (2) *want someone else to understand, enjoy, or believe it;* and (3) *say it as simply and directly as you can.*

Sensitivity to People and Situations

Have you ever listened to a speaker who, though he obviously was a person of integrity and knew his subject well, seemed oblivious to the fact that he was boring his auditors or in some way alienating or offending them? Perhaps he continued to talk long after their attention and interest had waned. Perhaps he told embarrassing stories, or trod on his hearers' religious scruples, or ridiculed their ethnic origins. Perhaps he employed a cold and dignified manner of delivery when warmth and informality were clearly called for.

In contrast, the competent communicator, in addition to having the assets of integrity, knowledgeability, self-confidence, and skill, is sensitive to the reactions of his listeners — their needs, beliefs, attitudes, and values — and to the demands of the occasion and the context in which he is speaking. He has a highly developed ability to read and adapt to the signs of attention or inattention, of agreement or disagreement, of approval or disapproval — in a word, the *feedback* which his audience gives to him. He has an acutely developed sense of what is and what is not appropriate to the ongoing interaction.

Sensitivity of this kind has been found to consist of a number of relatively independent variables and to differ considerably from individual to individual in much the same way that intelligence does.* Communication scholars have shown, however, that sensitivity can be improved through training and experience. Study in advance the constituency of your audience and the occasion for your speech; make a genuine effort to communicate; watch carefully the signals your listeners send to you as you talk; do not be afraid to turn from your speech plan in order to adapt to their reactions. Watch other speakers also, noting in particular how they succeed or fail in adapting to their hearers and the situation. In these ways you can begin to develop that sensitivity to persons and communicative contexts which is indispensable to success as a speaker.

AIDS TO PROGRESS IN SPEECH COMMUNICATION

Although the personal attributes of integrity, knowledge, self-confidence, skill, and sensitivity furnish the essential foundation upon which you must build, your progress as a speaker will be aided, as we have said, by a recognition of the need for and an understanding of certain rules and principles, by the systematic observation of other speakers, and by guided practice.

See Henry Clay Smith, Sensitivity to People (New York: McGraw-Hill Book Company, 1966), pp. 175–180; June Elizabeth Chance and Wilson Meaders, "Needs and Interpersonal Perception," Journal of Personality XXVIII (1960): 200–210; Victor B. Cline, "Ability to Judge Personality Assessed with a Stress Interview and Sound-Film Technique," Journal of Abnormal and Social Psychology L (1955): 193–197.

Understanding Basic Guidelines and Principles

The rules and principles of effective speaking, as embodied in a book of this kind or as presented in lectures or demonstrations by your instructor, represent the distilled experience of countless speakers over the course of many centuries. In addition, for the most part, they have been verified by established principles of psychology or logic and are, therefore, grounded in theory as well as in practice. When understood and applied, they provide convenient shortcuts to learning. They can help you avoid errors and keep you from developing habits that may require much labor and time to eradicate. Unlike the rules of a game which—when violated—always result in specified penalties, the rules of effective speaking are to be applied judiciously. Because each speaking situation gives rise, as we have seen, to a unique set of requirements, it is impossible to develop guides that will apply in all cases. What we *can* do at this point, however, is to focus attention on certain background materials which will give these principles a rationale and thus make them more understandable. First of all, if we can comprehend the *functions* of speech communication—what they are and how they work—we can perhaps better comprehend the principles by which they operate or are guided.

The Functions of Speech

Speech, as we have seen, performs numerous functions for us as human beings; but we shall concern ourselves with only four of the principal ones: (1) *to discover and identify the self*, (2) *to provide self-satisfaction*, (3) *to facilitate adjustment to the environment*, and (4) *to communicate with others in that environment.*

Using Speech to Discover and Identify the Self. If we do not possess a well-formed image of who we are, if we cannot discover our basic self-identity, the opportunity to develop our full potential as human beings is severely limited. It is almost as if we must know who we are in order to become what we can be. In infancy, the search for self-identity begins when the baby attempts to sort himself out from his environment. The world presents itself to the newborn child as a chaos. The startling sound of the doorbell or the blurred rush of an object past his field of vision are disconcerting occurrences because he cannot distinguish these external happenings from internal events. If the infant is to progress even to primitive rationality, he must impose upon the world outside himself some *ordering* of persons, objects, and events, and of the relationships among them.

The part which speech plays in effecting such ordering is crucial. Symbolic sound waves in the form of words allow the baby to label the elements of his environment: "mama," "tick-tock," "bye-bye," etc. These vocalized labels enable the baby to classify his experiences. But even more important, as he learns to classify and order his environment verbally, he also begins to distinguish himself as an entity. Words enable him to define and identify himself as well as to discriminate among his surroundings.

Not only in infancy, but throughout our lives we continue to use egocentric speech to learn more about ourselves. First-person pronouns preface and punctuate many of our utterances, and even the most humble adult finds it difficult to avoid frequent self-references.* We talk about ourselves because by monitoring our own messages we are able to learn who we are. Further evidence of the egocentric nature of our speech is the fact that we so continuously talk *to ourselves*—for the most part, fortunately, with our mouths closed. Such internal conversations are an aspect of our thinking processes. Through the medium of inner speech we ponder important questions, conduct internal debates, formulate plans for the future. In short, speech and thought are, for all practical purposes, inseparable.

Finally, our speech is egocentric in the sense that we so often assume that whatever we say will make perfect sense to our listeners, when in reality they do not possess the experiences, information, and attitudes necessary to understand or to appreciate our utterance. Unaware of the fact that they are not responding as we intend, we prattle on, confident that what seems so clear and evident to us will be equally clear and evident to them.

Egocentric speech, however, important though it is, is only one of many behavioral avenues to self-discovery. Our image of self is tentative and therefore subject to continuing verification. Much of our communication to others appears to be a test of that self-image. If, for instance, I make an assertion, behind it lurk a host of opinions, values, and attitudes: the basic stuff of the self. If listeners accept this assertion, they affirm the values and attitudes associated with it. Their acceptance, in effect, rewards the image of the self which—in speaking—I have projected through my message. Their positive response has confirmed the image of who and what I believe myself to be. Stated another way, our utterances are an extension of self; our audience reacts to this extension; and in reacting, it often has the power to confirm, modify, or negate the image we project. The speech occasion, in this regard, serves as a laboratory in which we explore and test our theory of self.

Too, we must remember that we do not present the same self to everyone. We have a different self—a different role to play—before each audience. We reveal, usually, a different self to, say, our father than that seen by the dean of the college, etc. Each audience and each situation place certain demands upon us, demands that give rise to certain expectations about how we should behave. It is, in large part, our speech behavior which enables us successfully to fulfill these

---

See Charles T. Brown and Charles Van Riper, Speech and Man (Englewood Cliffs, N.J.: Prentice-Hall, Inc., 1966), pp. 35–36. These authors report a study which found that in a sample of adult conversations the pronouns I, me, mine, and myself occurred in 30 to 40 percent of the remarks.

roles by presenting the self most appropriate to each situation.

Clearly, then, speech performs an important function in the discovery, development, and manifestation of our self-identity. Indeed, the role of speech here is so pervasive that we might conclude that the "self" is very largely a verbal creation.

Using Speech to Provide Self-Satisfaction. Although the human creature is capable of great sacrifices, generally he charts his life on a course designed to avoid pain and maximize pleasure. He is a reflective animal, concerned not with mere survival but with the *quality* of his survival. Here, too, speech performs a basic function. The sheer oral and aural activities of speaking are pleasurable. The infant makes sounds for the fun of it. Alone in his crib, he babbles and gurgles, exercising his vocal mechanism and thereby stimulating muscle activity in his stomach, chest, throat, and head. He not only hears the sound of his own voice, but he also feels the vibrations of his voice-producing mechanism in action. The stimulations are pleasurable.

Most of us outgrow infantile babbling, of course, but aspects of it linger on in adult behavior. Alone, we hum, we sing, and at times even talk aloud to ourselves because the activity and sound of our voice remain a source of pleasure. And, alas, many speakers do not confine such behavior to their private moments. We have all had the painful experience of suffering a speaker in love with the sound of his own voice, of having been trapped by a chatterer who cares little if he is understood or believed as long as he is allowed to keep up the din. Just as surely, we all sometimes are "guilty" of enjoying our own melodies, be they competent or crowlike.

Deriving self-satisfaction from speech, however, is not limited to voice production and reception. Often the enjoyment comes from the inner satisfaction of having executed a well-turned phrase, from making words and idea mesh gracefully. Few of us achieve eloquence, but we have all had the pleasure of putting "proper words in proper places." All of us, at one time or another, have said something "just right." And when we have, we have experienced an inner satisfaction, the pleasure of having produced something artfully.

Consider also the pleasures of conversation—something we talked about in detail in Chapter 2. Gab sessions in the dorm, coffee breaks at work, or "rapping" with a neighbor over a cold beer—these are just a few of the situations in which speech generates a pleasant camaraderie. Sometimes these and other social conversations may seem without point or order, a haphazard give-and-take. However, in the process of talking with each other we reduce our internal tensions, we draw each other out, we socialize. In a word, we become *human.* Very early we learn that the values of "just talking to each other" are considerable.

Perhaps the greatest pleasure which speech brings to man stems, however, from the understanding and agreement which our words sometimes find in an audience. We want to be understood; we want to be thought sound in our opinions, attitudes, and values. When our utterances are accepted, we are accepted. Thus it is that many a beginning public speaker suddenly loses his hesitancy to "make a speech" when he discovers that his listeners share his own interests or beliefs. Few speakers can ignore the pleasure of having attentive and responsive hearers. Some find their greatest moments of satisfaction when interacting with an audience. It may be just this pleasure which distinguishes the good teacher, the fluent trial lawyer, and the energized minister from the mediocre.

Using Speech to Facilitate Adjustment to Our Environment. We already have noted the role which speech plays in classifying and ordering our environment. Here we wish to call attention to a related function of speech: it assists us in *acquiring information* which helps us in further *adjusting* to our surroundings. We arrive on this planet in a state of complete ignorance, but very soon we set about remedying the situation. As small children, we constantly and aggressively seek information which will clarify the facts of our experience. From our earliest years onward we are interested in knowing about the world. As one psychologist has said: "We want to see, touch, know, and go out toward the world. . . . Anything new will be appraised as *good to know.*"[4] The role which speech plays in the investigation of our environment is crucial.

Well before the child reaches the age of two, he learns that his speech will elicit verbal behavior from others—verbal behavior that will tell him something about the world. In the simple act of seeing his favorite toy and declaring "Teddy," he may elicit from his father the response, "Yes, that's your bear." Through such simple declarations the child may have part of his knowledge of the world reinforced or may acquire information relevant to his basic needs. Soon the rising vocal inflection, which our ear associates with inquiry, and the interrogative formulas involving *who, what, when, where,* and *why* allow him to probe the universe in detail. He must know the name, cause, and time of all things. Nature has given him an exploratory impulse; speech provides the means to effect that exploration.

Throughout our lives speech thus helps us to explore, to investigate, and to understand. Most of us have had the experience of "kicking around" a subject in conversation. Suddenly, in the process of expressing ourselves, our ideas jell and fall into place; we gain an insight into the subject which we would not have gained had we remained silent. These moments of discernment demonstrate again the close relationship between thought and speech: talking about the subject seems to stimulate and to clarify our insights; in the challenge of discovering the right words, we somehow are led to the right thoughts. Indeed, this may be one of the principal advantages of a course in public speaking. In the very process of preparing and delivering a speech we may be led to a deeper understanding both of our self and of our topic.

Using Speech to Communicate with Others. Obviously, the self-knowing, self-sat-isfying, and information-acquiring functions of speech are important to our so-cial and intellectual development as human beings. However, as we demonstrat-ed in Chapter 1, speech is—above all—the instrumental process by which we communicate our knowledge, feelings, and convictions to others in our environ-ment. In our diagram of "A Speech Communication Transaction" on page 38, we depicted the central elements of this process as being (1) *speaker*, (2) *message*, and (3) *listener*—all encompassed and influenced by a social-physical context within which messages and responses to messages are channeled multi-directionally. It will be useful to our purpose here to "zero in" briefly on these central elements in order to understand more fully what happens when one person speaks to an-other in order to communicate information, to influence belief or action, or sim-ply to entertain and amuse. If we can visualize more specifically the chain of events involved in the ongoing dynamics of oral communication, perhaps we can—as we indicated at the outset of this section—better comprehend the princi-ples necessary to our progress as students and practitioners of speech.

Let us begin by reiterating a much-emphasized and extremely impor-tant principle: the act of speaking is *not* a linear, one-way process; it entails a se-ries of interacting elements, each *giving* and *receiving stimuli* and *responses to stim-uli.* The sound of your voice reaches your own ears as well as the ears of your lis-teners and causes you to talk louder, perhaps, or more slowly. Your listener reacts to your message by changes in facial expression or bodily posture, and in so doing he not only sends meaningful signals to you as a speaker, but also influ-ences his own attitude toward ideas you will be expressing later in your talk. Finally, because of what psychologists call "social facilitation," the reactions of an individual in an audience are influenced by the reactions of those sitting about him.* If they seem to be enjoying or believing what you say, he, too, tends to enjoy or to believe; if, however, they are reacting negatively, the chances are greater that he also will fail to respond as you desire.

The reactions and interactions described here are most apparent, of course, in the give-and-take of person-to-person and small group interaction. They are, however, equally present in the public speaking situation; and unless you are aware of them, you can scarcely hope to communicate your ideas and feelings fully and effectively in that setting.

Another way to understand the functioning and underlying principles of the speech process is to view it as a series of links in a "communication chain." The interaction between speaker and listener being *continuous*, the pro-cess of course has no ascertainable starting or stopping point. Even so, for the

---

See, in this connection, Solomon E. Asch, "Effects of Group Pressure upon the Modification and Distortion of Judgments," Group Dynamics: Research and Theory, ed. Dorwin Cartwright and Alvin Zander, 2nd ed. (New York: Harper & Row, Publishers, 1960), pp. 189–200.

sake of simplicity and increased understanding, let us arbitrarily "isolate" the variables in the process, look at them as if they were eight separate segments or links, and describe them as if they always occur and reoccur in the sequence which follows:

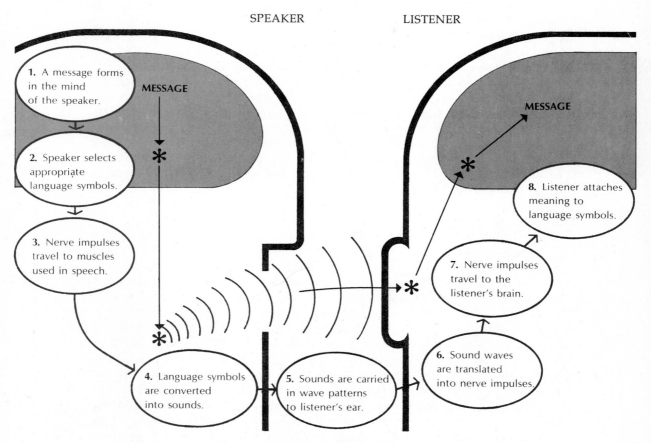

Figure 1. THE SPEECH COMMUNICATION CHAIN

(1) We begin with a *speaker* who has a *message* which he wishes to communicate to a listener. How he came to form this message—his prior activity—is of no concern to us at the moment; nor are we interested here in why the speaker wants to transmit his ideas to another person. We begin at the point where he has a message which he desires others to respond to in some way. (2) In order to communicate, the speaker must translate his ideas into *language sym-*

bols of some kind: words, phrases, sentences—in English or some other language.* As yet, however, these language symbols are mental concepts only; they have not emerged from the speaker's mind. To make these symbols audible, (3) nerve impulses from his central nervous system must actuate and control the complex systems of muscles used in speech—the muscles involved in breathing, the muscles of the larynx and the jaws, the tongue, the lips, etc.; and (4) these muscles must react in a coordinated movement to enable the speaker to produce the proper sounds.

But now these sounds are no longer words and sentences; they are merely disturbances in the molecules of air surrounding the speaker, a wave pattern of compressed and rarefied particles of gas. (5) The outward movement of these wave patterns through the air eventually strikes the eardrum of the *listener* and thus transmits to him the sounds made by the speaker. (6) In the ear of the listener, the waves of compressed and rarefied air are again translated into nerve impulses and (7) are carried to the brain by the auditory nerve. When this happens, the listener has "heard" the sounds; but he has not yet "understood" the speaker. As a final step, therefore, (8) he must recognize these *nerve impulses as language symbols*—words and sentences—and he must attach a *meaning* to them. Thus, what the listener hears arouses thought and feeling in him; he "responds," as we say, to the speaker's message.

From the foregoing descriptions, it is easy to see why speakers so often are misunderstood. A break or distortion *anywhere* along the chain of events which link the mind of the speaker with the mind of the listener will result in the transmission and/or reception of a message different from the one originally intended. Poor choice of language symbols by the speaker (link 2), poor articulation (links 3 and 4), interfering external noise (link 5), partial deafness (links 6 and 7), possession of an inadequate vocabulary or misinterpretation of the meaning by the listener (link 8)—a break at any of these points will result in an incomplete or distorted message. Similarly, a break in the chain of signals which the listener sends back to the speaker or which the speaker sends to himself will impair the communication process.

In view of these facts and complexities, the wonder is not that we sometimes misunderstand one another, but that we ever understand at all. Certainly, they point up the need for a clear understanding of the basic concepts and principles which underlie all of speech communication. They also demonstrate convincingly, we believe, the need for at least *some reasonably sound rules and guidelines*—matters which will be the central focus of Parts II and III of this book.

The "speaker" may, of course, use symbols other than verbal ones: facial expressions, gestures of the hands and arms, movements of the body, and the like. Moreover, he may use these either exclusively or in conjunction with verbal symbols. The essentials of the communication process remain the same, however, no matter what symbol system is employed.

You will find, we are sure, that empirically evolved and tested procedures can aid you significantly in communicative interaction. Learn them, we urge you, and follow them when there is no compelling reason not to do so. *Do not, of course, hold rules inviolate.* Depart from them whenever your good sense tells you that the subject you are treating, the audience you are addressing, or the situation in which you find yourself requires an alternate way of proceeding.

Improving Your Understanding of Speech Communication by Observing Other Speakers

A second important aid in learning to communicate more effectively is the careful observation of other speakers. Every time you have an opportunity to hear a speaker address an audience, take advantage of it. Go to hear poor speakers as well as good ones. Study the person's delivery and use of language. Notice how he organizes his ideas and develops his arguments. Observe the kinds of explanations, examples, illustrations, statistics, and comparisons that he chooses. Compare the speaker's performance with the rules and principles you have been taught and to which you have been exposed. To what extent does he exemplify them, and to what extent does he violate them? Do these violations make his speech more or less effective?

From among all of the speakers you listen to, pick out one or two whom you have a chance to hear frequently. Make a detailed study of what you consider to be their strengths and weaknesses. Decide if any of their methods would be good ones for you to adopt. If possible, question them about aspects of their speaking that particularly interest you. Do not take these persons or any others as models to be imitated in a servile fashion. Remember always that one of your greatest assets as a speaker is your own *individuality* and *distinctness as a person.* Learn from others, however, all that you can about the procedures and techniques upon which effective oral communication depends. You will find such observation an important source of information and guidance.

Practicing Communication Orally: First Classroom Speeches

Clearly, rules and observations will serve you well as aids to progress in speech communication, but they will be of little use if you do not take advantage of opportunities to apply what you are learning *in actual speaking situations.* This is why much of your time in this course very probably has been and will continue to be given over to *learning through oral practice.* In connection with Chapters 2 and 3, undoubtedly you have already been asked to involve yourself in unstructured and structured conversations and interviews and to participate in small group transactions. Subsequent chapters will present you with opportunities to read aloud exercises designed to improve the use of your voice and to engage in bodily activities intended to enhance your nonverbal communicative skills. The major thrust of your future practice efforts, however, very likely will be concentrated on *public speechmaking*. To this end, you will be asked to prepare and present to the class a number of speeches of various types and lengths.

To be of maximum usefulness, of course, practice must be systematic, and the various speech experiences in which you engage must be carefully prepared for. Although in later chapters we shall give detailed attention to all aspects of public speaking, including concepts and procedures, our present purpose is to help you lay the groundwork for your *initial* efforts and make your early practice more productive. With that in mind, let us note briefly the standard presentational methods or formats from which you may choose when speaking to an audience; a time-tested, seven-step procedure to follow when you are planning and preparing a formal, public speech; and three simple guides to on-the-scene message-delivery.

Presentational Methods of Speaking in Public

The ongoing, sustained nature of the public speech, its usually prescribed and comparatively lengthy duration, the preplanning and prestructuring requisites, the almost unvarying centrality of the speaker—these and other factors make the proper *method* of message-presentation for such speeches a matter of more complexity and concern than for any of the other forms of communication considered in this book. If you review your own observations and experiences, you will find that a speech may be:

1. Impromptu
2. Memorized
3. Read aloud from manuscript
4. Extemporized

The Impromptu Speech. For a speech of this kind, delivered on the spur of the moment, no specific preparation is or can be made. When you speak impromptu, you must rely entirely on your knowledge of the subject and the speaking skills you have at your command. The ability to speak impromptu is useful in an emergency; but, since a speech—to be really effective—must be preplanned and structured, the impromptu method should be restricted to those situations where your speaking could not have been anticipated. Too often the "moment" arrives without the necessary informed and inspired "spur." Whenever possible, therefore—even if you feel only that you *might* be called upon to speak—it is better to plan ahead than to risk the rambling, incoherent, fumbling presentation which the impromptu method so often produces.

The Memorized Speech. In this method, as its name implies, the speech is planned, structured, written out word for word, and then committed to memory. A few speakers are able to use this method effectively, but memorization usually produces a stilted, inflexible presentation. If you use it, you are likely to be either excessively formal or "oratorical," or you will tend to hurry through your speech, pouring out words without thinking of their meaning. When you attempt to memorize words, you will unavoidably concentrate on words rather than *ideas.* If you forget one phrase, you are in danger of losing the entire thread of your meaning and breaking the chain of communication you are trying to establish with your listeners. Worse, very probably you will sacrifice meaning for the empty utterance of symbols, and you will have largely destroyed the naturalness and spontaneity so fundamental to good interpersonal interaction.

The Speech Read Aloud from Manuscript. As in the case of the memorized method of presentation, the "manuscript" speech is written out word for word, but the speaker *reads* it aloud to his audience. If extremely careful wording is required — as in the President's message to Congress, for example, where a slip of the tongue or an imprecise phrase could undermine domestic or foreign policies, or in the presentation of scientific reports where exact and concise exposition is required — the manuscript method is appropriate, even necessary. Also, many radio and television speeches are "read" speeches because of the strict time limits imposed by broadcasting schedules. Viewed as a specialized method useful in certain situations, the ability to read a speech effectively is important. But you should not resort to it when it is neither useful nor necessary, for its use will almost inevitably diminish the freshness and spontaneity vital to meaningful oral communication. Finally, as we point out in the next chapter, the presentation of such speeches creates special problems in maintaining rapport with listeners, as well as in using nonverbal behaviors effectively.

The Extemporaneous Speech. Like the read-aloud and the memorized speech, the extemporaneous speech is carefully planned, systematically structured, and outlined in detail. There, however, the similarity ends. Rather than being written out word for word, it is "pre-phrased" aloud several times and thus practiced orally prior to presentation to an audience. Sometimes a complete draft is written out; more often, probably, it is not. If it is phrased in its entirety, the speaker does not read it aloud, nor does he commit it to memory. Substantially, all that is memorized is the *structure* or the *major-idea sequence.* Then, working from this sequence or outline (usually laid out before the speaker on 8½" × 11" paper), he practices *phrasing the speech aloud,* feeling perfectly free to express himself somewhat differently each time he "talks through" it. He uses the outline only to fix the order of the main ideas in his mind, and experiments with different wordings to develop the accuracy, conciseness, and flexibility of expression he desires.

144

Public speaking is by nature more structured and less spontaneous than other forms of speech communication. Even so, the presentation of speeches can range from impromptu, through extemporaneous and read-aloud, to memorized.

145

If you use the extemporaneous method carelessly, the result may resemble the impromptu speech—an unfortunate fact which sometimes leads to a confusion of these two terms. If you use the extemporaneous method properly, however, you can produce a speech that is nearly as polished as a memorized one and certainly more vigorous, spontaneous, and flexible. This is why, for general speech purposes, the extemporaneous method of delivery is superior to the manuscript method in most public communication situations. Without sacrificing solidity of content or cogency of organization, it makes possible easy adaptation to the exigencies of the speaking situation, enabling you to adjust readily and meaningfully to feedback from the audience. The extemporaneous speech, for example, may within reasonable limits be shortened or lengthened; ideas not understood when first stated may be repeated; and examples and other illustrative material may be altered as the need arises. In addition, when you are speaking extemporaneously, your delivery will usually have a naturalness, directness, and spontaneity which will render it more effective and which are almost impossible to achieve when reading a speech from manuscript. With few exceptions, the speeches you present in your speech class will probably be extemporaneous; but quite aside from this fact, you should strive to make it your preferred and most frequently used format.

PREPARING THE FORMAL SPEECH: SEVEN ESSENTIAL STEPS

What we shall say here is directed primarily to your immediate concern: the *preparation* of speeches for presentation in connection with your classwork. However, with minor modifications and/or elaborations, the procedure outlined in the following pages will prove useful in any situation where the careful preparation of a speech is called for.

When preparing a message for formal, public presentation, you are engaging in a threefold process:

First Phase: *Surveying the Problem.*
Second Phase: *Building the Speech.*
Third Phase: *Practicing for Oral Delivery.*

In each of these phases we tend to take certain specific steps with a view to achieving ultimately our overall goal or objective, as diagrammed in Figure 2, page 147. These seven distinct steps or tasks, you will find, need not always be performed in exactly the sequence indicated. Sometimes the subject or purpose of your speech will be assigned by your instructor. On other occasions you may gather material on several topics before you finally choose the one on which you are going to speak. As you gain additional experience you may, in fact, be able to dispense with one or more of the steps entirely or may develop a way of working that better fits your needs. For the present, however, and especially for the preparation of your classroom speeches, perform all of the steps suggested and take them in the order given. If you do, the result will probably be a more effective presentation than you otherwise would be able to make.

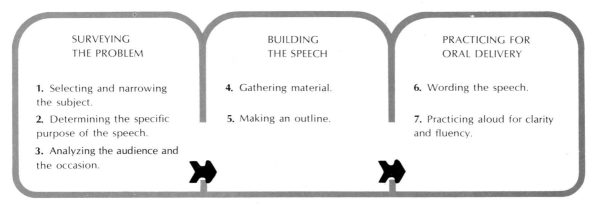

SURVEYING
THE PROBLEM

1. Selecting and narrowing the subject.

2. Determining the specific purpose of the speech.

3. Analyzing the audience and the occasion.

BUILDING
THE SPEECH

4. Gathering material.

5. Making an outline.

PRACTICING FOR
ORAL DELIVERY

6. Wording the speech.

7. Practicing aloud for clarity and fluency.

Figure 2. SEVEN ESSENTIAL STEPS IN SPEECH PREPARATION

Selecting and Narrowing the Subject

As we stressed earlier in the chapter, when you are free to choose the subject of your speech, begin by reviewing your own interests and knowledge. If possible, choose a subject you have learned about through personal experience or about which you can discover more than your audience already knows. Select subjects in which you are vitally interested and about which you have or can evolve fresh or original ideas. You will find that you not only will speak better on such subjects, but will have more poise and self-assurance when discussing them.

Remember, too, to narrow your subject so that it fits within the time limits you have been assigned. You owe it to your audience not to exceed them. More importantly, you will find that if you adapt your material to a predetermined time limit, you will generally make a better organized and more compelling speech. One of the commonest faults of beginning speakers is to select a topic too broad to be treated adequately in the time available.

When, therefore, you have settled upon a general subject, select some particular aspect or segment of it for your speech—no more than you can make clear or convincing in the time that you have. For a four- or five-minute talk, instead of discussing "How we can promote highway safety," tell "How seat belts save lives." Instead of explaining "How a big city newspaper operates," tell

"How local news is gathered." The narrower your subject, the more fully you can explain or prove the essential points and the more interesting you can make your speech by including many illustrative facts and stories.

Determining the Specific Purpose of the Speech

Too often a speaker arises to "say a few words" with no clear idea of his purpose in speaking. When this happens, his own time as well as that of his hearers usually is wasted. It is not enough to center your speech in a well-defined subject; *you also must have clearly in mind the exact reaction or response that you want from your audience.* You may wish them to *understand* a term or concept, to *believe* a proposition, to *take some definite action*, or merely to sit back and *enjoy* themselves. Frame your purpose into a clear, concise statement, such as the following: "Specific purpose: to explain the difference between *de jure* and *de facto* recognition." "Specific purpose: to prove that the sales tax is regressive." "Specific purpose: to secure contributions to the campus charity drive." "Specific purpose: to share with the audience some of my misfortunes as a Little League baseball umpire."

Think of each speech as an instrument for winning a definite response from your listeners. Your purpose, once you have determined it, should constantly be a guide to the selection and organization of the ideas and facts that constitute your speech.

Analyzing the Audience and the Occasion

A good speech not only reflects the interests and enthusiasms of the speaker, but is closely adapted to the audience and to the occasion on which it is given. Avoid topics which, though they may seem simple and clear to you because of some special experience or study, are too technical for the majority of your listeners. Also guard against imposing your own interests and enthusiasms upon others. The fact that you are an avid student of the social life of the Middle Ages or of Shakespeare's versification does not guarantee that other people will automatically share these interests.

Finally, if your talk is to be delivered as part of a speech course, make certain that it fulfills the assignment you have been given. Each of the speeches your instructor assigns will have a definite goal — to teach you how to organize ideas, to prove a point, to maintain interest, and the like. Always keep this goal in mind. Do not deliver a speech to inform when you are supposed to give a speech to persuade. Do not support your argument with explanation and examples when you have been instructed to use statistics.

Gathering the Speech Material

Having completed your survey of the problem by analyzing and determining the subject, purpose, audience, and occasion, you are now ready to move into the second phase of message-preparation: assembling the necessary materials with which to build your speech. Ordinarily, in the first phase you will have started by drawing together what you already know about the subject and deciding tentatively what ideas you want to include in its development. Nearly always, however, you will find that what you already know is not enough. You will need to gather additional information — facts, illustrations, stories, and examples — with which to develop, expand, and reinforce your speech. Using conversations and the kind of information-seeking interviews described in Chapter 2, you may acquire some of these data from persons who know something about the subject that you do not know. You may gather other materials from newspapers, magazines, books, and government documents, or from radio or television programs.* No matter how much time and labor may be involved, do your research thoroughly. Good speeches grow out of a full and deep knowledge of a subject, and are packed with the facts, figures, and examples which only long and careful study can produce.

Making an Outline

Early in your preparation, make a preliminary list of the points to be included in your speech and indicate very tentatively the arrangement of the central ideas. A complete outline, however, cannot be drawn up until all of the necessary supporting and enriching materials have been gathered. When you have assembled ample materials of these kinds, you should set down in final order the main points you expect to make, together with such subordinate ideas as are necessary to explain or to prove these points.

Later you will learn a number of organizational principles and specific patterns by which the ideas in a speech may be arranged. You will learn, too, the various forms an outline may take. For the present, remember two simple but important rules: (1) *arrange your ideas in a clear and systematic order;* and (2) *preserve the unity of your speech by making sure that each point is directly related to your specific purpose.*

Notice in the short sample outline below how the speaker covers all of the essential parts of the vocal mechanism. Observe also that instead of wandering off into a vague discussion of the characteristics of a pleasing voice or the

---

Oral and printed sources of speech materials are discussed at length in Chapter 10, pp. 288–294.

value of voice training, he holds strictly to his announced purpose of describing how speech is produced. Such clarity of organization, unity of subject matter, and tenacity of purpose will make the speech easy to understand and remember.

A SAMPLE OUTLINE

Specific purpose: To explain to the audience how speech is produced.

I. The human speech mechanism consists of four units or parts.
    A. The motor
        1. Consists of
            a. The lungs
            b. The ribs
            c. Certain muscles of the abdomen and thorax (and)
        2. Supplies the power necessary to produce sound.
    B. The vibrator
        1. Consists of
            a. The cartilages of the larynx or voice box
            b. The vocal folds (and)
        2. Produces the basic speech sound.
    C. The resonators
        1. Consist of
            a. The upper part of the larynx
            b. The throat
            c. The nasal cavities
            d. The mouth (and)
        2. Amplify the sound and give it body.
    D. The articulators
        1. Consist of
            a. The teeth
            b. The lips
            c. The tongue
            d. The soft palate
            e. The hard palate (and)
        2. Shape the basic speech sound into the vowels and consonants of the language.

II. In producing speech, these parts act in concert.
    A. The motor sends a stream of air up the trachea or windpipe.
    B. The vocal bands are set into motion by this air stream.
    C. The sound thus produced passes to the resonators.
    D. Finally, the resonated sound is formed by the articulators into recognizable syllables and words.

Wording the Speech

On certain occasions, as we have said, you may wish to write out your speech word for word and to read it from manuscript. This will be especially true if you are broadcasting your message on radio or television where precise timing is essential or if you are presenting complex technical or scholarly material. Generally, however, you will find it best to speak extemporaneously: plan your speech carefully, outline it in detail, but do not commit the words themselves to memory. Under this method, as we have suggested, use the outline to fix the ideas in your mind, and talk through the speech a number of times (preferably aloud), using the words that come to you at the moment. Continue to do this until you have achieved the desired facility in phrasing and fluency of expression. Each time you practice you will word your thoughts somewhat differently. Do not, however, let this worry you. What you are striving for is to master the sequence of ideas. When you have done this, the words or language necessary to express these ideas will in most instances begin to flow more readily and appropriately.

Practicing Aloud for Clarity and Fluency

Whether you are speaking extemporaneously or from manuscript, as a final step in your preparation, *practice your speech aloud whenever possible.* In this way you not only will get a better notion of how it will actually sound to the audience, but the experience of speaking the ideas aloud will also help you fix them more firmly in your mind. Stand rather than sit; move about as the ideas and their meanings "move" you. Take care, however, not to develop a planned set of gestures or movements, but keep your delivery as natural and conversational as possible. If you are practicing a speech to be read from manuscript, remember to glance up from the page frequently, for in actually delivering your talk you must maintain contact with your listeners.*

The amount of oral practice you will need depends largely on your ability, experience, and knowledge of the subject. You should not practice a speech so often that you become stale, but you must rehearse it frequently enough to fully establish the material in your mind. As a general rule, the less experience you have in speaking, the more oral practice you will require. Most students are inclined to practice too little rather than too much.

---

*In this connection, see "Special Problems in Delivering the Manuscript Speech," pp. 177–179.

It is hard to force the development and preparation of a speech. Good speeches, like stout trees, must grow over a period of time. Therefore, begin thinking about your subject and the desired audience response as soon as you know you are to speak. In this way you can best utilize your background of knowledge and fill in the gaps with additional material. Work on the speech as frequently as possible, even if only for a few minutes at a time. Your confidence will increase in direct proportion to your mastery of your material. To postpone beginning the preparation even of a classroom speech until the night before it is to be given is often to invite disaster.

THREE GUIDELINES TO EFFECTIVE SPEECH DELIVERY

Let's assume for the moment that you have prepared your speech carefully, are eager to communicate ideas that are interesting and important, and that you now stand before the class. "How," you ask, "should I *deliver* my message? What can I do that will help me communicate what I want to say *while I am saying it?*" Most of the rules for effective delivery, when reduced to their essence, are based upon three cardinal principles: (1) be natural; (2) look at your audience; (3) communicate with your body as well as your voice. If you begin now to let these guiding principles govern your delivery, you will later find it relatively easy to master the more advanced techniques of presentation.

1. Be Natural. Stand and move about in your usual manner—just as you would if engaged in an animated street-corner conversation with a friend. Avoid an excessively rigid posture, but don't slouch or lean on anything. Above all, do not assume an artificial, "oratorical" stance. When you are speaking, you want the attention of your listeners to be focused on the *ideas* you are expressing, not upon your delivery of them. Anything unnatural or unusual—anything that calls attention from matter to manner—is a distraction and should be avoided.

2. Look at Your Listeners. Do not gaze at the floor, the ceiling, or out the window. Obviously, unless you watch the faces of your listeners for clues to their reactions and responses, you will be unable to gauge the ongoing effectiveness of your interaction with them—to know whether, in fact, you are "putting your message across" or whether you should make some prompt and necessary adjustments. Moreover, people tend to mistrust anyone who does not look them in the eye; and if you fail to do that, they are likely to undervalue your ideas. And, finally, they nearly always listen more attentively if you look at them while you are speaking.

3. Communicate with Your Body as Well as Your Voice. Realize that as a speaker you are being *seen* as well as heard. Remember, as we have mentioned, that movements of the body, gestures of the arms and head, changes in facial expression and muscle tension — all help to clarify and reinforce your ideas. Keep your hands free so that when you feel an impulse to gesture, you can do so easily and naturally. Let other movements of your body also respond to the gestural impulse. Do not force these bodily communications, but do not hold them back when they seem appropriate and natural. Earnestly attempt to convey your ideas to others, and sooner or later you will be motivated to bodily responses of some kind, for such responses are an integral part of all forms of communication.

Developing good speech delivery is essentially a process of habit formation, and so it cannot happen overnight. Even these three simple principles may be difficult for you to put into practice at first. Do not be discouraged if your instructor needs to prod you concerning them. Eventually, given reasonable effort on your part, they will become habitual; and you will no longer need to concentrate upon them. What is important at this time is that you understand the principles of effective delivery. With these as a base, you can develop the necessary skills and can avoid practicing errors which you will later have to eradicate.

Here, in the closing chapter of Part I, we have focused primarily on those factors foundational to effective public speechmaking; we have tried to describe, at least briefly, what will be required of you as a competent communicator; and we have introduced — *only* introduced — what we consider to be the basic, specific procedures that you can profitably follow as you prepare and present your first speeches to the class. All of these matters will, of course, be accorded far more detailed and searching scrutiny in Part III, where we shall resume our consideration of the speechmaking process as it involves both the *preparation* and the *adaptation of speeches to audiences.*

By way of summing up Part I, we may appropriately take a concluding look at the chart on which, from time to time, we have been attempting to characterize the qualities and conditions inherent in the three forms of speech interaction which we have deemed basic: dyadic, small group, and public communication. The completed chart is shown on page 154.

Characterizing QUALITIES and CONDITIONS	DYADIC *person to person*	SMALL GROUP *all to all*	PUBLIC ADDRESS *one to many*	MASS COMMUNICATION *print and electronic; one or few to many*
Number of Persons	2	3–15	Many	Unlimited
Degree of Intimacy	High	Fairly high	Fairly low	Variable
Degree of Formality	Minimal	Minimal to medium	High— usually	Variable
Time Limits	Flexible	Pre-set— usually	Pre-set— usually	Fixed
Need for Prestructuring of Message	Minimum to medium	Increased— but flexible	Flexible	Maximum
Role of Nonverbal Factors in Projection of Message	Minimal	Moderate	Considerable— usually	Electro-Mechanical
Evidence of Communicator Purpose	Emerges quickly—usually	Fairly clear and strong	Specific, focused	Maximal
Alternation of Speaker-Listener Roles	Frequent	Frequent, but more restricted	None	None
Opportunities for Perceiving Listener Feedback	Maximal	Numerous and frequent	Comparatively few	None—of an immediate nature
Opportunities for Adjusting to Listener Feedback	Maximal	Numerous	Somewhat limited	None—of an immediate nature
Opportunities to Assess Fulfillment of Communicative Purpose	Numerous	Numerous and continuing	Restricted— in immediate sense	None at the moment. Later —good.
Opportunities for Mutual Exploration of Ideas	Many	Extensive	Restricted	None—usually

Figure 3. BASIC FORMS OF SPEECH COMMUNICATION: SOME GRADATIONAL QUALITIES AND INTERRELATIONSHIPS

A SAMPLE STUDENT SPEECH

The following speech by Joyce Miller, a senior at the University of Iowa, was prepared to fulfill an assignment similar to Speaking Assignment 3 at the end of this chapter. The students in a beginning public-speaking class were asked to present a three- or four-minute talk on a subject of interest to them and their classmates, and to supplement their previous knowledge of the subject with information drawn from at least three printed sources.

Mrs. Miller chose to discuss "Why Ice Floats," not only because it reflected one of her own interests as a chemistry major, but also because the subject met three other requirements of a good classroom speech: (1) it was something she could talk about with confidence; (2) it was appropriate to the occasion—the warm June afternoon on which the speech was delivered; and (3) it could be covered adequately in the time allotted. The specific purpose of the talk as stated on the prepared outline was: "To get my listeners to understand why ice floats."

In an effort to render a technical subject clear to a group of persons who had little or no previous background in science, Mrs. Miller developed her speech primarily through the use of comparisons, referring to such familiar things as Yogi Bear and a marching band. She also used examples liberally and took especial care to cast her explanation in language that was easy to understand.

The speech as a whole preserves a simple and unitary plan of development, and is closely related to the audience through the use of rhetorical questions and the frequent repetition of the word "we." In the next-to-the-last paragraph, an account of what happens as water is heated reinforces by contrast the explanation given earlier. Finally, a one-sentence conclusion neatly sums up the speech and reminds the audience of its central purpose.

On the whole, Mrs. Miller's speech is a good example of what an imaginative student can do in presenting a potentially complex subject to a general audience. Practicing on short speeches such as this one will provide you with the experience you will need eventually to handle talks that have many points and subpoints.

WHY ICE FLOATS[5]

Joyce Miller

On these hot summer days, there's nothing I like better than a tall glass of iced tea. Now, I'd be willing to wager almost anything that when I put an ice cube in my tea, it will float at the top of the glass rather than settle to the bottom. This shouldn't surprise any of you.

But do you know *why* ice floats? "That's easy!" you say. "Because ice is less dense, and therefore lighter than water." But why is ice less dense than water? We know that as a rule compounds expand when heated, and contract when cooled. We observe this phenomenon every time we look at a thermometer and see the mercury rise with the temperature. In very hot weather, the concrete on our highways expands until it buckles and cracks. On the other hand, butter and shortenings, gasolines and oils all contract when they solidify. Water, too, expands with heat and, upon cooling, contracts at all temperatures except for the range between 0° centigrade and 4° centigrade, where it acts in an exactly opposite manner. Why, then, is water so different from other compounds in this temperature range?

The answer to this question lies in a phenomenon known as *hydrogen bonding*. To understand hydrogen bonding, we must look at the structure of a water molecule. As you undoubtedly know, a molecule of water consists of two atoms of hydrogen and one atom of oxygen. The two hydrogen atoms are attached to the oxygen in such a way that they form an angle of approximately 105°. In fact, a molecule of water looks a little bit like Yogi Bear, his face being the oxygen atom and his two ears stuck out at the 105° angle being the hydrogen atoms.

Because oxygen is a larger atom than the hydrogen, and also for other reasons founded in chemical bonding theories, the oxygen side of the molecule has a slightly negative charge, while the hydrogen side bears a slightly positive one. Now, we all know that like charges repel and unlike charges attract. Therefore, the slightly negative oxygen side of one molecule is attracted toward the slightly positive hydrogen side of a neighboring molecule. This attraction between molecules is known as hydrogen bonding. Hydrogen bonding occurs to a certain extent in water at all temperatures; and heat must be applied to break these bonds, which explains the high boiling point of water when compared with boiling points of chemically similar compounds. When water turns to vapor, all the hydrogen bonds have been broken.

Picture, if you can, fifty members of a marching band standing in a tight group. They don't take up a great deal of space. But when the drum major blows his whistle and says, "Line up," everyone takes his place—with one man in front, one behind, and one on either side, and with a specified distance between them. Now the fifty members of the band are spread out and take up much more space.

The same thing happens in a group of water molecules when water is freezing. The drum major says, "All right, you molecules, line up," and they do. Each molecule of water now is surrounded by four other molecules arranged so that the oxygen atom of one molecule is next to the hydrogen atoms of its neighbor, thus forming a pyramid-shaped crystal with an empty space in the middle. As the ice thus spreads out and takes up more room, it becomes less dense and floats. The molecules begin lining up at a temperature of 4° centigrade and continue lining up until all the molecules are lined up at the temperature of 0° centigrade and the water is frozen. Actually, ice expands to a volume 9% greater than the volume of water. In other words, if you want to freeze 10 quarts of water in a closed container, it would be well to have a container with a volume of 11 quarts.

Finally, let us reverse the process by taking a piece of the ice out of our tea and applying some heat to it. As we do so, some of the hydrogen bonds will be broken and the molecules set free so that they can squeeze more closely together. As a result, the liquid becomes denser than the ice crystals it replaces. This process continues until the temperature of 4° centigrade is reached, the temperature at which water is the densest. At this point, the water begins to act as most other compounds do and expands with increasing temperature.

This is why the ice cube always floats in your glass of iced tea.

SOURCES OF DATA FOR "WHY ICE FLOATS"

L. B. Leopold, K. S. Davis, and the Editors of *Life*, "Water," *Life Science Library* (New York: Time, Inc., 1966).

W. J. Moore, *Physical Chemistry*, 3rd ed. (Englewood Cliffs, N.J.: Prentice-Hall, Inc., 1962).

C. R. Noller, *Textbook of Organic Chemistry*, 2nd ed. (Philadelphia: W. B. Saunders Company, 1958).

FOOTNOTES

[1] *Aristotle*, Rhetoric, *p. 1356a.*

[2] *A. Craig Baird and Franklin Knower*, General Speech: An Introduction, *2nd ed. (New York: McGraw-Hill Book Company, 1957), p. 114. Cf. Floyd I. Greenleaf, "An Exploratory Study of Stage Fright,"* Quarterly Journal of Speech *XXVIII (October 1952): 327; Franklin H. Knower, "A Study of Speech Attitudes and Adjustments,"* Speech Monographs *V (1938): 131; Howard Gilkinson, "Social Fears as Reported by Students in College Speech Classes,"* Speech Monographs *IX (1942): 144–145.*

[3] *Milton Dickens and William R. Parker, "Physiological, Introspective, and Rating Scale Techniques for the Measurement of Stage Fright,"* Speech Monographs *XVIII (November 1951): 259.*

[4] *Magda B. Arnold*, Emotion and Personality: Psychological Aspects *(New York: Columbia University Press, 1960), p. 200.*

[5] *Presented June 26, 1967. Text supplied through the courtesy of Mrs. Miller.*

Problems and Probes

1. Listen to at least two nationally known figures speak on television or in person. On the basis of the impressions thus gained, compare the two and try to formulate judgments as to their (a) integrity, (b) knowledge, (c) self-confidence, and (d) sensitivity to people and situations.

2. From your own experiences, give two or three examples of situations in which men or women have exerted influence over others because of their strong personal or ethical appeal. Did these persons have a comparably strong influence upon you personally? Why or why not?

3. Observe a lecture given in one of your classes and list as many evidences of feedback as you can. Include both negative (unfavorable) and positive (favorable) kinds. Describe three or four instances of how the speaker or speakers received and adjusted to this feedback.

4. Which factor—the speaker's knowledge of the subject or his or her skills in speech delivery—would you say is the more important in determining how the message will be received by an audience? Defend your answer.

5. Using any one of the three speech communication forms—dyadic, small group, or public—recall a circumstance in which one of the participants exhibited a high degree of sensitivity to the other person or persons and to the situation itself. Cite specific examples that suggest the importance and value of such sensitivity and adaptability.

6. Select a nationally known "celebrity" from the political or entertainment world—an individual whom you have seen and heard speak on a number of occasions and to whom you have a very strong reaction—either positive or negative. In terms of the communicative guidelines laid out by this chapter, describe and evaluate that speaker's characteristics. Include a thoughtful analysis of your reasons for reacting as you do.

7. With the aid of your instructor, select for detailed study a speech that has become important historically. Consider as possible sources *Famous Speeches in American History*, edited by Glenn R. Capp (Bobbs-Merrill, 1963); *The History of Public Speaking* by Robert T. Oliver (Allyn & Bacon, 1965); and *Contemporary American Speeches* by Wil A. Linkugel, R. R. Allen, and Richard L. Johannesen (Wadsworth, 1972). Answer as accurately and completely as you can the following questions:

    a. What had the speaker done *prior* to the delivery of the speech to establish the audience's confidence in his or her integrity, knowledge, and judgment?

    b. Can you find any information or evidence of what this speaker did *during* the presentation of the speech to further establish the above qualities?

    c. According to reports by observers, how did the skills of using the voice, language, and body help this speaker attain his objective?

8. At this point in the course, you have probably taken part in a number of different communicative activities: conversations, interviews, small group discussions, and the like. Refer to your Personal Speech Journal and look again at the inventory of your *speech needs and abilities* that you prepared at the conclusion of Chapter 1. Now enter in the Journal your views of yourself—written from an oral communication perspective, of course—and describe the extent and ways in which your speaking abilities and goals may have changed or been reinforced. You might use as a general guide in this analysis "The Characteristics of the Competent Communicator," which we considered on pages 124–133.

Oral Activities and Speaking Assignments

1. As a starting point for this assignment, try to imagine a more or less formal public speech situation. Analyze how you expect that you will feel as a speaker facing a small audience. Having done this, your next step is to choose a subject for a brief speech (three or four minutes in length). The chief criterion of your choice should be that talking on this subject will, you believe, be most likely to put you at ease as you speak to the other members of the class. Although in this chapter we have emphasized the importance of choosing a subject that will interest your audience, *for this particular assignment* choose a topic that YOU want to talk about because it interests you, and you feel you can talk about it knowledgeably.

After you have your instructor's "go ahead" on the chosen subject, proceed to prepare and practice this three- or four-minute speech in accordance with the "Seven Essential Steps" briefly outlined on pages 146–152 of this chapter.

2. Your instructor will call on you for a two-minute *impromptu* speech on a subject of his or her choice. When everyone has had a chance to participate in this activity, time will be allowed for an informal class consideration of some of the significant differences between the individual speeches presented in this impromptu exercise and those presented in Oral Activity Assignment 1 above.

3. Following the principles and procedures set forth in Chapter 4, prepare and present a three- or four-minute speech on a subject chosen by you and approved by your instructor. In the preparation, be sure to draw information from *at least three (3) printed sources* for the purpose of supplementing your personal knowledge of the subject. Narrow the focus of your

speech by selecting the one or two aspects of the subject that you feel would be of greatest interest and appeal to the other members of the class.

NOTE: Your instructor may or may not wish to involve you and the other members of the class in the *speech-evaluation process* until you have had several opportunities to develop further your confidence and skills in public-speech settings—something which you will be doing in Part Three. However, if your instructor feels that the class is—at this point in the course—sufficiently advanced to attempt evaluation of speeches, or for some other reason would like to introduce you to it, the "Public Speech-Evaluation Guide" on the facing page should prove useful. Full attention to the evaluative process will be given in Chapter 17, "Listening, Evaluation, and Ethical Judgment," pages 447–469.

Suggestions for Further Reading

David W. Addington, "The Effect of Vocal Variation on Ratings of Source Credibility," *Speech Monographs* XXXVIII (August 1971): 242–247.

Kenneth Anderson and Theodore Clevenger, Jr., "A Summary of Experimental Research in *Ethos*," *Speech Monographs* XXX (June 1963): 59–78.

Aristotle, *Rhetoric*, 1356a, "The Character of the Speaker as a Means of Persuasion"; 1378a, "A Certain Character in the Speaker."

A. Craig Baird, Franklin H. Knower, and Samuel L. Becker, *General Speech Communication* (New York: McGraw-Hill Book Company, 1971), Chapter IV, "The Speaker as a Person," pp. 37–44.

Waldo W. Braden and Mary Louise Gehring, *Speech Practices: A Resource Book for the Student of Public Speaking* (New York: Harper & Row, Publishers, 1958), Chapter II, "How Speakers Prepare Their Speeches," pp. 14–26.

John Hasling, *The Message, The Speaker, The Audience* (New York: McGraw-Hill Book Company, 1971), Chapter II, "Selecting Your Subject and Purpose," pp. 11–19.

Elliot R. Siegel, Gerald Miller, and C. Edward Wotring, "Source Credibility and Credibility Proneness: A New Relationship," *Speech Monographs* XXXVI (June 1969): 118–125.

A SPEECH EVALUATOR'S GUIDELIST

Speaker's Name: _____ *Speech Title:* _____

Evaluate the speech as it is presented by the speaker to an audience. Use for this purpose a Reactive Range of 1 ("Generally Excellent") to 5 ("Generally Ineffective"). Using the short guide-questions as a basis, react to each of the seven "Evaluative Factors." At the conclusion of the speech, formulate a general, overall Effectiveness Rating.

EVALUATIVE FACTORS	Reactive Range				
	1	2	3	4	5
CHOICE OF SUBJECT [Interested the speaker? Interested the audience? Stayed on it? Wandered or digressed?]					
PURPOSE OF THE SPEAKER [Clearly stated? Clearly implied? Vague or fuzzy? Emphasized response desired? Purpose achieved? Only partially fulfilled?]					
SPEAKER'S ANALYSIS OF AUDIENCE [Had given it thought? Attempted necessary adjustments? Needed more thought? Seemed oblivious to the problem?]					
ATTENTION TO SPEECH MATERIALS [Research was evident? Cited specific sources? Variety of materials created interest? All centered directly on speaker's subject and purpose?]					
ORGANIZATION AND PLAN OF SPEECH [Had clear, simple plan? Designed to accomplish speaker's purpose? Followed plan? Digressed from it? Stated and reiterated main ideas? Transitions from point to point?]					
THE WORDING OF THE SPEECH [Language simple? Concise? Meaning was always understandable? Sentences too involved? Rambling? Fragmentary? Used some vivid imagery? Routine? Imaginative? Overworked certain words and phrases? Vocabulary colorless? Limited?]					
PRACTICE AND PRESENTATION [Had obviously practiced phrasing and delivering speech? Needed more practice? Voice interesting to listen to? Too weak? Too harsh? Any distractive difficulties? Communicated with body? Often? Occasionally? Never? Talked *to* audience—or *at* it? Tried to establish real contact? Seemed at ease? Too tense?]					
GENERAL EFFECTIVENESS RATING					

Evaluator's Name: _____

PART TWO
Modes of Speech Communication:
Nonverbal and Verbal

5

USING THE BODY TO COMMUNICATE

MESSAGE DELIVERY AND THE COMMUNICATION PROCESS

The effectiveness of your speaking depends both on what you say and how you say it. Without solid content, you will not have anything worth communicating; without skill in delivery, you cannot transmit your thoughts clearly and forcefully to others.

According to a story which has come down through the centuries, the Greek orator Demosthenes, when asked for the most important ingredient of effective public speaking, replied, "Delivery." When asked for the second and third most important ingredients, his answer in each case remained the same. Good delivery, he declared, is that factor which above all others is crucial to the orator's success. *Delivery*, as we have been using the term in this text, refers to the manner in which a communicator presents a message, including the use of vocal and gestural activities. Although delivery is usually thought of with regard to a public speaker—and certainly in this context one's delivery is most easily observable—the concept applies to all forms of communication, dyadic and small group as well as public. Accordingly, as you study the material in this chapter and the ensuing one, you should recognize its relevance in all kinds of communicative situations.

In recent years a growing number of research studies have emphasized anew the important role that delivery plays in effective oral communication.* At the same time, experience has shown that good delivery is not something that can be achieved by learning and applying a predetermined set of rules. On the

---

*Paul Ekman, "Differential Communication of Affect by Head and Body Cues," Journal of Personality and Social Psychology II (November 1965): 726–735; Paul Heinberg, "Relationships of Content and Delivery to General Effectiveness," Speech Monographs XXX (June 1963): 105–107; Gerald R. Miller and Murray A. Hewgill, "The Effect of Variations in Nonfluency on Audience Ratings of Source Credibility," Quarterly Journal of Speech L (February 1964): 36–44; and B. G. Rosenberg and Jonas Langer, "A Study of Postural-Gestural Communication," Journal of Personality and Social Psychology II (October 1965): 593–597.

contrary, it comes from a thorough knowledge of subject matter, an earnest desire to communicate important ideas to others, and practice under the direction of a competent instructor who can help smooth out rough places and develop points of strength. In this chapter and the one that follows, therefore, we shall not present a body of rules—a list of do's and don't's—which you will be expected to memorize and to apply. Instead, we shall offer some general suggestions or guidelines which, if taken into careful account, may keep you from falling into certain nonproductive or distractive habits which may prove difficult to correct later. We shall also recommend a few basic principles which, if you understand them, will make the reasons for many of your instructor's comments and recommendations more readily apparent.

Since in the typical face-to-face speaking situation the speaker is seen as well as heard, a consideration of communicative delivery involves attention to two basic aspects or facets of the process: (1) what the listeners see or, as we shall call it, *the speaker's bodily behaviors* (the subject of the present chapter); and (2) what the listeners hear, or *the speaker's voice and how he uses it* (the subject of Chapter 6).

NONVERBAL DELIVERY: COMPONENTS AND REINFORCEMENTS

Among the many nonverbal signs and cues provided by a communicator and interpreted by listeners we must consider of predominant importance the speaker's physical aspect, bodily and gestural behaviors, and the facial mirroring of emotions and feelings. These nonverbal cues may be employed consciously and positively by the speaker to increase communicative impact and message effectiveness. Conversely, if through neglect or insensitivity the speaker's physical aspect and behaviors are such as to confuse or antagonize listeners, the import and impact of the message will almost certainly be weakened or, perhaps, lost entirely. We can advantageously, therefore, identify and examine more closely certain of these nonverbal projections and the audience response-reactions they are likely to engender; specifically: the speaker's *physical appearance*, *physical behaviors*, *posture*, *bodily movement*, and *gestures*. We can also beneficially consider some of the ways in which these nonverbal components may assist us in establishing visual contact and emotional bonding with our hearers and in reinforcing the delivery of our message-ideas to them.

The Physical Appearance of the Communicator

Almost at the instant the speaker appears—and well before he opens his mouth to speak—he inevitably communicates a great deal to his audience. Rightly or wrongly, fairly or unfairly, the listeners come immediately to certain conclusions about him; and these conclusions may ultimately prove crucial to his presentation and purpose. This is because, as we pointed out in preceding chapters, "appearances" make a difference in our society. We have been culturally conditioned to attach meanings and, often, unwarranted significances to a speaker's dress and personal aspect.

The clothing the speaker wears, the style of his hair, how well he is groomed, and the like, tell much about his personality and values, and thus cause an audience to form an opinion of him independent of what he says.* In particular, appearance is important because it provides listeners with their initial impression of the speaker and thus gives rise to an expectancy or set that may go far toward determining how the message as a whole is received. Unlike the actor, who always subordinates his own personal identity and deliberately assumes a role in which he portrays another person, the public speaker must retain his own identity and keep within reasonable bounds his adaptations of dress and appearance to suit a given speaking situation. Indeed, to do otherwise would be to violate the merited trust or integrity that is one of the speaker's most valuable assets. On the other hand, to pay no attention to how we look is to neglect a resource that may contribute significantly to the success of our speech.

The Physical Behavior of the Communicator

Just as audiences read meanings into a speaker's clothes and appearance, so are they quick to attach significance to the way he stands and walks, to his facial expressions and changes in muscle tension, to what he does with his head, arms, shoulders, and hands. Andrew H. Halpin, author of *Theory and Research in Administration*, writes:

> Communication embraces a broader terrain than most of us attribute to it. Since language is, phylogenetically, one of man's most distinctive characteristics, we sometimes slip into the error of thinking that all communication must be *verbal* communication.
>
> . . . .
>
> Unfortunately, the very nature of higher education forces all of us to place great store by the *word*, whether oral or written. What passes as education often consists of little more than having students regurgitate to the professor the same words that he has given them—untouched in the process by

---

*See, for example, N. Compton, "Personal Attributes of Color and Design Preferences in Clothing Fabrics," Journal of Psychology LIV (1962): 191–195; G. Thornton, "The Effect of Wearing Glasses Upon Judgments of Personality Traits of Persons Seen Briefly," Journal of Applied Psychology XXVIII (1944): 203–207.

human thought. But the language of words is only a fragment of the language we use in communicating with each other. We talk with eyes and hands, with gestures, with our posture, and with various motions of our body.[1]

All of us, whether we realize it or not, are constantly sending messages to others simply through the way we move or behave. Often a shrug of the shoulders, a sweep of the arm, a lift of the eyebrow, or a shuffling of the feet is more expressive than hundreds of spoken words. Moreover, investigators have found that there is a code or system of bodily movements which, within their customary contexts, are almost as consistent in meaning as language symbols and often are as readily understood. From our own experience in watching skilled dancers and pantomimists perform, we can well believe this to be the case.

Desirable Objectives for Communicating Nonverbally

If, then, as research tells us and as our own experience confirms, physical delivery is an important means of communicating ideas and feelings to others, at what broad physical/behavioral objectives should the speaker aim? Although they may be subdivided into a number of more specific aims or principles, two such objectives are basic and preeminent. First, when you are in a communication situation—with one other person, a few others, or many others—nothing in your appearance or behavior should distract the concentration of your listening audience, thus splitting their attention away from the facts and ideas you are presenting. And, second—as we emphasized in Chapter 4—the various parts of your body, instead of being stiff or restrained, should respond freely and naturally as changes in thought and feeling require. If, throughout the message, the attention of your listeners remains firmly fixed on *what* you are saying rather than on *how* you are saying it, and if the nonverbal aspects of your body work naturally along with your voice to clarify and reinforce the communication of your thoughts and feelings, your delivery is almost sure to be effective.

Speaker-Listener Contact Through Visual Bonding

In their classic study on nonverbal communication, psychologists Jurgen Ruesch and Weldon Kees assert: "All cooperative activities begin with the acknowledgement of the participants' perception of each other; this marks the signal for subsequent communicative exchanges."[2] We are all aware of the disturbing effect of conversing with someone who never "looks you in the eye." This feeling of remoteness and uncertainty is as prevalent in the small group and the public communication situation as it is in the person-to-person setting. At the outset of your speech, therefore—in fact, before you utter so much as a word—it is important that you establish contact with your listeners, that you make them feel you are aware of their identity as persons and intend to talk to them on a close personal basis. People respond unfavorably to a speaker who seems unaware of their presence or who appears to regard them as an undifferentiated mass of humanity.

In order to establish the kind of personal relationship that exists in informal conversation, look at your hearers for a few moments before you begin to speak, moving your eyes over the audience and letting them rest momentarily on a number of the persons present. In this way, besides establishing contact with your hearers, you also will be commanding their attention and giving them a brief opportunity to become acquainted with you.

Not only at the outset of a speech, however, is contact with your listeners important. Throughout the time you are talking, insofar as you can, you must make your individual listeners feel that you are talking directly to them. For this reason, as we have previously insisted, reading a speech or glancing at notes too frequently will almost invariably detract from your effectiveness as a communicator. Do as you would when conversing with a small group: pick out one person and talk to him or her directly for a few seconds, looking that individual in the eye as you do so; then shift to someone else. Be careful, however, to select people in all parts of the audience and to sustain the visual engagement with each one long enough to establish contact. In this way you will help your listeners feel that they are an integral part of the communication process.*

To achieve genuine audience contact, however, you must do more than merely look at your listeners; you must have, above all else, an earnest desire to *communicate* with them. Sometimes it is possible to look a person directly in the eye and yet have him think that your mind is miles away. In order to combat this impression, concentrate intently on both your message and your listeners' reaction to it. Study the individual reactions of your listeners as evidenced by their facial expressions and bodily postures. Make it evident to each person in your audience that you are interested in him as an individual and are eager to have him understand or believe the ideas you are presenting. By this means, you will establish *mental* as well as mere sensory contact with your audience.

The Posture of the Communicator: An Attitudinal Index

A speaker's posture is an index both of his attitude toward himself and of his attitude toward the persons he is addressing.** A rigid posture with the

---

*For an interesting treatment of nonverbal communication, and particularly eye behavior, see Flora Davis, "How to Read Body Language," Glamour (1969). Reprinted in Haig A. Bosmajian, ed., The Rhetoric of Nonverbal Communication (Glenview, Ill.: Scott, Foresman and Company, 1971), pp. 5–6.

**F. Deutsch, "Analysis of Postural Behavior," Psychoanalytic Quarterly XVI (1947): 195–213; W. James, "A Study of the Expression of Bodily Posture," Journal of General Psychology VII (1932): 405–436; Ruesch and Kees, Nonverbal Communication, p. 38.

head held stiffly erect, arms pressed to the sides, and muscles taut, signals tension or uncertainty on the part of the speaker. A posture that is excessively relaxed or slouchy signals indifference or an attempt to hide one's true feelings by a false appearance of nonchalance. Posture, particularly the position of the head and trunk, also has been found to vary, depending on whether one likes or dislikes the persons to whom one is talking, there being a tendency to turn or lean toward persons liked and away from those who are disliked or feared.

Contrary to the advice sometimes proffered, there really is no one best way to stand when delivering a public speech. If you appear alert and seem eager to communicate, if the way you stand is comfortable for you and does not call the attention of the audience away from the ideas you are presenting, then your posture will very probably be a satisfactory one.

Sometimes inexperienced speakers, because they are nervous and ill-at-ease, bounce up and down on their toes as they talk, or sway slightly from side to side. These behaviors, especially if habituated, distract the attention and, after a time, can become distinctly annoying to the audience. If you have such habits, your instructor undoubtedly will comment on them and offer some constructive suggestions concerning ways in which you can practice to direct your physical energies into purposive channels.

The Bodily Movement of the Communicator: Spatial Relationships

Movement, as we use the term here, refers to changing the position of your body in physical relationship to your hearers or co-communicators in a communicative interchange. Movement serves three important functions. First, movement is one of the speaker's best means of holding the attention of his listeners. The eye instinctively follows moving objects and focuses upon them. If you speak for minute after minute in exactly the same position, you may find your listeners gradually drifting away from you. By the simple expedient of making a slight movement or change of position, you may often revive their attention. Second, movement—because it represents a marked break or change in your delivery pattern—is a convenient way of "paragraphing" a message, of letting your listeners know that you are done with one idea or line of thought and are ready to begin another. Third, aside from its effects on the audience, movement performs important services for you as a speaker. As we explained in Chapter 4, because movement helps to work off the excess nervous energy generated by the challenge of the speaking situation, it is an excellent means of reducing tension and putting you more at ease. In addition, there is good reason to believe that movement, along with bodily activity in general, tends to stimulate thought and thus to improve fluency. Many persons, when faced with a problem or searching for an idea, get up and begin to pace about the room. This, they have found, helps them to think more effectively. In the same way that movement helps us when we are thinking or pondering a problem in solitude, it also may help us when speaking to an audience.

How much movement is desirable? When should one move? What errors or faults in movement should be avoided? *Purposiveness* and *appropriateness* are the key guidelines. Insofar as the amount and timing of movement are concerned, the answer is to follow your natural impulses. Move about when you feel a desire or need to do so. Obviously, you should try to make your movements as meaningful as possible and avoid aimless pacing back and forth. If, however, you are confident of yourself and your material and are earnestly trying to convey important ideas to your listeners, sooner or later you will feel a desire to change your physical position with reference to theirs. This, then, is the time to do so.

Remember also that in addition to moving about during the communication of your message, the way you walk to a position before your listeners and the way you leave it are important. Instead of ambling into position in a slovenly, meandering fashion, move briskly and purposefully. Let your manner suggest confidence; do not shuffle about timidly, as though you were afraid the audience might see or hear you. Once in position, as we already have suggested, do not begin to speak immediately. Take time to compose your thoughts and to look at your listeners; *then* begin to talk. When you have finished speaking, do not rush or sidle to your seat. Pause long enough to let your final words take full effect; then move away in a relaxed but dignified way, still keeping the degree of muscle tension you had as you finished speaking and still holding your eyes on your listeners. Avoid ruining the total effect of your message by an awkward or poorly timed entrance or exit.

Finally, not only when and how you move, but where you stand or come to rest in the communicative setting may enhance or impair the effectiveness of your message. In their study of nonverbal behavior which we referred to earlier, Ruesch and Kees point out that in appraising the friendliness and warmth of others, physical distance provides us with major clues. If you stand too close to persons, you may offend them by invading their sense of "privacy" or personal "space," whereas standing too far away frequently lends an air of indifference or impersonality to your talk.[3] In general, it is a good idea to speak from a position fairly close to your listeners; and when you come to a point you particularly want to emphasize, take another step or two forward. Except under very unusual circumstances, you should never back away from an audience. Nor, as a rule, should you stand behind a table, desk, or lectern that blocks the audience's view of you. Such objects not only restrict your movements, but they also erect major psychological barriers to full and free communication. In sum, the visual channel between you and your listeners must be kept constantly open.

The Gestures of the Communicator: Idea-Projection and Reinforcement

Gestures may be used to clarify or to emphasize the ideas in a message. By gestures we mean *purposeful* movements of some part of the body—head, shoulders, arms, or hands—to reinforce or demonstrate what is said. Fidgeting with coat buttons or aimlessly rearranging books or papers on the speaker's table are not gestures; they are not purposeful, and they distract rather than support the ideas you are expressing.

Gestures have aptly been described as "silent words."* They serve as abridgments and/or reinforcements for ideas, reactions, and states of affairs—as "shorthand" ways of communicating matters which it would take many words to express. A simple experiment will demonstrate how important gestures are to communication. Think of a location—a possible destination—several blocks away. Then try to give directions to a stranger who wants to find the place. Notice how necessary it is to point the way and to show turns in the route by movements of the hands, arms, or head. Or observe two persons in a heated argument and notice how often their hands come into play to emphasize the points they are making.

Besides their usefulness as shorthand methods of clarifying and stressing ideas, gestures—like other movements—are valuable in helping to capture and hold listeners' attention. Just as we watch more readily the speaker who occasionally changes his position rather than the one who remains rooted in a single spot, so we listen with greater attention to the communicator whose verbal and gestural messages coincide and reinforce one another. Unless a speaker compensates for the lack of gestures by unusually compelling ideas or rich and colorful language, listeners tend to respond sluggishly, even indifferently, to him and his message. On the other hand, a physically active speaker usually is able to stimulate more lively attention and sustain the interest of an audience. As we shall see in Chapter 12, movement—whether physical or psychological—is one of the basic factors of attention.

In emphasizing the importance of gestures, we are not implying that you should deliberately adopt a forceful, dynamic mode of delivery if as a person you are habitually quiet and reserved. Again, as in the case of movement, gestures should spring from an inner impulse and should be a natural and appropriate correlate to the ideas you are communicating. Do not decide in advance that at a certain place in your speech you will point your finger at the audience and, at another time, shake your fist. The effect will be, at best, mechanical; at worst,

---

*For an interesting discussion of the symbolism of gesture, see Maurice H. Krout, "The Symbolism of Objects and Movements," Introduction to Social Psychology (New York: Harper & Row, Publishers, 1942). Reprinted in Haig A. Bosmajian, ed., The Rhetoric of Nonverbal Communication (Glenview, Ill.: Scott, Foresman and Company, 1971), p. 25.

ludicrous. If gestures are to be effective, they always must reflect your inner states of earnestness, enthusiasm, or emotion.

Gestures of the Hands and Arms

All physical behaviors, of course—whether of the hands, arms, shoulders, or head—communicate ideas and feelings to others. Speech analysts have attempted, from time to time, to categorize gestural behaviors, especially as these behaviors involve the use of the hands and arms. For instance, distinctions are sometimes drawn between what are generally referred to as "conventional" and "descriptive" gestures.

Conventional gestures are signs or symbols which, though meaningless in themselves, have had meanings assigned to them by convention or custom. Commonly encountered codes or systems of conventional gestures include the hand-and-finger language of deaf-mutes, the arm signals of the football referee, or the cautionary or command arm motions employed by the platoon sergeant in directing his men under fire.*

Through long usage certain hand and arm movements employed by public speakers also have gradually acquired conventional meanings. Thus, the pointed finger is often interpreted as a sign of accusation or challenge; the clenched fist suggests strong feeling; an arm extended with the palm of the hand turned downward is a sign of rejection.

Descriptive gestures, as distinguished from conventional gestures, carry meaning not by common custom or agreement, but because they depict or describe more or less directly the idea to be communicated. A speaker, for example, may describe the size, shape, or location of an object by very specific movements of his hands and arms. He may show how vigorous a punch was by striking the air with his fist, the height of a younger brother by holding out his arm, or the details of a complicated manipulation of a toy by performing the manipulative motions required.

Certain scholars, notably Paul Ekman and Wallace V. Friesen, in their theoretically based classification of hand movements, refer to such gestures as *illustrators*, defining them as

> . . . those acts which are intimately related on a moment-to-moment basis with speech, with phrasing, content, voice contour, loudness, etc. Illustrators usually augment what is being said verbally, but they may contradict the verbalization or be used as a substitute for a word.[4]

---

*See Mario Pei, The Story of Language (New York: J. B. Lippincott Company, 1949) for some interesting facts concerning the history and use of conventional gestures as systems of sign language.

They distinguish the following eight types of illustrator-gestures:

batons: movements which accent or emphasize a particular word or
phrase
ideographs: movements which sketch the path or direction of thought
deictic movements: pointing to an object, place, or event
spatial movements: movements which depict a spatial relationship
rhythmic movements: movements which depict the rhythm or pacing of
an event
kinetographs: movements which depict a bodily action, or some non-
human physical action
pictographs: movements which draw a picture in the air of the shape of
the referent
emblematic movements: emblems used to illustrate a verbal statement,
either repeating or substituting for a word or phrase[5]

Although many hand gestures appear, at first glance at least, to fall readily into
one or another of these categories, many of them are really combinations of sub-
types. While such categories serve to emphasize the range and usefulness of gestural activities, obviously because of their spontaneous and image-evoking nature, descriptive gestures cannot be cataloged precisely. However, by watching
other speakers and drawing upon your own originality you may discover numerous variations and possibilities. Merely ask yourself, "How can I best make this
idea clear to my listeners?" Then use any descriptive hand-and-arm gestures that
occur to you, so long as they are reasonably dignified and in good taste.

Gestures of the Head and Shoulders

As you undoubtedly have observed, some people move the head and
shoulders a great deal when speaking, whereas others hold them practically still.
Persons of different races and nationalities also vary considerably in the amount
of head and shoulder action which they employ.

As in all other phases of bodily behavior, movements of this kind must
spring from an impulse to communicate and will vary in amount and character
according to the personality of the speaker and the nature of the subject he is
discussing. It is essential, however, to realize the important contributions they
may make to one's total speaking effectiveness.

Do not plan head and shoulder gestures in advance. Do not, on the
other hand, restrain or reject them on the false notion that they are improper or
that they will detract from your delivery. Use them to the extent that it is natural
for you to do so.

Body language includes facial and body gestures, obvious and subtle, deliberate and unintentional. Because it is frequently more universal in its interpretation than spoken language, nonverbal communication often can do more to enhance and emphasize a message than any words a speaker could utter.

Facial Expression: Emotional Reflection and Audience Feedback

Psychologist Albert Mehrabian has devised a formula to account for the emotional impact of a speaker's message. Words, he says, contribute 7 percent, vocal elements 38 percent, and facial expression 55 percent.[6] But not only are facial expressions powerful carriers of feelings; they communicate them with considerable accuracy, regardless of the cultural and educational backgrounds of the receivers. In a carefully controlled study made some years ago, Delwin Dusenbury and Franklin Knower found that despite significant differences among individuals and groups, the facial expression of emotional tendencies and attitudes often could be interpreted with a high degree of reliability.[7]

Here, as in so many other instances, however, the findings of research merely reinforce what is obvious. Facial expressions—especially when they form part of a total communicative context—reveal much about a speaker's convictions and feelings.* Do not plan facial expressions in advance of your message any more than you would plan gestures or the details of movement. If, however, you are well disposed toward your audience, are genuinely interested in the subject you are discussing, and are enthusiastic about communicating, your face will reflect your state of mind and will help greatly to support the ideas and feelings you express.

Characteristics of Effective Gestures

Although you can perfect your gestures only through practice, such practice will yield better results if you keep steadily in mind these characteristics: *relaxation, vigor and definiteness, proper timing,* and *adaptability and versatility.*

Relaxation. When your muscles are strained or tense, your gestures are almost sure to be jerky or awkward, and you cannot express yourself naturally. As we mentioned earlier, one of the best ways to break your tension is to move about— to take a few easy steps or unobtrusively to rearrange your notes or papers. To avoid stiffness and awkwardness during your first few moments in front of the audience, make a conscious effort to relax your muscles *before* you start to speak.

Vigor and Definiteness. Good gestures are alive and vigorous. Put enough force into them to make them convincing. A languid shaking of the fist is a weak support for a threat or challenge; an aimless or hesitant movement of the arm confus-

---

See, for example, Michael Argyle, Social Interaction (New York: Atherton, 1969) for a classification of the nonverbal areas; he lists, among others, facial and gestural movement and direction of gaze. See also Paul Ekman, Wallace V. Friesen, and Phoebe Ellsworth, Emotion in the Human Face: Guidelines for Research and an Integration of Findings (New York: Pergamon Press, Inc., 1972); and C. E. Izard, The Face of Emotion (New York: Appleton-Century-Crofts, 1971).

es rather than clarifies. Be energetic, yes; but be selective, too. Do not pound the table or saw the air constantly. Gestural exaggeration of minor points is incongruous. Vary the force and nature of your gestures, but be vigorous enough to project your conviction and enthusiasm.

Timing. The comedian often gets laughs from his audience by timing his gestures *improperly.* If, for example, you make a gesture after the word or phrase it was intended to reinforce already has been spoken, the result will be ludicrous. The stroke of the gesture—that is, the shake of the fist, the movement of the finger, or the break of the wrist—should fall exactly on, or should slightly precede, the point that is being emphasized. If you practice making gestures until they have become habitual and then use them spontaneously as the impulse arises, you will have no trouble synchronizing them effectively. Poor timing is the result of an attempt to use "canned" or preplanned gestures.

Adaptability and Versatility. Just because a certain type of gesture or movement is effective with one subject or with one audience, do not assume that it will suit all subjects and audiences. As observation will show, skillful communicators vary their physical behaviors according to the number and character of the persons they are addressing and the nature of the ideas they are communicating.

Generally speaking, the larger the audience, the larger and more pronounced the speaker's gestures will have to be. Conversely, restrained gestural action or slight changes in facial expression, while effective in dyadic or small group communication, may seem weak and indefinite to a large group of listeners. Subjects on which feelings run strong or which require crucial and immediate decisions usually motivate speakers to more vigorous bodily action than do subjects which are less moving or urgent. Some communicative contexts obviously call for dignity of movement as well as of expression, while others require more varied and enthusiastic activity. Be versatile. *Adapt.* Adjust your communicative manner to both subject and occasion. But in doing this, let your movements and gestures conform to your own personality as a speaker and as an individual. Remember that your best speaking always is done when you are most fully and naturally yourself.

NONVERBAL BEHAVIORS IN THE "MANUSCRIPT SPEECH": SOME SPECIAL PRESENTATIONAL PROBLEMS

When you read a speech from a manuscript or an excerpt from the printed page instead of speaking extemporaneously or from memory, you encounter certain problems in bodily movement and gestural behavior. Specifically:

1. Because you must look at your manuscript frequently, you will find it difficult to maintain close eye-contact with your listeners.
2. Because your manuscript usually lies on a table or a lectern, your bodily movement is restricted to the area about it.
3. Because you are reproducing orally ideas previously thought out and written down, you will probably experience little, if any, impulse to reinforce the expression of your ideas and feelings with gestures of the hands and arms.

There are, however, a few steps and precautions you can take to maintain at least a certain amount of visual bonding or eye-contact with your listeners, to compensate in part for imposed restrictions on bodily movement, and to make the most of the gestural range available to you.

Maintaining Eye-Contact

In order to maintain the best eye-contact possible under the circumstances, carefully consider these possibilities:

A. Prior to your appearance before an audience, prepare a cleanly typed, triple-spaced copy of your manuscript, free of inked-in changes or additions.

B. Divide your speech into many short paragraphs rather than a few long ones. As you conclude a given paragraph, raise your eyes from the manuscript, glance at the audience, and then return your attention to the next paragraph on the page. The indentations at beginnings of paragraphs will make it easier for you to locate the proper paragraph quickly and resume reading.

C. Practice reading your speech until by looking at the first few words of a sentence you are able to recall the remainder of it. In this way, you will only need to glance at your manuscript in order to catch the sentence as a whole and can spend most of your time watching your audience for visual bonding and evidences of feedback. Do not, however, memorize the speech in its entirety. This not only would be a waste of time, but will also seriously detract from the spontaneity and naturalness of your presentation.

D. Place your manuscript near the top of the speaker's stand or podium. Or, if you are holding it in your hand, keep it slightly below but near your eye-level. This will shorten the arc between the words on the manuscript and the eyes of your listeners and will make it much easier for you to look at the audience frequently without losing your place.

Compensating for Restricted Movement

Although your movements will be restricted, you can still move from one side of the speaker's stand to the other; you can move slightly forward and laterally in relation to your hearers; you can vary your postural stance somewhat from time to time. Even short moves will help you to hold the attention of your listeners and also to "paragraph" your speech and effect visual transitions in your material. In those few situations where, because of a microphone or television camera, you cannot move about at all, you must compensate for the lack of movement by more animated and meaningful facial expression, by judicious use of head and shoulder gestures, and by increasing the variety and tonal coloring in your voice.

Utilizing the Available Gestural Range

Free-swinging gestures usually seem inappropriate when you are reading a speech from manuscript, and in all probability you will not feel the impulse to make them. A few, more restrained gestures may be quite in order, however, especially if they are of a descriptive nature. Throughout, strive as earnestly as you can to get your audience to understand or to believe the ideas you are presenting. When you feel an impulse to use your hands, arms, shoulders, or head to help communicate or reinforce a point, let your body respond easily and naturally. Ordinarily, under these circumstances you will feel impelled to make at least a few gestures during the course of a long and vigorous manuscript speech. Moreover, you will be sure that your gestures will seem natural and appropriate to your listeners.

PRACTICING TO ACHIEVE SKILL IN NONVERBAL COMMUNICATION

In the beginning, you may find that although you recognize fully the role that responsive bodily behavior plays in communicating your ideas and feelings effectively to others, when you actually confront those others, you are restrained or immobile. This is because you still are not as much at home in the speaking situation as you should be. The only sure way to gain the ease in gestural activity and bodily responsiveness you desire is through practice.

Practicing to Achieve Skill in Nonverbal Communication 179

Therefore, speak and move and gesture as often as you can; and when you do move and gesture, do not be afraid to let yourself go for fear that you will do something wrong. If your instructor or classmates tell you that you are pacing aimlessly or are using too many gestures, make sure they do not really mean that your movements or gestures lack variety. Instead of reducing the amount of activity, vary it more. Later, after you have gained greater confidence in yourself, you may want to reduce the number of gestures you use, or to move about less frequently. For the present, however, move and gesture as the impulse directs you. With practice you will find that gradually the kind and amount of bodily activity appropriate to you, to your ideas, and to your particular communicative situation will come to you naturally. Your physical behavior as you face your audience will be forgotten and will, without conscious effort on your part, help to clarify and reinforce the ideas and feelings you wish to communicate.

In sum, regardless of the type of message or the form of its presentation, if you wish to enhance your skill in using nonverbal behaviors in communicative interaction, these are the avenues open to you: maintain meaningful contact and rapport with your listeners; assume an alert, yet comfortable posture; when you move, move purposefully; use vigorous, definite, and well-timed gestures; let your facial expression be mobile and responsive; and adapt your movements and gestures to the nature and number of your listeners and to the subject on which you are speaking. And, above all, practice . . . practice . . . *practice.*

FOOTNOTES

[1] *Andrew W. Halpin*, Theory and Research in Administration *(New York: The Macmillan Company, 1966), pp. 253–254.*

[2] *Jurgen Ruesch and Weldon Kees*, Nonverbal Communication: Notes on the Visual Perception of Human Relations *(Berkeley: University of California Press, 1964), p. 82.*

[3] *Ibid., p. 82. See also Edward T. Hall*, The Silent Language *(New York: Doubleday & Company, Inc., 1959), p. 163.*

[4] *Excerpts from "Hand Movements" by Paul Ekman and Wallace V. Friesen from the* Journal of Communication, 22 *(December 1972). Reprinted by permission of the authors and the International Communication Association.*

[5] *Ibid., p. 360.*

[6] *Flora Davis, "How to Read Body Language,"* Glamour *(1969). Reprinted in Haig A. Bosmajian, ed.,* The Rhetoric of Nonverbal Communication *(Glenview, Ill.: Scott, Foresman and Company, 1971).*

[7] *Delwin Dusenbury and Franklin H. Knower, "Experimental Studies of the Symbolism of Action and Voice— I: A Study of the Specificity of Meaning in Facial Expression,"* Quarterly Journal of Speech XXIV *(October 1938): 424–435.*

Problems and Probes

1. Recall the liveliest, most entertaining speaker you have heard recently. Make a list of the nonverbal behaviors and bodily actions which he or she used *purposefully* to project and/or reinforce the verbal elements of the speech. Make another list, including those nonverbal behaviors which the speaker used in ways that detracted from or interfered with his or her presentation. Which of these behaviors were the most irritating or disturbing to you personally?

2. "Body language" is a term that can be used to describe much of what is considered in this chapter. Drawing upon the Suggestions for Further Reading (pages 183–184), enlarge your understanding of this subject, and then prepare a two- or three-page report on an aspect of it that you were not heretofore aware of.

3. Make a concise, easy-to-follow list of the guides and suggestions regarding nonverbal behaviors in speech communication as they have been considered in this chapter. Take this list with you as you go to hear a speaker on the campus or in your community, and use it to check and evaluate the physical behaviors and nonverbal messages given off by this speaker during the course of his or her presentation. Note both strengths and weaknesses in the speaker's posture, movement, gestures, and contact with the audience. Observe particularly those statements emphasized with gestures and the kinds of gestures used for that purpose. Prepare a reasonably detailed report (written, oral, or both—as your instructor may indicate) on the "platform" behaviors of this speaker.

4. In this chapter the statement was made that words account for 7 percent, vocal elements 38 percent, and facial expression 55 percent of the emotional impact of an oral message. Defend or attack that assertion. In what speech situations would you expect these percentages to be largely valid? In what situations would you expect them to be probably not valid?

Oral Activities and Speaking Assignments

1. Pair off with another member of the class and sit silently facing each other for two minutes. Study your partner by reading his or her body language. Then discuss your impressions, citing specific examples of nonverbal behaviors and cues as the bases of whatever emotional reactions you may have experienced.

2. Holding your elbows well out from your body, keeping your wrists flexible, and moving your hands and arms vigorously, do the following exercises in sequence:

    a. Shake your arms and hands as if trying to get something loose from your fingers. Do this with your arms far out at the sides, up over your head, and out in front of you. Continue until all tension and stiffness are eliminated.

    b. While you are shaking your hands and arms, begin repeating the alphabet over and over—not in a monotonous rhythm, but as if you were actually talking in highly emotional language. Continue this "talking" while proceeding with Exercises c and d below.

    c. Gradually change from merely shaking your arms and hands to making more meaningful gestures: point your finger, reject an idea, drive home a point, etc. In making these various gestures, be sure to maintain the vigor and abandon of your hand and arm movements.

    d. Select a partner. Harangue each other by repeating the letters of the alphabet loudly and as though you were greatly excited. Keep up a vigorous flow of body language while you do this, both "talking" and gesturing at the same time.

3. Using descriptive as well as conventional gestures, try to communicate the following ideas silently—by means of physical actions alone:

    a. "Get out of here!"
    b. "Why, Tom (or Mary)! I haven't seen you for ages!"
    c. "If we're going to get what we want, we'll have to fight for it and fight hard!"
    d. "Cool it, will you? Give him a chance to explain."
    e. "Come here a minute, Jim, will you?"
    f. "Every penny I had is gone."

4. Without words, convey to the class a clear picture of each of the following:

    a. A nervous pedestrian crossing a street through heavy traffic.
    b. An irate motorist changing a tire on a hot day.
    c. A mother getting dinner and setting the table while trying in vain to keep a two-year-old out of mischief.
    d. A Christmas shopper trying to carry too many parcels, some of which start slipping.

e. A panhandler asking several different people for a coin for a cup of coffee.

5. Imagine yourself in one of the situations described below, and react spontaneously with whatever physical behavior seems natural. Speak out also if you feel impelled to do so.

    a. Someone has fired a gun just behind you.
    b. A child in front of you steps into the path of a fast-moving automobile.
    c. Someone has just slapped your face.
    d. Someone shouts to warn you of a heavy object about to fall on you.
    e. You are marooned on an island and are trying to catch the attention of the crew on a passing ship.
    f. A mob is bent on destruction; as the crowd goes past, you try to turn it in another direction.

6. Make a two- or three-minute speech explaining to the class how to do something, such as driving a golf ball, kicking a football, bowling, playing a musical instrument, or cutting out a dress pattern. Use movement and gestures to help make your ideas clear. Do not use the chalkboard or previously prepared diagrams.

7. Give a three- or four-minute speech on some subject that arouses your fighting spirit: dishonesty in advertising, cruelty to animals or children, bureaucratic red tape, campus injustices, unsympathetic officials or teachers, unfair course requirements, or the suppression of student-protest movements. Choose a subject that makes you genuinely angry, excited, or indignant. "Let yourself go" vocally and physically in denouncing the institution or practice. Be careful, however, to back up what you say with facts; do not pointlessly rant and rave or merely air a prejudice. You may make a point as strongly as you like, provided you are able to prove it. Remember to frame a specific purpose and to choose materials suitable to your listeners.

Suggestions for Further Reading

Ernest G. Bormann and Nancy C. Bormann, *Speech Communication: An Interpersonal Approach* (New York: Harper & Row, Publishers, 1972), Chapter V, "How to Improve Nonverbal Communication Through Body Language," pp. 83–98.

John W. Bowers, "The Influence of Delivery on Attitudes Toward Concepts and Speakers," *Speech Monographs* XXXII (June 1965): 154–158.

Haig A. Bosmajian, ed., *The Rhetoric of Nonverbal Communication* (Glenview, Ill.: Scott, Foresman and Company, 1971).

J. R. Davitz and L. J. Davitz, "Nonverbal Communication of Feeling," *Journal of Communication* XI (1961): 81–86.

Mark L. Knapp, *Nonverbal Communication in Human Interaction* (New York: Holt, Rinehart & Winston, Inc., 1972).

Erving Goffman, *The Presentation of Self in Everyday Life* (New York: Doubleday & Company, Inc., Anchor Books, 1959).

Edward T. Hall, *The Hidden Dimension* (New York: Doubleday & Company, Inc., 1966).

C. David Mortensen, *Communication: The Study of Human Interaction* (New York: McGraw-Hill Book Company, 1972), Chapter VI, "Nonverbal Interaction," pp. 209–253.

6
USING THE VOICE TO COMMUNICATE

After long experience in public life Benjamin Disraeli, the British states-man, declared, "There is no index of character so sure as the voice." It is true that often we tend to judge a person by his voice. A man whose voice is harsh or gut-teral may be regarded as crude and rough. A woman whose tones are sharp and nasal is thought to be a shrew. A thin, breathy voice, characterized by the fre-quent use of upward inflections, suggests a lack of conviction or decisiveness.

Of course, the conclusions we draw from vocal characteristics may some-times be incorrect. But correct or not, such judgments are important to the speaker because they color his listeners' attitudes toward what he is saying. Often a speaker's voice is the most important single factor in determining how his message is received; frequently it is among the major determinants.

In addition to projecting a desirable image, a good voice enables a speaker to make what he says clearer and more interesting. Listen to a child at a church or school program rattle off a poem or speak his lines in a play. Even though every word he speaks is clearly audible, his expression often is so drab and monotonous that the author's ideas are imperfectly conveyed. On the other hand, recall a play-by-play account of a football or baseball game broadcast by a skilled sports announcer. Did not the vividness of his description depend in large mea-sure upon the way he used his voice?

How can you as a speaker acquire an effective voice? As in bodily de-livery, improvement results chiefly from practice. Improper practice, however, may do more harm than good: repeatedly doing the wrong thing merely fixes a bad habit more firmly. To make practice worthwhile, you should first be acquaint-ed with the characteristics of a good speaking voice and with some of the methods by which these characteristics may be acquired. Then, with this information in mind, practice becomes more profitable and the goal of a good speaking voice easier to attain.

THE CHARACTERISTICS OF A GOOD SPEAKING VOICE

A good speaking voice has three essential properties: (1) it is reason-ably pleasant to listen to; (2) it conveys the speaker's ideas easily and clearly;

and (3) it is capable of expressing the fine shades of feeling and emotion which reveal the speaker's attitude toward himself, his subject, and his listeners. Technically, these three considerations are labeled *quality*, *intelligibility*, and *variety*. Let us consider them in order.

Voice Quality

The basic component of a good speaking voice is a pleasing tone or quality. This is the overall impression a voice makes on those who hear it— whether they regard it as harsh and strident, full and mellow, pleasant or annoying.

Sometimes, because a speaker's vocal mechanism is in a poor state of health or because it is habitually misused, his voice is excessively thin, husky, nasal, or breathy. In such cases, a special program of training under the direction of a competent instructor may be called for. Usually, however, by ridding himself of excessive tensions in the neck and throat area and learning to preserve a proper balance between oral and nasal resonance, a speaker gradually will acquire the best or optimum quality of which he or she is capable. A number of the exercises supplied at the close of this chapter will prove helpful in these respects.

Effect of Attitude and Emotion on Voice Quality

Because voice quality is so accurate as a mirror of attitude or state of mind, listeners usually are quick to detect whether a speaker is angry, happy, confident, fearful, or sad. Similarly, they are able to tell with a surprising degree of accuracy whether one is sincere or insincere in what he or she is saying. For these reasons, you should not attempt to vary the quality of your voice artificially or try to simulate an attitude or feeling you do not actually possess. Believe strongly in what you are saying, strive earnestly to make your ideas clear and convincing to your listeners, and in most instances you will find that your voice responds in the appropriate manner. Here, as in so many other aspects of the oral communication process, artificiality and insincerity nearly always are self-defeating.

Intelligibility

The intelligibility or understandability of your speech normally depends upon five separate but related factors: (1) the overall level of loudness at which you speak, (2) the duration of sounds within the syllables you utter, (3) the distinctness with which you articulate words and syllables, (4) the standard of pronunciation you observe, and (5) the vocal stress you give to a syllable, word, or phrase.

Adjusting the Loudness Level

Probably the most important single factor in rendering speech intelligible is the loudness level at which you speak as related to the *distance* between you and your listener and the amount of *noise* that is present.* Obviously, the farther away your listener is, the louder you must talk for him to hear you well. Most of us make this loudness-level adjustment unconsciously when projecting our voices over extreme distances; when we call to someone down the block or across a field, we have learned that we must shout in order to be heard. What we often forget is that a corresponding adjustment is required in conversations and other common forms of person-to-person interchange, where the listener is only a few feet away. You must realize also that your own voice will always sound louder to you (unless you are deaf) than to your listeners because your own ears are closer to your mouth than theirs are.

The sound of your voice diminishes rapidly as it travels from you. In fact, if it were not reflected from surrounding surfaces, listeners only a short distance away would hear but a fraction of its initial loudness.** This fact explains why it is important to hold a microphone or the mouthpiece of a telephone fairly close to your mouth or, if the microphone is of a type which picks up sounds at a greater distance, why you should be careful not to vary your distance from it. The effects of distance on the loudness of your voice cannot be too rigidly stated, however, because there are a number of modifying factors which also help determine the volume level at which you must talk. These include the surface of the walls—whether acoustically treated or made of smooth plaster—the number of people present, and the sound absorbency of their clothing.

In addition to distance, the amount of surrounding noise with which you must compete has an effect on the required loudness level. It is important to realize that even in normal circumstances some noise always is present. For example, the noise level of rustling leaves in the quiet solitude of a country lane (10

---

*The term loudness is here used synonymously with intensity because the former term is clearer to most people. Technically, of course, loudness—a distinct function in the science of acoustics—is not strictly synonymous with intensity. To explain the exact relationships between the two terms is beyond the scope of this book because the explanation involves many complicated psychophysical relationships. For a full discussion of these relationships, see Stanley S. Stevens and Hallowell Davis, Hearing: Its Psychology and Physiology (New York: John Wiley & Sons, Inc., 1938), p. 110 ff.

**The loudness of your voice—strictly speaking, its intensity—varies inversely with the square of the distance it travels from your lips. (Expressed mathematically, $1 \propto 1/D^2$.) Therefore, if it were not reflected from the walls and ceiling, your voice would be only one-sixteenth as loud twelve feet away as it is at a distance of three feet; and the listener fifty feet away would hear only a very tiny fraction of the original sound.

decibels*) is louder than a whisper six feet away. The noise in empty theatres averages 25 decibels, but with a "quiet" audience it rises to 42. In the average factory, a constant noise of about 80 decibels is likely to be characteristic. This is just about the same level as very loud speaking at a close range.

How can you determine the proper strength of voice to use in order to achieve sufficient loudness for the distance and noise conditions of a particular speech situation? While apparatus is available to measure the intensity of sounds with considerable accuracy, most of us do not have it and would not want to carry it around with us if we did. You can, however, always use your eyes to see if your auditors appear to be hearing you; or, even better, you can *ask* them. Get your instructor's advice on this point also. Ask your friends to report on the loudness of your voice as you talk in rooms of various sizes and under varying noise conditions. Listen to the sound of your voice so that you can begin to correlate your own vocal sensations with their reports. You will soon learn to gauge the volume you must use in order to be heard.

The proper loudness for talking into the microphone of a public address system introduces a different problem. Here the loudness of your voice will be affected by the type of microphone, the amplifying system, and the loudspeaker. No invariable rule can be given because equipment varies widely. You must, however, take the important precaution of trying out the equipment before you are scheduled to speak. Ask the technician in charge to advise you, and find out what signals he will use to tell you to talk louder or to move farther away from the microphone.

Syllable Duration

The second factor that affects a listener's ability to understand what you say is the duration of sound within the syllables you utter. Generally, a slower rate of speaking is more easily understood than a fast one, but merely slowing down is not enough. As we shall explain more fully later in this chapter, the rate of your speech depends on two elements: *quantity*, or the duration of sound within a syllable; and *pause*, or the silent interval between sounds. Experimental evidence seems to show that the intelligibility of speech—how much the listener hears accurately—depends more on syllable duration than on the overall rate of speaking. Thus a slow staccato utterance is not much more intelligible than a faster staccato utterance, but talking at a moderate rate *while prolonging the sounds uttered* improves intelligibility markedly.

This does not mean that everything you say should be spoken in a slow drawl. It *does* mean, however, that a rapid, "machine-gun" utterance often is

---

Loudness is expressed in decibels (db). Within certain acoustic limits, one decibel is roughly equal to the smallest difference in loudness which the ear can detect. Standard measurements for loudness are at distances of three feet unless otherwise noted.

hard to understand and should, therefore, be avoided. When the momentum of a fast-moving narrative is more important to your purpose than exact comprehension of every word you say, naturally you will want to speak with more speed. But when you want to be sure your listeners understand precisely what you are saying on some important point, take time to dwell on every significant word long enough to be sure it will be heard and understood.

Syllable duration is of especial importance when you are talking in a large hall, when you must be heard above a great amount of noise, or when the acoustics of the room produce a noticeable echo effect. Speakers who address mass meetings held out-of-doors, or who make announcements at a banquet where there is a clatter of dishes, have found that they must "stretch out" their syllables if they are to be understood. Even unaccented syllables (such as -ing in *going*) are drawn out longer than usual. The ringmaster at a circus or the announcer at a prizefight is not just trying to be different when he sings out, "L-a-a-d-i-e-s and ge-e-n-tle-m-e-en"; he has learned through experience that he has to prolong the sounds if they are to be understood. Similarly, pilots, in talking on the airplane intercom and in radioing the control tower, have found that sustained and slightly drawn-out syllables are much more easily understood above the noise of the engine. You will find the same thing true in talking over the telephone in a noisy office or shop.

Practice, then, until you can prolong your syllables without losing the rhythm and emphasis of your sentences; but be careful not to overdo this manner of speaking when neither noise nor distance requires you to do so. To assist you in this practice, suggestions and exercise materials are provided in the concluding section of this chapter, pages 211–212.

Distinctness of Articulation

Besides increasing the loudness of utterance and giving individual syllables greater duration, you may improve the intelligibility of your speech by exercising greater care in articulation. Good articulation is chiefly the job of the jaw, tongue, and lips. Only by using the muscles which manipulate these members with skill and energy can you achieve crisp, clean-cut speech. Some Oriental people move their jaws very little in speaking; in their language, so much of the meaning is conveyed by variation in pitch that scarcely any jaw movement is necessary. In English, however, failure to open the jaws adequately while speaking is a serious fault because meaning is largely conveyed by consonant sounds, and these cannot be made effectively unless the tongue is given enough room to move vigorously. Even vowel sounds are likely to be muffled if the jaws are kept immobile. As you talk, therefore, remember to move your jaws freely.

The tongue has more to do with the distinct formation of speech sounds than does any other organ. Even when the jaw is opened adequately, the sounds

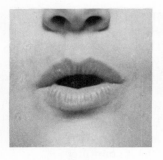
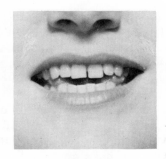
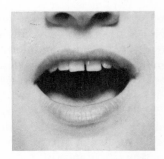

rose   **ch<u>ee</u>se**   **f<u>a</u>ther**

Contrasting movements, especially of the lips and jaw, produce and distinguish each of these vowel sounds from the others: the <u>o</u> in <u>rose</u>, <u>ee</u> in <u>cheese</u>, and <u>a</u> in <u>father</u>.

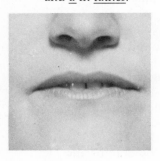
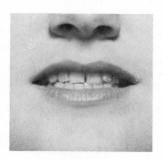
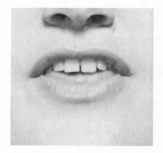

<u>v</u>eil   **<u>s</u>ee**   **<u>th</u>ing**

Note characteristic positioning of the articulators—particularly of the lips, tongue, and teeth—for proper formation of these sounds: <u>v</u> in <u>veil</u>, <u>s</u> in <u>see</u>, and <u>th</u> in <u>thing</u>.

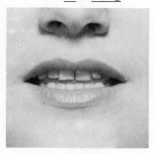
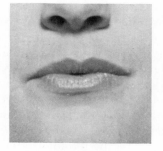
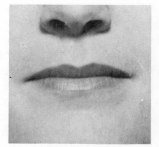

<u>l</u>ead   **<u>w</u>ear**   **<u>m</u>an**

Note modifications in the position of the lips and tongue for the formation of sounds represented by the <u>l</u> in <u>lead</u> and <u>w</u> in <u>wear</u>.

Prominent use of the articulators is required for formation of <u>m</u> in <u>man</u>.

190

produced cannot be sharp if the tongue lies idle or moves sluggishly. All the vowels depend partly on the position of the tongue for their distinctive qualities. Try saying "ee, ay, ah, aw, oor" and notice how the tongue changes its position. A great many consonant sounds, such as *d*, *th*, *ch*, *g*, and *k*, also depend upon the active movement of the tongue.

The lips, too, are important to distinct speech. If they are allowed to become lazy, the result will be a mumbled articulation, particularly of sounds such as *p*, *b*, *m*, and *f*, which depend chiefly on lip position. Of course, when talking directly into a microphone, we should avoid violent and explosive utterance of consonant sounds. However, in ordinary speaking—and especially in public speaking—we should use our lips more decisively to cut and to mold the sounds we make.

There also are many words in English that require special care and attention insofar as articulation is concerned. Experiments have shown, for example, that under most circumstances the word *fox* is more than twice as hard to understand as *dog*, and that six times as many errors of recognition are made on the word *nuts* as on *limeade.* And if the listeners in these experiments have never heard of foxes or nuts, the percentage of error is even greater because unfamiliar words usually are harder to understand than familiar ones.

The English language contains many words with different meanings but the same, or very similar, sounds: *one* and *won, for* and *four, sick* and *six,* and the like. Moreover, the acoustic difference between certain individual sounds often is too small for clear differentiation if all the other sounds in the word are the same. Thus it may be hard to understand the rapid utterance of such a phrase as "nine fine swine."

Careful articulation and lengthening the duration of syllables will help reduce misunderstandings of this kind. Especially when you talk on unfamiliar subjects requiring the use of terms—particularly technical terms—which are strange to your listeners, you must talk more slowly, prolong your syllables, and articulate more carefully. Wherever possible, try also to choose words that cannot be mistaken in context. In particular, be careful about using similar sounding words close together in sentences where the meaning of the first word may influence the meaning of the second. The story is told of a reporter who interviewed a farmer by telephone and reported in his newspaper that the farmer had just purchased "2008 pigs." The farmer had actually told him that he had bought "two sows and eight pigs." A difference of only one sound resulted in an error of 1998 hogs. Although errors of this magnitude do not often occur, frequently a listener may be confused about a certain word or sentence until something is said later in the discussion to clarify the point; and in the meantime the effectiveness of the intervening remarks may have been reduced. Be careful, therefore, to think of words in terms of the way they *sound* and not only of the way they look in print. Remember, it is what the listener *thinks* he hears that counts.

192

An unusual and ultimately successful experiment in voice training was the subject of the musical play My Fair Lady, *adapted from G. B. Shaw's* Pygmalion. *Months of lessons with Henry Higgins (Rex Harrison), professor of linguistics and phonetics, enabled Cockney flower girl Eliza Doolittle (Julie Andrews) to pass as a member of English gentility. Voice-training methods used by Professor Higgins included speaking with a mouthful of marbles to improve articulation and speaking into a lighted candle to improve breath control.*

Finally, enunciate to avoid indistinctness. Take time enough to get each sound out clearly instead of jumbling successive sounds together. *Take time to speak distinctly.* Later, as your jaw, tongue, and lips develop greater flexibility and precision, you can speed up—but never to the point of rushing.

Briefly, then, when you are talking, open your jaw wide; move your lips energetically; use your tongue vigorously; pay particular attention to words that are likely to be misunderstood or confused; and don't speak too fast. Practice the exercises for distinctness of articulation given at the end of this chapter, and be sure that you carry the results of this practice over into your daily conversation. It is possible, of course, to be so precise in your articulation that you seem affected, but the chances are that your fault lies in the other direction. Crisp and precise speech will create in your listeners considerable unconscious respect for you as a person.

The International Phonetic Alphabet: A Tool for Analyzing Articulation and Pronunciation*

As a student of speech, you should familiarize yourself with the International Phonetic Alphabet (IPA) and the ways in which it can assist you in improving your speech. Basically, a symbol is assigned to each speech sound; and these symbols, individually and in combination, are useful tools for analyzing pronunciation and articulation—your own as well as others'. Properly employed in listening, transcribing, and speaking, this phonetic guide can help you make certain that the nature and quality of your speech meet established norms.

On the facing page is an abridged version of the IPA. As you can see, the alphabet is divided into symbols for the *vowel*, *diphthong*, and *consonant* sounds. Many more symbols are required to represent and distinguish between individual speech sounds than are available in our conventional alphabet, particularly among the vowels. Sounds, for example, which are represented in spelling by the letter "a" require several phonetic symbols so that each may be distinguished. Another point to be noted is that in the sounds which are represented by "er" or "uh" the distinction must be made between accented and unaccented forms. Therefore, you will note that [ɝ], [ɜ], and [ʌ], which are used only in accented syllables, are regarded as separate sounds from [ɚ] and [ə], which appear only in unaccented syllables.

---

*For a more complete explanation of the phonetic alphabet, see John S. Kenyon and Thomas A. Knott, "Introduction," A Pronouncing Dictionary of American English (Springfield, Mass.: G. & C. Merriam Co., 1951). Also see Ralph R. Leutenegger, The Sounds of American English (Glenview, Ill.: Scott, Foresman and Company, 1963). For demonstrations of the phonemes, listen to Demonstration Exercises 1–3 in Voice and Articulation: Recorded Exercises, by Donald H. Ecroyd, Murray M. Halfond, and Carol Chworowsky Towne (Glenview, Ill.: Scott, Foresman and Company, 1966).

INTERNATIONAL PHONETIC ALPHABET

Symbol	Key Word	Pronunciation	Symbol	Key Word	Pronunciation
Vowels					
[i]	flee	[fli]	[ɔ]	thaw	[θɔ]
[ɪ]	sit	[sɪt]	[o]	no	[no]
[e]	mate	[met]	[ʊ]	good	[gʊd]
[ɛ]	fed	[fɛd]	[u]	suit	[sut]
[æ]	hat	[hæt]	[ɝ]	mercy	[ˈmɝsɪ] (*r* sounded)
[a]	ask	[ask] (as heard in	[ɜ]	mercy	[ˈmɜsɪ] (*r* silent)
		the East)	[ɚ]	mother	[ˈmʌðɚ] (*r* sounded)
[ɑ]	part	[pɑrt]	[ə]	rather	[ˈræðə] (*r* silent)
[ɒ]	wad	[wɒd] (as heard in		attack	[əˈtæk]
		New England)	[ʌ]	annul	[əˈnʌl]
Diphthongs					
[aɪ]	mile	[maɪl]	[ju]	union	[ˈjunjən]
[aʊ]	cow	[kaʊ]		mute	[mjut]
[ɔɪ]	employ	[ɪmˈplɔɪ]	[ɪu]	mute	[mɪut]
Consonants					
[p]	post	[post]	[h]	hat	[hæt]
[b]	bat	[bæt]	[tʃ]	chat	[tʃæt]
[t]	tale	[tel]	[dʒ]	jest	[dʒɛst]
[d]	duty	[ˈdjutɪ]	[m]	mute	[mjut]
[k]	cow	[kaʊ]	[m̩]	keep 'em	[ˈkipm̩]
[g]	gap	[gæp]	[n]	union	[ˈjunjən]
[f]	face	[fes]	[n̩]	mutton	[ˈmʌtn̩]
[v]	vine	[vaɪn]	[ŋ]	bang	[bæŋ]
[θ]	both	[boθ]	[l]	mile	[maɪl]
[ð]	then	[ðɛn]	[l̩]	handle	[ˈhændl̩]
[s]	sit	[sɪt]	[w]	wet	[wɛt]
[z]	zero	[ˈzɪro]	[hw]	when	[hwɛn]
[ʃ]	push	[pʊʃ]	[j]	yellow	[ˈjɛlo]
[ʒ]	measure	[ˈmɛʒɚ]	[r]	red	[rɛd]

Diphthongs are here considered as single speech sounds. Diphthong symbols, and such consonant symbols as [tʃ] and [dʒ], are regarded as single phonetic symbols. The diphthongs [ju] and [ɪu] often alternate (as in [mjut] and [mɪut]), with the same speaker sometimes using both forms. The symbol [ju] is a rising diphthong (the second element stressed more than the first), whereas [ɪu] is either a falling diphthong (first element stressed) or a level-stress diphthong.

As you study the accompanying chart, observe that key words containing sounds represented by specific symbols are transcribed into phonetic symbols in the pronunciation column. Accent marks are included with transcriptions of words of more than one syllable. Note, too, that the accent mark always *precedes* the accented syllable.

Acceptable Pronunciation

The fourth factor that contributes to the intelligibility of vocal utterance is adherence to an accepted standard of pronunciation. *If you fail to pronounce words acceptably, your listeners will not be able to grasp easily and quickly the meaning or significance of what you say.* Even if your words are recognized, any peculiarity of pronunciation is almost sure to be noticed by some of the people who hear you; and the mistake not only may distract their attention from your line of thought, but may also discredit your knowledge and authority as a speaker.

Standards of pronunciation differ, of course, sometimes making it difficult to know what is acceptable. Ordinarily, the best criterion is the usage of the educated people of your own community. For most words, a dictionary provides a helpful guide; but dictionaries can become outdated and for this reason should not be followed too slavishly. Moreover, most dictionaries do not take sufficient notice of *regional differences* in dialect. A native of Louisiana pronounces words differently from a person who lives in Montana, and the speech of a Chicagoan is easily distinguished from that of a Bostonian. The standard of an up-to-date dictionary, modified to agree with the usage of educated people in your community, should, therefore, be the basis of your pronunciation.

A common fault of pronunciation is to misplace the accent in words—to say "genu-*ine*," "*de*-vice," "the-*ay*-ter," "pre-*fer*-able," instead of the more accepted forms, "*gen*-uine," "de-*vice*," "the-ater," "*pref*-erable." Other errors arise from the omission of sounds (as in the pronunciation "guh'mnt" for *government*), from the addition of sounds ("athalete" for *athlete*), and from the substitution of sounds ("git" for *get*). Furthermore, as we know, the way words are spelled is not always a safe guide to pronunciation, for English words contain many silent letters (of*t*en, i*s*land, mor*t*gage), and many words containing the same combinations of letters require different pronunciations (b*ough*, r*ough*, thr*ough*; call*ed*, shout*ed*, gasp*ed*). In addition, the formality of the occasion exerts considerable influence. Many omissions acceptable in social conversation, informal interviews, or business conferences become objectionable in formal address. In television and radio broadcasting, careful pronunciation is particularly important. Because network programs are seen and heard throughout the nation, they tend to minimize regional differences in pronunciation and to foster a common standard across the country. In general, however, what is good pronunciation elsewhere is also good "on the air."

Do not be so labored and precise as to call attention to your pronunciation rather than to your ideas, but do not take this admonition as an excuse for careless speech. Avoid equally pronunciation that is too pedantic and that which is too provincial. Use your ears: listen to your own pronunciation and compare it with that of educated people in your community and with that of speakers on television and radio. If your pronunciation is faulty, record in your Personal Speech Journal or a notebook a list of the words you mispronounce, and practice their acceptable pronunciation frequently.

Vocal Stress

The intelligibility of a word or phrase often depends on how it is stressed. Consider the word *content*, and note the change of meaning produced by shifting the stress from one syllable to the other. The rules of stress, however, are by no means inflexible when words are used in connected speech. Emphasis and contrast often require the shifting of stress for the sake of greater clarity of meaning. For example, notice what you do to the accent in the word *proceed* when you use it in this sentence: "I said to proceed, not to recede." Many words change considerably in sound when they are stressed; especially is this true of short words such as pronouns, articles, and prepositions. For example, if you are speaking in a casual context, you might say, "I gave 'im th' book." But if you stress the third word, or the fourth one, you will say, "I gave *him* th' book," or "I gave 'im *the* book." In short, the requirements of contrast and emphasis, as well as the conventional rules of accent, influence the placing of stress in words.

Variety

Speech that is easily intelligible may yet be dull and monotonous to listen to. Moreover, it may fail to communicate to the audience the full measure of thought and feeling which the speaker wishes to convey. This often happens when the speaker's voice is not flexible enough to express the fine shades of attitude or emotion upon which accurate and pleasing expression depends.

How may you vary your voice so as to make it more lively or colorful and, at the same time, communicate your feelings and attitudes more precisely? How can you make important ideas stand out from those that are less significant? These are some of the questions with which we shall be concerned as we discuss in order the "vocal fundamentals" of *rate*, *force*, *pitch*, and *emphasis*.

Rate

Most persons speak between 120 and 180 words a minute; however, a uniform rate is not maintained with clocklike regularity. In normal speech, the speed of utterance corresponds to the thought or feeling the speaker is attempting to transmit. Weighty, complex, or serious ideas tend to be expressed more slowly; light, humorous, or exciting matters more rapidly. Observe how fast the sports announcer talks when he is describing a completed forward pass or a quick double play. In contrast, observe the slow, dignified rate at which a minister reads the wedding or burial service. A temperamentally excitable person tends to talk fast all of the time, while a stolid person characteristically talks in a slow drawl. The enthusiastic but poised individual who is in complete command of his material and of the speaking situation *varies* his rate, using this variation to convey the intensity of his convictions and the depths of his feelings. He tells a story, lays out facts, or summarizes an argument at a lively pace; but he presents his main ideas and more difficult points slowly and emphatically so that their importance may be fully grasped by the listener.

Pause. In addition to varying the rate of his utterance as changes in thought or mood require, the skilled speaker—whether in a dyadic, group, or public situation—knows how to use pauses effectively. *Pauses punctuate thought.* Just as commas, semicolons, and periods separate written words into thought groups, so pauses of different lengths separate spoken words into meaningful units. The haphazard use of pauses when you are speaking or reading a speech from manuscript, therefore, is as confusing to the listener as the haphazard use of punctuation in printed matter is to the silent reader.

Be sure that your pauses come between thought units and not in the middle of them. Moreover, when reading a speech aloud, remember that written and oral punctuation differ. Not every comma calls for a pause, nor does the absence of punctuation always mean that no pause is required. In extemporaneous speaking, pauses tend to fall naturally between thought groups. Here, as in the read speech, however, it is important to set off one idea from another clearly and definitely.

Often a pause may be used for emphasis. Placed immediately after an important statement, it suggests to your listeners: "Let this idea sink in." A pause before the climax of a story helps to increase suspense. A dramatic pause introduced at the proper moment may express the depth of your feeling more forcefully than words.

Many speakers are afraid to pause. Fearing they will forget what they want to say or that silence will focus attention on them personally, they rush on with a stream of words or vaguely vocalize the pause with *and-er-ah*. These random and meaningless syllables not only draw attention away from the ideas being expressed, but also are extremely annoying to the listener. Remember that a pause seldom seems as long to the hearer as it does to the speaker. Indeed, the ability to pause for emphasis or clarity is an indication of poise and self-control. Do not be afraid to pause whenever a break in utterance will help clarify an idea or emphasize an important point. Concentrate on the thought or emotion you are trying to convey and let your voice respond accordingly. But above all, when you do stop, stop completely. Do not fill the gap with *er, uh,* or *um.* These intrusive vocalizations defeat entirely the purposes a pause should serve.

Force

As we already have suggested, it is a basic responsibility of any speaker to use adequate vocal force or energy—to talk loudly enough to be heard easily. A certain amount of force also is needed if the communicator is to voice ideas and remarks with confidence and vigor. Talking too softly suggests that you are not sure of yourself or that you do not believe deeply in what you are saying. On the other hand, continuous shouting wears out an audience and dissipates attention. With force as with rate, variety should be your guiding consideration.

Degree. Variations in the force or energy of speech have as their primary purpose the adding of emphasis. By increasing the loudness of a word or phrase or by pointedly reducing its loudness, you may make an idea stand out as if it had been underscored. Moreover, changing the degree of force is an effective way to reawaken lagging interest. A drowsy audience will sit up quickly if a speaker suddenly projects an important word or phrase with sharply increased energy. Remember, however, that the effect is produced not so much by the force itself as by the *change* in degree; a sudden reduction may be quite as effective as a sharp increase.

While you are practicing to develop variety in vocal force or energy, take care not to alter the pitch and quality of your voice. The natural tendency for most speakers is to raise their pitch when they try to increase their loudness. You probably have noticed that when you shout, your voice is keyed much higher than when you speak in a conversational tone. This happens because the nerves which control the speaking mechanism tend to diffuse their impulses to all of the muscles involved, and the resulting general tension is likely to produce a higher pitch as well as more force. Sometimes this tension is so great that it simultaneously creates a harsh quality. Practice, however, should enable you to overcome this tendency. Just as you have learned to wiggle one finger without moving the others or to wink one eye without the other, so you can learn to apply force by contracting the breathing muscles without tightening the muscles of the throat and thus unnecessarily raising the pitch of your voice. A good way to begin is by repeating a sentence such as "That is absolutely *true!*" Hit the last word in the sentence with a greater degree of vocal energy and at the same time lower your pitch. When you are able to do this, say the entire sentence louder, and LOUD-ER, and *LOUDER,* until you can shout it without allowing your pitch to go up, too. As you practice, sustain the tone, use a long quantity, and try to maintain a full resonance. By learning to control the force of your voice, you will do much to make your speaking more emphatic and to convey to your audience an impression of power in reserve.

Pitch

Just as singers' voices differ, some being soprano or tenor and others contralto or bass, so do people in general vary in the normal pitch level at which they speak. Except when you are impersonating a character to embellish a story or an anecdote, it is best to talk in your normal pitch range. Otherwise, there is danger of straining your voice. Fortunately, you will find that there is considerable latitude within your normal range. In fact, few beginning speakers take advantage of the possibilities offered by their normal range. Instead, they tend to hit one level and stay there. Nothing reflects the animation and vivacity of speech so much as effective pitch variation. At this point, therefore, we shall discuss not only the *key,* or general level of pitch, but also changes in pitch—both the abrupt changes called *steps,* and the gradual changes called *slides.* We will note, too, how *melody patterns* emerge from these variations.

Habitual Pitch Level. As we have indicated, the habitual pitch level at which people speak varies considerably from person to person. Nearly everyone, however, can easily span an octave, and many people have voices flexible enough to vary more than two octaves without strain. Within this range, the key-level at which you habitually speak may create a very definite impression of you as a person. Ordinarily, a pitch that is continuously high suggests weakness, excitement, irritation, or extreme youth; a lower key-level suggests assurance, poise, and strength. For this reason, your customary pitch normally should be in the lower half of your natural range. In particular, be careful, when you are applying increasing degrees of force, not to let your voice get out of control, going to a higher and higher key until it cracks under the strain. If you feel tension, pause for a moment and lower your pitch. At times, of course, you will be excited, and your voice naturally will rise to a high key to match your emotion. Remember, however, that a somewhat restrained emotion makes a more favorable impression on listeners than does emotion which has gone completely out of control.

Steps and Slides. In connected speech, as we have suggested, pitch is changed in two ways: by steps and by slides. Suppose, for example, that someone has made a statement with which you agree and you answer by saying, "You're exactly right!" The chances are that you will say it something like this:

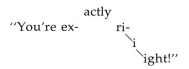

Notice that a complete break in pitch level occurs between the first and second syllables of the word *exactly.* This abrupt change in pitch is what we mean by a *step.* On the word *right,* however, a more gradual pitch inflection accompanies the production of the sound. Such a continuous change of pitch within a syllable is a *slide.* Both steps and slides may go upward or downward, depending on the meaning intended. Slides also may be double, the pitch going up and then down or vice versa, as when one says

$$\text{"O}\nearrow^{o}\searrow^{o}\nearrow^{o}\searrow_{\text{oh!"}}$$

to express the meaning, "I didn't realize that!"

In general, an upward step or slide suggests interrogation, indecision, uncertainty, doubt, or suspense, whereas a downward inflection suggests firmness, determination, certainty, finality, or confidence. Thus if you were to say, "What shall we do about it? Just this . . . ," a rising inflection in the question would create suspense; a downward inflection on the last phrase would indicate the certainty with which you were presenting your answer. A double inflection, as indicated by the example above, suggests a subtle conflict or contradiction of meaning, and is frequently used to express irony or sarcasm, or to convey innuendo. Steps and slides are primarily useful in communicating thought content rather than expressing emotional tone or color. By mastering their use, you will be able to make your meaning clearer and more precise.

All this does not mean that when you are about to speak to another individual or a group of individuals you should say to yourself: "This sentence requires an upward inflection," or "I shall use a *step* between these two words and a *slide* on that one." Such concentration on the mechanics of utterance would destroy communicative contact with your audience. Rather, in private and in class exercises, practice reading aloud selected passages which require pitch inflection and which encourage the habit of flexibility to grow in your speaking. Then, when you speak to others, your voice will tend to respond more or less appropriately and spontaneously to the ideas and moods you wish to convey.

Intonation Patterns. In all kinds of speech the rhythm and swing of phrase and sentence weave themselves into a continuous pattern of changing pitch. As the individual's thought or mood changes, the intonation pattern changes also. The use of a monotonous intonation pattern, however, is just as deadly as staying at one pitch level all of the time. Beware, therefore, of seesawing back and forth in a singsong voice. Avoid also the tendency of many inexperienced speakers to end nearly every sentence with an upward inflection. Assertions, when inflected in this way, sound more like *questions;* and you may sound doubtful even though you feel certain. A downward inflection at the close of each sentence is almost as bad, for it suggests an intolerance or dogmatism to which most listeners react unfavorably. If you can develop *variety of pitch inflection*, your melody pattern normally will adjust itself to the thought and mood you intend to express. Be careful, however, not to get into a vocal rut, unconsciously using the same pattern for everything you say.

Emphasis

Obviously, all forms of vocal variety help provide emphasis. Any change in rate, force, or pitch serves to make the word, phrase, or sentence in which the change occurs stand out from what precedes or follows it. This is true regardless of the direction of the change. Whether the rate or force is increased or decreased, whether the pitch is raised or lowered, emphasis will result. And the greater the amount of change or the more suddenly it is effected, the more emphatic will the statement be. In addition, emphasis is increased by pause and contrast: a pause allows the audience to "get set" for or to think over an important idea; contrast makes the idea seem more important than it otherwise would be.

Two warnings, however, should be noted: (1) Avoid *over*emphasis. (2) Avoid *continuous* emphasis. If you emphasize a point beyond its true value or importance, your audience will lose faith in your judgment. If you attempt to emphasize everything, nothing will stand out. Be judicious. Pick out the ideas that are really important and give them the emphasis they deserve.

THE IMPORTANCE OF PRACTICE

In this chapter we have suggested ways in which you can make your speech more intelligible and have reviewed the standard of pronunciation to which you should adhere. In addition, we have pointed out the importance of having a voice that is varied as well as clear, and have shown how variety depends upon a proper use of rate, force, pitch, and emphasis. Do not assume that you will be able to master in a day or a week all of the vocal skills that have been described. Take time to review and digest the ideas presented.

Above all, *practice*. Practice the exercises which are given in the following pages. Return to these exercises again and again, even after you have mastered them, so that your skills will not become rusty through disuse. Remember that any vocal skill, before it can be natural and effective with listeners, must be so much a habit that it will work for you without conscious effort when you begin to speak and will continue to do so more or less automatically throughout the utterance of your message.

EXERCISES FOR VOICE PRACTICE

Voice Quality

TO IMPROVE CONTROL OF BREATHING

1. Practice expelling the air from your lungs in short, sharp gasps; place your hand on your abdomen to make sure that there is a sharp inward contraction of the muscle wall synchronous with the chest contraction on each outgoing puff.

   a. Then vocalize the puffs, saying "hep!—hep!—hep!" with a good deal of force.

   b. In the same way, say "bah, bay, bee, bo, boo" with staccato accents and considerable vigor.

2. Fill your lungs; then exhale *as slowly as possible* until the lungs are empty. Time yourself to see how long you can keep exhaling without a break. (Note that the object here is not to see how much air you can get into the lungs but how slowly you can let it out.)

   a. Filling your lungs each time, vocalize the outgoing breath stream first with a long continuous hum, second with an *oo* sound, and then with other vowel sounds. Be careful not to let the sound become breathy; keep the tone clear.

   b. Place a lighted candle just in front of your mouth and repeat the series outlined above. The flame should just barely flicker.

3. On the same breath, alternate the explosive and the slow, deliberate exhalations outlined in Exercises 1 and 2. Practice until you can shift from one to the other easily both in silent breathing and in vocalized tones.

TO INDUCE RELAXATION OF THE THROAT

4. Repeat the following sequence several times in succession:
   a. Keeping your eyes closed and your neck and jaw muscles as relaxed as possible, raise your head easily to an upright position and then yawn with your mouth open as wide as possible.
   b. While your mouth is thus open, inhale deeply and exhale quietly two or three times; then intone "a-a-a-ah" very quietly.
   c. Say "m-m-a-a-ah" several times slowly, each time nodding the head forward gently and without tension.

TO IMPROVE THE QUALITY OF THE TONE

5. Intone the following words quietly at first, then louder, and louder; try to give them a ringing quality; put your fingertips on your nose and cheekbones to see if you can feel a vibration there. Avoid breathiness.

one	home	tone	alone	moan
rain	plain	mine	lean	soon
ring	nine	tong	moon	fine

6. Read aloud the following passages in as clear and resonant tones as you can produce. Be sure that you open your mouth wide enough and that you use only enough air to make the tones vibrate. Do not force the tone. If you notice any tension in your throat or harshness in your voice, go back to the preceding exercises and practice them until the tension and harshness disappear.

from APOSTROPHE TO THE OCEAN

Roll on, thou deep and dark blue Ocean, roll!
Byron

from THE RIME OF THE ANCIENT MARINER

Alone, alone, all, all alone,
Alone on a wide, wide sea!
And never a saint took pity on
My soul in agony.
Coleridge

from THE RAINY DAY

The day is cold and dark and dreary;
It rains, and the wind is never weary;
The vine still clings to the moldering wall,
But at every gust the dead leaves fall,
    And the day is dark and dreary.
    Longfellow

from LIBERTY

I have raised my head,
And cried, in thraldom, to the furious wind,
"Blow on!—This is the land of liberty!"
    Knowles

from RECESSIONAL[1]

God of our fathers, known of old,
    Lord of our far-flung battle-line,
Beneath whose awful Hand we hold
    Dominion over palm and pine—
Lord God of Hosts, be with us yet,
Lest we forget—lest we forget!
    Kipling

SELECTED PASSAGES FOR FURTHER PRACTICE

Some of the following selections are included because of the emotional tone they portray; others because of the vocal control they require. All of them, however, call for a clear, resonant quality for the best expression. Study them first for their meaning so that you are sure you understand what the author is saying. Then absorb the feeling; allow yourself to follow the mood of the writer. Finally, read the passages aloud, putting as much meaning and feeling into the expression as you can.

---

[1]*From* Rudyard Kipling's Verse: Definitive Edition *(British title:* The Five Nations*). Reprinted by permission of Mrs. George Bambridge, Doubleday & Company, Inc., Methuen & Co. and the Macmillan Co. of Canada.*

from THE CONGO[2]

Fat black bucks in a wine-barrel room,
Barrel-house kings, with feet unstable,
Sagged and reeled and pounded on the table,
Pounded on the table,
Beat an empty barrel with the handle of a broom,
Hard as they were able,
Boom, boom, BOOM,
With a silk umbrella and the handle of a broom,
Boomlay, boomlay, boomlay, BOOM.

Vachel Lindsay

from THE MAN WITH THE HOE[3]

Bowed by the weight of centuries he leans
Upon his hoe and gazes on the ground,
The emptiness of ages in his face,
And on his back the burden of the world.
Who made him dead to rapture and despair,
A thing that grieves not and that never hopes,
Stolid and stunned, a brother to the ox?
Who loosened and let down this brutal jaw?
Whose was the hand that slanted back this brow?
Whose breath blew out the light within this brain?

Edwin Markham

from THE BARREL-ORGAN[4]

There's a barrel-organ carolling across a golden street
    In the City as the sun sinks low;
And the music's not immortal; but the world has made it sweet
And fulfilled it with the sunset-glow;
And it pulses through the pleasures of the City and the pain
    That surround the singing organ like a large eternal light;
And they've given it a glory and a part to play again
    In the Symphony that rules the day and night.

Alfred Noyes

---

[2]*Reprinted with permission of Macmillan Publishing Co., Inc. from* Collected Poems *by Vachel Lindsay. Copyright 1914 by Macmillan Publishing Co., Inc., renewed 1942 by Elizabeth C. Lindsay.*

[3]*Copyright by the author.*

[4]*"The Barrel-Organ" (one stanza). Copyright 1906, 1909 by Alfred Noyes. From the book* Collected Poems, *Volume 1, by Alfred Noyes. Copyright 1913 by Frederick A. Stokes Company. Renewal 1941 by Alfred Noyes. Reprinted by permission of Hugh Noyes and J. B. Lippincott Company.*

from APOSTROPHE TO THE OCEAN

Roll on, thou deep and dark blue Ocean, roll!
    Ten thousand fleets sweep over thee in vain;
Man marks the earth with ruin—his control
    Stops with the shore;—upon the watery plain
    The wrecks are all thy deed, nor doth remain
A shadow of man's ravage, save his own,
    When for a moment, like a drop of rain,
He sinks into thy depths with bubbling groan,
Without a grave, unknelled, uncoffined, and unknown.
                                 Byron

DEATH, BE NOT PROUD

Death, be not proud, though some have called thee
Mighty and dreadful, for thou art not so;
For those whom thou think'st thou dost overthrow
Die not, poor Death; nor yet canst thou kill me.
From rest and sleep, which but thy picture be,
Much pleasure; then from thee much more must flow;
And soonest our best men with thee do go—
Rest of their bones and souls' delivery!
Thou'rt slave to fate, chance, kings, and desperate men,
And dost with poison, war, and sickness dwell;
And poppy or charms can make us sleep as well
And better than thy stroke. Why swell'st thou then?
One short sleep past, we wake eternally,
And Death shall be no more: Death, thou shalt die!
                               John Donne

    WIND IN THE PINE[5]

    Oh, I can hear you, God, above the cry
        Of the tossing trees—
    Rolling your windy tides across the sky,
        And splashing your silver seas
            Over the pine,
            To the water-line
        Of the moon.

---

[5]*From* Covenant With Earth: A Selection from the Poems of Lew Sarett. *Edited and copyrighted, 1956, by Alma Johnson Sarett. Gainesville: University of Florida Press, 1956. Reprinted by permission of Mrs. Sarett.*

Oh, I can hear you, God,
    Above the wail of the lonely loon—
When the pine-tops pitch and nod—
    Chanting your melodies
Of ghostly waterfalls and avalanches,
Swashing your wind among the branches
    To make them pure and white.

Wash over me, God, with your piney breeze,
    And your moon's wet-silver pool;
Wash over me, God, with your wind and night,
    And leave me clean and cool.
                Lew Sarett

GOD'S GRANDEUR

The world is charged with the grandeur of God.
    It will flame out, like shining from shook foil;
    It gathers to a greatness, like the ooze of oil
Crushed. Why do men then now not reck his rod?
Generations have trod, have trod, have trod;
    And all is seared with trade; bleared, smeared with toil;
    And wears man's smudge and shares man's smell: the soil
Is bare now, nor can foot feel, being shod.

And for all this, nature is never spent;
    There lives the dearest freshness deep down things;
And though the last lights off the black West went
    Oh, morning, at the brown brink eastward, springs—
Because the Holy Ghost over the bent
    World broods with warm breast and with ah! bright wings.
                Gerard Manley Hopkins

BY THE BIVOUAC'S FITFUL FLAME

By the bivouac's fitful flame,
A procession winding around me, solemn and sweet and slow—but first I
    note
The tents of the sleeping army, the fields' and woods' dim outline,
The darkness lit by spots of kindled fire, the silence,
Like a phantom far or near an occasional figure moving,
The shrubs and trees (as I lift my eyes they seem to be stealthily watching
    me),
While wind in procession thoughts, O tender and wondrous thoughts,

Of life and death, of home and the past and loved, and of those that are
        far away;
A solemn and slow procession there as I sit on the ground,
By the bivouac's fitful flame.

Walt Whitman

from FERN HILL[6]

Now as I was young and easy under the apple boughs
About the lilting house and happy as the grass was green,
        The night above the dingle starry,
                Time let me hail and climb
        Golden in the heydays of his eyes,
And honoured among wagons I was prince of the apple towns
And once below a time I lordly had the trees and leaves
                Trail with daisies and barley
        Down the rivers of the windfall light.

And as I was green and carefree, famous among the barns
About the happy yard and singing as the farm was home,
        In the sun that is young once only,
                Time let me play and be
        Golden in the mercy of his means,
And green and golden I was huntsman and herdsman, the calves
Sang to my horn, the foxes on the hills barked clear and cold,
                And the sabbath rang slowly
        In the pebbles of the holy streams.

All the sun long it was running, it was lovely, the hay-
Fields high as the house, the tunes from the chimneys, it was air,
        And playing, lovely and watery
                And fire green as grass.
        And nightly under the simple stars
As I rode to sleep, the owls were bearing the farm away,
All the moon long I heard, blessed among stables, the nightjars
        Flying with the ricks, and the horses
                Flashing into the dark.

Dylan Thomas

TO TEST THE INTELLIGIBILITY OF YOUR SPEECH

7. Following are twenty lists of sixteen words each which may be used in class to test whether your speech is intelligible to others.[7] Your scores will not be as accurate as if these tests were conducted under scientifically controlled conditions, but they will provide a measure of the relative intelligibility of your speech as compared with your classmates' and will show you what happens under various conditions. Proceed with the test as follows: (a) Read silently the list of words which is assigned to you. (b) Stand in a corner of the classroom with your back to the class. Read the first four words; then pause long enough for your classmates to write down the four words before going ahead to the next group of four words. Continue in this manner until you have read the complete list. (c) To determine your score, count the total number of words understood correctly by all listeners. Divide this total by the number which is the product of the number of listeners times sixteen (the number of words spoken). The result will be your percentage of intelligibility on this test.

a. Three, flap, switch, will——resume, cold, pilot, wind——chase, blue, search, flight——mine, area, cleared, left.

b. Iron, fire, task, try——up, six, seven, wait——slip, turn, read, clear——blue, this, even, is.

c. Nan, flak, timer, two——course, black, when, leave——raise, clear, tree, seven——search, strike, there, cover.

d. List, service, ten, foul——wire, last, wish, truce——power, one, ease, will——teeth, hobby, trill, wind.

e. Flight, spray, blind, base——ground, fog, ceiling, flame——target, flare, gear, low——slow, course, code, scout.

f. Tall, plot, find, deep——climb, fall, each, believe——wing, strip, clean, field——when, chase, search, select.

g. Climb, switch, over, when——this, turn, gear, spray——black, flare, is, free——runway, three, off, red.

h. Thing, touch, marker, sleeve——find, top, leave, winter——skip, free, have, beach——meet, aid, send, lash.

i. Try, over, six, craft——green, victor, yellow, out——trim, X ray, ramp, up——speed, like, believe, sender.

---

[7]*From a test used by Gayland L. Draegert in an experiment reported in* Speech Monographs, XIII, *50–53. Reprinted by permission of the* Speech Communication Association.

j. Dim, trip, fire, marker——wave, green, rudder, field——climb, to, plot, middle——speed, like, straight, lower.

k. Smooth, mike, four, catch——strip, park, line, left——leg, wheel, turn, lift——time, baker, orange, look.

l. Wake, other, blue, been——size, wish, black, under——field, down, empty, what——ship, strip, land, fire.

m. Leg, on, strip, leave——ground, trip, plot, area——speed, blue, will, ramp——wheel, blind, sector, nan.

n. Tail, when, through, at——climb, off, tower, rain——time, gear, cloud, pass——loaf, three, crash, direction.

o. Station, left, reply, read——final, blue, field, out——wind, west, marker, fire——tower, ground, gear, time.

p. Sighted, toward, finder, search——red, blind, each, weather——tall, after, while, wide——close, hole, mark, signal.

q. Neat, warm, beam, where——side, leader, bell, map——view, face, trap, well——seem, feed, clutch, vine.

r. Circle, beach, up, that——port, even, catch, pad——reach, heat, break, safe——still, put, enter, iron.

s. Chamber, wait, hair, open——wind, keep, sector, free——light, home, take, will——base, eleven, headphone, by.

t. Service, flat, have, on——bay, wait, fade, cold——tire, horn, bill, sad——feel, cave, set, limit.

TO DEVELOP AN ADEQUATE DEGREE OF LOUDNESS AND SYLLABLE DURATION

8. Practice saying the words in the above lists with a voice loud enough—

    a. to be barely understood (score below 50%) in a quiet classroom.

    b. to be perfectly understood in a quiet classroom.

    c. to be understood in a quiet classroom with your listeners' ears plugged with cotton (to simulate distance).

    d. to be understood above the noise of two, three, or four other students who are all reading aloud from different pages of the textbook.

9. Practice saying the words in the lists above with varying degrees of syllable duration under the conditions listed in the problem above.

10. Devise variations of these conditions with whatever recording or public address systems are available to your class.

11. Prepare sentences requiring precise understanding of the component words and practice saying them with the loudness and syllable length required for:

    a. a small group in a small room.
    b. a class in a fairly large lecture room.
    c. an audience in your college auditorium.
    d. a crowd in your football stadium.

Here are a few sample sentences to use:

"Just ten minutes from now, go in single file to room 316."

"In 1985, the population of Panama may be one and two fifths what it was in 1948."

"Hemstitching can be done by machine operation, using strong thread."

"Oranges, nuts, vegetables, and cotton are raised on the Kingston ranch."

TO INCREASE DISTINCTNESS OF ARTICULATION

12. Stretch the muscles of articulation:

    a. Stretch the mouth in as wide a grin as possible; open the mouth as wide as possible; pucker the lips and protrude them as far as possible.

    b. Stretch out the tongue as far as possible; try to touch the tip of the nose and the chin with the tongue tip; beginning at the front teeth, run the tip of the tongue back, touching the palate as far back as the tongue will go.

13. With vigorous accent on the consonant sounds, repeat "pah, tah, kah" several times. Then vary the order, emphasizing first *pah*, then *tah*, then *kah*. In the same way, practice the series "ap, at, ak" and "apa, ata, aka." Work out additional combinations of this kind, using different combinations of consonants and vowels.

14. Experiments have shown that the words grouped in fours below are easily mistaken for one another under conditions of noise interference.[8] Practice articulating them distinctly and precisely. Then with your back to the class and with three or four other students creating a noise by reading aloud from the textbook at the same time, read down one column or across one row, choosing one word at random out of each four. Announce

---

[8]*Taken from answer sheets for standardized tests developed by C. Hess Haagen, printed in* Intelligibility Measurement: Twenty Four-Word Multiple Choice Tests, *OSRD Report No. 5567 (P.B. 12050), issued by the Office of Technical Services, Department of Commerce, p. 21.*

before you start which column or row you are going to read from, pause briefly after each word, and have other members of the class put a check by the word they understood you to say. (Used in this way, the following list is not an accurate *test* of intelligibility, but it should provide interesting material for practice.)

	A	B	C	D	E	F
1	system	firm	banner	puddle	carve	offer
	pistol	foam	manner	muddle	car	author
	distant	burn	mother	muzzle	tarred	often
	piston	term	batter	puzzle	tired	office
2	heave	detain	scream	porch	fable	cross
	heed	obtain	screen	torch	stable	cough
	ease	attain	green	scorch	table	cloth
	eve	maintain	stream	court	able	claw
3	roger	pure	petal	vision	bubble	thrown
	rupture	poor	battle	bishop	tumble	drone
	rapture	tour	meadow	vicious	stumble	prone
	obscure	two	medal	season	fumble	groan
4	art	sponsor	game	cape	texture	eye
	heart	spotter	gain	hate	lecture	high
	arch	ponder	gage	take	mixture	tie
	ark	plunder	gang	tape	rupture	hide
5	comment	exact	made	process	glow	single
	comic	retract	fade	protest	blow	jingle
	cannon	detract	vague	profess	below	cycle
	carbon	attack	may	possess	low	sprinkle
6	bumper	cave	pier	divide	kitchen	baker
	number	cake	pierce	devise	mission	major
	lumber	cage	fierce	define	friction	maker
	lover	case	spear	divine	fiction	banker
7	gale	glamour	ward	leap	second	rich
	jail	slimmer	wart	leaf	suction	ridge
	dale	swimmer	wash	lease	section	bridge
	bail	glimmer	war	leave	sexton	grip
8	danger	enact	hold	crater	seaport	joy
	feature	impact	old	traitor	keyboard	going
	nature	relax	ode	trainer	piecework	join
	major	intact	hoed	treasure	eastward	dawn

15. Make a list of as many tongue twisters as you can find and practice saying them rapidly and precisely. Here are a few short examples to start on:

   a. She sells seashells on the seashore.
   b. National Shropshire Sheep Association.
   c. "Are you copper-bottoming them, my man?" "No, I'm aluminuming 'em, mum."
   d. He sawed six long, slim, sleek, slender saplings.
   e. Dick twirled the stick athwart the path.
   f. Rubber baby-buggy bumpers.
   g. "B — A, Ba; B — E, Be;
      B — I, Bi; Ba Be Bi;
      B — O, Bo; Ba Be Bi Bo"; etc.

16. Read the following passages aloud in a distinct and lively fashion; move the tongue, jaw, lips, etc., with energy:

To sit in solemn silence in a dull, dark dock
In a pestilential prison, with a lifelong lock,
Awaiting the sensation of a short, sharp shock,
From a cheap and chippy chopper on a big black block!

Gilbert and Sullivan

from FATHER WILLIAM

"You are old," said the youth, "and your jaws are too weak
   For anything tougher than suet;
Yet you finished the goose, with the bones and the beak—
   Pray, how did you manage to do it?"
"In my youth," said his father, "I took to the law,
   And argued each case with my wife;
And the muscular strength which it gave to my jaw
   Has lasted the rest of my life."

Lewis Carroll

from THE CATARACT OF LODORE
   "How does the water
Come down to Lodore?"
   My little boy asked me
   Thus once on a time;
And moreover he tasked me
To tell him in rhyme.

. . . .

The cataract strong
Then plunges along,
Striking and raging,
As if a war waging
Its caverns and rocks among;
Rising and leaping,
Sinking and creeping,
Swelling and sweeping,
Showering and springing,
Flying and flinging,
Writhing and ringing,
Eddying and whisking,
Spouting and frisking,
Turning and twisting,
Around and around . . .

And rushing and flushing and brushing and gushing,
And flapping and rapping and clapping and slapping,
And curling and whirling and purling and twirling,
And thumping and plumping and bumping and jumping;
And dashing and flashing and splashing and clashing;
And so never ending, but always descending,
Sounds and motion for ever and ever are blending,
All at once and all o'er, with a mighty uproar—;
And this way the Water comes down at Lodore.

Robert Southey

from THE PIRATES OF PENZANCE

I am the very model of a modern Major-General,
I've information vegetable, animal, and mineral,
I know the kings of England, and I quote the fights historical,
From Marathon to Waterloo, in order categorical;
I'm very well acquainted too with matters mathematical,
I understand equations, both the simple and quadratical,
About binomial theorem I'm teeming with a lot o' news—
With many cheerful facts about the square of the hypotenuse.
I'm very good at integral and differential calculus,
I know the scientific names of being animalculous;
In short, in matter vegetable, animal, and mineral,
I am the very model of a modern Major-General.

I know our mythic history, King Arthur's and Sir Caradoc's,
I answer hard acrostics, I've a pretty taste for paradox,

I quote in elegiacs all the crimes of Heliogabalus,
In conics I can floor peculiarities parabolous.
I can tell undoubted Raphaels from Gerard Dows and Zoffanies,
I know the croaking chorus from the *Frogs* of Aristophanes,
Then I can hum a fugue of which I've heard the music's din afore,
And whistle all the airs from that infernal nonsense *Pinafore*.

Then I can write a washing bill in Babylonic cuneiform,
And tell you every detail of Caractacus's uniform;
In short, in matters vegetable, animal, and mineral,
I am the very model of a modern Major-General.

Gilbert and Sullivan

TO ENCOURAGE ACCEPTABLE PRONUNCIATION

17. Make a list of words which you have heard pronounced in more than one way. Look them up in a dictionary and come to class prepared to defend your agreement or disagreement with the dictionary pronunciation. Here are a few words on which to start:

abdomen	creek	gauge	indict	route
acclimated	data	gesture	inquiry	theater
advertisement	deficit	grievous	recess	thresh
alias	drowned	humble	research	vagary
bona fide	forehead	idea	roof	yacht

SELECTED PASSAGES FOR FURTHER PRACTICE

18. Try to understand the significance of the following passages before you start practicing them. Then begin by reading them as you would before a small, quiet audience; next as you would need to do if the audience were large or there were considerable noise interference. Remember, however, that exaggerated precision, loudness, syllable duration, etc., beyond the amount clearly required for easy intelligibility in the actual situation will sound artificial to your listeners and is not good speech.

from THE WAR SONG OF THE SARACENS[9]

We are they who come faster than fate: we are they who ride early or late:
We storm at your ivory gate: Pale Kings of the Sunset, beware!
Not on silk nor in samet we lie, not in curtained solemnity die

---

[9]*"The War Song of the Saracens" from* Collected Poems *by James Elroy Flecker. Published by Martin Secker & Warburg Limited.*

Among women who chatter and cry, and children who mumble a prayer.
But we sleep by the ropes of the camp, and we rise with a shout, and we
    tramp
With the sun or the moon for a lamp, and the spray of the wind in our
    hair.

James Elroy Flecker

from ESSAY ON SELF-RELIANCE

    A foolish consistency is the hobgoblin of little minds, adored by little statesmen and philosophers and divines. With consistency a great soul has simply nothing to do. He may as well concern himself with his shadow on the wall. Speak what you think now in hard words, and tomorrow speak what tomorrow thinks in hard words again, though it contradict everything you said today—"Ah, so you shall be sure to be misunderstood." —Is it so bad, then, to be misunderstood? Pythagoras was misunderstood, and Socrates, and Jesus, and Luther, and Copernicus, and Galileo, and Newton, and every pure and wise spirit that ever took flesh. To be great is to be misunderstood.

Emerson

from THE SEA AROUND US[10]

    For the sea as a whole, the alternation of day and night, the passage of the seasons, the procession of the years, are lost in its vastness, obliterated in its own changeless eternity. But the surface waters are different. The face of the sea is always changing. Crossed by colors, lights, and moving shadows, sparkling in the sun, mysterious in the twilight, its aspects and its moods vary hour by hour. The surface waters move with the tides, stir to the breath of the winds, and rise and fall to the endless, hurrying forms of the waves. Most of all, they change with the advance of the seasons. Spring moves over the temperate lands of our Northern Hemisphere in a tide of new life, of pushing green shoots and unfolding buds, all its mysteries and meanings symbolized in the northward migration of the birds, the awakening of sluggish amphibian life as the chorus of frogs rises again from the wet lands, the different sound of the wind which stirs the young leaves where a month ago it rattled the bare branches. These things we associate with the land, and it is easy to suppose that at sea there could be no such feeling of advancing spring. But the signs are there, and seen with understanding eye, they bring the same magical sense of awakening.

Rachel L. Carson

[10]*Rachel Carson,* The Sea Around Us, *Oxford University Press, 1961, pp. 28–29.*

TO DEVELOP FLEXIBILITY IN VOCAL MANIPULATION

19. While repeating the alphabet or counting from one to twenty, perform the following vocal exercises (trying throughout to maintain good vocal quality and distinctness of utterance):

a. Beginning very slowly, steadily increase the speed until you are speaking as rapidly as possible; then, beginning rapidly, reverse the process.

b. Stretch out the quantity of the vowel sounds, speaking at a slow rate but allowing no pauses between letters or numbers; then shift to short quantity with long pauses. Shift back and forth between these two methods with every five or six letters or numbers you say.

c. Begin very softly and increase the force until you are nearly shouting; reverse the process. Then practice shifting from one extreme to the other, occasionally changing to a moderate degree of force.

d. Keeping the loudness constant, shift from an explosive application of force combined with a staccato utterance to a firm, smooth application of force.

e. Stress alternate letters (or numbers); then change by stressing every third letter, every fourth, etc.; then change back to alternate letters again.

f. Begin at the lowest pitch you can comfortably reach, and raise the pitch steadily until you reach the highest comfortable pitch; reverse the process. Shift back and forth suddenly from high to low to middle, etc.

g. Practice slides with the vowel sound *oh*. Try upward slides, downward slides, and those which are double — going up and down or down and up.

h. Using a half dozen letters or numbers, practice similar pitch changes in steps; then alternate steps and slides.

20. Vary the *rate* with which you say the following sentences in the manner indicated:

a. "There goes the last one."
   (1) Use long quantity, expressing regret.
   (2) Use short quantity, expressing excitement.
   (3) Use moderate quantity, merely stating a fact.

b. "The winners are John, Henry, and Bill."
  (1) Insert a long pause after *are* for suspense; then give the names rapidly.
  (2) Insert pauses before each name as if picking it out.
  (3) Say the whole sentence rapidly in a matter-of-fact way.

21. In the manner suggested, vary the *force* for the following:
  a. "I hate you! I hate you! I hate you!"
    (1) Increase the degree of force with each repetition, making the last almost a shout.
    (2) Say the second "*hate*" louder than the first, and the last one *sotto voce.*
    (3) Shout the first statement; then let the force diminish as if echoing the mood.
  b. "What kind of a thing is this?"
    Repeat the question, stressing a different word each time. Try not to raise the pitch, but to emphasize by force alone.
  c. "I have told you a hundred times, and the answer is still the same."
    (1) Make the statement a straightforward assertion, using sustained force.
    (2) Speak the sentence with a sudden explosion of force, as though you were uncontrollably angry.
    (3) Speak the sentence with deep but controlled emotion, applying force gradually and firmly.

22. Practice varying the *pitch* with which you say the sentences below, following the directions given:
  a. "I certainly feel fine today—that is, except for my sunburn. Now, don't slap me on the back! Ouch! Stop it! Please!"
    Begin confidently in a low key, successively raising the pitch level until the *please* is said near the top of your range. Repeat several times, trying to begin lower each time.
  b. "Oh, yes. Is that so?"
    Say this sentence as indicated in the following notations: Diagonal lines indicate *slides*; horizontal ones indicate a *level pitch*; and differences in height between the end of one line and the beginning of the next indicate *steps*. Each line represents one word.

    (1) ⎯⎺ ⎺⎯

    (2) ⎯╱⎯⎺╲

(3)

(4)

(5)

What are the different meanings thus conveyed?

   c. Say the sentence with varied pitch inflections so that it will mean as many different things as possible.

23. Practice reading aloud sentences from prose and poetry that require emphasis and contrast to make the meaning clear. Vary the pitch, rate, and force in different ways until you feel you have the best possible interpretation of the meaning. Here are some examples for practice:

   a. One of the most striking differences between a cat and a lie is that a cat has only nine lives. — *Mark Twain*

   b. So, Naturalists observe, a flea
     Has smaller fleas that on him prey;
     And these have smaller still to bite 'em;
     And so proceed ad infinitum. — *Jonathan Swift*

   c. I have waited with patience to hear what arguments might be urged against the bill; but I have waited in vain: The truth is, there is no argument that can weigh against it. — *Lord Mansfield*

   d. Gentlemen may cry, peace, peace! — but there is no peace. The war has actually begun! I know not what course others may take; but, as for me, give me liberty, or give me death! — *Patrick Henry*

24. Read the following passages so as to give the effect of climax: first practice the climax of increasing force, and then that of increasing intensity of feeling with diminishing force.

   a. There is no mistake; there has been no mistake; and there shall be no mistake. — *Duke of Wellington*

   b. Let us cultivate a true spirit of union and harmony . . . let us act under a settled conviction, and an habitual feeling, that these twenty-four States are one country. . . . Let our object be, OUR COUNTRY, OUR WHOLE COUNTRY, AND NOTHING BUT OUR COUNTRY. — *Daniel Webster*

TO INCREASE VOCAL VARIETY AND EMPHASIS

25. Clip a paragraph from a newspaper story describing some exciting incident and read it with appropriate vocal variety.

26. Memorize a section of one of the speeches printed in this book, as assigned by your instructor, and present it in such a way as to make the meaning clear and the feeling behind it dynamic.

27. Find an argumentative editorial or magazine article with which you agree or disagree. In your own words attack or defend the point of view presented, and do so with all the emphasis, contrast, and vocal variety of which you are capable.

SELECTED PASSAGES FOR FURTHER PRACTICE

Before you begin to practice a passage, study it carefully to understand its full meaning and determine its dominant mood. Some of the selections are light and fast moving; others are thoughtful and serious; at least one contains a marked climax. Avoid superficial or mechanical manipulation of the voice; read so as to make the meaning clear and the feeling contagious to your listeners. Effective reading requires that you practice enough in private so that before an audience you will not have to keep thinking of your voice, but will be able to concentrate on communicating ideas and feelings.

THE DISAGREEABLE MAN

If you give me your attention, I will tell you what I am:
I'm a genuine philanthropist—all other kinds are sham.
Each little fault of temper and each social defect
In my erring fellow-creatures, I endeavor to correct.
To all their little weaknesses I open peoples' eyes,
And little plans to snub the self-sufficient I devise;
I love my fellow-creatures—I do all the good I can—
Yet everybody says I'm such a disagreeable man!
    And I can't think why!

To compliments inflated I've a withering reply,
And vanity I always do my best to mortify;
A charitable action I can skillfully dissect;
And interested motives I'm delighted to detect.
I know everybody's income and what everybody earns,
And I carefully compare it with the income-tax returns;
But to benefit humanity, however much I plan,
Yet everybody says I'm such a disagreeable man!
    And I can't think why!

I'm sure I'm no ascetic; I'm as pleasant as can be;
You'll always find me ready with a crushing repartee;

I've an irritating chuckle, I've a celebrated sneer,
I've an entertaining snigger, I've a fascinating leer;
To everybody's prejudice I know a thing or two;
I can tell a woman's age in half a minute—and I do—
But although I try to make myself as pleasant as I can,
Yet everybody says I'm such a disagreeable man!
    And I can't think why!

Gilbert and Sullivan

STORM FEAR[11]

When the wind works against us in the dark,
And pelts with snow
The lower-chamber window on the east,
And whispers with a sort of stifled bark,
The beast,
    "Come out! Come out!"—
It costs no inward struggle not to go,
Ah, no!
I count our strength,
Two and a child,
Those of us not asleep subdued to mark
How the cold creeps as the fire dies at length—
How drifts are piled,
Dooryard and road ungraded,
Till even the comforting barn grows far away,
And my heart owns a doubt
Whether 'tis in us to arise with day
And save ourselves unaided.

Robert Frost

from A LETTER TO THE CORINTHIANS (1 CORINTHIANS, 13)

Though I speak with the tongues of men and of angels, and have not chari-ty, I am become as sounding brass, or a tinkling cymbal. And though I have the gift of prophecy, and understand all mysteries, and all knowledge; and though I have all faith, so that I could remove mountains, and have not charity, I am nothing. And though I bestow all my goods to feed the poor, and though I give my body to be burned, and have not charity, it profiteth me nothing. Charity suffereth long, and is kind; charity envieth not; charity

[11]*From* The Poetry of Robert Frost *edited by Edward Connery Lathem. Copyright 1934,* © *1969 by Holt, Rinehart and Winston, Inc. Copyright* © *1962 by Robert Frost. Reprinted by permission of Holt, Rinehart and Winston, Inc., Jonathan Cape Ltd., and the Estate of Robert Frost.*

vaunteth not itself, is not puffed up, doth not behave itself unseemly, seeketh not her own, is not easily provoked, thinketh no evil; rejoiceth not in iniquity, but rejoiceth in truth; beareth all things, believeth all things, hopeth all things, endureth all things. Charity never faileth: but whether there be prophecies, they shall fail; whether there be tongues, they shall cease; whether there be knowledge, it shall vanish away. For we know in part, and we prophesy in part. But when that which is perfect is come, then that which is in part shall be done away. . . . And now abideth faith, hope, and charity, these three; but the greatest of these is charity.

Paul, the Apostle

I WILL BE HEARD

I am aware that many object to the severity of my language; but is there not cause for severity? I will be harsh as Truth and as uncompromising as Justice. On this subject I do not wish to think, or speak, or write with moderation. No! No! Tell a man whose house is on fire to give a moderate alarm; tell him to moderately rescue his wife from the hands of the ravisher; tell the mother to gradually extricate her babe from the fire into which it has fallen — but urge me not to use moderation in a cause like the present. I am in earnest — I will not equivocate — I will not excuse — I will not retreat a single inch — and I will be heard.

William Lloyd Garrison

Suggestions for Further Reading

Donald Dew and Harry Hollien, "The Effect of Inflection on Vowel Intelligibility," *Speech Monographs* XXXV (June 1968): 175–180.

John Hasling, *The Message, The Speaker, The Audience* (New York: McGraw-Hill Book Company, 1971), Chapter IX, pp. 84–92.

Archibald Hill, "Some Speculations on Tempo in Speech," *Southern Speech Journal* XXXIV (Spring 1969): 169–173.

James C. McCroskey, *An Introduction to Rhetorical Communication* (Englewood Cliffs, N.J.: Prentice-Hall, Inc., 1968), Chapter XII, "Message Presentation: Oral Delivery," pp. 206–224.

Herbert F. Schliessen, "Information Transmission and *Ethos* of a Speaker Using Normal and Defective Speech," *Central States Speech Journal* XIX (Fall 1968): 169–174.

Stafford H. Thomas, "Effects of Monotonous Delivery on Intelligibility," *Speech Monographs* XXXVI (June 1969): 110–113.

PART THREE

Public Communication: Preparation and Adaptation to the Audience

7
CHOOSING SPEECH SUBJECTS AND PURPOSES

Determining the speech subject and purpose, analyzing the audience, substancing and supporting the major ideas of the speech, adapting it to listeners' beliefs and values and motivations, structuring the message-content for maximal impact and retrieval, phrasing for clarity and vividness of meaning, listening to and evaluating speeches, and applying ethical criteria—these are the central focus of Part Three. These concerns, as you will readily recognize, again involve (1) the assessment of the generative and conditional factors influencing the total speech-making situation; (2) building the speech, with the listeners or receivers always uppermost in mind; and (3) oral practice—this time with "live" audiences. Here in Part Three, we shall of course develop this process much more fully, with broader inclusion and a more detailed, in-depth treatment; and throughout our considerations will run a close and continuing concern for the *adaptational* processes and those listening and evaluative skills so essential to effective and productive human interaction. Although much of what we have to say in this and the remaining chapters of Part Three will bear most directly upon the preparational and adaptational procedures employed in *public* speech communication, it will also carry useful implications for and applicability to other forms of oral communication—notably dyadic and small group transactions.

In Chapter 4, "Public Speech Communication: Some Initial Concerns," you will recall that we surveyed—in very abbreviated form—the process of speech preparation as consisting, essentially, of the following steps: (*a*) selecting and narrowing the subject, (*b*) determining the speech purpose, (*c*) analyzing the audience and the occasion, (*d*) gathering the material, (*e*) making an outline, (*f*) working the speech, and (*g*) practicing aloud. In this chapter we return to two of these initial steps, namely: selecting a suitable subject for a speech and determining the purpose aimed at generating the response the speaker seeks from an audience.

GENERATING, SHAPING, AND INFLUENCING
THE TOTAL SPEECHMAKING ENTERPRISE

The Large Concerns . . .	The Chapters Involved . . .
Taking into account the listeners' interests, attitudes, beliefs, values, and motivations	7. Choosing Speech Subjects and Purposes 8. Analyzing the Audience and Occasion 9. Determining the Basic Appeals
Putting the speech together for maximum impact upon and retrieval-value for listeners	10. Locating and Classifying Speech Information 11. Supporting the Major Ideas 12. Selecting Material That Will Hold Attention 13. Adapting the Speech to the Audience: The Motivated Sequence 14. Organizing and Outlining the Speech 15. Beginning and Ending the Speech 16. Using Words to Communicate Meaning
Assessing the speech from the perspectives of the listener	17. Listening, Evaluation, and Ethical Judgment
Applying and practicing the principles of good speech communication for "live," in-class audiences	At chapter-ends: Classroom Speeches Oral Activities and Speaking Assignments

THE SUBJECT OF THE SPEECH

On many occasions, the subject of your speech will be determined for you—at least in part—by the group you are invited to address. You are, for instance, a water-resources expert asked to speak to a local service club on means of controlling pollution in a nearby river. Or, after an extensive trip through Eastern Africa, you are invited to describe for a women's study group the social and economic conditions as they now exist in some of the newly emerging nations in that area. At other times, of course, the subject on which you will speak is left to your discretion. *Nearly always, however, you will be free to select the particular phase or aspect of the subject you wish to emphasize.*

When confronted with the task of choosing a subject or determining which aspect of a more general topic to stress, beginning speakers frequently experience difficulty. Sometimes they choose a subject on which their background of knowledge or experience is glaringly inadequate. Often they fail to pay due attention to the obvious needs and interests of their audience, and they greatly underestimate the amount of time necessary to develop their message-ideas adequately. To avoid mistakes of this kind and to make the selection process more direct and systematic, observe the following guidelines:

Select a subject about which you already know something and can find out more. In speech, as elsewhere, there is no substitute for knowledge that is thorough and authoritative.

Select a subject that is interesting to you. If you are not interested in what you are talking about, you will find preparation a dull task; and your speaking is likely to be listless and ineffective.

Select a subject that will interest your audience. The more interest your listeners already have in the subject, the less you will have to worry about holding their attention when you speak. A subject may be interesting to an audience for one or more of the following reasons:

A. It vitally concerns their health, happiness, prosperity, or security.
B. It offers a solution to a recognized problem.
C. It is new or timely.
D. There is conflict of opinion concerning it.

Talk about something that is neither above nor below the intellectual capacity of your listeners. A speech about the value of a savings account in a local bank would be appropriate for an audience of grade-school children, but a discussion of the workings of the Federal Reserve System would not. On the other hand, do not underestimate the knowledge or capacity of your listeners by selecting a subject that makes you seem to be talking down to them.

Select a subject you can discuss adequately in the time at your disposal. In a ten-minute speech, do not attempt to review "The Causes and Consequences of the Vietnam War." Instead, describe some of the major decisions leading to our involvement, or discuss the terms of the settlement that resulted in our withdrawal.

In sum, remember that even though you are *assigned* a subject, you will probably still need to limit it—to select some phase or aspect that you can discuss effectively within the time limits you have been given.

THE TITLE OF THE SPEECH

Closely related to the subject of the speech, of course, is its *title*. The subject identifies the content of the speech: the problem to be discussed, the objects or activities to be described; the title is the *specific label* given to the speech—usually announced by the chairman—for the purpose of arousing the interest of the listeners. Hence, it is a sort of advertising slogan—a catchword, phrase, or brief statement which epitomizes the subject and spirit of the speech in an attractive or provocative form. When Ernest A. Jones, president of Mac-Manus, John & Adams, Inc., discussed the effects of advertising techniques in influencing the consumer's buying habits, he titled his speech "The Man with the Split-Level Head." A college orator, deploring the fact that students are often treated unsympathetically by teachers, called her speech "Walking Wounded." Another student, insisting that equality must encompass *all* areas of our society—personal as well as economic and political—chose the title "What Color Is Justice?" A third used the label "The Eleventh Commandment" for a speech denouncing what he perceived as a tendency to condone successful crime.

What, then, are the requirements of a good title? There are at least three: it should be relevant; it should be provocative; it should be brief. To be *relevant*, a title must be pertinent to the subject or to some part of the speaker's discussion of the subject. The relevancy of the title "The Eleventh Commandment" was made clear when the speaker pointed out that the commandments "Thou shalt not steal" and "Thou shalt not kill" had been supplemented by a new one, the eleventh, "Thou shalt get away with it." In this example, notice that while the title was not a prosaic statement of the subject, it clearly was pertinent to the idea the speaker sought to communicate. People do not like to be misled by a speaker's title any more than they enjoy false advertising.

To be *provocative*, a title should make the audience sit up and listen with anticipation and enthusiasm. Sometimes the speaker's topic is of such compelling interest that a mere, succinct statement of it is provocative enough. In most instances, however, you must find a more vivid or unusual phrasing. At the same time, of course, you must take care not to give away the entire content or message of the speech in the title—to provide *too much* advance information. Especially if the audience is hostile to your purpose, you must avoid wording your title in such a way as to make that purpose too obvious. To entitle a speech for a fraternity group "Why Fraternities Should Be Abolished" is provocative enough, but undiplomatic in the extreme.

Finally, the title of a speech should be *brief and simple*. Imagine the effect of announcing as a title, "The Effects on Non-Target Classmates of a Deviant Student's Power and Response to a Teacher-Exerted Technique." Such a title can only be excused when the discussion is a technical one to be presented before a professional audience that has a specialized interest in the subject. In circumstances of that nature, the precise denotation of the subject matter may be important. Even so, the title should be as short and simple as possible.

Usually the exact phrasing of the title can best be left until the speech has been completely built. To devise a title that is both relevant and provocative will be much easier after you have developed the central ideas of the your speech as a whole. The phrasing of the title has been considered here, rather than later, because of its close relation to the subject and purpose of the speech and not because it is something you must settle early in the process of speech preparation.

THE GENERAL ENDS OF SPEECH

Regardless of the subject or title, the aim of every speech—as we pointed out in Chapter 1—is *to win a reaction from the audience.* This purpose must never be lost sight of, for it lies at the basis of the entire process of speech preparation. What kinds of responses, then, do speakers in the public or one-to-all situations commonly seek to elicit?

There can be no doubt that the listener-reaction sought by an after-dinner speaker at a social banquet differs materially from that sought by a legislator urging the adoption of a bill, or that both of these desired responses differ from the response a college professor seeks when lecturing to a class. The first speaker wants his audience to *enjoy* themselves; the second wants them to *act*, to vote "aye"; the third wants them to *understand.*

Writers on practical speaking, from the classical period to the present, have grouped speech purposes into a few fairly definite categories and—for the last two centuries at least—have classified them according to the *kind of reaction* the speaker seeks from his listeners. Many such classifications, varying in scope and detail, have been used. The following one, listing four general purposes or ends of speech, should prove functional as well as convenient for your use.

General End		Reaction Sought
1. TO ENTERTAIN		*Interest and Enjoyment*
2. TO INFORM		*Clear Understanding*
3. TO PERSUADE		*Belief or Emotional Arousal*
4. TO ACTUATE		*Definite Observable Action*

Figure 1. THE FOUR GENERAL ENDS OF SPEECH

A *general end*, as the term is used here, denotes the broad category or type of response a speaker desires. It is the *outcome* for which he strives. Merely because your purpose falls largely within one of the four general ends, however, does not mean that you will be unconcerned with the others or that you can afford to neglect them. You will sometimes need to entertain or amuse during a speech to inform; you usually must inform in order to create belief; and you will ordinarily need to persuade in order to actuate—to stir your listeners to act as you desire. But one of these four general ends will be your major objective, and the others only contributory. For this reason you must take care that the contributory purposes do not detract from the central objective of the speech—that they are included *only when they advance the principal aim*, and only to the extent that they do so. Let us, therefore, briefly examine each of the general ends in its role as a *primary* aim.

To Entertain

The general end of a speech to entertain, divert, or amuse is to cause your listeners to enjoy themselves. To entertain is a frequent purpose of after-dinner speeches, but is by no means limited to such occasions. Often, a travel lecturer, although he or she may present informative material of a striking and unusual character, has as his or her primary aim to entertain or divert an audience. If, by informing, the lecturer creates an understanding of the subject, that is *contributory* to the major objective of the discourse. There are also many occasions of a dyadic or group nature when a speaker's legitimate objective is to generate enjoyment and delight for listeners, to afford them pleasure, or give them a "good time." If you are the speaker on such occasions, you may depend chiefly on humor, or merely present interesting anecdotes or curious bits of information. In any event, avoid heavy discussion and controversial issues; and if you do present facts and figures, offer them in a verbal setting that is unique and exceptional, something unlikely to be anticipated by your listeners. Always, in achieving a desired goal in speaking, you will find that vividness and originality of statement play an important part; but in speaking to entertain or amuse, they take on added significance.

To Inform

More than ever before—in this age of electronics, automation, and increasingly complex technologies of all kinds—we are under compulsion to inform and to be informed. *When, as a speaker, you try to clarify a concept or a process for one or more listeners, when you endeavor to define terms and relationships, or strive in other ways to widen the range of your auditors' knowledge, the objective of your speech will be to inform.* This is the purpose of the foreman who is showing a workman how to operate a new machine, of the teacher lecturing to a class, or of the county's farm agent explaining the results of tests carried on at an agricultural experimental station. Moreover, as we saw in Chapters 2 and 3, improved understanding of a subject or situation is frequently the purpose of persons engaging in an interview or coming together to discuss a topic or a problem.

All this does not mean, however, that clear explanation is useful only when speakers have the creation of understanding as their general goal. In a persuasive speech, for example, we can rarely induce an audience to accept a proposition that has not first been made completely clear. But in a speech which aims to inform, no particular belief or action is urged. The central purpose is to make the listeners understand and to provide them with the information needed for this understanding. To achieve this end, a speaker must relate new ideas to the existing knowledge of the listeners, must be sure that the structure of the message is clear in order to encourage greater retention of the information given, and must present an abundance of concrete examples and specific data so that the leading ideas of the message will be fully understood.

To Persuade

When your purpose is to alter the beliefs or deepen the convictions of your auditors, the general end of your speech will be to persuade. Many speeches have this as their general end. Political speakers urge their constituents to believe in the platforms and performances of their respective parties; attempts are made to create belief in the superiority of certain products, principles, or forms of government; philosophical hypotheses are debated pro and con; ministers call upon their congregations to dedicate themselves anew to the principles of their faith. In all these cases, however, where the general end of the talk is only *to persuade* (and not to actuate through persuasion), no overt act or performance is requested of the audience. They are merely asked to agree with the speaker. Many times, in fact, listeners are incapable of taking definite action because the authority for action lies with some other person or group. But they *can* form opinions by which to judge and sometimes change the actions of those who are in authority.

This important distinction can be drawn more sharply, perhaps, by the following example. A great many public speeches are made to the electorate, even in non-election years, about the foreign policy of the administration. The actual authority for controlling this policy lies with the President and with Congress, yet speakers outside the administration attempt to influence the beliefs of the ordinary citizen. Why? Because these beliefs, through the influence they can exert upon public opinion, ultimately will affect the government's foreign policies and help shape the nation's future course of action abroad. The immediate purpose of the speakers, however, is not to prompt performance, not to gain action in the form of voting, but to win agreement in belief. Later, of course, the candidates for President and Congress will speak on these same subjects in an attempt to actuate—to urge, to impel people to exert a direct influence on foreign policy by voting in a certain way in the fall elections. In the first case, the speaker's purpose is merely to persuade the audience; in the second, to secure action based upon persuasion—the purpose to which we now turn our attention.

To Actuate

When you wish not merely to influence the beliefs and feelings of your listeners, but to cause them to perform some definite overt act, the aim of your speech will be to actuate. This performance may be to vote "yes" or "no," to contribute money, to sign a petition, to form a parade and engage in a demonstration; or it may be any one of a hundred other types of observable public actions. Underlying and prompting this behavior, however, will be strong belief, aroused emotion, or both. For this reason the development of the speech which aims at producing action follows closely the methods suggested for speeches which seek simply to persuade. Sharply distinguishing the actuating speech, however, is the fact that it goes *beyond* the persuasive one; in it *you openly ask your listeners to perform some overt act at a specified time and place.* The relationship between the speech to persuade and the speech to actuate may be diagramed as follows:

When the general end of a speech is TO ACTUATE,
the speaker's purpose is

 to persuade as a necessary step toward causing the auditors to engage in some definite, observable behavior.

THE SPECIFIC PURPOSE OF THE SPEECH

In addition to a clearly defined general end or goal, a good speech also must have an *immediate* and *specific* purpose. *The specific purpose necessarily falls within the general one and states specifically and exactly what it is the speaker wishes the audience to enjoy, understand, believe, feel, or do.* The following examples will illustrate the relationship between the subject, the general end, and the specific purpose of various types of speeches:

1. *Subject:* The Trials and Tribulations of a College Dramatic Season.
   General end: To entertain.
   Specific purpose: To share with the audience some of the humorous situations that arose in the casting and production of the season's four plays.

2. *Subject:* Living in Outer Space.
   General end: To inform.
   Specific purpose: To help the audience understand some of the medical problems involved in living in outer space.

3. *Subject:* Built-in Automotive Safety.
   General end: To persuade.
   Specific purpose: To persuade the audience that car manufacturers should be required by law to design and build safer vehicles with less speed potential and smaller size.

4. *Subject:* Equality for All.
   General end: To persuade.
   Specific purpose: To cause the auditors to dedicate themselves anew to the principle of racial and social equality for all persons.

5. *Subject:* Health Insurance for College Students.
   General end: To actuate.
   Specific purpose: To get members of the student council to vote in favor of the group policy offered to the student body by the ABC Health Insurance Company.

Additional examples of a specific speech purpose might be to induce the audience to:

- laugh at the humorous mistakes found in examination papers (*entertain*).
- understand how safety matches are made (*inform*).
- believe in public ownership of electric utilities or renew their adherence to the basic principles of democracy (*persuade*).
- vote for Jones for congressman on November 4 (*actuate*).

Selecting the Specific Purpose: Determining Factors

If we think of communication as a behavioral response (direct activity), we will realize immediately that the selection of the specific purpose of a speech depends not only upon the speaker's own aims or wishes, but also upon the nature of the audience and the speaking occasion. In choosing and framing the specific speech purpose, therefore, keep in mind the following factors: the personal or ultimate aim of the speaker, the authority of the listeners or their capacity to act, the existing attitudes of the listeners, the occasion, and the time limits that are prescribed or imposed.

The Personal or Ultimate Aim of the Speaker

Suppose that an assistant vice-president of an electronics company is presenting a reorganization plan to his executive committee or board of directors. His *immediate* purpose is to secure the adoption of his plan; but his *ultimate* aim may be to increase his own reputation, authority, or salary. Keeping this in mind, he may modify his proposal somewhat, or he may strive to get someone else to urge its adoption so that the responsibility for it will not be entirely his own. A speaker's failure to consider his ultimate, as well as immediate, aim can sometimes be disastrous. Note what happened, for example, in the following circumstances. A campaign was started to raise funds for a union building for the student body of a large university. At a mass meeting of the senior class the members were asked to sign pledges to contribute a specified amount each year after graduation. High-pressure methods were used, and the students were even told that they would not be allowed to leave the meeting until they had signed. The next morning the college paper announced that the senior class had pledged itself 100 percent—the *immediate* purpose had been attained. But less than a third of these signers ever paid any money. Moreover, so much opposition was created by the high-pressure methods that it became difficult to obtain money from any other sources; and as a result, the entire project was delayed for several years. In sum, *do not try to win from your listeners an immediate, positive response which will have a negative effect upon your ultimate objective.*

The Authority of the Listeners or Their Capacity to Act

To demand of a group of students that they "abolish all required courses" would be foolish. They do not have the authority to take this action because the final word concerning course requirements is in the hands of the faculty. But students do have the right and the capacity-for-action to bring pressure on the faculty toward this end. A more logical and positively framed demand, therefore, would be "Petition the faculty to make all courses elective." As a speaker, *limit your request to an act lying within your listeners' range of authority.* Do not ask them to do something they would be unable to do even if they wanted to.

The Existing Attitudes of the Listeners

A group of striking workmen who believe they are badly underpaid and unfairly treated by their employer probably would be hostile to the suggestion that they return to work under the existing conditions. However, they might approve submitting the dispute to arbitration by a disinterested person whose fairness and judgment they respect. An audience hostile to the speaker's point of view might, as a result of only one speech, be convinced that "there is something to be said for his side of the question"; but the speaker would probably find it impossible to persuade them to take the positive action he or she desires. *Your purpose, in short, must be adjusted not only to the authority but also to the attitudes of your listeners.* Do not ask them for a response you cannot reasonably expect from persons holding their particular feelings or beliefs.

The Nature of the Speech Occasion

To ask people to contribute money to a political campaign fund might be appropriate at a pre-election rally, but to make such a request at a church dinner would be decidedly out of place. An athletic-awards ceremony is hardly the occasion on which to seek an understanding of safety devices for the home. The members of a little theater association would not want to engage in a discussion of finances between the acts of a play, though they might respond to a brief announcement urging their attendance at a business meeting where the budget would be discussed. The point we emphasize is this: *be sure that your purpose is adapted to the mood or spirit of the occasion on which you are to speak.*

The Time Limits of the Speech

You may be able in a few sentences to induce a hostile majority of your hearers to postpone action until a later time, but you almost certainly will need a much fuller verbal interchange or discourse in order to dislodge their fixed feelings and convictions. Similarly, if your subject is complex, you may be able to inform your audience about your proposal in a fifteen-minute speech—i.e., enable them to *understand* it—but you may require much more time *to convince* them of its desirability. In an hour you probably can provide an understanding of the basic political structure of the United Nations, with its various committees and agencies; but if you have only five minutes, you will almost certainly be more effective if you limit your effort to emphasizing the importance of one or two agencies and suggesting how to find out more about them. *Do not, therefore, attempt to achieve an outcome which is impossible to produce in the time available.*

Using the Specific Purpose as a Guide to Message Preparation

If you keep the foregoing factors in mind as you determine the specific purpose of your speech, your preparation will be off to a sound start. Moreover, a properly selected and limited purpose will serve as a useful guide throughout the remaining stages of your preparatory process. Write out your specific purpose in a clear, simple sentence and fix that sentence firmly in your mind. Whenever you encounter a fact or idea that will help advance you toward your goal, work it into your outline. Otherwise, forget about it, no matter how interesting or attractive it may be. By thus using a carefully framed purpose as the criterion for determining the relevance or irrelevance of possible speech materials, you can make certain that your talk will have unity and coherence, and that everything you say will be directed toward the precise response you seek.

SUBJECT CATEGORIES: AIDS TO CHOOSING SPEECH TOPICS

As we said earlier in this chapter, the beginning speaker often has difficulty in selecting a suitable speech subject. If you find yourself in this situation, we suggest that you study the following list of subject categories. They have proved helpful to others. These categories are not speech subjects; rather, they are *types or classes of material in which speech subjects may be found.* To decide upon a suitable subject for a public speech, consider them in terms of your own interests and knowledge, the interests of your audience, and the nature of the occasion on which you are to speak.

PERSONAL EXPERIENCE

1. Jobs you have held.
2. Places you have been.
3. Military service.
4. The region you come from.
5. Schools you have attended.
6. Friends and enemies.
7. Relatives you like—and dislike.

FOREIGN AFFAIRS

1. Foreign-policy aims.
   a. What they are.
   b. What they should be.
2. The implementation of policy aims.
3. History of the foreign policy of the United States (or of some other nation).
4. Responsibility for our foreign policy.
5. Ethics of foreign-policy decisions.
6. How foreign policy affects domestic policy.
7. War as an instrument of national policy.
8. International peace-keeping machinery.

DOMESTIC AFFAIRS

1. Social problems.
   a. Crime.
   b. The family: marriage, divorce, adjustments.
   c. Problems of cities.
   d. Problems of rural areas.
   e. Problems of races and ethnic groups.
   f. Problems of juveniles or the aged.
   g. Traffic accidents.
   h. Abortion.
   i. The drug culture.
   j. Sex mores.
   k. Pollution.

2. Economic problems.
   a. Federal fiscal policy.
   b. Economically deprived persons and areas.
   c. Fiscal problems of state and local governments.
   d. Taxes and tax policies.
   e. Inflation and price controls.
   f. International monetary affairs.

3. Political problems.
   a. Powers and obligations of the federal government.
   b. Relations between the federal government and the states.
   c. Problems of state and local governments.
   d. Parties, campaigns, and nominating procedures.
   e. The courts and court procedures.
      (1) Delays in justice.
      (2) The jury system.
   f. Congress versus the President.

   g. Democracy as a form of government — advantages and disadvantages.
   h. Careers in government.

THE ARTS

1. Painting, music, sculpture.
2. Literature and criticism.
3. Theatre, cinema, and the dance.
4. Government support of the arts.
5. The artist as a person.
6. History of an art form.
7. Censorship of the arts.

EDUCATION

1. Proper aims of education.
2. Recent advances in methods and teaching materials.
3. The federal government and education.
4. Courses and requirements.
5. Grades and grading.
6. Athletics.
7. Extracurricular activities.
8. Meeting the demand for education.
9. Fraternities.
10. Student marriages.
11. Students' role in educational decision making.
12. Parietal rules.

MASS MEDIA

1. Radio, television, and film.
2. The press.
3. Censorship of mass media.
   a. To protect public morals.
   b. For national security.
4. Use of mass media for propaganda purposes at home or abroad.

5. Ways to improve mass media.
6. Effects on children.
7. Cable television (CATV).

SCIENCE

1. Recent advances in a particular branch of science.
2. Science as method.
3. Pure versus applied research.
4. Government support of science.
5. History of science.
6. Science and religion.
7. Careers in science.

BUSINESS AND LABOR

1. Unions.
   a. Benefits and/or evils.
   b. Regulation of unions.
   c. "Right-to-work" laws.
2. Government regulation of business.

3. Ethical standards of business practice.
4. Advertising in the modern world.
5. Training for business.
6. Careers in business.
7. Blue-collar and white-collar status.
8. Wages: hourly or annually?
9. A guaranteed lifetime income.
10. Portable pensions.

PERSISTENT CONCERNS

1. "The good life" — what and how.
2. Man and God.
3. Beauty.
4. The ideal society.
5. Life-style — what it is and how to develop it.
6. Parents and children.
7. The tests of truth.
8. Love.
9. Discovering one's self.

In this chapter we have pointed out the importance of selecting a suitable subject and defining the general and specific purposes of your message. Moreover, we have suggested why these tasks should constitute the first two steps in your preparation. At the outset of your work on a speech, therefore, ask yourself the following questions and do not proceed until the answers are clear in your mind. Remember also that no one of these questions can be answered without simultaneous consideration of the others.

1. *What subject shall I talk about, and to what aspect of that subject shall I limit myself?*
2. *What general end shall I try to attain? Shall it be one of entertainment, information, persuasion, or actuation?*
3. *What specific response shall I seek from my audience? What is it exactly that I want them to enjoy, understand, believe, or do?*
   Finally, after you have finished building your speech in detail, ask yourself also this fourth question:
4. *How shall I phrase the title of my speech so that when it is announced, my audience will want to hear what I have to say?*

1. List at least five different occasions on which it might be appropriate to give a speech *to entertain*. (Remember that an entertaining speech is not necessarily a humorous one.) Also list five occasions on which a speech *to inform* might be called for. Do the same for speeches *to persuade* and *to actuate*. In class discussion, pool your suggestions with those of the other students and construct a master list of at least twelve occasions on which each type of speech might be used. Keep this list in your Personal Speech Journal for reference.

2. Select some subject with which you are familiar, one drawn from your major in college, from work experience, from travel, from your hobby, etc. Assume that during the semester you will be asked to present four five-minute speeches on this subject—one *to entertain*, one *to inform*, one *to persuade*, and one *to actuate*. Select and frame a specific purpose for each speech. Then repeat the experiment, but this time assume that in each case you will be presenting a fifteen-minute speech to a local service club. Let the other members of the class evaluate the appropriateness of your choices.

3. Read five printed speeches selected from such sources as *Representative American Speeches, The Speaker's Resource Book*, or recent issues of *Vital Speeches of the Day*. Try to determine the general and specific purpose of each speech and to evaluate how well these purposes have been fulfilled.

4. Select a speech from one of the above sources or one suggested by your instructor. Analyze the speaker's background and experience (this will probably require some research) and describe how these factors have seemingly influenced his or her choice of the general subject. Analyze, too, the speaker's general goal—to entertain, to inform, to persuade, to actuate— and his or her more specific purpose. Evaluate how successfully the speaker has related these to the audience. Was there any discernible difference between the stated purpose and what you sensed was the unspoken—possibly even subconscious—purpose? Describe how well the speaker has heeded the interests and needs of the audience and has gauged the amount of time necessary to develop his or her ideas. And, finally, comment on the title of the speech. Allowing for the fact that you are reading what was delivered orally, do you feel the overall effect was successful?

5. During a round of classroom speeches, jot down what you believe to be the specific purpose of each speech. At the close of the round, question the speakers to see if you have interpreted their purposes accu-

rately. In cases where the majority failed to grasp the speaker's purpose, decide at which link in the communication chain the breakdown or weakness has occurred. (Refer again to Chapter 4, pages 138–141.)

Oral Activity and Speaking Assignment

1. Select a subject with which you are well acquainted and about which you have much to say. Write a specific purpose for each of four or five speeches which you would like to give on this subject in your speech class. Select from these the purpose that seems best adapted to the interests of your classmates, and deliver a five-minute speech aimed at accomplishing this purpose. At the close of your speech, read aloud the specific purposes which you rejected, and let your classmates and instructor evaluate the appropriateness of your choice.

Suggestions for Further Reading

Bower Aly and Lucile F. Aly, *A Rhetoric of Public Speaking* (New York: McGraw-Hill Book Company, 1973), Chapter II, "Searching the Mind: Discovery," pp. 108–158.

Martin P. Anderson, Wesley Lewis, and James Murray, *The Speaker and His Audience* (New York: Harper & Row, Publishers, 1964), Chapter X, "Selecting Speech Subjects and Materials," pp. 214–240.

Aristotle, *Rhetoric*, 1358b–1359a.

Donald C. Bryant and Karl R. Wallace, *Fundamentals of Public Speaking*, 4th ed. (New York: Appleton-Century-Crofts, 1969), Chapter V, "Selecting Subjects," pp. 57–67.

Edward J. Corbett, *Classical Rhetoric for the Modern Student* (New York: Oxford University Press, Inc., 1965), Chapter II, "Discovery of Arguments," pp. 34–175.

Glen E. Mills, *Message Preparation: Analysis and Structure* (Indianapolis: The Bobbs-Merrill Company, Inc., 1966), Chapter II, "Selecting a Subject: Purposes and Types of Speeches," pp. 10–22.

Loren Reid, *Speaking Well*, 2nd ed. (New York: McGraw-Hill Book Company, 1972), Chapter V, "Choosing Subjects for Speaking," pp. 52–63.

8
ANALYZING THE AUDIENCE AND OCCASION

Talking to hear one's own voice may help to feed the ego or facilitate self-persuasion, but it is not to be confused with talking to communicate ideas to others. A basic assumption of most contemporary research and teaching is that speech communication is *audience-oriented*, whether that audience be one other person, a small group, or a formal public gathering. Short of seeking success by saying whatever others want to hear, a speaker has a responsibility to adapt his message to his audience and the specific occasion on which he speaks. The nature of the audience and the occasion should guide the selection of the subject matter and the specific purpose, the kinds of supporting materials, the pattern of organization, the language used, and the manner of vocal and physical delivery of the message.* Here in the opening pages of this chapter, we emphasize the importance of analyzing in advance the *audience* for whom the public speech is designed. In the closing section, we turn our attention to an analysis of the *occasion* on which it is to be presented. Throughout, we shall be concerned with useful means for effecting these analyses and with some of the ways in which they will influence the planning, preparation, and presentation of public communication.

THE AUDIENCE

The kinds of information about the audience which you will find relevant in preparing your message will be determined in part by your subject and by whether your aim is to inform, to entertain, to reinforce existing beliefs and attitudes, to alter beliefs and attitudes, or to induce overt action. One of the most important lessons you can learn as a speaker is to see things from the standpoint of your listeners. You must continually ask yourself: "How would I feel about this proposal if I were in their place?" "Would this argument sound reasonable to me if I had their experiences or expectations?" "Would this story interest me if I were the same age as they are?"

---

*For a more detailed discussion of the process and problems of audience analysis, see Paul D. Holtzman, The Psychology of Speakers' Audiences (Glenview, Ill.: Scott, Foresman and Company, 1970).

Factors in General Analysis of Audiences

Size

The larger the audience, the greater the diversity of attitudes and beliefs that are likely to be represented and, therefore, the more general and comprehensive your appeals must be. When addressing a large audience, you also must, as a rule, speak more loudly, use broader gestures, and enunciate with special care.

Age

Are the members of your audience approximately the same age, or of widely divergent ages? Age not only affects one's ability to understand, but also determines how far back a person's experience runs. Moreover, older persons tend to be less impulsive and more conservative than younger ones; and both groups may be somewhat skeptical, even contemptuous, of some of the values and attitudes of the other. In this regard, Aristotle's description of young men in the Fourth Century B.C. still seems pertinent for contemporary comparison:

> Young men have strong passions and tend to gratify them indiscriminately. . . . They are changeable and fickle in their desires. . . . Their lives are spent not in memory but in expectation. . . . Their hot tempers and hopeful dispositions make them more courageous than older men are. . . . They have exalted notions, because they have not yet been humbled by life or learnt its necessary limitations. . . . Their lives are regulated more by moral feeling than by reasoning; and whereas reasoning leads us to choose what is useful, moral goodness leads us to choose what is noble. . . . They think they know everything, and are always quite sure about it; this, in fact, is why they overdo everything.[1]

Sex

Is your audience a mixed one or all of the same sex? Men and women still tend to differ in the subjects which typically interest them. In addition, research rather strongly shows that "women are more persuasible than men."[2] However, attention has not specifically been given to the issue of whether such findings are due to biological differences or, as is more likely, to cultural conditioning of the female self-image as passive, pliant, submissive, and changeable. If cultural conditioning is indeed the major explanation, such research findings may become less frequent as we advance further into the era of Women's Liberation consciousness.

Occupation

Occupation often suggests the interests and types of knowledge that people are likely to have. You will, therefore, speak differently to a university faculty than to a labor union. In addition, a fair index of income-level can be gained from a knowledge of the principal occupations of your hearers — information which becomes especially significant if your message involves economic or social considerations, either directly or indirectly.

Education and Intellectual Level

Formal education and education which comes from experience are both important. A Chicago cabdriver may not have extensive formal training, but his broad knowledge of the ways of human nature and of the conditions in that city may be profound. Remember, therefore, to consider both the schooling and experience which characterize your hearers. The degree to which the level of education *may* serve as an index of the intelligence of your listeners is also an important consideration in trying to analyze their critical and interactive capacities. In general, people with high intelligence (in contrast to those with low intelligence) are better able to learn and remember, to sort out valid from specious arguments, and to see implications behind facts. They tend, therefore, to be influenced more by logical arguments and less by communication which relies on unsupported assertions or false, illogical, or irrelevant arguments.[3]

Membership in Organized Groups

Membership in social, professional, and religious groups often indicates both interests and prejudices. The Rotary Club, Knights of Columbus, Young Republican Organization, Black Panthers, National Organization of Women (NOW), and Students for a Democratic Society (SDS) — what do these organizations mean to you as a speaker? For purposes of audience analysis, they represent types of people, points of view, interests, and special aims which you must not fail to take into account as you plan and prepare your message. Whenever you find that a sizeable part of your audience is affiliated with some special group, you will have gained a valuable clue to their motivations and interests, and to the pressures and norms which peers may bring to bear on them.

Cultural and Ethnic Background

The American "melting-pot" ideal of cultural assimilation increasingly is being challenged by the ideal of a truly multi-ethnic society. And ethnic self-appreciation of heritage, contributions, and abilities is an increasing motivation for various societal groups. You would be well advised, for example, to discover whether members of your audience perceive themselves as Black, Negro, Chicano, Latino, Japanese-American, Chinese-American, American Indian, etc. The ethnic and cultural self-image held by your hearers will influence their interests and the assumptions they will use to evaluate the implicit or explicit appeals you make.

Factors Influencing Audience Attitudes Toward Speaker and Subject

Audience's Attitude Toward the Speaker

As we indicated earlier, the positive or negative perception which listeners have of a speaker's personal qualities plays a major role in determining whether they will accept the speaker's information, arguments, or proposal.* *Source-credibility*, *image*, and *reputation*—all are labels currently used to identify this concept of audience attitude toward you as a speaker. The Greeks, as we noted elsewhere, called this concept *ethos* and identified its three major elements as good sense, good character, and good will. Contemporary communication research has identified *expertness* and *trustworthiness* as the two most potent dimensions of speaker credibility.** You may see the expertness dimension at work when listeners, in assessing you as a person, make judgments about your competency, experience, and knowledge of the topic you are talking about. Trustworthiness is a quality which audiences will attribute to you if, from your speaking, you seem honest, dependable, sincere, and fair. To a lesser degree, researchers have identified a dimension often labeled *dynamism*, a quality having to do with how alert, energetic, firm-minded, and interesting your listeners judge you to be. Finally, on the grounds of informal observation at least, we would suggest also that listeners assess communicative good will by evaluating how friendly and likeable you appear to be and how much concern you show for others.

Obviously, then, when we look at these dimensions and the forces which tend to expand or decrease them, we recognize that *ethos* is a variable concept rather than a static one. Thus your *ethos* probably will vary from one audience to another and, indeed, even during the presentation of your speech to a given group of listeners. During your presentation, for instance, your *ethos* will fluctuate as your audience judges your use of evidence and reasoning, psychological ap-

---

*See Chapter 1, p. 14, and Chapter 4, p. 125.

**An excellent analysis of the nature and functioning of ethos, based on current research, is Kenneth E. Andersen, Persuasion: Theory and Practice (Boston: Allyn & Bacon, Inc., 1971), Chapter 12. A survey and extensive bibliography is Stephen Littlejohn, "A Bibliography of Studies Related to Variables of Source Credibility," Bibliographic Annual in Speech Communication: 1971 , ed. Ned A. Shearer (New York: Speech Communication Association, 1971), pp. 1–40.

peals, language, message organization, and vocal and physical delivery. At the conclusion of your speech, your *ethos* level will have derived from the interaction of your *reputation* (the audience's prior knowledge of your accomplishments, associations, views, and personality) with their *assessment of how well you actually perform* (their assessment of your competence) during the speech itself.

Although high *ethos* will not *guarantee* your success as a speaker, markedly low *ethos* usually will thwart your communicative effort. No matter how actually sound your program, accurate your information, or substantial your arguments, if the audience *perceives* you as incompetent, untrustworthy, bored, overly nervous, or aloof, your message probably will have little impact.

How does this analysis of audience attitude-in-process toward speakers apply directly and practically to what you can or may do during the delivery of your speech? What can you do in your presentation to increase the chances that your listeners will perceive your personal qualities as you like to believe they *actually* are? Suppose your analysis predicts that your listeners will be hostile toward you. Clearly, your first task as a speaker is to try to alter this attitude; and your chances of succeeding will be much greater if you can somehow *establish common ground with your hearers.* Often, this can be done by using one or more of the following methods:

1. Show a genuine friendliness, liking, and concern for your listeners.
2. Maintain an attitude of fairness, flexibility, modesty, and good nature.
3. Refer to experiences which you hold in common with them.
4. Point out your honest agreement with some of the cherished hopes, beliefs, attitudes, or values of your auditors.
5. Be honest and straightforward.
6. Demonstrate that you have genuine expertise and experience concerning the subject you are talking about.
7. Quote or indicate your association with persons whose *ethos* with the audience is high.
8. Avoid behaving in a conceited or antagonistic manner.
9. Use humor that is pertinent and in good taste, especially if it can be employed at your own expense.
10. Try to make sure that the nonverbal elements of your presentation reinforce rather than contradict or negate your verbal meaning.

Audience's Attitude Toward Speaker's Purpose and Role

If, with no preliminaries at all, you told the audience the specific purpose of your speech, what would be their attitude toward it? Would they approve, disapprove, or reserve judgment? Since the audience is seldom a homogeneous group, you can expect your listeners to have many different attitudes and to represent many different shades of opinion. Therefore, try to determine the *predominant* attitude and adapt your speech principally to it, while at the same time making allowances for any marked variations you anticipate from the minority.

If your general purpose is *to entertain* or *to inform*, your audience's attitude toward that purpose—as well as toward your subject—will be either interest or apathy. When your purpose is *to persuade,* your audience's attitude will be influenced by their feeling about the specific belief or action you advocate. They may be: (1) predisposed to respond as you desire; (2) favorably disposed, but not aroused; (3) apathetic; (4) interested in the situation, but uncertain what to think or do about it; (5) interested in the situation, but skeptical of your specific proposal because they doubt its workability, fear possible adverse effects, or prefer some other proposal; or (6) firmly opposed to any change from the present state of affairs.

What will be your audience's view of your *role* in speaking to them? What are their expectations concerning that role? They may expect different data, appeals, proposals, language, and delivery—depending upon whether they perceive your role to be that of leader, advisor, expert, novice, lecturer, entertainer, intruder, spokesman for them, spokesman for others, etc. To violate unnecessarily their role-expectations is to run unnecessarily the risk of failure.

If you are attempting to create concern for the nature and significance of a problem, do your listeners also expect you to offer a solution? Do they initially see the situation or the issues which prompt you to speak in the way that you do? Do your listeners believe—at the outset—that they have the power, authority, skill, money, or facilities to act concretely on your idea or proposal? These questions involve audience *attitudes,* and you should have the best possible answers before you face your listeners.

Audience's Knowledge of the Subject

Either through the accumulation of general data or through some special information which you may have discovered, you should be able to infer how much your audience already knows about the subject of your speech. Will they understand technical terms without explanation? Will an elementary discussion seem boring or trivial? What facts will be new, and what ideas and arguments might they dismiss as "the same old stuff"? For a speaker to imply by his remarks that he thinks his listeners ignorant or for him to assume a condescending manner toward them is not only bad manners and bad judgment, but is also a serious barrier to communication. An almost equally bad policy is to talk "over their heads." Try as well as you can to gauge the knowledge and understanding of the audience, and adapt your remarks accordingly.

Audience's Attitude Toward the Subject

Although, as we have mentioned, audiences sometimes are hostile or condescending, ordinarily they are either *interested* in a subject or *apathetic* toward it. Apathy usually is present when they see no connection between a subject and their own needs, satisfactions, and affairs. If, as a speaker, your analysis indicates that this will be the case, you will need to show your hearers that a significant and perhaps overlooked relationship *does* exist between what you have to say and the concerns of their lives. Conceding that they may not have been cognizant of this relationship, proceed quickly and skillfully to make them aware of it. Develop, emphasize, and dramatize the connection. Arouse their curiosity in some novel aspect of your subject. Utilize the most appropriate methods for capturing their attention.

Ours has been called "The Age of Apathy," and many people, including social psychologists, have speculated as to the validity and causes of this. It is true, as some say, that in our day of "instant information," important topics inevitably are discussed frequently and at length. Indeed, sometimes a subject has been publicly discussed so much that audience interest has declined to the point where they view the subject as a *trite* one to be avoided. Nevertheless, although audiences may perceive a topic as over-analyzed and over-discussed, you and others justifiably may—and should—continue to believe in its importance and insist upon talking about it. However, when you choose to speak on a subject that has long been in the public's mind and mouth, you must realize that your task of gaining and holding listeners' interest is greater than it might otherwise be. In preparing for this task, you will find some detailed advice and productive procedures in Chapter 12, "Selecting Material That Will Hold Attention."

The Role of Beliefs, Attitudes, and Values in the Audience's Acceptance of the Message

Fundamental Beliefs, Attitudes, and Opinions of Audiences

As soon as a child begins to receive impressions of his environment, he starts to form opinions and attitudes toward the persons and objects that compose or influence it. These opinions and attitudes may be modified by later experience; but by the time the infant has grown to adulthood, some of them have become the bases for firmly held beliefs and predictable conduct.*

The speaker who knows what settled beliefs and attitudes lie at the basis of his hearers' thinking can avoid arousing needless hostility and often can use these beliefs as pegs upon which to hang an argument or a proposal. A speaker also may avoid misunderstanding or negative judgment by being aware of the stereotyped perceptions and images reflected in beliefs, attitudes, and opinions. If a speaker can show how his ideas coincide with those already established in the minds of his audience, or how his proposal accords with one of their existing principles, often the chance of audience acceptance will be increased.

Finally, a crucial point to remember as you analyze your audience is that all beliefs and attitudes are not equally susceptible to change through speech communication. Be optimistic, of course. But you must also be *realistic* as you plan your speech in the light of knowledge gleaned about the audiences you will be addressing. Do not attempt to accomplish too much on the basis of your analysis. Remember that unexpected, uncontrollable "outside" events or countermessages from other communicators may possibly be at work in the minds of your hearers and so diminish the impact of what you plan to say. Moreover, your listeners may not possess the power or the means to make the changes you desire. Remember, too, that all *situations* are not equally amenable to change through speech communication. For example, no matter what you say, your audience may persist in what appears to be a virtually unshakable "frame of mind." However, underlying many of the established beliefs, attitudes, and behaviors characteristic of a society are what are often described as "the fundamental values"; and a brief examination of some of them should provide additional insights into why audiences think, react, and behave as they do.

Fundamental Values of Audiences

A *value*, as a type of belief, may be defined as a conception of the Good or the Desirable. Honesty, justice, honor, efficiency, progress, economy, courage, prudence, and patriotism are all examples of values. A value may function either generally as a goal motivating an individual's behavior or specifically as a stand-

---

*A belief *may be defined as any proposition or statement which one accepts as true, and which becomes accepted on such bases as evidence, authority, firsthand experience, faith, etc. An* attitude *can be defined as a predisposition, based on a set of beliefs, to respond positively or negatively to an idea, person, object, or situation. An* opinion *may be viewed as the verbal expression of a belief or attitude. As Daniel Katz points out in "The Functional Approach to the Study of Attitudes,"* Public Opinion Quarterly 24 (1960): 163–204, *beliefs and attitudes may serve a variety of psychological functions for those who hold them. Some beliefs and attitudes aid in maximizing rewards and minimizing punishments from those with whom a person must deal directly. Some protect a person from acknowledging harsh truths about himself or his environment. Other beliefs and attitudes reinforce an individual's self-concept and value system. Still others provide standards for structuring and making sense out of the chaotic experience surrounding the person.*

ard the person uses to assess the acceptability of means to ends. We might, for instance, recognize that a program is efficient and economical, but reject that program for being dishonest and inhumane. Dominant values for a person or group frequently are reflected in slogans or mottos: "Liberty, Equality, Fraternity"; "Duty, Honor, Country"; "Law and Order"; "Law and Order and Justice"; "Freedom Now!"; "All Power to the People!"; "Peace with Honor."

Centrality of Values in Motivation and Communication. Values are central to the lives of human beings and play a decisive role when we attempt to influence others. Richard M. Weaver, a rhetorical theorist and critic, observed that "It is the nature of the conscious life of man to revolve around some concept of value. So true is this that when the concept is withdrawn, or when it is forced into conflict with another concept, the human being suffers an almost intolerable sense of being lost."[4]

A social psychologist, Milton Rokeach, further emphasizes the impact of a value on the person committed to it:

. . . it becomes, consciously or unconsciously, a standard or criterion for guiding action, for developing and maintaining attitudes toward relevant objects and situations, for justifying one's own and other's actions and attitudes, for morally judging self and others, and for comparing self with others.[5]

The values to which your audience is committed thus are a major source of leverage for you as a speaker in any communication transaction. If your goal is to present information to increase the understanding of your listeners, you will have to consider whether they will perceive your message as *valuable*—as important, useful, relevant. If your goal is persuasion to reinforce or alter a belief or attitude, or to create overt action, you will have to consider whether the audience perceives your proposal as sanctioned by their relevant values—as harmonious with their basic value system. But a warning is in order. Do not assume that because a person or a group of persons say they are committed to a certain value they always will *act* in accordance with that value when and if you appeal to it. They may not *apply* a value to which they say they are devoted.

Hierarchies of Values. Values are not proved or disproved in the same way as "factual" matters are. We may measure the length of a table to show that it is indeed four feet long; but it is difficult, if not impossible, to measure precisely a person's degree of goodness, honesty, etc. As a culture or subculture develops, a given value becomes accepted as useful or functional for that group. Naturally, the sets of values which predominate may vary from one culture to another. For example, one culture may hold punctuality as a major value, whereas for another culture being on time may be of little concern.

Each of us develops his own value systems within some larger cultural set of values. We are committed to what may be a numerically small but nevertheless potent set of values. Usually we *rank* the values within our system into a rough hierarchy so that we "value" some values more than others. It has been argued, in fact, that "a particular audience is characterized less by values it accepts than by the way it grades them."[6] Note also, that in a specific situation several relevant values to which we are committed may come into conflict, thus forcing a choice of one value over another in making a decision. We may continue to believe in both values, but one temporarily is set aside in favor of the other. We may have to choose, in a given instance, honesty over efficiency, patriotism over self-concern, economy over education, or humaneness over frankness.

Value Frameworks Useful in Audience Analysis. Sociologists and others periodically attempt to formulate a reasonably accurate framework or categorization of the traditional or predominant values in contemporary American society. Such information about general value-orientations may aid you in several ways when you are analyzing your audience and preparing your message.

First, a value framework may serve as a backdrop against which you can project information about the value system of your specific audience. To what degree and in what ways do the major values held by your audience differ from predominant societal values? Is your audience unique, or is it typical in its value-orientation?

Second, knowledge of the uniqueness or typicality of your audience's value system may allow you to infer the ethical criteria with which they will judge the ethics of your proposal or of your supporting evidence, reasoning, and appeals. Whether you wish it or not, listeners formally or informally judge a speech in part by *their* relevant ethical standards for good and bad, right and wrong. We will direct additional attention to these and other judgmental standards in Chapter 17, "Listening, Evaluation, and Ethical Judgment."

Third, a value framework provides you a vantage point from which to evaluate the degree to which your audience's dominant values may have shifted over extended periods of time. In 1953, for example, Richard M. Weaver observed the following as major American values: *progress, factualness, scientificness, modernity, efficiency,* and *Americanism.*[7] How would you assess the meaning and potency of these values today?

Finally, knowledge provided by a value framework may alert you to potentially controversial issues in society. Where values collide, controversy, misunderstanding, dissent, and even revolution are generated. Are the values held by your audience in significant conflict with those you hold or those held by the established power structure in the relevant circumstance?

Audience reaction to a message is determined by a number of factors, including not only the demographic makeup of the audience as a whole, but also the attitudes, beliefs, and value-orientations of the individual listeners.

In the 1960s and early 1970s a variety of labels have been used to characterize the predominant value-orientations of American society: Puritan Ethic, Protestant Ethic, Establishment, Traditional, Middle American, Silent American, Old Culture, Consciousness II, Essentialist Stance, etc. Other labels are being used to mark the value-orientations seen as to some degree in conflict with the Establishment: Counterculture, New Culture, Hip Culture, Humanistic Ethic, Consciousness III, Existentialist Stance, and the like.

As a communicator whose business it is to understand listeners and to relate harmoniously and productively with them, you must be fully sensitive to these distinctions in value-orientations within our society. Unless you can recognize the significant differences, you cannot hope to cope effectively in a communicative sense with the conflicts and controversies such cultural discrepancies are almost certain to generate. Unless you can discover common ground between and among them, your best communicative efforts will almost surely be doomed to failure. To help forestall such an outcome, therefore, and to heighten your ability to draw some necessary distinctions as you plan and prepare to address your listeners, we offer the analyses shown below and on pages 256–257.

In attempting to isolate potentially controversial issues as they exist in value systems, let us look first at a framework which presumably describes the predominant or "Establishment" value-orientations of contemporary American society. The following overview has been extracted from a number of more extensive analyses, in particular those of sociologist Robin M. Williams.*

PREDOMINANT VALUE-ORIENTATIONS
IN CONTEMPORARY AMERICAN SOCIETY

Personal achievement. As demonstrated by the "success story," expansion, mastery, and ever-higher standard of living. Secular occupational success. Success in competition.

Activity and work. The belief, largely inherited from our Puritan past, that idleness is evil. Praise for the man of action.

Robin M. Williams, American Society: A Sociological Interpretation, 3rd ed. (New York: Alfred A. Knopf, Inc., 1970), Chapter 11. Williams has analyzed possible shifts in the saliency and intensity of his value-orientation categories in his "Changing Value Orientations and Beliefs on the American Scene," in The Character of Americans: A Book of Readings, rev. ed., Michael McGiffert, ed. (Homewood, Ill.: Dorsey Press, 1970), pp. 212–230. The Yankelovich public-opinion survey reported in Otis M. Walter and Robert L. Scott, Thinking and Speaking: A Guide to Intelligent Oral Communication, 3rd ed. (New York: The Macmillan Company, 1973), pp. 110–111, indicated that most Americans surveyed ascribed to the values of hard work, thrift, strength of character, organized religion, competition, private property, law and order, and compromise as essential for progress. See also Frank E. Armbruster, The Forgotten Americans: A Survey of the Values, Beliefs and Concerns of the Majority (New Rochelle, N.Y.: Arlington House, Inc., 1972).

Moral orientation. The tendency to view action in terms of ethical judgments. Honesty. Organized religion. Often our moralizations become split between theory and necessity.

Humanitarianism. That complex of values, such as charity, helping the underdog, and spontaneous aid in mass disasters. One could cite evidence to the contrary (wars, lynching, treatment of the American Indian), although there is a national norm of generosity.

Efficiency and practicality. Reverence for getting things done, for quantity and standardization, for orderliness and discipline.

Progress. The concept of change and forward movement.

Material comfort. A desire for material success, ease, and effortless gratification of desires.

Equality. A belief in the inherent value of the individual, in equality of legal rights and responsibilities, and in equality of opportunity.

Freedom. Independence of outside constraint. Moral autonomy in decision-making.

External conformity. Sensitivity to group pressures and sanctioned opinions.

Science and secular rationality. Esteemed as a tool for controlling nature. Interest in order, control, and calculability. Disciplined, functional, rational action. Pragmatic and efficient.

Nationalism/patriotism. American system is morally superior and should be adopted elsewhere. Two types : (1) *Totalistic*—demanding total and unquestioning allegiance to national slogans and symbols. "My country, right or wrong." "Love it or leave it." (2) *Pluralistic*—loyalty to national institutions and symbols insofar as they represent values that are of primary allegiance, such as freedom and equality.

Democracy. Freedom, equality, humanitarianism. Procedures for distributing power and settling conflicts. Key decision-makers should be elected; they should be subject to laws not of their own making; the people have a set of basic civil and political rights that cannot be voted away; and all citizens have a voice in major decisions affecting them.

Individual personality. High value on development of individual personality and protection of integrity of one's individualism. People not to be manipulated or exploited as tools. Resistance to conformity, racism, and excessive concern with success, efficiency, and material comfort.

Racism and related group-superiority themes. Ascription of worth and privilege to individuals on basis of race, social class, or related social category.

In contrast to the foregoing value-orientation framework, Philip Slater describes the choices that seem to him to characterize the potentially controversial issues existing between the Establishment's values and those of the Counter-culture. He points out that:

> The old culture, when forced to choose, tends to give preference to property rights over personal rights, technological requirements over human needs, competition over cooperation, violence over sexuality, concentration over distribution, the producer over the consumer, means over ends, secrecy over openness, social forms over personal expression, striving over gratification, Oedipal love over communal love, and so on. The new countercul-ture tends to reverse all of these priorities.[8]

By extracting from the works of Slater and others, we can build a second detailed framework that attempts to describe and contrast to an extent the value-orientations characteristic of the diverse individuals and groups often called collectively the "Counterculture":*

SOME VALUE-ORIENTATIONS OF THE COUNTERCULTURE

Participatory democracy. (More than representative democracy.) Direct self-determination of conditions by those directly affected. Decentraliza-tion of political power. Minimum institutionalism. Government inter-vention primarily to ensure civil rights and equality of opportunity. "Let the people decide."

Ethnic self-appreciation. Development of ethnic and cultural pride in heritage, accomplishments, and abilities rather than the assimilation or "melting-pot" ideal of American society.

Maximum self-expression. "Do your own thing." Vital for full self-actualization of individual potential.

Humaneness. Respect for each individual's unique worth regardless of status, race, accomplishment, etc. Social equality rather than acceptance of so-

---

*Philip E. Slater, The Pursuit of Loneliness: American Culture at the Breaking Point (Boston: Beacon Press, 1971), pp. 96–118; Mary H. Lystad, As They See It: Changing Values of College Youth (Cambridge, Mass.: Schenkman Publishing Co., Inc., 1973), pp. 1–15, 113–127; Richard Flacks, "The Liber-ated Generation: An Exploration of the Roots of Student Protest," in Black Power and Student Rebellion: Conflict on the American Campus, ed. James McEvoy and Abraham Miller (Belmont, Calif.: Wadsworth Publishing Company, Inc., 1969), esp. pp. 358–361; Kenneth Keniston, Young Radicals: Notes on Com-mitted Youth (New York: Harcourt Brace Jovanovich, Inc., 1968), pp. 272–290, 326–342; E. Joseph Shob-en, Jr., "The Climate of Protest," in Protest! Student Activism in America, ed. Julian Foster and Durward Long (New York: William Morrow & Co., Inc., 1970), esp. pp. 561–565; James W. Chesebro, "Cultures in Conflict—A Generic and Axiological View," Today's Speech 21 (Spring 1973): 11–20.

cial hierarchies. People more important than property. Attitudes of love, trust, kindness, and concern for others rather than domination, manipulation, exploitation, etc.

Frankness and honesty. "Tell it like it is." "Let it all hang out." Condemnation of role-playing, phoniness, insincerity, hypocrisy, and equivocation.

Community-identity and cooperation. (More than competition and self-reliance.) Sharing. Less value on the traditional family.

Enhancement of the emotional side of human existence. (With accompanying skepticism that "rationality" usually becomes rationalization or masks inhumanity.) Increased reliance on emotion, feeling, and moral "gut" reactions as bases for decisions and judgments. Trust in direct sensory experience over intellectual study. Promotion of emotional sensitivity and empathy in human interaction.

Economic socialism. (More than free-enterprise capitalism.) Assumption that sufficient economic resources exist to easily satisfy human needs (not assume that the world lacks enough resources to satisfy all human needs.

Reading and Reacting to Audience Feedback During the Speech Process

In the preceding pages, we have pointed out that despite all that may be said on the subject and all the advice that may be given, no prior analysis of your listeners is assurance against mistaken judgment. Moreover, as we have emphasized, the audience's attitude may—and very likely will—change even while you are speaking. For these reasons, it is important that you keep a close watch on the reactions of your listeners when your subject is announced and throughout the entire presentation of your speech. Positive feedback cues indicating understanding or acceptance by listeners may include such behaviors as a nod of the head, a smile, relaxed posture, applause, laughter, and—on rare occasions—a verbal "yes" or "right on." Negative feedback cues indicating apathy, fleeting attention, bewilderment, or disagreement may include such reactions as a facial scowl or frown, rigid or constantly shifting posture, whispering, vigorous shaking of the head, a hand gesture of dismissal, and—occasionally—booing or verbal heckling. Obviously, in all of your speaking experiences you must strive to develop a keen sensitivity to these signs and learn to adapt your remarks accordingly. In sum, *you must continue your analysis of your audience throughout the actual presentation of your speech* if you are to succeed in your communicative purpose of informing, entertaining, persuading, or actuating your listeners. This, in turn, requires sharp perception combined with a high degree of flexibility and such a thorough grasp of your subject that you will feel confident in making quick adjustments in your speech plan.

THE SPEECH OCCASION

Thus far in this chapter, we have emphasized the importance of studying and analyzing in advance the *audience* for whom the speech is designed. Let us now turn our attention to an analysis of the *occasion* on which it is to be presented and some of the ways in which the communicative situation influences the planning and preparation of the public speech. We can, perhaps, increase our understanding of these influences by asking some probing questions about (1) the *nature* of the public gathering which prompts the speechmaking, (2) the prevailing *social customs,* (3) *antecedent and ensuing events,* and (4) the *physical conditions* which will characterize the speech communication transaction in which you plan to engage.

Some Basic Analytical Questions

What Are the Nature of and Reason for the Occasion?

Is yours a voluntary or a captive audience? A voluntary audience attends a speechmaking event primarily because of their interest in the speaker or the subject: they have freely chosen to attend. A captive audience is required to attend, perhaps at the explicit instruction of the boss or under threat of a grade for course work. Or if you are speaking at a regular meeting of an organized group, members may feel group pressure to be present regardless of your speech. On certain occasions, you may address a chance gathering of people who have congregated spontaneously. In general, however, the more "captive" your audience, the less initial interest they will show and the greater will be their resistance to accepting your information or point of view.

Are people interested in learning more about your subject, in taking some positive action concerning it, or have they perhaps come to heckle or embarrass you? Are your subject and purpose in line with the reason for the meeting, or are you merely seizing the occasion to present some ideas which you think are important? Are you one in a series of speakers whom the audience has heard over a period of weeks or months? If so, how does your speech subject relate to those subjects which have been previously presented? These also are important questions you will need to answer when you are analyzing the occasion.

What Rules or Customs Will Prevail?

Will there be a regular order of business or a fixed program into which your speech must fit? Is it the custom of the group to ask questions of the speaker after his formal address? Do the listeners expect a formal or informal speaking manner? Will you, as the speaker, be expected to extend complimentary remarks to some person or persons or to express respect for some traditional institution or concept? A knowledge of these facts will help you avoid feeling out of place and will prevent you from arousing antagonism by some inappropriate word or action.

What Will Precede and Follow Your Speech?

At what time of day or night will your speech be given? Immediately after a heavy meal or a long program, both of which may induce drowsiness and retard interest? Just before the principal address or event of the evening? By whom and in what manner will you be introduced to the audience? What other items are on the program? What are their tone and character? All these things will, of course, influence the interest the audience may have in your speech. In some instances, you will be able to use the other events on the program to increase interest or belief in your own remarks; sometimes they will work against you. In any case, you must always consider the effect which the program as a whole may have on your speech.

What Will Be the Physical Conditions, the Audience-Speaker Environment?

Will your speech be given out-of-doors or in an auditorium? Is it likely to be hot, cold, or comfortable? Will the audience be sitting or standing; and if sitting, will they be crowded together or scattered about? In how large a room will the speech be given? Will an electronic public-address system be used? Will facilities be provided for the audio-visual reinforcements you will use, or must you bring your own? Will you be seen and heard easily? Are there likely to be disturbances in the form of noise or interruptions from the outside? These and similar environmental factors have an effect on the temper of the audience, their span of attention, and the style of speaking you will have to employ as you make adjustments to the speech environment or situation.

SOURCES OF DIRECT INFORMATION ABOUT AUDIENCES AND OCCASIONS

Now that you have an idea of some of the kinds of information about audiences and occasions which may prove relevant in your speech planning and presentation, we will mention briefly some of the concrete ways of obtaining that information. If possible, talk to the chairman or president of the group you are to address or to the person who invited you to speak. Try, if you can, to consult with several individual members of the group. You may discover useful clues to the group's prevailing interests, value frameworks, etc., by reading the literature they publish or the books that they themselves read and sanction, by watching television programs they regularly watch. The organization's constitution, minutes of past meetings, and scrapbooks of accomplishments may provide further insight into their beliefs, attitudes, and values.

If the group is a local affiliate of a national organization, your college library should be able to provide information concerning the nature of that national body. You might attend a prior meeting of the group or talk to a person who previously has spoken to them. If feasible, you might give your audience a pre-speech questionnaire—simple, brief, and neutrally worded—to tap their predispositions. In certain instances you may find it possible to consult the back files of the local newspaper or to make inquiries of the Chamber of Commerce. For data on general public beliefs, attitudes, and values, you should consult recent national public-opinion polls such as those published by Gallup, Roper, Harris, or Yankelovich.

In this chapter we have weighed some of the general and specific types of information about audiences and have posed some searching questions designed to help you in analyzing the occasions—the social contexts and physical settings—in which you will be speaking. We have suggested a few of the ways in which you may use the data thus derived and have considered some of the possible effects that such usage may have on listeners' acceptance or rejection of your message. Careful research of both a general and specific nature, we have said, can give you some—but by no means total—assurance that your predictions as to the character, knowledge-level, predispositions, values, and biases of an audience will prove reasonably reliable. Furthermore, we have emphasized that *while presenting your speech* you must constantly observe the reactions from your listeners and, when feedback so indicates, modify your message and your delivery accordingly.

Having been thus introduced at least to the processes involved in analyzing audiences, you should now be ready to extend and broaden that analysis in a somewhat different way and different direction—to determine what factors and forces there may be that are likely to *motivate* listeners to understand, believe, or act as you urge. What *motivational appeals* may you, as a speaker, make to your audience to accomplish the major purpose of your speech? On what are such appeals based? In the chapter that follows, we shall seek out some useful answers to these and related questions.

FOOTNOTES

[1]*Aristotle*, Rhetoric, trans. W. Rhys Roberts (New York: Modern Library, Inc., 1954), pp. 122–123. Chapters 12–14 of Book II of the Rhetoric *contain descriptions of the outlooks of young men, elderly men, and men in their prime.*

[2]*Marvin Karlins and Herbert I. Abelson*, Persuasion: How Opinions and Attitudes Are Changed, *2nd rev. ed. (New York: Springer Publishing Company, Inc., 1970), pp. 89–91.*

[3]*Ibid., pp. 97–99.*

[4]*Richard M. Weaver*, The Ethics of Rhetoric *(Chicago: Henry Regnery Company, 1953), p. 213. On the centrality of values to persuasion, see Ralph T. Eubanks and Virgil Baker, "Toward an Axiology of Rhetoric,"* Quarterly Journal of Speech *XLVII (April 1962): 157–168; Karl R. Wallace, "The Substance of Rhetoric: Good Reasons,"* Quarterly Journal of Speech *XLIX (October 1963): 279–287.*

[5]*Milton M. Rokeach*, Beliefs, Attitudes and Values: A Theory of Organization and Change *(San Francisco: Jossey-Bass, Inc., Publishers, 1968), p. 160. In fact, Rokeach contends that in the social-science study of communication, the processes of value formation and change (not attitude change) should be the central focus. Ibid., pp. 156–159.*

[6]*Chaim Perelman and L. Obrechts-Tyteca*, The New Rhetoric: A Treatise on Argumentation, *trans. John Wilkinson and Purcell Weaver (Notre Dame, Ind.: University of Notre Dame Press, 1969), p. 81.*

[7]*Richard M. Weaver*, The Ethics of Rhetoric *(Chicago: Henry Regnery Company, 1953), pp. 211–218. For a discussion of some other American value frameworks, see Wayne C. Minnick*, The Art of Persuasion, *2nd ed. (Boston: Houghton Mifflin Company, 1968), pp. 215–221.*

[8]*Philip E. Slater*, The Pursuit of Loneliness: American Culture at the Breaking Point *(Boston: Beacon Press, 1970), p. 100. There is some evidence, however, that the value conflicts between most parents and most of their children may not be as great as assumed. See the 1969 Yankelovich public-opinion survey reported in Otis M. Walter and Robert L. Scott*, Thinking and Speaking: A Guide to Intelligent Oral Communication, *3rd. ed. (New York: The Macmillan Company, 1973), pp. 110–111; Mary Lystad*, As They See It: Changing Values of College Youth *(Cambridge, Mass.: Schenkman Publishing Company, 1973), p. 121; Joseph Adelson, "What Generation Gap?" in* The Character of Americans: A Book of Readings, *rev. ed., Michael McGiffert, ed. (Homewood, Ill.: Dorsey Press, 1970), pp. 378–388. Adelson reminds us that the values of the large group of non-college youth and many college youths generally are closer to their parents' values than are the values of a highly visible subgroup of college young people.*

Problems and Probes

1. Assume you are an ecologist specializing in water-pollution control. Describe how you would present your subject to the following audiences: (*a*) the Chamber of Commerce, some members of which are manufacturers whose firms have emptied their wastes into a nearby river; (*b*) a high-school ecology class; (*c*) the League of Women Voters; (*d*) a church-sponsored club of retired men and women. Indicate the general and specific purpose of the speech that you would present in each of these four instances, and suggest the particular ideas that you would plan to incorporate in each of the separate speeches. Suggest an appropriate title for each speech.

2. How would you rank the following factors in terms of their importance in determining audience interests: predominant sex, educational level, region of the country in which the listeners live, occupation, age? Compare your ranking with those made by other members of the class and attempt to reach a consensus.

3. Select a suitable subject and use it to frame a specific purpose for a five-minute speech to persuade (*a*) an audience that is favorable but not aroused, (*b*) an audience that is interested but undecided, (*c*) an audience that is apathetic, (*d*) an audience that is hostile toward the proposition or recommendation, and (*e*) an audience that is opposed to any change from the present situation.

4. Come to class prepared to discuss the general topic, "The Ideal Physical Arrangements for a Public Speech." Consider such factors as the following: the size of the room in relation to the size of the audience; the arrangement of the chairs around the speaker's stand; the type of chairs in which the listeners sit; the distance between the speaker and the audience; the advisability of positioning the speaker on a platform that raises him or her above the level of the listeners; the acoustics; the lighting arrangements (houselights dark, spotlight on the speaker, etc.); the ventilation; and the decoration of the room in relation to the subject of the speech.

5. If, as a result of analysis, you find that your audience will be heterogeneous—that is, will contain persons of many different ages, occupations, educational levels, etc.—how should you plan to adapt your remarks? Should you attempt to find a subject or an approach broad enough to be of interest to all? Should you try to speak to the majority of your listeners and forget the rest? Should you divide your subject in such a way that different parts or aspects of it will appeal to different segments of your audience? Be prepared to defend your answer.

6. Locate a printed speech, or attend a speech in which the values, beliefs, and attitudes of the listeners are hostile or—at best—apathetic toward the purpose of the speaker. Analyze the speech to ascertain as best you can how the speaker has endeavored to overcome the hostility or apathy and get the audience to accept his or her purpose and message.

7. Restudy the discussion of *ethos* on pages 245–246. Defend or attack the statement that in recent years it has become increasingly difficult for a speaker to establish his or her *ethos* with an audience. Explain your position. In class, discuss this problem and try to agree upon two or three well-known, living, public personalities who exemplify a high degree of *ethos* or speaker credibility.

Oral Activities and Speaking Assignments

1. Hold a small group discussion (45–60 minutes in length) on the question: To what degree is the conflict in value-orientations between the

so-called Establishment and Counterculture serious, significant for communication, and reducible? As partial preparation, read the sources by Chesebro, Lystad, and Slater cited within this chapter and in Suggestions for Further Reading.

2. The student of speech communication can learn much about the principles of audience analysis by observing how such public-opinion pollsters as Dr. George Gallup analyze "the great American audience" to derive the samples upon which they base their predictions. Let several members of the class investigate these methods and report on them orally, either in individual presentations or in an informal discussion before the class.

Suggestions for Further Reading

Raymond A. Bauer, "The Obstinate Audience," *American Psychologist* (May 1964): 650–655.

Lloyd Bitzer, "The Rhetorical Situation," *Philosophy and Rhetoric* I (January 1968): 1–14.

James W. Chesebro, "Cultures in Conflict: A Generic and Axiological View," *Today's Speech* XXI (Spring 1973): 11–20.

Paul Holtzman, *The Psychology of Speakers' Audiences* (Glenview, Ill.: Scott, Foresman and Company, 1970).

Mary Lystad, *As They See It: Changing Values of College Youth* (Cambridge, Mass.: Schenkman Publishing Co., Inc., 1973).

Howard Martin, "Communication Settings," in *Speech-Communication: Analysis and Readings*, ed. Howard Martin and Kenneth Anderson (Boston: Allyn & Bacon, Inc., 1968), pp. 58–84.

Milton Rokeach, *The Open and Closed Mind* (New York: Basic Books, Inc., Publishers, 1960), Chapters I–IV, "The Theory and Measurement of Belief Systems," pp. 3–100.

Philip Slater, *The Pursuit of Loneliness: American Culture at the Breaking Point* (Boston: Beacon Press, 1970).

9
DETERMINING THE BASIC APPEALS

In the preceding chapter we emphasized the importance of analyzing your audience in order to ascertain—among other things—their beliefs, attitudes, opinions, and value-orientations.[1] In this chapter, we endeavor to build on that analysis and to probe even deeper into the *motivational foundations* underlying it. With respect to any particular subject on which you may be speaking, not only must you identify and assess the specific attitudes, beliefs, and values of your hearers, but you must also understand the motives that are likely to generate, control, and significantly influence any thinking, believing, and behaving they may do as a result of your speech.* Unless you can appeal to them in ways that will "motivate" their acceptance of the information you are giving or the proposal you are urging, your communicative effort is almost certain to fall short of its mark. Stated another way, the most carefully constructed and supported message is likely to fail unless it somehow affects the desires, drives, goals, or action-tendencies of the people who hear it.

MOTIVATION AND ATTITUDE-CHANGE: A FUNCTIONAL APPROACH

On the basis of our considerations in Chapter 8, in particular, we can make two key assumptions of vast importance to the communicator: (1) A significant proportion of the many manifestations of human behavior arise from peo-

---

*For purposes of this chapter, it is important to stress the interrelatedness of attitude, opinion, value, and belief. To facilitate your review of these concepts, we summarize the definitions provided by Richard V. Wagner and John J. Sherwood, The Study of Attitude Change (Belmont, Calif.: Brooks/Cole Publishing Company, 1969), p. 1, as follows: An attitude is often described as a predisposition of the human creature to react to and/or behave in a particular way toward a given object or element in his consciousness or in his environment. This reactive behavior is evaluative; that is, the behaver-reactor always attaches a value or set of values to the object or element. When the individual verbalizes or otherwise communicates an attitude, he expresses an opinion. A belief is generally thought of as being a highly intrapersonal conception of a supposed "reality," a subjective conviction of a perceived "truth." The strength of a belief is significantly affected by the number and nature of the values the believer attaches to it. In general, the greater the number and intensity of the values—or, as some say, belief-evaluations—connected with the belief, the stronger it is likely to be.

ple's perceptions of and attitudes toward objects, ideas, and other people and the values they attach to them;* and (2) one of the fundamental reasons why human beings communicate is to try to effect *attitude-formation* and *attitude-change* in others. If, as we are suggesting, a person thinks and behaves in accordance with his attitudinal predispositions, and if we can determine what those predispositions or inclinations are, we will have at least a partially valid and somewhat useful way to predict his responses to the ideas, positions, and propositions we desire to communicate to him.

Essentially, therefore, in the pages that follow we shall pursue what is commonly called a *functional approach* to attitude-change.** Simply stated, we are taking the view that human beings develop their attitudes and/or change them in accordance with and to the extent that they fulfill or frustrate their individual needs. *Attitude-formation* and *satisfaction of basic needs* are the dynamics by which the communicator can select and arrange the motivational appeals he will make to his hearers. They will help him determine ways in which he can most productively and—if necessary—persuasively formulate and phrase his ideas to ensure their motive strength and, we may hope, assure their favorable acceptance by others. In sum, by using the functional approach, we shall attempt to understand more completely why listeners hold the attitudes they do and how they may be influenced to form new ones or to change existing ones.

MOTIVES: SOME CONCEPTS AND CLASSIFICATIONS

Someone tells me that the only way I can find a job is to enlist the services of an employment agency, so I sign up and pay the fee required. Membership in Phi Beta Kappa, I'm told, will enhance my chances of gaining admission to the graduate school of my choice, so I begin to study harder. Because I am determined to make the varsity football squad, I work for long hours in the hot sun until every muscle aches and I am completely exhausted. In each of these instances my behavior has been *goal-directed:* some latent force within me has spurred me toward that behavior. An inner aim has *motivated* me to behave in a certain way; a deep-felt *need* or *desire* has impelled me to act.***

---

*See again Richard V. Wagner and John J. Sherwood, The Study of Attitude Change *(Belmont, Calif.: Brooks/Cole Publishing Company, 1969), esp. pp. 1–6.*

**D. Katz and E. Stotland, "A Preliminary Statement to a Theory of Attitude Structure and Change," in* Psychology: A Study of a Science, *ed. S. Koch, Vol. 3 (New York: McGraw-Hill Book Company, 1959), pp. 423–475.*

***For recent discussions of motives and the role they play in communication generally, see especially William V. Haney,* Communication and Organizational Behavior: Text and Cases *(Homewood, Ill.: Richard D. Irwin, Inc., 1967), Chapter 4; and Thomas M. Scheidel,* Speech Communication and Human Interaction *(Glenview, Ill.: Scott, Foresman and Company, 1972), pp. 208–224.*

Depending upon their era and particular point of view, psychologists have called such action-tendencies by different names: instincts, emotions, prepotent reflexes, purposive or wish-fulfilling impulses, inner drives, habitual action-tendencies, and other labels. There have been many arguments about the number of basic drives and the degree and extent to which they may be inborn or acquired through experience and habit. With the details of these arguments we are not concerned here. It is more important for us to note certain facts which are commonly agreed upon: (*a*) in all human beings there are certain universal action-tendencies — the organism has within it the capacity and tendency to move in different directions; (*b*) much human behavior is goal-directed in the way we have suggested above; and (*c*) while in some instances such behavior may be set into motion by the individual's own physiological or psychological needs, in other instances it may be triggered by the impetus or pressure put on the individual by his environment.

To translate this into the perspective of the public communicator, we may say that *the normal condition of the people in an audience is one of physical relaxation, mental inertia, and emotional equilibrium unless something has already happened to stir these people into motion or unless the speaker does so through the verbal and/or nonverbal appeal which he makes.* If, then, you are to accomplish the purpose of your speech, you must overcome the inertia of your listeners or counteract an opposite tendency by setting in motion some fundamental reaction which will move them in the direction of your purpose. You must puncture a hole in their apathy or opposition which will make them feel unsatisfied until they have reacted as you wish. But before you can do this, you must understand what these basic urges or reaction-tendencies are, and you must know how to arouse them and set them in motion.

For the purpose of simplicity we shall call the basic forces that motivate human conduct and belief *motive needs;* and, because these motive needs are so often combined in complex patterns and concealed from external observation, we shall call by the term *motivational appeals* the appeals to all the specific feelings, emotions, and desires by which the speaker may set the motive needs into action.

Some Classifications of Motive Needs

Basic human needs, as we have pointed out, have been classified in various ways, and no two lists agree entirely. Indeed, the only limit to such an enumeration is the infinite variety of human behavior itself. Of late, however, it has become popular to distinguish between "biological" and "psychological-social" needs, or between what are sometimes called "maintenance" (homeostasis-oriented) and "actualization" tendencies. In addition, greater importance is being attached to such social drives as the need for participation and belonging, "competence" in relation to one's environment, achievement, group approval, and the like. The important point to note here is that although psychologists are quite generally in accord that human behavior is prompted and, to a certain extent, controlled by certain essential physiological/biological/psychological needs, each authority tends to identify and classify these needs in somewhat different ways.

Abraham H. Maslow, however, is the psychologist whose list of basic need-categories is most often cited today; and a brief examination of his classification may enable us to walk on firmer and more fertile ground as we venture into the question of how, as communicators, we can go about the task of determining the basic appeals we will use in our speaking. In his *Motivation and Personality*,[2] Maslow presents the following categories of needs and wants which impel human beings to think, act, and respond as they do:

1. *Physiological Needs*——for food, drink, air, sleep, sex, etc.—the basic bodily "tissue" requirements.

2. *Safety Needs*——for security, stability, protection from harm or injury; need for structure, orderliness, law, and predictability in one's environment; freedom from fear and chaos.

3. *Belongingness and Love Needs*——for abiding devotion and warm affection with spouse, children, parents, and close friends; need to feel that one is a part of social groups; need for acceptance and approval.

4. *Esteem Needs*——desire for self-esteem based on achievement, mastery, competence, confidence, freedom, independence; desire for esteem of others (reputation, prestige, recognition, status).

5. *Self-Actualization Needs*——for self-fulfillment, actually to become what one potentially can be; desire to actualize one's capabilities; being true to one's essential nature; what a person *can* be he *must* be.

To these five categories Maslow has brought the highly significant dynamic of *prepotency*. These levels of human needs (especially in Western culture), as he has ordered them, function as a *prepotent hierarchy*. That is, lower-level needs must be largely (but not entirely) fulfilled before higher-level needs become operative. In the life of the individual, physiological needs must be largely satisfied before safety needs can operate or motivate with much force, and so on up the various levels of the hierarchy. A person caught in the daily struggle to satisfy the physiological and safety needs is likely to have little energy and "ambition" left to strive mightily for self-esteem or self-actualization. Of course, as individuals we tend to move upward and downward between one level and another as our life progresses or regresses; the ascent and/or descent is not necessarily steady or in a straight line in one direction or another. Perhaps the following diagram of the pyramidal "layering" or "stacking" of the five successive levels can help us to glimpse more readily and clearly this dynamic of the *prepotent hierarchy*.

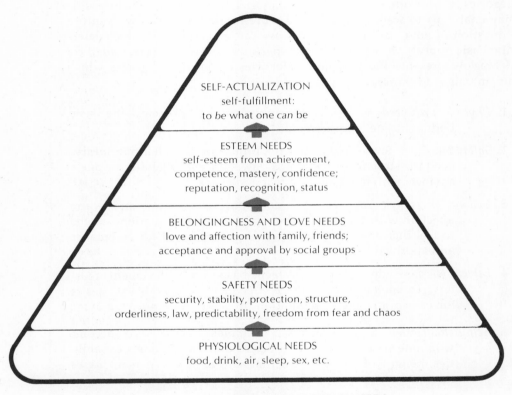

Figure 1. A HIERARCHY OF PREPOTENT NEEDS

Maslow also suggests two additional basic needs which he does not include in his hierarchy:

Curiosity Needs——to know and understand.

Aesthetic Needs——for order, beauty, symmetry, balance, etc.[3]

In particular, at this time you might mentally "file for future reference" Maslow's point that human creatures seem to feel a definite need for *symmetry* and *balance* in the worlds of their perceptions and cognitions. Around this need, psychologists and others appear to have built the so-called theories of "cognition balancing" and "cognitive dissonance" — matters which we shall encounter later, in Chapter 13, where we explore the *motivated sequence* as a method of adapting the speech structure to the thought processes of listeners.

Needs and Motives: Some Interrelationships

If, as Maslow and others claim, these are indeed the basic needs of humankind, then there are certain key questions to which we — as informative and persuasive communicators — need to seek answers. What forms, for instance, do these basic needs take when we want to communicate our ideas to others? In what specific ways do they influence aspects of our own thinking and behavior and — subsequently — the thinking and behavior of those with whom we would interact? How can these basic needs/wants/desires be "translated" into specific *motives*, into *motivational appeals* that we can make to our listeners?

At least a part of the answers to such questions may be found in the following assertions about the significant relationships between needs and motives — assertions which, if you think about them for a moment, will become more or less self-evident:

1. Arising from the foregoing categories of basic needs are the human impulses to act, *the* motives *which generate, shape, and continuously influence the thoughts people think, the words they utter, the decisions they make, the behaviors in which they choose or refuse to engage.*

2. The strength *of the motives generated by the various needs will vary from individual to individual. One person may value self-enhancement more than the avoidance of harm or injury; another may care more for self-fulfillment than for social acceptance or approval. Experience modifies the influence which the basic motive needs have upon people. Moreover, there are certain periods in a person's life when one or another of these needs "matures" and becomes most powerful. Furthermore, the immediate situation confronting the individual may call one of them into play more than any of the others. Regardless of such variations, however, motives play an unmistakably and exceedingly important role in shaping human behavior.*

3. Although motives often underlie and impel behavior, the cause-effect relationship is not always a direct *and* simple *one. The complexities of the human organism and the customs and mores of the society in which we live may prevent the immediate fulfillment of a fundamental need.*

4. *In such cases (and there are many), however, the underlying need and motivational force springing from it do not simply "disappear": they surface and make themselves manifest in a different form or forms. As a result, there develop a variety of* indirect *or "manifest" needs—needs which may represent only certain* aspects *or* segments *of a given motive or, in some cases, a combination of two or more motives. These indirect or manifest needs provide the grounds for what we shall here call* motive appeals. *The identifying and shaping of these appeals pose the crux of the challenge facing the effective communicator.*

5. *The choice and phrasing of the motivational appeals you make as a communicator should be* adapted to the beliefs, attitudes, and values *of your listeners.*

Obviously, the operation of motive needs is never a simple thing. Despite the cartoons we sometimes see, human beings do not wear push-buttons or wind-up keys in full view on their backs! The complexity of life prevents the easy and direct fulfillment of these desires. Experience produces a large variety of *composite desires*, combinations of the basic needs and motives as they relate to the concrete objects of our environment. *To these more specific and familiar patterns the speaker must make his motivational appeals.*

MOTIVATIONAL APPEALS: SOME TYPES AND IMPLICATIONS

Earlier in these pages we defined a *motivational appeal* as an appeal to some feeling, emotion, or desire by which the speaker may set the primary *motive needs* into motion. There are, of course, an infinite number of these specific human wants and needs, and any list of them must of necessity be incomplete and overlapping to some extent. The list which follows has both of these flaws, but nevertheless you may find virtue in its applicability and practicality. In it you will find the specific desires, drives, feelings, and sentiments to which motivational appeals have proved remarkably effective. You will find it, we believe, greatly worth your while to learn this list, to gain a thorough understanding of the meaning and import of each of the items listed, and to begin basing upon them your analysis of your listeners' attitudes, beliefs, and values and the major purposive points of your speech. This, in brief, is what we meant when we said on pages 264–265 that this chapter takes *a functional approach to motivation and attitude-formation/change.*

1. Achievement and Display.   *a*—Organizing.
2. Acquisition and Saving.   *b*—Building.
3. Adventure and Change.   6. Curiosity.
4. Companionship and Affiliation. 7. Deference.
5. Creativity.   8. Dependence.

9. Destruction.
10. Endurance.
11. Fear.
12. Fighting and Aggression.
    a — Anger.
    b — Competition.
13. Imitation and Conformity.
14. Independence and Autonomy.
15. Loyalty.
    a — To family (parental and filial love).
    b — To friends.
    c — To organizations and groups (clubs, colleges attended, companies worked for, etc.).
    d — To country, region, state, etc.
16. Personal Enjoyment.
    a — Of comfort and luxury.
    b — Of beauty and order.
    c — Of pleasant sensory sensations (tastes, smells, etc.).
    d — Of recreation.
    e — Of relief from restraint (sprees, protest marches, etc.).
17. Power, Authority, and Dominance.
18. Pride.
    a — Reputation.
    b — Self-respect.
    c — Sound judgment.
19. Reverence or Worship.
    a — Of leaders.
    b — Of traditions or institutions.
    c — Of a deity.
20. Revulsion.
21. Sexual Attraction.
22. Sympathy and Generosity.

Do not be disturbed by the fact that in this list certain wishes or desires appear to work at cross-purposes: fear against the drive for adventure, personal enjoyment against the desire for power and dominance, etc. Remember that the human being is an inconsistent and changeable creature who, at different times, may pursue quite different ends or goals. Also, as you study the list, make frequent comparisons with the items found in the "Predominant Value-Orientations in Contemporary American Society" (pages 254–256), and in "Some Value-Orientations of the Counterculture" (pages 256–257), as developed in Chapter 8.

Later on, in the present chapter, we shall consider some of the *methods* for making motivational appeals directly to listeners. Now, however, let us examine in greater detail each of the appeals included in the foregoing list.

Achievement and Display

Ordinarily, people want to do their best, although it may not always appear so. They yearn to achieve success or distinction of some kind. Usually, they are willing to work hard to accomplish tasks in which they can display their skill and expertise, to *do* or to *be* something that sets them apart, that makes others willing to acknowledge their uniqueness as a person. We are eager to exhibit our talents and want others to be aware of them. We try to say clever and witty things, to say things just to see how others will react.

The people who create and write advertising, like those who create and produce spoken messages, work to become expert users of motivational appeals. Although most mass-media advertising is as much visually as verbally oriented, many of the techniques for using the motivational appeals remain the same. Magazine advertisements on these pages have been structured around such appeals as loyalty, personal enjoyment, adventure, achievement and display, and fear. Try to identify the motivational appeals used in the advertising you see daily in magazines, newspapers, on television, or elsewhere.

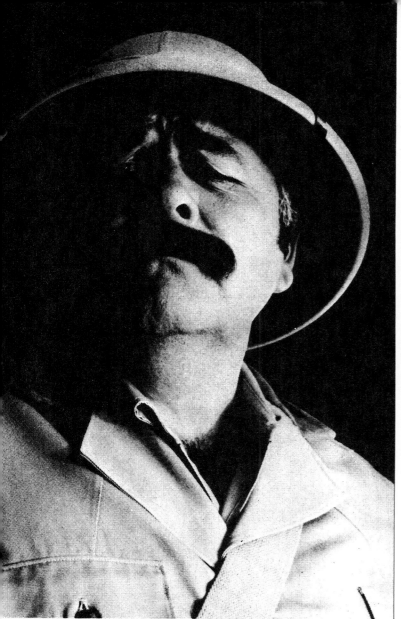

re's a little explorer in everybody...

And rrison keeps explorer cool comfortable rom homesite to campsite.

Before you set out to discover new places, discover GM-Harrison air conditioning. It can make exploring a lot more enjoyable. By keeping your camper cab cool and comfortable in summer. By removing dust, pollen and excess humidity. Scout up your Chevrolet or GMC Truck dealer and start your safari with a demonstration of GM-Harrison truck air conditioning.

Acquisition and Saving

Most of us like to earn money, to keep it, and to spend as little of it as we can in order to acquire the other things we want. Discount stores are filled with people trying to get as much as possible at the lowest price. Advertisements for airlines and resort hotels frequently feature special "off-season rates." But this want also extends to many things besides money. Stamp collecting, the keeping of dance programs or photo albums, the gathering of art treasures or rare books, and similar hobbies reflect this same tendency.

Adventure and Change

Nearly everyone likes the thrill of mild danger—the adventure of diving beneath the surface of the sea, of scaling a mountain, or of exploring strange lands and cities. Youngsters rarely climb the safest tree; roller coasters coin money because of the thrills they provide; some motorists drive as fast as possible even if they don't have to "get there quickly." When acquisition and adventure are combined—as in most forms of gambling, from slot machines to stock speculation—they provide especially powerful motivation. Basic to a yen for adventure is the longing for *change*. Change is the impetus that drives people to seek out new and different things, to meet other people. The ho-hum, humdrum routine of daily living stirs individuals to discover that which is novel, strange. Change gives them the courage to try new and different jobs, to participate in the latest fads, to "go" for the latest fashions.

Companionship and Affiliation

A few people prefer to be hermits, but most of us like company. We cross the street to walk with a friend rather than walk alone. We want to be a part of a friendly group, to share, to make strong attachments. We go to parties, join clubs, write letters to absent relatives, and prefer to live in a dormitory or share an apartment with friends. We like to affiliate ourselves with others who will reflect our beliefs and opinions. And, of course, the most tedious task becomes bearable if others are sharing it with us.

Creativity

We like to say, "I made this myself." The urge to create shows itself in many ways: in inventions, books, buildings, business organizations, and empires. In addition to the creative *arts* (painting, music, sculpture, etc.), this tendency takes two more general forms: *building* with physical objects such as bricks, steel, or wood; and *organizing* human beings into working units—political parties, business firms, athletic teams, and the like. This desire, for instance, motivates many campus and civic activities.

Curiosity

Children tear open alarm clocks to find out where the tick is, and adults crowd the sidewalks to gaze curiously at the celebrity passing by. But curiosity is not mere inquisitiveness or "nosiness," as is sometimes implied. It also provides the motivation of the experimentalist, the scholar, and—when curiosity is coupled with the love for adventure—of the explorer. Without curiosity, life would be dull and static.

Deference

There are times when most of us recognize the advantage of deferring to someone whose wisdom, experience, and expertise are greater than our own. It is this recognition which makes us open to suggestions from others, to find out what others think. We can sense the possible benefit of following instructions and doing what is expected of us. In the spirit of deference, we accept the leadership of others; we conform to custom; we even learn to praise other people.

Dependence

When people *over*-defer, especially for extended periods of time, they tend to develop a dependence. All are, of course, *born* dependent; and it is a feeling not altogether lost in adulthood. Whatever their age, people like to have others provide help when needed. When discouraged, they seek encouragement from others and expect them to be kind and helpful. In proper measure, dependence can be a healthy thing; overdone, it can quickly erode initiative and destroy other necessary drives and action-tendencies.

Destruction

In most of us there seems to be an occasional impulse to tear down, to break, to bulldoze over, to batter down, to cut to pieces—to destroy. Perhaps this urge springs from the desire to show our superiority, our dominance, over the object of our destruction and thus expand our ego. Or, again, it may arise from a desire to free ourselves from social and cultural restraints. In any event, we are all destroyers at times. Build a house of blocks for a baby, and he knocks it down. Let someone present a theory or an argument, and someone else delights in picking it full of holes and tearing it apart. There is always a crowd at a fire, and one of the reasons is the swift and awesome destruction by the flames.

Admittedly, this tendency is not entirely antisocial: after all, the old must be destroyed before the new can take its place. The critic who shouts "down with" a practice or an institution that merits oblivion sometimes performs a valuable service. But the speaker who would translate this drive into a motivational appeal should be mindful of Marc Antony's utterance at the conclusion of his impassioned speech to the Roman mob: ". . . Mischief, thou art afoot, take thou what course thou wilt!"

Endurance

Stick-to-itiveness in a highly mobile and "impermanent" age may seem something of an incongruity, but it is nevertheless a strongly motivating force for many people. There are still an ample number of individuals who—without great financial rewards or fanfare—keep steadily at a job until it is finished. "Work," they appear to be saying, "is its own reward." Usually, they insist on completing one particular job before tackling another. They "hang in there and keep pitchin'" at the problem even though they seem to be making no visible headway.

Fear

As a motive drive, fear has both positive and negative effects. It prevents us from doing things that bring peril, and it prompts us to protect ourselves when peril threatens. If the other person is bigger than I am, I hesitate to attack him; instead, I go home and put a lock on the door to keep him out. Physical injury, however, is by no means the only thing we fear. We are also afraid of losing our jobs, our property, our friends, our future. Especially do we fear the dangerous power of what is strange or hidden: *the unknown*. Witness stage fright. Fortunately, as practice makes us familiar with the circumstances of confronting an audience, this fear tends to diminish. (See again pages 127–131.) Conversely, if your *listeners* are the fearful ones, your first task is to reassure them—to allay their fears. Don't play upon them or exploit them.

Fighting and Aggression

Much has been spoken and written in an effort to explain why human creatures fight one another—why they engage in endless acts of aggression against each other. Here we shall concern ourselves with only two facets of this multifaceted manifestation of human conflict: *anger* and *competition*. Usually, people fight because their anger has been aroused by some opposing force or person. We become angry at people who cheat or insult us, challenge our ideas or values, destroy our property, or interfere with our rights or efforts. The form in which we fight back against these intrusions may vary all the way from physical attack to subtly destructive gossip, but it normally has for its purpose protecting our safety or restoring our self-esteem in the face of attack. Because society frowns on assault and battery, we generally tend to use more civilized and legal methods of responding—social ostracism, court action, and the like. But show any person that he is being cheated, insulted, or threatened, and he will likely become angry and fight back in one way or another.

The impulse to fight or to struggle also takes another form of expression in modern society, and this is *competition*. We enjoy matching wits and muscles with antagonists, even though we are not angry with them, for the sheer pleasure of the struggle or for the sake of demonstrating our superiority. Participation in games is based on this tendency, and many people argue or debate just for this reason. Business and scholastic rivalry are manifestations of the element of competition. The prevalent use of the phrase "We *beat* them" to indicate the winning of such competitive engagements suggests the "fighting" nature of the effort.

Imitation and Conformity

Both consciously and subconsciously, people tend to imitate others. From earliest childhood, all of us tend to emulate those whom we most greatly admire; and as we grow older, the range of the people, ideas, and behaviors we imitate steadily increases. When a new catch-phrase or colorful expression is heard on the campus, very quickly everyone begins to use it. We copy the garb, attitudes, actions, and even the pronunciations of other persons—especially of those we respect or envy. Tell your listeners how a famous person does something or has attained success, and they are likely to want to imitate that individual.

Do not suppose, however, that imitation is largely volitional; much of it is *imposed*. Oftentimes we may feel compelled to imitate—to *conform*—because of subtle or overt pressures from peers, parents, and professors. "They say" and "Everybody's doing it" are clearly conformative in their intent.

Independence and Autonomy

In spite of the tendency to imitate or conform, we do not like to lose our independence: we do not like to be *forced* to imitate. A woman's dress must be in style, but at the same time not exactly like any other dress. It must be unique. We do not like to be bossed about, to have to attend class, or to be prohibited from acting as we like. We insist upon autonomy: to be able to come and go as desired, to say what we think about things, to make our own decisions, to do things without regard for what others may think. If you can influence your hearers to believe they are doing something of their own volition, they will be much more likely to do it than if the act is forced upon them. Workmen have quit their jobs; members have resigned from clubs; nations have engaged in revolutions—all to maintain independence of action.

Loyalty

The feeling of loyalty, based upon an individual's tendency to identify himself with other persons or groups, sometimes provides very strong motivation. Often it is linked to such other appeals as affiliation and reverence. The strength of the loyalty appeal will vary, of course, with the degree to which the individual has become identified with the particular person or group of persons. Hence, a person's loyalty to family is usually stronger than loyalty to a college or a social club. A few of the more important types of loyalties are:

Loyalty to Family. Sometimes this is referred to as *parental love* or *filial duty.* Brothers may fight between themselves; but if an outsider attacks one of them, loyalty usually prompts both of them to forget their differences and stand shoulder to shoulder. Men buy insurance to protect their families; wives—traditionally at least—help their husbands succeed in a business or a profession. Parents stand by their children when they are in trouble.

Loyalty to Friends. We are willing to do things for close friends that we would not do for chance acquaintances. Similarly, people resent slurs upon their friends and are more likely to believe the opinions of their associates rather than those of strangers.

Loyalty to Groups or Organizations. Most persons feel a certain measure of loyalty to the school they attend, the organization or institution they work for, the social and political groups to which they belong. If the organizations or groups with which we are affiliated become the target of criticism or abuse, we speak out in their defense; if they undertake an activity or project, we endorse and support it.

Loyalty to Country, Region, State, or City. People, as a general rule, have an affection for the locale in which they live and work. Southerners are well known for their loyalty to the South; Westerners for their admiration of the West. When individuals travel, they enjoy meeting and talking with persons "from home." When the name of their city or state is mentioned by a politician or entertainer, they often cheer and applaud.

Personal Enjoyment

Pleasures are many and varied, and people usually act to prevent their curtailment or to enhance their effect. Among the pleasures almost universally desired we find the enjoyment of comfort and luxury, beauty and order, sensory satisfactions, and relief from restrictions and restraints.

Enjoyment of Comfort and Luxury. Most people prefer to sit on a soft chair rather than a hard one, to sleep in a warm bed rather than a cold one. They would rather fly than ride long distances in a crowded bus, and take a cab rather than walk through a heavy rain. They enjoy living in a comfortable home or stopping at a luxuriously appointed hotel with impeccable dining-room service. One reason why people work hard to earn money is to be able to enjoy the comfort and luxury it will buy for them.

Enjoyment of Beauty and Order. Most of us like to have things clean and neat, even if we may not always want to expend the effort to keep them so. In the beauty of autumn foliage, in the cadence of the surf, or in the creation of a skilled artist there is an aesthetic pleasure that cannot be paralleled. But even a neat outline, an orderly boiler room, or a well-pressed suit contributes to one's aesthetic satisfaction. More than one customer has bought an automobile because of its luxurious appointments and beautiful body lines rather than because of its economy or mechanical excellence.

Enjoyment of Pleasant Sensations. Sights, sounds, smells, tastes, and feelings which gratify the sense-perceptors—the eyes, ears, nose, the palate, and the rest—give special pleasure to most people. Obviously, the pleasures derived from comfort, luxury, beauty, and order are closely associated with this type, because they also are sensory in nature. But sensory pleasure exists even without beauty or luxury; it is more direct in its appeal. Regardless of the comfort, luxury, beauty, or orderliness of the environment in which it may be served, the *taste* of roast turkey on Thanksgiving gives pleasure. The smell and taste of a pipe filled with rare tobacco or of a bowl of steaming vegetable soup are further evidence of the sensory satisfactions we may experience.

Enjoyment of Recreation. Who does not like to relax and to play? Crowded golf courses, the steady stream of tourists to vacation spots, the popularity of certain television programs, and the enormous sale of paperback novels give an overwhelming answer. Everyone enjoys breaking away from work and engaging in interesting activities which have no serious purpose. Show your audience the *fun* they will have in doing a certain thing, and their impulse to do it usually will grow strong.

Enjoyment of Relief from Restraint. Have you ever listened to the laughter and shouts of children when they are dismissed from school on Friday afternoon? Similarly, college students appreciate a holiday as a relief from the restraints of hard study and regular class attendance. Note also the joyous attitude of the person who has just been allowed to break away from a rigid diet or who is being released after a long stay in the hospital. The tendency to seek relief from restraint is prevalent in almost everyone.

Power, Authority, and Dominance

Most of us like to exert influence over others. People have given up lucrative positions to enter government service at a much smaller salary. Why? Among other reasons, because their power over others may be increased, and they may be able to influence the course of events. Few persons will refuse appointment to a position that gives them a greater measure of authority. Show your listeners the additional power your proposal will bring to them or to the group or nation to which they belong. For many individuals, self-advancement means not only an increased income but also an increase in power and authority. Together these two appeals may become strongly persuasive.

Pride

One of the most powerful single appeals that can be made is to pride, especially when you are dealing with young people. A varsity letter has little intrinsic value, but an unbelievable amount of work will be done to earn one. Election to an honorary society has more importance to the average student than a cash award. But the influence of pride is not limited to the young; from childhood to old age, we are extremely careful to protect our egos.

Pride manifests itself in numerous ways, but we shall note only three of them here: in *reputation*, in *self-respect*, and in *sound judgment*. As between reputation and self-regard, the desire for the latter is the more fundamental, but in many practical situations the desire for a good reputation has a more tangible appeal. Reputation is the estimate others have of you; self-respect is the opinion you wish to have of yourself. Most of us find it difficult to have one without the other. To influence an audience, then, show them what effect your idea or proposal will have on their reputation, but be careful not to suggest something incompatible with their self-respect.

Nearly everyone has pride in the soundness of his judgment, too. Often we feel competent to judge not only our own motives and feelings and courses of action, but also those of others. The desire to be thought "right" in all matters is a temptation hard to resist. We enjoy also trying to predict outcomes and the behavior of others. Indeed, one of the major purposes of the present chapter is to sharpen predictive capabilities in that very direction. In using pride as a motivational appeal, you should remember that — regardless of its manifestation — it is a powerful and very personal force. If you let listeners know, for instance, that you consider their judgment both sound and important to your proposal, you are almost sure to earn a respectful hearing. Be careful, however, not to make your appeal to pride too obvious. And, above all, be *sincere*. "Smooth" flattery and oily compliments often evoke a negative rather than a positive reaction.

Reverence or Worship

There are times when all of us are aware of a sense of our own inferiority in relation to a superior person or thing. We defer or we revere. This sentiment shows itself in a feeling of humility and a willingness to subordinate ourselves. It takes three common forms: *hero worship*, or the deep admiration of other persons; *reverence for traditions and institutions*; and *worship of a deity*, whether it be conceived religiously or as a philosophical concept.

The first of these, hero worship, is particularly observable in children; but it also exists in numerous adults, especially in their admiration of business, political, or social leaders and sports heroes whose personal qualities have made a strong impression on them. Certain traditions and institutions also evoke strong feelings of reverence: we sit quietly and with bared heads at a funeral; the school song brings us to our feet; we respect the voting booth as a cornerstone of democracy. The feeling of worship for a deity has come down to us through the ages. It shows itself formally in religious ceremonies, but even persons who reject formal religion may be awestruck by the immensity of the heavens or the fury of a storm. Whether one is a Christian, Jew, Buddhist, Mohammedan, or atheist, this feeling of reverence is nonetheless real. At times an appeal to reverence or worship may add a great deal of persuasive force to the speaker's remarks. Conversely, of course, he wisely respects the heroes, traditions, and religious attitudes of the listeners, and avoids the antagonism which opposition to them may bring.

Revulsion

The fragrance of a flower garden attracts people; the odor of a refuse heap repels them. Just as pleasant sensory experiences evoke enjoyment, so unpleasant sensations and perceptions arouse disgust or loathing. By showing the unsanitary conditions in a city's slums, you may create sentiment to clean them up. If you can make people disgusted with graft and corruption in public office, they probably will vote to eliminate it. By picturing the horrors of war in bloody detail, you may influence hearers who could not be reached by reasoned arguments alone. While doing these things, however, beware of rendering your descriptions so gruesome that your speech itself becomes revolting. Restraint is required to make a description of repulsive conditions vivid enough to be impressive without, at the same time, offending the sensibilities of the listeners.

Sexual Attraction

In the vast majority of cases, men strive for the attentions of women, and women seek to attract men. The importance of this force in human life needs no emphasis here. Whenever an act or a declaration promises to make us more attractive in the eyes of the opposite sex or to remove an obstacle to that attraction, it usually gains our support. The taboos that society has placed upon sexual matters, however, require that the speaker use care in referring to them. Despite "the new morality" about which we hear so much, most audiences still react negatively to stories, anecdotes, or jokes which treat sex in vulgar or "off-color" ways, or to language too heavily freighted with sexual terms and innuendos. Yet the appeal to sexual attractiveness itself is strong; and when used with skill and the appropriate restraints, it also supports other appeals a speaker may employ.

Sympathy and Generosity

Just as we are likely to identify ourselves with the groups to which we belong or aspire to belong, so we tend to see ourselves in the plight of those who are unfortunate. This feeling of compassion for the unhappy or the unlucky, which we here call sympathy, makes us want to help them. We pause to aid a blind man or to comfort a crying child. Out of generosity we give money to feed people whose homes have been ravaged by flood, earthquake, or fire. As a speaker, you may influence your audience by rousing in them the sentiment of sympathy or pity. To do so, however, remember that you must make it easy for them to identify themselves with the unfortunate ones, to put themselves in the other persons' shoes. You cannot accomplish this with statistics and abstractions; you must describe specifically, sympathetically, and compassionately the individuals to whom you refer, and you must depict their plight vividly.

SOME METHODS FOR MAKING MOTIVATIONAL APPEALS TO LISTENERS

The specific motive needs fleetingly noted in the preceding pages are typical of those to which you may appeal in your efforts to influence the attitudes, beliefs, values, and actions of your listeners. Remember, however, that although these motivational appeals may be made singly, more often they are *combined*. In fact, as you studied the various possibilities, you probably noticed that in many of the examples some appeal other than the one being illustrated was present. Suppose you are urging students to attend college. You might tell them that doing so will enable them to "get ahead" in the world more quickly and easily. But what is actually involved in this statement? What *appeals*, specifically, are you using? You are, of course, focusing upon your listeners' desire for greater income, the power inherent in higher positions, and the pride of a recognized station in life. All of these — acquisition, power, pride — you have combined into a *cluster:* a single pattern called "getting ahead."

Or let us take another common experience. Suppose you are trying to persuade your friend to buy a suit or a dress. What would influence his or her decision to make the purchase? One thing would be the price — *saving;* another would be its comfort and appearance — the *pleasure* to be derived from beauty or luxury; another would be the style of the garment — *imitation;* or its individuality of appearance — *independence;* and, finally, a combination of these motivational factors would make an appeal to *pride:* Would other people think the dress or suit in good taste? Would they envy your selection? Some of these desires might be stronger than others, and certain ones might conflict with certain others, but all of them would influence your friend's decision. He or she would be likely to buy the suit or the dress consistent with the effectiveness of your appeal to these particular desires.

Clearly, then, because motivational appeals are so closely related, often you will find it advantageous to use them in combination — in clusters — rather than singly when building a speech. Note, however, that if you use an excessive variety, you may dissipate the effect you want. Usually, therefore, select the two or three appeals you think will have the greatest effect upon your listeners and concentrate on these, treating other appeals as secondary or incidental. Be sure also that you do not inadvertently use conflicting appeals — for instance, do not urge your hearers to do something because of the *adventure* involved while, at the same time, describing it so vividly that they come to *fear* the act or its consequences. To avoid such conflicts, select your appeals carefully and examine them for clarity and consistency.

Taking careful cognizance of the strength and interplay of motive appeals, a student who was urging classmates to participate in intramural athletics chose the following as the main points for a speech:

1. Concentrated study without exercise will make your mind stale and ruin your grades (*fear*).
2. By playing with others intramurally, you will make new friends (*companionship*).
3. Intramural competition may lead to a place on a varsity team (*power and pride*).
4. You will have a great deal of fun playing (*enjoyment*).

In the complete development of the speech, the student made incidental motive appeals to her hearers by introducing the idea of *imitation* through examples of those who had previously engaged successfully in intramural sports; she stimulated the desire for *competition*; she pointed out to her listeners that participation would signify *loyalty* to the membership of their group; and she emphasized that participation in intramural sports would help them to build strong and healthy bodies. The principal appeals, however, she directed to the motives incorporated in the four main points of her message.

Precautions for Making Motivational Appeals

You must, of course, develop skill, tact, and good judgment in your use of these appeals. *Do not be blatant, objectionably obvious, and patently aggressive.* These behaviors create resistance in listeners—not acceptance or commitment. Do not say, as an extreme example, "Mr. Harlow Jones, the successful banker, has just contributed handsomely to our cause. Come on, now. *Imitate* this generous man!" Or, "If you give to this cause, we will print your name in the paper so that your *reputation* as a generous person will be known by everyone." Instead, in making an appeal of this kind, respect the intelligence and sensitivities of your listeners and suggest—through the use of descriptions and illustrations of desired actions—that contributors will not only be associated with others in a worthwhile and successful venture, but they will also have the sincere appreciation of many who are less fortunate than they.

Remember, also, that people generally are reluctant to acknowledge, by word or action, certain motives which privately may exert a very powerful influence upon them: acquisition, fear, imitation, sexual attraction, self-pride, etc. Therefore, when you elect to use such appeals, be careful to present them objectively and tastefully, and—above all—supplement or combine them with *other* motivational drives or desires which your hearers will probably be less reticent to have others recognize as the causes of their actions.

From a functional standpoint, then, and to sum up the thrust of this chapter, *the choice and phrasing of your motivational appeals should always be adapted to the beliefs, attitudes, and value-orientations of your listeners.* Do not expect, however, to be able to accomplish this with complete success on your first—or even your tenth—speaking experience. This capability cannot come easily or overnight: it must be the product of painstaking analysis, much thought, and arduous practice. But mastery is worth the effort if genuinely effective communication is your goal.

Remember, too, that certain attitudes, beliefs, and values will be more deeply and firmly embedded than others in the thought and behavior patterns of your hearers. As we learned in Chapter 8, either as a result of personal experience or because of repeated assertions by parents, teachers, respected friends, or accepted authority figures, people tend to develop strong opinions concerning many aspects of their environment. They are "for" or "against" legalized abortion, censorship of the mass media, freedom of sexual behavior, or a reduction in defense expenditures. They consider policemen, politicians, nurses, businessmen, lawyers, and communists as all good or all bad, unreliable or trustworthy, ignorant or intelligent. They like or dislike popular music, flashy clothes, mathematics, and travel by automobile.

Crystallized attitudes and opinions of these kinds as we now know, are usually based on a combination of basic wants and sensed needs. In the beginning, no doubt, these wants and needs were real enough; but over a period of time, the major underlying motivation to fulfill them has been frustrated and submerged — but not without leaving what is often a tenaciously held attitude or opinion which, in turn, has become the dominating influence. Therefore, as we stated at the outset, *with respect to any particular subject and purpose about which you wish to speak, you must consider not only the controlling motives of your hearers, but also the specific attitudes, opinions, beliefs, and value-orientations into which these motives have developed.* By associating your ideas and proposals with the positive attitudes of your audience and by avoiding negative associations, you can make your appeals stronger, more direct, and — above all — more truly functional.

FOOTNOTES

[1]*Richard V. Wagner and John J. Sherwood,* The Study of Attitude Change *(Belmont, Calif.: Brooks/Cole Publishing Company, 1969), pp. 1–3.*

[2]*Adaptation of "A Theory of Human Motivation" (including data for Diagram "A Hierarchy of Prepotent Needs") in* Motivation and Personality, *2nd Edition, by Abraham H. Maslow. Copyright, 1954 by Harper & Row, Publishers, Inc. Copyright © 1970 by Abraham H. Maslow. By permission of the publishers.*

[3]*Ibid.*

Problems and Probes

1. Clip and bring to class ten magazine advertisements which contain one or more motivational appeals. Name each appeal, tell why you think it was selected to sell this particular product, and evaluate its effectiveness. Note that often a motivational appeal may be used in an illustration as well as in the text of an advertisement. Also note that illustration and text may be used to reinforce each other and the motivational appeal(s) of the advertisement as a whole.

2. In your opinion, which motivational appeals are best adapted to persuading an audience of young persons? Of older persons? Of men? Of women? Defend your answers.

3. Name some appeals that might well be combined to *strengthen* a persuasive effort. Then name several appeals which, if combined, might *work against* each other.

4. Under what conditions would you consider a motive appeal to the wants or desires of listeners an entirely ethical and legitimate means of persuasion? Under what conditions might such an appeal be unethical? In answering, consider the subject matter of the speech and the situation in which it is made, as well as the nature of the appeal itself.

5. Looking back at the oral activities and speaking assignments in which you've participated thus far in this class, evaluate in your Personal Speech Journal how successful you feel that you and your classmates have been in using motivational appeals. Using your class as a hypothetical audience, decide *in general* which appeals would probably be most effective and which ones would be least effective. Keep these in mind in future speech preparations for this course.

6. Assuming your speech class to be the audience, which motive appeals do you think would best support each of the following propositions? Which motive appeals probably would be most effective if you were opposing these same propositions?

> Fraternities and sororities should be abolished.
> Books and magazines should be censored to protect public morals.
> The United States should disarm unilaterally.
> Attend the movies regularly.
> Eat less and live longer.

7. If a speaker with whom you disagree attempts to persuade you through the use of motive appeals, how do you think the effect of that persuasion may best be combatted? By presenting appeals which work at cross-purposes with his (fear against self-enhancement, etc.)? By explaining to the audience the appeals with which he is trying to move them? By presenting evidence and arguments to the contrary? Why do you answer as you do?

8. In Chapter 8, Problem 6, you were asked to locate a printed speech or attend a speech in which the values, beliefs, and attitudes of the audience were hostile or—at best—apathetic to the purpose of the speaker and to analyze how the speaker endeavored to overcome the listeners' apparent reluctance to accept him and his message. Recalling that speech and your analysis, describe the motive appeals that the speaker used to win over his audience and make his points.

Oral Activity and Speaking Assignment

1. Present a three- or four-minute speech in which, through the combined use of two or three related motive appeals, you attempt to persuade your audience to a particular belief or action. (For example, combine *adventure*, *companionship*, and *personal enjoyment* to persuade them to take a conducted group tour of Europe; or combine *sympathy* and *pride* to elicit contributions to a charity drive.) At the conclusion of your speech, have one member of the class attempt to determine which motive appeals you were using. If there is any question about what these appeals were, explore with him and the rest of the class the reasons why they were not made clear. Consider also after each speech how the motive appeals could have been sharpened and strengthened.

Suggestions for Further Reading

Robert Bostrom, "Motivation and Argument," *Perspectives on Argumentation*, ed. Gerald R. Miller and Thomas R. Nilsen (Glenview, Ill.: Scott, Foresman and Company, 1966), pp. 110–128.

Roger Brown, *Social Psychology* (New York: The Free Press, 1965), Chapter XI, "The Principle of Consistency in Attitude Change," pp. 549–609.

Gary Cronkhite, *Persuasion: Speech and Behavioral Change* (Indianapolis: The Bobbs-Merrill Company, Inc., 1969), Chapter VII, "The Persuader's Choices," pp. 172–211.

Walter Fisher, "A Motive View of Communication," *Quarterly Journal of Speech* LVI (April 1970): 131–139.

Ralph N. Haber, ed., *Current Research in Motivation* (New York: Holt, Rinehart & Winston, Inc., 1966).

Abraham Maslow, *Motivation and Personality*, 2nd ed. (New York: Harper & Row, Publishers, 1970), Chapter IV, pp. 35–58.

Gerald R. Miller and Murray A. Hewgill, "Some Recent Research on Fear-Arousing Message Appeals," *Speech Monographs* XXXIII (November 1966): 377–391.

Ivan L. Preston, "Relationships Among Emotional, Intellectual, and Rational Appeals in Advertising," *Speech Monographs* XXXV (November 1968): 504–511.

10
LOCATING AND CLASSIFYING SPEECH INFORMATION

USEFUL SOURCES OF MESSAGE MATERIALS

To speak knowledgeably and clearly about a subject you will usually need to find out more about that subject than you already know, and in preparing for any communicative encounter — whether with one other person, a small group, or a large audience — you will need to review the pertinent information you have and to classify it. The purpose of this chapter is to suggest briefly the various sources from which the substance of your messages may be drawn and to explain a practical method for recording and classifying the materials you will need. Draw first, of course, upon your own personal knowledge and perceptions — the things that you yourself have observed and experienced.

Personal Experience

A good way to begin your search for speech materials is to jot down on a piece of paper everything you already know about the subject as a result of personal experience or observation. Then, insofar as possible, add to these data by further observation and/or personal experimentation. As we have already emphasized in Chapter 7, you can expect to speak best about people, ideas, and events that you know best; and you know best those things you have actually seen, heard, touched, tasted, smelled, or done. Even when your direct sensory experience with the subject cannot appropriately be cited in your message, it will sharpen your perspective or provide insight into the subject — something which almost invariably makes for greater clarity and vividness of expression. In short, make personal experience and observation your first and, whenever possible, your principal source of speech substance.

Often, of course, you will be called upon to speak about matters which have not fallen within the range of your personal experience and observation. At such times, you must look outside yourself for the necessary information. In these instances, there are several possibilities open to you: interviews with experts in the field, letters and questionnaires, publications of all kinds, radio, and television. We will turn our attention now to these various sources, and consider how you can use them to the best advantage in accumulating substantive materials for your speech messages.

Interviews

Beginning speakers often fail to realize that vast amounts of useful and authoritative information may be gathered merely by asking questions of the right persons.* If, for example, you expect to talk about interplanetary navigation, what better-informed and more convenient source of information could there be than a member of your college's astronomy department? Or if you are to discuss a problem in national or international affairs, why not talk first with a trained political scientist? Nearly all faculty members are willing to talk with you on questions pertaining to their special fields of interest. In your town or community also you usually will find one or more experts on nearly any topic you choose to speak about. Of course, you must avoid being bothersome or pushy in approaching these persons, and you must respect their time and schedules. But brief interviews, properly arranged and scheduled along the lines we recommended in Chapter 2, frequently can yield invaluable factual data; and, what is even more important, they can be a source of authoritative interpretations and opinions. As we have urged before, to save the time of the person you interview and to ensure getting the specific information you desire, make an appointment in advance, and prepare for the meeting by writing out the questions you particularly want answered.

During the interview itself, remember that your purpose is to obtain facts and judgments from the expert, not to argue with him by expressing your own views. If your opinions are asked for, state them, of course; but do so as briefly and as objectively as possible. At the same time, make sure that you understand the meaning and significance of the expert's remarks and make careful mental notes of his major ideas or arguments. Immediately after the interview, reduce these to a written record; and if you plan to quote the expert directly, give him an opportunity to verify the accuracy and completeness of the statements you attribute to him.

Even if an interview provides you with no facts or opinions that you can quote directly in your speech, it probably will give you a broader outlook on the problem and will suggest new sources of information. Do not, however, always limit yourself to interviews with experts. Try to find out also what the proverbial "man on the street" thinks. Such information, in addition to being used in your

---

*In this regard, review the material on the information-seeking interview in Chapter 2, pp. 49–55.

speech itself, often will provide you with guidelines for adapting your ideas to the persons in your audience.

Letters and Questionnaires

If it is impossible to talk with an expert directly, you can sometimes obtain information through correspondence. If you write to such a person, however, be sure that you make clear exactly what information you want and why you want it. Moreover, be reasonable in your request. Do not expect a busy individual to spend hours or days gathering facts for you. Above all, do not ask him for information that you yourself could find if you were willing to search for it. Write to an expert only after you have exhausted other resources available to you.

When there is controversy on some point and you want to get a cross section of the varying opinions, send a questionnaire to a number of people and compare their answers. This method is valuable, but has been somewhat overused. As a result, many people will merely discard a questionnaire, particularly a long one. Therefore, make your questions as easy to answer as possible, and keep the list of questions brief. Always enclose a stamped, self-addressed envelope for the reply. If you can find out an individual's name, address him personally instead of mailing your questionnaire to a general address.

Even in those cases, however, where the substance of your speech comes from questionnaires, interviews, and personal experience, it usually will have to be supplemented by *printed* data. The most abundant source of speech materials, of course, is printed matter—newspapers, magazines, and books.

Newspapers

Newspapers obviously are a useful source of information about events of current interest. Moreover, their feature stories and accounts of unusual happenings provide a storehouse of interesting illustrations and examples. You must be careful, of course, not to accept as true everything printed in a newspaper, for the immediacy and haste with which news is gathered sometimes makes complete accuracy impossible. Your school or city library undoubtedly keeps on file copies of one or two highly reliable papers such as *The New York Times*, *The Observer*, or the *Christian Science Monitor*, and probably also provides a selection from among the leading newspapers of your state or region. If your library has *The New York Times*, it probably has the published index to that paper also; and by using it, you can locate accounts of men and events from 1913 to the present. Another useful and well-indexed source of information on current happenings is *Facts on File*, issued weekly since 1940.

Magazines

An average-sized university library subscribes annually to thousands of magazines and periodicals. Among those of general interest, some—such as *Time, Newsweek,* and *U. S. News and World Report*—summarize weekly events. *The Atlantic* and *Harper's* are representative of a group of monthly publications which cover a wide range of subjects of both passing and permanent importance. Such magazines as *The Nation, Vital Speeches of the Day, Fortune,* and *The New Republic* contain comment on current political, social, and economic questions. Discussions of popular scientific interest appear in *Popular Science, Scientific American,* and *Popular Mechanics.* For other specialized areas, there are such magazines as *Sports Illustrated, Field and Stream, Saturday Review World, Better Homes and Gardens, Today's Health, National Geographic Magazine,* and *American Heritage.*

This list is, of course, merely suggestive of the wide range of materials to be found in periodicals. When you are looking for a specific kind of information, use the *Readers' Guide to Periodical Literature,* which indexes most of the magazines you will want to refer to in preparing a speech. Look in this index under various topical headings that are related to your subject. Similar indexes also are available for technical journals and publications.

Information concerning specific aspects of speech communication and related fields of study are contained in a variety of professional journals, prominent among them, these: *Theatre Crafts, The Journal of Communication, The Quarterly Journal of Speech, Southern Speech Communication Journal, The Speech Teacher, Speech Monographs, Theatre Quarterly, Educational Theatre Journal, Central States Speech Journal, Western Speech, Journal of Speech and Hearing Disorders, Journal of Broadcasting,* and *Today's Speech.* As a student of speech communication, you should find such journals especially useful. Your library may have some or all of them, as well as others in the same or related subject-matter areas.

Professional and Trade Journals

Nearly every profession, industry, trade, and academic field has one or more specialized journals. Such publications include: *American Academy of Political and Social Science Annals, American Economic Review, Quarterly Journal of Communication, American Medical Association Journal, Journal of Applied Psychology, AFL-CIO American Federationist, Trades Unionist, Coal Age, Educational Theatre Journal*, and others. These journals contain a great deal of detailed and specialized information in their respective fields.

Yearbooks and Encyclopedias

The *Statistical Abstract of the United States* is the most reliable source of comprehensive data on a wide variety of subjects ranging from weather records and birth rates to steel production and population figures. It is published by the federal government and is available in most libraries. Also useful as a source of facts and figures is the *World Almanac*, the *Book of Facts*, and — as previously mentioned — *Facts on File*. Encyclopedias such as the *Encyclopaedia Britannica* and *Americana Encyclopedia*, which attempt to cover the entire field of human knowledge in a score of volumes, are valuable chiefly as an initial reference source or for information on subjects which you do not need to explore deeply. Refer to them for important scientific, geographical, literary, or historical facts, and also for bibliographies of authoritative books on a subject.

Special Documents and Reports

Various government agencies — state, national, and international — as well as many independent organizations publish reports on special subjects. Among government publications, those most frequently consulted by speakers are the reports of Congressional committees or those of the United States Department of Labor or of Commerce. Reports on agricultural problems, business, government, engineering, and scientific experimentation are issued by many state universities. Such endowed organizations as the Carnegie, Rockefeller, and Ford Foundations, and such groups as the Foreign Policy Association, the League of Women Voters, and the United States Chamber of Commerce also publish reports and pamphlets.

Books on Special Subjects

There are few subjects suitable for a speech upon which someone has not written a book. As a guide to these books, use the subject-matter headings in the card catalog of your library.

General Literature

Wide reading in general literature provides a speaker with a wealth of illustrations and literary allusions which frequently can be used to illuminate an idea. Quick sources of apt quotations are Bartlett's *Familiar Quotations*, H. L. Mencken's *A New Dictionary of Quotations on Historical Principles from Ancient and Modern Sources*, Arthur Richmond's *Modern Quotations for Ready Reference*, George Seldes' *The Great Quotations*, and Burton Stevenson's *The Home Book of Quotations*.

Biographies

Detailed accounts of the lives of famous persons often furnish material for illustrating or amplifying ideas. *The Dictionary of National Biography* (deceased Britishers), the *Dictionary of American Biography* (deceased Americans), *Who's Who* (living Britishers), *Who's Who in America*, *Current Biography*, and similar collections contain biographical sketches especially useful in locating facts about famous people and in finding the qualifications of authorities whose testimony you may wish to quote.

Radio and Television Broadcasts

Lectures, debates, and the formal public addresses of leaders in business and government frequently are broadcast over radio and television; and many of these talks later are mimeographed or printed by the stations or by the organizations that sponsor them. Usually, copies may be obtained on request. If no manuscript is available and you are taking notes or making a tape as you hear the broadcast, listen with particular care in order to get an exact record of the speaker's words or meaning. Just as you must quote items from other sources accurately and honestly, so you are obligated to respect the remarks someone has made on a radio or television broadcast and to give that person full credit.

Obviously, you will not have to investigate all of the foregoing sources for every speech you make or for every conversation or discussion in which you participate. Your personal experience often will provide you with adequate knowledge, or you will need to locate only a few additional facts. Usually, however, a search among several outside sources will provide you with material that will make your speech more authoritative and interesting. Even though laborious at first, a careful investigation of these sources will be doubly valuable because you will be learning how to skim rapidly through a mass of material to pick out the important facts and ideas. This skill is valuable not only in preparing speeches, but also in every type of work where research into printed materials is required.

RECORDING THE SPEECH COMMUNICATION MATERIAL

Have you ever begun to tell a story only to find that the essential details have slipped your mind entirely? Or have you ever tried in vain to recall an important date or name? Since it is impossible to remember everything you read or hear, you must have some method for recording potential speech materials. Moreover, it is important that you *record immediately* any data which you think may later prove useful. All too often, to recover a fact or idea after a period of days or weeks, you must engage in a long and laborious search, and sometimes you lose the fact or idea forever.

Some persons prefer to keep their notes in notebooks, but for most research purposes notebooks are not as efficient as cards. Use a size that will best suit your inclination and purpose (3" × 5" is recommended), and carry a few of them in your pocket or briefcase for use whenever you encounter an idea you wish to preserve. Keep your completed cards permanently in a classified file where they will be easy to sort and rearrange when you begin to organize your speech. Moreover, statistics or quotations which you wish to present to your audience verbatim may be read directly and unobtrusively from the card itself.

In preparing notecards observe the following rules:

Place in the upper left-hand corner a subject heading which accurately labels the material recorded on the card. Such a heading will greatly facilitate the process of classifying and selecting when you begin to put your speech into final form.

Note in the upper right-hand corner the part or section of your speech in which the information on the card probably will be used. Will it help to develop or illustrate the problem with which you are concerned? Will it prove the soundness of the solution you propose? Will it point to certain benefits or advantages to be gained from acting according to your recommendations? If it is not possible to decide upon the proper classificatory label during the early stages of your speech preparation, leave the space blank to be filled in later.

Put only one fact or idea, or a few closely related facts or ideas, on each card. Unless you follow this rule, you will not be able to sort and classify the data properly, or to have at hand the specific information needed to develop a particular part of your talk.

Indicate verbatim quotations by quotation marks. In the first sample card (Figure 1, facing page), the note is a direct quotation and therefore carries quotation marks. Use direct quotations when they are sufficiently brief or when they

Evaluation of Intelligence
Tests

Soundness of Proposed
School Testing Program

   "The measurement of intelligence is psychology's most telling
accomplishment to date. Without intending to belittle other
psychological ventures, it may fairly be said that nowhere else--
not in psychotherapy, educational reform, or consumer research--
has there arisen so potent an instrument as the objective measure
of intelligence."

Richard Herrnstein, "I.Q.," The Atlantic, CCXXVII (September
1971), 45.

Figure 1. SOURCE-MATERIAL NOTECARD WITH DIRECT QUOTATION

Expenditures for Public
School Education

Problem: Need for Federal
Aid to Education

School year	Total	Total per Pupil
1929/1930	$ 2,316,790,000	$108
1939/1940	2,344,049,000	106
1949/1950	5,837,643,000	259
1951/1952	7,344,237,000	313
1953/1954	9,092,449,000	351
1955/1956	10,955,047,000	388
1957/1958	13,569,163,000	449
1959/1960	$15,613,255,000	$472
1961/1962	18,373,339,000	518
1963/1964	21,324,993,000	559
1965/1966	26,195,500,000	652
1967/1968	31,511,051,000	750
1968/1969	35,511,170,000	834
1969/1970	40,561,997,000	959

The New York Times Encyclopedic Almanac, 1971, ed. Lee Foster
(New York: The New York Times, 1970), p. 660.

Figure 2. SOURCE-MATERIAL NOTECARD WITH STATISTICS

state facts or ideas so clearly or forcefully that you probably will want to reproduce the original wording in your speech. Condense or paraphrase longer or less important statements; but in doing so, be sure to preserve the author's meaning.

Note at the bottom of the card the exact source from which the information is drawn. This point cannot be stressed too strongly. Often you will want to recheck a note for accuracy or completeness, or you may be called upon to verify the facts or figures you cite. For both of these reasons it is important that you have an exact record of the source from which you have drawn the information. (See Figure 2, page 295.)

CLASSIFYING THE MATERIALS COLLECTED FOR THE SPEECH

When you first begin to gather material, a simple topical method of classification usually is satisfactory. Group your notecards together according to the apparent similarity of the headings which you have placed in the upper left corner. As the number of cards increases, however, you will need a more systematic and somewhat more precise method. Here are a few possibilities:

Chronological method. You may classify your material on the basis of the time to which it refers — by years, by months, or by its relation to some fixed event.

Causal method. This method divides material relating to the apparent causes of a phenomenon from material relating to its probable effects.

Problem-solution method. Here the facts about a *problem* are put into one group, and the descriptions of the various *solutions* and the evidence which seemingly supports them are put into another.

Geographical method. When this method is used, the material is divided according to the communities, cities, counties, countries, states, or other localities to which it refers.

Begin by classifying your notes according to one of these methods or one equally appropriate to your purpose. Then as the carded data in any category become bulky or unwieldy, subdivide that class.

The value of classifying your material as you gather it is twofold. *First, you can see at a glance the kinds of information you lack and, in this way, can make your further investigations more purposeful. Second, the organization of the material into a speech is made much simpler if the material is in some reasonable order before the actual organizing process begins.* If you follow a systematic method of filing speech materials over a period of time, you will have a steadily growing mass of available information for future use.

The gathering, recording, and classifying of the data to be used in the speech comprise no small part of the total task of message preparation. Therefore, you will do well to begin your research early enough so that you have plenty of time to digest the information that you collect, organize it, and practice presenting it in its finished form.

Problems and Probes

1. Visit your college library and list the following:
   a. Five yearbooks or compilations of statistical data.
   b. Four encyclopedias, with some indication of the kind of information in which each specializes.
   c. Three technical or scholarly journals relating to your present or proposed major in college.
   d. Two indexes to periodical literature other than the *Readers' Guide*.
   e. Five biographical dictionaries.
   f. Two standard atlases of the world.
   g. Two reference works that list books in print.

2. Examine carefully selected cards in the card catalog of your library, and answer the following questions:
   a. How many times is each book listed in the catalog, and *how* is it listed?
   b. What information about the author is given on the catalog card?
   c. What information does the card give you about the book itself?

3. Without the help of the reference librarian, answer the following questions and name the sources in which you found the answers:
   a. How many miles of interstate highways have been completed to date?
   b. What was the size of the American expeditionary force in Europe during World War I? During World War II?
   c. Where did the governor of your state attend college?
   d. How many hits were collected by the baseball team that won the World Series in 1973?
   e. How did the senators from your state vote on the last military appropriations bill?
   f. Who is the author of *Future Shock?* Who is the publisher? Has the author written other books also? If so, what are their titles and when were they published?
   g. How many articles on trade with Africa were published during the first four months of 1971?

    h. How much does your state government contribute to the support of the schools in your community?

    i. What are five recent books on corporation finance?

4. Select a subject of some substance and scope on which you would like to give a classroom speech in the future.

    a. Jot down in proper note form all the pertinent information you already have on this subject.

    b. Indicate the firsthand observations you can make concerning it.

    c. List persons whom you could interview on the subject, and decide what questions you would ask each one.

    d. Devise a sample questionnaire on the subject and indicate the groups or individuals to whom it might be sent.

    e. Prepare a bibliography of printed materials on the subject, including (*a*) five references taken from an index to periodicals, and (*b*) five books found in the card catalog of your library.

5. Read selected articles or books on a subject of your choice; and, following the samples shown in Figures 1 and 2, page 295, prepare five or six notecards, at least one of which presents *statistics*, one *a direct quotation*, one *an indirect quotation*, and one *an illustration* or *example*.

6. On slips of paper write three questions beginning, "Where would you go to find out about _____?" Put these questions in a hat with those submitted by your classmates and take turns drawing them out and answering them.

7. Evaluate radio and television newscasts and public service programs as sources of speech materials, and be prepared to answer the following questions: What advantages do they have over printed sources? What disadvantages? What special rules or cautions should be observed when gathering materials from these sources?

Oral Activities and Speaking Assignments

1. Practice gathering speech materials through interviews. Use the following procedure: Select five or six persons in your speech class who because of work experience, travel, service in the armed forces, hobbies, or other personal involvement have acquired a considerable amount of knowledge concerning a certain subject. After your instructor has paired you with one of these individuals, *interview* him or her, following the suggestions set forth in this chapter and also in Chapter 2, pages 48–55. Make sure that

you have a series of questions planned in advance, that you interpret correctly the information you are given, that you record it accurately, and that you subsequently verify with the informant any statements which you might want to quote verbatim.

2. Prepare and present a five-minute speech on any subject that you believe will be of interest to your classmates. (Review Chapter 8, "Analyzing the Audience and Occasion.") In this speech, use material gathered from personal experience, from interviews, and from printed sources. In addition to the usual outline, hand to your instructor a dozen properly prepared notecards on which you have recorded the material gathered in interviews and from printed sources.

Suggestions for Further Reading

Ella V. Aldrich, *Using Books and Libraries*, 5th ed. (Englewood Cliffs, N.J.: Prentice-Hall, Inc., 1967).

Jacques Barzun and Henry P. Graff, *The Modern Researcher* (New York: Harcourt Brace Jovanovich, Inc., 1957), Chapter IV, "Finding the Facts," pp. 61–87.

Donald C. Bryant and Karl R. Wallace, *Fundamentals of Public Speaking*, 4th ed. (New York: Appleton-Century-Crofts, 1969), Chapter VI, "Finding and Handling Materials," pages 68–81.

Douglas Ehninger and Wayne Brockriede, *Decision by Debate* (New York: Dodd, Mead & Company, 1963), Chapter IV, "Obtaining Information: Personal Knowledge, Contacts with Experts"; Chapter V, "Obtaining Information: Printed Sources"; Chapter VI, "Recording and Filing Information."

Raymond L. Gordon, *Interviewing: Strategy, Techniques, and Tactics* (Homewood, Illinois: Dorsey Press, 1969), Chapter IV, "Interviewing Strategy"; Chapter V, "Techniques in Interviewing"; and Chapter VI, "Tactics in the Interview."

James D. Lester, *Writing Research Papers: A Complete Guide* (Glenview, Ill.: Scott, Foresman and Company, 1967), Chapter III, "The Library," pages 15–34.

Stephen A. Richardson, Barbara Snell Dohrenwend, and David Klein, *Interviewing: Its Forms and Functions* (New York: Basic Books, Inc., Publishers, 1965), Part III, "The Question-Answer Process."

Eugene E. White, *Practical Public Speaking*, 2nd ed. (New York: The Macmillan Company, 1964), Part II, "Preparing the Speech."

11
SUPPORTING THE MAJOR IDEAS

Most persons, especially when they are members of a sizeable audience, find it difficult to understand abstract ideas, bare and unadorned. Nor will they easily believe a proposition or act upon a proposal without stimulation or proof. Suppose, for example, that the purpose of your speech is to explain why devaluation of the dollar discourages imports or to prove that as a result of recent efforts social conditions in our inner cities have been materially improved. How is the average person likely to react to each of these ideas initially? In the first instance, he may very well say, "I do not understand why devaluation should affect imports. Please explain the relationship." In the second, he probably would say, "I doubt (or disbelieve) that social conditions in our inner cities have been materially improved. Please prove your statement."

These reactions would not occur because the hearer is dull or obstinate, but would reflect a human inability to comprehend abstract ideas and relationships without sufficient explanation or discussion, and a natural reluctance to accept a claim as true until appropriate evidence and reasoning have been offered on its behalf. Materials which provide the explanation and proof upon which understanding and belief rest are called *supporting materials.* Their purpose is to clarify, amplify, or establish as warranted the major ideas or contentions you wish to communicate. Without supporting material, the thoughts you present may be as well organized as the bones in a skeleton, but they will be equally bare and unappealing. The supporting materials are the flesh and blood which bring these ideas to life. The thought-skeleton of a speech must be there to give it unity and coherence, but it is the meat you put on that skeleton that gives it body and warmth and reality for your listeners. The leading ideas must be fleshed out with facts and examples that make them clear and convincing—with verbal materials that are concrete and specific—and, when appropriate, with such nonverbal supports as charts, diagrams, and models.

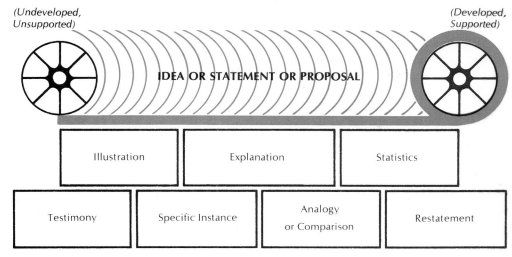

Figure 1. FORMS OF VERBAL SUPPORT FOR AN IDEA

VERBAL SUPPORTING MATERIAL: TYPES AND USES

In general, there are seven forms of verbal support which may be used to develop the ideas in a speech:

1. Explanation
2. Analogy or comparison
3. Illustration (detailed example)
   a. Hypothetical illustration
   b. Factual illustration
4. Specific instances (undeveloped examples)
5. Statistics
6. Testimony
7. Restatement

Often two or more of these forms are combined, as when statistics or examples are used within an illustration, or an analogy is offered by way of explanation. As you consider the following descriptions and analyses of these seven types of material, notice that the first three (explanation, analogy, and illustration), though they sometimes are employed as proof, are primarily useful in making an idea clear or vivid; while the next three (specific instances, statistics, and testimony) usually have as their principal function establishing and verifying the truth or importance of a contention the speaker wishes to prove. Restatement, as we shall learn, serves both purposes.

Explanation

By definition, an *explanation* is an expository or descriptive passage, the purpose of which is to make a term, concept, process, or proposal clear and intelligible.

Usually, explanation depends on simple exposition or description. It may, however, also proceed by showing the relationship between a whole and its parts, or may be reinforced by examples, statistics, or other forms of support. The first of these possibilities is illustrated by Mortimer J. Adler's attempt to make clear his conception of a liberal education.

Liberal education means two things essentially. On the side of the liberal arts, it means all the basic skills of the mind—the skills of reading and writing and speaking and listening, observing, measuring, and calculating; the skills essential to all forms of learning; the skills required for all forms of communication. And on the side of substance, liberal education means the humanities, which centuries ago would have been called "humane letters." By that, one does not just mean poetry or history, but even more philosophy and theology, and even the natural and social sciences when these are studied with a humane rather than a technical interest.

Let me explain this one step further. The humanities, as the word itself should suggest, represent the permanent and universal features of human life and society, which stem from the constancy of human nature itself—the powers and aspirations of man. Hence philosophy and theology are central and must be central in any humanistic education. As Cardinal Newman has taught us all, to be basically liberal, education must be through and through philosophical and theological.[1]

On the other hand, Dr. Marvin A. Block, former chairman of the AMA Committee on Alcoholism, introduced examples to help explain the factors present in disease:

Almost every disease depends for its existence upon factors whose recognition establishes its identity. There must be a host, whether an individual, a group, or an entire population; there must be a vector or causative agent, and there is also the immediate and overall environment which contributes to a greater or lesser degree to the host's ability to resist the onslaughts of the causative agents. The mere presence of the latter does not necessarily mean that the assaulted host will succumb. The built-in resistance of one host may be stronger than that of another, or it may be protective against one particular disease but not against another. The environment may be such as will either block or favor the eruption of a specific malady, depending entirely upon that environment's effect upon the causative agent—as in the case of infections—or upon the resistance of the individual as established through background and training and expressed in terms of physical health and endurance. Many other factors may combine with these to prepare a person or population for resisting any illness, or for overcoming it in its early stages without their ever being aware of its presence. This has been particularly so in the case of poliomyelitis. Many individuals have been found to have unknowingly contracted this dread disease and to have recovered from its early stages with no knowledge of what they had been through. Tuberculosis offers similar evidence of certain individuals having overcome the illness in its mild form without impairment of their general health and without ever having been aware of the true nature of their involvement.[2]

Finally, in explaining the problem created by an unfavorable balance of payments in the international market, James F. Oates, Jr., Chairman of the Board of the Equitable Life Assurance Society, depended chiefly on statistics:

But let me first review, very briefly, the problem we face with our balance of payments. For seven years, 1958 through 1964, the United States has continuously had a deficit in its international payments accounts. As you know, this means simply that the United States has, during each of these years, spent, loaned, or invested abroad more than foreigners have purchased, loaned, or invested in this country. The total accumulated deficit during these seven years amounted to $21 billion computed on the conventional basis. This deficit was financed by exporting roughly $7 billion of gold and $14 billion of dollar claims. The U.S. gold stock is now down to $14 billion, and outstanding dollar claims in the hands of foreigners exceed $30 billion.

Our failure to correct the deficit has opened to question the very integrity of the U.S. dollar, its role as a reserve currency, and the continued survival of the free world monetary system. So far this year we have lost $1.5 billion of gold. Unless this outflow is stopped, there will come a time when we can no longer provide gold for dollars at a rate of $35 per ounce.[3]

Valuable as explanation is in making ideas clear, two cautions must be observed in its use: First, *do not allow your explanations to become too long or involved;* and, second, *do not talk in vague or abstract terms.* Many an audience has been put to sleep by a long-winded explanation filled with unimportant or irrelevant details or by one conducted in language so vague and general that it was almost impossible to follow. Keep your explanations simple, brief, and accurate; combine them with other forms of supporting material so as to make your ideas concrete and specific. These are good rules to follow in all forms of communication, written as well as oral.

Analogy or Comparison

In an analogy or comparison, similarities are pointed out between something that is already known, understood, or believed by the listeners and something that is not. Thus you might explain the game of cricket by comparing it with baseball, or tell how a thermostat works by comparing it with a simple temperature thermometer.

At times, an idea also may be clarified by comparing it with something which, though quite different in nature, exhibits similar characteristics or relationships. Dr. Louis Hadley Evans, minister-at-large for the Presbyterian Church, used these brief analogies to distinguish between the terms *deist* and *theist*:

> To you the world is what: a clock or a car? Is it a huge clock, that God once made, that He wound up at the beginning and left it to run of itself? Then you are a *deist.*
>
> Do you believe that it is rather a car that God once made, but that does not run without His hand on the wheel, without His ultimate and personal control? Then you are a *theist.*[4]

The rapid rate at which new information is accumulated in the modern world and the rapid rate at which that information becomes outmoded were described by Peter G. Peterson, former president of Bell and Howell, by referring to a flooded river:

> In the space age, the flow of knowledge is as relentless and in a real sense as uncompromising as this spring's Mississippi River. It imposes on us the stiff and, in many ways, new requirement that we not merely adjust but that we *anticipate* the future.[5]

Still another analogy of the same type appears in a speech in which Albert Wass de Czege, a Hungarian writer, urged an American audience to preserve their freedom by accepting their responsibilities:

> If you want to live in your own home, you have to take care of the roof, paint the walls, watch for termites, and repair whatever needs to be repaired. If you are too lazy to do all that, you can live in an apartment, and in this case someone else will do all these things for you. However, the one who owns the building in which you decide to live will have the right to tell you what kind of pets you can have, how many children, and what colors you can use to paint your rooms.
>
> The same is true about your country. You can keep it a private home that suits your needs, your own way of life. Or you can concentrate it

into a huge apartment house in which the government will tell you how to live, as is done in the communist dominated countries. It is entirely up to you.[6]

Although analogies which compare things that are unlike—the world with a clock or a car, knowledge with rivers, your country with your residence, and so forth—may be excellent means of clarifying a point or making it vivid, they generally are of limited value as proof. For this purpose it is always more effective to employ comparisons of *like* phenomena—to argue, for example, that a system of one-way traffic on the downtown streets of City X would relieve congestion and promote safety because such a system has had these effects in City Y, or that a longer orientation period would improve the academic performance of freshmen students at College A because it has done so at College B. Note how a comparison of like phenomena—in this case, two state universities—was used to prove one of the claims advanced in a student speech by George Gruner:

> To show that an active and effective student government would help to reduce disciplinary problems at Iowa, we may refer to the experience of the university I attended before transferring here last fall—a school which, like Iowa, has between 15,000 and 16,000 students and which is a publicly supported state institution.
>
> Prior to reconstituting student government as a vital responsible force, the office of the dean at my former university handled more than 600 disciplinary cases each year. After putting new responsibility and authority into the hands of the students themselves, however, this number was cut by more than half, and the number of merely trivial or nuisance offenses decreased by about two-thirds. The dean himself attributed this reduction chiefly to the new sense of pride which a revitalized student government had given the students in their school.[7]

Because it attempts to base a conclusion on a single parallel instance, an analogy used as proof must meet a rigid test. And this is that the instances compared must be *closely similar in all essential respects.* Whether giving more authority to student government at Iowa would have the effect predicted, for instance, would depend upon the extent to which Iowa actually did resemble Mr. Gruner's previous school in size, composition of student body, administrative structure, and similarly pertinent qualities. Clearly, you could not infer that what worked in a small denominational college also would work in a large state university or that an effect achieved in a select private school also would be achieved in an institution whose student body is more varied. Do the similarities between the items or classes compared outweigh any differences that might be relevant to the conclusion you are drawing? This is the question that always must be asked when you attempt to use an analogy as proof for a contention or claim.

Illustration

An illustration is a detailed example cast into narrative form which serves to make vivid and concrete the idea it is intended to support. Sometimes it pictures the results that might be attained by adopting the proposal the speaker advocates; sometimes it describes in detail a case *typical* of the general conditions the speaker wishes to emphasize. In either case, it has two principal characteristics: (1) the illustration is in narrative form—recounts a happening or tells a story; and (2) the details of the story are vividly described. There are two principal types of illustrations: hypothetical and factual. The former describes an *imaginary situation;* the latter reports what *actually happened.*

Hypothetical Illustration

A hypothetical illustration, although it is an imaginary narrative, must be consistent with the known facts; it must seem probable or likely. The following is such an illustration:

> Let's put ourselves in the other fellow's place. If you got no satisfaction out of your job as employer, if you had no pride in the sense of accomplishment, if you didn't feel yourself a vital part of a dynamic organization, all the pay you would get would be money. Take away all those things that make up your compensation, and every one of you would demand that your pay be doubled, because money would be all that was left.
>
> Out in your shop a man comes to work at 7 A.M. He doesn't know too much about his job and almost nothing about his company or how his work fits into it. He works 8 hours and goes home—with what? His pay and nothing more. Nobody (except the union steward!) took much, if any, notice of him. Nobody complimented him if he did do well because nobody except a foreman *knows* whether or not he did well, and he realized *that* fact. Nobody ever flattered him by asking his opinion about something. In millions of cases nobody ever told him the importance of his work.
>
> At night he goes home to his family and neighbors—unimportant, with nothing to boast about or even talk about. But suppose the union calls a meeting to discuss a grievance—that workman can get up on his feet and sound off while people listen, he can be an officer with a title, he can boast to his family and friends how he "gave those big shots of the company what-for!" A strike vote is exciting!—Being a picket is important!—He gets looked at and talked about; he wears a badge!
>
> Again let's be honest. If you and I were in that worker's situation, wouldn't we do pretty much what he's doing?[8]

The hypothetical illustration is used principally to make an abstract idea or value vivid and concrete. It is particularly useful in explaining a complicated plan or outlining a complex state of affairs. Instead of merely listing the details, it takes a hypothetical person, yourself or a member of the audience, and envisions him going through the process of living and working under the conditions described. Note, for example, in the above illustration how the speaker causes his listeners to put themselves in the workman's place. For an additional example of this form of support, see again "Communication and Change," pages 4–7.

As a means of gaining clarity, the hypothetical illustration is useful because the speaker may arrange the details of his story to suit his purpose; as proof, however, it is of doubtful value simply because it *is* hypothetical.

Factual Illustration

A factual illustration, as we have said, is a narrative that describes in detail a situation or incident that has actually occurred. It is one of the most telling forms of support a speaker can use. Because details are brought into the story, the incident is made clear and vivid to the listeners; because the incident actually happened, the illustration frequently has high persuasive value. In the factual illustration which follows, note particularly how Donald Greve has employed the narrative method of development and how he has used direct discourse to lend interest and reality to the story:

> Pop Warner, a football coach, had a bunch of Indians on his football team. He tried to get them in shape. He had them doing calisthenics like all football players do. They didn't like it. He couldn't get them to do it. He didn't say all Indians were lazy because these boys didn't do the calisthenics to get in shape. Instead, Pop Warner went around and talked with some of the Indian parents to find out what could be done. With their help, he figured out a new way to motivate them. He loaded his Indian players on the school bus and went two miles away from the college. He put each one of the players off the bus and handed them a tow sack. He said, "Take this tow sack, go out there and catch two rabbits any way you want to. Then run back to town as fast as you can." They did it! They got in shape. He learned to motivate these fellows based on their background, not based on his. As a direct result, he had a nation's champion in his caliber of football teams. There was one fellow in particular, a 158-pound fullback who was not very big for a fullback, but was a great athlete. His name was Jim Thorpe. I doubt that Jim Thorpe could have become the outstanding athlete that he was if Pop Warner had not learned to motivate him based on his background.[9]

The same elements are present in this factual illustration used by Jack I. Straus, Chairman of R. H. Macy and Company, to show the importance of good customer relations. Notice that he describes a situation with which listeners can easily identify, thereby establishing common ground with them and enhancing the reality of his message.

Not long ago I received a complaint from a college professor's wife in Athens, Georgia. Our Davison division has a store there. It seems that this customer and her husband had gotten their signals mixed, and both had bought an item that they wanted, so one was returned for credit. I remember the price very well—$5.09. Instead of getting the credit, she was billed for $10.18. She paid $5.09, expecting the credit for the other on her next bill. P.S. She never got the credit so she started a correspondence that I am sure must have cost us at least $150 in labor, overhead, postage, and executive time. Finally, six months later, she sent the correspondence to me—the whole big bundle of it.

You can be sure that by the time any complaint gets to me, the customer is really hot. This one was exasperated almost to tears.

The minute I read her letter I phoned our division headquarters and said: "Pay the lady her $5.09 and apologize to her. Don't bother about the facts of the case now. But when you have apologized, check all the facts, and I'll bet you will find we made a mistake." They did as I suggested and sure enough we had made the mistake. We had not credited the item which had been returned.

But even if we had been right, what had we to gain by battling a customer—particularly on a university campus that provided most of our customers for our Athens store?

I say if we are right and the customer is wrong but we can't convince her, settle the matter promptly in her favor. Sure, there are deadbeats, but they're part of the cost of doing business. We could have paid off fifty questionable claims and still saved money in this case.[10]

Three considerations should be kept in mind when choosing a factual illustration to explain or support an idea. *First, is the illustration clearly related to the idea?* If you have to labor to show its connection, the illustration will be of little use. *Second, is it a fair example?* An audience is quick to notice unusual circumstances in an illustration; and if you seem to have picked an exceptional case, your description of it will not prove convincing. *Third, is it vivid and impressive in detail?* The primary value of an illustration is the sense of reality it creates. If this quality is absent, the advantage of using an illustration is lost. Be sure, then, that your illustrations are pointed, fair, and vivid.

Specific Instance

A specific instance is an undeveloped illustration or example. Instead of describing a situation in detail, it is merely referred to in passing. When time prevents the development of lengthy illustrations to clarify an idea or show the seriousness of a problem, you often may achieve the same result by mentioning a number of instances with which your listeners already are more or less familiar.

Observe how Lieutenant General V. H. Krulak employed such instances to dispel the idea that today, more than ever before, there is a premium on youth:

> We hear on all sides that 1972 is different from 1952; that today is the era of the young. . . . [But] haven't young people run the world ever since it began?
>
> The fact is, our youth actually matured earlier and took on responsibility younger a century ago than they do right now!
>
> In 1872, a seventeen-year-old girl who was not already married and raising a family was suspect. It was a rare young man indeed who was not busy supporting himself—and maybe a family—at eighteen. And there were few twenty-nine-year-old college students.
>
> In 1862, two-thirds of the colonels in the Confederate Army were under twenty-four.
>
> In 1790, John Adams [Quincy] was Secretary to our Ambassador to Moscow—at the age of 15.
>
> In 1880, the prize-winning design for the beautiful Liverpool Cathedral was created by a nineteen-year-old.
>
> In 1943, I polled the battalion I commanded and found that 60 per cent of them—all busy fighting the Japanese in their country's behalf—were teenagers.
>
> All of us know that Alexander the Great, Mozart, Bach, and Joan of Arc achieved great fame while still in their teens.
>
> And, as one thoroughly modern point, the fellow who declared just a few years ago that you should trust nobody over thirty has just had his thirtieth birthday![11]

To support her contention that American presidents have always been "targets of abuse," Ms. Louise Bushnell of the Public Information Department of the National Association of Manufacturers offered her listeners these instances:

> George Washington felt that critics treated him, and I quote, "no better than a common pickpocket." A Philadelphia newspaper . . . described [him] as "the man who is the source of all the misfortunes of our

country" . . . and said he had debauched and deceived the nation.

 Opponents of Andrew Jackson called him an adulterer . . . a gambler . . . a cockfighter . . . a bigamist . . . a Negro trader . . . a drunkard . . . a murderer . . . a thief and a liar!

 Though now largely forgotten, the attacks on President Lincoln equaled all those I have just mentioned in venom, and exceeded them in volume. He was subjected to a veritable drumfire of vicious, scurrilous vituperation. This included his wife, his long-dead mother, and her mother. It came from the North as well as the South. It came from some associates and thoughtless friends as well as foes. It did not die with him.

 President Grant had the nickname of "that Drunken Roustabout!" Coming closer to our own time . . . I do not have to tell you who was called "That man!" and, far more belligerently, "the Cripple" [Franklin Roosevelt]. President Truman did not escape and was known as "the Haberdasher" . . . and a tool of the Prendergast Machine![12]

If the names, events, or situations you cite are well known to your listeners, specific instances may provide strong support for a claim or contention. To an average American audience, for example, the assertion that many star athletes are black may be substantiated merely by mentioning the names of Karim Abdul Jabbar, Hank Aaron, or Leroy Kelly. On subjects with which the listeners are not familiar, however, or on which there are marked differences of opinion, it is well to supplement specific instances with more fully developed illustrations of a factual nature.

Statistics

 Not all figures are statistics; some are merely numbers. Statistics are figures used to show relationships among things: to point out increases or decreases, to emphasize largeness or smallness, or to show how one phenomenon is correlated with another. Because statistics are capable of summarizing great masses of specific facts or data, they are useful in making clear the nature of a complex situation as well as in substantiating a potentially disputable claim. In the following example, statistics are used primarily to prove a point:

 The Omnibus Crime Control and Safe Streets Act of 1968 that authorized expanded bugging and tapping also required full government reports to Congress detailing the annual costs, results, and number of wiretaps conducted. The reports have now been issued for the years 1968 to 1971, and they prove conclusively that wiretapping is at best of very little value.

Here are the facts:

In 1968, when there was no federal eavesdropping, state officials listened in on 66,716 conversations.

In 1969, when both federal and state officials eavesdropped, 173,-711 conversations were overheard.

In 1970, the amount of eavesdropping doubled to 381,865 conversations.

In 1971, at least 498,325 conversations were overheard, a jump of 30 per cent over 1970.

What were the results?

In 1968, out of 66,716 overheard conversations, *no* convictions were reported.

In 1969, out of 173,711 conversations, 294 convictions resulted.

In 1970, out of 381,865 conversations, 538 convictions resulted.

In 1971, out of at least 498,325 conversations, 322 convictions have resulted so far.

In the four years since the bill was passed, 93,080 people have been spied upon; and thus far, only 1,154 have been reportedly convicted — *barely more than 1 per cent.*[13]

Masses of figures or unusually large or small figures sometimes are difficult for an audience to comprehend. When you are speaking and have a problem of this kind, take time to "translate" the raw numbers into more immediately understandable terms, terms which are concrete and immediate rather than abstract and general. In the following passage, Dr. Warren Weaver, the well-known space scientist, used these examples to emphasize the huge ($30 billion) cost of our manned moon landings:

With that $30 billion we could give every teacher a 10 per cent raise for 10 years; endow 200 small colleges with $10 million each; finance the education through graduate school of 50,000 scientists at $4,000 a year; build 10 new medical schools at $200 million each; build and endow complete universities for more than 50 developing countries; [and] create three new Rockefeller Foundations with $500 million each.[14]

And, to help make clear the immense age of the earth, Richard Carrington, a science writer, gave the readers of the *Milwaukee Journal* this comparison:

If the earth's history could be compressed into a single year, the first eight months would be completely without life, the next two would see only the primitive creatures, mammals wouldn't appear until the second week in December, and no *homo sapiens* until 11:45 P.M. on Dec. 31. The entire period of man's written history would occupy the final 60 seconds before midnight.[15]

Other ways of making statistics more readily understandable include stating very large figures in round numbers (say "nearly 4,000,000," rather than "3,984,256"), breaking totals down on a per capita basis, writing figures on the chalkboard as you discuss them, pointing to prepared charts or graphs on which the data are presented, handing out mimeographed material summarizing the statistics you are presenting, and slowing down your rate of delivery.

When effectively and honestly interpreted, statistics are invaluable in explanation or proof. You must, however, be careful to avoid the misuses and fallacies to which they are prone. Remember that a median or mean can be a deceiving figure, since it tells little or nothing about any one of the individual items on which it is based. Remember, too, when drawing comparisons, that the units compared must actually be of the same sort; and that in order to establish a trend, the figures must cover a reasonably long period of time. There is an old saying to the effect that figures don't lie, but liars figure. Never let this be said of you.

Testimony

When a speaker cites verbatim the opinions or conclusions of others, he is using *testimony*. Sometimes testimony is offered merely to clarify or explain an idea; more often, it is intended to supply proof for an arguable claim.

An example of testimony used to clarify or explain is provided by Robert T. Oliver, Professor Emeritus of speech communication at Pennsylvania State University. In commenting on the difficulty of communicating with persons whose cultural backgrounds and value systems are different from our own, Professor Oliver said:

We can communicate with people in another culture only in terms that make sense to them. Prime Minister Nehru, on his visit to America in 1950, made the same point a bit more explicitly, and cogently enough to merit quotation. "If we seek to understand a people," he said, "we have to put ourselves, as far as we can, in that particular historical and cultural background. . . . One has to recognize that . . . countries and peoples differ in their approach and their ways, in their approach to life and their ways of living and thinking. In order to understand them we have to understand their way of life and approach. If we wish to convince them, we have to use their language as far as we can, not language in the narrow sense of the word, but the language of the mind."[16]

All testimony, whether used to explain or to prove, should meet the twin tests of *authoritativeness* and *audience acceptability*. In particular, when used to substantiate a claim, it should, insofar as possible, satisfy these criteria:

1. The training and experience of the person quoted should qualify him as an authority. He should be an expert in the field to which his testimony relates.

2. The statement of the authority should be based, whenever possible, on firsthand knowledge.

3. The judgment expressed should not be unduly influenced by personal interest; the authority should not be prejudiced.

4. The hearers should recognize that the man quoted actually is an authority. If they do not automatically accept him as such, they should be told why his opinion deserves respect.

The following passage from a student speech on water fluoridation employs testimony as proof. Observe that the speaker, Neal Luker, of the University of Iowa, chose as his authority a presumably unbiased expert in a position to know the facts firsthand, and that he was careful to state the authority's full title for his listeners:

Summing up experiments too numerous to mention and representing the best current professional opinion on fluoridation is the following statement by Dr. Nicholas Leone, Chief of Medical Investigation for the National Institute of Dental Research: "We know without question or doubt that one part per million in water supply is absolutely safe, is beneficial, and is not productive of any undesirable systemic effect in man."[17]

And here is how John Findley, speaking to a college audience, effectively integrated testimony and statistics as support for his contention that "individual votes per precinct often determine the outcome of an election":

As Tom Wicker of *The New York Times* wrote in 1968 about the 1960 Kennedy-Nixon election:

All history books record that Kennedy received 303 electoral votes to 219 for Richard M. Nixon. But electoral votes are determined by the popular votes . . . and in 1960, a shift of only 4,480 popular votes from Kennedy to Nixon in Illinois . . . and 4,491 in

Missouri, would have given neither man an electoral majority and thrown the decision into the House of Representatives. If an additional 1,148 votes had been counted for Nixon in New Mexico, 58 in Hawaii, and 1,247 in Nevada, he would have won an outright majority in the electoral college.[18]

When citing testimony, avoid the temptation to use "big names" simply because they are well known. A movie star may be famous for her beauty and appeal, but her statement about the nutritive value of a breakfast food is of little worth compared to the opinion of a dietician. The most reliable testimony always comes from subject-matter experts whose qualifications your listeners recognize and respect.

Restatement

This last form of support gains its strength from the power of repetition to clarify or persuade. Teachers, clergymen, and other speakers frequently repeat ideas in the hope that if they are not understood the first time, they will "sink in" by the second or third time. Advertisers spend thousands of dollars repeating the same message over and over in magazines, on billboards, and over radio and television. The possible danger, of course, is that such repetition will become monotonous. Restatement, properly understood, however, does not mean simple repetition; it means *saying the same thing two or more times, but saying it each time in a new and different way* in the hope that a listener who does not grasp or respond to the idea in one form will do so in another.

In a speech entitled "Leadership and the 'Sane Society,'" Dr. Ralph Eubanks, Chairman of the Department of Speech Communication at the University of West Florida, used restatement to make clear the kind of leader he thinks is required in modern America. Not satisfied with one restatement, Dr. Eubanks repeated his idea in three different ways:

> We must, among other things, create a new leadership in America. . . . The leader I shall define as one who can help his group conduct well the ancient search for "the good life in the good society." Put another way, a good leader for our times is one who can hold ever before the members of his group a truly human vision of themselves. In slightly different terms, he is one who can help his group find their way to honorable, human goals and can teach them how to "care for persons" in the process. In still different terms, he is one who can help us live up to the ancient definition of ourselves as *Homo Sapiens*, or Man the Wise.[19]

Note also how President Franklin D. Roosevelt used restatement to clarify and to gain emphasis in a "fireside chat" on his controversial plan to "pack the Supreme Court":

> Last Thursday I described the American form of Government as a three-horse team provided by the Constitution to the American people so that their field might be plowed. The three horses are, of course, the three branches of government—the Congress, the Executive, and the Courts. . . . Those who have intimated that the President of the United States is trying to drive that team, overlook the simple fact that the President, as Chief Executive, is himself one of the three horses.
> It is the American people themselves who are in the driver's seat.
> It is the American people themselves who want the furrow plowed.
> It is the American people themselves who expect the third horse [the Supreme Court] to pull in unison with the other two.[20]

These, then, are the seven forms of verbal support. Select them judiciously; use them generously, but discerningly. Avoid abstract, unsupported statements. Do not depend solely upon assertions of your own opinions. Express your views, by all means; but amplify and develop them by using *explanation, comparison, illustration, specific instances, statistics, testimony,* and *restatement.*

NONVERBAL SUPPORTING MATERIAL: TYPES AND USES

Thus far we have discussed only the various types of verbal material which may be used to clarify an idea or establish a claim—what may be said by way of explanation or proof. Equally important, sometimes even more important, are the *nonverbal* materials you can use for these same purposes. Maps, diagrams, charts, pictures, small working models, and even demonstrations with full-scale equipment often can make your presentation more effective.

For instance, if you are explaining how to use a complicated camera, your instructions will be clearer if you take an actual camera, show your listeners the parts that require adjustment, and demonstrate how to use it in taking different kinds of pictures. When the item to be demonstrated is too big to bring into the room where the speech is to be made, small-scale models may be substituted. Model airplanes, for example, are widely used to teach aerodynamics. The operation of a device, apparatus, or machine and the assembly of its interrelated parts can be made clearer by showing pictures or diagrams of the important pieces. Maps illustrate routes and distances and indicate the terrain of a given area. Statistical data can be clarified by column graphs or "pies"—circles cut into segments to show proportions. Slides and movies are extremely useful in showing learners how a task is to be carried out or a result accomplished.

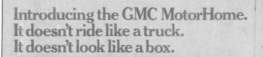

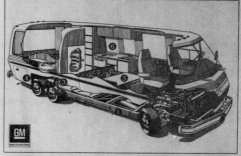

All forms of speech communication, especially small group and public, benefit from the use of nonverbal supporting materials. In the accompanying photographs we see scale models, chalkboard drawings, charts, diagrams, and the object itself used to reinforce messages in situations ranging from classroom lectures to mass-media advertisements.

317

Types of Nonverbal Support

The following list suggests the kinds of visual aids the thoughtful and imaginative speaker may use to support and enhance his ideas:

The object itself (for example, a metronome or a walkie-talkie).

Models, either small-scale models of large objects (a model racing car) or large-scale models of small objects (a model of the structure of a molecule). A working model has the added advantage of showing the operation of a device or apparatus, as well as its basic design.

Slides require projection equipment, and the darkened room obscures the speaker, but they usually add interest and promote understanding.

Movies require more equipment than slides, but have the advantage of showing action.

Maps should be large enough to be seen easily and should emphasize those details which relate to the point being made.

Chalkboard drawings should be completed before the audience assembles, but kept covered until the speaker is ready to refer to them. Be sure that the chalk marks are heavy enough to be seen by the entire group.

Graphs. Bar graphs show the relationship of two sets of figures. *Line* graphs show two or more variable facts. *Pie* graphs show percentages by a circle divided proportionately. *Pictorial* graphs show relative amounts by size or number of symbols.

Diagrams. Cutaway diagrams of an object display its inner workings as well as its external aspects. Diagrams which allow for a *three-dimensional* view are especially helpful.

Organization charts or *tables of organization* illustrate the parts and structure of a business, bureau, or agency.

For examples of some of these types of nonverbal supporting materials, see the photographs on pages 316–317.

Guides for Using Nonverbal Supporting Material

In using visual support for your speeches, be sure that you:

1. *Choose only objects and materials that are relevant.* The purpose of any nonverbal aid is to make an idea graphic for your audience. Irrelevant materials distract the viewers' attention from the idea you are discussing.

2. *Prepare all display materials before giving the speech.* Check to see that you have all the needed equipment, that chalkboard diagrams are complete, and that papers and books are arranged so they will be easy to handle. Practice using the visual aids as you rehearse your speech itself.

3. *Keep charts, graphs, and diagrams simple and clear.* Use ink in heavy broad lines and, where possible, in color to emphasize an important fact or feature. Make the displays large enough so that the entire audience can see them easily. Omit unnecessary details. A series of simple charts is better than a single complicated one.

4. *Place visual materials where they can be seen easily.* Stand well to the side of the display and use a pointer to indicate its different parts or aspects. When showing a model or other object, hold it so that your hands do not obscure it.

5. *Use nonverbal supporting materials at the proper psychological moment in the speech.* If your timing is faulty and the showing of the nonverbal support is not closely coordinated with the discussion, the chain of thought will be broken, and the aid will interrupt the continuity of the speech instead of clarifying the point at hand.

6. *Keep visual supporting material visible only when it is in use.* Keep it covered until you are ready for it, and put it out of sight when you have finished with it. If it can be seen when it is not in use, it will tend to distract the audience from the rest of your remarks.

USING SUPPORTING MATERIAL: THE SINGLE-IDEA SPEECH

Unless the subject of your speech is unusually complex, you probably will not use all of the various types of support in the development of every point. You will have to be *selective.* One idea may be supported, for instance, by explanation and comparison; another by statistics and quotation; a third by specific instances, and so on. In the discussion that follows, we shall attempt to demonstrate—among other things—some of the ways in which particular types of verbal and nonverbal supporting material can be selected and utilized to develop an idea in a speech. You will find in this a number of practical applications because many speeches have for their explicit purpose clarifying a single idea or proving one simple point. When this is the case, the structure of the message should be uncomplicated; and, of course, the forms of support should all bear directly upon the idea or point in question.

To organize and develop a single-idea speech is a comparatively simple process. After you have determined the thought you wish to explain or substantiate, you (1) *select a key idea* and (2) *support it strongly with verbal/nonverbal materials* that will (*a*) *explain* that idea or (*b*) *prove* it.

Selecting the Idea

To begin, decide on the exact idea you wish to explain or the claim you desire to prove. To be sure that you really have one point—and *only* one point—in mind, frame this idea or claim into a short, simple sentence; for example, "The death penalty is medieval." Focus on this single point throughout your entire speech. To clarify this point or to verify this claim is the *purpose* of your message. Do not wander off onto something else, no matter how interesting it may be.

With your purpose determined, assemble the supporting material best suited to achieving it, and arrange this material in a sequence or pattern that will be easy for listeners to understand and to follow. Keep clearly in mind whether you are trying to *explain* and *clarify* an idea or whether, on the other hand, you are attempting to *prove* a claim.

Using Supporting Material to Explain the Idea

If the purpose of your speech is to explain an idea, proceed as follows:

1. State in a short, simple sentence the idea to be explained.
2. Make it clear
   a. by explanation, comparisons, and illustrations;
   b. by using maps, diagrams, pictures, or models.
3. Restate the idea you have explained.

In the clarification (step 2 above), you may present the verbal and nonverbal supporting materials either separately or together. That is, you may tell your listeners and *then* show them; or you may show them *while* you are telling them. The following outline for a single-idea speech illustrates how supporting materials may be assembled to make an idea clear.

THE COUNCIL-MANAGER FORM OF CITY GOVERNMENT

I. *The council-manager form of city government is an efficient and effective way to handle municipal affairs because an elected "council" consisting of four or five citizens of the community hires a professionally trained administrator to carry out its directives.*

Statement of single idea.

A. The council confines its attention to policy matters.
   1. It passes ordinances.
   2. It appropriates money.
   3. It levies taxes.
   4. It arranges for bond issues.
B. The manager is responsible for all aspects of administration.
   1. He supervises the day-to-day operations of the various departments of government.
      a. He sees that laws and ordinances are properly enforced.
      b. He appoints, directs, and—if necessary—removes department heads and other city employees.
   2. He recommends to the council needed programs and improvements.
      a. His intimate knowledge of municipal affairs puts him in an excellent position to spot problem areas.
      b. His professional training prepares him to offer sound proposals.
   3. He maintains channels of communication with all segments of the community.
      a. He listens to complaints from individuals and groups.
      b. He delivers speeches and makes other public appearances.
      c. He prepares exhibits for informative and instructive purposes.

Explanation as a type of support.

II. Thomas Harrison Reed, a well-known municipal consultant, has likened the council-manager plan of city government to the organization of a business corporation.
   A. The council functions as a policy-determining board of directors.
   B. The position of the manager as principal administrator is similar to that of the company president.

Comparison as a type of support.

III. Professor George Buresh, author of *How Our Cities Are Governed*, declares, "Under the council-manager form of government, the council must answer to the people for policy, and the manager must answer to the council insofar as the implementation of policy is concerned."

Testimony as a type of support.

Using Supporting Material: The Single-Idea Speech 321

IV. The city-manager form of government and its relation to the more traditional commission form are shown in these diagrams:

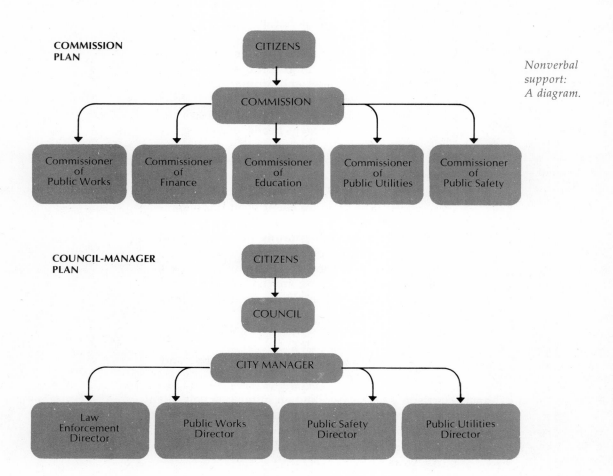

Nonverbal support: A diagram.

COMMISSION PLAN

CITIZENS

COMMISSION

Commissioner of Public Works | Commissioner of Finance | Commissioner of Education | Commissioner of Public Utilities | Commissioner of Public Safety

COUNCIL-MANAGER PLAN

CITIZENS

COUNCIL

CITY MANAGER

Law Enforcement Director | Public Works Director | Public Safety Director | Public Utilities Director

V. *The council-manager form of city government is an effective plan for administering municipal affairs because:*
    A. It provides a clear-cut organization.
    B. It fixes civic responsibility.
    C. It utilizes trained administrators.

Restatement of the single idea of the speech.

Using Supporting Material to Prove a Claim or Verify a Point

There are two common methods of assembling the types of support to provide proof for a single- or one-point claim: (1) the didactic method and (2) the method of implication.

The Didactic Method

In the didactic method, the claim to be proved is stated first, then the support or proof is presented, and finally the claim is restated as your conclusion. As the old parson explained, "I tell 'em what I'm *goin'* to tell 'em; I *tell* 'em; then I tell 'em what I *told* 'em." This is perhaps the clearest and often most effective method of organization. If the purpose of your speech is to prove or verify a point by the didactic method, proceed as follows:

1. State the point to be established.
2. Make it clear by explanation, comparisons, or illustrations.
3. Support it by additional factual illustrations, specific instances, statistics, and/or testimony.
4. Restate your point as the conclusion.

The Implicative Method

In the method of implication, the facts are presented first and then followed by a statement of the conclusion to which these facts lead. In other words, the implicative method is essentially the reverse of the didactic sequence: the claim comes at the *end* of the speech, and is stated only *after* the evidence which supports it has been set forth. This procedure, sometimes called the "natural" method of argument, coincides more nearly with the way we apparently reach conclusions when we are uninfluenced by another person. For this reason, the method of implication, though not quite so direct as the didactic arrangement, is sometimes more persuasive to an audience. It is, in fact, almost always to be preferred when listeners are *hostile* to the claim or conclusion you wish to establish. If the purpose of your speech is to prove or verify a point by the implicative method, proceed thus:

1. Present an analogy or illustration which *implies* the conclusion you wish to establish.
2. Present additional illustrations, instances, statistics, and testimony which point strongly to this conclusion without directly stating it.
3. Show how these facts lead inevitably to this conclusion; use as much explanation as necessary to establish the connection.
4. Explicitly state the conclusion which has thus been established.

Notice again that regardless of whether you use the didactic method of proof or the implicative method, three of the forms of support (explanation, comparison, and illustration) are primarily helpful in making an idea clear and vivid, whereas three others (instances, statistics, and testimony) function effectively to establish and verify the truth or importance of a claim. Restatement, of course, serves both to clarify and persuade, as well as to assist the listener in storing the idea in his memory and retrieving it later. As you study the sample speech outline below, note that the didactic method is being used. Also observe that if the general statement at the beginning of the outline is omitted, the sequence is then essentially the same as for the method of implication.

INSTRUCTION BY TELEVISION

I. *Classroom instruction by television is effective.* — General Statement

    A. Suppose this were to happen in your English literature class: — Hypothetical Illustration
        1. When you enter the room, there is a television set rather than an instructor in front of the class.
        2. On TV, however, you see the department's best teacher for the course you are taking.
        3. In other rooms, you discover, other classes are watching the same telecast.
            a. The students in each class can see and hear the identical lecturer and the teaching materials being used in all classes.
            b. The students in each class can obtain individual assistance when necessary.
        4. You realize that you will learn as much about literature as you would in a conventional class.
            a. Tests on appreciation of literature show this.
            b. Tests on comprehension of literature demonstrate the same result.

    B. Television has been used successfully in the Hagerstown, Maryland, public schools: — Factual Illustration
        1. Mathematics classes at nearly every grade level participated.
        2. Teachers, student ability, and other variables were controlled so that television was the only major difference in method.
            a. About half of the classes received instruction by television.
            b. The other half received regular instruction.

3. The students who received television instruction scored as high or higher on tests than those who had regular instruction.

C. The success of this experience has been repeated in a number of cases: *Specific Instances*
   1. Miami University of Ohio reported that students in TV sections and those in regular classes did equally well in subject-matter learning.
   2. The city of Chicago found similar results for high-school physics and algebra.
   3. In Cincinnati, high-school chemistry classes taught by TV were ahead of other classes.

D. A special committee headed by Arthur E. Traxler, of the Educational Records Bureau, and supported by the Fund for the Advancement of Education, reported figures that clearly show the effectiveness of television instruction: *Statistics*
   1. Experiments involving almost 27,000 students were conducted in several cities.
   2. Of 110 comparisons made in this study, 68 of them, or over 60%, showed that the groups instructed by television achieved higher scores than the other groups.

E. On the basis of studies such as these, experts have expressed their favorable views: *Testimony*
   1. Leslie P. Greenhill, associate director of Academic Research and Services for Pennsylvania State University, stated in the *National Education Association Journal:*
      a. "Results of TV research show that when the same teacher teaches in each situation, televised instruction is equivalent in effectiveness to face-to-face instruction."

F. Just as training films have assisted in teaching millions of men and women in the armed forces, so television can be useful in the classrooms of our schools. *Analogy*

II. *Subjects can be effectively taught by television.* *Restatement*

Not all single-idea speeches require as many different forms of support as were used in this sample outline. Most single-idea speeches also are briefer. This sample was given to show how a number of different types of support might be combined to achieve a single purpose.

In the preceding pages we have considered the substantive elements that you as a speaker may employ to explain, clarify, amplify, verify, or prove the major ideas in your messages. The verbal and nonverbal materials that you select and the uses to which you put them should be governed by the criteria of appropriateness and clarity. Above all, be sure that you provide sufficient support to make your leading ideas clear and convincing, and that this support speaks directly to the interests and concerns of your listeners.

A SAMPLE SPEECH

In the following speech by Clarence Yurk, a student at the University of Wisconsin-Milwaukee, a single idea or point is impressed upon the audience through a series of striking examples. When you have learned to develop one idea in this way, you will be ready to attempt speeches in which a number of different ideas must be put together into an integrated whole.

LOST: FOUR FRIENDS[21]

Clarence Yurk

In the last four years I have lost four friends.

During January of this year a friend of mine was driving on a highway late at night. Out of the darkness a car sped toward her. Her car was involved in a head-on collision and Gladys was killed. I lost a friend.

Four years ago a friend of mine scored thirty-eight points against Green Bay West in a high-school basketball game. That was on a Friday night. Two nights later the car in which he was riding slammed into a tree at ninety miles an hour. John was cut in half, and I lost another friend.

Two years ago Susie Hinz was killed. As usual, her mother picked her up after school and, as usual, they took the same side road home. They lived in the country. On that road they came upon a railroad crossing they had crossed a thousand times. However, on that particular day, because they had crossed the railroad crossing a thousand times and there wasn't a train scheduled for that time anyway, they started across the tracks without looking. A train smashed into their car at seventy miles an hour, dragging their car over a hundred feet. Susie was killed. I lost another friend.

All three of these accidents were a result of some form of carelessness. Let's go back over them again. As I said, Gladys was killed in a head-on collision. That means that either one or both of the cars involved crossed the centerline of the highway. One or both drivers were guilty of negligence.

John was killed in a car traveling at ninety miles per hour. Need I say more? That was foolishness.

Susie was killed because of inattentiveness. Had either she or her mother bothered to look before crossing those tracks they'd probably be alive today.

By this time you've probably guessed what I'm getting at. I'm talking to you about the age-old theme of "Drive Carefully." Oh, I know, you're probably saying, "Now look, Clarence, I heard this sermon a thousand times. What do you expect me to do?" There's *no reason* why you and I as college students should *ever* be guilty of negligence, foolishness, or inattentiveness. *Think* when you get behind the wheel of your car. If I can leave you with just one thought today, it's that. I want you to think when you drive. I don't know why it is, but a man can spend his whole day on the job thinking, or a college student can spend hours in a library, thinking, but when he gets into his car at night he completely forgets to think and relies entirely on natural instinct. A car is a two thousand-pound battering ram. That "tin lizzy" out there, or whatever affectionate name you've given it, kills more people in one year than we lost during the whole Korean conflict. *Think* when you drive. Always expect the unexpected. The shortstop for the Milwaukee Braves always expects the next play to come to him. That way he stays on his toes. You, too, should be on your toes when you drive. Always expect the unexpected. Always think.

Perhaps you've noticed by now that I said I lost four friends in four years and I've only told you about three. This afternoon I'm going to Sheboygan to attend a funeral. One of my best friends was killed in an auto accident on Tuesday. Gene was twenty-five, married, and had a seven-months-old son. What am I going to say to his wife?

Four friends in four years. At that rate, if I live to the age of seventy, I'm going to lose forty-five more friends. My definition of a friend is someone I know and like. *You* are all my friends.

FOOTNOTES

[1] *Excerpt from "A Liberal Education" by Mortimer J. Adler, delivered at the University of Portland (January 1963). Published in* Town and Country *(January 1963). Reprinted by permission of the author.*

[2] *From "Prevention of Alcoholism" by Dr. Marvin A. Block from* Vital Speeches of the Day, *Vol. XXXIX, (December 1, 1972). Reprinted by permission of Vital Speeches of the Day.*

[3] *From "Thinking Ahead in Federal Tax Policy" by James F. Oates, Jr., from* Vital Speeches of the Day, *Vol. XXXII, (December 1, 1965). Reprinted by permission of Vital Speeches of the Day.*

[4]*Excerpt from "Can You Trust God" by Dr. Louis Hadley. Reprinted by permission of the author.*

[5]*From "Help Wanted" by Peter Peterson from* Vital Speeches of the Day, *Vol. XXXI, (September 15, 1965). Reprinted by permission of Vital Speeches of the Day.*

[6]*From "The Golden Key to America" by Albert Wass de Czege from* Vital Speeches of the Day, *Vol. XXVI, (February 15, 1960). Reprinted by permission of Vital Speeches of the Day.*

[7]*"Let's Revitalize Student Government," delivered in an advanced course in public speaking at the University of Iowa, March 14, 1966.*

[8]*From "Effective Leadership for Better Employee Relations" by Charles J. Stilwell from* Vital Speeches of the Day, *Vol. XIV, (December 15, 1947). Reprinted by permission of Vital Speeches of the Day.*

[9]*From "The American Indian" by Donald Greve from* Vital Speeches of the Day, *Vol. XXXVI, (February 15, 1970). Reprinted by permission of Vital Speeches of the Day.*

[10]*From "Wanted: Concern for the Customer" by Jack I. Straus from* Vital Speeches of the Day, *Vol. XXXII, (December 1, 1965). Reprinted by permission of Vital Speeches of the Day.*

[11]*From "Our Freedom in a Changing World" by Lt. Gen. V. H. Krulak from* Vital Speeches of the Day, *Vol. XXXVIII, (August 1, 1972). Reprinted by permission of Vital Speeches of the Day.*

[12]*From "Integrity: What and How?" by Louise Bushnell from* Vital Speeches of the Day, *Vol. XXXIX, (November 1, 1972). Reprinted by permission of Vital Speeches of the Day.*

[13]*Excerpt from "Your Phone is a Party Line" by Ira Glasser and Herman Schwartz from* Harper's *Magazine, (October 1972). Copyright 1972 by Harper's Magazine. Reprinted from the October, 1972 issue by special permission.*

[14]*Cited by Arthur Krock of* The New York Times *News Service, in* The Des Moines Register, *December 1, 1965, p. 10.*

[15]*Quoted in* The Des Moines Register, *September 16, 1965, p. 6.*

[16]*"Culture and Communication" by Robert T. Oliver from* Vital Speeches of the Day, *XXIX (September 15, 1963). Reprinted with permission of the author.*

[17]*"Water Fluoridation," presented in an advanced public speaking class at the University of Iowa, May 13, 1963. Quotation taken from* Water Fluoridation: Facts, Not Myths *by Louis I. Dublin (Public Affairs Pamphlet No. 251), p. 15.*

[18]*From "Selecting the President" by John Findley from* Vital Speeches of the Day, *Vol. XXXVIII, (June 1, 1972). Reprinted by permission of Vital Speeches of the Day.*

[19]*From a speech before Annual Leadership Conference by Dr. Ralph Eubanks from* Vital Speeches of the Day, *Vol. XXIX, (May 15, 1963). Reprinted by permission of Vital Speeches of the Day.*

[20]Vital Speeches of the Day III (March 15, 1937): 349.

[21]*"Lost: Four Friends" by Clarence Yurk from* Speeches for Illustration and Example, *Scott, Foresman and Company, 1965. Reprinted by permission of Clarence Yurk and Goodwin F. Berquist.*

Problems and Probes

1. On each of three successive days, read carefully the editorials and signed columns in your local newspaper or in one of the larger metropolitan papers. Describe the supporting materials you find there. How well were these materials used to substantiate the writers' views? How often were opinions expressed without supporting evidence?

2. Read half a dozen recent public addresses in *Vital Speeches of the Day* or some other suitable source and tabulate the supporting materials employed by the speakers. Which of the forms of support is used most frequently? Which least frequently? Considering the subjects with which these speeches deal and the purposes at which they are aimed, try to explain why some forms of supporting material appear more frequently than others. For anthologies of recent speeches, see Carroll C. Arnold, Douglas Ehninger, and John Gerber, *The Speaker's Resource Book*, 2nd ed. (Scott, Foresman, 1966); Glenn Capp, *The Great Society* (Dickenson, 1968); Wil A. Linkugel, R. R. Allen, and Richard L. Johannesen, *Contemporary American Speeches* (Wadsworth, 1972). A number of recent speeches also are included in Goodwin Berquist, *Speeches for Illustration and Example* (Scott, Foresman, 1965).

3. Reexamine critically the supporting materials contained in the speeches you located in Problem/Probe 2. Find instances in which a given form of support seems to be appropriately and effectively used, and also locate instances in which it is inappropriate or poorly developed. Rewrite the latter passages so as to improve them.

4. During the next several rounds of classroom speeches, list and evaluate in your Personal Speech Journal the supporting materials used by each speaker. In doing this, be certain to keep in mind whether the purpose of a given speech is to explain and clarify a point or to establish a claim or conclusion. At the close of each day's speeches, in a brief oral consideration ascertain how closely the members of the class agree on the types of supporting materials employed and the degree of effectiveness with which they were used.

5. List five general subject-areas on which you would like to speak. For each of these areas, first frame a specific purpose suitable for a short, single-idea speech on this subject; and then frame a specific purpose suitable for a longer and more fully developed speech. Be ready to defend your choice of purposes and to tell why each is suitable for a single-idea development or for a more fully detailed, multi-point treatment.

6. Name some of the circumstances under which you probably would choose to organize a single-idea speech according to the didactic pattern and some of the circumstances under which you would select the method of implication. Include among these circumstances the nature of the subject, the attitude of the audience, the time available, etc.

7. Recall a number of the courses you have taken in high school and college, and thoughtfully review them in your mind. What uses did the instructors make of *visible* supporting materials in presenting the subject matter of these courses? Were such materials effectively used? Did the instructors take full advantage of the possibilities afforded by such supporting material? Cite several instances in which the instructors might have expanded or improved the visual presentation of the subject materials.

8. With the aid of your instructor, locate a number of speeches delivered before the year 1800. Compare the supporting materials used in these speeches with the supporting materials you examined for Problem/Probe 2 above. In what respects, if any, are they different? Compare the frequency of occurrence of the various forms of support in the two sets of speeches. From this comparison, try to draw some conclusions concerning changes in speakers' uses of supporting materials over a period of time.

Oral Activities and Speaking Assignments

1. In an interesting little book entitled *How to Lie with Statistics* (Norton, 1954), Darrell Huff explains some of the tricks and fallacies in statistical proof and tells how to guard against them. Read Huff's book and present to the class an oral report on the subject "Pitfalls in Statistics." Use appropriate visual aids as an integral part of your presentation. (*Note to instructor:* Various students may be assigned separate chapters of Huff's book and asked to present a series of reports.)

2. Following the suggestions offered in this chapter, prepare to present in class a two- or three-minute single-idea speech to inform, to persuade, or to entertain. For possible subjects, study the list of subject categories in Chapter 7, pages 237–239.

3. Present to the class a five-minute single-idea speech, the purpose of which is to explain or clarify a term, concept, process, plan, or proposal. Use at least three different forms of supporting material in developing your ideas and employ at least one chart, diagram, map, picture, or

other nonverbal support. To formulate an evaluation of the effectiveness of your speech, the instructor and the other students will consider the following: (*a*) adequacy of supporting material; (*b*) appropriateness of supporting material, both as to type and to substance; and (*c*) the insight and skill with which the supporting material is developed.

Suggestions for Further Reading

Donald C. Bryant and Karl R. Wallace, *Fundamentals of Public Speaking*, 4th ed. (New York: Appleton-Century-Crofts, 1969), Chapter VII, "Development of Materials in Informative Speaking," pp. 85–113.

Robert S. Cathcart, "An Experimental Study of the Relative Effectiveness of Four Methods of Presenting Evidence," *Speech Monographs* XXII (August 1955): 227–233.

William R. Dresser, "The Impact of Evidence on Decision Making," in *Concepts in Communication*, ed. Jimmie D. Trent *et al* (Boston: Allyn & Bacon, Inc., 1973), pp. 159–166.

William R. Dresser, "Effects of 'Satisfactory' and 'Unsatisfactory' Evidence in a Speech of Advocacy," *Speech Monographs* XXX (August 1963): 302–306.

James C. McCroskey, "The Effects of Evidence in Persuasive Communication," *Western Speech* XXXI (Summer 1967): 189–199.

Gerald R. Miller, "Evidence and Argument," in *Perspectives on Argumentation*, ed. Gerald R. Miller and Thomas R. Nilsen (Glenview, Ill.: Scott, Foresman and Company, 1966).

12
SELECTING MATERIAL
THAT WILL HOLD ATTENTION

In Chapter 9 we examined the various types of appeals a speaker may use to motivate his listeners to belief or action. In this chapter we shall see how he may hold their attention on the ideas he wishes to present.

Attention is a great deal like electricity: we don't know exactly what it is, but we do know what it does and what conditions bring it about. A baseball fan is sitting in the bleachers. The count is three and two. The pitcher settles himself on the rubber, winds up, and sends a fast ball sizzling over the plate. The umpire bawls, "Strike three! Yer out!" Only then does the spectator lean back, take a long breath, and notice what has been going on about him: the man who has been thumping him on the back, the sack of peanuts he has dropped, the threatening clouds that have suddenly darkened the sky, the scorecard he has crumpled in his excitement. What has happened? We say that this spectator was unaware of his surroundings because his attention was focused on the game. Those things to which he was paying attention controlled his thought and action so completely that everything else was forced into the background of his conscious perception. Attention, as this hypothetical illustration suggests, is "the psychological process of selecting only a portion of the available stimuli to focus upon while ignoring, suppressing, or inhibiting reactions to a host of other stimuli."[1]

THE NATURE OF ATTENTION

Although there appears to be no ideal definition of the attention process, psychologists have been able to single out some of the conditions that appear to affect it. Floyd L. Ruch and Philip G. Zimbardo, authors of *Psychology and Life*, suggest the following possibilities:

1. *Change.* Change, or contrast, is movement in any direction: from one place to another; from one intensity to another; from red to green; from

high to low; from moving to stationary. . . . A sudden shout in the middle of a quiet talk or a whisper from a man who has been shouting makes you "sit up and take notice." In other words, anything that is novel or unexpected is change of some sort and attracts your attention.

2. *Size*. Other things being equal, something large attracts attention better than something small. This is one factor favoring the full-page advertisement. Size, however, is only one of many interrelated factors determining the direction of attention. Even a large advertisement may suffer by its nearness to another—perhaps smaller—one which appeals more to the reader's interests or has a more striking use of color.

3. *Prepotency*. Stimuli of greater intensity are more potent than others in the same sensory modality. For example, high sounds are prepotent over low sounds; tickling is prepotent over broad, smooth pressure; and bright, saturated colors are prepotent over pastel shades. The latter is especially evident in the brilliant rows of laundry products, canned goods, baking mixes, and other products found in the supermarket.

4. *Repetition*. A weak stimulus frequently repeated may be as effective as a strong one presented once. But there is a limit to such effectiveness. If overdone, repetition can lead to monotony and complete loss of attention. Actors and actresses pay special attention to this phenomenon when trying to determine the optimal number of personal and TV appearances which will maintain public interest.

Experience shows that repeating a fundamental theme or motif with minor variations is more effective than repeating the original presentation exactly. Beethoven's Fifth Symphony illustrates this principle beautifully. Many radio and TV commercials are designed on this idea, their "jingles" being an ever-constant reminder that simple repetition with minor variations can work its way into your brain.

5. *Organic condition*. The stimulus that wins the competition for your attention is usually the one that relates to the strongest biological need operating at the moment. If you are hungry, stimuli related to food will attract your attention. If you are tired, stimuli related to resting will be most effective. Since sexual needs are frequently operating, it follows that sex-related stimuli may be used to call attention to any object with which they are paired—from convertibles to cigars.

6. *Interests*. People vary greatly in their attention to the same stimulation because a person's interests, like his organic condition, predispose him toward a particular response. For example, most people might not even notice a rather ordinary-looking rock on the ground. But it would certainly attract the attention of a "rock hound" who knew it to be a gemstone. The

objective stimulus is the same in both cases, but because people's interests differ, their attention and behavior vary accordingly.[2]

Some Interrelated Aspects of Attention

Psychologists and students of communication suggest that attention may be looked upon as having four concomitants or interrelated aspects:

1. An adjustment of the body and its sense organs.
2. Clearness and vividness of conscious experience.
3. A readiness to respond to stimuli—a set toward action.
4. Instability and impermanence.

Later in this chapter we shall look at a few of the special problems growing out of the unstable and impermanent nature of attention. Here we center our attention on the other aspects of it.

During the attention-paying process, bodily posture is adjusted, and the sense organs are "aimed at" the stimulus in order to gather and receive impressions from it more readily. Just as the robin cocks its head to listen for the worm underneath the sod, so people lean forward and turn their eyes and ears toward the object which captures their attention. You have only to call your friend by name, and he will turn toward you in order to attend to your remarks. By gaining the attention of your audience, then, you increase their capacity to hear what you say because they will have adjusted themselves physically to listen. (See in this connection Chapter 17, especially pages 447–453.)

Of greater importance to the speaker, however, is the second characteristic of attention—the fact that when we attend to or focus upon a stimulus, it becomes clearer and more vivid in our consciousness, while other equally strong stimuli seem to grow weaker or fade out altogether. This explains why the spectator at the ball game was unaware of so many of the things going on about him as long as his attention was focused on the game. Every moment of our lives innumerable stimuli impinge on our senses. We can hear the wind whistling, the birds calling, or the trucks rumbling; our clothing presses against our skin; a hundred different sights occupy the field of our vision. Why don't we notice them all? We do not—cannot—notice them all because of the selective nature of attention.

Research has shown that three factors are important in determining what we attend to. They are *motivation*, *learning*, and *expectation*. As we have noted, we focus on food when we are hungry, warmth when we are cold, or companionship when we are lonely. When the firecracker is lighted, we await the bang because we expect it. When reading a difficult assignment, we are able to attend to it in a way a small child could not because we have learned or been conditioned to study.* In all of these cases, the stimuli from the people and objects we attend to grow in strength and vividness, while other stimuli recede and become less influential. To the extent that you as a speaker can command the attention of your audience—can significantly influence their perceptions through selectivity of stimuli—the ideas you express will make a clearer and more vivid impression on them, while distracting sights and sounds or conflicting ideas will tend to recede into the background of their awareness.

Finally, as we suggested above, a set toward action accompanies attention. This involves both the factors of *expectation* and *readiness-adjustment*. We have a tendency, while attending to a series of stimuli, to "get set" to do something about them. Thus the driver of an automobile who pays attention to highway-safety signs has certain expectations regarding those signs and, therefore, "gets ready" to steer his car around a curve or to stop at an intersection. Similarly, assuming that what you say makes sense and contains the proper motivational appeals, the closer your listeners will pay attention to you and your message, the more likely they will be to behave as you suggest. As they listen, particularly if you give them clear and unmistakable "signs" as to the mental highway you are traveling, they will tend to "get set" to think or act as you propose and will be more disposed to do so without wavering or hesitation. It has been said that *what holds attention tends strongly to determine action.*** Certainly, speakers who do not attract and hold the audience's attention rarely generate the action they desire, and the most influential speakers are those who command the attention of their listeners.

Voluntary Versus Involuntary Attention

We must not assume, however, that paying attention is entirely a spontaneous and involuntary reaction of the listener, governed solely by what the speaker says. Many times we must force ourselves to concentrate on something which in itself does not attract us. A student, for example, because he is required to pass the course, may compel himself to focus his attention on a textbook assignment in spite of the distractions around him or to listen attentively to a dull classroom lecture. Necessity or some other strong motivation often leads us, as listeners, to exert this type of conscious effort in order to focus our minds on stimuli which are not attention-provoking in themselves.

See, for example, G. A. Miller, Language and Communication (New York: McGraw-Hill Book Company, 1951), p. 200; C. M. Solley and G. Murphy, Development of the Perceptual World (New York: Basic Books, Inc., Publishers, 1960), pp. 188, 194–195.

**For a classic discussion of this principle applied specifically to the problems of the public speaker, see James Winans, Public Speaking (New York: The Century Company, 1917), pp. 245–248; Lew Sarett and William Trufant Foster, Basic Principles of Speech (Boston: Houghton Mifflin Company, 1936), pp. 14–16.*

The attention which results from such conscious effort often is referred to as *voluntary* or *forced* attention, as distinguished from the *involuntary* or *effortless* attention paid to things which are striking or engaging in themselves. Audiences sometimes force themselves to listen to a speaker out of mere politeness or respect for his prestige or position. More often, however, such voluntary or self-compelled attention results from the listeners' feeling that the subject is important to them. Therefore, if your topic lacks natural or immediate interest, early in your speech make its importance and relevance so clear that your listeners will exert a voluntary effort to concentrate on your message.

The very fact that voluntary attention requires conscious effort by the listeners, however, also makes it tiring to them. To use the terminology of the psychologists, "It is accompanied by a mass of strain sensations" resulting, ultimately, in fatigue and boredom. Unless you want to tire your audience or risk having their interest wane as you go on, you cannot depend on their voluntary attention alone. Desirable as it is to give your listeners a reason at the start for paying voluntary attention, it is also your task as a communicator to ensure that as soon as possible their attention becomes effortless and involuntary. By choosing a subject that is intrinsically interesting or by using speech material which employs one or more of the factors of attention to which we have already alluded and which we are about to identify more specifically, you can make it easier for your audience to listen to you and focus attention on what you have to say.* In this way, voluntary attention on their part will become involuntary, effortless, and sustained; and your ideas will be left sharply impressed upon their minds.

THE FACTORS OF ATTENTION

If repeated often enough, the response we make to a particular stimulus becomes "learned"; it becomes a habit. We say we are "habituated" to it and that we no longer have to "think about" it. This has a strong implication for attention: the attention process involves *a breaking down of listener habituation.* People in audiences very quickly become habituated to the speaker—his appearance, his vocal rate and pitch, his gestural behavior, his modes of emphasis, etc. These are visual and auditory stimuli; and if the speaker makes no obvious

---

*Obviously, interest and attention are closely related. People not only pay attention to what interests them, but—conversely—what they pay attention to over a period of time tends to become interesting to them. Frequently a student begins a required course convinced that he is going to be thoroughly bored. After a while, however, the course begins to interest him and may actually arouse him to the point that he continues for many months or years to investigate the subject matter covered. Of utmost importance in a speech, therefore, is to capture the attention of the audience in the first place and to ensure that it gives the speaker's message a fair hearing. When this is done—if the speaker is skillful and the message worthwhile—interest probably will grow as the talk proceeds. (Note, however, the warning about the unstable nature of attention given on pp. 342–343.)

changes in them, his hearers will eventually habituate and no longer "attend" to them. Habituation, therefore, becomes — in a communicative sense — a major obstacle we must overcome when we try to *sustain* listeners' attention in a public speech. We, therefore, have a twofold problem: (1) what can we do to *attract* our hearers' attention; and (2) if we succeed in attracting it, how can we *hold onto it?* In regard to the latter, it seems reasonable to suppose that the same factors we use to gain attention in the beginning can be used also to sustain it. This is one reason why, throughout this book, we have emphasized and reemphasized the significance of *variation.* As we have observed, successive changes or variations in the stimuli we provide are almost sure to help us communicate more effectively.

What, then, are these stimuli and variations-of-stimuli that can help us capture and hold the attention of an audience? In Chapters 4, 5, and 6, we pointed out how purposive movement in relation to your hearers, varied and vigorous gestures, and an animated vocal delivery contribute to this goal. Obviously, too, your general reputation as a speaker and the degree of prestige accorded you by your listeners are extremely important. Here, however, we are concerned with the attention-gaining and attention-sustaining factors you can build into the content of the speech and its moment-to-moment presentation. What types of arguments or ideas tend more than others to command attention and hence to generate response? The *factors of attention* — those qualities of subject matter which usually capture the spontaneous attention of listeners — may be identified thus:

1. Activity and Movement.
2. Reality.
3. Proximity.
4. Familiarity.
5. Novelty.
6. Suspense.
7. Conflict.
8. Humor.
9. The Vital.

The influences of these factors overlap, of course; and frequently we will have to combine two or more of them to rivet and maintain attention. However, for convenience in analysis, let us consider them separately.

Activity and Movement

If you were standing on the sidewalk and two cars of the same make, model, style, and color were in your view, one parked at the curb and the other speeding down the street at seventy miles an hour, which one would you look at? The moving one, of course. Your speech likewise must move. Stories in which something happens have this quality. The more active or animated the ideas and events you talk about, the more intently people will listen. Instead of describing the structure of a machine, tell how it works — get the wheels turning, the parts moving, the pistons pounding. Show what happens step by step.

Moreover, your speech *as a whole* should move. Nothing is so boring as a talk that seems to get nowhere. Foreshadow your destination; set up some signposts pointing toward your goal. Make the movement of your speech clear to your audience by indicating when you are done with one point and are ready to advance to the next. Don't spend too much time on any single idea; keep pressing forward.

Reality

The earliest words a child learns are the names of "real" objects and of tangible acts related to them. This interest in reality — in the personal perception of the immediate, the concrete, the actual — persists throughout life. The proposition $2+2=4$, while true, is in itself so abstract that it holds little interest. Instead of talking abstract theory, talk in terms of real-life people, events, places, and tangible circumstances. Use pictures, diagrams, and charts. Tell not what happened to "a certain prominent physician of this city," but to Dr. Fred Smith, who lives at 418 Paine Street. Make good use of all the forms of verbal and nonverbal support we talked about in Chapter 11. Make your descriptions specific and vivid. Remember always that individual cases are more real than general classifications; actual names and places are more fascinating than impersonalized, generalized, or vague allusions.

Proximity

A direct reference to someone in the audience, to some object near at hand, to some incident that has just occurred, or to the immediate occasion on which the speech is being made usually will command attention. A reference to a remark of the preceding speaker or of the chairman creates a similar effect. A variation of the device is to call out the name of a member of the audience or make him or her the central character in a hypothetical illustration. Not only will this awaken anyone who happens to be dozing (heaven forbid!), but it will also tend to increase the attention-level of the other members. To single out one or more individuals establishes the audience *as individuals*; they are no longer an anonymous mass in which personal identities are lost. As Ruch and Zimbardo point out, "Individuating listeners is one of the most effective means of getting— and holding—attention. When you are talking to a single individual, looking him straight in the eye increases the likelihood that he will look back at you and listen to what you have to say."[3]

Familiarity

Many things—usually because they are near at hand—are familiar to us because of the frequency with which we meet them in our daily lives. Thus, knives and forks, rain, automobiles, toothbrushes, classes, and a host of other common objects and events are closely built into our experiences. Being so much a part of us, these and a multitude of other familiar things catch our attention. We say, "Ah, that is an old friend." But, as with old acquaintances, we become bored if we see too much of them and nothing else. In a spoken message, the familiar holds attention primarily when the speaker introduces it in connection with something unfamiliar or when he points out some fresh or unknown aspect of it. Stories about Lincoln and Washington, for example, are interesting because we are familiar with their characters; but we don't like to hear the same old rail-splitter or cherry-tree tales unless they are given a new twist or application.

Novelty

According to newspaper lore, when a dog bites a man, it's an accident; when a man bites a dog, it's news. In other words, we tend to pay attention to that which is new or unusual. This would appear to be the reverse side of the familiarity coin. Airplanes fly daily the thousands of miles from Chicago to Paris, but there is nothing in the papers about them unless one happens to crash, disappear, or set a speed record. Missile launchings have lost their novelty, and the exploration of space commands less attention than it did a mere two or three years ago. Nevertheless, the factor of novelty, if judiciously used, can be a potent force in arousing the attention of an audience. In selecting your materials, give particular consideration to two special aspects of it: (1) *size* and (2) *contrast*.

Size

Objects that are extremely large or extremely small attract our attention. People often are startled into attention by large numbers, especially if they are much larger than commonly supposed or are figures with which they are not familiar. In an address given at the University of Virginia, Henry W. Grady remarked, "A home that cost three million dollars and a breakfast that cost five thousand are disquieting facts."[4] Notice, however, that size alone is not sufficient; the size must be unusual or startling in comparison to what we expect or are already familiar with. Reference to a truck costing six thousand dollars or a bridge worth three million would hardly be striking. The New Yorker pays no attention to the skyscrapers, but the newcomer gets a cramp in his neck gazing up at the Empire State Building.

Contrast

At a formal dance, evening clothes pass unnoticed; but let a student come to class so dressed, and immediately attention centers on this fact. The student would have been equally conspicuous had he or she gone to the dance in gym clothes. Obviously, such extremes in attire are not recommended for the speaker; and, in any case, what is of primary concern here is the use of contrast in putting together and presenting the *content* of the speech. How much more compelling the facts mentioned by Grady become when he throws them into contrast with others: "Our great wealth has brought us profit and splendor, but the status itself is a menace. A home that cost three million dollars and a breakfast that cost five thousand are disquieting facts to the millions who live in a hut and dine on a crust. The fact that a man . . . has an income of twenty million dollars falls strangely on the ears of those who hear it as they sit empty-handed with children crying for bread."[5]

In utilizing the materials of novelty be careful, of course, not to inject elements that are so different or unusual that they are entirely unfamiliar. Remember that your listeners must at least know what you are talking about, or their attention will soon waver. They must be able to relate what you say to things they know and—preferably—have a degree of experience with. Best results are achieved by the proper combination of the new and the old, of the novel and the familiar. Note, too, that novelty may gain attention, but it will not necessarily hold it.

Suspense

Much of the fascination of a mystery story arises from uncertainty as to who committed the crime or, if known, whether the culprit will be caught. If the reader were to be told at once who killed the murdered man and how, why, and when the deed was done, probably the rest of the book never would be read. An effective advertisement, featuring a picture of a dividend check, declared: "The L. J. Smithson Company had been writing its balance in the red for two years, but last year it paid a dividend of twelve per cent." Immediately the reader wondered, "How did they do it?" and felt impelled to read on into the body of the advertisement to find out. Fewer people vote in what they know will be a one-sided election; the outcome is too predictable—there is no suspense. But the suspense of a close race arouses much interest. Hold the attention of your audience by pointing out results the cause of which must be explained, or by calling attention to a force the effect of which is uncertain. Keep up the suspense in the stories you use to illustrate your ideas. Mention some valuable information that you expect to divulge later in your speech but which first requires an understanding of the point you are now making. Make full use of the factor of suspense, but don't be so vague or mysterious that your listeners lose all hope of solving the riddle; give them a taste large enough to make them want to hear more, but make sure the suspenseful situation you are unfolding is important enough to the audience so that the suspense matters. Attention is seldom drawn by uncertainties which are trivial.

Conflict

The opposition of forces compels attention—especially if the listeners identify themselves with one of the contending sides. In a sense, conflict is a form of activity; but it is more than that—it is also a clash between competing desires or actions. Often conflict, like suspense, suggests uncertainty; but even when there is little doubt of the outcome, the combat itself draws attention. Football games, election contests, the struggle against the adverse elements of nature and disease—all these have an element of conflict within them, and people become interested when the conflicts are vividly described. For the same reason, controversy is more interesting than concurrence. A vigorous attack upon some antisocial force—be it gangsterism, graft, or child-neglect—will draw more immediate attention than an objective analysis of it, although the analysis might—in the long run—prove more effective or enduring. Describe a fight, show vividly the opposition between two factions, or launch a verbal attack on somebody or something, and people usually will listen to you. Be cautious, however, of sham battles. If you set up straw men and knock them down, the reality—and hence the effectiveness—of your message may be largely destroyed.

Humor

Laughter indicates enjoyment, and people pay attention to that which they enjoy. Few things, in fact, will hold an audience as well as the speaker's judicious use of humor. It provides relaxation from the tension often created by other factors of attention—conflict and suspense, especially—and thus reduces fatigue while still exercising a measure of control over the perceptions of the listener. Various types of humor and recommendations concerning their use will be discussed in Chapter 18, "The Speech to Entertain." For the present, however, note that the attention-holding power of humor is likely to be much stronger if you keep in mind two guidelines to which we have previously alluded: (1) *Be relevant.* Beware of wandering from the point under discussion. Any joke or anecdote you may use must reinforce rather than detract from the central idea of your speech. (2) *Use good taste.* Avoid humor on occasions where it would be out of place, and refrain from using those types of humor which might offend the sensitivities of your listeners.

The Vital

Finally, people pay attention to those things which affect their lives or health, their reputations, property, or employment. As we explained in Chapter 9, if you can show people that what you say concerns them or their families directly, they nearly always will consider your discussion vital and will listen intently. In a larger sense, the satisfaction of any of the basic drives or motives discussed in that chapter becomes a matter of vital concern to most persons. Even a danger to the life of someone else attracts listeners' attention because of their tendency to identify themselves with others. All of the other eight factors of attention are, of course, exceedingly important to communication; but this self-identification with the vital is indispensable. Always relate your comments and recommendations to matters which are vital to the existence, well-being, or happiness of your listeners.

The vital, humor, conflict, suspense, novelty, familiarity, proximity, reality, and activity and movement—these, in sum, are the magnetic "fingers" that beckon us to attention. These nine attention-attractors should be your constant guides when you are assembling, sorting out, and presenting ideas for a speech.

SUSTAINING ATTENTION: SOME PROBLEMS AND MATERIALS

As we pointed out in the beginning of this chapter, the essential nature of attention is to be *unstable* and *impermanent.* It tends to come and go or to flit from object to object in seemingly erratic and unpredictable ways. Our examination of the factors involved in generating it should have revealed, certainly, some of the reasons for this.

To explore this aspect of attention, try this simple experiment. Pick a spot on the wall or ceiling and attempt to focus your attention *solely* upon that spot for a full minute. In all probability, you will find this difficult or impossible to do. No matter how hard you try, after a few seconds you will find your attention wandering to another area of the wall or ceiling. You may, for example, become aware of another spot above or below or beside the spot you originally selected; you may think of your own bodily position; you may try to estimate how much of the minute has passed; you may even question the validity of the experiment itself. In all of these instances, and perhaps in others as well, your attention will have wandered from the spot on which you originally decided to concentrate.

This experiment should serve to demonstrate and reemphasize a very useful injunction: When preparing and presenting a speech, do not assume that all you need to do is catch the attention of your listeners in the first moments of your talk, and that their attention will then remain with you until you have finished. Realize instead that during the course of your message-presentation, your listeners' attention will come and go, will peak and lag. Consequently, you must be continuously concerned *throughout* your speech—in the opening, closing, and at all times *in between*—with bringing that attention back again and again to the ideas you wish to communicate.

As a concerned communicator, what—specifically—can you do to offset and, perhaps, compensate for the instability and impermanence of attention? Throughout this book we have been trying to supply a few of the answers: Vary your delivery. Relate your ideas to the needs, desires, attitudes, and values of your listeners. Support those ideas with sound and appropriate verbal and nonverbal substance. And, finally, as you select these materials, choose them carefully with a view to their *attention-generating* capabilities. In Chapter 15, for instance, where we consider specifically the matter of gaining the attention of your audience in the very beginning of your speech, we take particular note of the following:

1. Reference to the subject or problem.
2. Reference to the occasion.
3. Personal greeting or self-reference.
4. Rhetorical question.
5. Startling statement of fact or opinion.
6. Apt quotation.
7. Humorous anecdote.
8. Colorful illustration.

As you can readily see, such materials can prove especially valuable in helping to capture the attention of your listeners as you introduce yourself and your subject. And, of course, a number of them can be used also to create interest and hold the hearers' attention throughout the unfolding of your speech. Unless you succeed in holding the attention of your hearers on the ideas and materials you are communicating, you cannot hope to inform, instruct, or entertain them, let alone move them to belief or action.

A SAMPLE SPEECH

A graduate of John Marshall Law School and Chicago's Loyola University, The Honorable Edith S. Sampson, Circuit Court Judge of Cook County, Illinois, has been active in public life for most of her adult years and has served in numerous posts. Admitted to the Illinois Bar in 1927, she has been a referee in the Juvenile Court of Cook County and an assistant corporation counsel for the City of Chicago, and is one of the first black women in the United States to become an elected judge.

The following address was delivered by Judge Sampson at the 100th Annual Commencement ceremonies held at North Central College, Naperville, Illinois, on May 30, 1965—an occasion on which an honorary LL.D. degree was conferred on her. Note how the speaker has employed a number of the factors of attention—especially humor, familiarity, and the vital. Observe, also, how the easy, conversational style of the speech and its close adaptation to the audience help to sustain attention and interest.

CHOOSE ONE OF FIVE[6]

Edith S. Sampson

This degree that you have bestowed upon me out of your magnificent kindness is not just an honor. It's outright flattery—and I love it. Recognizing that it's impossible adequately to express my gratitude, I shall take the coward's way out and not even try.

Let me, instead, talk briefly to these graduates who have won their degrees the hard way instead of by the simple expedient of traveling from Chicago to Naperville.

You graduates have every right to expect penetrating words of profound wisdom from an LL.D., even when the doctorate is honorary.

You look for too much, of course, if you ask that I settle all affairs, both international and domestic, in anything under an hour. But I surely ought to be able to handle either one or the other of the side-by-side package without imposing too great a strain on your patience and your posteriors.

I should be able to untangle the enigma of Vietnam for you in 10 minutes and solve the Dominican problem in another 5. This would still give me, within a 20-minute limit, ample time to pronounce with authority on the assorted crises in the U.N., NATO, the Organization of American States, the Congo, Laos, Cambodia, Malaysia, Indonesia, India, and Pakistan.

Or, if I were to talk about the domestic scene, I should be able to sum up for you my definitive solutions to the problems of interracial relations, poverty, urban renewal, mass transportation, education—both higher and lower—organized crime, juvenile delinquency, the balance of payments, labor-management controversy, and what's to become of those dreadful people in Peyton Place.

If you wanted an analysis of the current state of art, literature, music, drama, and philosophy, you would have to give me another ten minutes.

Unfortunately, though, I am going to have to disappoint you, and I can only hope that you survive the sharp shock of disillusion. The degree that I've been given, precious as it is to me, did not endow me with instant wisdom.

As a result, I've been forced to fall back on a substitute for the all-revealing address that is your due today.

It's worse than that, really. Compounding what is already an offense, I'm going to present to you a multiple-choice test—the last of your college career.

The only consolations that I can offer in presenting the test are that it involves no bluebooks; you may consult texts freely; the test is self-scoring; and you have a lifetime at your disposal now to complete it.

This exam will be proctored, though. The proctors will be two—the community in which you live and, hardest taskmaster of all, your inner self.

The question: What do you do with your college education now that you have it—and now that it is beginning to become obsolete even as you sit here?

Choose one of five possible answers.

Choice One:

Put your diploma in a convenient drawer and close the drawer. Put whatever textbooks you've accumulated in a bookcase and close the bookcase. Put your mind to the dailiness of earning a satisfactory livelihood and close your mind.

I should warn you that it will take a bit of doing to follow this course with the rigor that it deserves.

You will have to take care not to read anything except, in the case of men, the sports pages or, in the case of women, columns of household hints.

You'll have to choose your friends with extreme care to make sure that you don't rub up against any stimulating personalities.

You'll have to build your own defenses against a world of complex realities that will insist on trying to intrude on you at the most inconvenient times.

But it can be done. I've known college graduates who have achieved it. They've wrapped themselves in an apathy so thick that they're in position to say in all truth, "No opinion," to any Gallup or Roper pollster who might question them on any subject.

It's a choice that's available to you. Choice one.

Choice Two:

Go forth into that waiting world, carefully assess the prevailing opinions, and then conform.

Forget this theoretical nonsense they've been feeding you here at North Central. What do professors and assistants and associates and instructors know about the real world anyway? Academics, all of them.

You'll have your degree. That certifies you're educated. Let it go at that.

This choice gives you more latitude than choice one.

You can scan the whole of the daily newspaper, as long as you make certain it's a newspaper that agrees with you and all other right-thinking citizens on all critical issues.

You can keep *Time* or *Newsweek*, *Life* or *Look* on the coffee table.

You can subscribe to the *Reader's Digest* and had better read at least some of it for conversational purposes.

You are even permitted, if you take this choice, to buy two books a year as long as you make sure they're best best-sellers. Reading the books is optional.

You don't have to be nearly so selective in making friends if you go this route instead of the first one. Just avoid the kooks—although that's easier said than done when what prevailing opinion recognizes as unmistakable kooks come in bewildering variety. But with a little caution you can easily manage.

After all, about 80, perhaps 85, per cent of the people with whom you'll come in contact fit nicely in this choice-two category. It isn't that they're particularly talented at blending into the background. They are the background.

You, too, can be a pillar-of-society conformist. No strain, no pain.

Well, almost no pain. The anguish of those moments in your middle age when you lie sleepless at 2 A.M. or 3 and wonder whatever happened to all your bright ambitions of college days—that anguish and those moments don't count too much.

Most of the time you can be comfortable with choice two, and who could ask for more than that?

One footnote at this point: Don't worry that your college degree will set you apart and make it impossible for you to be a really thorough conformist.

That was a slight danger in my day, but it's none at all now.

Ever since people have come to recognize the dollars-and-cents value of a college diploma as a passport to employment, more and more people have been going to college. Only the bigoted, narrow-minded people hold a degree against a person today, and the ranks of the conformists are filled with those who have had campus and even classroom exposure. B.A.'s, B.S.'s, masters, doctors—they can all live in the ticky-tacky houses.

Choice Three:

Refuse to relax into the commoner forms of conformity. Find yourself, instead, a clique of the elite, an "in" group, and conform yourself to it.

You might imagine, from that bare description of this choice, that this would be a difficult thing to do. It isn't at all.

There are just two requisites.

First, you must have a specialty of your own, some one field — or, better, part of a field — in which you're expert. It might be something in the arts — music before Vivaldi, for instance, or the epic poetry of Afghanistan. On the whole, though, it's better if your specialty is a little more practical, intellectual but money-making.

Then to the specialty, whatever it is, you add a dedication to everything that is advance guard and an amused contempt for everything else that isn't.

One thing you can't have if you go the third-choice way — at least not today — and that's a conviction that human beings and the history they have made and are making are important. Nothing is important really — nothing, that is, except your one staked-out small field of specialization.

A James Reeb is beaten to death for daring to assert in action the dignity of man. A Mrs. Liuzzo is shot, killed after the Selma to Montgomery march. Too bad.

But someone suggests that "The Cabinet of Dr. Caligari" isn't really such great shakes as a movie. This is monumental heresy. Tie him to the stake and put a torch to the faggots.

You must preserve the proper hierarchy of values, you see.

If you join the sort of "in" group I have in mind, your reading becomes constricted again, I'm afraid.

You mustn't read the daily papers, or at a minimum you mustn't admit it if you do. The Sunday *New York Times*, on occasion, can be tolerated, but no more than tolerated.

You may not read *Life*, *Look*, *Time*, *Newsweek*, or the *Reader's Digest*, not to mention such unmentionables as *Better Homes and Gardens* or *Family Circle*. Nothing more popular than *Scientific American*.

No best-sellers, of course — that goes without saying. It's much better to criticize Saul Bellow without having read *Herzog* all the way through, although you should read enough to be able to say it nauseated you so much you couldn't finish it.

This constriction of your reading is rather unfortunate in one way, really. You can't read things like the *New Republic*, or the *National Review*, or *Commentary*, or *Foreign Affairs*, or the *Bulletin of the Atomic Scientists*, or the *Reporter*, or anything of the sort. Those all deal with political and social and economic matters, you see, and an "in" conformist who attached importance to such matters would be drummed out of the corps. Serve him right.

Choice Four:

Choice four, though, offers an alternative for those who cannot erase their political-social-economic consciousness. Join an extremist group.

There is real effort involved in this at the very beginning. You have to study the various groups that present themselves and make your initial commitment.

The beauty of this choice, though, is that once you've made it, you can turn off your thinking and let yourself be carried by the forward surge of what is obviously a significant movement.

Say you link yourself to the far right.

Your enemies are immediately identified for you—Negroes, Jews, and Communists. Communists are easy to recognize—they're all the people who don't agree with you.

You know immediately what to oppose—fluorine in the water supply, income taxes, aid to foreign nations, the Supreme Court, movements for mental health, and any squeamishness about dropping nuclear bombs at will or whim.

You know immediately what to support—anything that the leaders of your group find good and pleasing, although unfortunately they find little that's either.

Say you link to the far left.

Your enemies are immediately identified for you—capitalists, the poor misled sheep of the middle class, and Fascists. Fascists are easy to recognize— they're all the people who don't agree with you.

You know immediately what to oppose—all business corporations, no exceptions; all Trotskyites; all deviationists; all revisionists; all efforts to help established governments resist Communist revolt.

You know immediately what to support—anything that the leaders of your group find good and pleasing, which is whatever the men in Moscow have smiled upon for the day.

What is so attractive about this choice four is that it requires no mental effort of you beyond the initial effort of making your selection. Yet it provides a wide-open emotional release [not] possible with any of the first three choices.

With choice four you can convince yourself that every action you perform has world-molding significance. In sharp contrast to the choice-three people, choice-four people are convinced that everything is important because everything links somehow to the cause.

Choice Five:

And then, finally, there's CHOICE FIVE. It's hard to state this one. About as close as I can come to it is this: Hang loose, but stay vibrantly alive.

This one's strenuous. This one's demanding.

Choice five would demand of you that you consider today's graduation no more than a pause to catch your breath before continuing the life-long job of education.

It would demand of you that you be your own unique best self. And there is no higher demand than that.

Choice five entails wide-ranging reading and deep-probing thought.

It calls for a contradictory thing—a mind that is constantly open to new facts that dictate change but at the same time is resolutely committed to what seems best at any given point of time.

It calls for human involvement, a compassionate concern for everyone on this fast-shrinking little planet of ours and for the generations to come.

It calls for the resolute rejection of all stereotypes and insists on the thoughtful examination of even the most widely held assumptions that are too easily taken for granted.

If only choice five involved only one thing or the other—thought or action—it would be ever so much easier. It doesn't, though. It involves both.

And as if that weren't bad enough, this choice usually brings with it a certain amount of inner ache, because this way is a lonely way.

Those who make choice four are caught up in a wave of fervent enthusiasm that is all the more compelling because there's so little of the rational in it. They have the company of their Birchite brothers or their Communist comrades.

Those who make choice three clump together with others of their kind to exchange small coins of comment about existentialism and Zen, the hilarious glories of Busby Berkley movies and the charm of Tiffany lamp shades.

Those who make choice two are protected by the great crowd of which they've so willingly, gladly made themselves an anonymous part, no different from every other anonymous part.

Those who make choice one deliberately dull their sensitivities. They are cud-chewing content to join the boys at the bar of a Saturday night or the girls at the bridge table Wednesday afternoon. They vegetate.

But those who make choice five are never fully comfortable.

They are nagged at by their realization that they could be wrong.

They're prodded by their recognition that they've still so much more to learn and even more than that to understand.

They're made restless by their knowledge that no matter how much they do, there's still ever so much more left to be done.

Choice-five people have to live constantly with an acceptance of the fact that there are no simple answers in this world because there are no simple questions.

This makes life exciting for them, challenging, at least intermittently rewarding. But comfortable? No.

I would not urge choice five on any of you graduates. It asks so much of you.

Any of the other four will see you through to age 60 or 65, retirement, and a modest pension. They might easily do better than that and make you rich. In dollars, that is.

Five is there, though—one of the multiple choices on the test.

If any of you in this class of '65 makes that fifth choice, I wish you'd let me know about it. You I'd like to know better than I possibly can just by having made a speech here.

You I would treasure even above the LL.D. with which North Central College has so graciously honored me—and that, you can believe me, is saying a great deal.

FOOTNOTES

[1] *Floyd L. Ruch and Philip G. Zimbardo,* Psychology and Life, *8th ed. (Glenview, Ill.: Scott, Foresman and Company, 1971), p. 267.*

[2] *Ibid., pp. 267–268.*

[3] *Ibid., p. 268.*

[4] *From an address by Henry W. Grady, presented to the Literary Societies of the University of Virginia, June 25, 1889.*

[5] *Ibid.*

[6] *"Choose One of Five" by Judge Edith S. Sampson from* Vital Speeches of the Day, *Vol. XXXI, (August 15, 1965). Reprinted by permission of the author.*

Problems and Probes

1. Find in the sample speeches in this book or in recent issues of *Vital Speeches of the Day* examples of each of the nine factors of attention considered in this chapter.

2. Listen to the commercials given on radio or television, and select five which you feel are probably effective in capturing and holding the attention of listeners/viewers. Write out the text of these commercial "messages"; identify the factors of attention employed in them; and, finally, decide which of the attention-getting and attention-holding techniques or devices would be useful to the public speaker and the participant in small group communication.

3. In which of the three forms of speech communication—dyadic, small group, or public speaking—do you expect to encounter the greatest difficulty in holding the listeners' attention? Develop a set of statements or reasons to support your conclusions convincingly.

4. From the pages of your daily newspaper and/or popular magazines, select five advertisements which seem to you to be particularly persuasive. Analyze them for the effectiveness with which they employ the factors of attention and the *skill* with which the copywriters have *phrased* the

advertising message so as to take maximum advantage of those factors. As a result of this analysis, carefully phrase five different statements which you as a public speaker could use to introduce a speech. Employ a different factor of attention in each statement, and remember that the purpose of the statement is twofold: (1) to *capture* listener interest and (2) to *hold* or *sustain* it.

5. Assume that you will be addressing an audience inclined to *drowsiness*. The time is late evening; the occasion is a formal banquet (the listeners have already eaten a heavy meal); and you are the fourth and final speaker on the program. Knowing these circumstances in advance, you have wisely decided to keep your remarks as brief and pointed as possible, limiting them to a ten-minute duration. Carefully devise three attention-"regaining" statements which, you believe, will be effective in awakening your listeners. Indicate at what intervals you will be uttering these "wake-up" statements.

6. Think back over your experiences of the past three days and select at least five instances in which you paid sustained attention to an object, process, or event: a classroom lecture, a book, a magazine, a television program, a visit to an art museum—for example. To which of these things did you pay attention *effortlessly* or *involuntarily?* To which of them did you have to pay *forced* or *voluntary* attention? What elements in the "involuntary" group especially attracted you? In the "voluntary" group, what particular elements or factors seemed to work against effortless attention?

7. Select three or four speech subjects which, you feel, would have little inherent interest-value for the other members of your speech class. Suggest how, through the use of factors of attention or similar devices, you could probably succeed in *making* these subjects of real interest to your hearers.

Oral Activities and Speaking Assignments

1. Perform the following experiment. After your instructor has placed a small white dot on an otherwise clean chalkboard, you and the other members of the class will sit in silence as you attempt to focus your attention *exclusively* on that dot for one full minute. At the end of that time, discuss the results of the test and what happened while it was taking place. Who, among you, was able to pay attention to nothing but the dot? How many of you were unable to keep your attention from wandering to something else—either tangible or intangible? As a result of the experiment and

the ensuing discussion, formulate some useful conclusions concerning the nature of attention and interest and the obligations of the speaker who hopes to attract and sustain them throughout the presentation of his or her message. (Reread pages 342–343, where a similar experiment was analyzed.)

2. Present a three- or four-minute speech in which you attempt to rivet the attention of the audience at the highest peak possible. Select a subject which in itself has exceptional interest-value, and use all of the materials, methods, and devices which we have considered in this chapter.

3. As a variation of the preceding assignment, deliberately "stack the cards" against yourself. Again present to the class a speech in which you attempt throughout to hold listeners' attention at the highest peak possible. This time, however, select a subject that has little or no inherent interest-value for your audience, and strive to make your speech as interesting and attention-commanding as you can.

Suggestions for Further Reading

Donald E. Broadbent, *Perception and Communication* (London: Pergamon Press, 1958).

J. Anthony Deutsch and D. Deutsch, "Attention: Some Theoretical Considerations," *Psychological Review* LXX (1970): 80–90.

Frank R. Hartman, "A Behavioristic Approach to Communication: A Selective Review of Learning Theory and a Derivation of Postulates," *Dimensions of Communication*, ed. Lee Richardson (New York: Appleton-Century-Crofts, 1969), pp. 127–132.

Barbara Lieb, "How to Be Influenced Discriminatingly," *Today's Speech* VII (April 1960): 24–26.

Floyd L. Ruch and Philip G. Zimbardo, *Psychology and Life*, 8th ed. (Glenview, Ill.: Scott, Foresman and Company, 1971), Chapter VII, "Awareness of the World We Live In," pp. 258–307.

Walter W. Stevens, "Attention Through Language," *Today's Speech* XI (November 1963): 23–25.

Hans Toch and Malcolm S. MacLean, Jr., "Perception and Communication: A Transactional View," *Audio-Visual Communication Review* X (1967): 55–77.

Magdalen D. Vernon, "Perception, Attention, and Consciousness," *Foundations of Communication Theory*, ed. Kenneth K. Sereno and C. David Mortensen (New York: Harper & Row, Publishers, 1970), pp. 137–151.

13
ADAPTING THE SPEECH STRUCTURE TO THE AUDIENCE: THE MOTIVATED SEQUENCE

Structuring, organizing, and outlining the speech—these are the primary concerns in this chapter and the one that follows. In the latter, we shall consider the rhetorical and compositional patterns by which to arrange substantive points and subpoints so as to ensure the validity and strength of their interrelationships. In the present chapter we consider how to *structure the speech psychologically:* how the psychological sequence of ideas within a speech can be adapted to the thinking processes of your listeners to help you gain the response you seek from them. Emphasizing further the ongoing, transactional relationships between speaker and listener, we view the structuring of the public speech as a *succession of steps* which, presumably, parallel and reinforce that process.

Remembering what we have said about the speech communication process and the transactional impulse which energizes it, it should be obvious that as a speaker you cannot simply "cram things down people's throats." You cannot force an audience to accept your ideas or compel listeners to decide or act against their will. Rather, you must *lead* and *guide* their thinking in ways that will cause them to respond willingly and naturally to the idea and intention you wish to communicate. You must, in short, build your speech with your hearers constantly in mind, and you must structure it so that the sequence of its major ideas corresponds with the way those hearers think their way through information and problems in order to arrive at understanding, belief, and/or action.

THE LISTENER'S MENTAL PROCESSES: SOME PSYCHOLOGICAL BASES

There is no guarantee, of course, that everyone—even in his most reflective moments—will always evaluate information, think through a problem, or arrive at a decision in exactly the same way. However, although individuals may vary to some extent, research has shown that most people seek a *consistency* or *balance* among their cognitions.* That is, when confronted with new knowledge, a contradictory or conflictive situation, or a problem that disturbs their normal orientation, they seek to *re-orient:* they look for ways to *re-balance;* they search for a *new solution.* As we emphasized when we talked about motivational appeals in Chapter 9, the desire for *order* is basic to humankind. When there is dissonance, we desire consonance. When something is *out* of order, we strive to put it back in. When something is out of balance, we try to restore equilibrium. When something seems inconsistent, we try to make it consistent. When we feel a need or want, we search for a way to satisfy it. In short, when anything throws people into a condition of disorganization or dissonance, they are motivated to adjust their cognitions and values, or to alter their behaviors in order to achieve a *new* state of balance. In making that adjustment, as psychologists Richard V. Wagner and John J. Sherwood point out, ". . . dissonance may be reduced by *selective exposure* to information about the dissonant elements."[1] A comprehension of the consistency concept in general, and the dissonance principle in particular, is fundamental to the overall understanding and successful use of the psychological sequence-structure we are proposing for the public speech.

The philosopher John Dewey drew upon this theory, as we mentioned in Chapter 3, to develop a description of the way in which most individuals, when confronted with a choice or a problem situation, systematically think their way through to a decision. *First,* Dewey said, they begin simply by recognizing the specific lack or disorientation which constitutes the problem at hand. *Second,* they examine the difficulty to determine its nature, scope, and implications. *Third,* they search for a new orientation in the form of a solution. *Fourth,* they compare and evaluate the possible solutions which occur to them. And, *fifth,* they select the solution or course of action which, upon the basis of the foregoing reflection, seems best.[2]

On first consideration, you might suppose that a listener's mental processes would vary according to the type of response the speaker asks him to make. You might assume that a response of *enjoying* or *being entertained* calls for a thought process different from that used in *understanding,* and that *believing* requires a mental pattern different from both. However, the fact of the matter is that the mental process that listeners go through in making various kinds of responses differs not so much in kind as in *completeness.* If the only reaction you ask from a listener is that he enjoy himself, the major thought-step he must take is to give attention to what you say. When your objective is to inform him, he must

---

*For a detailed explanation, see Leon Festinger, A Theory of Cognitive Dissonance (New York: Harper & Row, Publishers, 1957). Useful summaries of "balance" and "consistency" theories may be found in Thomas M. Scheidel, Speech Communication and Human Interaction (Glenview, Ill.: Scott, Foresman and Company, 1972), pp. 222–224.

still give you his attention; but now he must also take a second step—a step in which he becomes conscious of a need or desire to acquire new knowledge; and, in response to that need, he must understand, absorb, and relate to the information you are presenting.

To go a step further, let's suppose that you want to obtain from your listeners a response of *overt action*—to induce them to *do* something: sign a petition, make a contribution, join a protest march, vote for a specific candidate on election day. In this case, if your speech is to succeed, your listeners must not only (*a*) pay attention, (*b*) recognize a need to know, and (*c*) understand a proposal; they must also—through their thought process—(*d*) be convinced of the soundness and desirability of the recommended action, *and* they must be spurred on to (*e*) perform it. In short, the mental processes that lead the listener to each of the general ends of speaking are not actually different; instead, these processes are *cumulative*; their completeness and complexity are determined by the nature of the response you ask for.

The Motivated Sequence

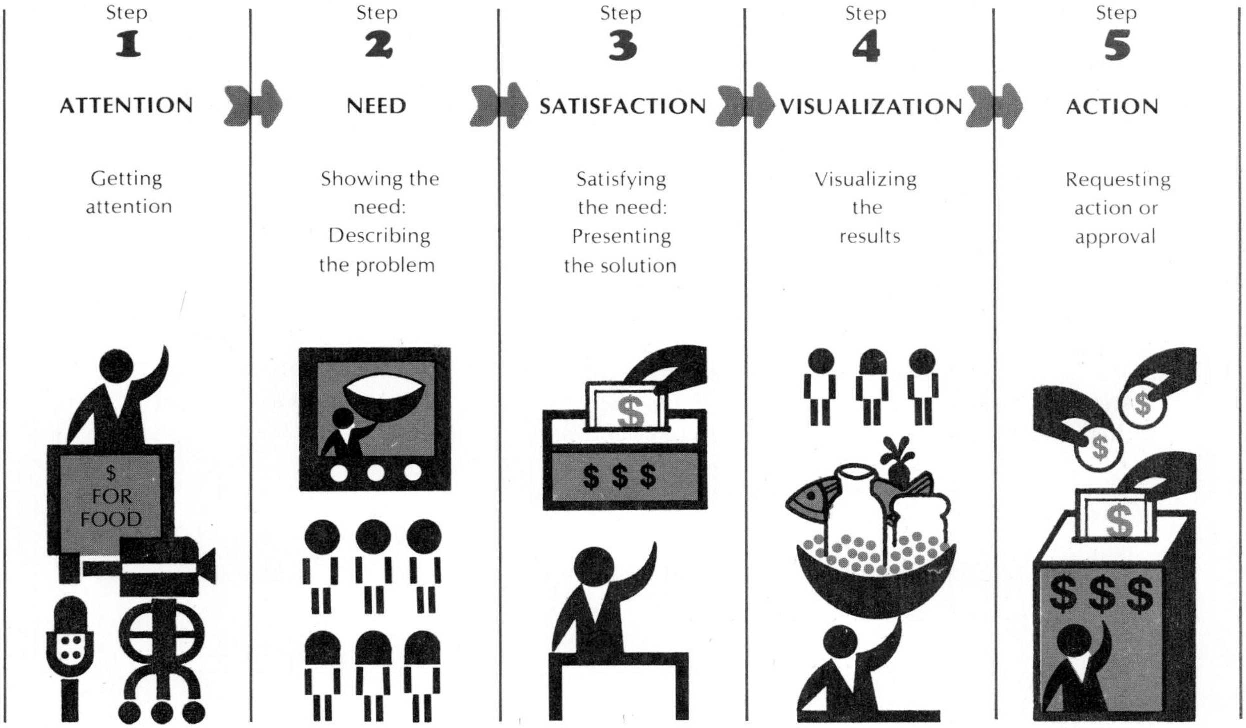

Step **1**	Step **2**	Step **3**	Step **4**	Step **5**
ATTENTION	NEED	SATISFACTION	VISUALIZATION	ACTION
Getting attention	Showing the need: Describing the problem	Satisfying the need: Presenting the solution	Visualizing the results	Requesting action or approval

Figure 1

THE MOTIVATED SEQUENCE

From the foregoing considerations, it seems reasonable to conclude that despite individual differences of temperament and cognitive capabilities, most listeners have thought processes that are surprisingly uniform—sufficiently uniform, at least, that they provide a practical basis for a standard pattern of speech structure. We call this pattern *the motivated sequence: the sequence of ideas which, because it follows the normal processes of human thinking, motivates an audience to respond to the speaker's purpose.*

As we shall see, the speaker may—if he chooses—use the motivated sequence as the backbone for all types of speeches, modifying it only by omitting or lengthening certain of the steps. Let us consider it first in its most complete form: that used when the communicator's purpose is *to produce action.* Although not a speech, the Maritz illustration on the facing page serves to exemplify how this motivational structuring works. Entitled "Motivated Men Made America Great," the advertisement appeared in *Fortune Magazine* and embodies the basic five-step progression and the essential features of the motivated sequence.

Notice that this advertisement has five distinct steps with the ultimate design of getting action: (1) your *attention* is caught; (2) you are made to feel a definite *need;* (3) you are shown a way in which this need can be *satisfied;* (4) the benefits of purchasing the Maritz service are *visualized;* and (5) *action* in the form of contacting a representative of the Maritz agency is called for.

With a similar end (to actuate) in view, we might use the same outline for a speech because the minds of human beings operate in much the same way whether confronted with the content of an advertisement or of an actuative speech. An audience must be guided through essentially the same steps: Attention must be diverted from other things and converged on what the speaker has to say; the listeners must be made to realize that a need exists; a method of satisfying this need must be presented and shown to be an effective one; the listeners must be helped to visualize the desirable condition which the solution will create; and, finally, they must be given instruction and guidance on how you want them to act or what you want them to believe.

The Five Steps in the Sequence

To each of these steps we shall assign a name indicative of its function:

1. Attention.
2. Need.
3. Satisfaction.
4. Visualization.
5. Action.

1. The beginnings of Abraham Lincoln's greatness can be found in his boyhood desire to learn. . . . With less than a year of formal education, "Honest Abe" overcame the obscurity of a bleak frontier environment to become a self-taught lawyer, a universally respected national leader, and our country's "Great Emancipator."

• • •

2. Countries need motivated men. Companies do, too, especially when their success depends on the extra effort of individual salesmen and entire sales organizations.

• • •

3. We help fill this need for companies in all industries.
Maritz is the only company in the United States engaged exclusively in the business of motivating men to sell. As specialists, we offer complete sales-motivation services including planning, program promotion, administration, and *follow-through.* All are offered in conjunction with distinctive merchandise and glamorous travel awards.

• • •

4. The combination causes salesmen to work harder, more intelligently, and more successfully. Their increased productivity improves sales and profits for the clients we serve.

• • •

5. Your Maritz Account Executive can tell you how we can help you develop new markets, open new territories, promote particular products, and achieve more sales with a sales-motivation program designed to meet your company's specific needs. We suggest that you contact him. He offers you the exclusive services of the leader in the field of sales motivation.[3]

With the names of these steps in mind, let us look again at the *Fortune* advertisement and extend our analysis of it, thus:

1. *Attention.* Using the interest factor of "the familiar," as explained in Chapter 12 (page 339), the communicator—in this case, the agency spokesman—attempts to capture attention by a brief description of Lincoln's strong motivation to succeed.

2. *Need.* A direct statement asserts that businesses, like countries, need motivated men.

3. *Satisfaction.* Because it specializes in all phases of motivation, the Maritz spokesman says his agency is well qualified to meet this need and can, therefore, ensure satisfaction.

4. *Visualization.* Benefits in the form of harder-working salesmen and greater sales and profits are pictured.

5. *Action.* The agency spokesman asks you to contact a Maritz account executive.

The Motivated Sequence Applied to Speeches to Actuate

Let us now consider a speech which, like the advertisement we have just examined, has *actuation* as its general end. Entitled "Nice People," it was prepared and presented in the annual contest of the Interstate Oratorical Association by Ms. Jan Bjorklund, Mankato State College, Mankato, Minnesota.

"NICE PEOPLE"[4]

Jan Bjorklund

What I am about to say, I have said before; so have many others in many other ways. And that's about it. A great deal has been *said*, but very little has been *done*, so this problem remains a problem. For this reason, I'd like to emphasize the words and the meaning of this speech, hoping that you will react from an understanding of these words. *Attention Step*

An epidemic of contagious disease is threatening the United States at this very minute: one so massive that a new case occurs every 15 seconds, for a total of 7,500 a day.[1] *Need Step*

All age levels are being victimized by this disease, but most selectively young people, ages 16 to 30. This epidemic is capable of spreading undetected inside the bodies of over 700,000 women, allowing them to continue a normal life, causing them no discomfort, no disability, no pain, while robbing them of their ability to bear children.[2]

All the while this disease continues to strike, to spread, and to slay, the means to cure it not only exist, but are relatively inexpensive, relatively simple to administer, and painless to the receiver.

Isn't it strange that our nation, one of the healthiest in the world, should allow such a disease to continue, to multiply into an uncontrollable epidemic? One would think that the halls of government would be echoing with the debate and discussion of possible courses of action to eradicate this festering blight. Yes, one could think that—until realizing this is not the case, due to the small and medically irrelevant fact that the disease in question is *venereal* disease.

In 1936, the Surgeon General of the United States Public Health Service, Thomas Parran, stated that the great impediment to the solution of the VD problem was that "nice" people don't have it.[3] Since then, the basis for this statement has disappeared. Oh, Freaks have it, and Blacks, and Jesus People, and urban disadvantaged, and poverty-stricken, and people on welfare: *they* all have it, all right! It's been called "their" disease. But is it theirs alone?

Berkeley, California, is a "nice" place to live. Within the city's limits, we find the University of California and many of its prominent faculty and students. Last year, 2,000 cases of gonorrhea were reportedly found there, too.[4]

Houston, Texas, is a "nice" place, too. Nice enough to attract attention and become the headquarters for our national space program. Last year it also attracted 1,266 cases of gonorrhea for every 100,000 inhabitants.[5]

Atlanta, Georgia, the cultural and commercial capital of the South, also leads the nation in the reported number of cases of gonorrhea. Last year it reported 2,510 cases for every 100,000 inhabitants.[6]

These are only the *reported* cases, estimated to be 25 percent of all cases, for only 1 out of every 4 cases is ever reported.[7]

This would mean that of the 100,000 inhabitants of Berkeley, California, approximately 8,000 contracted VD; that would be 1 out of 12!

This ratio isn't so crucial, though, when you compare it to that in some San Franciscan high schools where a student has 1 chance in 5 of contracting syphilis or gonorrhea before he graduates.[8]

Why? People neglect to get the proper treatment; or when they do, they don't name all their contacts, so the disease continues to spread.

According to *Today's Health* magazine, of the 4 out of 5 cases that are treated by private physicians, only 1 out of 9 is reported.[9] And of the many, many that go by unreported, I'd guess that 90 percent involve nice people.

Syphilis and gonorrhea are infectious diseases outranked in incidence only by the common cold.[10]

. . . .

Venereal disease is especially rampant among young people. As reported in *Newsweek*, January 24, 1972, at least 1 of every 5 persons with gonorrhea is below the age of 20.[12] Last year, over 5,000 cases were found among children between the ages of 10 and 14. Another 2,000 cases were found among children below the age of 9. Dr. Walter Smartt, Chief of the Los Angeles County Venereal Disease Control Division, states that the probability of a person acquiring VD before he reaches the age of 25 is about 50 percent. This would mean that of the number of us here in this room, one half of us have already or shortly will come in contact with VD. Where does that put you? Or me? It's always easy to say it can only happen to someone else, to the other person, but there is only one guarantee that it can't strike me or you.

And that one guarantee is abstinence. But in this day and age, that's hardly a likely possibility. We wouldn't think of stopping tuberculosis by stopping breathing, so how could we think of stopping venereal disease by stopping sex?

What is the solution? A number of suggestions have been made.

Satisfaction Step

First of all, in the opinion of many experts, syphilis could be brought under control by case-finding. However, in the last few years the number of case-finders has been reduced. The Federal Government is not supporting this effort.

Secondly, there is a deplorable inadequacy in both teaching and courses of instruction concerning VD. We need an educational effort at the earliest feasible age group. Looking at the ages of the patients coming into the clinics, we see we almost have to beat puberty.

Another possibility has been suggested by Dr. John Knox of Houston's Baylor College of Medicine. He predicts that a vaccine for syphilis could easily be developed in 5 years, but at the rate the government is putting out money, it will probably take 105 years.[13] A vaccine for gonorrhea, on the other hand, seems almost impossible at this point. There is a crying need for more research.

Visualization Step

I thought for sure that such a complex problem would require a complicated cure. However, I became aware of my mistaken thinking during a visit with my college physician, Dr. Hankerson. He informed me that syphilis and gonorrhea can be brought under control and cured by simple treatments of penicillin or similar antibiotics. If every American would have a regular checkup, and receive treatment if necessary, by 1973 we could begin to send venereal disease the way of typhoid, measles, polio, and the bubonic plague. If each of us would begin with a regular checkup, now.

Action Step

As you can see, it is a complex problem, and no one solution can completely eliminate it. What we need is a concerted drive that will encompass case-finding, support for an educational effort, and the search for a vaccine, along with the use of penicillin and other similar antibiotics.

But even if this does happen, the effort cannot be successful, for venereal disease will continue to spread as long as it is thought of as dirty and shameful. Dr. McKenzie-Pollock, former director of the American Social Health Association, made the following statement: "Once the public is aware and notified that syphilis and gonorrhea are serious factors in our everyday lives right now, the rest will follow."[14]

Very well, consider yourself *notified* . . . or are you one of those "nice people"?

[1]VD Fact Sheet—*1971, U.S. Department of Health, Education, and Welfare, Public Health Service, page 9.*   [2]*Today's Health, April 1971, page 16.*   [3]*Today's Health, April 1971, page 16.*   [4]VD Statistical Letter, *DHEW, February 1972, page 11.*   [5]*Ibid., page 4.*   [6]*Newsweek, January 24, 1972, page 46.*   [7]*Minneapolis Tribune, Wednesday, April 5, 1972, page 2A.*   [8]*Newsweek, January 24, 1972, page 46.*   [9]*Today's Health, April 1971, page 69.*   [10]*Sex and the Yale Student, Student Committee on Human Sexuality, 1970, page 51.*   [12]*Ibid., page 46.*   [13]*Ibid., page 49.*   [14]*Today's Health, April 1971, page 69.*

Observe that Ms. Bjorklund (1) called attention to her subject by piquing the curiosity of her hearers; (2) pointed out—by means of statistics, specific instances, authoritative testimony, and comparisons—the crucial need to bring venereal disease under control; (3) demonstrated—by means of offering a three-way solution—that this pressing need could be satisfied; (4) visualized briefly the results of carrying out the proposed solution; and (5) concluded by appealing for direct and immediate action in the form of a concerted drive.

As Ms. Bjorklund's speech demonstrates, the steps in the motivated sequence will not be of equal length in every speech, nor will they always be developed in the same way. Each situation must be handled separately. Sometimes one or more of the steps may be treated very briefly or omitted entirely. For instance, if your listeners already realize that a need exists—that something must be done—you do not have to dwell on the need step. You merely remind them of the urgency of the problem and show how your proposal will remedy it.

Figure 2. FUNCTIONAL RELATIONSHIP OF SEQUENTIAL STEPS TO SPEECH PURPOSES

Speech to:	*Attention*	*Need*	*Satisfaction*	*Visualization*	*Action*
Entertain	Step 1				
Inform	Step 1	Step 2	Step 3		
Persuade	Step 1	Step 2	Step 3	Step 4	
Actuate	Step 1	Step 2	Step 3	Step 4	Step 5

Moreover, the general end for which you are speaking will substantially modify your use of the motivated sequence. Indeed, only when the general end is *to actuate* are all five steps employed. The accompanying chart, "The Motivated Sequence Applied to Speeches to Actuate," is intended to emphasize this involvement and to help you set it in your mind, thus:

THE MOTIVATED SEQUENCE APPLIED TO SPEECHES TO ACTUATE

Step	Function	Audience Response
1. Attention Step.	Getting attention.	"I want to listen."
2. Need Step.	Showing the need: describing the problem.	"Something needs to be done (decided, or felt)."
3. Satisfaction Step.	Satisfying the need: presenting the solution.	"This is what to do (believe, or feel) to satisfy the need."
4. Visualization Step.	Visualizing the results.	"I can see myself enjoying the satisfaction of doing (believing, or feeling) this."
5. Action Step.	Requesting action or approval.	"I will do (believe, or feel) this."

These five steps again are illustrated in the following outline which a student drew up for a speech on fire prevention:

FIRE PREVENTION AT HOME

Attention Step

    I. If you like parlor tricks, try this:
        A. Place a blotter soaked in turpentine in a jar of oxygen.
        B. The blotter will burst into flames.
    II. If you have no oxygen jar around the house, try this:
        A. Place a well-oiled mop in a storage closet.
        B. In a few days the mop will burst into flames.

Need Step

> I. Few homes are free from dangerous fire hazards.
>> A. Attics with piles of damp clothing and paper are combustible.
>> B. Storage closets, containing cleaning mops and brushes, are dangerous.
>> C. Basements are often filled with dangerous piles of trash.
>> D. Garages attached to houses are danger spots.

Satisfaction Step

> I. To protect your home from fire requires three things:
>> A. A thorough cleaning out of all combustible materials.
>> B. Careful storage of such hazards as oil mops, paint brushes, etc.
>>> 1. Clean them before storing.
>>> 2. Store them in fireproof containers.
>> C. A regular check to see that inflammable trash does not accumulate.
> II. Clean-up programs show practical results.
>> A. Clean-up campaigns in Evansville kept insurance rates in a "Class 1" bracket.
>> B. A clean-up campaign in Fort Wayne helped reduce the number of fires.

Visualization Step

> I. You will enjoy the results of such a program.
>> A. You will have neat and attractive surroundings.
>> B. You will be safe from fire.

Action Step

> I. Begin your own clean-up campaign now.

Thus far, we have considered the motivated sequence only as it applies to speeches which ask for action. When, as in a speech to persuade, your general end is primarily to influence the beliefs of the audience, the fifth and final step in which you appeal for overt action may be omitted and the speech terminated with one of the types of conclusions to be discussed in Chapter 15 (pages 420–425).

The Motivated Sequence Applied to Speeches to Inform

The speech to inform requires only *three* steps: attention, need, and satisfaction—the need step showing the listeners why the information about to be presented is important to them, and the satisfaction step meeting the need by supplying the information itself, thus:

THE MOTIVATED SEQUENCE APPLIED TO SPEECHES TO INFORM*

Step	Function	Audience Response
1. Attention Step.	Getting attention.	"I want to listen."
2. Need Step.	Demonstrating the need to know.	"I need information on this subject."
3. Satisfaction Step.	Presenting the information itself.	"The information being presented helps me understand the subject more satisfactorily."

Here is how a student, giving instructions for rescuing drowning persons, used these three steps to structure an informative speech thus:

ROW—THROW—GO

Attention Step

    I. Holiday deaths by drowning are second only to auto accidents.

Need Step

    I. Every person should know what to do when a call for help is heard.
        A. This information may help you save a friend.
        B. This information may help you save a member of your family.

---

*For a more detailed discussion of the motivated steps in informative speeches, see pp. 492–502.

I. Remember three important words when someone is drowning: *row, throw, go.*
   A. *Row:* Look for boat.
      1. You can well afford to take a little time to look for a means of rowing to the rescue.
         a. Look for a boat.
         b. Look for a canoe.
         c. Look for a raft.
      2. Rowing to the rescue is always the wisest way.
   B. *Throw:* Look for a life buoy.
      1. See if you can locate something buoyant to throw to the person in distress.
         a. Look for a life buoy.
         b. Look for an inflated inner tube.
         c. Look for a board.
         d. Look for a child's floating toy.
      2. You can throw an object faster than you can swim.
   C. *Go:* As a last resort, swim out to the drowning person.
      1. Approach the victim from the rear.
      2. If you are grabbed, go underwater.
      3. Clutch the person's hair.
      4. Swim for shore.
II. Remember, when you hear the call for help:
   A. Look first for something in which to row.
   B. Look for something buoyant to throw to the victim.
   C. Swim out only as a last resort.

The Motivated Sequence Applied to Speeches to Entertain

And, finally, the speech to entertain may consist entirely of an expanded attention step, with the other four steps omitted, thus:

THE MOTIVATED SEQUENCE APPLIED TO SPEECHES TO ENTERTAIN

Step	Function	Audience Response
1. Attention Step.	Getting attention and retaining interest by providing entertainment.	"I want to listen, and I'll continue listening because I'm enjoying myself."

The brief outline below illustrates how one student structured an entertaining speech in this way by using humor in developing an extended attention step:

A TOAST TO THE APPLE

Attention Step

I. The apple should be our national fruit.
- A. Adam and Eve started our life of joy and confusion because of an apple.
- B. Apples saved the lives of our favorite childhood characters.
    - 1. The third little pig in the *Three Little Pigs* was saved from the wolf by an apple.
    - 2. Alex in the *Bear Story* was saved from starvation by eating the apples growing on the sycamore tree.
- C. Apples are the symbol of our early education.
    - 1. "A was an apple pie; B bit it; C cut it."
- D. Apples enter into our courtship songs.
    - 1. We sing to our sweetheart, "I'll Be with You in Apple Blossom Time."
    - 2. We then serenade her with "In the Shade of the Old Apple Tree."
    - 3. We warn her, "Don't Sit Under the Apple Tree with Anyone Else but Me."
- E. Our health may depend upon an apple.
    - 1. As the proverb says, "An apple a day keeps the doctor away."
- F. Johnny Appleseed is rightfully a national hero.

II. So here's to the apple—our national fruit!

From what has been said thus far, it should be apparent that these motivational divisions of a speech are *functional* in nature: that is, each part or step has a particular function to perform in influencing the mental processes of the listener. The ideas and supporting material included in each step, therefore, must be sufficient in amount and quality to perform the necessary function of that step. Moreover, the number of steps and the particular function of each must be modified to suit the general end of the speech. The chart on the following page summarizes the ways in which the motivated sequence is adapted to each of the general ends. *Study the chart carefully before going further.* You will then be ready to consider in greater detail how each step in the motivated sequence may be developed—the consideration to which we next turn our attention.

ADAPTATION OF THE MOTIVATED SEQUENCE TO THE GENERAL ENDS OF SPEAKING

Type of Speech	Instructive	Persuasive		Recreative	
General End	TO INFORM	TO PERSUADE	TO ACTUATE	TO ENTERTAIN	
Reaction Sought	Understanding (Clarity)	Belief (Internal)	Specific Action (Observable)	Interest and Diversion (Enjoyment)	
Attention Step	Draw attention to the subject.	Draw attention to the need.	Draw attention to the need.	(A) Draw attention to an interesting idea. Keep interest in it alive by a series of illustrations, anecdotes, and humorous treatment: relate these to things in which the audience is already interested. Organize as a single-idea speech. Stop while interest is still high.	(B) Draw attention to an absurd problem and entertain by an exaggerated treatment of it, thus burlesquing the entire motivated sequence as used in a serious speech to actuate; present the discussion in mock seriousness, with marked and obvious exaggeration.
Need Step	Show why the listeners need a knowledge of the subject; point out what problems this information will help them meet.	Present evidence to prove the existence of a situation which requires that something be decided and upon which the audience must take a position.	Present evidence to prove the existence of a situation which requires action.		
Satisfaction Step	Present information to give them a satisfactory knowledge of the subject as an aid in the solution of these problems; begin and end this presentation with a summary of the main points presented. (Normal end of the speech.)	Get the audience to believe that your position on this question is the right one to take, by using evidence and motivational appeals.	Propose the specific action required to meet this situation; get the audience to believe in it by presenting evidence and motivational appeals (as in the speech to persuade).	Omit last four steps of the motivated sequence.	
Visualization Step	Sometimes: briefly suggest pleasure to be gained from this knowledge.	Briefly stimulate a favorable response by projecting this belief into imaginary operation. (Normal end of the speech.)	Picture the results which such action or the failure to take it will bring; use vivid description (as in the speech to persuade).		
Action Step	Sometimes: urge further study of the subject.	Sometimes: arouse determination to retain this belief (as a guide to future action).	Urge the audience to take definite action proposed.		

THE STEPS OF THE MOTIVATED SEQUENCE

Now that we have viewed the motivated sequence as a whole and considered in some detail its actual application to the various types of public speeches, let us turn our scrutiny to the *individual steps*, noting in particular their internal structuring, the methods of their development, and the kinds of materials that may be used with good effect in each.

The Attention Step

As a speaker, your first task is, of course, to *gain attention*. But merely gaining attention is not enough: you must also gain *favorable* attention, and you must direct it toward the major ideas in your speech. Since we have devoted an entire chapter to the subject of attention (pages 332–352), we need not examine those factors further at this point; and because we shall consider in Chapter 15 the *materials* useful for gaining and sustaining attention, we shall merely enumerate them here, as follows:

1. Reference to the subject.
2. Reference to the occasion.
3. Personal greeting.
4. Rhetorical question.
5. Startling statement.
6. Quotation.
7. Humorous anecdote.
8. Illustration.

Frequently, you will use only one of these types of materials to develop the attention step of the motivated sequence, but you may also combine two or more of them. Remember, however, that except in the speech to entertain, the attention step is only a *means* to an end, not an end in itself. When speaking to inform, persuade, or actuate, be sure that your attention step leads naturally into the ensuing portions of your speech.

The Need Step

The kind of need step you develop will vary with the purpose of your speech and with the audience's attitude toward that purpose. For example, speeches to actuate often urge a change in existing conditions. In such speeches, the need step attempts to create dissatisfaction with things as they are in order to convince the audience of the desirability of altering them. Speeches to inform, on the other hand, require a need step in which the listeners are made to feel the limited scope of their knowledge of the subject and are helped to realize how important the missing information is to them.*

However, although adaptations to different kinds of situations and to various speech purposes clearly are called for, a good need step should—whenever possible—contain these four parts or elements: (1) *Statement*—a clear, concise statement of the need or problem. (2) *Illustration*—one or more detailed examples which illustrate it. (3) *Ramification*—additional examples, statistical data, testimony, and other forms of support to show the extent and seriousness of the need. (4) *Pointing*—a convincing demonstration of how the need directly affects the people addressed: their health, happiness, security, or other interests.

Let us put this method of development in outline form so that its essential structure is clear:

1. *Statement.* State the need (the specific lack or problem, or the importance of the information you will present to the audience).
2. *Illustration.* Relate one or more incidents to illustrate this need.
3. *Ramification.* Employ as many forms of support as are required to make the need convincing and impressive.
4. *Pointing.* Show the importance of the need to the particular audience you are addressing.

You will notice how closely this structure resembles that of a single-idea speech developed by the didactic method (page 323). This is because many need steps, taken by themselves, are really single-idea speeches; that is, they point out just one thing—need.

Some needs, of course, are complex and consist of more than one main aspect. In cases of this kind, develop each of these aspects separately and then draw them together to show their interrelation. The result will be similar to a series of single-idea speeches related to one another and tied together at the end.

Although usually desirable, it is not always necessary to use all four of the structural elements of *statement, illustration, ramification,* and *pointing* to develop the need step. You should always use the statement and the pointing, but you can omit the illustration and the ramification, depending upon the amount of detail required to impress the need on your listeners. But regardless of whether you use the complete fourfold development, only a part of it, or some other structure, you will find that the need step is one of the most important in your speech. This is because it is here that you must relate your subject to the vital concerns and interests of your audience.

For a more detailed development of the need step in speeches to inform, persuade, and actuate, see Chapters 19, 20, and 21.

The Satisfaction Step

As we have said, the purpose of the satisfaction step is to enable your hearers to understand the material you have chosen to explain or to get them to agree that the belief or action you propose is the correct one. The structure of this step differs somewhat, however, depending on whether the speech is informative or persuasive in nature. For this reason the satisfaction step for instructive speeches and the satisfaction step for persuasive and actuative speeches are discussed separately in the following paragraphs.

The Satisfaction Step in Speeches to Inform

When your purpose is to inform — to give the audience a clear understanding of some subject — the satisfaction step usually will constitute the bulk of your speech, and will present the information that was outlined as necessary in the need step. The development of this step customarily includes: (1) *an initial summary*, (2) *detailed information*, and (3) *a final summary*.

The *initial summary* gives a brief preview of the information you plan to present, and usually consists of an enumeration of the main headings around which you will group your facts and explanations. In this way, you make the direction of your discussion clear in advance. Obviously, the main points listed in this initial summary should parallel the order in which you intend to discuss them; otherwise, you will give your audience a false lead. Although not always called for, when a subject is complex or much information needs to be covered, an initial summary serves as an excellent guidepost for your listeners.

Next, the *detailed information* is presented; the main points mentioned in the initial summary are considered in turn, and the facts and explanations relating to them are grouped around these points in an orderly fashion. Use a consistent order of discussion, such as the time sequence, space sequence, etc. (See Chapter 14, pages 385–388.) In this way you can make sure that your speech moves along in a definite direction and that your audience does not get lost.

The *final summary* recapitulates the main points you have discussed, and reviews whatever important conclusions you have drawn from them. It is similar to the initial summary in structure, but is usually longer.

The development of the satisfaction step as used in informative speeches may, then, be outlined as follows:

1. *Initial summary.* Briefly state in advance the main ideas or points you intend to cover.
2. *Detailed information.* Discuss in order the facts and explanations pertaining to each of these ideas or points.

3. *Final summary.* Restate the main points or ideas you have presented, together with any important conclusions you have drawn from them.*

If presented as outlined above, your information will generally be clear and coherent.

The Satisfaction Step in Speeches to Persuade

When the purpose of a speech is to persuade or to actuate, five elements may be included in the satisfaction step: (1) *Statement.* Briefly state the attitude, belief, or action you wish the audience to adopt. (2) *Explanation.* Make sure your proposal is understood. Diagrams or charts often are useful here. (3) *Theoretical demonstration.* Show how the solution logically meets the problem pointed out in the need step. (4) *Practical experience.* Give actual examples showing that this proposal has worked effectively or that this belief has been proved correct. Use facts, figures, and the testimony of experts to support this conclusion. (5) *Meeting objections.* Forestall opposition by showing how your proposal overcomes possible objections which might be raised against it.

Again, as was the case with the elements in the need step, not all of the elements in the satisfaction step are required in every speech. Nor is it necessary that these elements always appear in the same order. For instance, objections can sometimes best be met by answers distributed strategically throughout the satisfaction step, at whatever points the questions are likely to arise. When developing the satisfaction step in speeches to persuade or to actuate, however, the first four elements — *statement, explanation, theoretical demonstration,* and *practical experience* — form a convenient and effective sequence, thus:

1. Briefly state the attitude, belief, or action you propose.
2. Explain it clearly.
3. Show how in theory it will meet the need.

Parallel Development of Need and Satisfaction Steps

In some speeches of a persuasive nature, the need step may have two or more important aspects. To give each of these aspects sufficient emphasis and to make your discussion clear, you may develop the need and satisfaction steps in a *parallel* order. First present one aspect of the need, and show how your proposal or information satisfies it; follow this same procedure with the second aspect; then the third aspect; and so on. This method weakens the cumulative effect of the motivated sequence, but the additional clarity often makes up for the loss.

---

*For a more complete consideration of these parts of the satisfaction step in a speech to inform, see pp. 495–497.

The following skeletal outlines, developed for the subject "Structural Safety in Airplane Design," illustrate the *normal order* and the *parallel order* for developing the need and satisfaction steps:

Attention Step

    I. I recently witnessed several interesting and frightening test flights.
        A. Vivid description of test flights.
        B. Vivid description of accidents.

Need Step

    I. The *body design* of a new airplane may have serious faults.
        A. Parts in the wing structures may be too heavy.
        B. The structures may not be strong enough to withstand strain.
   II. The *engine design* of a new airplane may have serious faults.

Satisfaction Step

    I. Test flights throw light on how the *body design* of a new airplane can be improved.
        A. They show up defects in the wing structures.
        B. By putting extra in-flight stresses on the airplane, they indicate the strength of the structures.
   II. Test flights throw light on how the *engine design* of a new airplane can be improved.
        A. They indicate engine reliability.
        B. They reveal general engine performance under great strains.

Visualization Step

    I. Through the help of test flights, there should be tremendous development in airplane engine and body design in the near future.

Action Step

    I. I therefore urge increased expenditures for test flights.

Attention Step

    I. I recently witnessed several interesting and frightening test flights.

Need and Satisfaction Steps
(First Aspect)

    I. Airplane *body design.*
        A. The body design of a new airplane may have serious faults.
            1. Parts in the wing structures may be too heavy.
            2. The structures may not be strong enough to withstand strain.
        B. Test flights throw light on how the body design can be improved.
            1. They show up defects in the wing structures.
            2. By putting extra strains on the airplane, they indicate the strength of the structures.

Need and Satisfaction Steps
(Second Aspect)

    II. Airplane *engine design.*
        A. The engine design of a new airplane may have serious faults.
        B. Test flights throw light on how the engine design of a new airplane can be improved.
            1. They indicate engine reliability.
            2. They reveal general engine performance under great strains.

Visualization Step

    I. Through the help of test flights, there should be tremendous improvement of and development in airplane design and body design in the near future.

Action Step

    I. I therefore urge increased expenditures for test flights.

Whether you use the normal order or the parallel order in the satisfaction step, you will, of course, always need to develop support for your statements by supplying an abundance of illustrations, statistics, quotations, and comparisons.

The Visualization Step

The visualization step, as we have said, is commonly used only in speeches to persuade or to actuate. Speeches to entertain or to inform ordinarily achieve their purpose by employing only the earlier attention, or attention, need, and satisfaction steps of the motivated sequence. (See again the chart on page 361.)

The function of the visualization step is to intensify desire: to help motivate the audience to believe, feel, or act. In order to do this, it projects them into the future. Indeed, this step might also be called the "projection" step, for its effectiveness depends upon the vividness with which it pictures the future or potential benefits of believing or acting as the speaker proposes. The visualization step may be developed in one of three ways: (1) by projecting a picture of the future that is *positive*, (2) by projecting a picture that is *negative*, or (3) by projecting first a negative and then a positive picture in order to show *contrast*.

The Positive Method of Developing the Visualization Step

When using the positive method, describe conditions as they will be in the future if the belief you advocate is accepted or solution you propose is carried out. Provide vivid concrete descriptions. Select some situation which you are quite sure will arise in the future, and in that situation picture your audience actually enjoying the safety, pleasure, pride, etc., which the belief or proposal will produce.

The Negative Method of Developing the Visualization Step

When using the negative method, describe the adverse conditions that will prevail in the future if the belief you advocate is *not* adopted or the solution you propose is *not* carried out. Graphically picture for your audience the danger or unpleasantness which will result. Select the most striking problems or deficiencies you have pointed out in the need step and demonstrate how they will continue unless your recommendations are adopted.

The Contrast Method of Developing the Visualization Step

The method of contrast combines the positive and negative methods. Use the negative development first, visualizing the *bad* effects that are likely to occur if your listeners fail to follow your advice; then introduce the positive development, visualizing the *good* effects of believing or doing as you urge. By means of this contrast, both the bad and the good effects are made more striking and intense.

Whichever methods you use, remember that the visualization step always must stand the test of *reality*. The conditions you picture must seem probable. In addition, you must *put your listeners into the picture*. Use vivid imagery: make them actually see, hear, feel, taste, or smell the things and benefits you describe.* The more vividly real you make the projected situation seem, the stronger probably will be their reaction.

The following example of a visualization step, developed by a student in a speech urging the use of fireproof materials in home construction, employs the method of contrast:

> But suppose you do build your home of the usual kindling wood: joists, rafters, and shingles. Some dark night you may awake from your pleasant sleep with the smell of acrid smoke in your nostrils, and in your ears the threatening crackle of burning timbers. You will jump out onto the cold floor and rush to wake up the household. Gathering your children in your arms, you will hurry down the stairs—if they are not already in flames—and out-of-doors. There you will watch the firemen chop holes in your roof, pour gallons of water over your plaster, your furniture, your piano. You will shiver with cold in spite of the blazing spectacle, and the plastic minds of your children will be indelibly impressed with fright. No fire insurance can repay your family for this horror, even though it may pay a small part of the financial loss.

> How much better to use *safe* materials! Then throughout the long winter nights you can dig down under the warmth of your bedclothes to sleep peacefully in the assurance that your house cannot burn, and that any fire which catches in your furnishings can be confined to a small space and put out. No more the fear of flying sparks. Gone the danger to your wife and children. Sleep—quiet, restful, and secure in the knowledge that the ''burning horror'' has been banished from your home.[5]

The Action Step

The action step characteristically occurs only in speeches to actuate, although at times something resembling an action step is used to fix more firmly

---

For a discussion of imagery, see pages 431–437.

the attitude or belief urged in a persuasive talk. Its function is to translate into overt action the desire created in the visualization step. There are many methods for developing the action step, but the one most frequently employed is to use one or more of the following types of material:

1. Challenge or Appeal.
2. Summary.
3. Quotation.
4. Illustration.
5. Statement of Inducement.
6. Statement of Personal Intention.

Be sure to keep the action step *short*. Someone has given the following rule for effective public speaking: "Stand up; speak up; shut up!" Insofar as the action step is concerned, we may modify this rule thus: "Clinch your major ideas; finish your speech briskly; and sit down."

The full motivated sequence, then, consists of five steps which correspond to the natural thought processes by which people come to enjoy, to understand, to believe, and to act. Our purpose in this chapter has been to explain the psychological principles upon which motivational structuring is based and to suggest why each of its steps is important in terms of the listener. In Part Four, we shall consider in detail the various ways in which the motivated sequence may be adapted to different *types* of speeches and speechmaking situations. Although speeches constructed on this psychologically dynamic basis are not automatically assured of success, we believe that they are more likely to accomplish their communicative purpose than those put together without regard for how listeners think, reason, and react.

There are, of course, other ways of organizing a speech. Probably the most prevalent of these alternatives is to divide the whole into the tripartite components of *introduction, body,* and *conclusion.* We have already given some attention to this method of organizing and outlining ideas and substantive points; and in the two chapters immediately following, you will be asked to give even closer consideration to it. There you will find that these traditional divisions of a speech are entirely compatible and, indeed, clearly interrelated with the steps of the motivated sequence. This compatibility and the interrelationships are presented in brief but graphic form in the chart which appears on the following page. We suggest that you give it careful study and analysis before moving on to Chapter 14.

THE RELATIONSHIP BETWEEN THE STEPS OF THE MOTIVATED SEQUENCE AND THE TRADITIONAL DIVISIONS OF A SPEECH

General ends	*Introduction*		*Body or discussion*		*Conclusion*	
To entertain	*Attention Step* Illustration or statement of the idea or subject.		*Attention Step* (continued) Further illustration or ramification of the idea or subject.		*Attention Step* (concluded) Final illustration, quotation, or restatement of the idea or subject.	
To inform	*Attention Step* Provoke curiosity in subject.	*Need Step* Show its relation to the listeners: why they need to know.	*Satisfaction Step* 1. Initial summary, outlining points to be covered to satisfy this need.	2. Detailed discussion of points in order.	*Satisfaction Step* (concluded) 3. Final summary: a recapitulation of the main points and of important conclusions.	
To persuade	*Attention Step* Direct attention to basic elements of the attitude or belief advocated.		*Need Step* Demonstrate that a need for decision exists and lay down criteria for judgment.	*Satisfaction Step* State the exact proposition you propose and offer reasons and motives to induce belief in it and its benefits.	*Visualization Step* Briefly make its desirability vivid through imagery.	*Action Step* Restate the proposition and recapitulate the reasons for acceptance.
To actuate	*Attention Step* Direct attention to—		*Need Step* Present conditions showing a need for action.	*Satisfaction Step* State proposed action and prove its workability and benefits.	*Visualization Step* Picture future conditions as a result of the action taken.	*Action Step* Appeal for or demand the specified action.

Note: Not everything listed above is always included. The chart is used merely to show the relationship between the two methods of organization.

FOOTNOTES

[1]*Richard V. Wagner and John J. Sherwood, eds.*, The Study of Attitude Change *(Belmont, Calif.: Brooks/ Cole Publishing Company, 1969), p. 17.*

[2]*For a more detailed examination of this particular thought process, see John Dewey, "Analysis of Reflective Thinking,"* How We Think *(Boston: D. C. Heath & Company, 1933).*

[3]*"Motivated Men Made America Great" from* Fortune Magazine *(January 1966). Reprinted by permission of Maritz, Inc.*

[4]*"Nice People" by Jan Bjorklund. Reprinted from* Winning Orations *by special arrangement with the Interstate Oratorical Association, Duane L. Aschenbrenner, Executive Secretary, University of Nebraska at Omaha.*

[5]*From a student speech by James Fulton.*

Problems and Probes

1. Find in *Vital Speeches of the Day* or elsewhere two persuasive speeches that are organized according to the motivated sequence. Analyze these speeches *structurally*, indicating at what points in each speech the successive steps begin. Are the need and the satisfaction steps arranged as suggested in this chapter? Is the positive, negative, or method of contrast used to develop the visualization step? Are any of the devices listed in this chapter used in the attention and need steps? If not, how are these steps developed in the speeches you are using for your analysis?

2. Using the two speeches from Problem/Probe 1, suggest, if you can, *alternative patterns* by which either or both of the speeches could have been structured differently. In your opinion, would this alternative structure have been preferable to that provided by the motivated sequence? Why or why not?

3. In *Vital Speeches of the Day* or some other appropriate source, locate a speech *to inform*—a speech not structured according to the motivated sequence. Rewrite this speech, making it conform to the three-step pattern of *attention*, *need*, and *satisfaction*. (*Note:* For purposes of this Probe, if—in your opinion—the speech does not contain suitable material for the attention and need steps, draw on your own resourcefulness and invention to supply it. Be careful, however, not to alter the essential subject matter of the speech or its basic purpose.)

4. Assuming that the members of your speech class will be your audience, select *a specific purpose* for a speech to persuade or to actuate. On the basis of that purpose, prepare a five-sentence plan or structure designed to elicit the desired response—*one sentence for each step in the motivated se-*

quence. In developing these sentences, keep in mind what we have said about selecting the major ideas for a speech, as discussed in this chapter.

5. Using the motivated sequence as a pattern, construct an outline for a speech urging support of a proposed reform in college life or administration, or in municipal, state, or national affairs. For this speech, prepare *three different visualization steps:* one using the positive method, one the negative method, and one the contrasting method. Also prepare *three different action steps:* one using inducement, one using a statement of personal intention, and one using one of the four other possibilities. (Review page 376 for a listing of these different types of action steps.) Which type of visualization step and which action step appear to be most effective for this particular speech ? Why?

6. In a book entitled *How We Think* (Heath, 1933), the philosopher John Dewey said that when a person reasons his way through a problem systematically or "reflectively," he characteristically does five things: (*a*) defines or delimits the problem, (*b*) analyzes the problem, (*c*) thinks of possible solutions, (*d*) makes a preliminary evaluation of these solutions by reasoning, and (*e*) verifies the most likely solutions empirically. After reading Dewey's detailed descriptions of these steps in reflective thinking and after reviewing what has been said in connection with them in Chapter 3 (pages 108–113) of this textbook, compare them with the steps in the motivated sequence as explained in this chapter. To what extent are the two processes alike? To what extent are they different? How do you account for these similarities and differences?

7. Defend (orally or in writing, as your instructor may require) the *logical* validity and the *psychological* validity of the motivated sequence. That is, point out why—both logically and psychologically—the *attention* step must begin the sequence, why *need* must precede *satisfaction*, why *action* appropriately follows *visualization*, etc. Would any other ordering of these five steps have equal logical and psychological validity?

Oral Activity and Speaking Assignment

1. Present in class a six-minute persuasive speech on one of the subjects listed below or on a subject upon which you and your instructor have agreed in advance. Build your speech on the pattern furnished by the motivated sequence. Develop a strong need directly related to the interests and desires of your listeners. Show through reasoning and examples how your proposal will satisfy this need. Use the positive, negative, or contrast-

ing method to build the visualization step. Close with a direct appeal for belief or action.

Strict gun-control laws should be enacted.

The sale of cigarettes should be controlled by law.

Go to church every Sunday.

Exercise to benefit your heart.

All college students should take at least three years of science (or mathematics, foreign language, etc.).

We should have a national repertory theatre.

Good books are a permanent source of satisfaction and pleasure.

Solve the problem of race relations.

How can we improve the quality of television programs?

We can conquer urban blight.

Give a fair deal to the farmer.

Remove the threat of strikes.

Improve college teaching.

Suggestions for Further Reading

W. Norwood Brigance, *Speech: Its Techniques and Disciplines in a Free Society*, 2nd ed. (New York: Appleton-Century-Crofts, 1961), Chapter VII, "The Architecture of Persuasion."

John Dewey, *How We Think* (Boston: D. C. Heath and Company, 1933).

Leon Festinger, *A Theory of Cognitive Dissonance* (New York: Harper & Row, Publishers, 1957).

Carl I. Hovland, Irving L. Janis, and Harold H. Kelley, *Communication and Persuasion* (New Haven, Conn.: Yale University Press, 1953).

James H. McBurney and Kenneth G. Hance, *Discussion in Human Affairs* (New York: Harper & Row, Publishers, 1950), Chapter VI, "The Steps in Reflective Thinking."

Richard V. Wagner and John J. Sherwood, eds., *The Study of Attitude Change* (Belmont, Calif.: Brooks/Cole Publishing Company, 1969), Chapter I, "The Study of Attitude Change: An Introduction," pp. 1–18; Chapter II, "The Functional Approach to the Study of Attitudes," pp. 19–39; and Chapter IV, "Cognitive Dissonance: Theory and Research," pp. 56–86.

Otis L. Walter, "Toward an Analysis of Motivation," *Quarterly Journal of Speech* XLI (October 1955): 271–278.

14
ORGANIZING AND OUTLINING THE SPEECH

Most speeches, as we have observed, contain a number of ideas. If they are to be communicated to your hearers with maximal, positive effect, those ideas must be well organized: they must be set forth in such an order as to reflect *the degree of their significance within the speech as a whole.* Whereas in Chapter 13 we considered how to adapt and structure what we say to the thinking processes of the listeners, in this chapter we are concerned with the rhetorical, compositional patterns by which you can arrange substantive points and subpoints so as to ensure the validity and strength of their interrelatedness—how you can cast your ideas into effective outline form. Careful organization of your speech ideas and materials will serve the dual purpose of helping you achieve a unified and fluid presentation while, at the same time, helping your audience comprehend more easily and retain more fully what you wish to communicate. Therefore, in the first part of this chapter we shall concentrate on the selection and arrangement of the major ideas and the supporting materials; then we will turn to the subject of outlining the speech—why the outline is a useful device in speech preparation, and how it can be a positive factor in facilitating meaningful public communication.

SELECTING THE MAJOR IDEAS FOR THE OUTLINE: KEY REQUIREMENTS

By the time your speech preparation has advanced to the point of final organization, you should have a fairly clear idea of what your major points will be. However, there are a few commonsensical rules or principles which should be followed in making this ultimate selection of major ideas. If a talk is to be successful, its major ideas should (1) be few in number, (2) be of equal scope or importance, and (3) cover all pertinent aspects of the subject treated. A closer look at these guidelines will demonstrate their importance.

Keep the Major Ideas Few in Number

Even the most intent and earnest listener has limited powers of attention and memory. Therefore, if you attempt to develop too many different ideas within a speech, it is likely that many of them will either be forgotten or pass unnoticed. Most audiences would be appalled by a speaker who announced, "This morning I am going to discuss with you fifteen important aspects of our trade with foreign nations," or "I am going to give you twenty-three reasons why marijuana should be legalized." Select at most three or four major ideas or arguments, and group the rest of your material as subpoints under these headings. Then even if the subpoints are forgotten, at least the chances are good that your listeners will go away with the crucial considerations fixed in their minds. Dwell on each major idea long enough so that people have a fair opportunity to grasp and consider it; reiterate this idea at several different points in your speech.

Keep Major Points of Equal Scope or Importance

Do not make the mistake of the student who argued against the abolition of tariffs on the grounds that such action would (1) threaten American manufacturers with a flood of cheap foreign goods, (2) mean a significant loss of revenue to our government, and (3) necessitate the rewriting of the syllabus used in the beginning economics course at his college. The last point was so obviously trivial in relation to the other two that he not only wasted precious minutes which might have been used to better effect, but actually made his entire speech—and, indirectly, himself—appear ludicrous.

Cover All Essential Aspects of the Subject

The major ideas of a speech should cover all important facets of the subject being discussed. Insofar as they fail to do so, the information the speech presents is incomplete, or the arguments it develops are less convincing than they might be. If a proposal has significant economic implications as well as social and political ones, be sure to include this fact. If the history of a subject is important to understanding it, do not disregard this area. When your speech is finished, all aspects of the subject which are relevant to your purpose should have been thoroughly explored. As we have urged, limit severely the number of major points or arguments you plan to communicate; but once you have limited them, be sure to treat each one as fully as the purpose of your speech and the nature of the occasion require.

PHRASING THE MAJOR IDEAS FOR THE OUTLINE: ESSENTIAL QUALITIES

The major ideas in a speech always should be stated clearly and emphatically. While illustrations, arguments, and other forms of support constitute the bulk of what you say, the statement of your main points ties these details together and points up their significance. Good speakers take particular pains to phrase their main points in such a way that the meaning will be clear, persuasive, and easily remembered by their listeners. To achieve this result, keep in mind four characteristics of good phrasing: *conciseness, vividness, motivational appeal,* and *parallelism.*

Conciseness

State your major ideas as briefly as you can without impairing their meaning. A simple, straightforward declaration is better than a complex one. Avoid clumsy modifying phrases or distracting subordinate clauses. State the essence of your idea in a short sentence which can be modified or elaborated as you subsequently present the supporting material, or phrase your point as a simple question to which your detailed explanations later will provide the answer. For example, "Our state taxes are too high" is better than "Taxes in this state, with one or two exceptions, are higher than present economic conditions justify." The second statement may present your idea more completely than the first, but it contains nothing that your supporting material should not clarify, whereas its greater complexity makes it less crisp and emphatic.

Vividness

Wherever possible, use words and phrases that are colorful and provoke attention. If your major ideas are worded in a dull and lifeless way, you cannot expect them to stand out and to be remembered. Since they *are* the main points, they should be phrased so that they *sound* that way. They should be the punch lines of your speech. Notice how much more vivid it is to say, "We must turn these rascals out!" than to say, "We must remove these incompetent and dishonest men from office." Remember, of course, that vivid phrasing can be overdone. The sober presentation of a technical report at a scientific meeting does not require the colorful language needed at a political rally; on the other hand, neither does it justify the ponderous, trite, and sterile jargon too often employed. Keeping in mind the nature of your subject and the occasion on which you are speaking, avoid equally a superficial and exaggerated vividness that seems merely to be straining for effect and a lifeless, dull wording that lacks strength and color.

Motivational Appeal

Whenever possible, word your major ideas so that they appeal to the wants and desires of your listeners.* Try to phrase your main points so that they rivet the attention of your listeners and impel them toward the belief or action you desire. Instead of saying, "Chemical research has helped improve medical treatment," say, "Modern chemistry helps the doctor make you well." Rather than asserting, "Travel by air is fast," declare, "Travel by air saves time." Remember that you not only are speaking about something, but *to somebody*. Your major ideas should be phrased so that they appeal to your hearers and remain linked to their thinking.

Parallelism

Try to use essentially the same sentence structure or similar phrasing for each point. Since your major ideas represent coordinate units of your speech, word them so that they sound that way. Avoid unnecessary shifts from active to passive voice or from questions to assertions. Whenever possible, use prepositions, connectives, and auxiliary verbs which permit a similar balance, rhythm, and direction of thought. Avoid wording a series of main points in this way:

I. The amount of your income tax depends on the amount you earn.
II. Property tax is assessed on the value of what you own.
III. You pay sales taxes in proportion to the amount you buy.

Instead, phrase them like this:

I. The amount you earn dictates your income tax.
II. The amount you own controls your property tax.
III. The amount you buy determines your sales tax.

Note that part of each statement in the series above ("The amount you . . . your . . . tax.") has been repeated, while the rest of the statement changed from point to point. Repetition of key words is often used in this way to intensify the parallelism. By imposing an order such as this on your message, you not only improve the phrasing of your main ideas, but you also make these ideas easier to remember—for you and your audience.

---

*Review the motivational appeals discussed in Chapter 9, pp. 270–282, and the factors of attention analyzed in Chapter 12, pp. 336–342.

Parallelism of phrasing—together with conciseness, vividness, and motivational appeal—will help make your major ideas stand out forcefully.

ARRANGING THE MAJOR IDEAS: SEQUENTIAL PATTERNS

When you get up to speak, an immediate and persistent problem will be to remember what you planned to say; and nothing will help you quite so much as having the major ideas of your speech arranged in a systematic sequence so that one leads naturally into the next. Moreover, your audience will follow your thoughts more easily, grasp them more firmly, and remember them longer if the pattern of your speech is clear. As is sometimes said, to hold the interest of your audience you must *"let your speech march!"* Your listeners should not get the impression that you are wandering aimlessly from point to point; you must make it evident to them that your ideas are closely related to one another and are "marching" toward completeness in a unified and orderly manner. There are several ways of selecting and arranging the points of a speech so as to accomplish this result: (1) *the time sequence*, (2) *the space sequence*, (3) *the cause-effect sequence*, (4) *the problem-solution sequence*, and (5) *the special topical sequence*.

Time Sequence

Begin at a certain period or date and move forward or backward in a systematic way. For example, the climate of a region may be discussed by considering the conditions which exist in the spring, summer, fall, and winter, respectively; methods for refining petroleum, by tracing chronologically the development of the refining process from the earliest attempts down to the present; the manufacture of an automobile, by following the assembly-line process from beginning to end. A time sequence may be appropriate to your subject no matter what your purpose in the speech may be. As in each of the instances above, however, it is often the most effective means of determining and arranging the major ideas in a speech to inform. Here is an example of time order used in an informative talk:

THE EARLY HISTORY OF TEXAS

I. Until 1822, Texas was under Spanish colonial rule.
II. From then till 1835, Texas remained a part of the Mexican Republic.
III. For the next ten years, Texas was an independent nation.
IV. In 1845, Texas became part of the United States.

Space Sequence

Arrange your material from east to west, from bottom up, from right to left. The density of population, for example, may be discussed according to geographical areas; the plans of a building may be considered floor by floor; or the layout for a city park may be explained by proceeding from entrance to exit. Different aspects of a problem or a solution also are sometimes arranged according to a space sequence. The following example shows a problem analyzed according to this spatial or "geographic" method:

OUR DECLINING SALES

I. New England sales have dropped 15 percent during the past year.
II. The Gulf States sales have dropped 10 percent.
III. The Great Lakes area sales have dropped 20 percent.

Cause-Effect Sequence

While a cause-effect sequence may be used to arrange the ideas in a speech to inform (as in explaining the relationship between a past and present event), it is more commonly found in speeches to persuade or to actuate. When you discuss certain forces and then point to the results these forces will produce, or when you describe conditions or events and then show what forces created them, you are dealing with causal relationships. Thus you might first describe a community's zoning ordinances and, second, try to prove that present conditions (good or bad) are the effect of those regulations. The number of individuals who commit crimes after they have served prison sentences can be reported, and then their criminal actions attributed to certain major causes—ineffective methods of rehabilitation, public misunderstanding, or others. A cause-effect argument may be arranged as follows:

THE RISING COST OF LIVING

I. Each year the cost of living increases. (A, B, C, etc.: cite examples and statistics.)
II. The causes of the increase are: (A, B, C, etc.: list and explain causes.)

Problem-Solution Sequence

Sometimes the major ideas of a speech may best be arranged according to a twofold plan: the description of a problem (or related problems) and the presentation of a solution (or solutions) to it. Thus you might describe the problems involved in building the Mackinac Bridge connecting the Upper and Lower Peninsulas of Michigan, and then explain how the problems were solved. Usually, however, this type of arrangement is applied to problems facing the immediate audience for which you wish to present a solution. For example, you might point to declining interest in an important campus activity and then try to convince your listeners that they should adopt one or more ways of reversing this trend. It is also possible to apply this method to discussions of future contingencies: for example, one could outline the ecological problems to be faced by the American public after twenty more years of increasing pollution, and then present suggested solutions. When this type of sequence is used with a multiple problem or solution, each of the two main divisions of your discussion must itself be arranged in an orderly way; and you may use one of the other sequences—time, space, or cause-effect—for this purpose. Here is an example of how one speaker employed the problem-solution sequence:

CONTROLLING CRIME

I. The problem of crime is constantly growing more serious.
   A. Serious offenses are more common.
   B. Juvenile crimes have increased alarmingly.
II. We must meet this problem in three ways:
   A. We must begin a crime-prevention program.
   B. We must strengthen our police force to insure speedy arrests.
   C. We must free our court procedure from politics.

Special Topical Sequence

Certain types of information are best presented in divisions which already are familiar to the audience. For example, financial reports customarily are divided into assets and liabilities. Institutions or agencies are described as clusters of related departments—for example, legislative, executive, and judicial. Objects or processes are explained as a series of parts or functions. Policies are considered in terms of advantages and objections, or of problems and solutions. A special topical order for a speech on democratic government, for example, might take this form:

DEMOCRATIC GOVERNMENT IS BEST

I. It guarantees legitimate freedom to the individual.
II. It reflects the will of the majority.
III. It deepens the citizen's feeling of responsibility.

Similarly, your points may be arranged to answer a series of questions known to be uppermost in the minds of the audience. Answer them directly and specifically. It would be foolish to diffuse the answers to these questions by adopting a different partition of the subject.

The fact that one of the above sequences may have been chosen for the major ideas of a speech does not prevent the use of another sequence for arranging the *subordinate* points. On no condition, however, should you shift from one method to another in ordering the main points themselves. The following outline will illustrate how two or more methods may be combined in ordering the main and subordinate points of a speech:

MAJOR INDIAN TRIBES OF THE WEST

I. Southwest.
    A. Apache.
        1. Early history.
        2. Contacts with explorers and settlers.
        3. Present conditions.
    B. Navaho.
        1. Early history, etc. (Develop chronologically, as above.)
    C. Pueblo. (Develop as above.)
II. Pacific coast.
    A. . . . etc.
III. Northwest.
    A. . . . etc.

Notice that in this outline the *space sequence* has been used for the main headings; the *special topical sequence* for subpoints A, B, and C; and the *time sequence* for sub-subpoints 1, 2, and 3.

ARRANGING SUBPOINTS AND SUPPORTING MATERIAL

After you have put the major ideas of your speech into a suitable sequence, you must decide how to arrange the subpoints and supporting material so that the *internal* structure of each of the principal units of your talk has orderliness and substance. It is important to repeat that this arrangement, this organization, has positive effects far beyond mere improvement in the quality of the prose of your speech. This order is the means by which you can more easily remember the points of your message at the time of delivery; and it is the means by which your co-communicators will "store" the arguments and information you present, and then — subsequently — retrieve or recall them.

Subordinating the Subpoints

A "string-of-beads discussion," in which everything seems to have equal weight — tied together, as it usually is, by "and-uh," "and next," "and then," "and so" — lacks contrast and purposeful movement and soon grows tiresome. If you emphasize everything, nothing will stand out as important. Regardless of how well you have chosen, arranged, and worded your major ideas, they will be lost unless your subpoints are properly subordinated to them. Therefore, avoid listing subpoints as if they were main points, and avoid listing under a main point items that have no direct relation to it. Here are some forms of subject matter that are commonly subordinate:

Parts of a Whole

Frequently a major idea concerns an object or a process which consists of a series of component parts; the subpoints then take up and treat those parts in order. For example, the grip, shaft, and head may be discussed as the parts of a golf club; or the number of churches in England, Scotland, Ireland, and Wales may be cited as subtotals of the aggregate number in the British Isles.

Lists of Qualities or Functions

When the main point describes the general nature of an object, process, or concept, the subpoints often list the qualities which contribute to that nature. If the main point suggests the purpose of some mechanism, organization, or procedure, the subpoints may list the specific functions it performs. Thus timbre, pitch, and loudness are qualities under which the nature of sound may be discussed; or the purpose of a police department may be made clear by citing its various duties or functions.

Series of Causes or Results

If you use the cause-effect sequence to arrange your major ideas, you will often find that neither cause nor effect is single. Separately, each of the several causes and results will then constitute a subpoint. Even when another type of sequence is used for the major ideas, a list of causes and results often forms the sub-items under this point. The causes of a crop failure, for instance, might be listed as drought, frost, and blight; or the results of proper diet could be given as greater comfort, better health, and longer life.

Items of Logical Proof

In a speech to persuade or to actuate, the subpoints should always provide logical proof of the idea they support. Often they consist of reasons or of coordinate steps in a single process of reasoning. When this is the case, you should be able to connect the major idea and subpoints with the word "because" (major idea is true *because* subpoints a, b, c, etc., are true); and, conversely, you should be able to use the word "therefore" (subpoints are true; *therefore* main point is true). Here is an example of this type of subordination: Strikes are wasteful because (*a*) workers lose their wages; (*b*) employers lose their profits; and (*c*) consumers lose the products they might otherwise have had.

Illustrative Examples

Many times the main point consists of a generalized statement for which the subpoints provide a series of specific illustrative examples. This method may be used both in exposition and in argument, the examples constituting clarification or proof respectively. Thus, the general statement that fluoride helps reduce tooth decay might have as its subpoints a series of examples citing the experience of those cities which have added fluoride to their drinking water.

These are by no means all of the categories of subordinate items, but these common types should serve to illustrate the general principle of subordination. Remember also that the same principle applies to further subordination under sub-subpoints. In longer and more detailed speeches you may have sub-subpoints and even sub-sub-subpoints. Do not let the process of subordination become too intricate or involved; but however far you go, keep your system of subordination clear and consistent.

Arranging Coordinate Subpoints

Usually there will be two or more subpoints under every major idea in your speech. Besides being subordinate to the major idea, these subpoints should be *coordinate* with each other. In what sequence, then, should they be arranged? Generally it is best to list them according to one of the types of arrangement given at the beginning of this chapter. Choose the sequence—time, space, causal, problem-solution, or topical—that seems most appropriate. You may want to use one of these sequences for the items under one major idea and a different sequence for those under another, but do not shift from one sequence to another *within* the same coordinate series. Above all, be sure that you do employ some kind of systematic order; don't crowd items in haphazardly just because they are subordinate points.

Supporting Subpoints

The importance of supporting material was emphasized in Chapter 11. The general rule is: *Never make a statement of a major point or a significant subpoint in a speech without presenting at least one of the forms of support to clarify, illustrate, or prove it.* Too often, speakers think that if they have set down several subpoints under every major idea, they have done enough. The fact is, however, that you can subdivide ideas all day without doing any more than add detail to the *structure* of your speech. The *substance* of what you say lies in the figures, illustrations, facts, and testimony introduced. The manner in which such material is used to support a point was fully discussed in connection with the single-idea speech and need not be repeated here.* While you may not always need as much support for each subpoint in your talk as was suggested there, remember that the more you have, the stronger the point will be.

We have now considered some of the principles and methods for the logical and coherent arrangement of ideas within a speech. Even with a thorough grasp of these methods, however, few persons can sit down with a mass of material and work out a suitable arrangement at first try. Test your general plan by putting your ideas into several different sequences. See which one seems to fit your material most naturally and best enables you to observe the rules for the selection and phrasing of major ideas. Time spent in this task will be of inestimable benefit not only in enabling your hearers to follow you more easily but also in helping you remember what you want to say.

PREPARING THE ACTUAL OUTLINE

When the major ideas of your speech have been selected and its basic pattern of organization determined, you are ready to begin making an outline. A carefully developed outline serves a number of essential functions. First, it lays out before you the entire structure of your speech so that you can see whether you have (*a*) fitted the parts together smoothly, (*b*) given each idea the emphasis it deserves, and (*c*) covered all important aspects of the subject. Second, it en-

---

*See again Chapter 11, pp. 319–326.

ables you to check on the adequacy and variety of your supporting materials. If you have failed to substantiate any of your leading ideas or have used only one or two forms of support throughout, your outline will reveal these deficiencies. Third, and finally, an outline will help you fix firmly in mind the ideas you wish to communicate and the order in which you plan to present them. By reading through your outline repeatedly, you can memorize the pattern or "geography" of your speech, with its principal headings and developmental materials, so that as you stand before your listeners you will recall how the speech "looks" as well as what it says. A visual "map" of this kind can be a valuable aid to memory.

Requirements of Good Outline Form

The amount of detail and type of arrangement you use in an outline will depend on the simplicity or complexity of your subject, the nature of the speaking situation, and your previous experience in speech composition. Any good outline, however, should meet four basic requirements:

1. *Each item in the outline should contain only one unit of information.* This is essential to the very nature of outlining. If two or three items or statements are run together under one symbol, the relationships they bear to one another and to other items in the outline will not stand out clearly. Compare these examples:

Wrong

I. Our city should conduct a campaign against the thousands of flies that infest it every year, breeding everywhere and buzzing at every kitchen door, because they spread disease by carrying germs and contaminating food, and because they can be eliminated easily by killing them with insecticides and preventing their breeding by cleaning up refuse.

Right

I. Our city should conduct a campaign against flies.
    A. Thousands of flies infest the city every year.
        1. They breed everywhere.
        2. They buzz at every kitchen door.
    B. Flies spread disease.
        1. They carry germs.
        2. They contaminate food.
    C. Flies can be eliminated easily.
        1. Widespread use of insecticides kills them.
        2. Cleaning up refuse prevents their breeding.

2. *The items in the outline should be properly subordinated.* Because a subordinate idea is a subdivision of the larger heading under which it falls, it should rank *below* that heading in scope and importance. It also should directly support or amplify the statement made in the superior heading.

Wrong

I. Radio is a direct benefit to humanity.
    A. It has saved many lives at sea.
II. It makes easier the spreading of news.
III. Present broadcasting methods are not as good as they might be.
    A. There are too many stations cluttering the air.
        1. Programs are becoming worse.
        2. There are too many disk-jockey programs and high-pressure sales talks.
    B. This is true even though a great many criminals have been tracked down by means of radio.

Right

I. Radio is a direct benefit to humanity.
    A. It has saved many lives at sea.
    B. It makes easier the spreading of news.
    C. It has aided in tracking down a great many criminals.
II. Present broadcasting methods are not as good as they might be.
    A. There are too many stations cluttering the air.
    B. Programs are becoming worse.
        1. There are too many disk-jockey programs.
        2. There are too many high-pressure sales talks.

3. *The logical relation of the items in an outline should be shown by proper indentation.* The greater the importance or scope of a statement, the nearer it should be placed to the left-hand margin. If a statement takes up more than one line, the second line should be indented the same as the beginning of the first.

Wrong

I. Shortening the college course to three years is not necessary.
    A. Provision is already made for students who are
unable to spend four years in college.
    B. Other parts of one's educational career can be cut short
with less loss than would result from this proposal.
        1. The preparatory-school course could be shortened.
        2. The course in professional school could be shortened.

I. Shortening the college course to three years is not necessary.
A. Provision is already made for students who are unable to spend four years in college.
B. Other parts of one's educational career can be cut short with less loss than would result from this proposal.
1. The preparatory-school course could be shortened.
2. The course in professional school could be shortened.

Right

I. Shortening the college course to three years is not necessary.
    A. Provision is already made for students who are unable to spend four years in college.
    B. Other parts of one's educational career can be cut short with less loss than would result from this proposal.
        1. The preparatory-school course could be shortened.
        2. The course in professional school could be shortened.

4. *A consistent set of symbols should be used.* One such set is exemplified in the outlines printed in this chapter. But whether you use this set or some other, be consistent; do not change systems in the middle of an outline. Unless items of the same scope or importance have the same type of symbol *throughout*, the mental "map" you have of your speech will be confused, and the chances of a smooth and orderly presentation impaired.

Wrong

I. There is a need for better traffic regulation.
    II. Figures show the extent of traffic-law violations:
        A. 300,000 motorists were arrested in New York last year.
        2. $1,000,000.00 was paid in fines last year by New York motorists.
            I. This is more than the total paid in all England, Scotland, and Wales.
            a. This amount would buy about 350 new automobiles at $3000 each.

Right

I. There is a need for better traffic regulation.
  A. Figures show the extent of traffic-law violations:
    1. 300,000 motorists were arrested in New York last year.
    2. $1,000,000.00 was paid in fines last year by New York motorists.
      a. This is more than the total paid in all England, Scotland, and Wales.
      b. This amount would buy about 350 new automobiles at $3000 each.

Types of Outlines

There are two principal types of outlines, each of which fulfills a different purpose — the *full-content* outline and the *key-word* outline. The former helps make the process of speech preparation more systematic and thorough; the latter serves as an aid to memory in the early stages of oral practice.

The Full-Content Outline

As its name implies, a full-content outline represents the complete factual content of the speech in outline form. Whether you use the traditional divisions of the speech (introduction, body, conclusion) or the steps in the motivated sequence (attention, need, satisfaction, visualization, action), each major component is set off in a separate section. In each of these sections, the major ideas are stated; and under them — properly indented and marked with the correct symbols — is put all the material used to amplify and support them. *Each major idea and all of the minor ones are written down in complete sentences* so that their full meaning and their relation to other points are made completely clear. Often, after each piece of evidence or supporting material, the source from which it was obtained is indicated, or these sources are combined in a bibliography at the end of the outline. Thus, when the outline has been completed, simply by reading it, the speaker or any other person can derive a clear, comprehensive picture of the speech as a whole. The only thing lacking is the specific wording to be used in presenting the speech and the visible and audible aspects of the speaker's delivery. The purpose of this type of outline is obvious. By bringing together all the material you have gathered and by stating it completely and in detail, you ensure thoroughness in the preparation of your speech.

To prepare a full-content outline requires much effort. It cannot be written offhand even by a person who has had a great deal of experience; the beginner should allow plenty of time for developing one. If you go about the task systematically, however, you can keep the time to a minimum.

The Key-Word Outline

The key-word outline has the same indentation and the same symbols as the full-content outline, but it boils down each statement to a key word, phrase, or—at most—a brief sentence that can be more easily remembered. By reading a key-word outline through several times from beginning to end, you will be able to fix the ideas of your speech firmly in mind and to recall them readily as you stand before the audience. Thus, it is an excellent aid to memory in the oral practice of your speech. Of course, to ensure accuracy you may read specific quotations or figures from notecards.

Steps in Preparing an Outline

An outline, like the speech it represents, should be developed gradually through a series of stages. While these stages may vary somewhat, depending on the work habits of the speaker, certain steps always should be included:

THREE SIMPLE STEPS IN PREPARING A GOOD OUTLINE

I. Select the subject and determine the general purpose of your speech.
   A. Limit the subject to fit the available time and to ensure the unity and coherence of your remarks.
   B. Phrase your specific purpose in terms of the exact response you seek from your listeners.
II. Develop a rough draft of your outline.
   A. List the main ideas you wish to cover.
   B. Arrange these main ideas into a systematic pattern, keeping in mind the steps in the motivated sequence (attention, need, satisfaction, visualization, action) appropriate to the type of speech you plan to present (informative, persuasive, etc.).
   C. Insert and arrange the subordinate ideas that fall under each main point.
   D. Fill in the supporting materials to be used in amplifying or proving your ideas.
   E. Check your rough draft to be sure it covers the subject adequately and carries out your specific purpose.
   F. If you are dissatisfied, revise your rough draft or start over.

III. Put the outline into final form.
    A. Write out the main ideas as complete sentences.
        1. State them concisely, vividly, and—insofar as possible—in parallel phraseology.
        2. Direct them to the needs and interests of your listeners.
    B. Write out the subordinate ideas either as complete sentences or as "key phrases."
        1. Be sure they are subordinate to the main idea they are intended to develop.
        2. Be sure they are coordinate to the other items in their series.
    C. Fill in the supporting materials.
        1. Be sure they are pertinent.
        2. Be sure they are adequate.
        3. Be sure to include a variety of types of support.
    D. Recheck the entire outline.
        1. It should represent good outline form.
        2. It should adequately cover the subject.
        3. It should carry out your speech purpose.

In order to see how this process may be followed in a specific situation, let us apply the principles we have just discussed to the selection and limitation of a subject, the development of a rough draft, and the preparation of an outline in final form.

Selecting the Subject and Determining the Purpose

Suppose your instructor has asked you to prepare a ten- to twelve-minute persuasive-type speech on a subject of current importance. Because in recent years shortages of gasoline, minerals, and lumber have emphasized anew the serious problems we as a nation face in husbanding our natural resources, you decide to address yourself to this topic. Moreover, because of the pressing nature of the problem, you believe that immediate *action* on the part of every citizen is required. Therefore, you decide that the general purpose of your speech will be *to actuate*.

Your broad subject area, then, is

THE CONSERVATION OF OUR NATURAL RESOURCES

and your general purpose is to move your hearers to

ACTION.

In the ten or twelve minutes you have to speak, however, you obviously will not be able to cover everything that might be said on so extensive a subject. Consequently, your first task is to narrow your topic. In thinking about how to do this, you consider selecting only one aspect of the problem to talk about — concentrating your attention on our shrinking reserves of oil, or of coal, or of water, or on the practices that are depriving us of much of our most productive farmland. After some thought, however, you realize that all of these facets of the problem are interrelated and that action on a broad front is called for. Therefore, in order to maximize the impact of your remarks, you decide to treat the problem as a whole, but to limit your subject by pointing out only the most dramatic facts you can discover concerning each type of resource. Moreover, by the time your preparation has reached this stage, a suitable title has occurred to you, and you have further decided the specific action you will urge is the formation of a Conservation Awareness Group in your community. So now you set down this title and state your specific purpose as follows:

OUR PLENTY IS NOT SO PLENTIFUL

(*Specific purpose:* To induce my hearers to take the initiative in forming a Conservation Awareness Group in this community.)

Developing the Rough Draft

In determining the scope of your subject and framing your specific purpose, you already have made a preliminary selection of some of the principal ideas to be dealt with in your speech. Now you set these points down on paper to see how they may be modified and fitted into a coherent sequence. Initially, your list might look something like this:

> Waste in gas-well drilling.
> Loss of valuable farmlands.
> Contributions of scientific research.
> Abandoned copper mines.
> Constantly increasing demand for resources of all kinds.
> Harnessing the Colorado River.

This list covers a number of things you want to be sure to include, but the order is random, and you realize that your present stock of information on the subject is inadequate. Therefore, you begin to gather additional data; and as you find ideas you wish to include, you distribute them under the various motivated-sequence heads of a speech to actuate: Attention, Need, Satisfaction, Visualization, and Action. You also begin to distinguish between main ideas and subordinate ones, and to group these into appropriate units. Finally, you sketch in the necessary supporting materials in the form of statistics, comparisons, specific instances, etc., testing these materials for pertinence and variety.

At this point, examine your rough draft carefully to be sure (1) that you have included all the ideas you want to cover; (2) that you have not unbalanced your discussion by expanding unimportant items too greatly or skimping on important ones; (3) that in ordering your ideas you have followed the principles of systematic arrangement and subordination; and (4) that you have assembled a sufficient amount of pertinent and varied supporting material. When you are satisfied on these matters, you are ready to cast your outline into final form.

Putting the Outline into Final Form

This task consists, in part, of examining what you have already done and of adjusting the details. Sometimes you may want to combine or rearrange certain of the points as they appear in your rough draft, or perhaps you will even decide to drop several of them. In addition, you will now need to restate all of the major ideas in your outline as complete sentences—sentences that convey your meaning clearly and exactly—and to see that your outline meets the requirements listed on pages 392–395. To do this, begin by working on the main points, rephrasing each until it is clear and vivid. Then, taking each main point in turn, work on the subordinate ideas that fall under it, striving for proper subordination and coordination. Finally, make certain that the supporting materials are set forth in the most economical and effective way.

The Technical Plot: Testing Your Outline

In analyzing the completed outline to discover possible gaps or weaknesses, it frequently is helpful to work out a *technical plot* of your speech. To make such a plot, lay the completed outline beside a blank sheet of paper; and on this sheet, set down opposite each unit a statement of the devices used in developing it. Where you have used statistics in the outline, write the word *statistics* in the technical plot, together with a brief statement of their function. In like manner, indicate all of the forms of support, attention factors, types of imagery, motive appeals, and methods of development you have employed. The complete outline of "Our Plenty Is Not So Plentiful" (pages 400–406) includes a technical plot for your examination.

Used as a testing device, a technical plot can help you determine whether your speech is structurally sound, whether there is adequate supporting material, whether you have overused one or two forms of support, and whether the appeals you plan are adapted to the audience and occasion. Many speeches, of course, do not need to be tested this thoroughly; and experienced speakers often can make an adequate analysis without drafting a complete technical plot. For the beginner, however, there is no more effective way of checking the structure of a speech and testing the methods used to develop it.

The following example shows the complete outline for the speech on conservation drawn up in final form and with an accompanying technical plot. For illustrative purposes, all items in the outline are stated as complete sentences. Such completeness of detail may be desirable when the occasion is an especially important one or the speaker has difficulty framing thoughts extemporaneously. Usually, however, as we have said, it is sufficient to write out only the main ideas as complete sentences and to state the subordinate ideas and supporting materials as key phrases.

OUR PLENTY IS NOT SO PLENTIFUL

FULL-CONTENT OUTLINE   TECHNICAL PLOT

Attention Step

I. Do you know that our most vital natural resources are being seriously depleted while demands for them are doubling or tripling?
    Startling statements of fact

    A. Hans H. Landsberg reports that by 2000 A.D. our need for industrial energy and metals will be tripled; for lumber, nearly tripled; and for farm products and fresh water, nearly doubled.

    B. At projected levels of future consumption, our crude-oil reserves will last less than 50 years.

    C. By the end of this century we will be consuming forest products faster than they can be replaced.

    D. Every day we lose more water than we use — an average of 19 billion gallons — by evaporation from open storage areas alone.

    E. Each year a billion tons of earth are washed down the nation's rivers in the form of eroded topsoil.

II. You may be directly affected by this drastic depletion of resources.
    Statements relating subject to listeners

    A. Conservationists warn of increasing difficulty in obtaining food, energy, and materials.

        1. Diminishing supplies of wood, coal, and oil will mean less fuel for your home.

2. Evaporation, erosion, and sedimentation will create serious scarcities of food and water.
    B. Shortages will create higher costs.

III. A natural catastrophe of this sort can be prevented only by a wise conservation program.

Transition to need step

Need Step

I. Three principles are vital to any conservation program:
    A. We must make the most of what we have.
    B. We must renew whatever resources we can.
    C. We must do whatever we can to preserve the balance of nature.

Criteria of sound conservation program

II. In the past, these "musts" have been ignored.
    A. Irreplaceable metals and oils have been wasted.
        1. Petroleum and petroleum products have been mercilessly exploited.
            a. Estimates of the amount of known crude-oil supplies left unrecovered in the developed oil fields range as high as 83 percent.
            b. As late as 1948, losses of gas in well-drilling and extraction-processing in Texas alone were greater than the entire volume of gas shipped out of that state.
        2. Copper mines have been abandoned before the ore was exhausted.
            a. It is now too expensive to reopen the water-filled shafts.
            b. We are being forced to import more and more copper.
        3. Stuart Chase says that the avoidable waste in mining coal in the United States is 35 percent, compared to 5 to 10 percent in Europe.
    B. Principles vital to conservation have been too long ignored.
        1. Early settlers, like some Americans of more recent times, looked upon America as inexhaustibly wealthy, with resources to squander.

General statement of need

Supporting examples and statistics

Historical examples

a. When cotton fields became sterile, farmers simply moved to new land.

b. Within 50 years after the pioneers moved into the Western states in the nineteenth century, 700 million acres of grass west of the Mississippi had been destroyed.

c. Later, overexpansion of crop acreages to capitalize on high prices denuded much of the Great Plains and led to the Dust Bowl of the 1930s.

d. Up to now, lumber companies assumed a never-ending supply of high-grade timber.

2. This lack of foresight set in motion a vicious cycle of spoilage: *Results of past neglect*

   a. With the forests went the protective soil covering of decayed leaves and pine needles.

   b. Rain and melted snow rushed down the hillsides instead of being gradually absorbed by this cover.

   c. Precious topsoil was carried away by the surging waters.

      i. The torrents eroded gullies in the farmlands.

      ii. The silt thus formed polluted the water supply.

C. Even today we continue to disregard the interrelation of natural resources. *Recent examples and statistics*

   1. Baltimore taxpayers are paying for the poor farming methods in the upper river valleys of Maryland:

      a. Sediment from the farms clogs the harbor.

      b. Over the years, the city has paid more than 17 million dollars to dredge 111 million cubic yards of sediment.

   2. What happened in Decatur, Illinois, is another glaring example:

      a. In 1922, Decatur built a two-million-

dollar dam across the Sangamon
River.
    b. By 1946, silt had deprived the
reservoir of 26 percent of its capacity.
    c. The city had not taken heed of the
shift to intertilled crops in the
watershed area.
        i. Corn and soybeans had
replaced hay, grass, and
grain.
       ii. Lack of close-growing crops
had increased erosion
at the rate of 4000 tons
annually for each average
farm.
    d. Decatur was forced to invest more
money to reestablish its water
supply.
  3. Mighty Lake Mead above Hoover Dam has
been filling with 137,000 acre-feet of
sediment annually since this world's third-
largest artificial lake and the dam were
completed in 1936.

III. It is high time we fully observed the principles vital to
conservation.

*Statement
summarizing need
step*

Satisfaction Step

  I. A threefold program is the only way to meet the urgent need:
    A. We must establish programs for river valleys.
    B. We must observe modern forestation and farming
practices.
    C. We must support programs of scientific research.

*Requirements of
sound
conservation
program*

 II. Such programs satisfy the three "musts" for effective
conservation:
    A. By establishing valley programs, we can restore and
maintain the balance of nature.
      1. Forests should be restored in watershed areas.
        a. Such watershed erosion-control
would prevent floods.
        b. Such a program would also reduce

*First requirement
considered*

*Support by
explanation*

downstream sediment significantly, as shown by the 33 percent reduction in the Lake Waco, Texas, watershed, and the 78 percent reduction in the Lake Newman, Georgia, watershed.

  2. Below watershed areas, dams should be constructed.

    a. They would prevent floods in the lower valley.

    b. They would maintain water supply.

    c. They would furnish electric power.

  3. Below the dams, land can be reclaimed for cultivation.

    a. Arid land can be made productive by irrigation.

    b. Fertility can be maintained by growing the proper crops.

B. By applying modern methods of forestry and farming, we can produce more and still replenish the land.

  1. According to an NEA report, 70 million acres can be cleared, drained, or irrigated to make productive farmland.

  2. The quality of the soil can be improved.

    a. Crop rotation would prevent excessive erosion and restore nitrates.

    b. Proper fertilization would increase productivity.

  3. Reforestation can supply the necessary lumber and protect the soil.

C. With programs of scientific research, we can extend our valuable mineral resources.

  1. The most efficient methods of extracting and refining can be worked out.

  2. New mines and oil fields can be located.

  3. Synthetics can be developed for the time when we run out of natural resources.

III. Specific results already obtained guarantee the success of such an overall program.

  A. Harnessing the Colorado River has resulted in benefits for the whole valley.

Second requirement considered

Support by statistics and explanation

Third requirement considered

Support by explanation

Practicability (workability) of programs recommended

1. Hoover Dam has conquered the floods which once threatened the Imperial and Yuma Valleys.
2. Farmers in these valleys now irrigate their lands.
3. Navigation above and below the dam has been extended and improved.
4. According to the Department of the Interior, the dam produces electrical energy at the rate of 4 1/3 billion kilowatt-hours a year.
    a. By May 31, 1987, the end of the 50-year repayment period, Hoover Dam will have returned twice the entire Boulder Canyon power production allocation of $130 million.
    b. The dam returns more than $290,000 to the United States Treasury each month.

B. Startling results have been achieved from farming with modern conservation methods.
1. In a study reported by the NEA, the average annual increase for 4 million acres under conservation was 36 percent.
    a. Farmers grew 1,300,000 more bushels of corn on 32,000 fewer acres.
    b. Their average income was $4.90 per acre higher than that of other farmers.

C. Scientists and engineers have made important contributions to conservation and development of resources.
1. Chemical film coatings have been developed to lessen evaporation from water surfaces in open storage areas.
2. The Bureau of Mines has developed a way to make potassium, formerly imported from Germany, out of potash rock.

Visualization Step

I. If we don't stop destructive practices now, catastrophe can result.

Support by examples and statistics

Appeals to fear

A. In some instances, industry will decline for lack of raw material. (Description of ghost town.)
B. Although the chance of a killing famine in the U.S. is remote, certainly food or water shortages are grim possibilities.
C. Weakened economy can lower our resistance to possible enemy invaders.

II. By developing valley projects, by renewing the soil and forests, and by supporting further scientific research, we can abolish those threats to our nation's welfare.

Appeal to security and well-being

Action Step

I. An effective conservation program demands the full cooperation of each citizen.

Program of action recommended

A. We can begin right here in this community by joining together to form a Conservation Awareness Group.

Practicability of action called for

1. Such groups exist in many cities.
2. They are successfully attacking conservation problems in their areas.

B. We must act today, not tomorrow.

Pressing need for action stressed

1. The problem exists here and now.
2. The problem is constantly getting worse.

II. Sign up on the form I am circulating.

Specific overt action called for

A. You will derive satisfaction from helping to preserve our crucial resources.
B. You will be serving not only yourself, but future generations as well.

Appeals to self-satisfaction and to future benefits

Problems and Probes

1. Using as a source this textbook, recent issues of *Vital Speeches of the Day*, or other sources suggested by your instructor, select three speeches for organizational analysis. Make a complete outline of each. Which one of the three was easiest to outline? Which was the most difficult? How do you account for these differences? Reexamine the speech most difficult to outline, and rework it so that it will fall into good outline form more readily.

2. One of the chief purposes of outlining is, of course, to help ensure clarity; and clarity emerges more readily when messages or speeches

are made up of more or less complete units of thought and when relevant ideas are arranged in clearly recognizable groups. In this chapter we have suggested a number of *sequential patterns* by which the arrangement of thoughts and ideas can be more easily grasped: *time, space, cause-effect, problem-solution, special topical,* etc. Other writers cite "organizing principles" as means of arranging thoughts and ideas, for example, the principle of *proximity,* the principle of *similarity,* the principle of *continuity,* and the principle of *totality.* Interrelate the sequential patterns with these four organizing principles.

3. Develop a demonstration outline on a subject with which you are quite familiar and in which you are very much interested. In it, demonstrate your understanding of (*a*) the correct subordination of points, (*b*) the correct use of indentation, and (*c*) the correct use of number-letter symbols.

4. Make a technical plot for each of the speeches you outlined for Problem/Probe 1 or for three similar speeches. Using the technical plot as a guide, evaluate each speech in terms of the following qualities: (*a*) adequacy of supporting material, (*b*) variety of supporting material, (*c*) use of the factors of attention, (*d*) and use of motivational appeals.

5. For a speech entitled "Make Reading Your Hobby," rearrange the following points and subpoints in proper outline form:

> Low-cost rental libraries are numerous.
> Reading is enjoyable.
> It may lead to advancement in one's job.
> Books contain exciting tales of love and adventure.
> Many paperback books cost only 75¢ to 95¢.
> People who read books are most successful socially.
> Reading is profitable.
> One meets many interesting characters in books.
> Nearly every town has a free public library.
> Through books, one's understanding of human beings and the world is increased.
> The new and stimulating ideas found in books bring pleasure.
> Reading is inexpensive.

Oral Activities and Speaking Assignments

1. For presentation to your class, prepare a five- to seven-minute speech on a subject of your choice. As a part of your preparation, draw up a

detailed outline of this speech and also a complete technical plot in accordance with the sample form provided in this chapter. Hand your speech outline and technical plot to your instructor at least one week before you are scheduled to present the speech itself. The instructor will check these materials and return them to you with suggestions for possible improvement. Following these suggestions, carefully rewrite both the outline and the technical plot, and hand the improved versions back to your instructor just before you begin your actual presentation of the speech.

2. Your instructor will provide you and the other members of the class with a random listing of twenty-five uses of a paper clip. Organize this random list in accordance with one or more of the sequential arrangements or patterns which have been suggested in this chapter, or in accordance with some other useful organizing principle which you have discovered in the Suggestions for Further Reading provided below. Read your organized list aloud to the members of the class; identify the organizational pattern or principle(s) you employed, and explain why you believe it to be the most appropriate for the purpose.

Suggestions for Further Reading

Loren J. Anderson, "A Summary of Research on Order Effects in Communication," *Concepts in Communication*, ed. Jimmie D. Trent *et al* (Boston: Allyn & Bacon, Inc., 1973), pp. 128–138.

K. C. Beighley, "A Summary of Experimental Studies Dealing with the Effect of Organization and of Skill of Speakers on Comprehension," *Journal of Communication* II (1952): 58–65.

Carl I. Hovland, Irving L. Janis, and Harold H. Kelley, *Communication and Persuasion* (New Haven, Conn.: Yale University Press, 1953).

Marvin Karlins and Herbert I. Abelson, *Persuasion: How Opinions and Attitudes Are Changed* (New York: Springer Publishing Co., Inc., 1970), Chapter II, "How to Present the Issues," pp. 5–40.

Glen E. Mills, *Putting a Message Together*, 2nd ed. (Indianapolis: The Bobbs-Merrill Co., Inc., 1972).

R. Wayne Pace and Robert R. Boren, *The Human Transaction: Facets, Functions, and Forms of Interpersonal Communication* (Scott, Foresman and Company, 1973), Chapter V, "Clarifying Our Own Messages," pp. 133–183.

Ernest Thompson, "Some Effects of Message Structure on Listeners' Comprehension," *Speech Monographs* XXXIV (March 1967): 51–57.

15
BEGINNING AND ENDING THE SPEECH

THE IMPORTANCE OF PLANNING AND PREPARATION

All too often speakers who devote much labor to planning and preparing the body of a message pay little or no attention to its introduction or conclusion. They prefer, apparently, to leave these vital parts to the inspiration of the moment. Unfortunately, the needed inspiration is not always forthcoming; and, as a result, they introduce their otherwise carefully planned remarks in haphazard, fumbling fashion to an audience that quickly grows bewildered or bored. Or, similarly, they bring an otherwise polished speech to a weak, ineffectual close because they have not *planned* a clear and satisfying conclusion.

As we have repeatedly emphasized in these pages, to communicate successfully, the continuous and overriding thrust of your message-making effort should be devoted to choosing and developing the major ideas you want your listeners to carry away with them. Obviously, these ideas must be worked out in some detail before you can intelligently determine how best to *lead into them* and how to *tie them together* most tellingly at the end. But it is folly to leave the opening and closing of your message to mere chance. In an effective speech, *each* part or division—beginning, body, and conclusion—has a vital role to play. If it is to play that role well, each must be the product of thoughtful planning and preparation.

How you choose to open and close a speech depends, usually, on three interacting factors:

> *The subject*——the central idea or ideas you wish to communicate.
> *The purpose*——the reason or objective you have in speaking.
> *The listeners*——the people whose acceptance and/or understanding you seek.

To choose wisely in terms of these factors and make them work for you, you will need to know first some of the standard methods—the means—for beginning and ending a message and to familiarize yourself with some of the useful types of materials upon which to draw. In this chapter, therefore, we shall examine these methods and briefly exemplify these materials. We shall consider also how to adapt the introduction and the conclusion to the speech purpose and the audience, and how to join them meaningfully to the body or substance of the message.

BEGINNING THE SPEECH

As we have emphasized, you must sustain the audience's attention *throughout* the presentation of your speech; but at the beginning your principal task is to *capture* that attention. Your entire message must, of course, be built upon one or—usually—more of the attention-generators that we identified in Chapter 12. However, the need for these "generators"—the necessity for choosing just the right one or combination of them in order to magnetize the attention of your hearers—is nowhere more urgent than in your introduction. Nowhere in your speech is there a greater necessity for novelty, reality, activity, or humor. But to gain mere attention is not enough: you must also earn the good will and respect of those with whom you wish to communicate. In many situations your reputation or the chairperson's introduction will create a favorable attitude toward you; and when this is the case, you need only be sure to start your talk in a confident but tactful manner. When, however, you are unknown to your listeners or are confronted by hostility, distrust, or skepticism, you must immediately take steps to overcome this handicap.

Another important function of the introduction is to indicate the specific topic you wish to discuss and to lead your hearers easily and naturally into a consideration of it. A good introduction, therefore, has three goals: *to win attention, to gain good will and respect*, and *to pave the way for the body of the speech.*

Methods and Materials for Beginning the Speech

To attain these results speakers frequently use one or more of the following methods:

1. Refer to the subject or problem.
2. Refer to the occasion.
3. Extend a personal greeting or make a personal allusion.
4. Ask a rhetorical question.
5. Make a startling statement of fact or opinion.
6. Use an apt quotation.
7. Relate a humorous anecdote relevant to a topical point.
8. Cite a real or hypothetical illustration.

Reference to the Subject or Problem

When you are sure that your audience already is interested in the problem or subject you are to discuss, it often is enough merely to state the topic succinctly and then plunge at once into your first main point. The very speed and directness of this approach suggest an eagerness to present your ideas and to press for understanding or belief. For example, a speaker recently began a talk to college seniors with this brief and forthright statement: "I'm going to talk to you about jobs: how to get them and how to keep them." In his now-famous "Des Moines speech" criticizing television coverage of news events, former Vice-President Spiro Agnew also opened with a direct reference to the subject:

> Tonight I want to discuss the importance of the television news medium to the American people. No nation depends more on the intelligent judgment of its citizens. No medium has a more profound influence over public opinion. Nowhere in our system are there fewer checks on vast power. So, nowhere should there be more conscientious responsibility exercised than by the news media. The question is: Are we demanding enough of our television news presentations? And are the men of this medium demanding enough of themselves?[1]

An additional example of an introduction by reference to subject and problem is provided by Phyllis Jones Springen in a speech entitled "The Dimensions of the Oppression of Women":

> When I was asked to speak on "The Dimensions of the Oppression of Women," I laughed. "Oppression" is such an ugly word. Our chairman must have been thinking of those Arab countries where women can't vote and where a woman can be forced to marry any man her father selects, but in the United States women are hardly "oppressed." But as I began to do my research, I quit laughing. There exists a tremendous amount of legal and economic discrimination against the American woman. Much of it is subtle and, therefore, hard to recognize.[2]

A reference to the subject is a good way to begin a speech when the audience is friendly toward the speaker or already is interested in the subject to be discussed. When listeners are hostile, however, such a beginning lacks the elements of *common ground* and *ingratiation* upon which acceptance depends. Nor does it in itself contain the curiosity-provoking qualities desirable in the opening of a speech to an apathetic audience. When used in the latter situation, therefore, it must be combined with one or more of the factors of attention and with material specifically designed to arouse interest. How this may be done is illustrated by the opening of a speech delivered by Father Theodore M. Hesburgh, president of the University of Notre Dame:

> I wish to address you this evening on the subject of science and man. It is a fair assumption that the majority of this audience knows much more about science and technology than I do. This being so, one might wonder why I do not drop the first part of my title of science and man. This is why: I shall not pretend to make any startling revelations in the field of science and technology; but I do want to consider this twin reality in conjunction with man and his actual world. What I have to say may not be popular, but then I never have found this to be a good reason for not saying something that should be said. Anyway, most statements that are popular and safe are also generally dull. This you should be spared.[3]

Reference to the Occasion

Speeches may sometimes best be begun by referring to the occasion which prompts their delivery. On October 18, 1964, President Lyndon Johnson began a nationwide radio-television address by referring to the events which had occasioned it:

> My fellow Americans: On Thursday of last week, from the Kremlin in Moscow, the Soviet government announced a change in its leadership. On Friday of last week, Communist China exploded a nuclear device on an isolated test site in Sinkiang. Both of these events make it right that your President report to you as fully and as clearly and as promptly as he can. This is what I mean to do this evening.[4]

Personal Greeting or Self-Allusion

At times, a warm and personalized salutation from the speaker or a pleasurably recalled earlier association with the audience or the scene serves as an excellent starting point. This is particularly the case if the speaker occupies a high-status position and has considerable prestige in the eyes of the audience. Dr. Grayson Kirk, president of Columbia University, began a speech at the centennial celebration of the University of Denver, with these words:

> It is a pleasure to be in Denver once more, to visit again this university where I taught one happy summer, and to have the opportunity to renew so many longstanding and precious friendships. Actually, I tend, in retrospect, to associate this institution with one of the major changes in the direction of my life. It was here that I enjoyed my last full-time teach-

ing—though I did not know it at the time—because immediately after my return from that pleasant summer here I was invited to become Provost of Columbia, a decision that, once made, brought my teaching days to a close. Now that I am here again, who knows but that when I go back to New York, there might be a strong campus opinion developed in favor of my return to teaching. If this should be the case, then I think I ought to come back here and start where I left off in 1949.[5]

A personal reference of a somewhat different type was used by General Eisenhower to open a speech in Detroit in 1952, when he was campaigning for his first term as President. He began by saying:

Ladies and gentlemen, I think sometimes my military training may not have been as thorough as it could have been, because one of the principles of military life is never to be surprised. I am touched, astonished, and surprised this morning, and I expect it is due to deliberate intent on the part of my associates, now normally labeled as political advisers.

They get some inkling of the way I get tired of my own voice, and so I think they conceal from me at times that I am expected to battle again with one of these microphones.

In any event, as you know, I am scheduled for two talks here today. For a simple fellow like myself, that is quite a chore.[6]

Finally, the way in which a personal-reference type of introduction may be used to gain a hearing from a hostile or skeptical audience is shown by Anson Mount, Manager of Public Affairs for *Playboy* magazine, in a talk presented to the Christian Life Commission of the Southern Baptist Convention:

I am sure we are all aware of the seeming incongruity of a representative of *Playboy* magazine speaking to an assemblage of representatives of the Southern Baptist Convention. I was intrigued by the invitation when it came last fall, though I was not surprised. I am grateful for your genuine and warm hospitality, and I am flattered (though again not surprised) by the implication that I would have something to say that could have meaning to you people. Both *Playboy* and the Baptists have indeed been considering many of the same issues and ethical problems; and even if we have not arrived at the same conclusions, I am impressed and gratified by your openness and willingness to listen to our views.[7]

A personal reference or self-allusion should, of course, be modest and sincere. If it is otherwise, it may gain the attention of the audience, but it is unlikely to establish rapport and good will. Beware, however, of being *overly* modest or apologetic. Avoid saying, "I don't know why your organization picked me out to talk on this subject when others could do it so much better," or "The man who was to speak to you couldn't come, and so at the last minute I agreed to speak, but I haven't had much time to prepare." To introduce yourself and your message with self-denigrating allusions of this sort tends to defeat your basic communicative purpose by suggesting that neither you nor your message are worthy of attention. Be cordial, sincere, and modest, but not apologetic.

In these first three types of speech beginnings which we have analyzed—reference to subject or problem, reference to occasion, and personal greeting or self-allusion—you may have noticed that the factor of *common ground* seems to be a predominating concern. In these three types of speech introductions, the speaker is trying very hard to associate his or her experiences with those of the listeners, to tie his or her past or perspectives to those of the hearers. This thread of common ground runs throughout the fabric of speech communication, and it can be an effective and cohesive force in your message.

Rhetorical Question

To ask a rhetorical question—a question to which no immediate and direct answer is sought—is another effective means of introducing the central idea of your message. One or more such questions, especially if they are well phrased and strike swiftly and cleanly at the very core of your subject or purpose, will prompt your hearers to seek an answer in their own minds and stimulate them to think about the subject which you as the speaker wish to develop. If I ask you a sensible question, very probably you will react by (*a*) trying to formulate an answer or (*b*) at the very least, feeling that it deserves an answer or that one will be forthcoming.

In beginning his discussion of fire hazards in campus buildings, a student pointedly asked: "What would you do if a fire should break out downstairs while I am talking and the stairway collapsed before you could get out?" Rhetorical questions of this kind are especially effective if they impinge on some immediate interest of the listener or deal with a problem of widespread concern. Indeed, if you are presenting your proposal in problem-solution terms, by posing a series of rhetorical questions you may thus lead your audience to formulating an answer or series of answers by which they themselves will arrive at the solution you are advocating.

Here is how Dick Montgomery, a student at the University of Iowa, used two rhetorical questions to open a classroom speech on the trimester plan:

How would you like to graduate from college in three years? How would you like to be able to get out into the world and begin earning money while gaining valuable experience a year sooner than is now possible? You could do this if Iowa adopted the trimester plan.[8]

Jacques Piccard, the well-known marine scientist, when introducing a lecture on the pollution of the oceans, led more gradually and somewhat more elaborately into a rhetorical inquiry:

> Everywhere we hear of pollution, of ecological problems, and of environmental disasters. In every newspaper we read that the sea is about to die, that the atmosphere is poisoning our lungs, that mankind itself may disappear within one or a few generations. Pollution has become the great problem in our century. And as always when a big subject becomes fashionable, all the most dangerous exaggerations are carefully mixed up with the most realistic facts. What should we believe? What should we fear? What is the role played in this by the oceans? I would like to analyze the general problem with you and try to see what can be done to increase the chances of human survival.[9]

Startling Statement

Another method of opening a speech consists of jarring the audience into attention by a startling statement of fact or opinion. H. A. Overstreet has appropriately called this the "shock technic."[10] Clarence Darrow, the trial lawyer, demonstrated the considerable impact of the startling statement when he began a lecture to the prisoners in Cook County Jail in Chicago with these assertions:

> The reason I talk to you on the question of crime, its cause and cure, is because I really do not in the least believe in crime. There is no such thing as a crime as the word is generally understood. I do not believe there is any sort of distinction between the real moral condition of the people in and out of jail. One is just as good as the other.[11]

Whether you are using a startling statement as the sole method of beginning a speech or are combining it with other methods, keep in mind that to rivet your listeners' attention, you will have to phrase your assertions with special care and as strikingly as possible. In both the phrasing and the selecting of ideas to be presented, however, you must be careful to avoid obvious sensationalism — shock solely for the sake of shock. Nor should you use materials which, because they are questionable factually, over-exaggerated, or in poor taste, impair the listeners' respect for your integrity and good judgment. The objective is to invite and attract their *favorable* attention, not to alienate them.

Pertinent Quotation

If properly chosen and presented, a quotation may be an excellent means of introducing a speech. The characteristics of simplicity and succinctness in the choice of a quotation are highly desirable. At the beginning of a speech, the speaker is usually still unknown to the listeners; and they have to adjust to his vocal characteristics, his delivery, etc. Frequently, the audience is still settling down, adjusting their seats, or looking at their programs. Thus, if the speaker chooses a quotation that is long or complex, the members of the audience may not adjust in time to hook on to the relevance or pertinency of the speaker's later remarks.

A pertinent or particularly apt quotation, or a portion of it, may also be used from time to time *during* the speech to reflect, restate, echo, or emphasize its overall structure—to remind the audience that this quoted passage, or the idea it contains, continues to be applicable to the speech as a whole. Thus it helps to heighten the listeners' concentration on the speaker's theme and purpose. Finally, a quotation which is used as the beginning of a speech may be used again in the conclusion; or if one verse of a poem is used to start a speech, another verse or the rest of the poem may appropriately be used to end it.

Observe the way J. Carroll Bateman, president of the Insurance Information Institute, opened an address on the public-relations aspects of the insurance business:

> An embittered Voltaire put into the mouth of Candide the question: "If this is the best of all possible worlds, what then are the others?" Two centuries later, the American novelist James Branch Cabell added cynically: "The optimist proclaims that we live in the best of all possible worlds; the pessimist fears this is true."
>
> We live in a world—i.e., the American society—that *appears* to offer more security than was ever offered by any society in history; and yet, as we look around us, it does not appear to be a very secure place.[12]

Jon P. Peterson of the University of Wisconsin used a single, more extended quotation to introduce his Northern Oratorical League speech entitled "The Alienated Majority." He opened with this passage from Dickens:

> "It was the best of times, it was the worst of times; it was the age of foolishness, it was the age of reason; it was the epoch of belief, it was the epoch of incredulity; it was the season of light, it was the season of darkness; it was the spring of hope, it was the winter of despair. We had everything before us, we had nothing before us; we were all going direct to heaven, we were all going direct the other way."
>
> Thus Charles Dickens described the time of the French Revolution. But we may apply his comments to our own times; for we, too, are in the midst of a revolution: a revolution of our youth; a youth no longer silent, no longer afraid, no longer unchallenged.[13]

Humorous Anecdote Relative to the Major Point or Purpose of the Speech

Another often-used — and often-abused — way to begin a speech is to tell a funny story or relate a humorous experience. A most emphatic word of caution is in order here, however: be sure that the story or experience you recount will amuse the audience and that you can tell it well. If your opening falls flat (and an unfunny or irrelevant story may do just that), your speech will be off to a poor start. If the story has no apparent connection with the circumstance or context of the message, at the very least your audience will be perplexed; if your story is poorly told, your *ethos* may plummet and cost you their respect; if your story is off-color and offends their sensibilities, you will have alienated them at the very outset of your speech. It is imperative, therefore, that an introductory anecdote be relevant and appropriate to your *subject*, your *purpose*, and your *audience*. A joke or a story that is unrelated to these important concerns wastes valuable time and channels the attention and thoughts of your listeners in the wrong direction.

Exercise care, too, in the *manner* in which you tell your story or recount a humorous experience. The speaker who "tries to be funny" rarely is. Very few people enjoy listening to a smart aleck. Tell your tale simply and clearly, letting a quiet sense of humor and enthusiasm shine through. Take the general attitude: "I rather enjoy the humor and good fun of this joke, and I'm hoping you will share a measure of that enjoyment with me." And, above all, if you insist upon laughing at your own jokes, at least give the audience a chance to laugh first. Harold B. Gores, president of Educational Facilities Laboratory, used the following humorous anecdote with good effect to open a lecture at Stanford University:

Let me begin with an ancient story. Once upon a time the people of the valley heard a great noise coming down from the hills. As you would expect, a committee was formed to go up into the hills to see what was making all the racket. In due course the committee came to a clearing in whose center was a great contraption producing a great noise and large quantities of dust, and presided over by a local character named Zeke.

"What is this thing?" asked the chairman of the committee. "It's a stonecrusher," Zeke replied. "Are you crushing any stones, Zeke?" the chairman asked. "No," replied Zeke. "Well," said the chairman, "isn't that rather wasteful?" And Zeke replied, "I guess it is, but you see it takes all my time and energy to run the damn thing empty."

This has been the trouble in our city schools. It has taken all our time and energy to run them empty. There's never been the money and therefore not the energy to prepare for problems before they break upon us. Typically, city schools have not beaten the gun anticipating new problems. Rather, and typically, they have simply reacted to the sound of the shot.[14]

Real or Hypothetical Illustration

Still another method of starting a speech is to use a vivid, rather detailed narrative-illustration of the central point or thrust of your message. Especially useful in this connection are *real-life* incidents and stories taken from history, literature, or daily newspapers. Several brief incidents presented in a series can add a dramatic effect to the beginning of a speech. Equally valuable for this purpose—but sometimes more difficult to originate or evolve—are *hypothetical* illustrations: imagined or suppositional interpretations of events having the quality of implied parallelism with actual ones. Fables and parables may be included in this category. Again, as in the case of the startling statement, quotation, or humorous anecdote, be sure that the introductory illustration you use is *interesting in itself* and that it *connects closely with the central idea of the speech* that is to follow it.

In criticizing certain aspects of our present system of criminal justice, Dr. William A. Stanmeyer, associate professor of law at Georgetown University, led off with this real-life incident:

> On July 2, 1972, four-year-old Joyce Ann Huff, a beautiful little girl, to judge by the newspaper photos, happily went out to play in the yard of her home in Los Angeles County. She played awhile, her mother occasionally glancing out at her from the kitchen a few feet away. Joyce Ann was an innocent child, full of love and promise and expectation on this bright summer day. Her parents were hardworking citizens with no enemies in the world.
>
> Neither Joyce Ann Huff nor her mother noticed a yellow 1966 Chevrolet carrying three men roll up the street and pause while a man in the back seat took aim with a shotgun at the little girl. But they heard a thunderous explosion as the shotgun drove forty-two pellets into Joyce Ann's body and drove her soul forever from the face of this earth. Spattered with blood, Joyce Ann died within five minutes in the arms of her sobbing mother.
>
> Witness identification enabled the police to arrest the three. The prime suspect had previously been arrested for: attempted murder, assault with a deadly weapon, robbery, burglary, arson, and narcotics charges. The motive this time appeared to be, "for the thrill of it," and the UPI wire-service story was entitled, "Police Arrest 2 for Shotgun 'Joy' Killing of Girl, 4."
>
> What, if anything, under our present system of criminal justice, will happen to the murderers? One may ask: What happened to Charles Manson? What happened to Richard Speck? What happened to Sirhan Sirhan? What would happen in the United States, if the murders at the Munich Olympics happened here, rather than in Germany?[15]

Perry Prentice, retired vice-president of Time, Incorporated, used an illustration drawn from historical records to begin a talk delivered at a conference on housing and urban development:

> If you will pardon a brief digression from this afternoon's subject, I'd like to devote my first 81 seconds to the sad fate of King Louis XIII of France, who died at the age of 41 on December 4, 1642, moaning that he was much too young to die and angrily (and quite correctly, I suspect) protesting that he was being killed by his doctors. Within a year they had bled him 47 times, purged him 215 times, and dosed him with 212 different remedies from a pharmacopia which included the left foot of a tortoise, the urine of a lizard, some elephant's dung, a mole's liver, blood drawn from the right wing of a white pigeon, elixir of quicksilver, and elixir of arsenic. The doctors don't seem to have had any idea what the King's ailment was, so lacking a diagnosis they tried everything, and if a mild dose didn't work, they tried a stiffer dose; and if that didn't work, they tried something else — until at last the King died, and it was too late to try on him the other 1748 potions in their pharmacopia.
>
> Now I realize that you did not come here to listen to such sad stories of the death of Kings, so let's forget for a while how the doctors killed the King of France 330 years ago and get straight to the point of what we today are doing to cure or not to cure today's housing problems and today's urban problems.[16]

Actual and hypothetical illustrations, relevant humorous anecdotes, pertinent quotations, startling statements, rhetorical questions, personal greetings and self-allusions, and references to the speech subject, problem, or occasion — these, then, are eight useful ways of beginning a speech. Sometimes one method may be used alone; at other times, two or more of them will work more effectively in combination. Notice, for example, how Professor Lester Thonssen brings together an illustration, a personal reference, and a reference to the occasion in opening a commencement address at Huron College:

> In his essay on "The Anthropology of Manners," Edward T. Hall, Jr., tells of a tribesman who came to a prearranged spot in Kabul, the capital of Afghanistan, to meet his brother. But he couldn't find him. So he left, giving instructions to the local merchants where he might be reached if his brother showed up. Exactly a year later, the tribesman returned to the same place in Kabul, and sure enough, there was his brother. It seems that the brothers had agreed to meet in Kabul on a certain day of a certain month at a particular place, but they failed to specify the year.
>
> My plans have been like those of the tribesman. Often I've agreed

to meet friends on a return to the campus at commencement time, but the year was never definitely set. Now thirty-two years after graduation—a disturbingly grim statistic—I'm honored and privileged to keep an appointment on this important occasion in the life of a fine institution.[17]

Whatever method or methods you use to begin a speech, remember that besides gaining attention you must also lead the minds of your listeners easily and naturally into your subject. Remember, too, that you must gain their good will and respect for you as a person.

ENDING THE SPEECH

The principal function of any method used to end a speech is to focus the thought and feeling of the hearers on the central theme developed during the presentation of your ideas. Clarity, conciseness, and a sense of climactic concentration and unifying completeness characterize the genuinely effective conclusion. *Summary* and *decisive restatement* or *reiteration* are the major means by which it is usually achieved. If you present a single-idea speech, that idea must be restated at the end in a manner that will make your meaning clear and forceful.* If your speech is more complex, you must bring its most important ideas together in a condensed and unified form that points unmistakably to their overall significance, or else suggest the action or belief to which these ideas lead.

In addition to bringing the substance of the speech into final focus, a good ending should leave the audience in the proper mood. If you expect your listeners to express vigorous enthusiasm, you must stimulate that feeling by the way you close. If you want them to reflect thoughtfully on what you have said, your conclusion should encourage a calm, judicious attitude. Decide whether the response you seek requires a mood of serious determination or good-humored levity, of warm sympathy or cold anger, of objective deliberation or vigorous immediate action. Then plan to end your message in such a way as to generate that mood, to create that frame of mind.

Finally, remember that the end of a speech should convey a sense of *completeness* and *finality*. Nothing annoys an audience so much as to think the speaker has finished, only to have him go on again. Avoid false endings. Tie the threads together so that the pattern of your speech is brought to completion; deliver your concluding sentence with finality—and then stop. If you bring the central theme into sharp focus, create the proper mood, and close with decisiveness, you will be more likely to achieve the purpose for which you speak.

---

*See pp. 317–326, where the single-idea speech is discussed.

Methods and Materials for Ending the Speech

To achieve these results in ending a speech, speakers frequently employ one or more of the following methods:

1. Issue a challenge or an appeal to listeners.
2. Summarize major points or ideas.
3. Provide an appropriate quotation.
4. Epitomize with a thematic illustration.
5. Offer an additional inducement for accepting or acting upon the speaker's proposal.
6. Express the speaker's personal intention or endorsement.

Challenge or Appeal to Listeners

When using this method, appeal openly for belief or action, or remind your listeners of their responsibilities in achieving a desirable or beneficial goal. Such an appeal should be vivid and compelling, and should contain within it a suggestion of the principal ideas or arguments you have presented in your speech. Note how Louis B. Lundborg, chairman of the Bank of America, employed this kind of conclusion in his keynote address to a National Convocation on World Hunger:

> The task before us is great indeed. It will require ingenuity and patience. We will have to bring to our efforts humility before the magnitude of the problems to be solved, but determination in the light of the importance of the task. Therefore, let us so conduct ourselves over the next few days that the world can say that at this time and in this place the talking ended and the action began. Thank you.[18]

In the political arena, challenge-appeal conclusions are used frequently. Note, for instance, how Hubert Humphrey concluded the speech announcing his candidacy for the Democratic nomination for President by combining a stirring challenge with an epitomizing quotation drawn from Victor Hugo:

> My fellow Americans, we are the people of today; we are the people of the future. And it is to the future that we look and aspire.
> The future has several names. For the weak, it is the impossible. For the faint-hearted it is the unknown. For the thoughtful and the valiant, it is the ideal. The challenge is urgent. The task is large, the time is now. On to victory![19]

Summary of Major Points or Ideas

A summary conclusion reviews the main ideas of the message and draws whatever inferences may be implicit in the speech material as a whole. In a speech to inform, a summary ending is nearly always appropriate because it restates and helps you to impress upon the listeners those ideas which you especially want remembered. In a speech to persuade, a summary conclusion provides a final opportunity to reiterate your principal arguments and appeals.

As part of his conclusion to a speech delivered at Aquinas Junior College in Nashville, Tennessee, and entitled "What the Future Demands," Guilford Dudley, Jr., an insurance executive, used this summary:

> Let me try to wrap all that I have said to you into a tight little ball before we get into the discussion period. . . .
>
> We have accented the need for a profound understanding of the impact of accelerating change and global shrinkage. . . .
>
> We have discussed not so much a reorientation of our values as a need to reorient the roles of the various parts of our society in working toward the common goals.
>
> We have noted that our vision must encompass the fact that our goals are no longer fixed by physical limitation, though our achievements may be limited by our lack of will.
>
> And finally we have stated that the profile of tomorrow's business executive must include raw courage.
>
> We have spoken of very basic things, like the need to be multilingual. We have moved into philosophical discussions in our awareness that more and more daily problems and challenges present themselves in moral terms.[20]

Pertinent Quotation

A quotation, either poetry or prose, may be used to end a speech if it bears directly on the central idea you have been trying to communicate, or if it strongly suggests the attitude or action you wish your listeners to take. A few lines of poetry, for instance, can often provide in figurative, climactic language the theme or essence of your message. A few words of quoted prose, especially if carefully chosen to encapsulate or envision the fulfillment of your speech purpose, can lend both color and authority to your conclusion.

Elmer W. Lower, president of ABC News, in addressing the Buffalo, New York, chapter of Sigma Delta Chi, national journalism fraternity, used a quotation to provide a striking and forceful conclusion to a speech entitled "Racial Stress and the Mass Media":

Experienced, responsible news executives, reporters, editors, and producers, as they have in this country since it was founded, still must exercise their own seasoned judgment in reporting and editing the news. In all of our history the mass media have never failed the public in time of stress. I am sure they will not do so now.

We are indebted to William Allen White, the great journalistic sage of the Kansas plains, for this counsel. And I quote:

"You say that freedom of utterance is not for time of stress, and I reply with the sad truth that only in time of stress is freedom of utterance in danger. No one questions it in calm days; only when free utterance is suppressed is it needed; and when it is needed, it is most vital to justice."[21]

How a challenge may be combined with a quotation to conclude a speech effectively is illustrated by Charles Schalliol, a student at Indiana University, in an intercollegiate oration on the subject of air pollution:

In spite of any action the government and industry take, a large part of the responsibility must rest with the public. If public sentiment ignores the existence of air pollution as criminal, little will be done. We must alert Americans to the consequences inaction will cause . . . no one is free from America's greatest criminal. If we ignore air pollution it will loom ever larger. In the words of Professor Morris B. Jacobs, former director of the Department of Air Pollution Control, "It is now time to end this plague. Time to look beyond narrow vested interests, to awaken from slumbering too long—and save ourselves. We had better act now. It will soon be too late."[22]

Epitomizing Illustration

Just as an illustration which epitomizes your leading ideas may be used to open a speech, so may an illustration of this type be used at the close. A speech-ending illustration should be both *inclusive* and *conclusive:* inclusive of the main focus or thrust of your speech, conclusive in tone and impact. And also like the illustration used as a speech-opener, it may be either actual or hypothetical. Dr. Samuel B. Gould, president of the Educational Broadcasting Company, concluded a speech to the students and faculty of Hunter College as follows:

Whatever the career and whatever the task, it deserves what is best and finest in us. . . . B. J. Chute, the writer, tells a wonderful story about a small child who watched a sculptor working on a slab of marble. Day after day, the child watched and the sculptor worked. And then, at last, there came a day when the child drew his breath and looked at the sculptor in amazement and said, "But how did you know there was a lion in there?"

To know there is a lion in one's mind, and finally to produce it— that is success. That is the flavor for our daily bread, the closest we shall ever come to human happiness.[23]

Additional Inducement

Sometimes a speech may be concluded by quickly reviewing the most important ideas presented in the body of the talk and then supplying one or two additional reasons for accepting the belief or taking the action proposed. Observe how Miss Linda Mast combined the methods of summary and added inducement in the conclusion of a speech urging use of seat belts in cars:

All in all, you will find that buying seat belts for your car and using them is a worthwhile investment. As I have shown, they are a great aid in saving lives and preventing serious injuries; having them in your car may enable you to pay less insurance; and wearing them will make travel more comfortable and enjoyable. The few arguments which may be raised against seat belts do not outweigh their advantages, but only show how indifferent most people are to their own safety and well-being. Even if you are willing to take chances with your own life, however, you owe this additional security to your family and friends. Install seat belts in your car today![24]

Expression of Personal Intention or Endorsement

A statement of personal feeling or of intention to act as your speech recommends is another convincing method of concluding your message. It is particularly valuable when your prestige with the audience is high, but you may also employ it with strong effect in other circumstances. Perhaps the most famous example of this method of closing a speech is the declaration attributed to Patrick Henry: " . . . As for me, give me liberty or give me death!" In a contemporary setting, Senator Paul Fannin of Arizona demonstrated the strength of the personal-intention conclusion in a speech presented to students in a management-training course sponsored by the General Electric Company:

I may not agree that everything is right about our present system, but I surely think it is better than anything we could import. I see no major government on the world scene today that I would care to swap for ours. So I shall continue to work on improving this system, to make right those things that are wrong with it, and to preserve those time-tested, honorable principles that are the foundation of our national success.[25]

In sum, then, the choice of materials, the methods by which you will present them, and the hoped-for impact of your message depend greatly on the positive interaction of your subject, your purpose, and the predispositions of your listeners. It would be folly, therefore, to leave any part of your speech to mere chance. Clearly, *each* part—beginning, body, and conclusion—has a vital role to play in achieving your communicative goal. If it is to play that role well, you must plan each part thoughtfully, carefully select the most appropriate materials for each, and integrate *everything* into a truly cohesive whole.

FOOTNOTES

[1] From "Des Moines Speech" by Spiro Agnew from Vital Speeches of the Day, Vol. XXXVI, (November 15, 1969). Reprinted by permission of Vital Speeches of the Day.

[2] From "The Dimensions of the Oppression of Women" by Phyllis Jones Springen from Vital Speeches of the Day, Vol. XXXVII, (February 15, 1971). Reprinted by permission of Vital Speeches of the Day.

[3] Excerpt from speech by Father Theodore M. Hesburgh, President of the University of Notre Dame, from Representative American Speeches: 1962–1963, published by the H. W. Wilson Company. Reprinted by permission of the author.

[4] Representative American Speeches: 1964–1965, ed. Lester Thonssen (Bronx, N.Y.: The H. W. Wilson Company, 1965), p. 46.

[5] From "Responsibilities of the Educated Man" by Dr. Grayson Kirk from Vital Speeches of the Day, Vol. XXX, (May 1964). Reprinted by permission of Vital Speeches of the Day.

[6] New York Times, June 15, 1952. Reprinted in Speeches for Illustration and Example, ed. Goodwin Berquist (Glenview, Ill.: Scott, Foresman and Company, 1965), p. 193.

[7] Excerpt from Speech by Anson Mount from Contemporary American Speeches, 3rd Edition, by Wil A. Linkugel, R. R. Allen, and Richard Johannesen. © 1973 by Wadsworth Publishing Company, Inc., Belmont, California 94002. Reprinted by permission of the author and the Christian Life Commission.

[8] Text supplied by Mr. Montgomery and his instructor, Mr. Donovan Ochs.

[9] From "How Modern Technology Is Endangering Our Lives" by Jacques Piccard from Vital Speeches of the Day, Vol. XXXIX, (January 1, 1973). Reprinted by permission of Vital Speeches of the Day.

[10] Harry A. Overstreet, Influencing Human Behavior (New York: W. W. Norton & Company, Inc., 1925), p. 120.

[11] "Address to Prisoners in Cook County Jail," in Attorney for the Damned, ed. Arthur Weinberg (New York: Simon and Schuster, Inc., 1957), p. 3. Reprinted with permission of the publisher.

[12] From "The Best of All Possible Worlds" by J. Carroll Bateman from Vital Speeches of the Day, Vol. XXXIV, (December 15, 1967). Reprinted by permission of Vital Speeches of the Day.

[13] Excerpt from speech, "The Alienated Majority" by Jon P. Peterson. Delivered at the University of Iowa, March 4, 1968. Reprinted by permission of the Northern Oratorical League and through the courtesy of the League's secretary, Robert Kemp.

[14] From "The Schoolhouse in the City" by Harold B. Gores from Vital Speeches of the Day, Vol. XXXIII, (October 1, 1967). Reprinted by permission of Vital Speeches of the Day.

[15] From "Urban Crime: Its Causes and Control" by Dr. William A. Stanmeyer from Vital Speeches of the Day, Vol. XXXIX, (January 1, 1973). Reprinted by permission of Vital Speeches of the Day.

[16] From "Our Housing and Our Cities" by Perry Prentice from Vital Speeches of the Day, Vol. XXXIX, (March 1, 1973). Reprinted by permission of Vital Speeches of the Day.

[17]*Excerpt from "The Anthropology of Manners" by Lester Thonssen from* Representative American Speeches, *1958–1959, ed. Lester Thonssen. (Bronx, N.Y.: The H. W. Wilson Company, 1959), pp. 132–133. Reprinted by permission of the author.*

[18]*From "The Agribusiness Approach: Problems and Opportunities" by Louis B. Lundborg from* Vital Speeches of the Day, *Vol. XXXIII, (October 1, 1967). Reprinted by permission of Vital Speeches of the Day.*

[19]*From an address delivered before guests at a luncheon at the Shoreham Hotel, Washington, D.C., and broadcast nationwide by radio and television, April 27, 1968. Text from* Des Moines Sunday Register, *April 28, 1968, p. 4-G.*

[20]*From "What the Future Demands" by Guilford Dudley, Jr. from* Vital Speeches of the Day, *Vol. XXXIV, (April 1968). Reprinted by permission of Vital Speeches of the Day.*

[21]*From "Racial Stress and the Mass Media" by Elmer W. Lower from* Vital Speeches of the Day, *Vol. XXXIV, (November 1, 1967). Reprinted by permission of Vital Speeches of the Day.*

[22]*"The Strangler" by Charles Schalliol. Reprinted from* Winning Orations *by special arrangement with the Interstate Oratorical Association, Duane L. Aschenbrenner, Executive Secretary, University of Nebraska at Omaha.*

[23]*Excerpt from "A Flavor of Our Daily Bread" by Samuel B. Gould. Reprinted by permission.*

[24]*Presented at the University of Iowa, January 15, 1963. Text supplied by Miss Mast and her instructor, Mr. Donovan Ochs.*

[25]*From Speech by Paul Fannin from* Vital Speeches of the Day, *Vol. XXXIV, (May 1, 1968). Reprinted by permission of Vital Speeches of the Day.*

Problems and Probes

1. Select fifteen or twenty speeches from recent issues of *Vital Speeches of the Day, Representative American Speeches,* or one of the sources suggested in the Problems and Probes of earlier chapters. Classify the various ways in which these speeches begin and end. Are certain types of beginnings and endings used more frequently than others? Do some types seem to be more common in speeches to inform and others more common in speeches to persuade? What types appear most frequently in speeches delivered on special occasions—anniversaries, dedications, farewells, etc.?

2. Select ten of the beginnings and endings cataloged in Problem /Probe 1. Evaluate these in terms of their suitability to (*a*) the speaker's purpose, (*b*) the subject matter of the speech, and (*c*) the nature and attitude of the audience (insofar as you are able to determine them). Which of the beginnings and endings could have been improved? How?

3. After listening to one or more of the following types of speeches, evaluate the beginning and ending which the speaker used in (*a*) a classroom lecture; (*b*) a church sermon; (*c*) a television address; (*d*) remarks made at a fraternity, sorority, or dormitory council meeting. In reporting your evaluation, supply sufficient information about the speaker and speaking situation so that someone who was not present could understand why you evaluated a particular beginning or ending as you did.

4. Work out at least two alternative means for beginning and ending a talk to members of your speech class on one of the following subjects:

The ROTC program	Primitive culture
Career opportunities	The problems of our cities
Water-pollution control	Pesticides — pro and con
The Counterculture	Life from a test tube
VISTA	The Equal Rights Amendment
Legislative reapportionment	The amateur investor
The Third World War	New faces in the films

Oral Activities and Speaking Assignments

1. Select a subject toward which the members of your speech class probably will hold one of the attitudes described on page 247 — favorable, but not aroused; apathetic; interested, but undecided; hostile to any change, etc. Prepare and present a five-minute speech on this subject. Be sure that the introduction or beginning is specifically adapted to the probable attitude of the audience.

2. Present a five-minute speech on a subject of interest to the members of your speech class. Conclude it with an ending designed to leave the audience in one of the following frames of mind: (a) thoughtful or reflective, (b) emotionally aroused or excited, (c) determined to take the action you propose.

Suggestions for Further Reading

Aristotle, *Rhetoric*, 1414b–1415a, " The Proem or Introduction"; and 1419b–1420b, "The Epilogue."

Quintilian, *Institutio Oratoria*, IV. 1, "The Prooemium or Exordium."

Richard Whately, *Elements of Rhetoric*, ed. Douglas Ehninger (Carbondale, Ill.: Southern Illinois University Press, 1963), "Of Introductions and Conclusions," pp. 168–174.

Eugene E. White, *Practical Public Speaking*, 2nd ed. (New York: The Macmillan Company, 1964), Chapter VIII, "Developing the Introduction of the Speech"; and Chapter IX, "Developing the Conclusion of the Speech."

16
USING WORDS
TO COMMUNICATE MEANING

In Chapters 13 and 14 we examined the psychological structuring and the compositional organization of your speech materials. Further, we discussed how this structuring and organization lay the groundwork for the full-content outline. Even the most complete organizational outline, however, does not provide a complete or finished talk. The problem of phrasing the ideas in vivid and compelling language and of making clear and graceful transitions from one point to another still confronts you. In this chapter we will be scrutinizing the words and phrases in which you couch your message. We shall consider some of the principles that underlie the effective use of words, and we shall offer specific guidance for their selection and arrangement.

ACCURACY OF MEANING

Precise meaning can be expressed only if words are carefully chosen. The man who tells the hardware clerk that he has "broken the hickey on his hootenanny and needs a thing'ma-jig to fit it," expresses his meaning vaguely; but his vagueness is only a little greater than that of the orator who proclaims, "We must follow along the path of true Americanism." The sentiment obviously is to be admired, but just what does this statement mean? Remember that words are only symbols which stand for meanings and that your listener may attach to a symbol a meaning different from the one you intend. *Democracy*, for example, does not mean the same thing to a citizen of the United States that it does to a citizen of Soviet Russia. An *expensive* meal to a college student may seem quite moderate in price to a wealthy man. A mode of travel that was *fast* in 1867 seems painfully slow a century later. The *United States* today is not the same as it was in the days of George Washington—in area, in population, in industry, or even in much of its governmental structure. Nor, for that matter, are all the members of a general class alike: Frenchman A differs from Frenchmen B and C; one Chevrolet may be old and rusty, another is new and shiny. Students of general semantics* continually warn us that words in themselves are not objects or qualities or operations, but only *symbols* for these things. Many grave errors in thinking and communication arise from treating words as if they were the actual conditions, processes, or objects to which they refer, and accordingly fixed and timeless in meaning.

If, therefore, you think there is the least chance that your audience may misinterpret what you say, define your words in more concrete or immediate terms.** Notice, for example, how Elliott V. Bell in the following passages makes clear what he means by *structural unemployment* and *fiscal policy:*

> "Structural unemployment" is just another name for what we used to call technological unemployment except that it has a broader meaning. It means not merely the unemployment that results when, for example, a textile plant is fitted out with labor-saving machinery and hand-workers are displaced by automation. It also means what happens when the old textile plant in New England is abandoned and the new automated plant is erected in North Carolina. It means what happens when homes and factories switch from coal to oil. Coal miners in West Virginia or Pennsylvania lose their jobs. Even if there are unfilled jobs elsewhere, the miners may not be able or willing to move away and learn new skills. . . .
>
> "Fiscal policy" is a term that is often used and seldom defined. By it I mean all of the taxing, spending, and borrowing operations that the Government conducts—all of the ways in which the Federal Establishment puts money into the national economy or takes money out ot it.[1]

A speaker concerned about how his audience may interpret his remarks will, in definitions and elsewhere, choose words which express the exact shade of meaning he intends to convey. Although dictionary definitions are not sure guides to the meaning which any particular listener will attach to a word, they do represent the commonly accepted usages stated as precisely as possible. The careful speaker, therefore, will refer to his dictionary constantly to verify or correct his choice of words. He will note and observe in his speech the distinctions dictionaries make among related words, such as *languor, lassitude, lethargy, stupor,* and *torpor.* He may even use a book of synonyms (such as Roget's *Thesaurus*)

For a more extended treatment of the subject, see Irving J. Lee, Language Habits in Human Affairs *(New York: Harper & Row, Publishers, 1941); Wendell Johnson,* People in Quandaries *(New York: Harper & Row, Publishers, 1946); Doris B. Garey,* Putting Words in Their Places *(Glenview, Ill.: Scott, Foresman and Company, 1957); and Roger Brown,* Words and Things *(Glencoe, Ill.: The Free Press, 1958).*

**A discussion of various methods of definition will be found on pp. 497–499.*

in an attempt to select words which exactly express his meaning. For example, among the synonyms for the verb *shine* are: *glow, glitter, glisten, gleam, flare, blaze, glare, shimmer, glimmer, flicker, sparkle, flash, beam.* The English language is rich in subtle variations of meaning. To increase the precision of your expression, make use of this variety in your choice of words.

SIMPLICITY

No matter how accurately a word or phrase may express a speaker's meaning, it is useless if the audience cannot understand it. For this reason, expression not only must be exact, but must be clear and simple. "Speak," said Lincoln, "so that the most lowly can understand you, and the rest will have no difficulty." This rule is as valid today as when Lincoln uttered it; and because modern audiences as created by the electronic media are vaster and more varied than any Lincoln dreamed of, there is even more reason for contemporary speakers to follow it. Say "learn" rather than "ascertain," "*after-dinner* speech" rather than "*postprandial* speech," "large" rather than "elephantine." Never choose a longer or less familiar word when a simpler one will do. As the Roman teacher Quintilian said, "Speak not so that you will be understood, but so that you cannot possibly be misunderstood."

In particular, choose words that are short and concrete over those that are longer and more abstract. Herbert Spencer illustrates the importance of this advice in his *Essay on Style* by comparing two sentences:

(1) "In proportion as the manners, customs, and amusements of a nation are cruel and barbarous, the regulations of their penal code will be severe." — How much better to have said —
(2) "In proportion as men delight in battles, bullfights, and combat of gladiators, will they punish by hanging, burning, and the rack."

Billy Sunday, the famous evangelist, has given us another example of the same point:

If a man were to take a piece of meat and smell it and look disgusted, and his little boy were to say, "What's the matter with it, Pop?" and he were to say, "It is undergoing a process of decomposition in the formation of new chemical compounds," the boy would be all in. But if the father were to say, "It's rotten," then the boy would understand and hold his nose. "Rotten" is a good Anglo-Saxon word and you do not have to go to the dictionary to find out what it means.[2]

Use short words; use simple words; use words that are concrete and specific; use words with meanings that are immediately obvious. The able speaker, regardless of the range of his experience, invariably devotes painstaking attention to matters of simplicity, specificity, and vividness in the actual phrasing of his speech.

APPROPRIATENESS

A third requirement is that your language be appropriate to the subject on which you are speaking and to the situation in which your speech is delivered.

Serious or solemn occasions call for diction that is restrained and dignified; light or joyful occasions, for diction that is informal and lively. Just as you would never use slang in remarks at a funeral service or in a speech dedicating a church or memorial, so you should never phrase a humorous after-dinner speech in a heavy or elevated style. Suit your language to the spirit and tone of the occasion; be dignified and formal when formality is expected and light and casual when informality is called for. The good speaker is one who can sense what the situation requires, and can vary his style accordingly.

IMAGERY

We receive our impressions of the world around us through our senses of sight, smell, hearing, taste, and touch. In order to get an audience to experience the object or state of affairs you are describing, you must, therefore, appeal to their senses. But you cannot punch them in the nose, scatter exotic perfume for them to smell, or let them taste foods which are not present. The only senses through which you as a speaker can reach them *directly* are the visual and the auditory: they can see you, your movements and your facial expressions; and they can hear what you say.

Despite this limitation, however, you can *indirectly* stimulate all of the senses by using language that has the power to produce imagined sensations in a listener, or which causes him to recall images he has previously experienced. The language of imagery falls into seven classes, or types, each related to the particular sensation that it seeks to evoke.

Types of Imagery

The seven types of imagery are:

1. Visual (sight)
2. Auditory (hearing)
3. Gustatory (taste)
4. Olfactory (smell)
5. Tactual (touch)
   a. Texture and shape
   b. Pressure
   c. Heat and cold
6. Kinesthetic (muscle strain)
7. Organic (internal sensations)

Visual Imagery

Try to make your audience actually "see" the objects or situations you are describing. Mention size, shape, color, movement, and the relative position of one part or element to another. Notice how C. P. Snow uses visual imagery to emphasize his point that we should help people in the underdeveloped countries "live as long as we do and eat enough." He says:

> We are sitting like people in a smart and cozy restaurant and we are eating comfortably, looking out of the window into the streets. Down on the pavement are people who are looking up at us, people who by chance have different colored skins from ours, and are rather hungry. Do you wonder that they don't like us all that much? Do you wonder that we sometimes feel ashamed of ourselves, as we look out through that plate glass?[3]

And in the following description, note how Ivan T. Sanderson has combined the precise details of the physical appearance of sea elephants to produce a striking word picture:

> Even a photograph cannot give a true picture of these fabulous and ridiculous creatures. Not only are they immense, males growing to eighteen feet in length and as much as fifteen feet in girth, but this sex is adorned with an eighteen-inch trunk that normally flops down over the mouth but which is also connected with the nasal passages and can be inflated and raised almost straight up. Worse still, these animals are clothed in very short sparse greyish brown hair, which they moult once a year and in doing so not only lose their fur but also their whole outer skin; they are then bright pink and present the most grotesque and revolting appearance, especially when they lounge around on shore in great misshapen, heaving masses under a hot sun, moaning, groaning, gurgling and roaring. They live on cuttlefish, seaweed, and shellfish and are fairly agile in the water but spend a lot of time on land. The great bulls heave their immense bulk up

gently sloping beaches and into the tussocky tall grass of the islands they most prefer and then go to sleep. Nothing is quite so alarming as to stumble up against one of these animals at such a time since they come "unstuck" with a veritable explosion and rise to full height, blowing and snorting.[4]

Auditory Imagery

Make the audience hear not only what you say but also the sounds which you are describing. In the following example, Tom Wolfe vividly describes the opening of a stock-car race:

Then the entire crowd, about 4,000, started chanting a countdown, "Ten, nine, eight, seven, six, five, four, three, two," but it was impossible to hear the rest, because right after "two" half the crowd went into a strange whinnying wail. The starter's flag went up, and the 25 cars took off, roaring into second gear with no mufflers, all headed toward that same point in the center of the infield, converging nose on nose.

The effect was exactly what one expects that many simultaneous crashes to produce: the unmistakable tympany of automobiles colliding and cheap-gauge sheet metal buckling.[5]

Loren Eiseley employs both auditory and visual imagery to describe the moment after a raven has killed and eaten a nestling:

The sound that awoke me was the outraged cries of the nestling's parents, who flew helplessly in circles about the clearing. The sleek black monster was indifferent to them. He gulped, whetted his beak on the dead branch a moment and sat still. Up to that point the little tragedy had followed the usual pattern. But suddenly, out of all that area of woodland, a soft sound of complaint began to rise. Into the glade fluttered small birds of half a dozen varieties drawn by the anguished outcries of the tiny parents.

No one dared to attack the raven. But they cried there in some instinctive common misery, the bereaved and the unbereaved. The glade filled with their soft rustling and their cries. They fluttered as though to point their wings at the murderer.[6]

Sounds vary in loudness, pitch, and rhythm, as well as in quality. By calling attention to these details, you can create a more vivid auditory image.

Gustatory Imagery

Help your audience imagine the taste of what you are describing. Mention its saltiness, sweetness, sourness, or its spicy flavor. Observe how Charles Lamb in his "Dissertation upon Roast Pig" describes that delicacy:

There is no flavor comparable, I will contend, to that of the crisp, tawny, well-watched, not over-roasted, *crackling*, as it is well called—the very teeth are invited to their share of the pleasure at this banquet in overcoming the coy, brittle resistance . . . the tender blossoming of fat . . . the lean, not lean, but a kind of animal manna—or, rather, fat and lean . . . so blended and running into each other, that both together make but one ambrosian result . . . too ravishing for mortal taste.[7]

Olfactory Imagery

Make your audience smell the odors connected with the situation you describe. Do this not only by mentioning the odor itself but also by describing the object that has the odor or by comparing it with more familiar ones, as shown in this example:

As he opened the door of the old apothecary's shop, he breathed the odor of medicines, musty, perhaps, and pungent from too close confinement in so small a place, but free from the sickening smell of stale candy and cheap perfume.

Tactual Imagery

Tactual imagery is based upon the various types of sensation that we get through physical contact with an object. Particularly it gives us sensations of *texture* and *shape*, *pressure*, and *heat* and *cold*.

Texture and Shape. Enable your audience to feel how rough or smooth, dry or wet, or sharp, slimy, or sticky a thing is.

Pressure. Phrase appropriate portions of your speech in such a way that your auditors sense the pressure of physical force upon their bodies: The weight of a heavy trunk borne upon their backs, the pinching of shoes that are too tight, the incessant drive of the high wind on their faces.

Heat and Cold. These sensations are aroused by what is sometimes called "thermal" imagery.

The following passage by Loren Eiseley well illustrates the use of tactual imagery:

I thought of all this, standing quietly in the water, feeling the sand shifting away under my toes. Then I lay back in the floating position that left my face to the sky, and shoved off. The sky wheeled over me. For an instant, as I bobbed into the main channel, I had the sensation of sliding down the vast tilted face of the continent. It was then that I felt the cold needles of the alpine springs at my fingertips and the warmth of the Gulf pulling me southward. Moving with me, leaving its taste upon my mouth and spouting under me in dancing springs of sand, was the immense body of the continent itself, flowing like the river was flowing, grain by grain, mountain by mountain, down to the sea.[8]

Kinesthetic Imagery

Kinesthetic imagery relates to muscle strain and movement. Word portions of your speech in such a way that your audiences may feel for themselves the stretching and tightening of their tendons, the creaking in their joints:

> He climbed two thousand feet above the black sea, and without a moment for thought of failure and death, he brought his forewings tightly in to his body, left only the narrow swept daggers of his wingtips extended into the wind, and fell into a vertical dive.
> The wind was a monster roar at his head. Seventy miles per hour, ninety, a hundred and twenty and faster still. The wing-strain now at a hundred and forty miles per hour wasn't nearly as hard as it had been before at seventy, and with the faintest twist of his wingtips he eased out of the dive and shot above the waves, a gray cannonball under the moon.[9]

Organic Imagery

Hunger, dizziness, nausea—these are a few of the feelings organic imagery calls up. There are times when an image is not complete without the inclusion of specific details relating to these inward feelings. Be careful, however, not to offend your audience by making the picture too revolting. A fine taste is required to measure the detail necessary for vividness without making the image so gruesome that it becomes either disgusting or grotesque. Observe the use made of organic imagery by H. G. Wells:

> That climb seemed interminable to me. With the last twenty or thirty feet of it a deadly nausea came upon me. I had the greatest difficulty in keeping my hold. The last few yards was a frightful struggle against this faintness. Several times my head swam, and I felt all the sensations of falling. At last, however, I got over the well-mouth somehow and staggered out of the ruin into the blinding sunlight.[10]

A somewhat different kind of organic imagery is used by Tom Wolfe:

All the faces come popping in clots out of the Seventh Avenue local, past the King Size Ice Cream machine, and the turnstiles start whacking
away as if the world were breaking up on the reefs. Four steps past the
turnstiles everybody is already backed up haunch to paunch for the climb
up the ramp and the stairs to the surface, a great funnel of flesh, wool, felt,
leather, rubber and steaming alumicron, with the blood squeezing through
everybody's old sclerotic arteries in hopped-up spurts from too much coffee
and the effort of surfacing from the subway at the rush hour.[11]

Using Imagery

These, then, are the seven types of imagery: *visual*, *auditory*, *gustatory*,
olfactory, *tactual*, *kinesthetic*, and *organic*. Victor Alvin Ketcham called them " The
Seven Doorways to the Mind," doorways which the speaker must open with his
words if he expects his audience to understand or believe him. As Professor Ketcham pointed out, *"People differ in the degree to which they are sensitive to different
types of imagery."*[12] The public speaker is wise, therefore, to employ as many
types as possible.

In employing imagery you should be aware of three considerations: (1)
the difference between produced and reproduced images, (2) the principle of reference to experience, and (3) the importance of detail in creating accurate and
vivid word pictures.

Produced and Reproduced Images

There are two types of images: one based on the memory of a single
experience, the other produced by putting together in a new pattern the details
of several different experiences. If I describe the football game which you attended yesterday, I may be able to *reproduce* a fairly complete image of the experience
which you had; if, however, I describe a cricket match—a sport which you have
never seen—by putting together details of clothing, action, and sound which you
have experienced in other circumstances, I can *produce* a new image in your
mind. Of the two types, new (or produced) images obviously are the harder to
create. In drawing them, take time to picture each part of the object or scene fully
and to show exactly how it relates to the whole. When carefully developed, however, produced images can become vivid and can stimulate the imaginations of
the listeners almost as well as reproduced ones.

The Principle of Reference to Experience

Words as symbols are effective in direct proportion to the strength of
the experiences with which they are associated. Some words create stronger

images than others; for example, *wrench* is more vivid than *pull* simply because stronger sensations have been associated with it. For the man who has never seen a *dirigible*, the word creates at best an indistinct picture; you must use language with which he is familiar or make comparisons to experiences which are common to him. Notice, for example, how much more vivid the image becomes when you say that the dirigible is like a "huge, elongated football, painted silver, moving slowly through the air."

The Principle of Detail

Remember, finally, that while you can speak only one word at a time, a large number of different and detailed sensations normally are received simultaneously. If you are to create a vivid image, you must take time to describe all aspects of an object or event. The importance of details in making ideas vivid has been noted by Barbara W. Tuchman, the historian:

> At a party given for its reopening last year, the Museum of Modern Art in New York served champagne to five thousand guests. An alert reporter for the *Times*, Charlotte Curtis, noted that there were eighty cases which, she informed her readers, amounted to 960 bottles or 7,680 three-ounce drinks. Somehow through this detail the Museum's party at once becomes alive; a fashionable New York occasion. One sees the crush, the women eyeing each other's clothes, the exchange of greetings, and feels the gratifying sense of elegance and importance imparted by champagne—even if, at one and a half drinks per person, it was not on an exactly riotous scale. All this is conveyed by Miss Curtis' detail."[13]

Observe how the Atlanta editor, Henry W. Grady, used details to create a picture of the defeated Confederate soldier in the following passage from his famous address, "The New South":

> Let me picture to you the footsore Confederate soldier, as, buttoning up in his faded gray jacket the parole, which was to bear testimony to his children of his fidelity and faith, he turned his face southward from Appomattox in April, 1865. Think of him as, ragged, half-starved, heavy-hearted, enfeebled by wounds and exhaustion—having fought to exhaustion—he surrenders his gun, wrings the hands of his comrades in silence, and, lifting his tear-stained and pallid face for the last time to the graves that dot the old Virginia hills, pulls his gray cap over his brows and begins the slow and painful journey.[14]

LOADED WORDS

Many words—even some of the shortest and simplest ones—contain within themselves not only a denotative or dictionary meaning but, in addition, an aura of implied or connotative meaning. Because such words are thus "loaded," they have a strong effect on the reactions of an audience. Observe the different responses that you yourself make to the following: *man, fellow, guy, person, savage, cheapskate, piker, chiseler, sportsman, father, dad, baron, miser, dictator.* Although each of these words denotes a human being, what different types of human beings they suggest and how strongly some of them convey approval or disapproval!

Because of the responses which they can call up, loaded words must be used with caution. When employing them, be sure you can answer these two questions affirmatively: Does the audience understand the meaning I intend to convey? Do I have sound facts and reasoning to support my position so that the words I use are justified? Select words which will add vividness to your speaking, but take care to employ them accurately and fairly.

Meaning Derived from Associations

Many words become "loaded" as a result of experiences with which they are associated. After the repeal of national prohibition, for example, places where liquor was sold came to be called *taverns* in order to avoid the unpleasant mental image associated with the old saloon. The word *politician* suggests to many people a scheming, dishonest man, making promises which he does not expect to keep and uttering pious platitudes while he secretly accepts illegal pay from "special interests"—a picture repeatedly painted by cartoonists and novelists and by opposing politicians. Yet the intrinsic meaning of the word denotes only one who is occupied in the management of public affairs or who works in the interest of a political party.

Since different people have different experiences, the connotation of a word may vary greatly, and you must always be tactful in adapting it to your particular audience. Shoe clerks, for example, tell a woman: "Madam, this foot is slightly smaller than the other," instead of "That foot is bigger than this one." Observe in the following example how Dr. Ernest Tittle, in his description of words as such, uses words freighted with meaningful associations:

There are colorful words that are as beautiful as red roses; and there are drab words that are as unlovely as an anaemic-looking woman. There are concrete words that keep people awake; and there are abstract words that put them to sleep. There are strong words that can punch like a prize-fighter; and weak words that are as insipid as a "mama's boy." There are warm, sympathetic words that grip men's hearts; and cold, detached words that leave an audience unmoved. There are warm, sympathetic words that lift every listener, at least for a moment, to the sunlit heights of God; and base words that leave an audience in the atmosphere of the cabaret.[15]

Meaning Derived from the Sound of the Word

Some words gain a particular value from the very sounds they contain. Such words as *hiss, crash, rattle, slink, creep, bound, roar* suggest by their sound their exact meaning. The poems of Edgar Allan Poe and of Vachel Lindsay abound in words of this kind — *clanging, tinkle, mumbo-jumbo.* As H. A. Overstreet has said, "There are words that chuckle; words that laugh right out; words that weep; words that droop and falter."[16] A proper appreciation of the sound values of words will help make your speaking clearer and more vivid.

TRITENESS

Words and expressions which are powerful or vivid in themselves may be rendered ineffective and colorless by overuse. A once-powerful phrase is stripped of its significance by thoughtless repetition and serves only to display a lack of originality in the person who uses it. Thus, when one says that he "sat down to a sumptuous repast placed on a table loaded with delicacies," he not only is violating the rule of simplicity but is using worn-out phrases as well. The words *gorgeous, fabulous, terrific,* and others have been so overworked that they have lost their original effectiveness. Figures of speech in particular are likely to become trite; avoid such expressions as "slept like a log," "dead as a doornail," and "pretty as a picture." On the other hand, beware of grotesque combinations and mixed metaphors. The speaker who described a dump heap as a "picturesque eyesore" was original but ludicrous, as was the man who remarked that "The years roll on, drop by drop." Note in contrast the appropriateness of this figurative statement by Justice Learned Hand:

Liberty lives in the hearts of men and women. When it dies there, no constitution, nor court, nor law can save it.[17]

Note also the strength and freshness of Yale President A. Whitney Griswold's comparison of the free mind and the unfree mind:

The mind that is unfree, the mind that is possessed, the mind that is indoctrinated or forced does not learn. It copies. Discovery is the true essence of learning. The free mind travels while the unfree simply looks at the maps. The unfree mind locks the doors, bars the shutters, and stays at home.[18]

SLANG

Slang words and phrases may on certain occasions be both acceptable and effective. They can add succinctness and color. In fact, when a slang phrase is inherently precise or vivid, it may eventually become standard usage. Usually, however, slang is only temporary and weak. College slang especially tends to become trite and to substitute one word for a variety of more specific and effective ones. A young woman, for example, is "cool" or "with it," but so is a football game, a chocolate soda, a dance, a class lecture, or a pair of shoes. To use slang for a particular effect is permissible, but to use it merely to avoid the search for more precise words is slipshod and results in weak or meaningless expressions.

CONNECTIVE PHRASES

Unlike written compositions, material which is spoken cannot be divided into units by paragraph indentations or by underlined headings. Instead, the relationships between the points of a speech must be made clear by the wording itself.

Preliminary and final summaries are useful in mapping out for the audience the road you intend to follow and in reviewing your speech at its close. But you must also set up signposts as you go along to assist your audience in following you. For this purpose, you will find a variety of connective phrases useful. The following list contains some of the more common ones:

Not only . . . but also . . .
In the first place . . . The second point is . . .
In addition to . . . notice that . . .
More important than all these is . . .
In contrast to . . .
Similar to this . . . is . . .
Now look at it from a different angle . . .
This last point raises a question . . .
You must keep these three things in mind in order to understand the
    importance of the fourth . . .
What was the result of this . . . ? Just this: . . .

Clarity often depends upon the effectiveness of a speaker's connective phrases. Expand your list of such phrases and use them to make easy, smooth transitions from one point to another.

BUILDING A VOCABULARY

In order to choose words that are accurate, clear, appropriate, and vivid, a speaker must have a large and constantly growing vocabulary. Wide reading, close observation of the language used by cultured people, even the systematic attempt to "use a new word every day" — all of these methods are helpful in vocabulary development. It is equally important, however, to put into active use the vocabulary you already possess. Most people know the meanings of ten times as many words as they actually use. Work to transfer the words from your recognition vocabulary to your active vocabulary. Effective speakers are noted not for the large number of words they use but for the skill with which they combine the simple words of the average man's vocabulary to state even complicated ideas vividly and precisely.

A SAMPLE SPEECH

Examine the use of language and imagery in the following classroom speech by Miss Ann E. Bogaard, a sophomore at the University of Iowa. How well do you think Miss Bogaard met the criteria of accurate, simple, appropriate, and vivid expression? What criticisms do you have of this speech? What changes, if any, would you make in the development of her central idea? in her choice of words and images?

YOU — A SPONGE?[19]

Ann E. Bogaard

Suppose it's raining outside and you want to collect rain water, so you go out with a ketchup bottle; it's obvious that you're not going to collect much rain. You'd have much better luck with a wide-mouthed jug or even a basin.

This afternoon I'm going to persuade you — NOT to be a ketchup bottle, not even to be an ordinary basin; but I'm going to persuade you to be a sponge in a basin.

All of us are constantly in the "rain" of ideas, impressions, sights, sounds, personalities, and happenings. We are bombarded with these things simply because we are alive and because we are part of a complex world. Now let's get on with specifically what I mean by a "sponge."

A basin is a container that holds something; the world is a basin. A sponge in a basin absorbs the material or the something that the basin contains; *I* am a sponge! Not only do I absorb from my environment, but under the slightest pressure of being squeezed—if I am a real sponge—I will release and give back part of what I absorbed.

The *what* of being a sponge is mainly this: being an individual with an open mind that is flexible and receptive to change—not a mind that is restricted to the narrow dimensions of a bottleneck. Suppose the farmer had been a ketchup bottle, stubbornly resisting the changes in industrialization and mechanization. Where would we be today? But the farmer was a sponge, applying change and progress for the benefit of mankind.

Now that you know what a sponge is, let's ask the question, "Why a sponge?"

There are two basic reasons why I want to be a sponge. The first reason is that by being a sponge, I can benefit myself. I have to live with myself; and, therefore, I want to be fit to live with myself. I exist as a miracle and so do you. If this miracle is going to be a sponge, I must first understand and learn about *me*. I must know myself and to mine own self be true. The second reason logically follows: by being a sponge, others will benefit. Charity, kindness, love, sympathy, and knowledge for and of my brother can lead to nothing but understanding and peace. The oppressed, the downtrodden, and the destitute of this world can *live*, if *I* will be a sponge.

Maybe I've already persuaded you to be a sponge, but I'm not going to stop now. I want you not only to think like a sponge, but to act like a sponge. We've talked about the "what" and "why" of being a sponge; now comes the most difficult part: "how" to be a sponge.

Let's take a few examples and ask a few questions. If the questions seem to prick your conscience a bit, let them. We are all college students; are you a ketchup bottle in class, or a sponge? Most of us are members of a religious community; do you put on your suit of piety for an hour on Sunday morning, or do you wear your religion every day of the week? You are a member of a family; what do you give to your family which helps make "house" a "home," or is home just a place where you eat and sleep?

A sponge is an active participant in life, not just a spectator on the sidelines. He gives of himself, he shows emotion, he expresses himself, and he stands for something! A sponge must be trained to be aware, conscious, and observant, and at the same time be open and receptive.

Being a sponge is an abstract concept—a concept which has no charts, facts, or figures to back it up, but I believe in this concept with all my being. What about you there, standing in the rain? Are you a ketchup bottle? Do you stand there with your umbrella up, shielding and protecting you from the rain? Or is there the possibility that now you'll be a sponge with me?

FOOTNOTES

[1] *From "Economic Outlook" by Elliott V. Bell from* Vital Speeches of the Day, *Vol. XXVII, (June 1, 1961). Reprinted by permission of Vital Speeches of the Day.*

[2] *Quoted in J. R. Pelsma,* Essentials of Style *(New York: Crowell Collier and Macmillan, Inc., 1924), p. 193.*

[3] *From "The Moral Un-Neutrality of Science,"* Representative American Speeches, *1960–1961, ed. Lester Thonssen (New York: The H. W. Wilson Company, 1961), p. 53.*

[4] *From* Living Mammals of the World *by Ivan T. Sanderson. Published by Doubleday, 1955.*

[5] *Reprinted with the permission of Farrar, Straus & Giroux, Inc., International Famous Agency and Tom Wolfe from* The Kandy Kolored Tangerine Flake Streamline Baby *by Tom Wolfe, copyright © 1963, 1964, 1965 by Thomas K. Wolfe, Jr., copyright © 1963, 1964, 1965 by New York Herald Tribune, Inc.*

[6] *From* The Immense Journey, *by Loren Eiseley. Copyright © 1957 by Loren Eiseley. Reprinted by permission of Random House, Inc.*

[7] *Charles Lamb, "A Dissertation upon Roast Pig,"* The Complete Works and Letters of Charles Lamb *(New York: Modern Library, Inc., 1935), pp. 110–111.*

[8] *From* The Immense Journey, *by Loren Eiseley. Copyright © 1957 by Loren Eiseley. Reprinted by permission of Random House, Inc.*

[9] *Reprinted with permission of Macmillan Publishing Co., Inc. and Turnstone Press Ltd. from* Jonathan Livingston Seagull *by Richard Bach. Copyright © 1970 by Richard D. Bach.*

[10] *H. G. Wells, "The Time Machine,"* The Complete Short Stories of H. G. Wells *(London: Ernest Benn Limited, 1927), p. 59.*

[11] *Reprinted with the permission of Farrar, Straus & Giroux, Inc., International Famous Agency and Tom Wolfe from* The Kandy Kolored Tangerine Flake Streamline Baby *by Tom Wolfe, copyright © 1963, 1964, 1965 by Thomas K. Wolfe, Jr., copyright © 1963, 1964, 1965 by New York Herald Tribune, Inc.*

[12] *From "The Seven Doorways to the Mind" in* Business Speeches by Business Men, *ed. William P. Sandford and W. H. Yeager (New York: McGraw-Hill Book Company, 1930).*

[13] *From "History by the Ounce" by Barbara W. Tuchman from* Harper's Magazine, *(July 1965). Reprinted by permission of Russell & Volkening, Inc. as agents for the author. Copyright © 1965 Harper's Magazine Company.*

[14] *Delivered at the New England Society Dinner in New York City, December 22, 1886.*

[15] *From a commencement address by Ernest F. Tittle, delivered at the Northwestern University School of Speech, June, 1924.*

[16] *H. A. Overstreet,* Influencing Human Behavior *(New York: W. W. Norton & Company, Inc., 1925).*

[17] *Quoted in a speech "The Bold Go Toward Their Time," by William C. Lang, printed in* Vital Speeches of the Day *XXVII (March 15, 1961): 333–334.*

[18] *Ibid.*

[19] *Presented August 3, 1965. Supplied through the courtesy of Ann E. Bogaard Howard.*

Problems and Probes

1. As an exercise in choosing language that is appropriate for different speech situations, study the following groups of words and decide whether the individual words or phrases are (*a*) appropriate for any speech situation, (*b*) appropriate for informal speech situations, (*c*) appropriate for formal situations. Be prepared to defend your decisions regarding these terms:

> hoggish, greedy, gluttonous
> drunk, intoxicated, soused, inebriated, tight, blotto, pie-eyed
> falsehood, whopper, lie, fib, misrepresentation, untruth
> crabby, ill-tempered, cross, quarrelsome, grouchy
> savory, appetizing, delicious, tasty, scrumptious
> laughable, funny, amusing, ludicrous, hilarious, killing
> a capricious elderly man, a queer old duck, a nutty old character, an eccentric old man, a strange old fellow, a crazy old geezer

2. List two or more meanings for each of the following words:

fast	right	slip
fair	top	cut
race	hot	dope

Add to this list at least ten other multiple-meaning words.

3. Find a shorter and simpler word to express each of the following:

maintain	designate	culmination
escalate	perturbation	tenacious
partition	holistic	funereal
investigation	tautology	preferential

4. Make a list of ten neutral words or expressions. Then for each word in this list find (*a*) a "loaded" synonym which would cause listeners to react favorably toward the object or idea mentioned and (*b*) a "loaded" synonym which would cause them to react unfavorably toward the same object or idea. (EXAMPLE: *neutral word*—"old"; *complimentary synonym*—"mellow"; *uncomplimentary synonym*—"senile.")

5. Pick out five "loaded" words or phrases in the speech by Ann Bogaard, pages 441–443, and indicate whether each carries a favorable or unfavorable connotation. What would be a neutral synonym for each of these loaded terms?

6. Read a recent issue of *Vital Speeches of the Day* to find (*a*) passages that illustrate particularly good word choice (i.e., passages in which the

words are accurate, simple, and appropriate), and (*b*) instances of the skillful use of connective words and phrases.

7. Read one or more speeches by each of the following: Edmund Burke, Daniel Webster, Abraham Lincoln, and Adlai Stevenson. Compare the wording in these speeches, giving special attention to (*a*) accuracy of word choice, (*b*) simplicity, (*c*) appropriateness, (*d*) imagery, and (*e*) the use of loaded language.

8. Expand to twenty or more the list of connective phrases given on page 440.

9. What connective phrase might you use to join (*a*) a major idea with a subordinate one, (*b*) a less important idea with a more important one, (*c*) two ideas of equal importance, (*d*) ideas comparable in meaning, and (*e*) contrasting or opposing ideas?

10. Using varied and vivid imagery, describe orally or in writing one of the following:
      Sailboats on a lake at sunset
      Goldfish swimming about in a bowl
      Traffic at a busy intersection
      Sitting in the bleachers at a football game in 15° weather
      The hors d'oeuvre table at an expensive restaurant
      The city dump
      A symphony concert

11. List examples of imagery taken from several magazine advertisements and/or television commercials.

Oral Activities and Speaking Assignments

1. Describe orally in class a personal experience or an event you have recently witnessed—for example, a traffic accident, the crucial moment in a basketball game, a memorable meal, big city noises. Employ vivid imagery in an effort to stimulate your listeners to relive this experience or event with you.

2. Write a four- to six-minute speech to be presented from manuscript. Revise the manuscript several times to be sure that (*a*) the words and expressions you choose are accurate, simple, and appropriate; (*b*) wherever possible, you have employed live and vivid imagery; (*c*) you

have used loaded words skillfully but ethically; (*d*) you have avoided trite expressions; and (*e*) your connective phrases are clear and graceful. In presenting the speech, observe the suggestions for reading a speech from manuscript as described on pages 177–179 in Chapter 5.

Suggestions for Further Reading

Hubert G. Alexander, *Meaning in Language* (Glenview, Ill.: Scott, Foresman and Company, 1969).

J. L. Aranguren, *Human Communication* (New York: McGraw-Hill Book Company, 1967), Part III, "The Sociology of Communication: The Content," pp. 137–205.

Jane Blankenship, *A Sense of Style: An Introduction to Style for the Public Speaker* (Belmont, Calif.: Dickenson Publishing Company, 1968).

Kenneth Boulding, "Introduction to 'The Image,'" *Dimensions in Communication: Readings*, ed. James H. Campbell and Hal W. Hepler (Belmont, Calif.: Wadsworth Publishing Company, 1970), pp. 26–35.

William V. Haney, *Communication and Organizational Behavior*, 3rd ed. (Homewood, Ill.: Richard D. Irwin, Inc., 1973), Chapters VI–XV.

Wendell Johnson and Dorothy Moeller, *Living With Change: The Semantics of Coping* (New York: Harper & Row, Publishers, 1972).

Bardin H. Nelson, "Seven Principles of Image Formation," *Dimensions of Communication*, ed. Lee Richardson (New York: Appleton-Century-Crofts, 1969), pp. 53–60.

I. A. Richards, *The Philosophy of Rhetoric* (New York: Oxford University Press, Inc., 1936), Chapter III, "The Interinanimation of Words"; and Chapter V, "Metaphor."

John R. Searle, *Speech Acts: An Essay in the Philosophy of Language* (Cambridge: Cambridge University Press, 1969).

17
LISTENING, EVALUATION, AND ETHICAL JUDGMENT

Too often it is assumed that the speaker bears the major, if not the entire, responsibility for effective communication. But as we have stressed repeatedly, speech communication is a two-way transaction *between* speaker and listener, not a one-way action of speaker *on* listener. Obviously, then, effective and accurate listening is not only an important ability but also an integral part of the total process. Listeners must make a concentrated effort to understand what they hear. They must decide whether the speaker's recommendations are useful and his conclusions probable. They must judge whether the contentions are fairly stated and adequately proved. Listeners must assess both the ethics of the speaker's purpose and proposal and the ethics of the communicative techniques he employs. Finally, if they are to enjoy or appreciate the speaker's ideas, listeners must relate them to their own standards of taste and humor. Because of these varied obligations, the task of the listener is fully as demanding as that of the speaker. Because of the transactional nature of the speech communication process, the ability to listen well is just as important as the ability to speak well. Without the one, there would be little need for the other.

LISTENING

In a given day, *more than 40 percent* of the time which the average adult spends in communication activity is spent in listening.* Despite this large allocation of time, most human beings listen inefficiently. After listening to a ten-minute lecture, for example, students could remember accurately only about *50 percent* of what was said; after two weeks or more, accuracy of recall dropped to about *25 percent*.** If these figures are typical, a great many of us are not meeting

---

*See the studies reviewed by Larry L. Barker, Listening Behavior *(Englewood Cliffs, N.J.: Prentice-Hall, Inc., 1971), pp. 3–4.*

**For details, see the studies reported by Ralph G. Nichols, *"Do We Know How to Listen? Practical Helps in a Modern Age,"* The Speech Teacher X *(March 1961): 120.*

seriously the responsibilities that communicative listening involves. As a listener-participant in the oral communication process, you sometimes must do *more* than your share by concentrating on a dull presentation of a significant message or by making internally your own structure for ideas randomly scattered by the speaker, and thus compensate for his inadequacies. Moreover, as a listener you are obligated to assist the speaker by providing *useful feedback:* usually, you are expected to react overtly in ways which will help him present his message more easily and accurately. You can do this by making sure that your verbal and non-verbal reactions (*a*) can be seen and heard by the speaker; (*b*) clearly and accurately communicate your intended meaning; (*c*) are ordinarily made immediately; (*d*) are appropriate for the speaker, the subject, and the occasion; and (*e*) are not so profuse that they confuse the speaker.[1] Two experts on the listening process, Ralph G. Nichols and Leonard Stevens, have concluded:

> It seems that we shall eventually come to believe that the responsibility for effective oral communication must be equally shared by speakers and listeners. When this transpires we shall have taken a long stride toward greater economy in learning, accelerated personal growth, and significantly deepened human understanding.[2]

Listening is, of course, a complex communication skill, and the ability to listen can be improved. As we pointed out in Chapter 4 (pages 139–140), it involves, among other things, acute hearing: the conversion of sound waves by the ear mechanisms into nerve impulses sent to the brain where they are converted into symbols to which meaning is attached. But there is much *more* to the listening process than that. In addition to acute hearing, effective listening involves the interpretation of overt and covert meanings, the making of inferences about speaker intent, the analysis and evaluation of the message, and reaction to what the speaker says. If, as we believe, listening can indeed be improved, how can we go about it? We suggest that you can become a better listener if you:

1. Recognize and practice to *rid yourself of inefficient listening habits;*
2. *Get ready* to listen;
3. Learn to listen in order to *appreciate* what you listen to; and
4. Listen to *understand* what you hear.

Inefficient Listening Habits

On some occasions each of us probably has engaged in certain thought—or thought*less*—patterns and certain internal-response behaviors. Such patterns and behaviors, when indulged in frequently and/or for lengthy periods of time, tend to become faulty, self-distractive, inefficient listening habits and thus hinder the listener's full concentration on and selective response to the speaker's message.* Let us consider briefly a few of these nonproductive or negating habits. These habits, we should emphasize, are by no means limited to public communication; they seem to deter listeners from their purpose whenever and wherever human beings congregate and attempt to interact.

Private planning. While the speaker is talking, some listeners become engrossed in their own problems and in planning solutions and forthcoming activities: what they will have for dinner, what they will say to the boss or a spouse, what they will say to the speaker if they get the chance, etc. They cannot, of course, listen attentively to the speaker while doing their private planning.

Self-debating. A listener tends to carry on a continuous, private argument with himself or herself about the soundness and worth of what the speaker is saying. Often the auditor will engage in a lengthy, silent argument with himself as to the comparative strengths and weaknesses of the message rather than merely noting that an aspect or element of it is questionable and delaying full evaluation until later.

Yielding easily to distractions. These distractions take innumerable forms: loud noises or uncomfortable conditions in the environment, daydreams about being in more pleasant and preferred circumstances, etc. A fleeting word, a half-heard phrase, a glimpsed image, or some other stimulus will trigger a lengthy recall of past personal experiences. Inattention to the speaker is the inevitable result.

Avoiding difficult listening. Too many of us like to avoid complex or challenging subjects. We prefer to say, "Oh, that's not for me," and close our ears. When we do this, however, we lose valuable opportunities to *exercise* our concentrative skills and thereby improve our listening abilities.

Prematurely dismissing a subject as uninteresting. We should realize that some rather dry subjects are nevertheless important and that a knowledge of them can become valuable to us personally. Rather than "shutting off" the speaker, focus patiently on what he or she is saying, recognizing as you do so that the real relevance of the topic may not emerge until the speaker is well into the subject.

Being overly critical of the speaker's delivery and physical appearance. Sometimes we are unnecessarily harsh in our internal criticism of the speaker's

---

This discussion of inefficient listening habits is adapted in part from Larry L. Barker, Listening Behavior (Englewood Cliffs, N.J.: Prentice-Hall, Inc., 1971), pp. 61–66; and from Ralph G. Nichols and Leonard A. Stevens, Are You Listening? (New York: McGraw-Hill Book Company, 1957), pp. 89–112.

mode of dress, or his vocal and bodily delivery, or other nonverbal factors. We allow ourselves to be "turned off" by these negative impressions and thus obscure the necessity of evaluating the intrinsic merits of the message itself. Nonverbal elements are significant, of course; but if we are to listen well, we must give close attention to *both* the verbal and the nonverbal elements.

Listening just for isolated facts. Too often we listen only for the "bits and pieces" of a speech—only the "things that interest us." At such times, we tend to ignore the substance as a *whole* and overlook the structural relationships and emphases accorded the various parts. In other words, we fail to get the entire picture. If we fall into this habit, we are usually trying to remember or write down every detail, fact, and example used by the speaker rather than focusing on understanding the major ideas or arguments which the speaker is trying to develop *by means of* such materials. We need to look for the organizational reasons why he or she may have *selected* particular items to illustrate a main idea.

Allowing emotionalism to hinder listening. Often people react positively or negatively and in a strong manner to certain emotionally laden words or ideas. Positive attitudes triggered by a specific word or phrase may cause us to lower our evaluative standards and thereby produce an uncritical, unreflective response. Negative attitudes so triggered may lead us to reject—without fair and total judgment—*everything* the speaker says. Note, however, that this definitely does not mean that listeners *never* should respond emotionally to a message or become empathically involved. Emotions are a valid part of human experience. We simply should be *aware* of the nature of our own individual emotional tendencies and not allow them to affect adversely our reception of a message.

Allowing basic convictions or prejudices to hinder listening. A very human tendency is to allow prejudices; stereotypes; and basic beliefs, attitudes, values, and motives to impair the accuracy of our understanding or fairness of evaluation. The admonition to "know thyself" is directly applicable to effective listening.

Being dogmatic. A closed-minded person with a tunnel vision of *the* truth does not strive to *understand* various or conflicting viewpoints preliminary to judging their acceptability. The dogmatist usually does not wait to "hear the speaker out" before evaluating and deciding.

Mental "wool-gathering," internal debate, giving in to distractions, dodging subjects and materials difficult to listen to, premature evaluation of subject and speaker, trying to "absorb" isolated facts rather than the whole, emotional distortion, prejudice, and dogmatism—these, then, are the chief "culprits" in causing us to be poor listeners. To rid ourselves of resultant inefficient habits, we need to learn to listen with both an open ear and an open mind.

Getting Ready to Listen

As we have observed in all forms of oral communication, the good listener—like the good speaker—has a specific purpose he wishes to achieve by participating in the communicative transaction. This purpose may be (1) *to learn*—to acquire new information and points of view; (2) *to judge or evaluate* the worth of the ideas and arguments presented; or it may be simply (3) *to enjoy*. Although one of these purposes is usually primary, good listening often includes all three. Under no circumstances, however, is the good listener passive and indifferent; he has a *reason* for listening and, therefore, approaches the listening situation with a positive rather than a negative attitude. He listens because he wants to, not because he has to.

In order to achieve his purpose, whenever possible the good listener prepares himself in advance for the speech or lecture he is going to attend. He studies the topic to be discussed, finds out what he can about the speaker and his beliefs, and investigates the group or organization by which the talk is sponsored. When he arrives at the place where the speech is to be given, he seats himself where he can see and hear easily, and throughout the program remains alert both physically and mentally. Finally, when the talk is over, he reviews what was said, discusses the ideas with his friends or—if possible—with the speaker himself, and studies the subject further. In this way, he is able to receive maximum benefit in return for the time and effort he has expended.

Listening for Appreciation

If the speaker's purpose is to entertain rather than to inform or persuade, your purpose as a listener may be simply to derive enjoyment from his speech. Under such circumstances you usually can increase your pleasure and appreciation by following these suggestions:

1. *Relax physically and mentally.* Sit in a comfortable, relaxed position. Insofar as possible, free your mind from other interests and from vexing problems and worries.

2. *Cultivate a receptive attitude.* Do not spoil your pleasure by being too analytical or hypercritical. This does not mean that you should be completely undiscriminating, but that you should view the speaker in a warm and friendly light and should anticipate with pleasure the speech he is about to present.

3. *Use imagination and empathy.* Instead of holding back, enter into the spirit of the occasion freely and fully. Give your imagination enough

play so that you can join with the speaker in reliving the events or experiences he relates. If you can imagine yourself a participant in the situations described, their vividness will be enhanced and your pleasure in the speech will grow accordingly.

Listening for Understanding

Sometimes your primary purpose as a listener is to learn new facts, more clearly understand an idea or viewpoint, or more fully comprehend a subject which now seems vague or confused to you. When that is the case, you may benefit from the following guides:

1. *Identify the speaker's major or leading ideas, and concentrate closely on each as it is expressed.* Unless you take care to identify each major idea as it is stated and to separate it from the developmental material that is associated with it, you may fail to grasp the speaker's dominant thesis or point of view and may carry away from the listening experience nothing more than a confused mass of data. In other words, as we have emphasized, don't fall into the inefficient habit of listening "just for the facts." Besides identifying each major idea as such, you should concentrate closely on each idea as it is stated. Such concentration not only will help you grasp its full significance, but also will increase your chances of remembering it later.

2. *Identify the structure or arrangement of the major ideas.* Determine whether the speaker is organizing his material according to one or more patterns, such as chronological, spatial, cause-effect, problem-solution, motivated sequence, conclusion-proven-by-data, or data-leading-to-conclusion. By identifying and bearing in mind the speaker's organizational approach, you will be able to follow his explanations more easily and remember his main points more accurately. If a speaker does not provide a clear pattern, if the speech is rambling and disorganized, as a listener you may have to attempt to structure the ideas into some pattern meaningful to you.

3. *Examine critically the details used to develop and support the major ideas.* As you identify each major idea and observe how it fits into the pattern of the speech as a whole, note also the materials by which this idea is exemplified or supported. What additional light is thrown on the idea by the illustrations or comparisons which the speaker supplies? Does this piece of explanation or that set of statistics point up some implication or inference that you have previously overlooked? Do certain of the speaker's quotations confirm or throw doubt on the

idea as originally presented? Are the scope, pertinence, and importance of the idea significantly modified by the supporting data? By asking such questions, you can appreciably increase your comprehension of the idea and its place in the speech.

4. *Relate the major ideas to your own previous knowledge and interests.* Try to determine *why* the information presented by the speaker should be important to you or *why* you should want to make it a permanent part of your storehouse of knowledge. The speaker may be offering answers to a question important to you, presenting information about a subject on which you are largely uninformed, or providing fresh insight concerning knowledge you already possess. What is the relation of the information to your needs and goals? In what ways can the information be used or applied? Where does this new material fit within the context of information which you already consider worthwhile? Where and how might you obtain additional material on the subject?

EVALUATION

Evaluative listening includes the skills necessary to listen effectively for understanding and comprehension, but it goes beyond. Frequently evaluative listening seeks to assess speech communication which has *persuasion* as its primary purpose. When your aim is to *evaluate* speech communication, you will strive for something approaching a total assessment of communicative strengths and weaknesses, societal worth, effectiveness, and ethics of the speech and its presentation. This, clearly, is a complex and often subjective task. To help structure the evaluative process, we shall raise and discuss a number of questions. In this way we hope to identify potential dimensions for evaluation which you may apply, if appropriate, to whatever speech you are assessing. Try to find answers to the following lines of inquiry:

1. *What seem to be the speaker's general and specific purposes?* To entertain, to present information and increase understanding, to reinforce existing beliefs and attitudes, to change beliefs and attitudes, or to secure overt action? To what degree is the purpose appropriate for the speaker, audience, and occasion? For a persuasive speech, consider whether its intent is conciliation and identification, shock and arousal, or confrontation and alienation. How might factors in the occasion or prevailing ideological climate have influenced the speaker's purpose and/or methods? To what in particular does the speaker seem to be responding? Given the audience and relevant circumstances, does the speaker's purpose seem realistic and achievable?

2. *How does the speaker arouse and maintain your attention and interest?* In the content, language, and delivery, are such interest-factors as conflict, suspense, curiosity, action, novelty, and humor capitalized upon? Is interest heightened through analogies, narration, vivid descriptions, contrasts, factual and hypothetical examples, and illustrations?

3. *Does the speaker try to make sure that you, as a listener, clearly understand the message as intended?* Do you know exactly what the speaker is asking of you, and concretely how he intends to implement that idea or proposal? Judge whether ideas are presented accurately and clearly and whether extremes of complexity and simplification are avoided. If ambiguity seems employed intentionally, what factors inherent in the subject or occasion might account for it? What patterns of organization does the speaker use to promote unity and clarity? If the speech lacks structure, is this due to speaker ineptness or is there some justification for it? To promote understanding, how does the speaker employ such devices as repetition, restatement, association with the familiar, examples and illustrations, questions and answers, statistics, and definitions? How does the speaker employ audiovisual aids and vocal and physical delivery to increase understanding? If appropriate, does the speaker adequately answer the basic questions of who, what, where, when, how, and why?

4. *Do you view the speaker's proposal (idea, belief, policy) as reasonable?* Consider how he uses evidence and reasoning to demonstrate that the proposal actually will work, will solve the problem, will be efficient, and will not be too costly. Assess the soundness of the factual examples, expert testimony, literal analogies, statistics, and cause-effect reasoning that he employs. Is the proposal feasible despite such potential limitations as minimal finances, time, or manpower?

5. *Do you feel there is a legitimate connection between the speaker's idea or purpose and your relevant needs, motives, and goals?* Do you see a personal stake in the outcome? Has the speaker exaggerated the connection or appealed to irrelevant needs?

6. *Is the speaker's idea consistent with your relevant beliefs and attitudes?* If not, is there reason for you to reexamine some of your related beliefs and attitudes?

7. *Is the speaker's idea sanctioned by your relevant values?* How does it measure up to your conceptions of The Good or The Desirable? Does the speaker's idea conflict in any way with your basic values? Are

the values you are using to judge the proposal the most appropriate ones?

8. *What do you perceive as the speaker's attitude toward you as a listener?* What is the speaker's view of your personal worth or abilities? Consider in what ways and to what degree the content of the speaker's message, the language, and the delivery reflect any of the following attitudes toward you: respect, sincerity, humility, aloofness, objectivity, self-aggrandizement, coercion, aggressiveness, deference, defensiveness, conciliation, or any one of the countless other attitudes with which a speaker might view his listeners.

9. *Do you perceive the speaker as a credible source on this subject?* To what degree and in what ways do you view the speaker as expert, competent, experienced, educated, trustworthy, sincere, dependable, honest, energetic, personable, committed, concerned, and friendly? How and to what extent has the speaker's credibility fluctuated during the presentation of his speech? What factors of content and delivery contributed to your assessment of credibility? Is the speaker *representing* a credible person or group?

10. *Can you discern any unstated assumptions in the speech?* What unspoken basic beliefs, values, premises, stereotypes, etc., implicitly undergird the speaker's ideas? Why, possibly, should these assumptions have been made explicit? Do you agree with these assumptions? How do these assumptions reflect the speaker's conception of reality, truth, knowledge, religion, goodness, or the essential nature of humankind? Is the speaker actually a spokesperson employed by some person or group?

11. *In what ways does the speaker's language usage (style) contribute to clarity and persuasiveness?* Consider whether the language is appropriate for the speaker, audience, subject, and occasion. Examine the communicative function served by stylistic resources such as repetition, restatement, rhetorical question, comparison, contrast, parallel structure, antithesis, alliteration, analogy, metaphor, imagery, personification, or narration. Do any stylistic devices seem ornamental or "added on" for display? Consider the following guidelines which have been suggested for evaluating language usage:

What does the speaker's style reveal about him personally or about his view of his audience? How do his language choices compare with those he might have made? What stylistic alternatives did he seem to have and why might he have made the choices he did? If the speaker's language is militant and abrasive, why might he have made this choice? If so-called obscene words are used, what might be their function and impact? Does he rely heavily on any particular stylistic device? If so, why? If use of metaphors is a major stylistic characteristic, are they trite or fresh? Is there a dominant or thematic metaphor woven throughout the speech? Does the speaker rely heavily on "god terms" or "devil terms," on concepts with intense positive or negative denotations and connotations? Remember, also, that public tastes in rhetorical style vary from era to era and even between different audiences in the same era. For the particular speech you are analyzing, consider what might be the most appropriate standards of stylistic judgment.[3]

12. *Do the nonverbal elements in the speech reinforce or conflict with the speaker's verbal meaning?* Does the speaker's vocal and physical delivery tell you one thing and the speaker's words another? If so, which should you believe and why? How do elements of the speaker's delivery contribute to clarity and persuasiveness?

13. *What function does the speech seem to serve in some larger campaign of communication or in the activities of a particular social movement?* Is the speech a major effort to be supplemented by other modes of communication? Is it one in a planned series of addresses on the topic? Is the central communicative thrust on this topic being carried out through other modes and channels with this speech as only a minor part of the total program?

14. *As best you can determine, what were the effects or consequences of the speech?* This is, of course, a very large question requiring comprehensive answers. In evaluating such outcomes, there are numerous complexities; for example:

First, one must remember how hard it is to determine exact and certain causal connections between a specific speech and later outcomes. And an effect may be the result of a number of rhetorical and non-rhetorical events. You may attempt to assess the effects of a speech by noting the impact on the immediate audience, the long-term impact on the policies and ideology of society at large, the impact on persons in positions of public-opinion leadership, the impact on experts, the reactions of news-media reporters; and whether the speaker's aim has been achieved, whether the speaker's ideas have been verified by later historical events, or whether the audience's expectations and desires have been met. . . . Finally, you may want to consider the influence of a speech on the speaker himself. Did it enhance or lower his *ethos* or image? How did this speech affect his subsequent rhetoric and actions? Did he in any way become trapped by his own rhetoric?[4]

ETHICAL JUDGMENT*

"Ethical questions have always been closely linked with the persuasive process. Each time an individual asks the factual question 'How can I persuade?' he has some obligation to ponder the concomitant value query 'Is it ethical for me to employ this particular means of persuasion?' "[5]

Ethical Perspectives

Ethical issues are inherent in all speech communication whether it aims to persuade the listener or to influence his comprehension, understanding, and level of knowledge. In seeking either to inform or persuade, the speaker attempts to influence the other person or persons; and in so doing, he makes conscious choices concerning the specific ends he will seek and the communicative techniques he will use to achieve those ends. These criteria of possible effects on other human beings and the speaker's choice of ends and means point to a number of significant, potential ethical issues in human behavior. Even if a speaker or listener chooses to ignore ethical judgments entirely, *potential* ethical issues nevertheless inhere in most speech communication. Necessarily, therefore, *ethical evaluation* becomes one of the final and most important steps in the complete assessment of a speech.

What, then, are some of the possible standards and basic issues relevant to ethical evaluation? From what vantage points can we usefully view an assessment of this kind? We suggest four pertinent *ethical perspectives:*

1. The Philosophical or Ontological Perspective.
2. The Political Perspective.
3. The Dialogical Perspective.
4. The Situational Perspective.

* This section on ethical judgment is significantly revised and adapted from Richard L. Johannesen, "Perspectives of Ethics in Persuasion," in Charles U. Larson, Persuasion: Reception and Responsibility (Belmont, Calif.: Wadsworth Publishing Company, Inc., 1973), Chapter 9. Revision and adaptation with permission of the author and publisher.

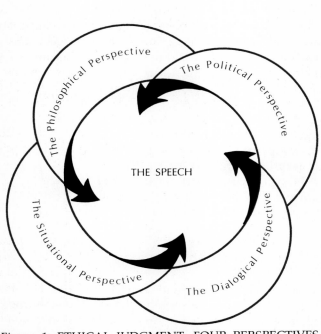

Figure 1. ETHICAL JUDGMENT: FOUR PERSPECTIVES

That is, in assessing the ethics of a speech, we may ask, "What are the philosophical, political, dialogical, and situational *implications* of this particular speech?" As classifications, these perspectives are not mutually exclusive, nor are we offering them in any order of preference. We shall attempt to define them as we proceed to examine each one briefly.

The Philosophical Perspective

This perspective focuses on the essential nature of man, those unique characteristics which set humankind apart from other living creatures. What characteristics and qualities make man essentially man? If we can identify them, we have one yardstick or standard by which to judge the ethics of specific communication techniques. The philosophical perspective assumes that uniquely human attributes should be enhanced so as to promote fulfillment of the individual's potential. In assessing a speech from this vantage point, we try to determine the degree to which a speaker's appeals and techniques either foster *or* undermine the development of a fundamental human quality or characteristic. Included among the characteristics suggested as marks of "being human" are: the capacity and compulsion to utilize symbols; the need for understanding; the capacity to reason; the ability to *generate* knowledge through communication;

and the capacity for conscious, free, informed, responsible choice-making.

Any one of these attributes could be used to judge the ethics of a speech. Using the philosophical perspective, for example, Henry Weiman and Otis Walter take the position that: "Rhetoric, if it is to be ethical, must create conditions favorable to expansion of symbolism and mutual understanding and control."[6] Based on the assumption that a unique capacity of humans is their ability to *create* knowledge *in* the actual process of communication, Robert Scott contends that ethical communication follows three guidelines: (*a*) toleration of divergent views and the right of others to self-expression; (*b*) conscious effort at maximum participation in a communication transaction; and (*c*) intent to achieve good consequences coupled with accepting responsibility for all consequences so far as they can be known.[7]

The Political Perspective

The political perspective concentrates on the implicit or explicit values and procedures fundamental to the health and growth of a specific political system. When these essential political values have been identified, they can be used as standards for judging the ethics of the means and ends of communication within that particular political system. Each different system could embody different values which could lead to different ethical assessments of a given speech.

Within the context of American representative democracy, Karl Wallace identifies the essential values as belief in the dignity and worth of the individual, faith in equality of opportunity, belief in freedom, and belief in each person's ability to understand the nature of democracy.[8] Citizens should promote freedom of speech, wide dissemination of information, and width and diversity of communication channels. To be ethical, Wallace says, communicators must recognize that during presentation they are the sole source of argument and information; they must select and render fact and opinion fairly; they must reveal the sources of their information and opinion; and they must respect diversity of argument and viewpoint.

Thomas Nilsen analyzes both values and procedures basic to American democracy.[9] Crucial *democratic values*, in his opinion, are belief in the enhancement of the human personality; acceptance of reason as an instrument of personal and societal development; and self-determination through free, informed, rational, and critical choice. Necessary *democratic processes* include: unrestricted debate and discussion; varied forms of public address, parliamentary procedure, and legal procedure; freedom of inquiry, criticism, and choice; and publicly defined rules of evidence and tests of reasoning. In Nilsen's judgment, then, ethical speech communication — viewed from the political perspective — is that which (1) provides adequate information, diversity of views, and knowledge of alternatives and their possible consequences; (2) provides rational debate on controversial issues, freedom of expression, and constructive criticism; and (3) exemplifies civility, fair play, and high quality in content and language.

The Dialogical Perspective

In this perspective, the attitudes held by each of the participants in a speech communication transaction are an index of the ethical level of that communicative encounter. Some attitudes (characteristic of dialogue) are held to be more fully human, humane, and facilitative of personal self-fulfillment than are other attitudes (characteristic of monologue).*

Communication as dialogue is characterized by such attitudes as honesty, concern for the welfare and improvement of others, trust, genuineness, open-mindedness, equality, mutual respect, empathy, humility, directness, lack of pretense, non-manipulative intent, sincerity, encouragement of free expression, and acceptance of others as unique individuals with intrinsic worth regardless of differences in belief or behavior. Communication as monologue, in contrast, is marked by such qualities as deception, superiority, exploitation, dogmatism, domination, insincerity, pretense, personal self-display, self-aggrandizement, distrust, coercion, possessiveness, condescension, self-defensiveness, judgmentalism which stifles free expression, and viewing others as manipulable objects.

The techniques and presentation of a speaker, then, may be scrutinized to determine the degree to which they reveal *ethical dialogic attitudes* or *unethical monologic attitudes* toward listeners. Paul Keller and Charles Brown suggest this kind of ethic for interpersonal speech communication.[10] In their view, loyalty to rationality or some conception of universal truth is a less important consideration than the degree to which a speaker is sensitive to freedom of choice for listeners. For example, from this perspective, they ask: is the speaker willing to accept an audience response contrary to the one he is seeking? Keller and Brown believe that the speaker is unethical to the degree that he develops hostility toward the audience or in some way tries to subjugate it.

The Situational Perspective

From the situational perspective, an evaluator—in order to make an ethical judgment—employs only the elements of the specific communication situation at hand.** Criteria drawn from broad philosophical, political, or dialogical

---

*For a general analysis of communication as dialogue and monologue, see Richard L. Johannesen, "The Emerging Concept of Communication as Dialogue," Quarterly Journal of Speech LVII (December 1971): 373–382.

**See, for example, Edward Rogge, "Evaluating the Ethics of a Speaker in a Democracy," Quarterly Journal of Speech XL (December 1959): 419–425; Saul D. Alinsky, Rules for Radicals (New York: Random House, Inc., 1971), pp. 7, 11–12, 24–47, 79.

viewpoints are minimized; universal standards are avoided. The situational or contextual factors relevant to making an ethical judgment may include: the role or function of the speaker for the specific audience; expectations held by the listeners; their ethical standards; the urgency for implementing the speaker's proposal; extent of audience awareness of the means being used by the speaker to achieve his purpose; and goals and values held by the audience.

Using the situational perspective, the evaluator could argue that unlabeled hyperbole or exaggeration is ethical in a political speech, but unethical in a classroom lecture; that imperiled national survival might justify techniques that at other times would be unethical, or that an acknowledged leader has the responsibility in some situations to rally support and could, therefore, employ emotional appeals which circumvent the rational process of making choices. The situational perspective might also justify a speaker's use of guilt-by-association, innuendo, and unfounded name-calling if the audience both recognizes and approves the use of such techniques.

The situational view of ethics generates some controversial issues, of course. For example, should ethical criteria be more stringent for communication aimed at children than at adults? Should ethical standards for speech communication be higher in peacetime or in time of declared war? Should ethical guidelines vary for communication in different fields: advertising, education, politics, religion, etc.? Is the use of so-called obscene words ethical in some public communication situations, but not in others?*

Typically, clear communication of intended meaning will be one major aim of an ethical speaker, whether that speaker seeks to enhance listeners' understanding of a subject or tries to persuade them toward a particular belief or action. In certain situations, however, speakers may feel justified in *creating ambiguity* in the minds of an audience. Intentional ambiguity might, for instance, characterize an international diplomatic negotiation, a political news conference, or a speech to entertain. In these and similar situations, a speaker might use the technique to promote the listeners' psychological participation in the communicative transaction, to broaden the latitude for a revision of his position in subsequent dealings, or to generate uncertainty or double meaning for the sake of evoking a humorous response.**

A person employing a situational perspective to make an ethical assess-

---

*See, in this connection, Haig Bosmajian, "Obscenity and Protest," in Dissent: Symbolic Behavior and Rhetorical Strategies (Boston: Allyn & Bacon, Inc., 1972), pp. 294–306; and J. Dan Rothwell, "Verbal Obscenity: Time for Second Thoughts," Western Speech XXX (Fall 1971): 231–242.

**See, for example, Robert T. Oliver, Culture and Communication (Springfield, Ill.: Charles C. Thomas, Publisher, 1962), pp. 65–69; B. Aubrey Fisher, "The Persuasive Campaign: A Pedagogy for the Contemporary First Course in Speech Communication," Central States Speech Journal XX (Winter 1969): esp. 297–298.

ment of a speech might argue that at least some of the dialogical attitudes, such as honesty, frankness, and truthfulness, depend on the circumstances of the specific speaking situation. Or, in a given circumstance, a concern for the psychological welfare of others could take precedence over an attitude of total frankness.

Speakers whose aim is persuasion usually seek to generate between themselves and their listeners an outcome variously described as consensus, agreement, or identification. But in some situations speakers feel justified ethically in *promoting conflict, unrest,* and *tension* in order to awaken society to a problem, to expose the true nature of an opponent, or to illustrate the inadequacy of more traditional modes of public communication and decision-making.*

Judgmental Questions

With some understanding of the philosophical, political, dialogical, and situational perspectives, we can now approach a few of the many difficult and significant issues related to ethical judgments of speech communication. In an attempt to highlight these issues, we pose the following questions:

To what degree should ethical standards for judging speech communication be relative, flexible, and situation-bound, or inflexible, universal, and absolute? Surely the more absolute our criteria, the easier it is to render simple, clear-cut judgments. But in matters of human behavior and public decision-making, the ethics of persuasive ends and means seldom are simple. In making ethical evaluations of persuasion, therefore, we probably should avoid snap judgments, carefully examine the relevant circumstances, determine the perspective(s) most appropriate to the instance, and consider the welfare of all involved.

In assessing speech communication, do the ends justify the means? To say that the end does not *always* justify the means is different from saying that ends *never* justify means. The speaker's goal probably is best considered as one of a number of potentially applicable criteria from among which the most appropriate standards or perspectives are selected. Under some circumstances, such as threat to physical survival, the goal of personal security temporarily may take precedence over other criteria. In general, however, mature ethical assessments are best made by evaluating the ethics of the speaker's techniques apart from the worth of the speaker's goal. In essence, to the extent that we can do so, we should sepa-

---

*Franklyn S. Haiman, "The Rhetoric of 1968: A Farewell to Rational Discourse," in Contemporary American Speeches, 3rd ed., Wil A. Linkugel, R. R. Allen, and Richard L. Johannesen, eds. (Belmont, Calif.: Wadsworth Publishing Company, Inc., 1972), pp. 133–147, esp. pp. 143–147; Herbert W. Simons, "Persuasion in Social Conflicts," Speech Monographs 29 (November 1972): 227–247, esp. 238–240.

rate *what* the speaker says from *how* he says it. Then strive to judge *separately* the ethics of his techniques and of his goals. In some cases, we may find ethical devices employed to achieve an unethical goal; in other cases, unethical techniques may be aimed at an entirely ethical goal.

Are the so-called "propaganda devices" uniformly to be judged as inherently unethical? Writers in propaganda analysis frequently list such devices as name-calling, glittering generality, transfer, testimonial, plain-folks, card-stacking, and bandwagon. Awareness of these techniques, however, does not constitute a sure guide to exposure of unethical persuasion. Certainly, the ethics of at least some of them depends on how they are employed in a given context. For example, the plain-folks technique of stressing humble origins and modest backgrounds which the persuader and audience share may not be uniformly unethical. In his "whistle-stop" speeches to predominantly rural, Republican audiences during the 1948 Presidential campaign, Democrat Harry Truman typically used the plain-folks appeal to establish common ground in introductions of his speeches. His purpose was to establish rapport with his hearers, and he did not rely on the device for proof in the body of his speeches. But if a politician relied primarily on the plain-folks appeal as *pseudo-proof* in justifying the policy he advocated, such usage could be condemned as unethical.

Is the use of so-called "emotional appeals" in a speech inherently unethical? Our culture traditionally has viewed with suspicion public expression of emotion and a speaker's attempt to capitalize on it. Recent research on persuasion, however, suggests that receivers of persuasive messages find it difficult to categorize appeals or supporting materials as either emotional or logical in exactly the same manner that the persuader intends. One audience may view an appeal as being emotional; another audience may consider it logical. A given technique, such as a set of statistics indicating high probability of falling victim to cancer during one's lifetime, may be perceived as possessing both logical and emotional components. In brief, neither so-called logical nor emotional appeals are inherently unethical, but depend largely on manner and circumstance of usage.

However, if we wish to evaluate the ethics of a persuasive technique which we perceive as emotional appeal, the following guideline may prove useful. Assuming that the appeal is ethical in light of other relevant perspectives, the "emotional" device is ethical if it has sound evidence and reasoning to support it. The speaker could present this support as he makes the persuasive appeal, or he could have the support available for presentation if a critical listener requests it. Moreover, the emotional appeal is ethical if the audience is asked to view it not as proof or justification, but as the expression of the persuader's internal emotional state. Generally the emotional appeal is unethical when it functions as pseudo-proof giving the appearance of evidence, or if it functions to short-circuit the receiver's capacity for free, informed, responsible choice.

THE STUDENT AS CLASSROOM SPEECH CRITIC

In addition to comprehending, appreciating, and evaluating a speaker's ideas, as a student of speech you have the special task of studying his manner, method, and materials. In so doing, you can improve your listening and observational skills, develop your ability to judge good speaking, and—at the same time—note ways to improve your own speech.

To analyze a speech thoroughly, you would have to consider many points—in fact, nearly all the topics covered in this book. Obviously, that would be a long and difficult task. Begin, therefore, by trying something less comprehensive. Each time you hear one of your classmates speak, center your attention on only a few closely related aspects of his talk—preferably on those matters which have been stressed in the particular assignment he is fulfilling. Later you will be able to make your analyses more complete as you learn to judge concurrently a larger number of speaking behaviors and aspects of the speech.

A convenient basis to use in criticizing speeches is the "Checklist and Index for Evaluation and Improvement of Student Speeches" printed inside the back cover of this book. Remember, however, that your critical analysis of a speech should not be limited merely to pointing out defects or weaknesses. Both you and the speaker can also learn much about good speaking by giving positive attention to the strong points of the speech and its presentation.

If your instructor asks you to evaluate one of the speeches given in class, divide your criticism into three steps. *First*, point out what was good about it; even the very worst attempts usually have something good that can be said about them. *Second*, tactfully suggest how the speech might have been improved. *Third*, indicate one or two specific aspects the speaker should work on the next time.

Do not hesitate to offer thoughtful criticism when it is invited. In a situation where all are trying to learn together, the objective comments of fellow students seldom can be offensive. Learn also to accept criticism with good grace. After all, hearing and heeding the comments of your hearers is one of the best ways to improve your speaking.

As aids to classroom speech evaluation, you and—possibly—your instructor may wish to utilize one or both of the following Speech Evaluation Forms.* Depending upon the purpose, audience, and occasion for the speech you are assessing, some of these criteria or dimensions may be considered more significant and relevant than others.

---

*Speech Evaluation Form 1 developed by Richard L. Johannesen and first published in Contemporary American Speeches, 3rd ed., Linkugel, Allen, and Johannesen, eds., pp. 21–22. Reprinted in slightly revised form by permission of the author and publisher. Speech Evaluation Form 2 adapted by Richard L. Johannesen from a form used in the Fundamentals of Speech course, Department of Speech and Drama, University of Kansas, during the early 1960s.

CONTENT:
_____central purpose?
_____main ideas?
_____supporting ideas?
_____content suitable?
_____worthwhile?
_____interesting?

INTRODUCTION:
_____techniques used?
_____gain attention?
_____create good will for speaker and topic?
_____lead smoothly into main subject of speech?
_____challenge or arouse audience?

ORGANIZATION (of Body):
_____what type?
_____clear?
_____logical?
_____unified?
_____appropriate to subject?
_____transitions?
_____lack of organization necessarily a defect?

LOGICAL APPEALS:
_____type and adequacy of reasoning (inductive, causal, analogical, deductive, etc.)?
_____factual examples?
_____expert testimony?
_____valid statistics?
_____clear explanations?
_____evidence and reasoning used ethically?

STYLE (Language Usage):
_____clear?
_____simple?
_____appropriate to speaker, audience, occasion, and subject?
_____rhythm?
_____impressive?
_____interesting?
_____use of stylistic devices such as repetition, restatement, rhetorical question, parallel structure, antithesis, alliteration, comparison, contrast, allusions, analogy, metaphor, simile, imagery, personification, illustrations, narration, etc.?
_____language used ethically?

PSYCHOLOGICAL APPEALS:
_____appeals to relevant emotions, motives, drives, and desires?
_____appeals to basic beliefs, interests, attitudes, and values?
_____appropriate humor?
_____use of suggestion?
_____allusions to deity?
_____vivid imagery?
_____appeals used ethically?

SPEAKER'S CREDIBILITY (_Ethos_ or Image):
_____expertness?
_____trustworthiness?
_____dynamism?
_____character?
_____sincerity?
_____competence?
_____friendliness?
_____experience?
_____education?
_____personal appearance?
_____raised or lowered by the speech?

CONCLUSION:
_____techniques used?
_____summary type?
_____convey sense of finality? leave audience in proper mood?
_____final appeal for central belief or action sought?

DELIVERY:
_____reinforce the speaker's verbal meaning?
_____body movement?
_____forceful and meaningful gestures?
_____facial expression?
_____clear, correct pronunciation?
_____voice (force, rate, pitch, quality)?
_____any distracting mannerisms?

EFFECT:
_____speaker achieved immediate purpose?
_____long-range purpose?
_____impact of speech in addition to speaker's intent?
_____effects desirable (morally, socially useful, etc.)?
_____use any "unethical" means to achieve purpose?

SPEECH EVALUATION FORM 2: DIMENSIONS FOR IMPROVEMENT

Name of Speaker _____ Subject _____

The items checked below indicate that you need:

SPEAKER DELIVERY

_____a slower rate of speaking

_____more warmth and friend-liness

_____more sincerity

_____more vitality and energy

_____more overall poise

_____more directness and con-sistent eye-contact

_____to be less notebound

_____better posture

_____to eliminate distracting mannerisms

_____to move about more

_____more expressive and ap-propriate gestures

_____more pitch variation and tone color

_____more vocal force and pro-jection

_____a greater change of pace in rate

_____to be more distinct and precise in articulation and enunciation

_____improved pronunciation

_____to avoid your "uh's" and "er's"

LANGUAGE

_____to define your terms

_____to be more precise in your phrasing and choice of words

_____to be more concise; you tend to be wordy

_____to watch your grammar

CONTENT

_____to be better prepared

_____a better choice of subject

_____a more refined subject to fit the time limit

_____better evidence

_____more concrete support for your points

_____to develop ideas more fully

_____to use more illustrative materials to bring out the meaning

_____more attention-getting and interest devices

_____to show more originality in your speeches

ORGANIZATION

_____a more imaginative intro-duction

_____a more appropriate intro-duction

_____better transitions

_____to show a more logical progression of ideas

_____to skeletonize the develop-ment of your speech

_____to clarify central purpose

_____to improve organization of individual points

_____a better conclusion

AUDIENCE

_____to be more sensitive to listeners' feedback

_____to adapt speech more to situation and audience

FOOTNOTES

[1]*Adapted from Larry L. Barker*, Listening Behavior *(Englewood Cliffs, N. J.: Prentice-Hall, Inc., 1971), pp. 124–125.*

[2]*Ralph G. Nichols and Leonard A. Stevens*, Are You Listening? *(New York: McGraw-Hill Book Company, 1957), pp. 221–222*

[3]*Excerpts from* Contemporary American Speeches, *3rd Edition, by Wil A. Linkugel, R. R. Allen, and Richard Johannesen.* © *by Wadsworth Publishing Company, Inc., Belmont, California 94002. Reprinted by permission.*

[4]*Ibid., p. 20. Reprinted by permission.*

[5]*Gerald R. Miller and Michael Burgoon*, New Techniques in Persuasion *(New York: Harper & Row, Publishers, 1973), p. 104.*

[6]*Henry N. Wieman and Otis M. Walter, "Toward an Analysis of Ethics for Rhetoric,"* Quarterly Journal of Speech *XLIII (October 1957): 266–270.*

[7]*Robert L. Scott, "On Viewing Rhetoric as Epistemic,"* Central States Speech Journal *XVIII (February 1967): 9–17.*

[8]*Karl R. Wallace, "An Ethical Basis of Communication,"* Speech Teacher *IV (January 1955): 1–9.*

[9]*Thomas R. Nilsen, "Free Speech, Persuasion, and the Democratic Process,"* Quarterly Journal of Speech *XLIV (October 1958): 235–243; Nilsen*, Ethics of Speech Communication, *2nd ed. (Indianapolis: The Bobbs-Merrill Company, Inc., 1974), esp. pp. 10, 18, 41, 43, 105.*

[10]*Paul W. Keller and Charles T. Brown, "An Interpersonal Ethic for Communication,"* Journal of Communication *18 (March 1968): 73–81.*

Problems and Probes

1. In your Personal Speech Journal, make an objective analysis of yourself as a listener. Note both your strong and your weak points. Are you objective in your attitude? Are you able to pay close attention over a period of time? Are you usually alert physically and mentally? When you have completed your analysis, lay out a specific program for improving your listening ability. In doing this, consult again the suggestions for constructive listening set forth in this chapter (pages 447–453) and examine such additional sources as your instructor may suggest.

2. With several other members of your class, attend a speech or lecture held on the campus or in the community. Attempt to determine (a) the speaker's specific purpose, (b) his major headings, and (c) the nature and adequacy of his supporting material. Compare your findings with those of others in your class who attended the same speech event.

3. List various factors in the physical surroundings which make good listening difficult—distracting noises, uncomfortable temperature or humidity, unsatisfactory seating arrangements, etc. Tell what you as a speaker or program chairperson can do to eliminate such problems.

4. At the next speech or lecture you attend, seat yourself where you can observe closely the reactions of various members of the audience as they listen to the ideas presented. How many appear to listen intently throughout the talk? How many seem to let their attention wander or not to listen at all? What cues or signs of a physical nature lead you to conclude that some persons are listening more intently or more consistently than others? Does the speaker give any indication that he is aware of and responsive to audience feedback? If the speaker loses the audience's attention, how does he or she attempt to recapture it?

5. During a round of classroom speeches, make an outline of each talk as it is delivered. Pay particular attention to setting off the major ideas from the supporting material and to following the rules for proper subordination. (Review Chapter 14, "Organizing and Outlining the Speech," pages 381–406.) As a test of your listening ability, compare your outlines with those drawn up by the speakers themselves.

6. Should the criteria of "tactfulness" be included or excluded as an ethical criteria for assessing speech communication? Consider also the meaning of such concepts as candor, frankness, appropriateness, etc.

7. Read pages 125–164 in Saul Alinsky's *Rules for Radicals*. Using two of the four ethical perspectives discussed above (philosophical, political, dialogical, situational), present your assessment of the ethics of the tactical rules Alinsky advocates.

8. Read a speech in *Vital Speeches* or in Linkugel, *et al.*, *Contemporary American Speeches*, 3rd ed. Write a three- or four-page evaluation of that speech applying the standards discussed in this chapter.

9. In your Personal Speech Journal, refer again to the analysis you prepared for Problem/Probe 7 in Chapter 1. Since writing that analysis, presumably you have intensively studied and practiced both speech preparation and delivery. Would you now agree or disagree with your earlier assessment of that particular speech? Write a two-page reevaluation or expansion of that previous assignment.

Oral Activities and Speaking Assignments

1. Present a five-minute oral evaluation of a speech previously presented by one of your classmates. Identify both strengths and weaknesses by applying three or four of the standards discussed in this chapter which you feel are most appropriate for the speech you are judging.

2. During one or two class periods hold a small group discussion among four to six people in which the following question is probed: "How ethical were the techniques of persuasion employed by the major candidates in the most recent national presidential campaign?" Be sure the discussants clearly identify the ethical perspectives they employ.

Suggestions for Further Reading

Kenneth E. Andersen, *Persuasion* (Boston: Allyn & Bacon, Inc., 1971). Chapters 16 and 17 explore issues of ethics in persuasion.

Larry L. Barker, *Listening Behavior* (Englewood Cliffs, N. J.: Prentice-Hall, Inc., 1971).

John W. Bowers and Donovan Ochs, *The Rhetoric of Agitation and Control* (Reading, Mass.: Addison-Wesley Publishing Company, Inc., 1971). Presents a framework for evaluating the rhetoric of protest.

Karlyn Kohrs Campbell, *Critiques of Contemporary Rhetoric* (Belmont, Calif.: Wadsworth Publishing Company, Inc., 1972). Examines theoretical perspectives for evaluating rhetoric and presents case studies of criticism.

Robert Cathcart, *Post Communication: Criticism and Evaluation* (Indianapolis: The Bobbs-Merrill Company, Inc., 1966).

Richard L. Johannesen, "Perspectives on Ethics in Persuasion," in Charles U. Larson, *Persuasion: Reception and Responsibility* (Belmont, Calif.: Wadsworth Publishing Company, Inc., 1973), Chapter 9.

Richard L. Johannesen, *Ethics and Persuasion: Selected Readings* (New York: Random House, Inc., 1967).

Wil A. Linkugel, R. R. Allen, and Richard L. Johannesen, eds., *Contemporary American Speeches: A Sourcebook of Speech Forms and Principles*, 3rd ed. (Belmont, Calif.: Wadsworth Publishing Company, Inc., 1972). A collection of thirty-five speeches, including twelve by students, suitable for evaluation.

Ralph G. Nichols and Leonard A. Stevens, *Are You Listening?* (New York: McGraw-Hill Book Company, 1957).

Thomas R. Nilsen, *Ethics of Speech Communication*, 2nd ed. (Indianapolis: The Bobbs-Merrill Company, Inc., 1974). A provocative synthesis of political, philosophical, and dialogical perspectives for judging the ethics of speech communication.

Carl Weaver, *Human Listening: Processes and Behavior* (Indianapolis: The Bobbs-Merrill Company, Inc., 1972).

PART FOUR

Public Communication: Types and Occasions

18
THE SPEECH TO ENTERTAIN

Many speakers give little thought to the speech to entertain. Consequently, when they attempt this type of presentation, often they succeed only in boring their listeners. On the surface, developing a good speech to entertain, amuse, or divert seems easy. Actually, however, this is far from the case. Much practical experience, as well as a knowledge of principles and methods, is necessary if you are to present a genuinely entertaining or amusing speech.

A common notion about the speech to entertain is that it must be funny, and certainly humor is a basic ingredient in many speeches of this kind. But it is wrong to believe that only funny speeches are entertaining. Accounts of travel experiences or descriptions of unusual people or out-of-the-ordinary events may also prove highly entertaining. In fact, almost anything that would provide interesting conversational material for the persons addressed may be used to entertain an audience.

Moreover, it should be observed that whether entertainment is provided through humor or through novelty, it is not confined solely to this type of speech. As you have no doubt observed many times, novelty and humor are often called for in other types of speaking situations also. Audiences that have been fatigued by a prolonged discussion of a complicated problem commonly welcome a few moments of relaxation. Humor is useful in relieving the tensions that result when opposing ideas or values come into sharp conflict or in winning the favor of a skeptical or unfriendly group of listeners. Remember, therefore, that many of the suggestions offered in this chapter can be applied to other kinds of speeches as well as to the speech to entertain.

TYPICAL SITUATIONS FOR SPEECHES TO ENTERTAIN

Speeches for entertainment or diversion are given on many and varied occasions, including: (1) *Club meetings.* Organized groups—religious, social, and political—may arrange sessions that are frankly for the purpose of diversion and amusement, and these may include speeches. (2) *Dinners.* The after-dinner speech is undoubtedly the most common type of speech to entertain. Certainly it is the best known, the most abhorred when poorly done, and the most enjoyed when cleverly presented. (3) *Parties.* Social occasions, such as anniversary celebrations and reunions, sometimes offer the opportunity for an amusing speech. When the gathering is large, a special program frequently is arranged to include speeches to entertain.

THE PURPOSE OF THE SPEECH TO ENTERTAIN

As has already been implied, the purpose of a speech to entertain is to provide those present with an enjoyable listening experience, to give them the same sort of pleasant relaxation they might find in a lighthearted social conversation, or in a popular novel, play, or movie.

THE SPEECH TO ENTERTAIN: SOME CHARACTERISTICS OF CONTENT AND DELIVERY

Even when one's principal purpose is to provide entertainment or diversion, it often is desirable to inject at least one or two serious ideas near the close of the speech. Froth alone can become tiresome, and too much humor unrelieved now and then by a more serious moment soon loses its effectiveness. Underlying your lightheartedness, therefore, there may well be something more substantial—some sentiment of loyalty or appreciation for the group addressed, or a glance at the more serious side of the subject discussed. Similarly, speeches recounting humorous personal experiences or adventures normally should contain at least one or two serious elements. These elements, however, must never be allowed to predominate; their function is only to provide a contrast to the entertaining qualities of the talk or to give the listeners a simple, worthwhile thought to carry away with them.

Have a central idea or theme around which your speech is built. The speech to entertain, like speeches of other types, always should "make a point" and should have the unity and coherence that come from the development of a single theme.

Be optimistic. A speech to divert is not the place to unload your troubles, to be argumentative, or to paint a dark picture of the future—unless, of course, you are obviously doing it in jest. Be optimistic and lighthearted; let the troubles of tomorrow take care of themselves.

Avoid a complicated arrangement of ideas. Don't make your audience strain to understand you. Develop your speech around one or two simple ideas that can be grasped easily. Be sure, however, that these few points have in them something novel, provocative, or original.

Sprinkle stories and illustrations liberally throughout your speech. Don't rely on "canned" jokes alone. Humorous anecdotes and tales of your own experiences or the adventures of someone else also will serve to illuminate your ideas and should be used generously. Unless you are clever at turning phrases, avoid too much discussion between your illustrations and descriptions; let one story lead naturally into another, each serving to bring out the theme around which your speech is built. But see that your tales are to the point; never "drag them in by the heels."

Let good nature, geniality, and vitality dominate your presentation. Insofar as delivery is concerned, remember that you cannot encourage enjoyment in others unless your manner suggests that you yourself are enjoying the situation. Be genial and good-natured—this is of great importance—but beware of appearing as though you are forcing your merriment. Do not put on the sickly grin of the boy who vowed that the more he was thrashed, the harder he would laugh. On the other hand, stay clear of the scowling determination of the overzealous reformer. As Mr. Dooley, the character created by Finley Peter Dunne, put it, "Let your spakin' be light and airy." Be quick and alert, lively and animated; above all, don't let your speech drag or your voice become drab and monotonous. Over three centuries ago, Milton expressed the proper mood for a speech to entertain in these lines:

> . . . bring with thee
> Jest, and youthful jollity,
> Quips and cranks and wanton wiles,
> Nods and becks and wreathed smiles . . .
> Sport that wrinkled care derides,
> And laughter holding both his sides,
> Come, and trip it as ye go,
> On the light fantastic toe. . . .[1]

Your delivery, then, should reflect the same mood as your ideas—lightness of touch, good humor, novelty, and the spirit of fun or enjoyment.

SOME USES AND FORMS OF HUMOR

Since humor is appropriate in many types of speeches and on many kinds of occasions, the public speaker should learn to use it effectively. Reaction to humor, you will have observed, ranges all the way from the inward chuckle to the loud guffaw. You do not have to make your listeners roar with laughter, but at least try to loosen them up to the point of smiling. There are a number of ways to do this, but fundamental to all of them are a spirit of fun on the part of the speaker and an ability to see and portray the incongruity of situations, events, and ideas. It is *things out of their expected order* which, as a rule, cause us to laugh. A huge man on a big horse is not funny, but the same man astraddle a small, balky donkey is likely to bring a smile to the face of even the most matter-of-fact person.

But, you may ask, how can a speaker put into practice this principle of sensing and portraying the incongruous? He can begin by familiarizing himself with some of the characteristics of humor in order to understand its possible impact upon an audience. What is comic or witty can be analyzed in many different ways, but the public speaker may find it useful to note briefly a few of the various forms in which humor manifests itself.* Consider, for example, the following:

1. Exaggeration or overstatement.
2. Puns or plays on words.
3. Poking fun at authority or dignity.
4. Burlesque or parody.
5. Unexpected turns.
6. Unusual or eccentric traits of people.

Exaggeration or Overstatement

Often you can add humor to your speech and at the same time put your point across to the audience by a skillful use of exaggeration or overstatement. For example, there was the cynic who said of a famous Hollywood sex symbol: "She has broken so many homes she's listed in the Yellow Pages under 'Demolition Contractors'" (Earl Wilson in *The Des Moines Register*); while a sadly underpaid worker cryptically complained to his tight-fisted boss: "I'm so underpaid I'm the only man I know who can cash his pay check on the bus." (*St. Louis Globe-Democrat.*) Pride of ancestry is a frequent prompter of overstatement. A well-to-do society matron was fond of tracing her lineage back to William the Conqueror. After listening patiently and at some length, a skeptical friend inter-

---

*Note: *In this chapter, a number of the specific examples of humor and novelty—jokes, puns, and human-interest anecdotes—have been adapted from items found in newspapers, magazines, and books, in street-corner conversations with friends, and in commuter camaraderie with strangers. To pinpoint the precise origin of a quip or jest or funny tale is often difficult, if not impossible; but in those instances where it has been possible to make note of a source, this has been done.*

rupted sarcastically, "Actually, I suppose your ancestors were with Noah on the Ark." "Certainly not," retorted the dowager disdainfully. "My family had a boat of its own."

Exaggeration is, of course, the basis of humor in many "tall tales." In *The Jokeswagen Book*, edited by Charles Preston, there is the instance of the distinctly different Texan who preferred to drive a Volkswagen instead of a Cadillac. An affluent colleague asked scornfully if the Volks was air-conditioned. "No," shrugged the Texan, "but I always keep a couple of cold ones in the refrigerator." And Harry Karns (*Garden City*, N.Y., *Newsday*) calls attention to the enterprising photographer who took a picture of the mythical monster of Scotland's Loch Ness. He flew down over the creature and shot the photo from his flying saucer.

Puns and Plays on Words

"Show me a squirrel's home," says the punster, "and I'll show you a nutcracker's suite." ("Trade Winds," *Saturday Review*.) Frequently, laughter may be provoked by using words which have a double or extended meaning or which sound like other words with a different meaning. John Ciardi describes a girl as "certainly the best idea any boy has had to date." (*Saturday Review*.) A wag has defined a race horse as an animal that can take several thousand people for a ride at the same time. (*Baltimore Sun*, reprinted in *The Des Moines Register*.) And you have probably heard of the human cannonball who informed the proprietor of the circus that he had decided to retire from the act. "But you can't quit now," protested the disconcerted owner. "After twenty years—where would I ever find another man of your caliber?"

Sometimes, to give punch to a pun, a speaker may embroider the build-up a bit. Consider, for instance, the high cost of living. The soaring price of meat has put the finer cuts beyond the reach of many a family budget, and countless cost-conscious wives have had to invent innumerable ways to cook what is euphemistically called "ground beef." One harried husband insists that his mate has prepared hamburger in so many different ways—and disguised it so ingeniously—that every night at dinner his four hungry children peer suspiciously at the meat course and solemnly intone, "How *now*, ground cow?" And finally there was the disgusted telephone user who grumbled at Ma Bell: She gives us "princess phones and peasant service." (Earl Wilson in *The Des Moines Register*.)

Poking Fun at Dignity or Authority

People like to see someone take a dig at those who are on top and, even more, at those who mistakenly think they are. It is human nature to resent insincerity or affectation and to enjoy pricking the balloon of pomposity. Cornelia

Otis Skinner tells of a giddily garrulous countess who, in trying to impress the French actor Lucien Guitry, burbled, "You know, I simply talk the way I think." "Yes," replied Guitry wearily, "but more often." (*Elegant Wits and Grand Horizontals.*) An anecdote making the rounds in political circles involves Sargent Shriver when he was handling both the Peace Corps and the poverty programs. Paul Bell, head of the Corps' office in Central America, sent Shriver a memo asking him to approve the nomination of a Washington attorney to direct activities in Guatemala. Not knowing the lawyer and uncertain of his qualifications, Shriver returned Bell's request with a pointed question: "What does your man know of Guatemala?" Equally pointed was Bell's second memo to the millionaire administrator: "Very little, Sarge. But what do you know about poverty?" Politicians have, of course, always been fair game for jokesters. Senator Leverett Saltonstall describes a New England town meeting which was being held to consider the purchase of a chandelier. A venerable citizen stood up to protest the expenditure. "In the first place," he said, "there ain't one of us that can spell it. In the second place, there ain't nobody here that can play it. And in the third place, we need a new light fixture a whole lot more than we need a chandelier." (Walter Trohan, "Washington Scrapbook," *The Chicago Tribune.*)

There are times when this form of humor is neatly reversed, and the dignitary or "authority" turns the barb back upon the belittlers or fun-pokers, thus delivering the climactic *bon mot* himself. Eugene Exman relates the incident of a farewell dinner given in honor of a crusty, cantankerous British publisher who, at seventy, was about to retire. There were the usual testimonial speeches; and the old fellow's associates, overjoyed at the prospect of his departure, outdid each other in voicing elaborate—but insincere—praise. When the moment came for the aged gentleman to acknowledge the empty accolades, he rose, gazed shrewdly around at the assembled guests, and innocently remarked, "I had no idea I was held in such high esteem. I shall stay on."

On occasion, the public speaker may find it useful to poke fun at his *own* dignity. In addressing a graduating class at the University of Iowa, W. Willard Wirtz, former Secretary of Labor, commented that "Commencement speakers have a good deal in common with grandfather clocks: standing usually some six feet tall, typically ponderous in construction, more traditional than functional, their distinction is largely their noisy communication of essentially commonplace information."

Burlesque or Parody

The chief characteristic of burlesque consists of treating absurd situations seriously or serious situations absurdly. Insomnia has been defined as "a condition sometimes caused by an upset stomach, but more often by an upset wife," and a hypocrite described as "a person who preaches by the yard but practices by the inch." ("Comic Dictionary," *The Des Moines Register.*) Matty Simmons tells what happened when two middle-aged society women—overfed, overdressed, and overexpansive—met on a street in fashionable Palm Beach. One pointed to the enormous gem glittering at her throat and gushed grandly, "My dear! This is the world-famous Plotkin diamond." "I've heard of the Hope diamond," exclaimed her dazzled and envious friend, "and the curse that goes with it. I've also heard of the Koh-i-noor diamond. But of the Plotkin diamond—never." "Not only is this one of the biggest and most expensive diamonds in the world," persisted its proud possessor, "but it has its own curse that goes along with it—Mr. Plotkin!" (*Diner's Club Magazine.*)

A frequently used variation of burlesque is the *parody* or *take-off* on an idea or situation which is ordinarily treated with seriousness. A sense of incongruity can be developed by describing absurdities in the dignified language usually reserved for serious subjects, or by treating minor problems as if they were complicated and important. Despite the fact that each year thousands of eligible teen-agers are clamoring to enroll in some of our more prestigious colleges and universities, public-relations officials continue to feel compelled to describe these institutions in the most glowing and utopian terms. According to prevalent press agentry, the ideal college ought to be both rural and urban, both small and large, and stand upon a hill near a river or a lake—from which eminence it can look fondly back upon the traditions of a glorious past and eagerly forward to the experimental joys of the future. In parodying this picture, the late president of Vermont's Bennington College, William Carl Fels, wrote of his institution as follows: "It is a small, rural, private, experimental women's college of high quality which emphasizes the development of the individual. It shares the cultural advantages of New York, Boston, and Montreal. Its hill is moderately high. From it on a clear day, you can just see, beyond the toilet-paper factory, the historic Walloomsac River flowing northward away from Williamstown, where there is a small, rural, private, experimental college of high quality for well-rounded men." (*Columbia University Forum II.*)

Unexpected Turns

Lead your audience to believe that you are going to say the normal or anticipated thing; then say the opposite—or at least what your listeners do not expect. Woody Allen recounts taking a girl to a drive-in movie and finding it disappointing because "every time we started to neck, we fell off my bicycle." (Earl Wilson in *The Des Moines Register.*) *The New Yorker* reports the reply of a bartender when congratulated on the opening of a new bar in Boston's Symphony Hall, "Thank you, Sir. The community has accepted the additional bar most graciously." Paul Lowney tells of a man who was bitten by a dog and was later informed by the physician that he had rabies. The victim snatched pencil and paper and began to scrawl rapidly. The doctor, hoping to reassure him, said soothingly, "Don't worry about making out your will. I'll pull you through." "This isn't my will," snapped the man. "It's just a list of the people I'm going to bite." (*The World's Funniest Offbeat Humor,* 1966.) In the Soviet Union, where the unexpected seems to occur but rarely, this story was told: When Stalin realized he was dying, he summoned his successor, Nikita Khrushchev, clutched his hand, and whispered conspiratorially, "I've prepared two letters. When you find yourself in hot water over domestic difficulties, open the first one. When you're in real trouble—when your enemies are plotting against you and demanding your life's blood—open the second." Later, when Nikita found himself in the throes of an economic crisis, he opened the first letter. It read: "Blame everything on me." Khrushchev promptly denounced Stalin as a murderer and a tyrant. In 1964, when the bitter struggle for power raged anew and the big showdown came in the Kremlin, Khrushchev opened Stalin's second letter. Its pointed instruction: "Prepare two letters." (Matt Weinstock in *The Los Angeles Times.*) Equally illustrative of the unexpected twist is the comment of the fashion designer who declared, "Nothing can replace the modern swimsuit—and it practically has." Or the safety expert who described America as "a land whose motto is 'In God We Trust,' and whose people prove it by the way they drive." ("Comic Dictionary," *The Des Moines Register.*)

Repartee that is truly witty is a genuine rarity; but when it does occur, it is almost sure to hinge upon a sudden or unexpected turn of phrase. Marshall McLuhan, widely heralded for his authorship of *The Gutenberg Galaxy* and *Understanding Media* and for his trenchant but not always closely connected comments on modern communication, lectured on these matters at Kendall College. In introducing Mr. McLuhan, Charles Benton, president of Encyclopaedia Britannica, Inc., referred to one of the lecturer's books as "a string of pearls without the string." Retorted McLuhan, "Pearls are a great deal harder to come by than string." (Virginia Kay, "Dateline Chicago," *Chicago Daily News.*)

Unusual or Eccentric Traits of People

Describe some person's idiosyncrasies, or illustrate peculiarities which seem to be characteristic of certain classes of people. It has been said, for instance, that a politician is a man with an answer for everything—and everybody. Asked at a press conference what he thought of the proposal to limit to one quart the amount of liquor American tourists may bring back from foreign countries, an Illinois senator replied, "I'd make it a pint. We have a big distilling industry in my state, and it pays a million dollars a day in revenue tax." "But, Senator," his questioner protested, "foreign countries don't have pints." "Then let them buy pint bottles from us," countered the politician. "We also have a big glass-making industry in my home state." (*The Chicago Tribune.*)

The traits, trials, and triumphs of children provide a limitless source of humor. Some years ago the *Associated Press* carried the report of the floor nurse in a Salt Lake City hospital. She was trying to speak via the intercom to a patient in the children's ward — a youngster who had never been hospitalized before and was unfamiliar with the electronic device. After several attempts failed to produce an answer from the child's room, the nurse spoke rather firmly, "Answer me, Jimmy. I know you're there." A few seconds later, a tiny, quavering voice responded, "Wh-what do you w-want . . . Wall?" (As reported in *Reader's Digest.*) From Dorchester, England, *United Press International* relayed this story of a child's-eye view of a tonsillectomy: "When they wheeled me into this big room, I saw two lady angels, all dressed in white. Then two men angels came in. One of the men angels looked down my throat and said, 'Lord! Look at this child's tonsils!' And the Lord looked and said, 'My heavens! I'll take them out at once!'" (*Reader's Digest.*)

Somewhat more precocious, perhaps, was the six-year-old who had just completed his first day in the second grade at a very progressive school. At dinner that night, the boy abruptly asked his parents, "What is sex?" Startled, the mother and father managed to stammer out a somewhat involved explanation of the birds and the bees. The puzzled youngster pulled a school questionnaire from his pocket and asked, "But how am I going to put all that information in this tiny little square marked 'Sex'?" This may have been the same youth who, when he became a high-school student, was asked by his exasperated teacher if he ever listened to the voice of conscience. Came the reply: "I don't know. What channel is it on?"

Mothers and little old ladies, too, often have endearing and enduring charms for an audience. Florence Horner tells this story about her mother. "While others were busy at various household activities of debatable importance, my mother began washing walls. 'Well,' she announced to the rest of the family at suppertime, 'I've got four walls done and a little start on the ceiling.' We craned our necks dutifully, and there on the gray ceiling, spelled out in spick-and-span white, was the message: 'HELP!'" (*Reader's Digest.*)

Many college students are getting married these days, and they seem to undertake the financing of the combined marital and educational ventures with a courage that borders on the breathtaking. *Changing Times*, The Kiplinger Magazine carried a story illustrating this point. The mother of a married coed was asked by a neighbor how the newlyweds were getting along. "Oh, they're ecstatically happy," the mother declared with pardonable pride. "They've just returned from a month in Nassau, and they've leased a new apartment. My daughter's buying all new furniture for it, of course. And as soon as she and her husband are settled, they're going to buy a car." "Goodness," exclaimed the neighbor, "your son-in-law must be doing awfully well!" "He certainly is," agreed the mother. "He's getting straight A's."

In the foregoing pages we have illustrated only a few of the many ways in which the incongruities and absurdities of life may prove humorous. Your ability to use the humorous, the novel, and the exciting in your speeches depends in large measure upon your ability to see the contrasts, the inconsistencies, and the incompatibilities of people and events around you. Watch for the unexpected and the unusual. Often a minor mishap of word or action that occurs just before you begin to speak will furnish you with a spontaneous bit of humor or human interest. And if you don't take your speech too seriously—if you throw off your cares and enjoy the experience—even as you talk you will probably think of quips, novel touches, and exciting anecdotes you can introduce.*

ORGANIZATION OF THE SPEECH TO ENTERTAIN

A speech to entertain may be organized in a number of ways, but two methods have proved especially helpful to beginning speakers. The first is to employ the pattern for the single-idea speech, as described in Chapter 11; the second is to mock or burlesque the five-step motivated sequence.

Using the Pattern of the Single-Idea Speech

When you use this method, your speech will consist of a series of illustrations, anecdotes, or humorous contrasts following one another in rapid order.

---

*Special Note: *Among the many collections of anecdotes and humor which may be of interest and use to the student speaker are A. K. Adams, ed.,* Home Book of Humorous Quotations *(New York: Dodd, Mead & Company, 1968); Oren Arnold,* Arnold's Sourcebook of Family Humor *(Grand Rapids, Mich.: Kregel Publications, 1972); Joseph M. Braude,* Speaker's Encyclopedia of Stories, Quotations, and Anecdotes *(Englewood Cliffs, N. J.: Prentice-Hall, Inc., 1964); various compilations by Bennett Cerf, including* The Laugh's on Me *and* Laugh Day *(Garden City, N. Y.: Doubleday & Company, Inc., 1959 and 1962, respectively);* 10,000 Jokes, Toasts, and Stories, *ed. Lewis and Faye Copeland (Garden City, N. Y.: Doubleday & Company, Inc., 1965); Maxwell Drake,* Speaker's Handbook of Humor *(New York: Harper & Row, Publishers, 1956); Evan Esar,* Twenty Thousand Quips and Quotes *(Garden City, N. Y: Doubleday & Company, Inc., 1968); William R. Gerler,* Executive's Treasury of Humor for Every Occasion *(West Nyack, N. Y.: Parker Publishing Company, 1965); George Q. Lewis and Mark Wachs,* The Best Jokes of All Time and How to Tell Them *(New York: Hawthorn Books, Inc., 1966); Paul B. Lowney,* The World's Funniest Offbeat Humor *(Seattle, Wash., 1966); and Herbert V. Prochnow and Herbert V. Prochnow, Jr.,* A Dictionary of Wit, Wisdom, and Satire *(New York: Harper & Row, Publishers, 1962).*

Among the numerous magazines and periodicals which carry witty sayings, entertaining anecdotes, and human interest stories are Saturday Review/World, Reader's Digest, The New Yorker, Saturday Evening Post, Changing Times, Diner's Club Magazine, The American Legion Magazine, Farm Journal, Time, Newsweek, Coronet, *and* Pageant. *Similar material will also be found in the press reports, editorial pages, and feature sections of such newspapers as* The New York Times, The Chicago Tribune, The Chicago Daily News, The St. Louis Globe-Democrat, The Los Angeles Times, *and* The Garden City (N. Y.) Newsday. *As you no doubt have noted, a number of the examples in this chapter were adapted from items drawn from the foregoing sources.*

Each item, however, should refer in some way to one central idea or theme; and the individual elements should be integrated into a coherent whole. For the implementation of the single-idea type of organization, this simple step-by-step procedure will prove practical:

1. Tell a story or give an illustration.
2. Point out the essential idea or point of view expressed by it, and around which you intend to unify the details of your speech.
3. Follow with a series of additional stories and illustrations, each of which amplifies or illuminates the same central point. Arrange these items so as to maintain a balance of interest or humor. Avoid grouping all of the funniest or most appealing material in one spot, and particularly beware of a let-down at the end. Save an especially striking, humorous, or novel anecdote for the last.
4. Close with an unusual restatement of the central idea you have elaborated or illuminated. At this point also bring in whatever serious or sobering statement you may wish to make.

By developing your speech in this way, you not only will entertain your listeners, but you will also make it easy for them to remember the ideas in your talk.

Burlesquing the Motivated Sequence

When you use this second method of organizing a speech to entertain, the structure of your talk will contain all five steps of the motivated sequence; but these steps will mock or burlesque the corresponding steps as used in serious persuasion. The pattern of such a method may be arranged thus:

The attention step. Begin your speech with a reference to the occasion, an allusion to an unusual incident, or a humorous story or anecdote. The incident, story, or anecdote should illustrate the central point of your talk and should lead naturally into the theme you wish to develop.

The need and satisfaction steps. Present a serious problem (such as making income meet expenditures), but exaggerate its seriousness beyond reasonable proportions; and then offer an absurd or humorous solution or point out how absurd a commonly mentioned solution is. Introduce a series of amusing or unusual anecdotes to amplify the absurdity of your problem or solution, or to show the incongruity between them.

The visualization step. By adding an exaggerated picture of the conditions your solution will bring about, heighten the absurdity already developed in the preceding steps.

The action step. Close your speech swiftly by burlesquing an exorbitant demand for action, by telling a story to illustrate the irony of your argument, or by summarizing the "vital" points in your speech. Make this final touch short and amusing.

Two final cautions: First, when giving a speech to entertain, *don't talk too long.* Nothing spoils humor or human interest so much as dragging it out. Bring your speech to a point; illuminate that point for a moment; then sit down. Unless you are the only speaker, five or ten minutes ought to be your limit. Second, as we have emphasized from time to time, *be sure your humor is in good taste.* If it leaves a sting or a feeling of embarrassment or shame, you will not have created good feeling.

SAMPLE SPEECHES

In this chapter we have examined some of the uses—and misuses—to which public speakers put humor and novelty in an effort to make speeches entertaining, amusing, or diverting. We have also made some suggestions regarding the purposes, characteristics, content, organization, and delivery of such speeches. We conclude these considerations with two sample speeches: "A Case for Optimism" by Douglas Martin, and "A Funny Thing Happened to Me on the Way to the White House" by the late statesman Adlai Stevenson. With the former we have included some marginal notations; for the latter we urge you to undertake your own analysis, basing it on ideas and principles presented in the preceding pages.

A CASE FOR OPTIMISM [2]

Douglas Martin

I'm sure you have heard the verse that runs:

'Twixt optimist and pessimist
The difference is droll:
The optimist sees the doughnut,
The pessimist, the hole.

Poem embodying analogy used as opening

The longer I live, the more convinced I am of the truth of this poem. Life, like a doughnut, may seem full, rich, and enjoyable, or it may seem as empty as the hole of a doughnut. To the pessimist, the optimist seems foolish, but

Statement

who is foolish—the one who sees the doughnut or the one who sees the hole?

Somebody else pointed out the difference between an optimist and a pessimist this way: An optimist looks at an oyster and expects a pearl; a pessimist looks at an oyster and expects ptomaine poisoning. Even if the pessimist is right, which I doubt, he probably won't enjoy himself either before or after he proves it. But the optimist is happy because he always is expecting pearls. *Analogy*

Pessimists are easy to recognize. They are the ones who go around asking "What's good about it?" when someone says "Good morning." If they would look around, they would see *something* good, as did the merchant whose store was robbed. The day after the robbery, a sympathetic friend asked about the loss. "Lose much?" he wanted to know. "Some," said the merchant, "but then it would have been worse if the robbers had got in the night before. You see, yesterday I just finished marking everything down 20 per cent." *Anecdotes*

There is another story about a shoemaker who left the gas heater in his shop turned on overnight and upon arriving in the morning struck a match to light it. There was a terrific explosion, and the shoemaker was blown out through the door almost to the middle of the street. A passerby who rushed up to help inquired if he were injured. The shoemaker got up slowly and looked back at the shop which by now was burning briskly. "No, I ain't hurt," he said, "but I sure got out just in time, didn't I?"

Some writers have made fun of that kind of outlook. You may recall the fun Voltaire made of optimism in *Candide:* "Optimism," he said, "is a mania for maintaining that all is well when things are going badly." A later writer, James Branch Cabell, quipped: "The optimist proclaims that we live in the best of all possible worlds; the pessimist fears this is true." *Testimony pro and con*

These writers, I suppose, couldn't resist the urge to make light of optimists; but I, for one, refuse to take *them* seriously. I like the remark by Keith Preston, literary critic and journalist, "There's as much bunk among the busters as among the boosters."

Optimism, rather than the cynicism of Voltaire, is the philosophy I like to hear preached. There was a little old lady who complained about the weather. "But, Melissa," said her friend, "awful weather is better than no weather." So quit complaining, I say, and start cheering; there is always something to cheer about. And quit expecting the worst. An optimist cleans his glasses before he eats his grapefruit. · *Illustrations*

Give in to optimism; don't fight it. Remember the doughnut and, as Elbert Hubbard advised: *Restatement*

As you travel on through life, brother,
Whatever be your goal,
Keep your eye upon the doughnut
And not upon the hole.

A FUNNY THING HAPPENED TO ME
ON THE WAY TO THE WHITE HOUSE[3]

Adlai Stevenson

A funny thing happened to me on the way to the White House!

The fact was, of course, that the General [President Dwight D. Eisenhower] was so far ahead we never even saw him. I was happy to hear that I had even placed second. But no one will say, I trust, that I snatched defeat from the jaws of victory.

Which reminds me that four years ago, occupying the seat I occupy tonight, was another great governor [Governor Thomas E. Dewey of New York, unsuccessful Republican candidate for President in 1944 and 1948]—excuse me, the governor of another great state—some say the second greatest state in the Union. What just happened to me had just happened to him. In fact, it had just happened to him for the second time.

But did he despair? He did not. He said to himself—if I may take a newspaper man's license and tell you what a man says to himself—he said: "If I cannot be president myself, I can at least make somebody else president." Which, blast his merry heart, he proceeded to do. Look at him now. He's as contented as the cat that swallowed the canary, or should I say, the Cabinet.

At that Gridiron dinner just four years ago, the newly elected governor of Illinois [Stevenson had been elected governor of Illinois in November 1948] sat down there with you common people—which reminds me that I rather enjoy talking over your heads—at last! I was happy and carefree and had nothing to worry about; nothing except the organization of a new Administration to clean up the state of Illinois after the long years of the usual Republican misrule.

I, a Democrat, had just been elected governor by the largest majority ever received in Republican Illinois. And here I am, four years later, just defeated by the largest majority ever received in Democratic America.

I had not planned it that way. I had wished to continue as governor of Illinois, there to erect a shining temple of administrative purity and political probity. But the gods decreed otherwise—after meeting in the Chicago Stockyards [Site of the 1952 National Democratic Convention]. Mindful of the Chinese maiden's philosophical acceptance of unwanted and aggressive attentions, I concluded to accept my fate gallantly and joyfully.

Now I content myself that it is all for the best. After all, didn't Socrates say that the duty of a man of real principle is to stay out of politics? So you see I'm delighted that the sovereign people have put an even higher value on my principles than I did.

I am happy that almost 27 million voted for me. I was a little baffled by the emergence of that word "egghead" to describe the more intelligensiac members of that lunatic fringe who thought I was going to win. I am happy to note you have refrained from saying of the eggheads that the yolk was on them.

I enjoyed the campaign — in spots. There were times, I confess, when I was afraid I wouldn't die, times when I felt I wouldn't do it to a dog. Let me add, by the way, that, like every red-blooded American patriot, I own a dog. [In a speech defending himself from charges of having received unreported campaign funds, Richard Nixon, the Republican candidate for Vice-President in 1952, referred poignantly to his dog Checquers.] It was not a campaign contribution. And I think the General would say to me that·there are times when he wishes he was in my shoes — you see I had them fixed. [A widely circulated photograph of Stevenson with his legs crossed showed a hole in the sole of one of his shoes.]

As to my future: Well, there are those like the man who changed the sign on his car after the election from "Switched to Stevenson" to "Switched, Bothered and Bewildered," who feel that I should devote my classic talents to the welfare of mankind by frequent talking.

Then there is another smaller group who insist that God and/or the election has appointed me the scourge of the Republican Party. And finally there is the much smaller group that feels that it is not wholly unworthy or improper to earn a living. My sons are numbered in the latter group.

But despite anything that you may have read or written, there are some plans of action that I have definitely rejected. I have declined an invitation to become president of the National Association of Gagwriters. And I will not go into vaudeville. It is equally definite that I will not become manager of the Washington Senators — I mean Clark Griffith's, not Mr. Taft's.

I have great faith in the people. As to their wisdom, well, Coca-Cola still outsells champagne. They may make mistakes. They do sometimes. But given time they correct their mistakes — at two- or four-year intervals.

I have faith in the people — and in their chosen leaders: men of high purpose, good will and humble hearts, men quite prepared to stand aside when the time comes and allow even more humble men to take over.

FOOTNOTES

[1] *From "L'Allegro" by John Milton; lines 1 – 4, 7 – 10.*

[2] *Based in part on material taken from* Friendly Speeches *(Cleveland: National Reference Library).*

[3] *"A Funny Thing Happened to Me on the Way to the White House" by Adlai Stevenson. Reprinted by permission of Harold Ober Associates Incorporated.*

Problems and Probes

1. Identify the various forms of humor used in the sample speeches on pages 483–486.

2. Listen to three of the more popular comedy programs on television, and compare the types of humor that are employed. In what respects are the same methods or devices used to generate laughter? What, in each case, seems to be unique about the program? To what extent are humorous effects dependent on the personality of the "star" or "stars" and upon the particular way in which they deliver their lines? By watching these programs, what may the public speaker learn *not* to do when giving a humorous speech?

3. Consider the following topics for entertaining speeches:

You can't take it with you.
How to swallow a pill.
What this country really needs ____ ____.
Gentlemen prefer blonds—and brunettes and redheads.
There's many a slip 'twixt the cup and the lip.
Professors I have known.
Campus traditions in the year 2000 A.D.
My solo flight in an automobile.

For which of these topics would you recommend the single-idea method of organization? For which would you recommend a burlesque of the motivated sequence? Why?

4. Name three advantages of introducing humorous or entertaining material into speeches on serious subjects. Then name three dangers which must be avoided when doing this. Explain each advantage and danger briefly.

5. It is frequently said that the single most important rule to observe when presenting a humorous speech is to be sure that the audience laughs *with* you and not *at* you. Explain this rule and tell why it is important. How may the speaker see to it that he is laughed *with* rather than *at?*

6. Using the anthologies and other sources we have cited earlier, locate the text of a speech the purpose of which is to entertain, but which is not basically humorous.

7. Devise five appropriate titles for entertaining speeches which would not be heavily dependent upon humor to achieve their major purpose.

Oral Activity and Speaking Assignment

1. Prepare and present a four- or five-minute speech to entertain. For your subject, select a topic from those listed below or in Problem 3 above; or devise one of your own. Use either the single-idea pattern of organization or a burlesque of the motivated sequence as explained in this chapter. Work particularly for a light and amusing style and manner of delivery. Exaggerate ideas as much as you like, inject quips and anecdotes, and poke fun at others; but also be certain that your humor (a) is relevant to the central idea of the speech, (b) is in good taste, and (c) is in no way cruel or malicious. Suggested subjects:

Life in the army (at camp, on the farm).
The art of "reaching" for the check.
Seeing our friends at the zoo.
Measuring up to a too-good first impression.
Counting sheep and other sleep-inducing devices.
Rediscovering Tom Swift (or any other fictional character).
Parkinson's Law at work in colleges.
Out of step with the "in" crowd.
Love at first slight.
We, the fat people.
TV movies I've slept through.

Suggestions for Further Reading

Richard W. Armour, *Writing Light Verse and Prose Humor* (Boston: The Writer, Inc., 1971).

Jeffrey H. Goldstein and Paul E. McGhee, eds., *The Psychology of Humor* (New York: Academic Press, 1972).

John Y. T. Greig, *The Psychology of Laughter and Comedy* (New York: Cooper Square Publishers, 1969).

Wilma Grimes, "The Mirth Experience in Public Address," *Speech Monographs* XXII (November 1955): 243–255.

Kenneth G. Hance, David C. Ralph, and Milton J. Wiksell, *Principles of Speaking* (Belmont, Calif.: Wadsworth Publishing Company, Inc., 1962), Chapter XV, "Speaking to Entertain."

Harry Levin, *Veins of Humor* (Cambridge, Mass.: Harvard University Press, 1972).

Jacob Levine, *Motivation in Humor* (New York: Atherton Press, 1969).

19
THE SPEECH TO INFORM

An important function of speech is to provide us with a means of communicating knowledge. Through speech one person is able to give others the benefit of his learning and experience. In this chapter we shall discuss some of the principles a speaker should observe if he is to convey information clearly and interestingly.

TYPES OF INFORMATIVE SPEECHES

Informative speeches take many forms. Three forms occur so frequently, however, that they merit special mention: (1) *Oral reports:* scientific reports, committee reports, executive reports, and similar informational accounts. Experts who engage in research projects announce their findings. Committees carry on inquiries and report their results to the parent organization. Teachers, representatives of fraternal groups, and businessmen attend conventions and then share with others the information they have obtained. (2) *Oral instructions:* class instructions, job instructions, and instructions for special group efforts. Teachers instruct students in ways of preparing assignments and performing experiments. Supervisors tell their subordinates how a task should be carried out. Leaders explain to volunteer workers their duties in a fund-raising drive or an antipollution campaign. For convenience, such instructions often are given to a group of persons rather than to single individuals and, even when written, may need to be accompanied by oral explanations. (3) *Informative lectures:* public lectures; class lectures; and lectures at meetings, study conferences, and institutes. People often are invited to share information or knowledge with groups interested in receiving it. Many informative talks are given each week before businessmen's luncheon clubs and women's study groups. Instructors present lectures daily on every college campus, and visiting speakers appear before church groups, conventions, and business and professional institutes.

THE PURPOSE: TO INFORM AND INSTRUCT

As you will recall from the discussion in Chapter 7, the main purpose of a speech to inform is to make certain that the audience understands clearly and fully the ideas presented. Hence, you should not view such a speech as an opportunity to parade your knowledge. You should not try to see how much ground you can cover in a given time; rather, you should try to help others grasp and remember the essential facts or ideas you present.

But while its primary purpose is to teach, an informative speech need not be dull and dry. Because people absorb information more easily when it interests them, a secondary purpose of this type of speech is to make your information interesting to your listeners. Be sure, however, that this secondary purpose *remains* secondary. Too often a speaker rambles from one interesting point to another without specifically relating them to each other or to his central theme. Remember that your principal duty is to make the conclusions of your report clear, to have your instructions understood, or to ensure a proper grasp of the content of your lecture.

THE MANNER OF SPEAKING INFORMATIVELY

The manner in which you deliver an informative speech will depend almost entirely upon your subject and audience and upon the degree of formality required by the speaking occasion. In general, however, talk slowly enough to be understood and rapidly enough to hold interest. If you speak too fast, you will confuse your listeners; if your rate of speaking is too slow, it will put them to sleep. The more difficult the information is to grasp, the more slowly you should proceed; but on the first sign of inattention, speed up a little.

THE INFORMATIVE SPEECH: TREATMENT OF CONTENT

Organize and Relate Your Material Carefully

*Clear organization is the first essential.** To be sure your speech is organized clearly, remember the following rules: (*a*) Do not have too many main points. If possible, reduce your ideas to three or four principal topics, and then group the remaining facts *under* these main headings. (*b*) Make clear the logical relation between your main points. Keep moving in the same direction; don't

---

For a more detailed treatment of this subject, review carefully Chapters 13 and 14, pp. 353–408.

jump back and forth from one point to another. (*c*) Make your transitions obvious. As you pass from one main topic to the next, let your audience know about it. In a discussion of several different sports, for example, if you start to talk about football and then turn your attention to baseball, say so definitely. Otherwise, your hearers may think that you are still talking about football. If necessary, enumerate your points: "First, second, third," etc.

Use Concrete Data——Don't Be Abstract

In addition to having a clear structure, a speech to inform also must be "meaty"—that is, packed with facts, figures, examples, and explanations. When presenting this data, however, two cautions always need to be kept in mind. First, *in your concern for accuracy of detail, do not sacrifice clarity.* Many rules and principles, for example, have exceptions. In presenting such material, however, do not impair your listeners' understanding by an excessively detailed discussion of the exceptions. Or, as we said earlier, when discussing statistics (see pages 310–312), whenever feasible present figures in round numbers in order that the smaller digits may not prevent a comprehension of the larger one. Say "a little over two million" rather than "2,001,397." If extreme accuracy is essential, as in a financial statement or engineering survey, accompany your speech with a written report in which the detailed figures and facts are presented. Second, *use charts, graphs, and printed material whenever appropriate and helpful.* Your audience will often understand a point better if they can see it at the same time they are hearing it. A diagram of a machine makes its operation easier to explain; columns and pied circles render proportions clearer; drawings and photographs may speak a hundred words. (At this point, review the discussion of visual aids, pages 315–317.)

Avoid Dullness——Use Humor or Vivid Imagery

There is a limit to any person's capacity for absorbing facts. Recognizing this, the wise speaker uses vivid phrasing and includes occasional bits of humor to enliven, humanize, and enrich his factual materials. (Review pages 431–435, where various forms of imagery are discussed.)

Connect the Unknown with the Known

People learn new things by associating them with what they already know. If you are talking to a group of farmers on new developments in feedlot management, compare the methods you are presenting to existing practices and procedures. An educator speaking to a manufacturer's convention on the problems of higher education presented his information in terms of *raw material, casting, machining, polishing,* and *assembling.*

THE ORGANIZATION OF THE INFORMATIVE SPEECH

In organizing a speech to inform, do not plunge at once into the detailed information you wish to present. As we have previously emphasized, you must *lead* the thoughts of your listeners rather than force them. Nor can you expect people to be interested in a subject unless they see how it somehow affects them. In most instances, therefore, you will need to prepare your listeners' minds for what you are going to say. To do this, you must first gain their *attention* and show them why they *need* to know about your subject.

Attention Step

When you are sure that the subject of your speech is of interest to the audience, usually you can attract attention simply by referring to your theme. But when your listeners are not vitally concerned with the subject or are not aware of its importance to them, you may have to use a startling statement, an unusual illustration, or one of the other standard methods for catching attention at the beginning of a speech (see pages 410–420).

Need Step

Although it should be short, the need step in a speech to inform is exceedingly important. Informative speakers often fail because they assume that their listeners are waiting to seize the "pearls of knowledge" their speeches contain. Unfortunately, this is not always the case. Unless you are certain of their interest in advance, show your audience why the information you are to present is valuable to them — why it is something they need to know or even to act upon. If you suggest how the information you provide will help them get ahead, save money, or do their work more quickly and easily, they will be eager to listen.

Develop the need step of your speech by including these elements:

1. *Statement.* Point out the importance of your subject and the listeners' need to be better informed concerning it.

2. *Illustration.* Present one or more stories or examples which illustrate the importance of the need or demonstrate its significance and timeliness.

3. *Reinforcement.* Provide as many additional facts, figures, or quotations as are required to make the need convincing and impressive.

4. *Pointing.* Show how your subject directly relates to the interests, well-being, or success of your hearers. Say, in effect: "This information vitally concerns *you* because . . ."

There will be times, of course, when the information in your speech is not of a practical or workaday variety—something which directly affects the health, happiness, or prosperity of your listeners. When this is the case, you may be able to use the element of suspense or curiosity in building your need step. A noted chemist, for example, began a lecture by telling of an unusual murder case. He made his audience wonder who the guilty man was and then proceeded to show how, through the use of certain chemical tests, the man was identified and convicted.

Satisfaction Step: The Information Itself

Having captured the attention of your listeners and shown them why they "need" the information you are about to present, you are ready to offer the information itself. This is done in the satisfaction step—the step in which you answer or "satisfy" the need you have created.

Select and Arrange Your Points Systematically

The satisfaction step usually is the longest part of a speech to inform, and may comprise from three fourths to nine tenths of the whole. In this step you must exercise the greatest care to organize your material clearly, for nothing is quite so confusing as information presented in a careless or unsystematic way.

As we emphasized in Chapter 14, there are several standard patterns or sequences useful in the organizing and outlining of almost any speech, the chief ones being: (1) the *time sequence*, (2) the *space sequence*, (3) the *cause-effect sequence*, (4) the *special topical sequence*, and (5) the *problem-solution sequence*. Because these patterns also provide some practical ways of organizing the satisfaction step of the informative speech, we urge you to review the textual descriptions of them on pages 385–388, and to analyze the sample outline for each of them, as shown below:

1. *Time Sequence:* FLIGHTS IN SPACE

I. The first space flight was made on April 12, 1961, by Major Yuri Gagarin of the Soviet Air Force.
II. On May 5, 1961, Alan Shepard became the first American to enter space.
III. Astronauts Neil Armstrong and Edwin Aldrin set foot on the moon on July 20, 1969.
IV. The final flight of the $25 billion Apollo Project occurred on December 11–14, 1972, when Astronauts Eugene Cernan and Jack Schmitt explored the mountainous side of the moon.

2. *Space Sequence:* PRINCIPAL AMERICAN DIALECTS

I. Eastern dialect is heard chiefly in New England.
II. Southern dialect is heard in former Confederate states.
III. General American dialect is common west and north of these two areas.

3. *Cause-Effect Sequence:* AIR POLLUTION

I. Motor vehicles, industrial plants, and home incinerators discharge large amounts of waste material into the atmosphere.
II. This discharge has created a serious air-pollution problem in most of our cities.

OR

3a. *Cause-Effect Sequence:* AIR POLLUTION

I. Most of our major cities face a serious problem of air pollution.
II. Important causes of this problem are the vapors discharged from motor vehicles, industrial plants, and home incinerators.

4. *Special Topical Sequence:* SOURCES OF VITAMINS

I. Vitamin A is found in butter, fortified margarine, and vegetable oils.
II. B-complex vitamins come from bread, flour, and cereals.
III. Vitamin C is supplied by citrus fruits, tomatoes, and raw cabbage.

5. Problem-Solution Sequence: THE DRUG PROBLEM

I. The drug problem today is a serious one.
    A. The use of "hard drugs" is increasing.
    B. Children of grade-school age often are the victims of unscrupulous "pushers."
    C. Attempts to control the international traffic in drugs have failed.
II. Students of the problem believe that in order to achieve a solution three courses of action are necessary.
    A. Congress must pass stiffer regulatory legislation.
    B. Narcotics-control agencies must be strengthened.
    C. The schools must mount a massive antidrug campaign.

Maintain a Consistent Arrangement

On no condition should you shift from one order to another in presenting the *main* points of an informative speech. Sometimes, however, it will be convenient to present the subordinate ideas in a pattern different from that used for the main heads.

Develop Your Satisfaction Step in Three Phases

In order to unify the presentation of your information and make it easier to understand and follow, you often will find it useful to begin the satisfaction step of an informative talk with an *initial summary*, then to provide the *detailed information*, and finally to review your main points in a *closing summary*.

1. *The initial summary.* As its name suggests, the initial summary consists of a brief enumeration of the main points you expect to cover. Its purpose is to help your hearers grasp the plan of your discussion as a whole, as well as see the relation one idea bears to another. For example, if you were going to explain the organization of athletic activities on your campus, you might begin your satisfaction step in this way:

> In order to make clear the organization of athletic activities on our campus, I shall discuss, first, the management of our intercollegiate sports; second, our intramural program; and third, the class work in physical education.

Note how such a preview was used by Whitney J. Oates, chairman of the Council of Humanities at Princeton University, in an address on "Philosophy as the Center of Liberal Education":

I propose first to sketch briefly the role of philosophy, as I see it, in history, in literature and the arts, the social sciences and the natural sciences, in other words, those subjects which constitute, broadly speaking, the traditional content of liberal education. And I shall conclude with a discussion of other ways in which philosophy reveals its significance in the intellectual life.[1]

The order in which you list the main points in your initial summary obviously should follow the same sequence you intend to use in your detailed discussion; otherwise you will confuse your listeners by setting up a guidepost which points in a direction different from the road you actually will take. Properly developed, an initial summary will help your audience follow your discussion and will help them see the relation of each point to the whole.

2. *The detailed information.* This information is presented next, covering in order the main points enumerated in your initial summary. Explanations, facts, comparisons, and other information should be grouped around each main point in a systematic fashion and, when possible, amplified and illustrated by maps, pictures, tables, demonstrations, or other visible or audible aids to understanding. As you move from one main point to the next, be sure you make clear that you are doing so. Use freely connective sentences or phrases to emphasize the shifts (see pages 440–441). At all times be sure that your audience knows where you are and in what direction your discussion is heading. Follow a consistent plan of arrangement as you proceed, and amplify your points with an abundance of supporting material, both verbal and nonverbal (pages 300–323).

Reports and instructions usually require special patterns of organization. For *research reports*, begin with a clear statement of the hypothesis to be tested or the problem to be investigated; second, give a brief review of previous research on the subject; third, explain the materials used, the apparatus employed, or the literary or historical sources investigated; fourth, describe the procedure followed in the study; and finally, summarize the data or results obtained. For *other types of reports*—such as those resulting from committee discussions, financial operations, travel, or direct observation—first, state the nature or scope of the subject to be covered; second, review the sources from which material was gathered: discussion, observation, written records, etc.; and third, set forth the salient points discovered as a result of the inquiry.

When the purpose of an informative speech is to *give instructions*, it usually contains: first, an overall statement of the nature and purpose of the operation to be performed; and, second, an explanation of each step in that operation *in the order in which it is to be taken.* The discussion of each step also may include the reason for it, the materials or tools or special information required, and the precautions to be observed. Frequently, in giving such talks, the speaker may pause after explaining each step in the process, inviting questions from his listeners or testing their understanding as he goes along.

Regardless of the subject or specific purpose of an informative speech, or how it may be treated in the satisfaction step, remember that its main objective is to secure a clear and thorough understanding on the part of your audience. The detailed information, therefore, must be clearly organized and fully amplified with concrete and specific supporting material.

3. *The closing summary.* In this summary, tie together the information you have presented, in order to leave your audience with a unified picture. This may be done by restating your main points and reviewing any important conclusions or implications which have grown out of your discussion. The closing summary is similar to the initial one, but is usually somewhat longer. Notice the difference between this closing summary and the initial summary (see page 495) for the speech on athletic activities:

> From what I have said, you can readily see that the three main divisions of our athletic system are closely related to one another. The intercollegiate sports serve as the stimulus for developing superior skill as well as a source of revenue for financing the rest of the program. Our intramural system extends the facilities for physical recreation to a large part of our student body — three thousand last year. And our physical education classes not only serve in training men and women to become the coaches of the future, but also act in systematically building up the physical endurance of the student body as a whole and in giving corrective work to those who have physical defects. The work of these three divisions is well organized and complete.

Define Important Terms

In addition to the initial summary, the detailed information, and the closing summary, the satisfaction step of a speech to inform sometimes requires a fourth element — the *definition of important terms.* There is no fixed point at which such definitions should be introduced; but when they relate to the whole body of information to be presented, they are most frequently given either just before or just after the initial summary.

The purpose of a definition is to clarify an obscure term or to establish a special meaning which you wish to attach to a particular word or phrase. Therefore, any means which will accomplish such an end may be employed. Usually, however, you will find yourself using one of the following methods:

Dictionary definition. Put the term or concept to be defined into a general class or category and then carefully distinguish it from the other members of this class. ("An apple is a *fruit* that is *red* and *round* and *hard* and *juicy.*" "Man is a *rational* animal.")

Etymology. Clarify meaning by telling the history of a word—the elements from which it is derived. (*"Propel* comes from the Latin *pro* meaning *forward* and the Latin verb *pellere* meaning *to drive.* Therefore, a propeller is an instrument which drives something forward.")

Negation. Clarify the meaning of a term or concept by telling what *it is not.* ("By *socialism* I do not mean *communism,* which believes in the common ownership of all property. Instead, I mean . . . .")

Example. Clarify by mentioning an actual example or instance of what you have in mind. ("You all have seen the Methodist church on Maple Street. This is what I mean by English Gothic architecture.")

Use in a context. Occasionally the best way to clarify the meaning of a term or concept is actually to use it in a sentence. (*"Hopping* is a slang term for *very* or *exceedingly.* For instance, if I say, 'He was *hopping* mad,' I mean that he was angry indeed.")

Study the following passages in which the speaker attempts to define a word or concept used in the speech. Note that the methods of definition outlined above are employed, but additional methods are used as well.

When I speak of "speech" this morning, I have always in mind the full range of Man's speech behavior—the act of utterance, the symbol system of spoken language, the integration of matter and manner in spoken discourse, and dramatic communication in which discourse among characters is a central means of furthering the dramatic action.[2]

By "provincial" I mean here something more than I find in the dictionary definitions. I mean more, for instance, than "wanting the culture or polish of the capital" . . . and I mean more than "narrow in thought, in culture, in creed. . . ." I mean also a distortion of values, the exclusion of some, the exaggeration of others, which springs, not from lack of wide geographical perambulation, but from applying standards acquired within a limited area to the whole human experience; which confounds the contingent with the essential, the ephemeral with the permanent.[3]

What is this thing called hemophilia? Webster defines it as "a tendency, usually hereditary, to profuse bleeding even from slight wounds." Dr. Armand J. Quick, Professor of Biochemistry at Marquette University and a recognized world authority on this topic, defines it as "a prothrombin consumption time of 8 to 13 seconds." Normal time is 15 seconds. Now do you know what hemophilia is?[4]

Most people use the word *Blues* to mean any song that is "blue" or torchy or lowdown or breast-beating—like "Stormy Weather," for example. But "Stormy Weather" is not a Blues, and neither is "Moanin' Low," nor "The Man I Love," nor even "The Birth of the Blues." They are all popular songs.

The Blues is basically a strict poetic form combined with music. It is based on a rhymed couplet, with the first line repeated. For example, Billie Holiday sings:

"My man don't love me, treats me awful mean;
Oh, he's the lowest man I've ever seen."

But when she sings it, she repeats the first line—so it goes:

"My man don't love me, treats me awful mean;
I said, my man don't love me, treats me awful mean;
Oh, he's the lowest man I've ever seen."

That is one stanza of Blues. A full Blues is nothing more than a succession of such stanzas for as long as the singer wishes.[5]

Concluding the Informative Speech

When you have presented your information and created an understanding of it, you will have attained your purpose. Ordinarily, therefore, the closing summary as given at the end of the satisfaction step concludes an informative speech. There are times, however, when you may wish to encourage further interest in the subject you have been discussing—that is, when you want to actuate as well as simply inform. In such cases, add to the summary a few words suggesting that your listeners apply what they have learned, or recommend books and articles in which they can find a further consideration of the matter. Then close quickly with a sentence of appreciation for their attention or a few remarks aimed at motivating the behavior or study you recommend.

A Sample Outline

The following full-content outline, prepared by Douglas Nigh, suggests one way to organize materials in a speech designed to inform or instruct:

I. No form of away-from-home entertainment is more widely popular than the movies.
  A. Throughout the world, people flock to watch movies.
  B. In the United States, despite the inroads of television, movies are still popular.
II. My purpose is to sketch developments which made this form of entertainment possible.

Gaining attention.

I. The story of the birth of the movies is worth telling.
  A. It forms an interesting chapter in the history of science and invention.
  B. It anticipates the development of an art form.
  C. It shows how far the modern sound and color film has advanced from humble beginnings.
II. As college students who frequent the movies, you should have a special interest in their early history.
  A. This knowledge will enable you to gain a better perspective of the motion picture industry as it exists today.
  B. This knowledge will also deepen your appreciation of the motion picture as an art form.

Showing the listeners why they need to know.

I. I shall discuss five developments which, together, are responsible for the movies as we know them today: a new theory of human vision, the beginnings of the science of photography, improved methods and materials for action photography, the devising of projection techniques, and the utilization of movies to tell a story.
  A. Explorations into the nature of vision were made by Peter Mark Roget.
    1. Roget's theory, presented before the Royal Society in London in 1824, maintained that "the image of a moving object is retained by the eye for a fraction of a second longer than it actually appears" [*Collier's Encyclopedia*].

Satisfying the need to know: presenting the information. (Initial summary.)

(Detailed information.)

2. Roget developed this theory after observing actions through a venetian blind.
3. Roget's theory led to experiments in viewing rapid movement of still images.
4. Mechanisms based on Roget's theory were limited to the animation of hand-drawn phases of motion.

B. The development of the science of photography led to attempts to view photographs of subjects in phases of motion.
1. In 1861, Coleman Sellers patented a machine that mounted posed-action photographs on a paddle wheel for viewing.
2. In 1870, Henry R. Heyl showed a series of action photographs through a "magic lantern" projecting device.
3. In 1877, two other Americans used a battery of 24 cameras in sequence to photograph a racehorse in action.

C. Better methods and materials for action photography were developed next.
1. In 1899, George Eastman developed a celluloid filmstrip.
   a. It was flexible and would not break or buckle.
   b. Its high-speed emulsion permitted photography of continuous action by one camera.
2. Thomas A. Edison used Eastman's film in his camera, the Kinetograph.

D. Projection techniques to permit viewing of the motion pictures were devised.
1. The earliest and most important of these was Edison's Kinetoscope, a peep-show device, patented in 1891.
   a. The Kinetoscope was first used publicly in penny arcades in 1894.
   b. A customer saw a loop of filmed moving picture lasting about 50 seconds.
2. Another important projector was Thomas

Armat's Vitascope, presented publicly in a
New York music hall in 1896.

    a. An entire audience was permitted
       to see films at the same time.

    b. Some of the films shown were
       those used in the penny arcades.

E. Movies as we know them were born when they
began to tell a story.

  1. In early moving pictures, the story was
    nonexistent.

      a. Films were bits of vaudeville action
        or examples of trick shooting.

      b. Some pictures, taken with portable
        hand-cranked cameras, showed fire
        engines or trains in motion, or
        crowds out for a stroll.

  2. By 1899, George Méliès of France began to
    link brief scenes to form a narrative.

  3. In 1903, Edwin S. Porter produced *The Great
    Train Robbery.*

      a. It introduced disjunctive editing:
        events did not follow a strict
        chronological sequence.

      b. It transformed movies into a
        widely accepted form of
        entertainment.

      c. It was on the program at the
        opening of the first moving-picture
        theater — a nickelodeon in
        Pittsburgh.

II. The history of the birth of the movies is the history of five
major developments:

  A. Roget supplied the theory of vision.

  B. The development of photography spurred other
men to apply Roget's theory to the new science.

  C. George Eastman and Thomas Edison gave us the
film and camera needed for action photography.

  D. Projection techniques enabled us to see moving
pictures on a screen.

  E. *The Great Train Robbery* ushered in an era of
moving pictures as entertaining narratives.

*(Final
summary.)*

A BASIC STRUCTURAL OUTLINE FOR THE INFORMATIVE SPEECH

From the sample outlined above, you will observe that the organization of a speech to inform or instruct will have a skeleton outline somewhat like this:*

SUBJECT: _____

SPECIFIC PURPOSE: _____

I. (Opening statement) _____.   *Gaining*
    A. (Support) _____.   *attention.*
        1. (Details) _____.
        2., etc. (Details) _____.

II. (Statement of purpose) _____.

I. (Statement of need for information) _____.   *Showing the*
    A. (Support) _____.   *listeners why*
        1. (Details) _____.   *they need to*
        2., etc. (Details) _____.   *know.*
    B. (Support) _____.
        1. (Details) _____.
        2., etc. (Details) _____.

II. (Pointing statement relating to audience) _____.
    A. (Support) _____.
    B., etc. (Support) _____.

I. (Statement of subject, including initial summary) _____   *Satisfying the*
_____.   *need to know:*
                                                                        presenting the
                                                                        information.

Note that the skeleton outline provides for details under supporting statements. Such details, although generally omitted from the streamlined outline on "The Birth of the Movies," are essential to the complete development of your speeches.

A. (Statement of first main division of the
    subject) _____.

      1. (Support) _____.

          a. (Details) _____.

          b., etc. (Details) _____.

      2. (Support) _____.

          a. (Details) _____.

          b., etc. (Details) _____.

B., C., etc. (Statements of other main divisions of

        subject, supported by subordinate ideas

        and details) _____.

II. (Final summary statement) _____.

    A. (First main division of subject summarized _____

    _____.

    B., C., etc. (Other main divisions of subject

    summarized) _____.

*Restating and
reinforcing the
information.*

SAMPLE SPEECHES

The student speech which follows was prepared to fulfill an assignment in a beginning public-speaking course at the University of Iowa, and was delivered on June 20, 1967. The students were instructed to present a three-minute informative talk on a subject of interest to themselves and their classmates, and to organize their material in a clear, easy-to-follow fashion. In accordance with this directive, Mr. Dennis Ragan chose an old and familiar topic, but treated it in a novel way. He was careful to distinguish between the two major causes of "backaches" and to explain each by comparisons and examples. Throughout, his ideas are expressed clearly and economically; and the speech "moves ahead" well. In the opening sentence, attention is caught by a rhetorical question addressed directly to the listeners, and the central idea of the speech is restated at the close.

BACKACHES[7]

Dennis Owen Ragan

Does your back ever hurt? If it does, don't feel you are alone. The majority of the people in the world suffer from backaches of one kind or another, either chronically or occasionally.

Backache sufferers give many reasons for their aches and pains. They may say that they are due to improper lifting and carrying, nervous tension, over-exertion, lack of exercise, or any one of a host of others. These are all valid causes, but they are secondary in nature. The primary cause of the two main types of backaches man suffers from is the fact that he walks upright on two feet.

The first common type of back trouble man suffers from is the slipped disc and its associated vertebral and spinal nerve pain.

Since man walks upright, all his weight is directed downward onto his feet, with the spine acting as a supporting rod for his back. This condition heavily compresses the vertebrae and the cartilaginous pads or discs between them. A sudden wrong move or a fall can cause a disc to slip out of position. This results in the vertebrae rubbing together or pinching the spinal nerves which lie within the vertebrae. Those of you who have slipped a disc know the intense pain this causes.

The other common type of back trouble is strain of the muscles of the back.

In an animal that walks on four feet, the line of gravity (by this term I mean an imaginary line drawn through the animal perpendicular to the ground in such a way that equal amounts of the animal's weight lie both in front of and behind the line) lies just behind the animal's shoulders. The animal's organs hang suspended in and supported by the rib cage. The four feet support the bodily weight (especially the front legs, since this is where most of the weight is), with no strain being placed on the back muscles.

Man's line of gravity lies about two inches in front of his spine. Thus, most of his viscera and body weight are in front of his spine, causing him to be front-heavy, with a tendency to fall forward. Since he does walk upright, his rib cage cannot support his organs. They have a tendency to drop forward and down. In order to prevent either of these conditions from happening, the stomach muscles must pull the viscera up and back toward the spine for support and balance.

The secondary causes I mentioned earlier now come into play. If for any reason the stomach muscles are weak and cannot do their job, the back muscles have to take over. They must hold the viscera up and maintain balance as well as keep the spine stiff and the body erect, which is their normal function. The muscles of the back were not designed for this extra load, and severe back-muscle strain can result.

The biological sciences teach us that evolution has so specialized man that he stands at the head of the animal kingdom. As far as his back is concerned, however, he might be better off to be standing at the head of the animal kingdom on four feet instead of two.

The following speech was delivered by Professor Robert T. Oliver of Pennsylvania State University at the Annual Convention of Toastmasters International held in New York City on August 20, 1965. After a combined attention and need step, Professor Oliver developed his subject in a roughly chronological order, and concluded his speech with a direct reference to the audience. Throughout, the information presented is animated and enlivened in such a way that the speech impresses and inspires at the same time that it informs.

Professor Oliver is a Past President of the Speech Communication Association and the author of many books and articles in the fields of speech and international relations.

THE INFLUENCE OF PUBLIC SPEAKING IN AMERICA: BUILDING BLOCKS IN A FREE SOCIETY[8]

Robert T. Oliver

We meet together today as fellow workers in the development of one of the greatest of human arts — the realm of public speaking. Just as has always been true since ancient times, we recognize the enormous importance of the spoken word in the development of individual personality and in the effective functioning of democratic society.

Man is above all a languagized mammal. Individuals and communities are at their civilized best when there is a free and skilled development of public discourse. We all have moods, of course, when speech seems cheap and we insist that we prefer deeds to words, action to talk. But we realize this means preferring what one man can do by himself to what many can accomplish when working together in a cooperative enterprise. Language, and especially oral language, is the great instrument of human cooperation. *Community*, *communion*, and *communication* are inevitably closely related.

Winston Churchill, with a rifle in his hands, crouched behind an earthen rampart along the Dover Coast, might have repelled two or three Nazi invaders.

But this same Winston Churchill, speaking with his matchless oratory, was able to marshal the global resources and inspire the will to victory that toppled Hitler's empire and preserved the democratic civilization of the Anglo-American world.

In American history, public speaking has been important in two closely related achievements—the development of individual leaders and the growth of the ideas, ideals, and institutions which characterize our nation.

The debating societies, the Friday afternoon programs in our public schools, and such special occasions as Fourth of July celebrations did much to awaken and enlarge the minds and the spirits of men and women who arose to leadership throughout our history. Henry Ward Beecher, America's greatest preacher, traced his intellectual awakening to the speech class taught by John Lovell in Mt. Pleasant Academy, in Amherst, where for the first time he encountered a kind of teaching that was less concerned with the input of information into his mind than with the outflow of influence from his whole personality. Henry Clay attested that whatever he was and whatever he achieved he owed to his early and constant training in the art of public speaking. Andrew Johnson could not even read and write at the time of his marriage, but he educated himself by hiring a boy to read aloud to him the great orations of Burke, Fox, Erskine, and Pitt while he worked busily at his sewing in his tailor shop. Lucy Stone left her farm home to enter Oberlin College where, as a mere girl, she was not allowed to give speeches but prepared herself for leadership as an eloquent advocate of women's rights by sitting as a mute auditor in a young men's public speaking class. Woodrow Wilson wrote his first published essay on oratory and organized a debating society because he was convinced that skill in speech was the basic requirement for intellectual development and personal leadership. Such examples could be multiplied from the whole scope of our national history.

The earliest immigrants came to our shores from European homelands that were described by the French émigré Michel Guillaume de Crèvecoeur, in his *Letters from an American Farmer*, as "a continual scene of sore affliction or pinching penury." They came as debtors and peasants, as political refugees and religious dissenters. They came in poverty but in hopefulness and with pride. And while they built their homes and laid out farms, they also constructed meeting houses and invented the Town Meeting as a place in which to talk out their community problems through discussion and debate.

It was in these Town Meetings, and in the churches which preached spiritual individualism, and in the colonial legislatures—especially those in Massachusetts and Virginia—that our new nation was born.

We read with proper pride of the courage of the Minute Men at Concord and Lexington, but the doughty and eloquent John Adams raised the right question and proposed the right answer when he said: "What do we mean by the

American Revolution? Do we mean the American War? The Revolution was effected before the war commenced. The Revolution was in the minds and hearts of the people. . . . This radical change in the principles, opinions, sentiments, and affections of the people was the real American Revolution.''

In a real sense, the American Revolution was talked into being. It began in the homes, and taverns, and churches, and town meetings of the thirteen colonies—where our ancestors were learning to solve their own problems in their own way, rather than to await directions from overseas.

It began in the legislature of Massachusetts, where James Otis and Sam Adams were pouring out ''inflammatory speeches'' to support a propaganda principle that Adams well understood: ''Put your adversary in the wrong and keep him there.''

It began in St. John's Church, in Richmond, where the Virginia colonial assembly was in session on March 23, 1775, when a red-headed farmer-lawyer from the backwoods arose and electrified the delegates with a torrent of eloquence—reminding his listeners that ''We have petitioned, we have remonstrated, we have supplicated . . . and we have been spurned, with contempt, from the foot of the throne.'' Then Patrick Henry launched into his memorable peroration: ''What is it that gentlemen wish? What would they have? Is life so dear, or peace so sweet, as to be purchased at the price of chains and slavery? Forbid it, Almighty God! I know not what course others may take, but as for me, give me liberty or give me death!''

A listener reported that ''When he sat down, I felt sick with excitement. Every eye yet gazed entranced on Henry. It seemed as if a word from him would have led to any wild explosion of violence.'' There was no applause when this, one of America's greatest speeches, was finished. Only silence; no reply—just the vote, which set Virginia by the side of Massachusetts and assured the Revolution of eventual success.

Without eloquent and effective speech, this nation would never have been formed. Then through discussion and debate our basic institutions were devised and our guiding national policies were developed. This is how it was—through the democracy of free speech, skillfully used.

The Constitution was formulated in the course of a long summer of group discussion. Sometimes the delegates were so discouraged that they might have gone home with their task uncompleted, but George Washington quietly addressed them, saying: ''If we offer to the people something that we do not ourselves approve, how can we afterward defend our work? Let us raise a standard to which the wise and the honest may repair. The event is in the hands of God.''

The Constitution was ratified in a series of State Conventions, in the thrust and parry of great debate. We now had our fundamental instrument of government, but any nation needs more than laws. We needed also a sense of greatness and a dedication to the purpose courageously established by our founding fathers. We needed to create traditions and to establish high goals. This function of nation-building was performed with great artistry and effect largely through the oratory of Daniel Webster.

Webster was a public speaker of wide range and great skill, who was effective in the Congress, in the law courts, at public gatherings, and on ceremonial occasions. He became the greatest interpreter of the Constitution and the chief defender of the federal union against the threats of nullification and secession. But his greatest role was interpreting the meaning of Americanism in the early years of our history when the American people had not yet savored the magic of the phrase, "our pioneer ancestors." It was Webster who imprinted the glories of our frontier heritage so vividly in our national consciousness that it is personal and real even to our most recent immigrants.

One of Webster's greatest speeches was given at Plymouth, in December, 1820, while he was still a young man, to celebrate the courage and idealism of the Pilgrims. In it he explained the commemorative function which great public speaking may perform:

> It is a noble faculty of our nature [he said] which enables us to connect our thoughts, our sympathies, and our happiness with what is distant in place or time; and, looking before and after, to hold communion at once with our ancestors and our posterity. Human and mortal though we are, we are nevertheless not mere insulated beings, without relation to the past or the future. Neither the point of time, nor the spot of earth, in which we physically live, bounds our rational and intellectual enjoyments. We live in the past by a knowledge of its history; and in the future, by hope and anticipation. By ascending to an association with our ancestors, by contemplating their example and studying their character, by partaking their sentiments and imbibing their spirit, by accompanying them in their toils, by sympathizing in their sufferings and rejoicing in their successes and their triumphs, we seem to belong to their age, and to mingle our existence with theirs.

After Webster had concluded his depiction of the deeds and personalities of our New England forebears, the hardheaded publisher George Ticknor, who was in the audience, reported that he returned to his room, "never so excited by public speaking before in my life. Three or four times I thought my temples would burst with the gush of blood. . . . When I came out I was almost afraid to come near him. It seemed to me as if he was like a mount that might not be touched and that burned with fire. I was beside myself, and am so still."

By great oratory the reform movements of abolitionism, and women's suffrage, and prohibition, and internationalism were launched. By still other oratory the Southern States propagated their theories of state rights. And such great speakers as Webster, Henry Clay, William Henry Seward, Stephen A. Douglas, and Abraham Lincoln sought to prevent, and did in fact delay, the advent of Civil War.

One of the most effective speeches from this period in our history was delivered in the relatively remote confines of the Pennsylvania Assembly, and its actual words were not reported or preserved. The speaker was Thaddeus Stevens, a club-footed, beetle-browed, dark-haired lawyer-legislator from Lancaster. The year was 1835, and Pennsylvania was about to repeal the free public school system, which had been in effect for a year. Newspapers and the public opposed free schools because they meant higher taxes. The Senate had already voted to abolish them, and the Assembly was about to concur.

Then Thaddeus Stevens arrived, late for the session, from Lancaster. He found himself almost alone in favor of free schools. Nevertheless, in a torrent of ironic eloquence, in which he charged that Pennsylvanians were more solicitous for their hogs than for their children, he proved so persuasive that the Senate reversed its earlier vote, and the Assembly ratified the free school system by a two-thirds vote. As the historian Richard N. Current attested, "No one questioned that Stevens' eloquence was responsible for this about-face."

One of the most courageous speeches in American history was not immediately successful, but in retrospect it proved to have a great and beneficent influence. This was the address by Thomas Corwin of Ohio in the Senate of the United States. On February 11, 1847, he denounced the war with Mexico and demanded that the United States make peace on the basis of returning to Mexico all the southwestern territories which our arms had won.

"It is idle, Mr. President," he thundered, "to suppose that the Mexican people would not feel as deeply for the dismemberment and disgrace of their country as you would feel for the dismemberment of this Union of ours. . . . If I were a Mexican, I would tell you, 'Have you not room enough in your own country to bury your dead men? If you come into mine, we will greet you with bloody hands, and welcome you to hospitable graves.'"

It is not surprising that now, more than a hundred years after Corwin's death, his name and his eloquent plea for generous justice, remain a strong pillar supporting the friendship of Mexico and the United States.

Of all the many orators who have pleaded and planned for the unity and harmony of the diverse groups which comprise this far-flung nation, none has spoken with greater eloquence or has left a finer heritage of leadership than Abraham Lincoln. One of the greatest of his statements, spoken just a few days before his death, is needed today as it was needed then, to heal sectional bitterness and to unite bitter adversaries in the common cause of national loyalty. The passage to which I refer is the conclusion of Lincoln's second inaugural:

With malice toward none, with charity for all, with firmness in the right as God gives us to see the right, let us strive on to finish the work we are in, to bind up the nation's wounds, to care for him who shall have borne the battle and for his widow and his orphan, to do all which may achieve and cherish a just and lasting peace, among ourselves, and with all nations.

From the long roll of distinguished American orators, there are many to choose, and I must omit them only with regret. There are Robert Green Ingersoll and Henry Ward Beecher, iconoclast lecturer and liberal preacher, who together did much to free American religion from the fear of hellfire and to substitute love and service. There are the great lawyers, Rufus Choate, Jeremiah Black, William Evarts, and Clarence Darrow, who humanized the law and who helped to extend its protection to broader spheres and to every class. There are the great reformers, Frederick Douglass, Theodore Weld, Ralph Waldo Emerson, John B. Gough, Lucretia Mott, and Frances E. Willard, who fought for human freedom, and temperance, and women's rights. There are the evangelical political leaders like William Jennings Bryan, Theodore Roosevelt, Robert M. LaFollette, and Woodrow Wilson, who raised the moral tone of political campaigning.

No other nation in history has matched the United States in platform eloquence. And the reason is clear. We have needed free and skilled public speaking in order to develop and deepen our self-governing democracy. The free platform is even more important than the free ballot box as a bastion for personal and public liberties.

There is one more thing I should like to say in conclusion. It is not only the great and splendid orations that signalize the true contributions of public speaking in American life. All through our history, in local communities, in Friday afternoon programs in the country schools, and in the many debating societies, ordinary men and women learned as they acquired skill in speech that their own opinions and their own feelings were matters of weight and influence in their communities.

The teaching and the learning of public speaking have been among the principal building blocks in the structure of our free society. And so it remains today. The man or woman who gains the understanding and ability to stand erect and to communicate deeply held convictions on matters of public concern is a better human being and a more constructive citizen.

This is the true measure of the influence of public speaking in the history of the United States. It has made and it still is making multiple thousands of us to be more effective human beings than we otherwise could hope to be.

To this ideal, Toastmasters International, with its scores of thousands of members, has made and is making and will continue to make an enormous contribution. Toastmasters Clubs and members deserve the gratitude of all who value democracy and treasure individualism, and of all who believe in the disciplined and liberal values of the study of effective speech.

FOOTNOTES

[1] *Liberal Education, ed. F. L. Wormald (Washington, D. C.),* Bulletin of the Association of American Colleges I *(May 1964): 213.*

[2] *Carroll C. Arnold, "Speech as a Liberal Study," in* The Speaker's Resource Book, 2nd ed., *Carroll C. Arnold, Douglas Ehninger, and John C. Gerber, eds. (Glenview, Ill.: Scott, Foresman and Company, 1966), p. 2.*

[3] *T. S. Eliot,* On Poetry and Poets. *Copyright 1945, 1957 by T. S. Eliot (New York: Farrar, Straus & Giroux, Inc., and London: Faber and Faber, Ltd.), "What Is a Classic?"*

[4] *Ralph Zimmermann, "Mingled Blood," in* Winning Orations of The Interstate Oratorical Association. *Reprinted by permission of The Interstate Oratorical Association. Also in* The Speaker's Resource Book, *p. 98.*

[5] *From* The Joy of Music, *copyright © 1959 by Leonard Bernstein. Published by Simon and Schuster, Inc. Lyrics from "Fine and Mellow" by Billie Holiday. © Copyright Edward B. Marks Music Corporation. Used by permission.*

[6] *Prepared by Douglas Nigh; assembled from material in the* Encyclopaedia Britannica, Encyclopaedia Americana, *and* Collier's Encyclopedia.

[7] *Reproduced by permission of Mr. Dennis Owen Ragan.*

[8] *"The Influence of Public Speaking in America: Building Blocks in a Free Society" by Robert T. Oliver from* Vital Speeches of the Day, XXXI *(October 1, 1965). Reprinted with permission of the author.*

Problems and Probes

1. List at least ten different situations in which an informative speech is called for. To what extent do you think the same principles of content and organization apply in each of these situations, and to what extent must special modifications or adaptations be made?

2. Make a study of one particular type of informative speaking— the classroom lecture, the expository sermon, the oral report, the informative radio or television address. After reading and listening to a number of speeches of this kind, prepare a paper in which you comment on the special problems of organization or presentation which seemed to occur. How were these problems solved in the speeches you studied?

3. Outline an informative speech reprinted in a recent issue of *Vital Speeches of the Day,* and note the psychological structuring-devices employed by the speaker. What method has he or she used to gain attention? Does the speaker show the listeners why they need to know the information he or she is going to present? Is there an initial summary?

4. Analyze the use made of the *factors of attention* in at least three informative speeches. Are some of the factors used more frequently than others? Which seem to you to be most effective?

5. Indicate and be prepared to defend your choices of the types of arrangement (time, space, cause-effect, problem-solution, or special topical sequence) which you think would be most suitable for an informative speech on each of the following subjects:

> The campus parking situation
> Facilities of the college library
> The fraternity tradition
> Censorship of the press
> Our city government
> Political problems of Southeast Asia
> Stamp collecting as a hobby
> Principles and policies of public taxation
> The Head Start program

6. Drawing upon your observations as a listener, discuss the role that the speaker's delivery plays in conveying information clearly and interestingly. Can you cite examples where delivery definitely helped or hindered the speaker in these respects?

7. Select a principle of physics, chemistry, biology, or a similar science and describe how you might explain this principle to: (*a*) a farmer, (*b*) an automobile repairman, (*c*) a twelve-year-old newsboy, (*d*) a lawyer. Write a paragraph in which you make this particular principle clear to one of the above.

8. Recall several informative speeches (classroom lectures, instructional talks given at military reserve-unit meetings, directions to groups of employees, etc.) in which the speaker used visual aids to help communicate the ideas. What kind of visual aid (chart, map, working model, etc.) did he or she employ? What type of material (statistics, operational procedures, etc.) was the aid used to present? Was the aid used separately or simultaneously with oral explanation? Did the speaker handle it effectively? Did it help to communicate the idea it was intended to develop, or did it distract from that idea? If the aid was poorly chosen or ineffectively handled, how could its use have been improved? (For a discussion of the various types of visual aids and the rules governing their use, review pages 315–317 in Chapter 11.)

9. In the following speaking assignment, evaluate your classmates' speeches, using either of the two Speech Evaluation Forms in Chapter 17. If time permits, your conclusions and those of some of the other evaluators may be discussed in class. In any case, use the forms to focus your attention on the various aspects of the content and delivery of the speech.

Oral Activity and Speaking Assignment

1. Prepare a speech to inform for presentation in class. Using one of the topics suggested below or a similar topic approved by your instructor, select and narrow it appropriately. Use whatever visual aids you think will improve your presentation. Follow the rules of organization and development set forth in this chapter. Suggested topics:

New wonder drugs
Contemporary American writers (artists, musicians)
Teaching machines and programmed learning
The Federal Communications Commission
How to learn through better listening
The use of visual aids in speaking
Advances in automation
Medical problems of space travel
Recent advances in automotive engineering (or design)
Changing perspectives in American foreign policy
Military lessons of the Vietnam War
Transportation problems of our major cities
The physical and psychological effects of LSD

Suggestions for Further Reading

A. Craig Baird, Franklin H. Knower, and Samuel L. Becker, *General Speech Communication* (New York: McGraw-Hill Book Company, 1971), Chapter XX, "Informational Speaking," pp. 289–302.

W. A. Mambert, *Presenting Technical Ideas: A Guide to Audience Communication* (New York: John Wiley & Sons, Inc., 1968).

Thomas H. Olbricht, *Informative Speaking* (Glenview, Ill.: Scott, Foresman and Company, 1968).

Charles R. Petrie, "Informative Speaking: A Summary and Bibliography of Related Research," *Speech Monographs*, XXX (June 1963): 79–91. Reprinted in *The Rhetoric of Our Times*, ed. J. Jeffrey Auer (New York: Appleton-Century-Crofts, 1969), pp. 237–254.

Loren Reid, *Speaking Well*, 2nd ed. (New York: McGraw-Hill Book Company, 1972), Chapters XIV–XVII, pp. 204–268.

Raymond S. Ross, *Speech Communication: Fundamentals and Practice*, 2nd ed. (Englewood Cliffs, N. J.: Prentice-Hall, Inc., 1970), Chapter XIII, "Presenting Information," pp. 134–159.

20
THE SPEECH TO PERSUADE

We live today in a complex society. No longer can one person working alone accomplish a task of any magnitude. Others also must be convinced that the task is worthwhile and agree to lend their support and encouragement. In the preceding chapter we explained how a speaker may organize and present ideas when seeking to increase the knowledge or understanding of the listeners. In this chapter we shall explain how to organize and present ideas when one's purpose is to persuade — to alter the listeners' existing beliefs or attitudes or to instill new ones.

SITUATIONS REQUIRING PERSUASION

Sooner or later almost everyone is faced with the task of persuading others. Consider only three typical situations: (a) *The job-seeking interview.* As we pointed out in Chapter 2, when you are being interviewed by a prospective employer, one of your basic aims is to persuade the interviewer that you are well qualified to fill the position in question. (b) *The business conference.* The executive committee of a business or corporation constantly must make decisions concerning the management of the organization. In the course of its deliberations, officers present reports and urge their acceptance, subcommittees offer recommendations for future actions, and individuals advocate or oppose policies. (c) *Public meetings.* Countless speeches to persuade are given at political rallies and mass meetings. "Communication and Change," the hypothetical illustration with which we opened this book, emphasized the part such speeches play in effecting change on the local level.* On the state and national scenes also, meetings are held at which policies are criticized, reforms advocated, and candidates for office supported or attacked.

---

*See pp. 4–7.

THE PURPOSE: TO SECURE BELIEF

When speaking to persuade, your ultimate aim is to induce your listeners to believe the claim or proposition you are advancing or to win their support for the policy you propose. You are, in effect, setting forth a proposal for your listeners' consideration and, if you are successful, their acceptance. In order to achieve this goal, however, you must, as a rule, keep two subsidiary or intermediary puposes in mind: (*a*) to provide your listeners with *a motive for believing or acting*—show them how the endorsement of your claim or proposition will, for example, remove an existing evil or contribute in some way to their happiness, power, profit, or pride; and (*b*) to convince them of the factual correctness, moral soundness, or inherent practicability of the claim or proposition you advance.*

ANALYZING THE CLAIM

Before beginning to construct a speech to persuade, it is important that you yourself have clearly in mind the purpose you wish to achieve. Basically, there are three kinds of claims or propositions which you may either advocate or oppose. They are called *claims of fact*, *claims of value*, and *claims of policy*.

Claims of Fact and Value

If you were attempting to persuade your listeners that "assembly-line workers suffer mental depression" or that "price controls on raw agricultural products result in shortages," you would in each case be presenting a factual claim—asserting that a given state of affairs exists or that something is, indeed, the case. When confronted with a claim of this sort, two questions are likely to arise in the mind of a thoughtful listener:

1. *By what criteria or standards of judgment should the truth or accuracy of this claim be measured?* If you were asked to determine a person's height, you would immediately look for a yardstick or other measuring instrument. Listeners likewise look for a standard when judging the appropriateness of a factual claim. In the first of the examples given above, before agreeing that assembly-line workers do experience mental depression, the members of your audience would almost certainly want to know what you as a speaker mean by that term. In the

---

*At this point, you will find it useful to review Chapter 9, "Determining the Basic Appeals." Review also Chapter 11, "Supporting the Major Ideas," since the forms of support there described provide the characteristic means for proving the "factual correctness, moral soundness, or inherent practicability" of a claim.

second example, they would, no doubt, demand a definition of "shortages." Does it mean "the disappearance, for all practical purposes, of a given kind of food" or merely "less of that food than everyone might perhaps desire"? Against what standard, precisely, is the accuracy of the claim to be judged?

2. *Do the facts of the situation fit the criteria as thus set forth?* Is it a fact that all, or at least a reasonable majority of, assembly-line workers experience those feelings or symptoms which you have previously defined as constituting "mental depression"? Does the amount of produce and other raw agricultural products presently on supermarket shelves fall within the limits set by the speaker's definition of "shortages"? If you can first get your listeners to agree to certain standards or measurements for judgment and then present evidence to show that a given state of affairs meets these standards, you will, in most instances, be well on your way toward winning their belief.

The establishment of criteria through definition or other means is also important when analyzing a claim of a valuative nature—one which asserts that something is good or bad, desirable or undesirable, justified or unjustified. Is desirability to be judged in terms of the cost entailed or of the service rendered? Is something justified as long as it is legal, or should a stricter test of morality be applied? Sometimes it is well to pick out two or three different criteria which together cover all possible bases for judgment.* For example, in determining the quality of a particular college, you might consider such factors as the distinction of the faculty, the adequacy of its physical plant, the success of its students in graduate school, and the reputation it enjoys among the general public.

Claims of Policy

You are dealing with a typical claim of policy when you urge your audience to approve propositions of the following kinds: "Federal expenditures for pollution control *should be* tripled." "The student senate *should have* the authority to dismiss students from the university." "The speed limit in this state *should be* reduced to fifty miles an hour." In each instance, you are asking your audience to endorse a proposed "policy" or course of action. In analyzing a policy claim, four subsidiary questions are relevant:

1. *Is there a need for such a policy or course of action?* If your listeners do not believe that a change is called for, they are not likely to approve your proposal.

2. *Is the proposal practicable?* Can we afford the expense it would entail? Would it really solve the problem or remove the evil it is designed to correct?

---

*See again "Ethical Judgment," pp. 457–463.

Does it have a reasonable chance of being adopted? If you cannot show that your proposal meets these and similar tests, you can hardly expect it to be endorsed.

3. *Are the benefits your proposal will bring greater than the disadvantages it will entail?* People are reluctant to approve a proposal that promises to create conditions worse than the ones it is designed to correct. Burning a barn to the ground may be a highly practicable and efficient way to get rid of rats, but it is hardly a desirable one. The benefits and disadvantages that will accrue from a plan of action always must be carefully weighed along with considerations of its basic workability.

4. *Is the proposal superior to any other plan or policy?* Listeners are hesitant to approve a policy if they have reason to believe that an alternative course of action is more practicable or will bring greater benefits.

In analyzing a policy which you intend to urge upon an audience, consider, then, these four questions: Is such a policy needed? Would it prove practicable? Would the advantages outweigh the disadvantages — the benefits offset the losses? Is it better than any reasonable alternative? Determine the criteria to apply in arriving at answers and see if the available evidence meets them. Observe how this procedure was applied in developing the outline "Our Plenty Is Not So Plentiful," in Chapter 14 (pages 400–406).

THE ORGANIZATION OF THE SPEECH TO PERSUADE

The motivated sequence, as outlined in Chapter 13, provides a basic pattern for the speech to persuade, whether your aim is to win belief in a claim of fact, a claim of value, or a claim of policy. Let us see how it may be applied in each case, beginning with a claim of fact.

Seeking Belief or Disbelief in a Claim of Fact

Before constructing a speech designed to persuade an audience of the truth or accuracy of a factual claim, make sure that the claim in question cannot be settled by other more direct and effective means. Often differences concerning matters of fact may be resolved by personal observation, by looking in a reliable reference source, or by conducting a controlled experiment. It would, for example, be absurd to give a speech aimed at proving it is or is not raining outside, that the distance between Cleveland and Chicago is approximately three hundred miles, or that the fruit in a given basket is contaminated. The first of these questions can be settled simply by looking out the window, the second by consulting a road map, and the third by making the appropriate chemical tests.

But now consider these questions: "Is China gaining on us in the missile race?" "Do the countries of Southeast Asia resent United States interference in their internal affairs?" "Is Jones guilty of murder as charged?" Although these questions, too, raise issues of a factual nature, for one reason or another satisfactory answers cannot be arrived at by observation, by the checking of reference works, or by conducting an experiment. While data gathered from such sources could contribute in a major way to the judgment that is made, in the end we must rely upon our own informed opinion—must reason from the best facts available to what appears to be the correct conclusion. It is on questions of this second type that speeches in support of factual claims become necessary and may appropriately be made.

Although departures sometimes are required by the nature of the subject or by the situation in which you find yourself, generally in a speech on behalf of a factual claim you may employ the steps in the motivated sequence in the following way:

1. Secure the *attention* and *interest* of the listeners.
2. State clearly the claim you are advancing and show why a judgment of its truth or validity is *needed*. Do this either by pointing out (*a*) why the matter at hand concerns the listeners personally or (*b*) why it concerns the community, state, nation, or world of which they are a part.
3. *Satisfy* the need developed in the preceding step by advancing what you believe to be the correct judgment and offer evidence and argument in support of your view.*
4. *Visualize* for your listeners what they will gain by accepting the judgment you recommend or the evils or dangers they will incur by rejecting it.
5. Appeal for *action*—for the acceptance of your proposal and a determination to adhere to it.

These steps are illustrated in the following skeleton outline:

OUR STUDENT GOVERNMENT

I. State University has one of the oldest and most widely   *Attention*
imitated systems of student government in the entire nation.
    A. It was founded in 1883, when student government
        was almost entirely unknown.
    B. Many of the leaders of our state and nation gained
        their first practical administrative experience as
        campus officers.

---

*In addition to using the forms of support, you may employ the types of reasoning described on pp. 525–527.

II. Has our student government, once a free and powerful institution, become a mere tool of the dean of men and the university administration? *Statement of Question*

I. This is a question of vital importance to each of us. *Need*
    A. The prestige of the university is at stake.
    B. Our freedom as students to govern ourselves and conduct our own affairs is endangered.

I. In recent years the dean of men and other administrative officers of the university have encroached upon the rights and powers of our student government to an alarming extent. *Satisfaction: Statement of Claim*
    A. All actions of the Student Senate must now have administrative approval. *Supporting Evidence*
    B. The budgets of student organizations must be approved and their accounts audited by the university treasurer's office.
    C. The election of class officers is conducted under the supervision of the dean.

I. Unless we are all aware of these serious encroachments upon our traditional rights as students and consider steps to oppose or counteract them, further encroachments will almost certainly occur. *Visualization: Warning of Future Evils*

I. Make these facts known to your fellow students. *Action*
II. Resolve that student government will once again be a strong and vital force on this campus.

If your purpose is to oppose a factual claim advanced by another (in this case, to prove that the administration has *not* infringed upon student rights and privileges), proceed in exactly the same way, except to offer a negative rather than an affirmative claim at the beginning of the satisfaction step and present evidence and argument that justify this stand.

Seeking Belief or Disbelief in a Claim of Value

Whereas claims of fact assert that something is so, claims of value, you will recall, assert that something is good or bad, desirable or undesirable, justified or unjustified. Typical claims of value are: "Quotas on the export of agricultural products are unfair to the farmer." "Big-time athletics are detrimental to the best interests of college students." "Harry Truman was one of our greatest presidents."

When advancing a valuative claim, with a view to convincing your listeners that they should agree with your estimate of a person, practice, institution, or theory, you may adapt the basic pattern of the motivated sequence as follows:

1. Capture the audience's *attention* and *interest.*

2. Make clear that an estimate concerning the worth of the person, practice, or institution is *needed.* Do this by showing either (*a*) why such an estimate is important to your listeners personally or (*b*) why it is important to the community, state, nation, or world of which they are a part. With the *need* made clear, set forth the criteria on which an appropriate estimate must rest.

3. *Satisfy* the need developed in the preceding step by advancing what you believe to be the correct estimate and by showing how this estimate meets the criteria specified.

4. *Visualize* the advantages that will accrue from agreeing with the estimate you offer or the evils and dangers that will follow from endorsing an alternative.

5. Appeal for *action* — for acceptance of the proposed estimate and a determination to gain it.

Each of these basic steps is present in the following speech outline:

THE VALUES OF INTERCOLLEGIATE DEBATING

I. In recent years intercollegiate debating has come under strong attack from many quarters.

    A. Philosophers and social scientists charge that debate is a poor way to get at the truth concerning a disputable matter.

    B. Educators charge that debate teaches the student to approach a problem with an "either-or" attitude, thus causing him to develop habits of contentiousness and dogmatism rather than of fact-centered objectivity.

Attention

I. How we evaluate debate is important to each of us for at least two reasons:

    A. As students, we help support the debate program on this campus because a portion of our activity fee is allocated to the Debate Society.

    B. As citizens in a democratic society, we are

Need:
Evaluation
Necessary

concerned because the method of decision-making employed in intercollegiate debating is essentially the same as that employed in the courtroom and the legislative assembly.

II. As is true of any extracurricular activity, there are two important criteria by which debate may be evaluated: *Criteria*
    A. Does it develop abilities and traits of mind that will aid the student in his course work?
    B. Does it develop abilities and traits of mind that will be of value in later life?

I. The experience of many years has shown that debate is valuable in both respects. *Satisfaction: Evaluation Provided*
    A. Debate helps students do better work in their courses.
        1. It teaches them to study a subject thoroughly and systematically.
        2. It teaches them to analyze complex ideas quickly and logically.
        3. It teaches them to speak and write clearly and convincingly.
    B. Training in debate is of value in later life.
        1. It teaches courtesy and fair play.
        2. It develops self-confidence and poise.

I. Picture serious students of debate in the classroom and in their post-college careers. *Visualization*
    A. As students, they will know how to study, analyze, and present material.
    B. As business or professional persons, they will be better able to meet arguments and to express their views in a fair and effective manner.

I. Remember these facts whenever you hear the value of intercollegiate debating questioned. *Action*
    A. The contribution debate training makes to business or professional success has been eloquently affirmed by many thousands of prominent men and women who were themselves debaters in college.
    B. We should encourage and support this worthwhile activity in every way we can.

A speech opposing a claim of value (for instance, a speech intended to prove that debating does *not* provide desirable and useful training) may be developed acccording to the same general pattern. In this case, however, instead of showing that debate meets the criteria outlined in the need step, you would show that it *fails* to meet them. The visualization step then might assert that college debate experience is not merely useless to a person in business or professional life, but actually harmful.

Seeking Belief or Disbelief in a Claim of Policy

When your purpose is to induce your listeners to endorse a claim of policy, the motivated sequence may follow closely the pattern outlined in Chapter 13, thus: (1) secure *attention;* (2) assert that because of existing deficiencies or evils there is a *need* for some action; (3) provide *satisfaction* for this need by presenting a remedy which will remove the evils or deficiencies; (4) *visualize* the benefits to be obtained from believing or acting as you propose; and (5) request *action* in the form of an endorsement of the proposal you advance.

Opposing Endorsement of a Proposition of Policy

When opposing a policy ("We should *not* deprive freshmen of the right to own and drive cars") also try to capture attention, but then proceed by denying any or all contentions embodied in steps (2), (3), and (4), above. Thus you may argue: (2) There is no need for such a policy; things are perfectly all right as they are. (3) The proposal is not practicable; it could not be made to work. (4) Instead of bringing benefits or advantages, the proposed policy would actually introduce new and worse evils; it would be unfair, difficult to administer, etc.

Sometimes all three of these contentions may be combined when developing a speech in which you oppose a policy. On other occasions you will find that only one or two of them apply, and your speech will be limited accordingly. Proof beyond reasonable doubt on any of the three, however, will cause an earnest listener to reject a proposal because, obviously, no one wants to adopt a policy that is not needed or is impracticable or productive of new problems and evils. Proof beyond reasonable doubt on all three contentions constitutes the strongest possible case that can be made against a proposed change.

Here is a skeleton outline of the main points of a speech in which an action is opposed on the grounds that it is unneeded, impracticable, and undesirable. For purposes of simplification, the attention step and supporting material have been omitted.

I. The turnpike from Ashton to Waterton, proposed by the Governor's Committee on Highways, is not needed. *Not Needed*
  A. The existing highway connecting the two cities is only three years old and is in excellent condition.
  B. Automobile traffic between Ashton and Waterton, instead of increasing, has actually decreased 6 percent during the last decade.

II. Even if the proposed turnpike were needed, it could not be built at this time. *Impracticable*
  A. State funds for road construction are at an all-time low.
  B. Borrowing for road construction is difficult and costly in the present bond market.

III. Finally, even if such a turnpike were both needed and possible, its construction would be undesirable. *Undesirable*
  A. It would impose a serious hardship on owners of motels, filling stations, restaurants, and other businesses along the present highway.
  B. The suggested route would spoil the Ashton State Park.

THE MANNER OF SPEAKING FOR THE SPEECH TO PERSUADE

No one style of delivery is suitable to persuasive speaking in all of its forms. For obvious reasons, your manner in talking to a single individual or to a small group of businessmen in an executive meeting will be different from your manner in addressing a large audience at a public gathering. Moreover, your delivery before an apathetic audience will differ from your delivery before either an interested group or a hostile one. In general, however, a straightforward, energetic presentation that suggests enthusiasm without seeming to be overemotional is effective in creating belief.

THE CONTENT OF THE SPEECH TO PERSUADE

Concrete Facts and Vivid Illustrations

When speaking to persuade, avoid generalities and abstractions. Use facts and figures that are within the experience of your listeners. Incidents that are recent, common, or particularly striking are usually powerful in attaining conviction. No other single approach is likely to be as effective as presenting facts, pertinent facts — and then more facts. Review the forms of support discussed in Chapter 11 and use them consistently and throughout.

Sound, Logical Reasoning

Regardless of how much detailed and concrete evidence you present, a speech will not carry strong conviction unless your reasoning is sound. A brief consideration of the three most frequently used forms of reasoning is therefore important.

Reasoning from Example

This form of reasoning consists of drawing conclusions about a general class of objects after studying one or more individual members of that class. For instance, if a housewife is in doubt about the flavor of the apples in a bushel basket, she may bite into one of them to test its flavor. If it tastes all right, she reasons on the basis of this sample that all the apples in the basket have a good flavor. Or perhaps, if she is skeptical, she may dig down to the bottom to find out if all the apples seem to be the same. This sort of reasoning is employed in much of our thinking, whether the point at issue is big or little. Scientific experiments, laboratory tests, the determination of social trends — all of these are based upon reasoning from example. Reasoning of this sort should be tested by asking the following questions:

1. *Is the sample extensive enough to support the conclusion offered?* One robin does not make a spring, nor can two or three examples prove that a broad or general claim is incontestably true.

2. *Are the examples chosen fairly?* To show that something is true in New York, Chicago, and Boston — all large cities — does not prove it also is true in smaller towns throughout the country.

3. *Are there any outstanding exceptions?* One well-known instance which differs from the general conclusion you urge may cause doubt unless you can show that this instance is the result of unusual or atypical circumstances.

Reasoning from Axiom

This form of reasoning consists of applying an accepted rule or principle to a specific situation. For example, it is generally conceded that by buying in large quantities one may get merchandise more cheaply than by buying in small lots. When you argue that discount stores save money because they purchase goods in large quantities, you are, therefore, merely applying this general rule to a valid specific instance. Reasoning from axiom may be tested as follows:

1. *Is the axiom, or rule, true?* For many years people believed the world was flat. Many assertions which pass for true are only prejudices or superstitions. Before applying an axiom, make sure of its validity. Remember also that no matter how true a principle may be, you cannot base an argument upon it unless you can first convince your audience of its truth.

2. *Does the axiom apply to the situation in question?* A rule that is itself true or valid may be improperly applied. For instance, to argue, on the basis of the above-mentioned principle, that discount stores buy goods more cheaply than individual merchants is warranted; but to argue on this same basis that the customer can always buy goods from discount stores at lower prices is not valid. Additional proof would be required to establish this further contention.

Reasoning from Causal Relation

When something happens, we assume that it must have had a cause; and when we see a force in operation, we realize that it will produce an effect. A great deal of our reasoning is based on this relationship between cause and effect. The rate of violent crime goes up, and we hasten to lay the blame on drugs, bad housing, public apathy, or inept public officials. We hear that the star on our football team is in the hospital with a broken ankle, and we immediately become apprehensive about the results of Saturday's game. We reason from known effects to inferred causes, and from known causes to inferred effects. There is perhaps no other form of reasoning so often used by speakers, nor is there any form of reasoning which may contain so many flaws. Test causal reasoning for soundness by asking:

1. *Has a result been mistaken for a cause?* When two phenomena occur simultaneously, it sometimes is hard to tell which is the cause and which the effect. Do higher wages cause higher prices, or is the reverse true?

2. *Is the cause strong enough to produce the result?* A small pebble on the track will not derail a passenger train, but a large boulder will. Be careful that you don't mistake a pebble for a boulder.

3. *Has anything prevented the cause from operating?* If a gun is not loaded, pulling the trigger will not make it shoot. Be certain that nothing has prevented the free operation of the cause which you assume has produced a given situation.

4. *Could any other cause have led to the same result?* Note that at the beginning of the section, four different, possible causes were listed to account for the

increase in violent crime. Each one of these causes is cited — by some persons — as the *sole* cause. Be sure that you diagnose a situation correctly; don't put the blame on the wrong cause nor all the blame on a single cause if the blame should be divided among several causes.

5. *Is there actually a connection between the assumed cause and the alleged effect?* Sometimes people assume that merely because one thing happens immediately after another, the two are causally connected. Do not mistake chronology for cause. Developing a pain in your back shortly after you have eaten strawberries doesn't mean that the pain was caused by the strawberries. Do not mistake a coincidence for a true cause-effect relationship.

SPECIAL TECHNIQUES OF THE SPEECH TO PERSUADE

The most important characteristic of a good speech to persuade — indeed, more important than all the other characteristics put together — is that it be *listener-oriented*. Always speak with your auditors in mind. You cannot sell a person an automobile just because you like it; you must approach each individual on the basis of his or her own needs and desires. Nor can you induce a group of people to believe or act as you want them to unless you understand how they view your proposal. In no other type of speech is a thorough analysis of your listeners quite so important. You must find out all that you can about them: their likes and dislikes, their attitude toward your subject, their habits, and patterns of thought. Put yourself in their place and look at the problem as they look at it. With the standpoint of the audience constantly in mind, utilize to the utmost the following special methods or techniques:

Appeal to the Dominant Motives of the Audience

Your speech not only must exhibit sound, logical reasoning and include many concrete facts and vivid illustrations; it must also contain effective appeals to *the motives for human action* (see Chapter 9). You must convince your audience that their basic desires will be better satisfied if they do what you propose. You may, for example, prove that they are losing money under present conditions or that they will save money by approving your plan, but underlying all this proof is the appeal to acquisition or saving.

Identify Your Proposal with Existing Beliefs

Find out what your listeners' attitudes and beliefs are; and, if possible, show that your proposal embodies these attitudes and beliefs. For example, if they believe that saving money is important, show how your proposal will have this effect. If they believe in preserving the environment, show that your plan embodies this ideal. If they are opposed to publicly supported day-care centers, show how your proposal will discourage them. You will usually be able to find ways of linking your proposition with at least some of your audience's attitudes, beliefs, and values. Even when your plan is in direct opposition to an existing belief, you may be able to offset the disadvantage by balancing this belief against an equally strong conviction that is in your favor.

Use the "Yes-Response" Technique

Do not begin your speech with an idea your listeners will find difficult to accept. Instead, start with ideas you think they will approve of. If you can first draw them into a pattern of agreeing with you and put them into a receptive and positive frame of mind, you will reduce their resistance to less favorable arguments. A speaker, trying to persuade a group of stockholders to vote for a mining merger, began by saying, "I know you have a lot of objections to this plan, but you're all wrong about it." A much better beginning would have been: "I am sure you are interested in getting the greatest return on your investment consistent with safety." The speaker then could have shown how the merger would produce this result.

Use the "This-or-Nothing" Technique

Try to show the impossibility of believing or doing anything other than what you propose. People often reject a proposition because they have not been made to realize that it is the best one possible. By showing that there are only (let us say) three available courses of action, two of which are undesirable, you will cut off all avenues of "escape" except the one you advocate. Thus, if you explain that the only alternatives to bankruptcy are heavy borrowing and curtailment of operating expense, you may—by showing the impossibility of further extension of credit—secure approval for your program of reduced expenditures.

In sum, then, when speaking to persuade, approach the subject from the standpoint of your listeners, present concrete facts and vivid illustrations which are within their experience, use sound reasoning, appeal to their dominant motives, identify your proposal with their existing beliefs, employ the "yes-response," and use the "this-or-nothing" technique. Remember always that although people should be convinced chiefly through logical reasoning and evidence, they often *act* in a certain way largely because they *wish* or *desire* to do so. Most of us, for example, are concerned for the safety of our families and ourselves, but we seldom take active steps to ensure this safety until we experience an actual threat to our well-being—an epidemic, fire, flood, or shortage of food or water supply. Together with logic and evidence, therefore, you must employ vivid descriptions which appeal to the basic desires and emotions which underlie your hearers' logic.

Appeals to the emotions are particularly important in the visualization step; in fact, this step should always be descriptive and should usually contain strong emotional inducements. Elsewhere in your speech, an occasional vivid example will add a dynamic quality to your argument which sound logic alone will not produce. Except in the visualization step, however, do not substitute emotional appeals for logic and evidence—use both. Make your logical arguments vivid and compelling, and you will have the essence of an effective speech to persuade.

ADAPTING THE ORGANIZATION OF THE SPEECH TO THE AUDIENCE ATTITUDE

Earlier in this chapter we examined several of the more common forms of the speech to persuade, and we saw that in each case the five-step structure of attention, need, satisfaction, visualization, and action provided a basic pattern of organization. The detailed development of any particular speech to persuade as it will actually be delivered, however, must depend on the audience's attitude toward the speaker's claim or proposal. Therefore, as a final step in our study of speaking to persuade, let us consider some of the attitudes an audience may display toward a claim, and the adaptations which the speaker must make to each.*

Audience Interested in the Situation but Undecided

Some audiences are conscious that a problem exists or a decision is called for, but they are uncertain as to the belief they should adopt or the course of action they should pursue. In such cases, your primary purpose is to get them to agree that your claim is correct or that your proposal is the best one possible.

Attention step. Since the audience already is interested in the question, the attention step may be brief. Often it consists of a direct reference to the matter to be decided. At other times it may be a short example or story. When using this second method, however, take care to center your listeners' attention on the

---

*Review the discussion of audience attitudes on pp. 245–248.

heart of the matter rather than on side issues or irrelevant details. Focus their thinking on fundamentals by excluding all but the central issue under consideration.

Need step. Review briefly the background out of which the need for a decision has grown. Summarize its historical development if this will help your hearers understand the situation more clearly. Also, describe in a few words the situation as it now exists, and show why an immediate decision is imperative. Finally, set forth the standards or criteria which a sound decision must meet.

Satisfaction step. This will usually be the most important, and probably the longest, part of your speech. State your claim, or outline the plan of action you wish your hearers to adopt, and define any vague or ambiguous terms. Show specifically how what you recommend will satisfy the criteria outlined in the need step. Proceed to demonstrate the advantages to be gained by accepting your proposition and why it is superior to any possible alternative. Prove each of your contentions with an abundance of facts, figures, testimony, and examples.

Visualization step. Make this step rather brief in relation to the rest of the speech. Be vivid and persuasive, but don't exaggerate. Project the audience into the future by painting a realistic picture of the desirable conditions which will be brought about by approving your claim or supporting your proposal—or the evils that will result from a failure to do so.

Action step. Restate in clear and forceful language your request for belief or for endorsement of the plan you advocate. Recapitulate briefly the principal arguments and appeals presented earlier in the speech.

Audience Interested in the Situation but Hostile to the Proposal

Sometimes audiences are conscious that a problem exists or that a question must be decided, but are opposed to the particular belief or plan of action you wish them to accept. Often this hostility is based either on a fear that some undesirable result will accompany the proposed action or on a positive preference for an alternative belief or policy. Sometimes the hostility is a reflection of deeply ingrained prejudices. In any case, your goal must be to overcome existing objections and ensure the acceptance of your ideas.

Attention step. This step is similar to the attention step for a speech to an undecided audience. However, since you know there will be hostility toward your proposition, you should try, first of all, to conciliate your audience and win a hearing. Approach your subject indirectly and gradually. Concede whatever you can to your listeners' point of view; establish common ground by emphasizing areas of agreement; minimize or explain away differences. Make your listeners feel that you are genuinely interested in achieving the same results they are.

Need step. Attain agreement on some basic principle or belief, and use this principle as the criterion by which to measure the soundness of the proposition you advance. Otherwise, develop this step as you would for an audience that is interested but undecided.

Satisfaction step. Show specifically how the proposed belief or plan of action meets the criterion established in the preceding step. Offer strong and extensive proof of the superiority of your claim to any other proposition which you have reason to believe your listeners may favor. (But do not imply that you know they favor such an alternative; if they become aware of that, you may have to combat their embarrassment in admitting they have made a mistake.) Otherwise, develop this step in the same way you would if you were addressing an undecided audience.

Visualization and action steps. If you have been successful thus far, your listeners should be in the same frame of mind as the audience discussed previously — that is, interested in the question but undecided about what to think or do. The development of your speech from this point on, therefore, will follow the pattern outlined for that type of audience, but will provide special emphasis on the visualization, or benefits, step.

Audience Apathetic to the Situation

In contrast to the two audiences just discussed — the undecided and the hostile audiences — apathetic audiences are not interested in the subject at all. They say, "What's it to me?" "I should worry about this? That's up to George." Obviously, with such persons your main object is to make them realize that the matter at hand *does* affect them — that they must assume a direct responsibility for arriving at a proper decision concerning it.

Attention step. Overcome apathy and inertia by touching briefly some matter that is related to your listeners' self-interest. Present one or two striking facts or figures, and use vivid phraseology to show the audience how their health, happiness, security, prosperity, chances for advancement, and other personal concerns are directly involved.

Need step. With interest thus aroused, proceed to demonstrate fully and systematically how the question under discussion affects each individual member of the audience. Relate the problem to them by showing: (*a*) its direct and immediate effect upon them; (*b*) its effects on their families, friends, business interests, or the social and professional groups to which they belong; (c) its probable future effects.

In showing these effects, employ the strongest possible evidence—specific instances and illustrations, striking statistics, strong testimony—and emphasize little-known or startling facts and conditions. This step will nearly always need to be longer in a speech to an apathetic audience than in a speech directed to listeners who are interested but undecided or listeners who are interested in the situation but hostile to the claim advanced. It will also require more impressive proof and more energetic delivery. From this point on, however, you may develop your speech in the same manner as for an audience that is interested but undecided.

Audience Hostile to Belief in the Existence of a Problem

If listeners are hostile because they do not believe that a problem exists or that a decision is called for, you must combat this disbelief at the outset, or your speech will have little chance of success.

Attention step. Place yourself on a common footing with the audience in the first few minutes by the use of common ground or the yes-response. Recognize their point of view, and admit whatever merits it may have, without in any way detracting from your own. As early as possible, gain agreement on an acceptable criterion by which to judge the claim or proposal you intend to advance. Support this criterion by quoting the testimony of persons who are respected by your listeners—if possible, persons from among their own number.

Need step. Show at some length exactly how your audience's present belief or existing situation violates the criterion laid down in the preceding step and therefore must be corrected. Since this is the point concerning which your hearers are skeptical or uninformed, use facts, figures, and especially testimony to establish your contention. Be careful, however, that you do not exaggerate. Instead of stilling opposition, stretching the facts will only strengthen the resistance of your listeners.

After convincing your hearers that their present belief or condition violates the criterion agreed upon, you may develop the rest of your speech as you would if you were addressing an audience that is interested in the question, but hostile to the proposal.

Finally, in planning a persuasive speech for an audience that is essentially hostile, remember that there will be times when you will find it helpful to develop the need and satisfaction steps in *parallel order*—a procedure we explained in Chapter 13 (pages 371–374). When this developmental order is used, each aspect of the need is discussed individually, together with that particular part of the claim or proposal which will satisfy it. The division of points may often be made according to the criteria advanced as a basis for judgment. Thus, you might first consider the "cost" criterion—that is, the desirability of adopting a proposal that will prove as economical as possible—and then show how your proposition meets this test. Next, you might present certain social or cultural criteria and demonstrate that your proposal satisfied each of these also. Finally, you might indicate the desirability of having a plan that is flexible enough to meet changing conditions and show that your proposal has this quality, too. In this way, you may develop your complete case in appropriate, parallel segments.

Real-life audiences, obviously, are seldom as clear-cut and uniform in their attitudes as our considerations in this chapter would seem to suggest. But if you can determine the attitudes, beliefs, and values of the majority or of the more influential members of an audience, you can usually develop an effective persuasive speech by following one of the four plans we have outlined in the foregoing pages—or by employing variations or combinations of them. Whatever method of organization you choose to follow, however, always keep in mind *the attitude of your listeners toward your proposition*. Always speak from the point of view of the people who are sitting before you.

SAMPLE SPEECHES TO PERSUADE

The following speech, delivered to the Young Men's Lyceum of Springfield, Illinois, on January 27, 1837, not only provides an excellent example of Abraham Lincoln's early style, but it also concerns itself with the same basic problems of "law and order" with which we continue to be concerned today. Lincoln, as we know, loved the logic of the law and was fascinated by its far-ranging search for fairness and justice, by the dramatic confrontation it affords both sides of an argument, and by its demand for precise meaning of words—a cause for which he was a lifelong advocate.

His speech, "The Perpetuation of Our Political Institutions," reflects the general plan of the motivated sequence, opening with an *attention step* that establishes common ground, and dividing the *problem (need) step* into the subunits of statement, illustration, ramification, and pointing (see pages 534–537). The *satisfaction* (or *solution*) *step* has a clearly defined statement of the policy recommended and a section in which objections are recognized and answered (see pages 537–540). Although the *visualization step* is brief, it is developed by the method of contrast (see page 540) and follows closely from the solution. The *action step* is brief, but challenging, and provides a strong climax.

As you read the speech, ask yourself in what respects it seems dated and in what respects it would be suitable for presentation to a present-day audience. Does the dated quality lie principally in the language? In the arguments and appeals? In the supporting materials? How could the speech be rewritten to be even more applicable to the temper and tone of our time?

THE PERPETUATION OF OUR POLITICAL INSTITUTIONS[2]

Abraham Lincoln

In the great journal of things happening under the sun, we, the American people, find our account running under date of the nineteenth century of the Christian era. We find ourselves in the peaceful possession of the fairest portion of the earth as regards extent of territory, fertility of soil, and salubrity of climate. We find ourselves under the government of a system of political institutions conducing more essentially to the ends of civil and religious liberty than any of which the history of former times tells us. We, when mounting the stage of existence, found ourselves the legal inheritors of these fundamental blessings. We toiled not in the acquirement or establishment of them; they are a legacy bequeathed us by a once hardy, brave, and patriotic, but now lamented and departed race of ancestors. Theirs was the task (and nobly they performed it) to possess themselves, and through themselves us, of this goodly land, and to uprear upon its hills and its valleys a political edifice of liberty and equal rights; 'tis ours only to transmit these—the former unprofaned by the foot of an invader, the latter undecayed by the lapse of time and untorn by usurpation—to the latest generation that fate shall permit the world to know. This task gratitude to our fathers, justice to ourselves, duty to posterity, and love for our species in general, all imperatively require us faithfully to perform.

ATTENTION STEP

Common Ground

How then shall we perform it? At what point shall we expect the approach of danger? By what means shall we fortify against it? Shall we expect some transatlantic military giant to step the ocean and crush us at a blow? Never! All the armies of Europe, Asia, and Africa combined, with all the treasure of the earth (our own excepted) in their military chest, with a Bonaparte for a commander, could not by force take a drink from the Ohio or make a track on the Blue Ridge in a trial of a thousand years.

NEED (OR PROBLEM) STEP

At what point, then, is the approach of danger to be expected? I answer, If it ever reach us, it must spring up amongst us; it cannot come from abroad. If destruction be our lot, we must ourselves be its author and finisher. As a nation of freemen we must live through all time, or die by suicide.

I hope I am over wary; but if I am not, there is even now something of ill omen amongst us. I mean the increasing disregard for law which pervades the

Statement

country—the growing disposition to substitute the wild and furious passions in lieu of the sober judgment of courts, and the worse than savage mobs for the executive ministers of justice. This disposition is awfully fearful in any community; and that it now exists in ours, though grating to our feelings to admit, it would be a violation of truth and an insult to our intelligence to deny. Accounts of outrages committed by mobs form the everyday news of the times. They have pervaded the country from New England to Louisiana; they are neither peculiar to the eternal snows of the former nor the burning suns of the latter; they are not the creature of climate, neither are they confined to the slaveholding or the non-slaveholding States. Alike they spring up among the pleasure-hunting masters of Southern slaves, and the order-loving citizens of the land of steady habits. Whatever, then, their cause may be, it is common to the whole country.

It would be tedious as well as useless to recount the horrors of all of *Illustration* them. Those happening in the State of Mississippi and at St. Louis are perhaps the most dangerous in example and revolting to humanity. In the Mississippi case they first commenced by hanging the regular gamblers—a set of men certainly not following for a livelihood a very useful or very honest occupation, but one which, so far from being forbidden by the laws, was actually licensed by an act of the legislature passed but a single year before. Next, Negroes suspected of conspiring to raise an insurrection were caught up and hanged in all parts of the State; then, white men supposed to be leagued with the Negroes; and, finally, strangers from neighboring States, going thither on business, were in many instances subjected to the same fate. Thus went on this process of hanging. . . .

Turn then to that horror-striking scene at St. Louis. A single victim only was sacrificed there. This story is very short, and is perhaps the most highly tragic of anything of its length that has ever been witnessed in real life. A mulatto man by the name of McIntosh was seized in the street, dragged to the suburbs of the city, chained to a tree, and actually burned to death; and all within a single hour from the time he had been a freeman attending to his own business and at peace with the world.

Such are the effects of mob law, and such are the scenes becoming more and more frequent in this land so lately famed for love of law and order, and the stories of which have even now grown too familiar to attract anything more than an idle remark.

But you are perhaps ready to ask, "What has this to do with the perpet- *Ramification* uation of our political institutions?" I answer, "It has much to do with it." Its *(developed by* direct consequences are, comparatively speaking, but a small evil, and much of *Explanation)* its danger consists in the proneness of our minds to regard its direct as its only consequences. *Abstractly* considered, the hanging of the gamblers at Vicksburg was of but little consequence. They constitute a portion of population that is worse than useless in any community; and their death, if no pernicious example be set by it, is never a matter of reasonable regret with anyone. If they were annually swept from the stage of existence by the plague or smallpox, honest men would perhaps be much profited by the operation. Similar, too, is the correct reasoning in regard to the burning of the Negro at St. Louis. He had forfeited his life by the perpetration of an outrageous murder upon one of the most worthy and respectable citizens of the city; and had he not died as he did, he must have died by the sentence of the law in a very short time afterward. As to him alone, it was as well the way it was as it could otherwise have been. But the example in either case was fearful. When men take it in their heads today to hang gamblers or burn murderers, they should recollect that in the confusion usually attending such transactions they will be as likely to hang or burn someone who is neither a gambler nor a murderer as one who is, and that, acting upon the example they set, the mob of tomorrow may, and probably will, hang or burn some of them by the very same mistake. And not only so; the innocent, those who have ever set their faces against violations of law in every shape, alike with the guilty fall victims to the ravages of mob law; and thus it goes on, step by step, till all the walls erected for the defense of the persons and property of individuals are trodden down and disregarded. But all this, even, is not the full extent of the evil. By such examples, by instances of the perpetrators of such acts going unpunished, the lawless in spirit are encouraged to become lawless in practice; and having been used to no restraint but dread of punishment, they thus become absolutely unrestrained. Having ever regarded government as their deadliest bane, they make a jubilee of the suspension of its operations, and pray for nothing so much as its total annihilation. While, on the other hand, good men, men who love tranquillity, who desire to abide by the laws and enjoy their benefits, who would gladly spill their blood in the defense of their country, seeing their property destroyed, their families insulted, and their lives endangered, their persons injured, and seeing nothing in prospect that forebodes a change for the better, become tired of and disgusted with a government that offers them no protection, and are not much averse to a change in which they imagine they have nothing to lose.

Thus, then, by the operation of this mobocratic spirit which all must admit is now abroad in the land, the strongest bulwark of any government, and particularly of those constituted like ours, may effectually be broken down and destroyed—I mean the attachment of the people. Whenever this effect shall be produced among us; whenever the vicious portion of a population shall be permitted to gather in bands of hundreds and thousands, and burn churches, ravage and rob provision-stores, throw printing presses into rivers, shoot editors, and hang and burn obnoxious persons at pleasure and with impunity, depend on it, this government cannot last. By such things the feelings of the best citizens will become more or less alienated from it, and thus it will be left without friends, or with too few, and those few too weak to make their friendship effectual. At such a time, and under such circumstances, men of sufficient talent and ambition will not be wanting to seize the opportunity, strike the blow, and overturn that fair fabric which for the last half century has been the fondest hope of the lovers of freedom throughout the world.

I know the American people are much attached to their government; I *Pointing* know they would suffer much for its sake; I know they would endure evils long and patiently before they would ever think of exchanging it for another,—yet, notwithstanding all this, if the laws be continually despised and disregarded, if their rights to be secure in their persons and property are held by no better tenure than the caprice of a mob, the alienation of their affections from the government is the natural consequence; and to that, sooner or later, it must come. Here then is one point at which danger may be expected.

The question recurs, "How shall we fortify against it?" The answer is *SATISFACTION* simple. Let every American, every lover of liberty, every well-wisher to his pos- *(OR SOLUTION)* terity swear by the blood of the Revolution never to violate in the least particular *STEP* the laws of the country, and never to tolerate their violation by others. As the patriots of '76 did to the support of the Declaration of Independence, so to the *Statement* support of the Constitution and laws let every American pledge his life, his property, and his sacred honor—let every man remember that to violate the law is to trample on the blood of his father, and to tear the charter of his own and his children's liberty. Let reverence for the laws be breathed by every American *Explanation* mother to the lisping babe that prattles on her lap; let it be taught in schools, in seminaries, and in colleges; let it be written in primers, spelling books, and in almanacs; let it be preached from the pulpit, proclaimed in legislative halls, and enforced in courts of justice. And, in short, let it become the political religion of the nation; and let the old and the young, the rich and the poor, the grave and the gay of all sexes and tongues and colors and conditions, sacrifice unceasingly upon its altars.

While ever a state of feeling such as this shall universally or even very generally prevail throughout the nation, vain will be every effort, and fruitless every attempt, to subvert our national freedom.

When I so pressingly urge a strict observance of all the laws, let me not *Explanation* be understood as saying there are no bad laws, or that grievances may not arise for the redress of which no legal provisions have been made. I mean to say no such thing. But I do mean to say that although bad laws, if they exist, should be repealed as soon as possible, still, while they continue in force, for the sake of example they should be religiously observed. So also in unprovided cases. If such arise, let proper legal provisions be made for them with the least possible delay, but till then let them, if not too intolerable, be borne with.

There is no grievance that is a fit object of redress by mob law. In any case that may arise, as, for instance, the promulgation of abolitionism, one of two positions is necessarily true—that is, the thing is right within itself, and therefore deserves the protection of all law and all good citizens, or it is wrong, and therefore proper to be prohibited by legal enactments; and in neither case is the inter-position of mob law either necessary, justifiable, or excusable.

But it may be asked, "Why suppose danger to our political institutions? Have we not preserved them for more than fifty years? And why may we not for fifty times as long?"

We hope there is no sufficient reason. We hope all danger may be over-come; but to conclude that no danger may ever arise would itself be extremely dangerous. There are now, and will hereafter be, many causes, dangerous in their tendency, which have not existed heretofore, and which are not too insig-nificant to merit attention. That our government should have been maintained in its original form from its establishment until now is not much to be wondered at. It had many props to support it through that period, which now are decayed and crumbled away. Through that period it was felt by all to be an undecided exper-iment; now it is understood to be a successful one. Then, all that sought celeb-rity and fame and distinction expected to find them in the success of that experi-ment. Their all was staked upon it; their destiny was inseparably linked with it. Their ambition aspired to display before an admiring world a practical demon-stration of the truth of a proposition which had hitherto been considered at best no better than problematical—namely, the capability of a people to govern them-selves. If they succeeded, they were to be immortalized; their names were to be transferred to counties, and cities, and rivers, and mountains; and to be revered and sung, toasted through all time. If they failed, they were to be called knaves, and fools, and fanatics for a fleeting hour; then to sink and be forgotten.

They succeeded. The experiment is successful, and thousands have won their deathless names in making it so. But the game is caught; and I believe it is true that with the catching end the pleasures of the chase. This field of glory is harvested, and the crop is already appropriated. But new reapers will arise, and they too will seek a field. It is to deny what the history of the world tells us is true, to suppose that men of ambition and talents will not continue to spring up amongst us. And when they do, they will as naturally seek the gratification of their ruling passion as others have done before them. The question then is, Can that gratification be found in supporting and maintaining an edifice that has been erected by others? Most certainly it cannot. Many great and good men, suf-ficiently qualified for any task they should undertake, may ever be found whose ambition would aspire to nothing beyond a seat in Congress, a gubernatorial or a presidential chair; but such belong not to the family of the lion, or the tribe of the eagle. What! think you these places would satisfy an Alexander, a Caesar, or a Napoleon? Never! Towering genius disdains a beaten path. It seeks regions hith-erto unexplored. It seeks no distinction in adding story to story upon the monu-ments of fame erected to the memory of others. It denies that it is glory enough to serve under any chief. It scorns to tread in the footsteps of any predecessor, however illustrious. It thirsts and burns for distinction; and if possible, it will have it, whether at the expense of emancipating slaves or enslaving freemen. Is it unreasonable, then, to expect that some man possessed of the loftiest genius, coupled with ambition sufficient to push it to its utmost stretch, will at some time spring up among us? And when such a one does, it will require the people to be united with each other, attached to the government and laws, and generally intelligent, to successfully frustrate his designs.

Distinction will be his paramount object; and although he would as willingly, perhaps more so, acquire it by doing good as harm, yet, that opportunity being past, and nothing left to be done in the way of building up, he would set boldly to the task of pulling down. Here, then, is a probable case, highly dangerous, and such a one as could not have well existed heretofore.

Another reason which once was, but which, to the same extent, is now no more, has done much in maintaining our institutions thus far. I mean the powerful influence which the interesting scenes of the Revolution had upon the passions of the people as distinguished from their judgment. By this influence, the jealousy, envy, and avarice incident to our nature, and so common to a state of peace, prosperity, and conscious strength, were for the time in a great measure smothered and rendered inactive, while the deep-rooted principles of hate, and the powerful motive of revenge, instead of being turned against each other, were directed exclusively against the British nation. And thus, from the force of circumstances, the basest principles of our nature were either made to lie dormant, or to become the active agents in the advancement of the noblest of causes — that of establishing and maintaining civil and religious liberty.

But this state of feeling must fade, is fading, has faded, with the circumstances that produced it.

I do not mean to say that the scenes of the Revolution are now or ever will be entirely forgotten, but that, like everything else, they must fade upon the memory of the world, and grow more and more dim by the lapse of time. In history, we hope, they will be read of, and recounted, so long as the Bible shall be read; but even granting that they will, their influence cannot be what it heretofore has been. Even then they cannot be so universally known nor so vividly felt as they were by the generation just gone to rest. At the close of that struggle, nearly every adult male had been a participator in some of its scenes. The consequence was that of those scenes, in the form of a husband, a father, a son, or a brother, a living history was to be found in every family — a history bearing the indubitable testimonies of its own authenticity, in the limbs mangled, in the scars of wounds received, in the midst of the very scenes related — a history, too, that could be read and understood alike by all, the wise and the ignorant, the learned and the unlearned. But those histories are gone. They can be read no more forever. They were a fortress of strength; but what invading foemen could never do, the silent artillery of time has done—the leveling of its walls. They are gone. They were a forest of giant oaks; but the all-restless hurricane has swept over them, and left only here and there a lonely trunk, despoiled of its verdure, shorn of its foliage, unshading and unshaded, to murmur in a few more gentle breezes, and to combat with its mutilated limbs more ruder storms, then to sink and be no more.

They were pillars of the temple of liberty; and now that they have crumbled away, that temple must fall unless we, their descendants, supply their places with other pillars, hewn from the solid quarry of sober reason. Passion has helped us, but can do so no more. It will in future be our enemy. Reason—cold, calculating, unimpassioned reason—must furnish all the materials for our future support and defense. Let those materials be molded into general intelligence, sound morality, and, in particular, a reverence for the Constitution and laws; and that we improved to the last, that we remained free to the last, that we revered his name to the last, that during his long sleep we permitted no hostile foot to pass over or desecrate his resting-place, shall be that which to learn the last trump shall awaken our Washington.

VISUALIZATION STEP (Briefly developed by Method of Contrast)

Upon these let the proud fabric of freedom rest, as the rock of its basis, and, as truly as has been said of the only greater institution, "the gates of hell shall not prevail against it."

ACTION STEP (OR CONCLUSION)

The student speech which follows was prepared by Mr. Richard Marvin. As we have emphasized before, the personal experiences of a speaker, presented either by themselves or in combination with information and judgments drawn from others, always furnish a potential source of speech materials (see pages 288–290). When these experiences are in some way unusual or dramatic, they may create a credibility and persuasiveness which could not otherwise be achieved.

Mr. Marvin's speech, calling for prison reform and asking for a more constructive attitude toward ex-convicts on the part of society, was delivered in a contest conducted by The Interstate Oratorical Association. By referring to things which he himself learned and to situations he had personally experienced, he was able to develop both the *problem* and the *solution steps* of his speech in a particularly striking way. Moreover, the frank announcement of his own past, as made during his first few seconds before the audience, piques the attention and causes the hearer to anticipate with interest the ideas to be presented in the body of the talk.

MAN'S OTHER SOCIETY[3]

Richard Marvin

When you look at me, it is easy to see several similarities between us. I have two arms, two legs, a brain, and a heart just like you. These are my hands, and they are just like yours. Like you I also have wants and desires; I am capable of love and hate. I can laugh and I can cry. Yes, I'm just like you, except for one very important fact — I am an *ex-con.*

The word *ex-con* is a rough word. It means that I committed a crime, was arrested, convicted of Misapplication of Federal Funds, sentenced, and served time. For eleven months and eleven days I was part of Man's Other Society.

On June 16, 1959, I was sentenced to a term not to exceed two years in a federal institution. I was taken to the United States Federal Penitentiary, Terre Haute, Indiana, where I stayed for two months. I was then transferred to the Federal Correctional Institution at Sandstone, Minnesota, where I served until my parole was granted.

You have read about prison life in books and periodicals. You have seen in the movies and on television, dramatizations concerning prison activity. Maybe you have wondered — What is it really like? I no longer wonder. I have served time. I know what it is like to live behind prison bars.

Until a person has his freedom taken from him, he can never fully appreciate how precious it really is. Think what it means to go for a walk, a long walk in one direction — to be able to take your car and drive through the countryside — to pick up a child, hold him in your arms, and listen to his childish chatter — to reach into your pocket and take a nickel — to gaze upon the third finger of your left hand and to see your wedding ring. These are some of the things which you cannot have in the prison community.

How many of you know that as an inmate in a federal institution I was allowed to write three letters a week, to an approved correspondent? Did you know that I could spend five hours per month visiting with my family, or that I was allowed to receive one package a year, at Christmas time; and it had to be of a certain size, weight, and could contain only specific items?

During my three-hundred-and-forty-six days as an inmate I saw many things. I met men I never knew existed before. My dorm mates were murderers, rapists, and dope addicts. You name them and I dormed with them. I had the opportunity to talk with them and to hear the very twisted thoughts which they had.

During this period of time I also learned many things. I can go out on the parking lot, take your car, start it, and I don't need your keys. I have acquired the ability whereby I can take my bare hands and kill you, just like this. I know more ways of taking your money from you than I can possibly remember. I have become an accomplished poker player, and believe me when I say that I can deal from the bottom of the deck with the best of them.

Oscar Wilde put it this way in his poem entitled "Ballad of Reading Gaol":

> The Vilest deeds like poison weeds,
> Bloom well in prison air,
> It is only what is good in Man,
> That wastes and withers there.

Now you may be thinking: Well, what did he expect; he asked for it, didn't he? And you are right; I got exactly what I deserved. I am ashamed of having done time, but I did; and although I would give my right arm to be able to turn back the pages of time, it cannot be done. The purpose of the prison, however, is not only to confine a man, but it also has the obligation to take that individual and return him to society as a rehabilitated human being. Does the taking of a man's wedding ring from him, allowing him to write three letters a week, or allowing him to visit with his family but five hours a month—do these things aid in rehabilitation of an inmate? The answer is NO. They do not.

It is easy to stand here and criticize the prison community, especially after one has done time in it. Criticism of this nature, however, bears with it very little validity, unless the person making the accusations stands ready to propose a program that will eliminate the evils to which he objects.

The problems of the prison are many and they are varied. In my estimation, however, there is one that stands out above all others. It concerns itself with the mistaken idea, which still persists, that there is a direct relationship between the seriousness of a man's crime and his potential for rehabilitation. William Krasner, a noted writer in the field of criminology, states that the dominant correctional philosophy is that the penitentiary is a kind of purifying flame into which the sinner must be thrust and held until he is punished, purged, or consumed. Mr. Krasner then goes on to say that society fails to realize that the prison door swings both ways, and unless a man dies in the institution he will some day return to society.

The program which I propose consists of three steps, and if they are followed, they will go a long way toward elevating rehabilitation to its proper position in the field of prison operation.

Step number one—segregation. The first-time offenders will have to be segregated from the general prison population. Once a man has become institutionalized, it is almost impossible to change him. I recall a young man I met in Sandstone who was twenty-seven years old. His life of crime began when he was sixteen; and in the eleven years that followed, he spent a total of less than six months in free society. He did time in five different state and federal prisons. Then there was the man who was sentenced the same day I was. He was fifty-one years of age and in the past twenty-seven years had spent less than two years as a free man. I could give you many other examples that would illustrate the fact that the prison is not returning men to society in a reformed condition. I am not trying to get you to believe that all of us criminals are reformable. You know and I know that is not so. What I am saying is that the best chance for rehabilitation lies with that first-time offender provided he can be kept from association with the time-hardened inmate.

Step number two—social education. You would be surprised at the number of men who enter the institution with the idea that society owes them a living. Unless this attitude is changed in the institution, he will return to society in the same frame of mind. This part of my program demands very careful planning so that the desired results can be achieved.

Step number three—educate society. In order for this program to be accomplished, society will have to be made to realize that an inmate is a human being. Father Clark of St. Louis, Missouri, who has been called the "Hoodlum Priest" because of his work with released prisoners, gives the following point of view on how society treats the released inmate. He says: "We boycott him all the way down the line—economically, socially, morally. It's very tough to get a job, own a home, lead any kind of normal life. The unions don't want him; the bonding companies and Armed Forces won't have him." Society will have to be willing to accept him upon his release; and, even more important, they will have to be willing to provide him with gainful employment.

To succeed, this program needs the interest of the general public. How many of you know what goes on behind the walls of your state institutions? How is the inmate treated? Is the correctional program of a progressive nature? Do the prison and the personnel therein provide an atmosphere that is conducive to rehabilitation? These are questions that need answers. Unless we are willing to take an active interest in this problem, rehabilitation will always occupy a position of secondary importance rather than being the number-one goal of prison operation.

In June of this year I will receive my Baccalaureate Degree with a Bachelor of Science in Education. I hope to join the Federal Prison System as an Assistant Director of Education in one of its thirty-two federal institutions. There I will be given an opportunity to set up and conduct a program of social education. I am one of the lucky ones. For everyone like me there are hundreds who are allowed to fall by the wayside because of the indifference of society. I ask of you to keep in mind that the prisoner doesn't need your sympathy, and he doesn't need your charity, but he does need your help, and this he needs most desperately. The Bible puts it in no uncertain terms when it tells us that you should do unto others as you would have them do unto you, for you are your brother's keeper.

FOOTNOTES

[1]Selections from Lincoln's Addresses, Inaugurals and Letters, *ed. Percival Chubb (New York: The Macmillan Company, 1925), pp. xvi–xvii.*

[2]*Originally printed in the* Sangamo Journal, *February 3, 1838.*

[3]*Reprinted by permission of Mr. Jimmie D. Trent, Executive Secretary, Interstate Oratorical Association.*

Problems and Probes

1. Recall a persuasive speech that you have heard recently. Reconstruct as completely as possible the speech and the situation in which it was delivered. Describe the nature and purpose of the gathering, the initial attitude of the audience, the type of claim the speaker advanced, the methods he used to develop and support it, and the extent to which he made adjustments to the listeners' attitudes, beliefs, and value-orientations. Finally, estimate the probable effect the speech had in influencing the audience to accept his claim or proposal.

2. With several other members of your class, arrange to attend a meeting at which one or more speeches to persuade are presented (an intercollegiate debate, a political rally, or a meeting of the student senate). Using the analytical bases in Problem/Probe 1, prepare a joint report describing the event and its effectiveness.

3. Find in some suitable source a speech centering on a claim of policy, another on a claim of fact, and a third on a claim of value. Outline each of these speeches carefully. How do they compare in structure with the patterns of development recommended on pages 518–524? Give reasons for any major departures from those patterns.

4. Turn in to your instructor four claims of fact which cannot be settled by observation, experimentation, or direct recourse to printed data and which, therefore, would make subjects for speeches to persuade.

5. Make a list of five of your personal beliefs or convictions that might provide suitable subjects for speeches on claims of policy. Compile a similar list for speeches on claims of value.

6. Listen to a speech to persuade—a speech delivered in a face-to-face situation or on television—and comment on the speaker's skill in using verbal and nonverbal communication. Did the speaker's delivery aid him or her in achieving conviction among the listeners? Explain how and why.

7. Which of the two following methods do you think is more likely to ensure full and lasting persuasion: (*a*) impressing your listeners with a motive for believing what you want them to believe or (*b*) showing them the logic of your proposal by presenting well-supported information and well-reasoned arguments? Discuss your choice.

8. On pages 527–529, we considered some of the special techniques especially useful in the speech to persuade. Examine five or six speeches of this type, and find as many examples of these techniques as possible. Evaluate the effectiveness with which each of these devices is used.

9. Find in any suitable printed source several speeches having instances of each of the forms of reasoning described on pages 525–527. In each of these instances, how well does the reasoning meet the tests listed on those pages?

10. Study several newspaper editorials to determine the forms of reasoning used in them. In each case, apply the appropriate test to determine how valid the reasoning is. Do the same for a number of advertisements clipped from magazines, and also for several television commercials.

11. With your instructor's help, locate a historically important speech that was delivered to an audience exhibiting one of the attitudes described on pages 529–533 (interested but undecided, interested but hostile to the proposal, etc.). Study the speech to determine the means the speaker employed to adapt his or her arguments and appeals to the particular audience attitude. How well would you say the speaker succeeded?

Oral Activities and Speaking Assignments

1. Conduct a class discussion on the ethics of persuasion. (See again Chapter 17, pp. 457–463.) Consider these questions, among others: What methods and appeals may legitimately be used in effecting persuasion? What methods and appeals should always be avoided? Are there any circumstances in which a person not only has the right, but the obligation to undertake to persuade others by any means at his or her disposal?

2. Choose a subject for a six-minute persuasive speech. In making your choice, consider the subject possibilities which you developed for Problems/Probes 4 and 5 above and also those listed below. Build your speech on the pattern provided by the motivated sequence. Develop a strong need

directly related to the interests and desires of your listeners. Show through reasoning and examples how your proposal will satisfy this need. Use the positive, negative, or contrasting method to build the visualization step (see again pages 374–375).

Conquering urban blight
A fair deal for the farmer
Controlling the use of addictive drugs
Improving race relations
Bridging the "generation gap"
Raising the level of television programs
Teaching children to read
Religion and life
Reforming the undergraduate curriculum
The protection of human rights
Government programs for the poor
Improving our mental hospitals
Meeting the increased cost of public education
Protecting the consumer

Suggestions for Further Reading

Kenneth E. Andersen, *Persuasion: Theory and Practice* (Boston: Allyn & Bacon, Inc., 1971).

Erwin P. Bettinghaus, *Persuasive Communication*, 2nd ed. (New York: Holt, Rinehart & Winston, Inc., 1973).

Gary Cronkhite, *Persuasion: Speech and Behavioral Change* (Indianapolis: The Bobbs-Merrill Company, Inc., 1969).

Marvin Karlins and Herbert I. Abelson, *Persuasion: How Opinions and Attitudes Are Changed*, 2nd ed. (New York: Springer Publishing Company, Inc., 1970), Chapters III, IV, and V, pp. 41–106.

Daniel Katz, ed., *Public Opinion Quarterly* XXIV (Summer 1960). Special edition on attitude change.

Charles U. Larson, *Persuasion: Reception and Responsibility* (Belmont, Calif.: Wadsworth Publishing Company, Inc., 1973).

Roger E. Nebergall, "The Social Judgment-Involvement Approach to Attitude and Attitude Change," *Western Speech* XXX (Fall 1966): 209–215.

Thomas M. Scheidel, *Persuasive Speaking* (Glenview, Ill.: Scott, Foresman and Company, 1967).

21
THE SPEECH TO ACTUATE

Unlike the speech to persuade, which attempts to alter the beliefs of the listeners or to renew their enthusiasm for a conviction already held, the speech to actuate seeks an immediate, overt response from the audience. It asks people to commit themselves on the spot by signing a petition, making a contribution, standing up to be counted, going out on a strike, engaging in a protest march—in other words, not only thinking or believing something, but taking definite *action* on it.

SITUATIONS REQUIRING SPEECHES TO ACTUATE

Any situation in which it is appropriate to call for immediate action, rather than mere mental resolution or the intention to act at some indefinite time in the future, provides a suitable occasion for a speech to actuate. Hence such speeches frequently are given in *deliberative* or *legislative bodies* by persons who wish other members to vote for a motion they have introduced or to support a program they favor. *Speeches presented at political rallies* or *mass meetings, lawyers' pleas before juries*, and *evangelistic sermons* are common examples of this type of talk. The characteristics of *immediacy* and *overt action by listeners* are, then, the distinguishing marks of the speech to actuate.

THE PURPOSE: TO MOVE LISTENERS TO ACTION

While the purpose of a speech to actuate is to elicit from the audience some form of specific behavior, the request for this action usually will fall on deaf ears unless the listeners first are convinced of the need and the practicability of the proposal and are moved to act upon it. Therefore, the two *secondary* or intermediate purposes of a speech to actuate are (1) to persuade and (2) to motivate the audience.

In those cases where the behavior requested must continue over a period of days or weeks, it is especially important that the speaker persuade the audience of the need and practicability of the proposed course of action. The determination and enthusiasm which the listeners feel as the speaker concludes may dissipate rapidly when they come out on the cold street corner where they are to hand out literature or when they encounter the rebuffs of the first persons to whom they attempt to sell tickets. In all types of persuasive speaking, the speaker has the obligation to support recommendations with sound evidence and valid arguments. In a speech to actuate, however, such support is more than a question of ethics; it is indispensable for attaining the action the speaker seeks.

THE MANNER OF SPEAKING FOR THE SPEECH TO ACTUATE

A speech to actuate usually calls for a relatively forceful or dynamic manner of delivery. This does not mean that you must shout and wave your arms wildly. It does mean, however, that your delivery must be animated and must mirror an inner intensity of belief and feeling. You cannot stir an audience to action unless your own enthusiasm and commitment to the cause are evident.

Above all, avoid the actions of a demagog or rabble-rouser. In presenting a speech to actuate, your most important personal assets are integrity, sincerity, and balance of judgment. Make it evident that you have thought long and carefully about the course of action you recommend; be honestly enthusiastic; pattern your vocal and physical delivery on the model of a well-informed and responsible individual who is genuinely aroused. A delivery of this type can be highly effective in moving people to action.

CHARACTERISTICS OF THE CONTENT OF ACTUATIVE SPEECHES

As we already have suggested, the speech to actuate is closely related to the speech to persuade, differing only in the fact that it attempts to translate belief or feeling into immediate, overt behavior. For this reason, its contents will be similar to the contents of a persuasive speech. Evidence and reasoning must be infused with powerful motivation and vivid imagery, and the leading ideas must be expressed in striking and concrete language. Be ever alert for opportunities to cast your proposal into an appropriate catch-phrase or to throw ideas into dramatic contrast.

THE ORGANIZATION OF THE SPEECH TO ACTUATE

In organization, the speech to actuate makes full use of each of the steps in the motivated sequence, the ideas being developed and arranged in accordance with those steps, as follows:

Attention Step

Although the attention step of a speech to actuate is usually short, it is extremely important. If people are to be motivated to act, everything in your speech, from the very first words to the very last, must drive strongly and steadily at generating the behavior you desire. Moreover, what you say as you begin should contribute directly toward clarifying the action you propose. Do not waste time by telling a funny story that has only a marginal bearing on your purpose, or by reading a quotation which—though timely and interesting—might point the audience in a different direction. Be brief, but be direct and forceful. From the very first moment, begin to build toward the specific action you wish your hearers to take.

Need Step

If the audience already is aware of the need for the action you recommend, review that need briefly, perhaps adding one or two illustrations which show its urgent nature, and remind your listeners of significant ways in which it affects them. When, on the other hand, the audience is unaware of the need or does not recognize its full scope and importance, develop the need step at some length and with strong emphasis. Use the four speech elements described earlier in connection with the motivated sequence; namely:

1. *Statement.* State clearly the specific need or problem which requires action.
2. *Illustration.* Give one or two examples which further clarify this need.
3. *Ramification.* Employ as many forms of support as may be required to make this need convincing and impressive.
4. *Pointing.* Show how your listeners are involved—how their health, security, happiness, etc., are directly affected.

Satisfaction Step

Combine solid proof of the practicability of your proposal with strong motivation for doing as you recommend. Show that the action you are urging actually will raise the money, produce the improvement you claim, or remove the evils that you decry. Support your contention by showing that similar actions have had these results in the past, or are now having these results in other states or communities. Give facts and figures. Take full advantage of the human wants or needs described in Chapter 9. Show how the action you advocate will be easy to perform, or relatively cheap, or will bring prestige to the person or group performing it. Fit your motivational appeals to the listeners you are addressing. If security is their dominant motive, show how your proposal will satisfy it. If they value self-enhancement or freedom of action, emphasize how your plan can help them realize those desires. Be ethical, of course, in your use of motivational appeals, and always aim at people's nobler desires rather than their baser drives. But, within these limits, *motivate your audience as strongly as you can.* Logical arguments can produce the conviction that sustains action once it is under way; strong motive appeals, however, are needed to arouse people from their apathy and prompt them to action in the first place.

Visualization Step

Use the positive or joint rather than the negative method for developing the visualization step, as explained on pages 374–375. If you tell an audience how bad things will be if they do not act as you urge, that description must support your proposal directly; otherwise it may crystallize negative or inhibitory ideas in their minds. On the other hand, a positive description of benefits, especially when projected in vivid and compelling language, clarifies the goal toward which the proposed action is directed and is itself a strong motivating factor.

Action Step

The action step must continue the strong motivation which you launched in the satisfaction and visualization steps, and it must review the arguments which prove your proposed action necessary and practicable. *In addition*, the action step should contain *a clear and sufficiently detailed statement of exactly what you want the listeners to do or exactly where they should go to do it.* All too often speakers get their audiences aroused and determined to act, but fail to give them precise directions for carrying out the action. Sometimes the listeners do not know exactly where to go to register or vote, or the hours at which the polling places will be open. They may not know exactly where to send their contributions or how to address the envelope. They are sometimes left with only a vague impression concerning the corner on which the mass rally is to be held or the hour at which they are to assemble.

Even with the best of intentions, most individuals are remiss about initiating the inquiries which will bring them the needed information. They tend to say, "Yes, I must find that address, but I am so busy today that I will wait until tomorrow." The trouble is that one "tomorrow" follows another, and the matter continues to drift. To help ensure action, then, make such inquiries unnecessary.

Before concluding your speech, state fully and explicity—repeating information you have given in earlier steps if necessary—exactly what you want done, and exactly where, when, and how to do it. Remember: *what, where, when, how*—and *now*. When your hearers are armed with this information, they are much more likely to act as you want them to.

A SAMPLE OUTLINE

The following outline was prepared for a student speech, "Filtering Our Industrial Waste," by Howard Brown and presented by him to an audience presumed to be the Board of Directors of the Central Fibre Products Company. As the company's production engineer, Mr. Brown urged the purchase of new equipment. Note how he has used the principles and methods described in this chapter in an attempt to move his audience to action.

FILTERING OUR INDUSTRIAL WASTE

Attention Step

    I. The decision we reach today can mean greater profit for Central Fibre or a continuation of our practice of literally throwing money down the drain.

Need Step

    I. Our present waste-disposal method is seriously inadequate.
- A. We need to diminish the amount of stream pollution caused by the waste water of our plant.
  1. Pressure has been brought under National Law #3972 and a corresponding state law by the State Board of Sanitation.
  2. The pollution we cause is equivalent to that of a city of 60,000 population.
- B. We are letting substantial profits drain into the Wabash River.
  1. Every minute we discharge water containing from three to twelve pounds of minute usable fiber.
  2. Every day we pump 15,500,000 gallons of water which we heat, use, and discharge into the river.
     a. This water carries with it countless B.T.U.'s we have added.
- C. In short, our disposal is both illegal and inefficient.

II. We need a practical solution of this problem that will meet the following requirements:
   A. The discharged water must be brought within the standards required by state and national laws.
   B. The system must be reliable in operation.
   C. It must be economical.
   D. It should reduce our present waste.
   E. If possible, it should help improve the quality of our product.

Satisfaction Step

I. The installation of an Oliver Vacuum 8 × 10 Saveall in our mill will solve our problem.
   A. The Saveall would be conveniently located at the west end of the machine room in our mill.
      1. Here it would be close to the machines, screens, digestors, and beaters.
   B. Here is the way it operates:
      1. This oversize flow sheet shows the simplified operation of the Saveall in paper-mill use. (Show and explain chart.)
      2. These detailed working drawings and actual photographs of the Saveall show how it has been installed at other mills. (Show drawings and pictures.)
   C. The Saveall will meet the requirements of a practical solution:
      1. It will reduce our stream pollution below the legal limits allowed by statute. (Read specifications and guarantee.)
      2. The Oliver Filter Company is a very reliable firm of worldwide reputation.
         a. The Saveall was designed for paper-mill use.
         b. Savealls are being used successfully by 1300 paper mills in all parts of the world.
      3. The plan is economical.
         a. The original cost of the Saveall will be $75,000.
         b. Since servicing is done by the Oliver Company, upkeep will be small.
         c. Added labor costs will be nil.

4. The Saveall in a short time will pay for itself in the amount of fiber recovered.
   a. The Terre Haute Paper Company reports a saving of 660 tons of fiber last year.
   b. The Tama, Iowa, mill has shown a 900-ton saving per year.
5. By reusing the "white" or clear water processed by the Saveall, higher grade products can be made.
   a. The Terre Haute mill has produced better products.
   b. The Tama mill also improved the quality of its products.

II. The Oliver Saveall is a practical and economical solution to our problem.

Visualization Step

I. By installing an Oliver Saveall, we can save an average of 5 pounds of fiber per minute—7 tons a day.
   A. At $15 a ton, in one day our saving would be $105.
   B. In less than two and one-half years the Saveall will have paid for itself. (Show graph of cumulated savings vs. cost.)

II. The clear water we use will be free of river refuse.
   A. This will speed up production.
   B. It will give us a better grade of product.

III. We shall be free from danger of legal action because of stream pollution.

Action Step

I. I recommend we order the Oliver Saveall immediately.
   A. The law demands action on our part.
   B. An Oliver Saveall will meet that demand and at the same time will end the flow of thousands of our dollars down the Wabash.

A SAMPLE SPEECH TO ACTUATE

In the following address, Thomas J. Watson, Jr., Chairman of the Board of International Business Machines Corporation, presents a strong plea for a national program of medical care. The occasion was "Industrial Day at Mayo," a meeting of the Mayo Foundation, Rochester, Minnesota, November 19, 1970. Included in the audience were supporters of the Foundation — executives from seventy major areas and national companies — and former President Lyndon B. Johnson, who was also one of the speakers.

The organization of the materials reflects in an interesting way how the motivated sequence may be used to build an actuative speech. To gain the *attention* of his audience, Mr. Watson employs a series of rather startling statements. He then establishes the *need* with a series of short, hard-hitting facts and specific instances. In the *satisfaction* step, he contrasts "socialized medicine" with medical-care-as-usual and points out the urgency of effecting a compromise between the two. After a *visualization* of what is not happening — but ought to be — he calls forcefully for concerted *action*, pleading with his prestigious audience to "build a bonfire of persuasion — to speak out, to demand change, and not stop pushing for action until we get the legislation we need," and closing on a powerful note that action must be taken *now*. Although demarcation lines between successive steps are not always sharply drawn and some overlapping is evident, in many ways this address is a well-conceived and well-organized speech to actuate.

MEDICAL CARE[1]

Thomas J. Watson, Jr.

Let me start by asking a question that this great medical center brings to mind: How would you like to live in a country which — according to the figures available in the United Nations — during the past two decades has dropped from seventh in the world to sixteenth in the prevention of infant mortality; has dropped in female life expectancy from sixth to eighth; has dropped in male life expectancy from tenth to twenty-fourth; and which has bought itself this unenviable trend by spending more of its gross national product for medical care — $1 out of every $14 — than any other country on the face of the earth? *Attention Step*

You know the country I am talking about: Our own USA, the home of the free, the home of the brave, and the home of a decrepit, inefficient, high-priced system of medical care.

Just look for a moment at what some of the figures mean. They mean that in infant mortality we have been overtaken by France, the UK, and Japan; that in male life expectancy we have been overtaken by France, Japan, West Germany and Italy. *Need Step*

I know experts can disagree over our precise international standing. And I realize that medical problems in the United States, Europe and Japan are not identical.

But the evidence overwhelmingly indicates that we are falling down on the job, heading in the wrong direction, and becoming as a nation a massive medical disgrace.

Now, it may seem undiplomatic to stand here under the banner of the Mayo Clinic and make an accusation like that.

I know American medicine has scored many brilliant triumphs—the magnificent record of this institution outstanding among them, including the Mayo Brothers' pioneer work in surgery; and the discovery and use of cortisone, which brought Doctors Kendall and Hench of Mayo the Nobel Prize; the work of Dr. Jonas Salk, who made one of the most significant and heartwarming discoveries in history; of Dr. Bela Schick in eliminating diptheria; and of many others.

We have an outstanding record of individual achievement across the whole medical spectrum.

But despite all that, when I look up at the international scoreboard, I can come to only one conclusion: We are failing to fulfill adequately for all our people the first right set down in the Declaration of Independence—the right to life.

What do we have to do to restore that right to every man, every woman, every child in America?

First, as the Carnegie Commission said last month, I believe we have to beef up our arsenal: Train more doctors, more nurses, more paramedics; bail our medical and dental schools out of their present deep financial troubles; break ground for new hospitals and clinics; in a word, spend more money.

We Americans are great on that.

Show us a shortage—of airplanes or tanks or trucks or scientists or engineers or satellites—and we'll fix it.

And I believe we can do that kind of job just fine in medicine.

Second, we must build into the system better management, better organization, more incentives to increase productivity and cut inefficiency.

I find it shocking, for example, that comprehensive prepaid group practice, which has repeatedly delivered better care at lower costs, encounters legal roadblocks in more than half our states.

I find it shocking to read of Americans living in backwoods towns and city slums without a doctor or a dentist or a clinic.

I find it shocking that as 30,000 highly trained medical corpsmen return to civilian life every year—many from the field of battle—they too often discover, if they want to enter medicine as a career, that they have just one job open to them—hospital orderly.

We cannot continue to live with facts like these. We have to overhaul the system.

But as we do so, we should begin simultaneously to do the third part of the job: Put health care within reach of everyone in America.

And that means putting it within the reach of the poor.

I do not really believe, of course, that you can ever make the poor rich and the rich poor. But I do think we should have a floor for each American below which he cannot fall, and I believe this applies not only to his economic status, but also to his medical status.

For the plain fact is that under our present medical system, the poor suffer by far the most.

Moreover, if a person happens not to be white, the picture is even bleaker.

A nonwhite infant can expect to live six years less than a white infant.

The nonwhite infant mortality rate is the white rate multiplied by *two*.

The nonwhite maternal death rate is the white rate multiplied by *four*.

To me, all this adds up to a completely unacceptable situation, which I think is un-American, undemocratic and unfair.

How do we correct it, and extend coverage for medical bills to everyone?

Not just through tinkering with our present system of paying for health care.

Not just through trying to stretch the umbrella of private health insurance, which, despite its costliness, still doesn't come close to covering Americans today.

No, we need a far more thoroughgoing reform.

And that brings us up against that old taboo — "socialized medicine."

I completely believe in the American free-enterprise system. But when the system clearly fails to produce a much needed good, I think we should not flinch from looking to some sort of Government intervention to get the job done.

Satisfaction Step

Frequently in the past, we have faced up to such a requirement with new legislation: on workmen's compensation, child labor, the reduction of the work week, unemployment insurance, and social security.

I believe we face today the same kind of moment of truth in medicine.

And I believe we have only one choice before us that will work: some very new form of national health insurance.

Twenty-one years ago, we looked at national health insurance when President Truman urged it, and we rejected it.

And in 1949 we rejected it in part because of arguments like this which appeared that year in the June issue of the magazine of the American Medical Association under the title: "Wake up, America!"

The private profession of medicine is taking rapid strides toward the solution of this problem (of medical aid for the poor). Voluntary, prepaid hospitalization and professional insurance plans now protect 50 million Americans. . . . The American people enjoy a state of good health unequaled in the world today.

As a dyed-in-the-wool free trader, free enterpriser, and hater of bureaucracy, I accepted that argument in 1949, and I bet nearly everyone else in this room did, too.

But on the evidence—particularly the international evidence—I cannot accept it in 1970.

We need a dedicated and total effort to find a way to build a floor under each citizen of this country that assures much better quality and equality of medical services for all.

Visualization Step

A variety of plans have been advanced to this end in the Congress, by representatives of government, labor, business and the medical profession; but none of these plans is moving very fast, and our problem is compounding.

We do not need national health insurance as a political football in 1972.

We need a new national health insurance law, and we need it now—in the next session of the Congress. Indeed, I hope the Administration will put this at the top of its priority list for 1971.

To get that legislation, the partisans of varying plans—in the Congress, the American Medical Association, the AFL-CIO—must get together and compromise their differences.

Action Step

And to speed such compromise, I believe all of us as citizens—and I dare to include doctors—should start now to build a bonfire of persuasion—to speak out, to demand change, and not stop pushing for action until we get the legislation we need.

We can take pride in our system of universal public education, social security, and works laws.

The time has now arrived for us to have a system of universal public medicine in which we can also take pride.

A national program, of course, is not a panacea in itself. But as we look toward some sort of governmental approach to this problem, let us remember that the plans in Britain and the Scandinavian countries have proved very successful in keeping those countries in the front rank internationally. And certainly they have provided better medical service for all of the people than the systems they supplanted. To me, this is a tremendously compelling argument for keeping an open mind as we look for a solution.

Not long ago, on a visit to the California Institute of Technology, I read these words on a student poster: "Our age is characterized by the perfection of means and confusion of goals."

The goal before us in medicine is clear.

But we shall reach it only by doing what we have always done with our magnificent American system: fearlessly facing its faults, cutting them away, replacing them with something better, and moving on.

I think that same truth comes pounding through to us in the restless, pioneering lives of the Mayos—a truth which should guide and inspire us as we undertake the tough and crucial job which lies ahead: Bringing the fullness of American medical care to all the American people.

We must begin it now.

As the wealthiest, most powerful, best educated nation in the world—a people with a heroic history of pioneering and justice and compassion—I believe we can do no less.

FOOTNOTE

[1]*"Medical Care" by Thomas J. Watson, Jr. Address delivered on "Industrial Day at Mayo," a meeting of the Mayo Foundation, Rochester, Minnesota (November 1970), from* Representative American Speeches: 1970–1971, *published by The H. W. Wilson Company. Reprinted by permission of the author.*

Problems and Probes

1. Radio and television commercials, as well as advertisements in newspapers and magazines, are of course aimed at actuating listeners or readers. Compare the actuative methods and strategies used by the mass media with those recommended in this chapter for the public speaker. What similarities do you detect? In what way are the methods and strategies different? Describe special modifications and adaptations that might "work" usefully. Identify some actuative methods used by television and newspapers which are not used in face-to-face communication.

2. Formulate some statements of the ethical standards to which advertisers presumably adhere in their attempts to actuate buyers. Try to evaluate those standards. For instance, do advertisements in newspapers and on television usually give the full and unbiased information upon which intelligent action should be based? If not, in what respects and with what frequency do they appear to fall short? Would you agree or disagree with this statement: "Those attempts to actuate which are guided by high ethical and moral standards are, in the end, always more persuasive than those which are not"? Why do you answer as you do?

3. A leader of the French Revolution is reported to have looked out the window one day and said: "There goes the mob on their way to the palace. I must hurry to place myself at their head, for I am their leader." What implications does this statement have for speakers who seek to actuate audiences?

4. If you were presenting a speech to actuate, would you encourage questions and comments from the audience at its completion or would you discourage them? Defend your answer.

5. What motive appeals would you employ if you were attempting to induce an audience of college students to take the following actions: (*a*) contribute to the campus charity drive, (*b*) enlist in the Army, (*c*) study harder, (*d*) give up their automobiles, (*e*) have an annual physical examination, (*f*) learn to speak Russian, and (*g*) drop out of college?

6. Comment on this statement: "Most men act out of desire rather than reason; they only use reason to justify to themselves what they want to do anyway." Use the remark to formulate at least three valid and useful recommendations regarding speaker-listener relationships.

7. Devise a slogan or catch-phrase which you might use in a speech to actuate your hearers to respond positively to each of the following proposals:

> Work for the college student's right to vote in local elections.
> Participate actively in clean-up, paint-up week.
> Make an appointment for a dental checkup today.
> Enroll in a rapid-reading course.

Oral Activity and Speaking Assignment

1. Present a five-minute speech to actuate, the purpose of which is to persuade the members of your speech class to sign a petition requesting the alteration of an unpopular rule or the correction of an undesirable situation on the campus or in your community. Select a rule or situation which actually exists—not an imaginary or fictional one. Show your listeners why they should be concerned; explain why a petition of this kind has a good chance of influencing the authorities in charge; point out the advantages to be gained from acting as you recommend, etc. Use carefully reasoned arguments, strong motivation, and vivid and compelling language. Your delivery should conform to the suggestions offered in this chapter. At the close of your speech, pass the petition among the members of the class for signatures. You might, for example, urge your audience to sign a petition requesting one of the following changes:

> Graduating seniors should be excused from final examinations.
> The student government should be given complete control over "activity fees."
> Campus food service should be improved.

All curfew restrictions for men and women should be lifted.

Parking meters should be installed on X Street.

City garbage pickup should be put on a twice-a-week schedule.

Advertising sound trucks ought to be prohibited in the area of the campus.

The college should establish a cooperative bookstore (or grocery, or gasoline station).

Landlords renting to students should conform strictly to anti-discrimination laws.

The community should enter at once upon a plan of environmental protection.

Suggestions for Further Reading

Kenneth E. Andersen, *Persuasion: Theory and Practice* (Boston: Allyn & Bacon, Inc., 1971).

John W. Bowers and Donovan J. Ochs, *The Rhetoric of Agitation and Control* (Reading, Mass.: Addison-Wesley Publishing Company, Inc., 1971).

Gary Lynn Cronkhite, "Logic, Emotion, and the Paradigm of Persuasion," *Quarterly Journal of Speech* L (February 1964): 13–18.

B. J. Diggs, "Persuasion and Ethics," *Quarterly Journal of Speech* L (December 1964): 359–373.

Ted Robert Gurr, *Why Men Rebel* (Princeton, N.J.: Princeton University Press, 1970), Chapter VII, "The Communication of Aggressive Symbols," pp. 223–229.

Paul D. Holtzman, *The Psychology of Speakers' Audiences* (Glenview, Ill.: Scott, Foresman and Company, 1970), Chapter V, "Listener Motivational Factors," pp. 50–65.

Stephen Kosokoff and Carl W. Carmichael, "The Rhetoric of Protest: Song, Speech, and Attitude Change," *Southern Speech Journal* XXXV (Summer 1970): 295–302.

Paul E. Reid, "A Spectrum of Persuasive Design," *Speech Teacher* XIII (March 1964): 87–95.

Thomas M. Scheidel, *Persuasive Speaking* (Glenview, Ill.: Scott, Foresman and Company, 1967).

Herbert Simons, "Persuasion in Social Conflicts: A Critique of Prevailing Conceptions and a Framework for Future Research," *Speech Monographs* XXXIX (November 1972): 227–247.

22
SPECIAL TYPES OF SPEECHES
AND PUBLIC DISCUSSIONS

From the preceding chapters of Part Four, you have no doubt correctly concluded that speeches to inform, to persuade, and to actuate are the three types of one-to-many communication that you will most often be called upon to make. Many situations, however, require *special* types of speeches and presentations. You may have to introduce a visiting speaker or welcome a distinguished guest. You may be asked to pay tribute to an individual or a group, to nominate a candidate for office, or to present a good-will speech on behalf of your business or profession. In this chapter we shall consider briefly these special types of speeches, noting in each case the purpose toward which the speech is directed, the manner in which it should be delivered, the kinds of ideas it may contain, and the principles by which it is to be organized. In these special types of public communication, as we shall note, the motivated sequence again has certain useful applications. The chapter concludes with a brief consideration of the various forms of public discussion, including debate, and suggests how they may be adapted to the mass communication media of radio and television.

SPEECHES OF INTRODUCTION

Speeches of introduction usually are given by the person who arranged the program or by the chairperson or president of the group to be addressed. Sometimes, however, they are presented by another person who, because of personal association or professional interests, is especially well acquainted with the featured speaker.

Purpose and Manner of Speaking

The *purpose* of a speech of introduction is, of course, to create in the audience a desire to hear the speaker you are introducing. Everything else must be subordinated to this aim. Do not make a speech yourself or air your own views on the subject. You are only the speaker's *advance agent;* your job is to sell him or her to the audience. This task carries a twofold responsibility: (1) You must arouse listeners' curiosity about the speaker and/or subject, thus making it easier for him or her to get the attention of the audience. (2) You must do all that you reasonably can to generate audience respect for the speaker, thereby increasing the likelihood that listeners will respond favorably and positively to what he or she says or asks.

When giving a speech of introduction, your *manner of speaking* should be suited to the nature of the occasion, the closeness of your acquaintance with the speaker, and the speaker's prestige. If you were introducing a justice of the United States Supreme Court, for instance, it would hardly be appropriate to poke fun at him. Nor would this approach be tactful if the speaker were a stranger to you or if the occasion were serious and dignified. On the other hand, if you are presenting an old friend to a group of associates on an informal occasion, a solemn and dignified manner would be equally out of place. The difficulty is that many people know only *one* method: either they present every speaker with ponderous dignity regardless of the occasion and circumstance, or they make the introduction by telling a joke. Neither of these methods is "bad" in itself, but each should be used only in its proper place.

Regardless of the formality or informality of the occasion, a speech of introduction should always reflect sincere enthusiasm. Suggest by the way you talk about the speaker that you yourself are eager to hear him or her. Be careful, however, not to overdo it. Your audience usually will be able to sense if your enthusiasm is counterfeit or forced. If you have no real interest in the speaker, develop one — or ask someone else to make the introduction.

Formulating the Content of the Speech of Introduction

The better known and more respected a speaker is, the shorter your introduction can be. The less well known he or she is, the more you will need to arouse interest in the speaker's subject or build up his or her prestige. In general, however, observe these principles:

Do not talk about yourself. You may be tempted to express your own views on the subject or to recount anecdotes about your own experiences as a speaker. Avoid these self-references because they call attention to you rather than to the speaker.

Talk about the speaker. Who is he? What is his position in business, education, sports, or government? What experiences has he had that qualify him to speak on the announced subject? Build up the speaker's identity, tell what he knows or has done, but do not praise his ability as a speaker. Let the speaker *demonstrate* his communicative skills.

Emphasize the importance of the speaker's subject. For example, in introducing a speaker who is going to talk about the oil industry, you might say: "All of us drive automobiles in which we use the products made from petroleum. A knowledge of the way these products are manufactured and marketed is, therefore, certain to be valuable to our understanding and perhaps to our pocketbooks."

Stress the appropriateness of the subject or of the speaker. If your town is considering a program of renewal and revitalization, a speech by a city planner is likely to be timely and well received. If an organization or firm is marking an anniversary, the founder should—appropriately—be one of the speakers. Reference to such information is obviously in order and serves to relate the speaker more closely to the audience.

Organizing the Speech of Introduction

In a long and formal speech of introduction, you may wish to employ all five steps in the motivated sequence. Usually, however, one of the following abbreviated forms will suffice. Create attention and arouse interest by plunging directly into the (1) *need step*, in which you state the importance of the subject to the audience, and follow with the (2) *satisfaction step*, in which you state in sharply abbreviated form why the speaker is qualified to speak on this subject; then close with the (3) *action step*, in which the actual presentation of the speaker is made.

Sometimes who the speaker is may be more important than the subject he is going to discuss. In such instances, create attention by beginning with the (1) *satisfaction step*, in which you state the facts about the speaker, especially facts that are not ordinarily known or those that are of particular significance to the occasion; then proceed to the (2) *action step*, in which you present the speaker and make a brief announcement of his or her subject.

When time is short or the speaker is so well known that extreme brevity is desirable, gain attention by your salutation, "Ladies and Gentlemen," "Members of the Izaak Walton League," etc.; then move at once to the *action step*: a brief announcement of the speaker's name, position, and subject.

Under all circumstances, remember that the four primary virtues of a speech of introduction are *tact, brevity, sincerity,* and *enthusiasm.*

SPEECHES FOR COURTESY: WELCOMES, RESPONSES, ACCEPTANCES

Most persons active in business or civic life are, at one time or another, called upon to give a speech for courtesy either on their own behalf or on behalf of a group or organization they represent. Knowing what to say on such occasions can, of course, be a valuable asset.

Typical Situations Requiring Speeches for Courtesy

Speeches for courtesy commonly are given to fulfill one of three obligations: (1) *To welcome visitors or new members.* As a matter of courtesy, the presiding officer of an organization or one of its prominent members voices a greeting and extends a welcome to guests or newcomers. At a convention where persons from many places are gathered, the mayor of the host city or the president of the local branch of the organization welcomes the visiting delegates. (2) *To respond to a welcome or greeting.* An individual or group thus welcomed generally is expected to express appreciation for the greeting. (3) *To accept a gift or award.* When someone is given an award for an accomplishment or for a service rendered, usually it is appropriate for him to express his appreciation in a brief speech of response.

Purpose and Manner of Speaking for Speeches for Courtesy

The speech for courtesy has a double purpose: first, to express a genuine sentiment of hospitality or gratitude on the part of the speaker; and, second, to create good feeling in the audience. The success of such a speech, therefore, often depends in large part upon whether the listeners feel that the speaker's remarks are appropriate to the situation. When guests are present or acknowledgments are due, the audience expects the proper courtesies to be extended. Just as the courtesies of private life put people at ease, so public acts of courtesy create good feeling in an audience.

Suggest by your *manner* that you are genuinely pleased to extend or acknowledge the welcome, or to receive the award. In probably no other type of speech is there so great a temptation to repeat with oratorical flourishes a series of flowery platitudes. Resist this temptation. Speak sincerely and honestly.

Formulating the Content of the Courtesy Speech

Keep these guidelines in mind:

Indicate why you are speaking. Identify the circumstances out of which your speech arose. Name the visitors you are greeting or the guests you are welcoming. Mention the significance of the occasion for the persons being honored, for the group you represent, or for yourself.

Indicate for whom you are speaking. When you are acting as spokesman for a group, make clear that the greeting or acknowledgment comes from everyone and not from you alone.

Present complimentary facts about the person or persons to whom you are extending the courtesy. Review briefly the accomplishments or qualities of the person or group you are greeting or whose gift or welcome you are acknowledging.

Illustrate—do not argue. Present incidents and facts that make clear the importance of the occasion, but do not be contentious. Avoid areas of disagreement. Do not use a speech for courtesy as an opportunity to air your personal views on a controversial subject or to advance your own policies. Rather, express concretely and vividly the thoughts which probably are already in the minds of your listeners.

Organizing the Speech for Courtesy

Speeches for courtesy seldom require more than three of the steps in the motivated sequence. At times, only the satisfaction step—the actual greeting or expression of appreciation—is present. A need step is superfluous because from the very nature of the situation the audience naturally expects an act of courtesy to be performed. An action step is unnecessary because the speaker is not calling on the listeners for action. If all three of the remaining steps—attention, satisfaction, and visualization—are included, they may be developed thus:

Attention step. The opening may consist of a brief reference to the occasion, to the person or group addressed, or to the group for which you are spokesman. If you are accepting a gift or award, you may appropriately begin by referring to the donor of the gift or to the conditions under which the award is being made. Such references at the beginning of your speech should, however, be brief and should lead directly into the satisfaction step.

Satisfaction step. The bulk of the speech consists of the satisfaction step—the actual performance of the act of courtesy. In a speech of welcome or response, this step may be amplified by one or both of the following types of materials: (1) complimentary facts about the host, guest, or donor; and (2) facts about the group you represent—who it is that joins you in the welcome or response, the eagerness with which you have looked forward to the occasion, the preparations that have been made, or the nature of the program to follow.

When acknowledging a gift or award, mention may be made of the conditions under which the achievement was made, the persons who aided in carrying the project to a successful conclusion, and the appreciation felt for the recognition granted.

Visualization step. Again depending on the circumstances, the function of the visualization step in a speech for courtesy is to suggest anticipated pleasure in having the guests present, in being present as a guest, or in using the gift or award and remembering the donors of it. Many times, instead of forming a separate part of the speech, visualization is included in the discussion of the various points in the satisfaction step—a kind of parallel treatment. In either case, an expression of anticipated pleasure always should be included. At the end of the visualization step, close with a sincere reiteration of the greeting or acknowledgment.

All of these steps, we emphasize, will not always need to be used in speeches of this kind. The order of the steps also may vary with the situation. What is important is that your remarks leave the audience with a feeling that the demands of the situation have been met with good taste, sincerity, and warmth.

SPEECHES OF TRIBUTE: MEMORIALS, DEDICATIONS, FAREWELLS

A speaker may be called upon to pay tribute to another person's qualities or achievements. Such occasions range from the awarding of a trophy after an athletic contest to a eulogy at a memorial service. Sometimes tributes are paid to an entire group or class of people—for example, teachers, soldiers, or mothers—rather than to an individual.

Typical Situations Requiring Speeches of Tribute

Memorial services. Services to pay public honor to the dead usually include a speech of tribute or *eulogy*. Ceremonies of this kind may honor a famous person and be held years after his or her death. Witness, for example, the many speeches paying tribute to Abraham Lincoln down through the years since his death. More often, however, a eulogy honors someone personally known to the audience and recently deceased.

Dedications. Buildings, monuments, parks, etc., may be constructed or set aside to honor a worthy cause or to commemorate a person, a group of persons, a significant movement, an historic event, or the like. At their dedication, the speaker says something appropriate about the purpose to be served by the memorial and about the personage(s), event, or occasion thus commemorated.

Farewells. In general, speeches of farewell fall into one of three subcategories: (1) When a person retires or leaves one organization to join another or when anyone who is admired leaves the community where he has lived, the enterprise in which he has worked, or the office he has held, public appreciation of his fellowship and his accomplishments may be expressed by an associate or colleague in a speech befitting the circumstances. (2) Or, the individual who is departing may use the occasion to present a farewell address in which he voices his gratitude for the opportunities, consideration, and warmth afforded him by his co-workers and, perhaps, calls upon them to carry on the traditions and long-range goals which characterize the office or the enterprise. In both of these situations, of course, verbal tributes are being paid. What distinguishes them, basically, is whether the retiree or departing one is *speaking* or is being *spoken about*. (3) More rarely, when an individual—because of disagreements, policy-differences, organizational stresses, etc.—decides to resign or sever an important or long-standing association with a business or governmental structure, in a message of farewell he may elect to present publicly the basis of the disagreement and the factors prompting his resignation and departure. Public figures, particularly in politics, have from time to time used this form of farewell with a measure of success and satisfaction. Used thus, the form becomes, in part at least, a speech of self-defense or *apologia*.* A noteworthy case in point was General Douglas MacArthur's address to Congress ("Old Soldiers Never Die") following his dismissal by President Harry Truman.

Presentation of awards. Frequently, awards are presented to groups or individuals for outstanding achievements or meritorious service. Public notice often is taken, and the presentation calls for appropriate remarks from a speaker.

Purpose and Manner of Speaking for the Tribute Speech

The *purpose* of a speech of tribute is, of course, to create in those who hear it a sense of appreciation for the traits or accomplishments of the person or group to whom tribute is paid. If you cause your audience to realize the essential worth or importance of that person or group, you will have succeeded. But you may go further than this. You may, by honoring a person, arouse deeper devotion to the cause he represents. Did he give distinguished service to his community? Then strive to enhance the audience's civic pride and sense of service. Was he a friend to youth? Then try to arouse the feeling that working to provide opportunities for young people deserves the audience's support. Create a desire in

---

Note that dictionaries, in general, differentiate between apology and apologia. As Webster's Seventh New Collegiate Dictionary, for example, points out: "APOLOGY now commonly applies to an expression of regret for a mistake or wrong with implied admission of guilt or fault; like APOLOGIA it may be used to imply not an admission of guilt or error but a desire to make clear the grounds for some belief or course of action." For an insightful and thoroughgoing analysis of this type of speech, see B. L. Ware and Wil A. Linkugel, "They Spoke in Defense of Themselves: On the Generic Criticism of Apologia," Quarterly Journal of Speech LIX (October 1973): 273–283.

your listeners to emulate the person or persons honored. Make them want to develop the same virtues, to demonstrate a like devotion.

When making a speech of tribute, suit the *manner* of speaking to the unique aspect of the circumstance. A farewell banquet usually blends an atmosphere of merriment with a spirit of sincere regret. Dignity and formality are, on the whole, characteristic of memorial services, the unveiling of monuments, and similar dedicatory ceremonies. Regardless of the general tone of the occasion, however, in a speech of tribute avoid high-sounding phrases, bombastic oratory, and obvious "oiliness." These hollow elements will quickly dampen or destroy its effect. A simple, honest expression of admiration presented in clear and unadorned language is best.

Formulating the Content of Speeches of Tribute

Frequently, in a speech of tribute a speaker attempts to itemize all the accomplishments of the honored person or group. Such enumeration lacks impact because, in trying to cover everything, it emphasizes nothing. Plan, instead, to focus your remarks, as follows:

Stress dominant traits. If you are paying tribute to a person, select a few aspects of his personality which are especially likeable or praiseworthy, and relate incidents from his life or work to illustrate these distinguishing qualities.

Mention only outstanding achievements. Pick out only a few of the person's or group's most notable accomplishments. Tell about them in detail to show how important they were. Let your speech say, "Here is what this person (or group) has done; see how such actions have contributed to the well-being of our business or community."

Give special emphasis to the influence of the person or group. Show the effect that the behavior of the person or group has had on others. Many times, the importance of people's lives can be demonstrated not so much in any traits or material accomplishments as in the influence they exercised on associates.

Organizing the Speech of Tribute

Ordinarily you will have little difficulty in getting people to listen to a speech of tribute. The audience probably already knows and admires the person or group about whom you are to speak, and listeners are curious to learn what you are going to say concerning the individual or individuals to be honored.

Attention step. Your task, therefore, is to *direct* the attention of the audience toward those characteristics or accomplishments which you consider most important. There are three commonly used ways to do this: (1) Make a straight-forward, sincere statement of these commendable traits or achievements or of the influence they have had upon others. (2) Relate one or more instances which vividly illustrate them. (3) Relate an incident which shows the problems faced by your subject, thus leading directly into the need step.

Need step. The speech of tribute contains no real need step in the sense of demonstrating a problem confronting the audience. The tribute subsequently paid in the satisfaction step may be heightened, however, by emphasizing obstacles overcome or difficulties faced by the person or group being honored. This serves to bring into focus the traits or achievements which you wish to commend. John Kennedy's energetic life-style, for example, became the more noteworthy when contrasted with some of his severe illnesses and physical reverses of his earlier career.

A slightly different method is to point out not the personal problems of the person to whom tribute is paid but the problems of the organization which it was his official responsibility to meet or, in a still larger sense, the problems of society which his accomplishments helped solve. Thus an account of the extent and seriousness of the smoke-pollution problem in a large city might precede a tribute to the women and men who developed and enforced an effective smoke-control plan.

Satisfaction step. The lengthiest part of a speech of tribute usually will be the satisfaction step, for it is here that the tribute is actually paid. Relate a few incidents which show how the problems, personal or public, which you have outlined in the need step were met and surmounted. In doing this, be sure to demonstrate at least one of these three things: (1) How certain admirable traits — vision, courage, and tenacity, for example — made it possible to deal successfully with these problems; (2) how remarkable the achievements were in the face of the obstacles encountered; (3) how great the influence of the achievement was on others.

Visualization step. In the preceding step, you will have enumerated the traits or achievements of the person (or group) being honored. In the visualization step, then, try to bring all of these together so as to create a vivid composite picture of the person and his or her accomplishments. It will help you to achieve this if you: (a) *Introduce an apt quotation.* Try to discover a bit of poetry or a literary passage which fits the person or group to whom you are paying tribute, and introduce it here. If you use this method, however, commit the passage to memory so that you do not falter in presenting it. Also, be sure that the quotation is not too long or flowery. (b) *Draw a picture of a world (community, business, or profession) inhabited by such persons.* Suggest how much better things would be if more people had similar qualities. (c) *Suggest the loss which the absence of the indi-*

vidual or group will bring. Show vividly how much he, she, or they will be missed. Be specific: "It's going to seem mighty strange to walk into Barbara's office and not find her there ready to listen, ready to advise, ready to help."

Action step. Frequently, no action step is used in a speech of tribute. When it is, it will vary with the occasion somewhat as follows: *Eulogy*——suggest that the best tribute the audience can pay the person they are honoring is to live as that person did or to carry on what he or she has started. *Dedication*——suggest the appropriateness of dedicating this monument, building, or whatever, to such a person or group, and express the hope that it will inspire others to emulate their accomplishments. *Farewell*——extend to the person or persons who are going away the best wishes of those you represent, and express a determination to carry on what they have begun. Or, if you yourself are saying farewell, call upon those who remain to carry on what you and your associates have started.

By following the foregoing principles and procedures with reasonable care and discernment, you should be able to devise a useful framework upon which to build a speech of tribute. To complete your speech, however, you will need to fill in this outline with vivid, illustrative materials and develop the whole message sensitively to suit the mood of the occasion. Note how this has been done in the three sample speeches which follow—a *eulogy*, a *dedicatory speech*, and a *speech of farewell*—and analyze the approach and the particular kinds of illustrations employed by the speaker in each instance.

SAMPLE SPEECH: A EULOGY

This short but vividly phrased speech eulogizes Vergil I. Grissom, Edward H. White II, and Roger B. Chaffee, members of the Apollo Test Crew who perished in a fire aboard the command module on January 27, 1967, during a countdown rehearsal. The eulogy was written and presented by Eric Sevareid on CBS Evening News, January 31, 1967, and in a number of respects is an excellent example of the memorial address.

EULOGY FOR THE ASTRONAUTS[1]

Eric Sevareid

Grissom and White and Chaffee—mortals who aspired to the moon and eternal space—were returned to the earth today from which they came and to which we all belong.

They had lived life more intensely in a very few years than most of us do in our lifetimes and they shall be remembered far longer.

They were among the men who wield the cutting edge of history and by this sword they died.

Grissom and Chaffee were buried near the grave of Lieutenant Thomas Selfridge, the first American military pilot to be killed in an airplane crash, nearly sixty years ago. Then, the air above the ground was as unfamiliar as the space above the air.

The men who go first are accounted heroes and rightly so, whatever the age, whatever the new element and horizon. Space, said the late President Kennedy, is our new ocean and we must sail upon it.

It was truly the hazards of the unknown oceans and territories that took the lives of earlier heroes, like Magellan or Captain Cook, men who went first and were killed by inhabitants of the Pacific.

It was not precisely the unknown hazards of space that killed our astronauts; it was the hazards of fallible man's calculations. It was not a technical failure; all technical failures are human failures. It was the familiar, never totally escapable failure of the human brain to cope with the complexities it has arranged.

A slight miscalculation, a single slip, then a spark, a flame and the end of three remarkable products of those infinitely more complex mysteries, genetic inheritance and environment. The processes that occasionally produced personalities like Grissom and White and Chaffee—men who are brave but not brash; proud but not self-conscious; thoughtful but not brooding. Men of a health, a wholeness, we all aspire to but so few attain.

We are told they will be replaced. This only means that other such men will take their places. The three cannot be replaced. There never was a replaceable human being.

SAMPLE SPEECH: A DEDICATION

The following remarks were made by Mr. Harold Haydon at the unveiling of "Nuclear Energy," a bronze sculpture created by Henry Moore and placed on the campus of the University of Chicago to commemorate the achievement of Enrico Fermi and his associates in releasing the first self-sustaining nuclear chain reaction at Stagg Field on December 2, 1942. The unveiling took place during the commemoration of the twenty-fifth anniversary of that event. Mr. Haydon is Associate Professor of Art at the University, Director of the Midway Studios, and art critic for the *Chicago Sun-Times*.

By combining specific references to the artist and his work with more general observations concerning the function of art and man's hopes and fears in a nuclear age, Mr. Haydon produced a dignified and thoughtful address, well suited to the demands of the occasion.

THE TESTIMONY OF SCULPTURE[2]

Harold Haydon

Since very ancient times men have set up a marker, or designated some stone or tree, to hold the memory of a deed or happening far longer than any man's lifetime. Some of these memorial objects have lived longer than man's collective memory, so that we now ponder the meaning of a monument, or wonder whether some great stone is a record of human action, or whether instead it is only a natural object.

There is something that makes us want a solid presence, a substantial form, to be the tangible touchstone of the mind, designed and made to endure as witness or record, as if we mistrusted that seemingly frail yet amazingly tough skein of words and symbols that serves memory and which, despite being mere ink blots and punch-holes, nonetheless succeeds in preserving the long human tradition, firmer than any stone, tougher than any metal.

We still choose stone or metal to be our tangible reminders, and for these solid, enduring forms we turn to the men who are carvers of stone and moulders of metal, for it is they who have given lasting form to our myths through the centuries.

One of these men is here today, a great one, and he has given his skill and the sure touch of his mind and eye to create for this nation, this city, and this university a marker that may stand here for centuries, even for a millennium, as a mute yet eloquent testament to a turning point in time when man took charge of a new material world hitherto beyond his capability.

As this bronze monument remembers an event and commemorates an achievement, it has something unique to say about the spiritual meaning of the achievement, for it is the special power of art to convey feeling and stir profound emotion, to touch us in ways that are beyond the reach of reason.

Nuclear energy, for which the sculpture is named, is a magnet for conflicting emotions, some of which inevitably will attach to the bronze form; it will harbor or repel emotion according to the states of mind of those who view the sculpture. In its brooding presence some will feel the joy and sorrow of recollection, some may dread the uncertain future, and yet others will thrill to the thought of magnificent achievements that lie ahead. The test of the sculpture's greatness as a human document, the test of any work of art, will be its capacity to evoke a response and the quality of that response.

One thing most certain is that this sculpture by Henry Moore is not an inert object. It is a live thing, and somewhat strange like every excellent beauty, to be known to us only in time and never completely. Its whole meaning can be known only to the ever-receding future, as each succeeding generation reinterprets according to its own vision and experience.

By being here in a public place the sculpture "Nuclear Energy" becomes a part of Chicago, and the sculptor an honored citizen, known not just to artists and collectors of art, but to everyone who pauses here in the presence of the monument, because the artist is inextricably part of what he has created, immortal through his art.

With this happy conjunction today of art and science, of great artist and great occasion, we may hope to reach across the generations, across the centuries, speaking through enduring sculpture of our time, our hopes, and fears, perhaps more eloquently than we know. Some works of art have meaning for all mankind and so defy time, persisting through all hazards; the monument to the atomic age should be one of these.

SAMPLE SPEECH: A FAREWELL

On October 10, 1973, Spiro T. Agnew resigned as Vice-President of the United States. Five days later, on October 15, in a telecast from Washington, D.C., carried by all of the major networks, Mr. Agnew delivered the following speech to the American people. It is presented here as an example of a speech of special historical interest. Study it. Analyze it. You will find that it illustrates a number of the principles we have discussed in this section.

ADDRESS TO THE AMERICAN PEOPLE[3]

Spiro T. Agnew

Good evening, ladies and gentlemen.

Nearly five years ago, and again last year, you gave me the greatest honor of my life by electing me Vice-President of the United States. I do not want to spend these last moments with you in a paroxysm of bitterness, but I do think there are matters relating to my resignation that are misunderstood. It is important to me and, I believe, to the country, that these misconceptions be corrected.

Late this summer, my fitness to continue in office came under attack when accusations against me, made in the course of a grand jury investigation, were improperly and unconscionably leaked in detail to the news media. I might add that the attacks were increased by daily publication of the wildest rumor and speculation, much of it bearing no resemblance to the information being given the prosecutors. All this was done with full knowledge that it was prejudicial to my civil rights. The news media editorially deplored these violations of the traditional secrecy of such investigations; but at the same time, many of the most prestigious of them were ignoring their own counsel by publishing every leak they could get their hands on.

From time to time, I made public denials of those scurrilous and inaccurate reports and challenged the credibility of their sources. I have consistently renewed those denials, last doing so at the hearing in the United States District Court. There, in response to the statement of the prosecutor's case, I stated that, with the exception of my decision not to contest the 1967 tax charge, I flatly and categorically denied the assertions of illegal acts on my part made by the Government witnesses. I repeat and emphasize that denial of wrongdoing tonight.

Notwithstanding that the Government's case for extortion, bribery, and conspiracy rested entirely on the testimony of individuals who had already confessed to criminal acts and who had been granted total or partial immunity in exchange for their testimony against me, their accusations, which are not independently corroborated or tested by cross-examination, have been publicized and broadcast as indisputable fact. This has been done even though such accusations are not a provable part of the single count of tax evasion which I saw fit not to contest and which was the only issue on which I went to court.

Up until a few days ago, I was determined to fight for my integrity and my Office, whatever the cost. The confidence that millions of you expressed encouraged me, and no words can convey the appreciation that my family and I will always feel for your outpouring of support.

However, after hard deliberation and much prayer, I concluded several days ago that the public interest and the interests of those who mean the most to me would best be served by my stepping down.

The Constitutional formalities of that decision were fulfilled on last Wednesday, when I tendered my resignation as Vice-President to the Secretary of State.

The legal sanctions necessary to resolve the contest—sanctions to which I am subject like any other citizen under our American system—were fulfilled that same day when I pleaded *nolo contendere* and accepted the judgment of a Federal court for a violation of the tax laws in 1967 when I was Governor of Maryland.

While I am fully aware that the plea of *nolo contendere* was the equivalent of a plea of guilty for the purpose of that negotiated proceeding in Baltimore, it does not represent a confession of any guilt whatever for any other purpose. I made the plea because it was the only quick way to resolve the situation.

In this technological age, image becomes dominant; appearance supersedes reality. An appearance of wrongdoing, whether true or false in fact, is damaging to any man — but, more important, it is fatal to a man who must be ready at any moment to step into the Presidency.

The American people deserve to have a Vice-President who commands their unimpaired confidence and implicit trust. For more than two months now, you have not had such a Vice-President.

If I had remained in office and fought to vindicate myself through the Courts and the Congress, it would have meant subjecting the country to a further agonizing period of months without an unclouded successor for the Presidency. This I could not do — despite my tormented verbal assertion in Los Angeles.

To put his country through that ordeal of division and uncertainty would be a selfish and unpatriotic action for any man at the best of times. At this especially critical time, with a dangerous war raging in the Middle East and with the Nation still torn by the wrenching experiences of the past year, it would have been intolerable.

So I chose instead not to contest formally the accusations against me. My plea last week in court was exactly that — not an admission of guilt, but a plea of "no contest" done to still the raging storm — delivering myself for conviction in one court, on one count — the filing of a false income tax return for 1967.

But in addition to my Constitutional and legal responsibilities, I am also accountable to one other authority — that of the people themselves. Tonight I would like to try briefly to give you the explanation that you rightly should have.

A few words about government contractors and fund-raising appear to be in order:

At every level of government in this country — local, state, and national — public officials in high executive positions must make choices in the course of carrying out architectural and engineering projects undertaken for the public good. Because they involve professional people, these are negotiated and non-bid awards. Competition is fierce, and the pressures for favoritism are formidable.

Now I am sure that you realize that public officials who do not possess large, personal fortunes face the unpleasant but unavoidable necessity of raising substantial sums of money to pay their campaign and election expenses.

In the forefront of those eager to contribute always have been the contractors seeking non-bid State contracts.

Beyond the insinuation that I pocketed large sums of money, which has never been proven and which I emphatically deny, the intricate tangle of criminal charges leveled at me, which you have been reading and hearing about during these past months, boils down to the accusation that I permitted my fund-raising activities and my contract-dispensing activities to overlap in an unethical and an unlawful manner. Perhaps, judged by the new, post-Watergate political morality, I did; but the prosecution's assertion that I was the initiator and gray eminence in an unprecedented and complex scheme of extortion is not realistic. Portraying the prosecution's witnesses, who have long been experienced and aggressive in Maryland politics, as innocent victims of illegal enticements from me is enough to provoke incredulous laughter from any experienced political observer.

All knowledgeable politicians and contractors know better than that. They know where the questionable propositions originate; they know how many shoddy schemes a political man must reject in the course of carrying out his office.

What makes my accusers, self-confessed bribe-brokers, extortionists and conspirators, believable — and their stories have been treated as gospel by most of the media — particularly when they have been encouraged to lessen their punishment by accusing someone else?

Let me reiterate here that I have never — as County Executive of Baltimore County, as Governor of the State of Maryland, or as Vice-President of the United States — enriched myself in betrayal of my public trust. My current net worth, less than $200,000, is modest for a person of my age and position. Every penny of it can be accounted for from lawful sources. Moreover, my standard of living throughout my political career has been demonstrably modest and has been open to public scrutiny during my public life. In the government's recitals against me, there are no claims of unexplained personal enrichment.

But if all of this is true, you well might ask why I did not resign and defend myself in court as a private citizen. I did consider that very seriously. But it was the unanimous judgment of my advisors that resignation would carry a presumption of guilt sufficient to defeat a defense on the merits. I'm afraid what I have been reading and hearing persuades me they were right.

By taking the course of the *nolo* plea, I have spared my family great anguish and, at the same time, have given the President and the Congress the opportunity to select on your behalf a new Vice-President who can fill that Office unencumbered by controversy. I hope to have contributed to focusing America's attention and energies back to where they belong — away from the personal troubles of Ted Agnew and back on the great tasks that confront us as a Nation.

As the country turns back to those tasks, it is fortunate indeed to do so under the leadership of a President like Richard Nixon.

Since events began to break in August, the President has borne a heavy burden in his attempt to be both fair to me and faithful to his oath of office. He has done his best to accommodate human decency without sacrificing legal rectitude.

He has said to me in private exactly what he has stated in public, that the decision was mine alone to make. Having now made that decision, I want to pay tribute to the President for the restraint and the compassion which he has demonstrated in our conversations about this difficult matter. The reports from unidentified sources that our meetings were unfriendly and even vitriolic are completely false.

I also want to express to the President and to all of you my deep regret for any interferences which the controversy surrounding me may have caused in the country's pursuit of the great goals of peace, prosperity, and progress which the Nixon Administration last year was overwhelmingly reelected to pursue.

Yet our great need at this time is not for regret, which looks to the past, but for resolve, which faces up to the future. The first challenge we face as a Nation is to summon up the political maturity that will be required to confirm and support the new Vice-President.

Under the newly applicable 25th Amendment to the Constitution, for the first time in our history, in the event of the President's death or disability his successor will be someone chosen by the President and confirmed by the Congress, not someone elected by the people.

In choosing Gerald Ford, the President has made a wise nomination. The Republican House leader has earned the respect of the entire Congress, as well as those in the Executive Branch who have come in contact with him during his long and distinguished career. Jerry Ford is an eminently fair and capable individual— one who stands on principle, who works effectively and non-abrasively for the achievable result. He will make an excellent Vice-President, and he is clearly qualified to undertake the highest office should the occasion require it.

After the Vice-Presidency is filled, the next question for Americans will be whether we are able to profit from this series of painful experiences by undertaking the reforms that recent tragedies cry for.

Will recent events form the crucible out of which a new system of campaign financing is forged, a system in which public funding for every political candidate removes any opportunity for evil or the appearance of evil? I sincerely hope so.

Will the furor about campaign contributions dramatize the need for state and local governments across the country to close the loopholes in their laws which invite abuse or suspicion of abuse in the letting of lucrative contracts to private businesses? Again, I hope so. I remember closing one such loophole regarding the awarding of insurance contracts when I was County Executive of Baltimore County.

Will my nightmare-come-true bring about a healthy self-examination throughout our criminal-justice system aimed at stopped prejudicial leaks? Will the prosecutors be restricted and controlled in their ability to grant immunity and partial immunity to coax from frightened defendants accusations against higher targets?

Certainly, these procedures need closer supervision by the courts and defense counsel. As things now stand, immunity is an open invitation to perjury. In the hands of an ambitious prosecutor, it can amount to legalized extortion and bribery. Again, I would hope that such reforms might result.

If these beneficial changes do flow from our current national trauma, then the suffering and sacrifice that I have had to undergo in the course of all this will be worthwhile.

But regardless of what the future may bring, nothing can take away my satisfaction of having served for some fifty-seven months as the second highest constitutional officer of the greatest Nation on earth — a satisfaction deriving not from what I did, but from what was done for me by millions of fine men and women whose beliefs and concerns I tried to articulate, and from what was done around me by a great President and his Administration in advancing the cause of peace and well-being for this country and all mankind.

I believe that America has always thrived on adversity, and so I can foresee only good ahead for this country, despite my personal sorrow at leaving public service and leaving many objectives incomplete.

Under this Administration which you have chosen and in which I have been privileged to serve, the longest war in America's history has been brought to an honorable end; and we are within reach of the best chance for lasting peace that the world has had in a century and a half. Both the abundance and the quality of American life are pushing to new highs.

Our democracy with its balanced Federal system, its separation of powers, and its fundamental principles of individual liberty, is working better than ever before. Our Bicentennial in 1976 will be marked by a chance for the electorate to choose among an unusually fine group of potential leaders.

These are America's strengths and her glories, which no amount of preoccupation with her weaknesses can obscure.

Every age in American history has had its political crises and upheavals. They all must have seemed like massive earthquakes to those who stood at the epicenter of the movement, but they all left the foundations of the Republic secure and unshaken when history moved on.

The resignation of a Vice-President, for example, is insignificant compared with the death of a President, particularly one so great as Lincoln, but I cannot help thinking tonight of James Garfield's words to an audience in New York just following the announcement that Lincoln had died.

Garfield, who was later to be President himself, was only a young Army officer at the time of that great tragedy in 1865, but he saw clearly where this country's strength lay, and he expressed it all in these few words to the frightened crowd: "Fellow citizens! God reigns, and the Government at Washington still lives."

I take leave of you tonight, my friends, in that same sober but trusting spirit. God does reign—I thank Him for the opportunity of serving you in high Office, and I know that He will continue to care for this country in the future as He has done so well in the past. The Government at Washington does live—it lives in the pages of our Constitution and in the hearts of our citizens, and there it will always be safe.

Thank you, good night, and farewell.

SPEECHES OF NOMINATION

Closely related to the speech of tribute is the speech to nominate. Here, your main *purpose* is to review the accomplishments of some person whom you admire. This review, however—instead of standing as an end in itself—is made to contribute to the principal goal of the speech: obtaining the listeners' endorsement of the person as a nominee for an elective office.

In a speech of nomination, your *manner of speaking* generally will be less formal and dignified than when you are giving a speech of tribute. It should, however, be businesslike and energetic. In general, the content of the speech will follow the pattern already described; but the illustrations and supporting materials should be chosen with the intent to show the nominee's qualifications for the office in question. Although the speech to nominate has certain special requirements, fundamentally it is a speech to actuate. Organize it, therefore, as follows:

In the *attention step*, announce that you arise to place a name in nomination. In the *need step*, point out the qualifications needed for success in the office; enumerate the problems that must be met, the personal qualities that are called for. In the *satisfaction step*, name the person you are nominating, and show that he or she has these qualifications. Point to the individual's training, experience, success in similar positions, etc. In the *visualization step*, picture briefly the accomplishments which may be expected if your nominee is endorsed and elected. Finally, in the *action step*, formally place the name in nomination and urge audience endorsement and support.

Sometimes the naming of the nominee is part of the attention step. This is a good practice if the audience is favorably disposed toward the person being nominated. However, if there is some doubt about their attitude, wait until the satisfaction step to reveal the name. In this way, by first showing the particular fitness of the person you may avoid unnecessary hostility.

As you probably have observed, in political conventions the name of a proposed candidate often is withheld until the very end of the nominating speech in order to heighten the drama of the situation and to avoid premature demonstrations. This practice should not, however — except in very special circumstances — be used elsewhere. In most situations, before you come to the concluding phase of your speech, most of your listeners probably will guess whom you are talking about anyway. As a mere trick of rhetoric, the device is too obvious to be genuinely effective.

Not all nominations, of course, need to be supported by a speech. Frequently, the person nominated is well known to the audience, and his or her qualifications are already appreciated. Under such circumstances, the simple statement, "Mr. Chairman, I nominate Jane Citizen for the office of treasurer," is all that is required.

SPEECHES TO CREATE GOOD WILL

Every speech seeks an affirmative response from the audience, but the type of speech now to be considered has as its principal aim the generating of good will. Ostensibly, the objective of a good-will speech is to inform. Actually, however, it seeks to enhance the listeners' appreciation of a particular institution, practice, or profession — to make the audience more favorably disposed toward it. By skillfully blending facts with indirect arguments and unobtrusive appeals, the speaker attempts to develop a positive attitude toward his subject. In short, the speech of good will is a mixed or hybrid type: it is an informative speech with a strong, underlying persuasive purpose.

In recent years, speeches of good will have played an increasingly important role in the public-relations programs of many business firms. For instance, more than 1800 speeches of this type were made in a single year by representatives of one large, Chicago-based corporation. But business firms are not alone in this practice. Schools, churches, and governmental agencies — to name only a few — also employ speeches of good will as a means of winning public approval and support.

Typical Situations Requiring Speeches for Good Will

There are numerous situations in which good-will speeches are appropriate, but the three which follow may be considered typical:

Luncheon meetings of civic and service clubs. Gatherings of this kind, being semisocial in nature and having a "built-in" atmosphere of congeniality, offer excellent opportunities for presenting speeches of good will. Members of such groups—prominent men and women from many walks of life—are interested in civic affairs and in the workings of other people's businesses or professions.

Educational programs. School authorities, as well as leaders of clubs and religious organizations, often arrange educational programs for their patrons and members. At such meetings, speakers are asked to talk about the occupations in which they are engaged and to explain to the young people in the audience the opportunities offered and the training required in their respective fields. By use of illustrations and tactful references, a speaker may—while providing the desired information—also create good will for his or her company or profession.

Special demonstration programs. Special programs are frequently presented by government agencies, university extension departments, and business organizations. For example, a wholesale food company may send a representative to a meeting of nutritionists to explain the food values present in various kinds of canned meat or fish products, and to demonstrate new ways of preparing or serving them. Although such a speech would be primarily informative, the speaker could win good will indirectly by showing that his or her company desires to increase customer satisfaction with its products and services.

Purpose and Manner of Speaking in the Speech for Good Will

As we have seen, then, the *real* and the *apparent* aims of a speech of good will are different. Insofar as the audience is concerned, the purpose may appear to be primarily informative. From the speaker's point of view, however, the purpose also is persuasive. By presenting information, he trys in subtle, unobtrusive ways to gain support for the profession or organization he represents.

Three qualities—modesty, tolerance, and good humor—characterize the manner of speaking appropriate for good-will speeches. Although the speaker will be talking about his own vocation and trying to make it seem important to his audiences, he should never boast or brag. In giving a speech of this type, let the facts speak for themselves. Moreover, show a tolerant attitude toward others, especially competitors. The airline representative, for instance, who violently attacks trucking companies and bus lines is likely to gain ill will rather than good. A courteous, positive attitude accompanied by a tactful presentation of the forward-looking and beneficial things his company has done will be much more effective. Finally, exercise good humor. The good-will speech is not for the zealot or the crusader. Take the task more genially. Don't try to force acceptance of your ideas; instead, show so much enthusiasm and good feeling that your listeners will respond spontaneously and favorably to the information you are providing.

In addition to speeches that entertain, inform, persuade, or actuate are the special types of public communication which as students and practitioners we are often required to present. Included in this category are the after-dinner speech, the acceptance speech, the dedication and commencement address, and the good-will speech.

Formulating the Content of the Speech for Good Will

In selecting materials for a good-will speech, keep these suggestions in mind: *Present novel and interesting facts about your subject.* Make your listeners feel that you are giving them an "inside look" into your company or organization. Avoid talking about what they already know; concentrate on new developments and on facts or services that are not generally known. *Show a relationship between your subject and the lives of the members of your audience.* Make your listeners see the importance of your organization or profession to their personal safety, success, or happiness. Finally, *offer a definite service.* This offer may take the form of an invitation to the audience to visit your office or shop, to help them with their problems, or even an expression of your willingness to answer questions or send brochures.

Organizing the Speech for Good Will

The materials we have just described may be organized into a well-rounded speech of good will in accordance with the following steps:

Attention step. The purpose of the beginning of your speech will be to establish a friendly feeling and to arouse the audience's curiosity about your profession or the institution you represent. You may gain the first of these objectives by a tactful compliment to the group or a reference to the occasion that has brought you together. Follow this with one or two unusual facts or illustrations concerning the enterprise you represent. For instance: "Before we began manufacturing television parts, the Lash Electric Company confined its business to the making of phonograph motors that would never wear out. We succeeded so well that we almost went bankrupt! That was only fifteen years ago. Today our export trade alone is over one hundred times as large as our total annual domestic business was in those earlier days. It may interest you to know how this change took place." In brief, you must find some way to arouse your listeners' curiosity about your organization.

Need step. Point out certain problems facing your audience—problems with which the institution, profession, or agency you represent is vitally concerned. For instance, if you represent a radio or television station, show the relationship of good communications to the social and economic health of the community. By so doing, you will establish common ground with your audience. Ordinarily the need step will be brief and will consist largely of suggestions developed with only an occasional illustration. However, if you intend to propose joint action in meeting a common problem, the need step will require fuller development.

Satisfaction step. The meat of a good-will speech will be in the satisfaction step. Here is the place to tell your audience about your institution, profession, or business and to explain what it is or what it does. You can do this in at least three ways: (1) *Relate interesting events in its history.* Pick events which will demonstrate its humanity, its reliability, and its importance to the community, to the country, or to the world of nations. (2) *Explain how your organization or profession operates.* Pick out those things that are unusual or that may contain beneficial suggestions for your audience. This method often helps impress upon your listeners the size and efficiency of your operation or enterprise. (3) *Describe the services your organization renders.* Explain its products; point out how widely they are used; discuss the policies by which it is guided—especially those which you think your audience will agree with or admire. Tell what your firm or profession has done for the community: people employed, purchases made locally, assistance with community projects, improvements in health, education, or public safety. Do not boast, but make sure that your listeners realize the value of your work *to them.*

Visualization step. Your object here is to crystallize the good will that the presentation of information in the satisfaction step has created. Do this by looking to the future. Make a rapid survey of the points you have covered or combine them in a single story or illustration. Or, to approach this step from the opposite direction, picture for your listeners the loss that would result if the organization or profession you represent should leave the community or cease to exist. Be careful, however, not to leave the impression that there is any real danger that this will occur.

Action step. Here, you make your offer of service to the audience—for example, invite the group to visit your office or plant, or point out the willingness of your organization to assist in some common enterprise. As is true of every type of speech, the content and organization of the speech for good will sometimes need to be especially adapted to meet the demands of the subject or occasion. You should, however, never lose sight of the central purpose for which you speak: to show your audience that the work which you do or the service which you perform is of value to them—that in some way it makes their lives happier, more productive, interesting, or secure.

PUBLIC DISCUSSIONS: FOUR TYPES

In Chapter 3 (pages 88–116) we considered the principles and methods of small group communication—that type of discussion in which from three to twelve persons engage in a relatively informal interchange of facts and opinions in order to learn more about a particular subject, solve a problem, or formulate a decision. On many occasions, however, when group consideration of a matter is desirable or urgent, the number of persons is so large that small group procedures are impractical. In these situations, if communication is to be of maximum meaning and value, modifications of the methods and plans described in Chapter 3 are clearly called for. These modifications produce four types of discussion which may be collectively described as *audience-oriented* or *public discussion* in order to distinguish them from small group interchange. They are: (1) the *panel discussion*, (2) the *symposium*, (3) the *open forum*, and (4) the *public debate*.

The Panel Discussion

When a group is too large to engage in effective discussion or its members are not well enough informed to make such discussion profitable, a panel of individuals—from three to five, usually—may be selected to discuss the topic for the benefit of the others, who then become an audience. The discussants in this special panel are chosen either because they are particularly well informed on the subject or problem and can supply the information needed for understanding or action, or because they represent divergent views on the matter at issue. The members of the panel, under the direction of a leader, discuss the subject or problem more or less according to the procedures and guidelines previously set forth for small group discussion. Following this interchange among the panel members, they usually invite questions and comments from the audience.

The Symposium

A second type of audience-oriented or public discussion is the symposium. In this format, several persons—again from three to five, usually—present short speeches, each focusing on a different facet of the subject or offering a different solution to the problem under consideration. Especially valuable when recognized experts with well-defined points of view or areas of competence are available as speakers, the symposium is the discussion procedure usually employed at large-scale conferences and conventions.

Various modifications of the panel and the symposium are possible, and sometimes the two formats may be successfully combined. Frequently, the set speeches of the symposium are followed by an informal interchange among the speakers; and then the procedure is "thrown open" to involve audience questions, comments, and reactions. The essential characteristic of both the panel and the symposium, however, is that a small number of persons carry forward the discussion of a subject or problem while a larger number of persons listen.

The Open Forum

As it is generally planned and conducted, the open forum consists of a single, relatively long speech or lecture followed by a communicative situation in which—under the direction of the speaker or a chairperson—the listeners raise questions and make statements of their own. In one important respect, however, the open forum differs from the usual persuasive public speaking situation: instead of the speaker's trying to influence the direction and outcome of the listeners' thinking—winning from them a carefully predetermined response—he plans his remarks with the specific purpose of stimulating them to ask questions and make comments from the floor. The aim of an open-forum speech, in short, is to cause the listeners to think for themselves rather than simply to inform or persuade them. As a result, the success of a speech made in the open forum is measured not by products sold or votes won, but rather by the extent and vigor of the discussion it generates and encourages.

The Public Debate

Debate as a mode of public discussion may take one of two basic forms: (1) One or more persons may be assigned to act as advocates for a given proposal or point of view and asked to present and defend it against advocates for the opposing position or point of view. Or (2) the group as a whole may arrive at a decision by debating a question under the rules of parliamentary procedure.

Both forms of debate require considerable technical knowledge of the method employed, as well as a thorough understanding of the question being considered. Moreover, they work best in those decision-making situations where *only two alternatives* for choice or action are available.* Every citizen should, however, be acquainted with the basic rules of parliamentary procedure (see pages 588–589) and should be aware of the rights and opportunities which these rules guarantee.** Furthermore, each citizen should recognize that debate between spokesmen for competing points of view—whether it occurs in the legislative chamber, the courtroom, or on the political campaign platform—is perhaps the basic instrument by which we arrive at public choices and decisions in a democratic society.

---

*For full treatments of debate as a mode of public discussion, see Austin J. Freeley, Argumentation and Debate: Rational Decision Making, 3rd ed. (Belmont, Calif.: Wadsworth Publishing Company, Inc., 1971); Douglas Ehninger and Wayne Brockriede, Decision by Debate (New York: Dodd, Mead & Company, 1963); Wayne Thompson, Modern Argumentation and Debate: Principles and Practices (New York: Harper & Row, Publishers, 1971).

**For a comprehensive treatment of the rules and procedures governing parliamentary debate, see Robert's Rules of Order Newly Revised (Glenview, Ill.: Scott, Foresman and Company, 1970).

PARLIAMENTARY PROCEDURE FOR HANDLING MOTIONS

Classification of motions	Types of motions and their purposes	Order of handling	Must be seconded	Can be discussed	Can be amended	Vote required[1]	Can be reconsidered
Main motion	(To present a proposal to the assembly)	Cannot be made while any other motion is pending	Yes	Yes	Yes	Majority	Yes
Subsidiary motions[2]	To postpone indefinitely (to kill a motion)	Has precedence over above motion	Yes	Yes	No	Majority	Affirmative vote only
	To amend (to modify a motion)	Has precedence over above motions	Yes	When motion is debatable	Yes	Majority	Yes
	To refer (a motion) to committee	Has precedence over above motions	Yes	Yes	Yes	Majority	Until committee takes up subject
	To postpone (discussion of a motion) to a certain time	Has precedence over above motions	Yes	Yes	Yes	Majority	Yes
	To limit discussion (of a motion)	Has precedence over above motions	Yes	No	Yes	Two-thirds	Yes
	Previous question (to take a vote on the pending motion)	Has precedence over above motions	Yes	No	No	Two-thirds	No
	To table (to lay a motion aside until later)	Has precedence over above motions	Yes	No	No	Majority	No
Incidental motions[3]	To suspend the rules (to change the order of business temporarily)	Has precedence over a pending motion when its purpose relates to the motion	Yes	No	No	Two-thirds	No
	To close nominations[4]	[4]	Yes	No	Yes	Two-thirds	No
	To request leave to withdraw or modify a motion[5]	Has precedence over motion to which it pertains and other motions applied to it	No	No	No	Majority[5]	Negative vote only
	To rise to a point of order (to enforce the rules)[6]	Has precedence over pending motion out of which it arises	No	No	No	Chair decides[7]	No
	To appeal from the decision of the chair (to reverse chair's ruling)[6]	Is in order only when made immediately after chair announces ruling	Yes	When ruling was on debatable motion	No	Majority[1]	Yes
	To divide the question (to consider a motion by parts)	Has precedence over motion to which it pertains and motion to postpone indefinitely	[8]	No	Yes	Majority[8]	No

						Two-thirds	Negative vote only
	To object to consideration of a question	In order only when a main motion is first introduced	No	No	No	Chair decides	No
Privileged motions	To divide the assembly (to take a standing vote)	Has precedence after question has been put	No	No	No	No vote required	No
	To call for the orders of the day (to keep meeting to order of business)[6,9]	Has precedence over above motions	No	No	No	Chair decides[7]	No
	To raise a question of privilege (to point out noise, etc.)[6]	Has precedence over above motions	No	No	No		No
	To recess[10]	Has precedence over above motions	Yes	No[10]	Yes	Majority	No
	To adjourn[11]	Has precedence over above motions	Yes	No[11]	No[11]	Majority	No
	To fix the time to which to adjourn (to set next meeting time)[12]	Has precedence over above motions	Yes	No[12]	Yes	Majority	Yes
Unclassified motions	To take from the table (to bring up tabled motion for consideration)	Cannot be made while another motion is pending	Yes	No	No	Majority	No
	To reconsider (to reverse vote on previously decided motion)[13]	Can be made while another motion is pending[13]	Yes	When motion to be reconsidered is debatable	No	Majority	No
	To rescind (to repeal decision on a motion)[14]	Cannot be made while another motion is pending	Yes	Yes	Yes	Majority or two-thirds[14]	Negative vote only

[1] A tied vote is always lost except on an appeal from the decision of the chair. The vote is taken on the ruling, not the appeal, and a tie sustains the ruling.

[2] Subsidiary motions are applied to a motion before the assembly for the purpose of disposing of it properly.

[3] Incidental motions are incidental to the conduct of business. Most of them arise out of a pending motion and must be decided before the pending motion is decided.

[4] The chair opens nominations with "Nominations are now in order." A member may move to close nominations, or the chair may declare nominations closed if there is no response to his inquiry, "Are there any further nominations?"

[5] When the motion is before the assembly, the mover requests permission to withdraw or modify it, and if there is no objection from anyone, the chair announces that the motion is withdrawn or modified. If anyone objects, the chair puts the request to a vote.

[6] A member may interrupt a speaker to rise to a point of order or of appeal, to call for orders of the day, or to raise a question of privilege.

[7] Chair's ruling stands unless appealed and reversed.

[8] If propositions or resolutions relate to independent subjects, they must be divided on the request of a single member. The request to divide the question may be made when another member has the floor. If they relate to the same subject but each part can stand alone, they may be divided only on a regular motion and vote.

[9] The regular order of business may be changed by a motion to suspend the rules.

[10] The motion to recess is not privileged if made at a time when no other motion is pending. When not privileged, it can be discussed. When privileged, it cannot be discussed, but can be amended as to length of recess.

[11] The motion to adjourn is not privileged if qualified or if adoption would dissolve the assembly. When not privileged, it can be discussed and amended.

[12] The motion to fix the time to which to adjourn is not privileged if no other motion is pending or if the assembly has scheduled another meeting on the same or following day. When not privileged, it can be discussed.

[13] A motion to reconsider may be made only by one who voted on the prevailing side. It must be made during the meeting at which the vote to be reconsidered was taken, or on the succeeding day of the same session. If reconsideration is moved while another motion is pending, discussion on it is delayed until discussion is completed on the pending motion; then it has precedence over all new motions of equal rank.

[14] It is impossible to rescind any action that has been taken as a result of a motion, but the unexecuted part may be rescinded. Adoption of the motion to rescind requires only a majority vote when notice is given at a previous meeting; it requires a two-thirds vote when no notice is given and the motion to rescind is voted on immediately.

PLANNING THE PUBLIC DISCUSSION: SOME GUIDELINES

For public discussion, no less than for small group communication, careful planning is essential. As you plan, keep the following suggestions in mind:

Select the type of discussion that best fits your subject and purpose. The various types of public discussion—panel, symposium, open forum, and debate—vary in their usefulness, depending on the subject to be discussed and the purpose to be served by the discussion. Panels, for example, tend to be especially suited to study or learning situations, whereas debates are better adapted to making decisions and agreeing on courses of action. Panel discussions are a good format for exploring subjects on which options for choice have not yet crystallized, whereas symposia and debates work best when the options already are clear. In choosing the method for a public discussion, consider first the subject or problem to be examined and the purpose to be served.

Make use of the discussants' specialized knowledge. Whatever the type of discussion you decide to employ, be sure to take advantage of the specialized knowledge and background of the participants. Although no person's remarks ought to be limited to a single field, each participant should be given full opportunity to set forth those facts and state those opinions which he or she is best qualified to express. Unless you and your group provide this opportunity, the very purpose of selecting a small number of persons to probe and discuss the subject for the benefit of a much larger number is likely to be undermined.

When planning a symposium, divide the topic among the various speakers. Each speaker may be assigned a particular phase or aspect of the subject; or one speaker may present the problem, and each of the others may set forth one possible solution. Additional arrangements may be suggested by the subject to be considered. In all cases, however, work out some reasonable distribution of responsibilities in advance, and be sure that each participant fully understands what they are.

In choosing the type of discussion to be used and the plan to be followed, keep in mind the relative prestige of the participants. If certain persons on a panel or symposium enjoy considerable prestige in the eyes of the audience, their views may so overweigh the opinions of others that a balanced and thoughtful consideration of the subject is impossible. Under such circumstances, avoid the danger of a hasty or biased decision by providing for the full and equal presentation of all points of view.

Be flexible. Do not let any of the suggestions presented in this chapter take the place of your own good sense and judgment in planning a particular discussion. Be guided, yes, by what has been said in these pages; but, above all, know thoroughly the subject to be considered, find out all you can about the persons who will participate, study the audience that will be present, form a clear idea of the purpose the discussion is intended to serve, and then select a type of discussion format and develop a plan or agenda to fit and accommodate these circumstances. What is important, really, is the *result*—not the procedure.

BROADCASTING THE PUBLIC DISCUSSION

As you are doubtless fully aware, public discussions and debates of all kinds are prominent on the program schedules of the electronic media. Some of these discussions, such as "Meet the Press," "The Advocates," "Issues and Answers," and "Wall Street in Review," are regularly scheduled by the television networks. Other discussion programs are organized on a special basis to consider and analyze a particular event or development: an important presidential address, a far-reaching legislative proposal, a startling scientific discovery, etc.

Television and radio discussions are not, however, confined to the networks. They are also broadcast in large numbers by local stations; and on these programs, high-school and college students, clergymen, and civic and business leaders of the community are frequently asked to participate.

There are two important considerations which participants in a broadcast discussion should keep in mind. *First*, the discussion is not primarily carried on for the benefits of the discussants themselves, but for the listening and/or viewing audience whose informational backgrounds, attitudes, and interests must constantly be remembered. *Second*, because of the restricted time limit, the broadcast discussion needs to be planned and controlled so as to focus on a single, relatively narrow theme or purpose. Except for these considerations, however, radio and television discussions—whether informative or argumentative, whether conducted as panels or symposia or debates—should be as much like other public discussions as possible. In televised programs, of course, the discussants must be seated on one side of the table or, depending on the number and positions of the cameras employed, in some other manner so that the faces instead of the backs of the speakers will be visible to viewers. Generally, what is good public discussion elsewhere is also good discussion on television.

Preparing the Broadcast Discussion

Unlike the telecast or radiocast of a speech, discussions that are to be broadcast should not be written out and read from a script.* Instead, for both ra-

---

For a discussion of the manner of speaking for radio and television broadcasts, see Chapter 23, pp. 599, 602–607.

dio and television presentation, as for on-the-scene audiences, a discussion plan should be outlined in advance. On this outline should be the names of the participants who will be responsible for introducing certain points. Also listed should be the principal ideas to be brought out during each phase of the discussion. This information enables the leader to know in advance the general direction the discussion will take and to move it along so that it can be completed in the time available for the broadcast. The outline should, however, provide for as much flexibility as possible and should not commit participants in advance to positions or points of view.

Practicing the Broadcast Discussion

Frequently, and especially when the participants are inexperienced, a practice session held before the time of the actual broadcast may prove useful. This practice or rehearsal may immediately precede the broadcast, or it may be scheduled several days in advance of it. In either case, by this means the ice is broken; the discussants become acquainted with the microphones, cameras, and lights; and there is an opportunity to explore each individual's information and point of view. Finally, in a practice period of this kind, the leader has a chance to gauge the temper of his group and decide how he may maximize the contribution of each participant.

Practice sessions must not, of course, continue to the point where the participants become "stale" or the interchange loses it spontaneity and naturalness. When properly limited in number, however, or when new material is required for consideration at each successive session, such run-throughs are a valuable means of getting the group warmed up and breaking down the barriers of strangeness or "mike fright" that may detract from the public discussion once it is on the air.

FOOTNOTES

[1] "Eulogy for the Astronauts" by Eric Sevareid. Copyright 1967 by Eric Sevareid, reprinted by permission of Harold Matson Co., Inc.

[2] "The Testimony of Sculpture" by Harold Haydon. First appeared in The University of Chicago Magazine, (January 1968). Reprinted by permission of Mr. Harold Haydon and The University of Chicago Magazine.

[3] Address to the American People by former Vice-President Spiro T. Agnew, October 15, 1973. Reprinted by permission.

Problems and Probes

1. Assume that you are to act as chairperson on one of the following occasions (or on some similar occasion):

A school assembly celebrating a successful football season.
A student-government awards banquet.
A special program for a meeting of a club to which you belong.
A student-faculty mass meeting called to protest a regulation issued by the dean's office.

In your role as chairperson, (a) plan a suitable program of speeches, entertainment, etc.; (b) allocate the amount of time to be devoted to each item on the program; (c) outline a suitable speech of introduction for the featured speaker or speakers; (d) prepare publicity releases for the local newspaper; (e) arrange for press coverage, etc. Work out a complete plan, one that you might show to a steering committee or a faculty sponsor.

2. Using as a basis one of the speeches reprinted in this textbook, assume that you are to introduce the speaker to a campus audience. Make an outline of a suitable speech of introduction, employing the appropriate steps in the motivated sequence.

3. Interview the faculty member who serves as chairman of your campus lecture committee, or a faculty member who frequently introduces visiting lecturers or artists. Try to determine what his conception of a good speech of introduction is and what rules or principles he tries to follow when introducing speakers.

4. One of the most famous speeches of dedication ever delivered by an American was presented by Daniel Webster at the laying of the cornerstone of the Bunker Hill Monument, June 17, 1825. After studying this speech, decide whether it would be appropriate in style and manner for a present-day audience. Why or why not? (See W. M. Parrish and Marie Hochmuth, eds., *American Speeches* [New York: Longmans, Green and Co., 1954], pages 101–121. Also frequently reprinted elsewhere.)

5. Find a printed speech of courtesy—welcome, response, or acceptance. Outline this speech and prepare a written report commenting on its general content and organization. Indicate those steps in the motivated sequence that the speaker used and those that he or she omitted, along with the possible reasons for those omissions.

6. Select as an example of a speech of tribute either Lincoln's Gettysburg Address or Pericles' Funeral Oration. (Both have been reprinted many times; your instructor will help you locate a good text.) Note the

methods which the speaker employed to communicate his message. In what sense was the speech addressed directly to the audience? In what sense was it addressed to all people in all ages?

7. You were told in this chapter that the good-will speech is usually an informative speech with a hidden persuasive purpose. Describe various circumstances under which you think the informative element should predominate in this special type of speech, and then describe other circumstances in which the persuasive element should be emphasized. In the second case, at what point would you say that the speech becomes openly persuasive in purpose?

8. List several specific situations other than radio or television broadcasts in which a *panel discussion* might be the most appropriate form of communication to use. List other non-broadcasting situations in which the *symposium* probably would be more suitable. And, finally, list a number of non-broadcasting situations in which the *open forum* would be appropriate.

9. Assume that, as a part of a mythical National Student Week, you have been asked to arrange on your campus a panel, symposium, open forum, or debate to which all students and faculty members will be invited. Select a subject that you think would be of interest to such an audience. Indicate whom you would ask to participate. Where and when would you hold the meeting? How long would it last? In each case, be prepared to defend your answer.

10. Select and watch one of the weekly television discussion shows on which persons from government, business, or the professions are questioned by a panel of newspaper reporters ("Meet the Press," "Face the Nation," or "Issues and Answers," etc.). To what extent do the formats and procedures used on these shows adhere to the principles of group discussion outlined in this chapter? In what respects do these shows depart from the methods and ideals of discussion as here described? Do you think that these departures make them more or less effective means for considering a current problem? How do the departures contribute to capturing and maintaining audience interest? Evaluate how well the participants followed the general rules for good discussion. (Review the guidelines suggested in Chapter 3, pages 91–106.) If there was a moderator or leader, how effective was his or her control and direction? Analyze several of the participants for the qualities you found particularly appealing or decidedly unappealing. Use the "Discussion Checklist" on page 118 to facilitate your analysis.

Oral Activities and Speaking Assignments

1. For the remainder of the semester, your instructor will appoint student chairpersons to preside over successive rounds of classroom speeches. Each student will serve as chairperson for one day; his or her duties will include arranging the speeches in a suitable order, introducing the speakers, keeping the program moving on time, preserving order, presiding over question-and-answer interchanges, etc. The chairperson will be graded on the basis of how well these tasks are performed.

2. Prepare a three-minute speech of courtesy suitable for one of the following occasions:

> Welcoming a distinguished alumnus to a fraternity or sorority banquet.
> Welcoming newly initiated members into an honorary society.
> Responding to a speech welcoming your group or delegation to a neighboring campus.
> Accepting an award for athletic or scholastic achievement.
> Accepting an office to which you have been elected.
> Presenting a gift to a faculty member on his retirement.

3. Prepare a five-minute speech paying tribute to:

> A man or woman important in national or world history.
> Someone in your home community who, though he or she never gained fame, contributed in a significant way to the success, well-being, or happiness of many others.
> A group of volunteers who participated in a successful or unsuccessful charity drive.
> A team of scientists who have just completed a successful project.
> A faculty member who has long served as a fraternity or sorority or campus-activity adviser.
> The highest ranking student in your class.
> An outstanding athlete or team which has received state or national recognition.
> An officer of a student organization who has served long and well.
> Founders of an organization for civic betterment.

4. Prepare for delivery in class a five-minute good-will speech on behalf of a campus organization to which you belong. (You may substitute a national organization, such as the Boy Scouts or Y.W.C.A., if you wish.)

Select new and little-known facts to present; pay particular attention to maintaining interest at a high level; keep your arguments and appeals indirect; and show tact and restraint in your speaking manner. Be prepared to answer questions after your talk is completed.

5. Assume that a prominent alumnus has given your college a new classroom or union building and that it is to be named after him. Prepare and present a short dedicatory speech which would be suitable for presentation on the day the edifice is opened for public use.

Suggestions for Further Reading

Otto F. Bauer, *Fundamentals of Debate: Theory and Practice* (Glenview, Ill.: Scott, Foresman and Company, 1966).

Ralph Borden Culp, *Basic Types of Speech* (Dubuque, Iowa.: Wm. C. Brown Company, Publishers, 1968).

J. H. C. Green, *Speak to Me* (Indianapolis: The Bobbs-Merrill Company, Inc., 1962), Chapter IX, "May I Present?" pp. 67–70.

Ralph A. Micken, *Speaking for Results* (Boston: Houghton Mifflin Company, 1958), "To Make an After-Dinner Speech," pp. 198–199.

William J. Pfeiffer and John E. Jones, *A Handbook of Structured Experiences for Human Relations Training*, 3 vols. (Iowa City: University Associates Press, 1971).

Raymond S. Ross, *Speech Communication: Fundamentals and Practice*, 2nd ed. (Englewood Cliffs, N.J.: Prentice-Hall, Inc., 1970), Chapter XIII, "Special Occasion Speaking," pp. 233–250.

Eugene E. White, *Practical Public Speaking* (New York: The Macmillan Company, 1964), Chapter XV, "Speeches of Special Types," pp. 343–368.

23
ADAPTING SPEECHES
TO RADIO AND TELEVISION

The public speaker today needs a general knowledge of broadcasting techniques. Any man or woman in business, a profession, or a position of community leadership may be called upon to speak over the local radio or television station. The purpose of this chapter, therefore, is to point out the most important differences between face-to-face speaking and speaking over the air to an unseen audience, and to suggest briefly how the principles and procedures previously presented may be adapted to the broadcasting situation.* You will observe that, although important differences do exist, many of the same fundamental principles apply; and, more often than not, what is effective speaking before a visible audience is also effective over the air.

THE PURPOSE OF A BROADCAST SPEECH

Television and radio speakers hope, of course, to reach a larger audience than could be gathered together in person at one place. This motivation aside, however, there is no great difference between the purposes of broadcast speeches and the purposes of the types of speeches discussed in the preceding chapters. Like other speakers, radio and television speakers attempt to entertain, to inform, to persuade, or to actuate; they introduce other speakers, express welcomes, debate public issues, pay tributes, and attempt to gain good will. Your purpose in talking before a visible audience may also be your purpose when you broadcast. And with some modifications, the same characteristics of speech content and delivery and the same methods of speech organization are utilized.

---

*For purposes of this discussion, the term "broadcast" will be used inclusively to mean both the "telecast" and the "radiocast."

THE RADIO AND TELEVISION AUDIENCE

The radio and television audience is sometimes called "universal" because anyone who has a receiving set within the power range of the station may be listening. The audience is likely to be composed of persons of both sexes and of all ages, creeds, occupations, interests, and degrees of intelligence. Only the hour of the broadcast, the location of the station, and the special nature of the program are limiting factors. Surveys have shown that women listeners and viewers predominate during the morning and early afternoon hours when husbands are at work and children at school. Children give their attention mainly in the late afternoon and early evening; men listen or watch during the evenings and on Sundays. At mealtime the audience for a public speech is likely to be varied; but it may be small because most people prefer musical programs or brief announcements (markets, news, weather, etc.) at this time. Insofar as location is concerned, a metropolitan station tends to draw a larger urban audience; and a station in a smaller city, a larger rural audience. However, the more powerful stations and the networks reach every kind of community. Some stations cater to certain types of listeners and viewers, and some program series are specifically designed for certain groups. College stations, for example, direct many programs to students and faculty.

An important characteristic of radio and television audiences is that the listener or viewer is usually alone or is in a small, intimate group. Although the audience as a whole may be large, the persons comprising it are not gathered in a mass but are scattered about in living rooms, offices, automobiles, and the like. While each individual no doubt is aware that others are watching or listening to the same program, he is primarily attuned to his own surroundings and expects the speaker to talk to him in a conversational manner suited to that environment.

Two further facts need to be remembered: (1) listeners or viewers can easily turn off a broadcast at any time, and (2) they are likely to have many distractions. People hesitate to make themselves conspicuous by leaving an audience while a speaker is talking directly to them in person, but they feel no hesitation about tuning out a radio or television speech. In addition, anyone trying to pay attention to a broadcast speech is likely to be surrounded by distracting noises—the baby's crying, the clatter of dishes, a conversation at the other end of the room, or the roar of traffic. To compete with these distractions, the broadcast speech must have a high degree of interest value.

TYPES OF BROADCAST SPEECHES

Broadcast speeches fall into two principal classes: (*a*) those made without an audience present and (*b*) those given before a studio audience or broadcast from an auditorium or assembly hall. In the former, the speaker has only an unseen audience; in the latter, he confronts two audiences, one of which is physically present and another which he can only imagine.

Broadcasts Without an Audience Present

When you speak from the studio for the broadcast audience only, it is like conversing with a friend over a telephone. To develop the conversational rapport called for in this situation, some speakers address the announcer when he is in the same room; or they speak directly to a friend who has come to the studio with them.

Broadcasts With an Audience Present

When you address an audience that is actually sitting before you, the radio listeners and television viewers are allowed, as it were, to "listen in." Your broadcast audience knows that an actual audience is present, and they do not mind your talking in a manner appropriate to formal public speaking rather than to informal conversation. They imaginatively project themselves into your presence and in a sense become part of the crowd at the dinner or in the auditorium. If the broadcast is over radio only, you may help your listeners acquire this feeling by referring to the audience before you or to the occasion which has brought the group together. A ripple of audience laughter or applause also will help the radio listener feel more a part of the immediate situation. Although you owe primary attention to those you are addressing face to face, do not forget the radio and television audience entirely; even in this situation the content and structure of your speech and, to some extent, your manner of speaking should be modified for the broadcast situation.

THE MANNER OF SPEAKING FOR RADIO

In presenting a radio speech, remember that your listeners cannot see you and, therefore, that you cannot give them visual cues by means of gestures, facial expression, and bodily movement. Nor will you be able to employ visual aids in explaining or proving an idea. All meaning must be communicated by means of *the voice alone:* attention must be gained and held, thoughts made clear, and action generated through the use of rate, inflection, and vocal force.

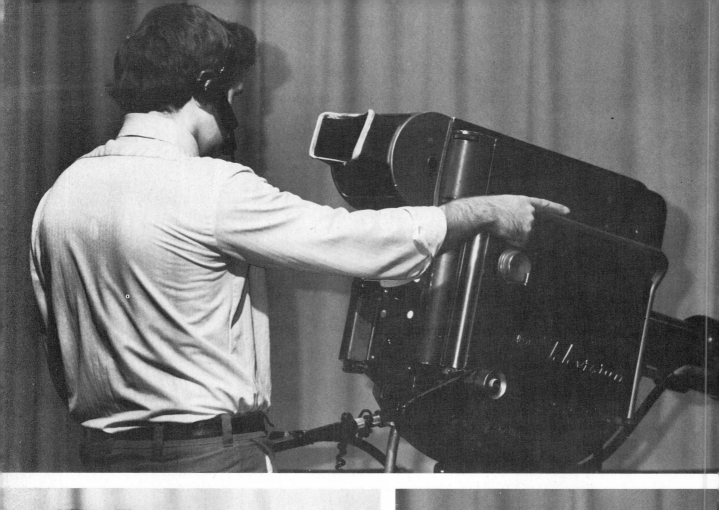

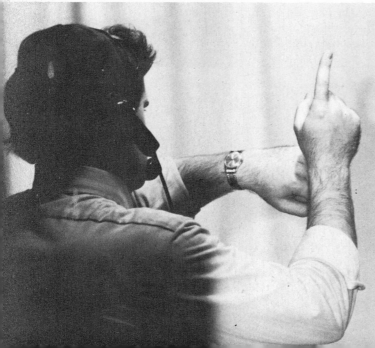

Television directors must rely heavily upon nonverbal communication to relay messages and information to speakers during telecasts and taping sessions. Shown in these photographs are some of the more commonly used signals. Opposite page, top: *Begin talking.* Lower left: *One more minute air time.* Lower right: *Cut (stop talking).* This page, top: *Cut (station break).* Center: *Commercial coming.* Bottom: *Five more minutes air time.*

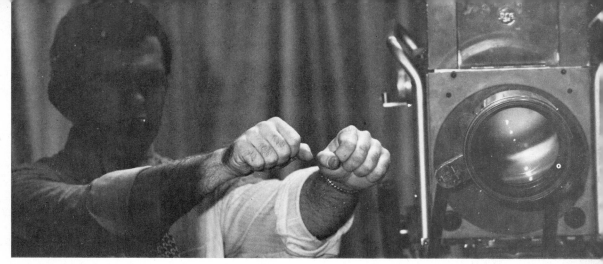

Using the Microphone

Many different types of microphones are available for radio and television use. Some pick up sound equally well from all directions; others pick up those sounds made directly in front of them, but do not pick up as well those made beside, above, or behind them. Ask the announcer or the technician in the studio how far from the microphone you should stand or sit, and from what angle you should speak into it. Ask also about the volume level at which you should talk.

The loudness of the sound picked up by most microphones varies inversely in approximate geometric ratio to the distance of the microphone from the source of the sound. To illustrate, if you speak with the same degree of force, a sound picked up at a distance of one foot will be four times louder than a sound picked up at a distance of two feet. Therefore, to avoid fading or increasing the volume, always remain approximately the same distance from the microphone. Especially when you have an audience as well as a microphone in front of you, do not move about too freely. Hand, lapel, and chest microphones have been developed in order to give the speaker more mobility; but you still may produce an uneven volume if you turn your head too often or move too far from the microphone. In the studio, the temptation to move is not so great; if you are seated or standing comfortably, you are likely to remain still. However, if you are reading your material from a manuscript, be careful not to bob your head because this movement may cause the volume to fluctuate markedly.

Most radio equipment is extremely sensitive; and for this reason, sudden increases in volume will produce "blasting," an effect similar to that created by hitting the keyboard of a piano with a clenched fist—a crash of sound rather than a clear tone. The engineer in the control room can, within reason, modulate the volume of your voice, building it up or toning it down; but he cannot anticipate every sudden change. Therefore, keep your vocal force reasonably even.

Amateurs commonly make two mistakes which result in sounds that are intensified by the sensitivity of broadcasting equipment. The first is *rattling or rustling papers close to the microphone.* Any sound in the studio is amplified over the air; therefore, at its worst, paper rustling may sound like the rapid firing of a gun, the flapping of an awning in an angry wind, or the crushing of an orange crate into kindling. At the very least, it will make your listeners aware that you are reading your remarks, and thus destroy the illusion of direct communication. If you use a manuscript, choose soft paper, unclip it before you approach the microphone, and lay each sheet aside quietly when you have finished reading it. You will, moreover, create less noise by resting your manuscript on the table or speaker's stand rather than holding it in your hand. (A note of caution: *Check the pages of your manuscript before the broadcast to make sure they are in the correct order.* No pause seems as long as that which occurs when you turn to page three and find page four.) The second common mistake *is tapping the microphone or table.* This, too, may be only a slight noise in the studio, but a loud one over the air. Avoid drumming on the table or thumping it for emphasis; let your gestures be noiseless.

Because broadcasting equipment amplifies sound and because radio listeners focus their attention entirely upon your voice, the distinctness of your speech and the accuracy of your pronunciation are especially important. Errors and crudities that might pass unnoticed on the platform will be very noticeable over the air. Do not, however, talk so carefully that your speech sounds artificial. To speak in an overly precise manner is almost as bad as to speak indistinctly, for it calls attention to the utterance rather than to the thought. Try to avoid both extremes.

Another point to consider is that the quality of a speaker's voice often is changed in transmission. In general, high-pitched voices are less pleasant over the radio, whereas those of moderately low pitch are sometimes improved in the process of broadcasting. The best way to check the effect of transmission on your voice is to have *an audition* or to make *a tape recording* of the broadcast so you can listen to yourself. The fact that you can talk conversationally before the microphone and do not have to increase vocal force in order to project to an audience should improve the quality of your voice, since most people have better vocal quality when they speak in a quiet and relaxed manner. Keep the resonating passages open, however. The silence of the studio and the lack of direct audience response may cause you to forget you are communicating and allow your voice to become flat and colorless. In articulation, pay particular attention to the sibilants — sounds such as *s, z,* and *sh.* Some microphones minimize the problem, but the high frequencies of these sounds tend to produce a whistling or hissing when they are given too much emphasis. If you have trouble with sibilants, learn to subdue your production of them or, at the very least, use sparingly words in which these sounds occur in stressed positions.

Compensating for the Lack of Visual Cues

The visual cues a speaker gives his audience add emphasis, convey additional meaning, help hold attention, and fill in gaps left by pauses. When, as in radio speech, the burden is thrown entirely on the voice, variety of vocal expression is more than a valuable asset; it is essential. Review the section in Chapter 6 which deals with rate and pitch (pages 198–202); practice the exercises given there to develop vocal flexibility (pages 218–220). As we have already warned, however, avoid sudden changes in vocal force.

When broadcasting by radio, you should speak at a fairly rapid rate. This does not mean that you have to rush, but it does mean that you cannot allow your speech to drag. Take particular care to avoid long pauses. In a face-to-face speaking situation, you sometimes can emphasize a point by standing silent, holding your listeners' attention by your facial expression and the apparent tension of your body; all this is lost to the radio listener; he gets only silence. In radio speaking, therefore, pauses must be used sparingly and must be of minimal duration. When speaking directly and in person to an audience, a speaker may pause to search for the exact word to express his thought: he is thinking it out with his listeners, and they are seeing him do it. On the air, such pauses may suggest that the speaker is ill-at-ease and unprepared.

Because groping for words is a major sin in radio broadcasting, most people write out their speeches word for word and read them from manuscript. This procedure not only ensures their knowing what to say next, but also makes it certain that they will finish on time. There is one disadvantage, however: Some people cannot write with the informality of oral style; and even when they can, they have difficulty reading aloud in a conversational manner. But this disadvantage can be overcome with practice. Experts almost unanimously advise using a manuscript for a radio speech and learning to read from it naturally.

When preparing for a broadcast speech, then, practice reading your manuscript aloud. Do not read it for the first time as you stand before the microphone and address your audience. Master or alter difficult sound combinations in advance. Become so familiar with your material that you can ad-lib if you happen to lose your place or misplace a page. Above all, practice reading with a mental image of your listeners before you; make your reading sound like talk. Do not stress unimportant words, such as *the*, *of*, and *to*. Avoid both a monotone and an artificial inflection.

THE MANNER OF SPEAKING FOR TELEVISION

Unlike radio broadcasting, telecasting permits your audience to see you while you talk. Therefore, your appearance, facial expression, and movement help convey your thought just as they do when you are speaking to an audience face to face. In fact, the way the television camera picks up your image, especially in close-ups, makes your appearance and movement even more important than when you address audiences in person.

Although you need not depend on your voice alone when speaking on television, neither can you talk exactly as you would if you were facing only an immediate audience. Instead, your voice and movements must conform to limitations imposed by the microphone and camera.

Generally, you will find that the suggestions we have given for using the microphone and avoiding distracting noises are pertinent to television as well as to radio broadcasts. In addition to observing these directions, however, you also must adapt to the distractions of the heat and brilliance of the television studio's dazzling lights, to the movement of the cameras on their booms or dollies, and to the restriction of your movement within the area upon which the lights and cameras are focused. And, throughout, this adaptation must seem natural. Avoid equally a stunned or disconcerted appearance and a tendency to "play to the gallery."

The technical aspects of television are changing rapidly, and facilities at different stations vary considerably. Hence, each time you broadcast you probably will need special advice from the directors and technicians in order to adapt your presentation to prevailing conditions. For this reason, the following discussion omits detailed instructions and includes only suggestions which are fairly universal in their application.

Adapting Vocal Delivery for Television

While many of the vocal requirements of radio broadcasting apply equally to television, important differences should be noted. Since, when speaking on television, you are seen as well as heard, you can talk more slowly and can pause longer for transitions or emphasis. When a program is broadcast over both radio and television, however, pauses should not be too long nor the rate of speaking too slow.

In telecasts, be careful also to maintain a quiet, conversational manner. Especially in intimate studio surroundings, remember that you are conversing with your listeners as a guest in their homes. Vocal variety and emphasis are needed; but a tone that is too excited, an excessively rapid rate, or an overassertive inflection may be offensive.

Adapting Movement and Appearance to the Television Camera

The adjustment of the television camera's lens and its distance from the speaker determine how much of his body will be shown. Moreover, the camera's position determines the angle from which the speaker is viewed. Usually, to provide variety, camera angles and distances are changed during the broadcast. Often more than one camera is used, the broadcast pick-up shifting from one to another so that the picture changes from a distant view to a close-up or from a front to an angle shot; or the camera is moved so that the angle shifts gradually. If an audience is present, the camera may go from speaker to audience and back again. The director will instruct you ahead of time where you are to stand or sit, and how far you may safely move without getting beyond the focal depth or angle of the camera or outside of the lighted area. If you intend to use visual aids, be sure they are placed where the camera can include them.

The effect which televising has upon colors, textures, and patterns requires special attention to make-up and clothing. The bright lights cause the normal reddish color of the lips to fade out and the usual shadows around the eyes and nose to disappear, so that the face appears flattened. Hence, make-up is necessary to ensure that facial color and contour will look natural. Make-up also must be used to reduce glare (perspiring skin or a bald head may gleam unless toned down with dull grease paint or panchromatic powder) and to obscure blemishes or stubble (a man's shaven face may appear dirty and unkempt unless basic make-up is applied). Finally, clothes must be chosen so as to give life to the image without creating bizarre effects.

Adapting Movement and Appearance to the Type of Broadcast

Earlier in this chapter we discussed the difference between radio broadcasts in the studio without an audience and broadcasts with an audience present. In television, this difference is particularly important. If an audience is present, you will be expected to talk to your listeners, not to the camera. Your posture, movements, and gestures must be adapted to the people immediately before you.

The studio telecast without an audience present is more intimate. Here, as we have said, you must think of yourself as talking to your listeners in their living rooms. Occasionally, you may stand while speaking, especially if you have something to point out or to demonstrate. More often, however, you will be seated at a desk or in a large, comfortable chair. In either case, your movements should be suited to easy, animated conversation. Stand or sit in a relaxed manner. Change your position from time to time, and use your hands to emphasize and clarify your statements. Now and then, lean forward slightly to emphasize important ideas. Your gestures, however, should be somewhat restrained; move the hand and forearm in a relatively small arc and avoid declamatory mannerisms. Look at the camera, but do not stare at it continuously. Above all, do not rely heavily on a manuscript or notes. If you must read all or part of your speech, you may be able to arrange for the use of a Teleprompter. This device puts a copy of your speech, in large type, on or near the camera. Thus, even though you are reading, you can maintain fairly good eye contact with the viewers.

Using Visual Aids on Television

Television makes possible the use of all types of visual aids to illustrate and substantiate the content of a speech. Maps, charts, pictures, models, and even short sequences from motion pictures add variety and life to a presentation. Sometimes large-scale visual aids are placed beside or behind the speaker so that he can point to them as he talks. Frequently, small pictures or miniature models are picked up by a separate camera. When broadcasting with an audience present, you may not be able to use these devices extensively; but when broadcasting from a studio, you usually can employ them with good effect. In fact, you may be able to organize your entire talk around a series of visual aids especially devised to portray your ideas.

PRINCIPLES OF CONTENT AND ORGANIZATION OF THE BROADCAST SPEECH

Although the principles of speech development presented in previous chapters apply to both radio and television speeches, some of them deserve special emphasis. In particular, bear in mind the following suggestions:

Fit Your Talk to the Exact Time Limit

Most stations operate on a schedule that is adhered to with only thirty seconds' leeway; if a program runs overtime, it is cut off. Moreover, programs start on schedule; therefore, allow yourself plenty of time to get to the studio and to catch your breath before you begin speaking. Remember, too, that your speech will comprise only a *part* of the program. If you are given a fifteen-minute "spot," you will not have a full fifteen minutes available because announcements and introductory remarks will consume part of that time. Find out how many minutes actually are yours and what kinds of signals will be given to indicate how the time is going. Without realizing it, many people talk faster in a studio than elsewhere and therefore tend to finish ahead of schedule. Prepare for this eventuality by having an additional illustration or story which can be inserted near the end of your speech if you see that you are getting through too early. Prepare also to cut a paragraph or two, should this become necessary. "Backtime" your speech by noting on the manuscript or Teleprompter copy at what point you have one or two minutes of material remaining. If, near the end of the broadcast, the clock shows that you have too much or too little time, adjust your remarks accordingly.

Make Your Appeals as Universal as Possible

Remember that all kinds of people may be listening and observing. Relate your appeals to their everyday experiences and try to interest as many of them as you can.

Use lively, concrete material. Avoid abstract theorizing; listeners will tune you out unless you make your speech come alive with stories, illustrations, and comparisons.

Employ as many factors of attention as possible. In choosing ideas, give special emphasis to *the vital*—use materials related to the impelling needs and desires of many people; to *activity* and *reality*—use materials characterized by movement and concreteness; and to *suspense*—arouse curiosity or expectation that some valuable information will be presented later. (Review the factors of attention, pages 336–342.)

Give your speech a sense of continuous movement and development. A radio or television talk must never bog down or ramble. Keep your listeners aware that you are getting somewhere, that you have an objective and are moving steadily toward it.

Make Your Speech Easy to Follow

In addition to these extra incentives to paying attention, special aids to understanding often are needed by listeners who are not present in the room:

Use simple (but not childish) wording and sentence structure. Avoid technical terms where common ones will do; but if you must use technical terms, explain them. Also avoid flowery, over-elegant language and long, complex sentences. Do not, however, talk down to the audience.

Use simple speech organization. Intricate patterns of organization and lengthy chains of reasoning have no place in a broadcast talk. Rarely is there time to make complex arguments clear; and because you cannot see your listeners, you cannot tell whether they understand. A few main points, clearly related and simply supported, should furnish the basic structure of your speech.

Make your transitions clear. When you move from one idea to another, indicate this fact by a sentence or two or by a distinct change of rate or pitch. In a television broadcast, you can indicate transitions by movement or a gesture; but over the radio, your voice and language must do this work. Do not allow your transitions to become stereotyped; vary them and keep them informal. Do not overwork such terms as "In the first place" and "Second"; they seem too stilted. You might say instead, "It's too costly, for one thing," "There's no need to labor that point," or "But let's look at something else for a minute."

In this chapter, we have presented a few of the principles to keep in mind when you prepare a speech for broadcasting. Seek opportunities to apply them as often as possible. Also, by listening to some of the many speeches which are given each week on radio and television, observe how others apply these principles.

Problems and Probes

1. On three or four consecutive days, listen to a popular television newscaster and attempt to determine those aspects of vocal and physical delivery upon which his effectiveness depends. Report on your findings.

2. Compare the newscaster studied in Problem 1 with another popular newscaster. Are the same factors of effectiveness present in both? If not, how do the two men chiefly differ? To what extent is it possible to recommend a single standard or ideal style of delivery which all television newscasters should follow?

3. Compare one of the television newscasters studied in Problems 1 or 2 with a well-known radio newscaster. How do the techniques of the radio speaker differ from those used by his colleague on television? If the two men were to exchange media, would either or both of them lose some of their effectiveness?

4. Analyze critically a speech delivered over radio or television, paying particular attention to (*a*) the suitability of the subject for a broadcast speech, (*b*) the speaker's diction and sentence structure, (*c*) the organization of the talk, (*d*) the variety and vividness of the supporting materials.

5. Select either a speech to inform or a speech to persuade which you presented in class earlier this term; and, observing the rules of good television speaking as described in this chapter, adapt it to a manuscript suitable for a ten-minute presentation on television.

6. Interview the manager or program director of a local radio or television station to get his ideas concerning the nature of an effective broadcast talk. Ask him also to explain to you some of the special rules and restrictions which a radio or television speaker must observe concerning libel and ethical responsibility of public utterance. Review pages 49–55 and 457–463, and then write a report on the results of your interview.

Oral Activities and Speaking Assignments

1. Prepare and present from manuscript a ten-minute informative or persuasive speech especially adapted for radio or television. In choosing

and developing a subject and in wording and delivering your speech, observe insofar as possible the various recommendations set forth in this chapter, and check the timing. If possible, deliver the speech over a closed-circuit radio or television hookup. In case the necessary equipment is not available, the radio-speaking situation can be simulated roughly by having the speaker talk from behind a screen. (*Note:* Subject to your instructor's approval, you may use the manuscript which you prepared for Problem/Probe 5 above.)

2. Prepare in manuscript form a five- or ten-minute summary of campus or community news suitable for broadcast. Present this summary to the class either face to face while you are seated at a table, or deliver it over a closed-circuit television or radio hookup. Ask your classmates to comment in particular on your manner of delivery.

Suggestions for Further Reading

Samuel L. Becker and H. Clay Harshbarger, *Television: Techniques for Planning and Performance* (New York: Holt, Rinehart & Winston, Inc., 1958).

Elihu Katz and Paul Lazarsfeld, *Personal Influence: The Part Played by People in the Flow of Mass Communication* (Glencoe, Ill.: The Free Press, 1964).

Elihu Katz, Martin L. Levin, and Herbert Hamilton, "Traditions of Research on the Diffusion of Innovation," *Foundations of Communication Theory*, ed. Kenneth K. Sereno and C. David Mortensen (New York: Harper & Row, Publishers, 1970), pp. 342–364.

Sherman P. Lawton, *Introduction to Modern Broadcasting: A Manual for Students* (New York: Harper & Row, Publishers, 1964).

Marshall McLuhan, *Understanding Media: The Extensions of Man* (New York: McGraw-Hill Book Company, 1966).

Everett M. Rogers and Floyd Shoemaker, *Communication of Innovations* (New York: The Free Press, 1968).

Wilbur Schramm, *Men, Messages, and Media* (New York: Harper & Row, Publishers, 1973).

Wilbur Schramm and D. F. Roberts, *The Process and Effects of Mass Communication*, rev. ed. (Urbana, Ill.: University of Illinois Press, 1971).

R. M. W. Travers, et al., *Research and Theory Related to Audiovisual Information Transmission* (Salt Lake City: Bureau of Educational Research, University of Utah, 1966).

The authors and publisher gratefully acknowledge the contributions of the following teachers who responded to a questionnaire based on their use of and experiences with the Sixth Edition of Principles and Types of Speech *and thereby provided much practical guidance in the preparation of this new edition.*

Thomas J. Aylward

Clarence H. Baxter, Jr.
Paul W. Beardsley
Catherine Beaty
Winton H. Beaven
Mrs. Jo Bennett
Mr. Val Bettin
David J. Blackim
Lucy Blandford
David J. Blossom
Robert L. Bohlken
Marcus H. Boulware
Dudley Boyd
Harold J. Bruxvoort
Thomas L. Burbridge

G. W. Cartwright
Daniel D. Chesla
L. R. Chudomelka
David A. Cornell
Rachael M. Crowe

Lawrence Davis
Bobbie Morrow Dietrich

Dorothy J. Edwards
Maude Edwards
J. Harold Ellens

Lana Freeman

Randy K. Gascoigne
Josephine W. Gatz
Betty George

Harry B. Gooch
Thelma B. Goodwin
Yvonne Goulet
Lorelei F. Guidry

Vera T. Hahn
Jean Harper
Charles L. Hayes
T. R. Hayes
Bob W. Heath
David B. Hill
Ray W. Hindman
Sandra Hoffmann
Mrs. Phyllis Holstein
Alzara Hooker

Theodore O. H. Karl
Patrick C. Kennicott
Grant Kilpatrick

Bill Lassett

Vera Malton
O. G. Manion
Virginia McAlister
Athel V. McCombs
Thomas J. McGrath
Rhoda Riber Mones
Melvin P. Moorhouse
Creston D. Munger

James Newburger

Gerald S. Owen

Nina Parlain
J. O. Pierson
James E. Pirkle
Mrs. William Preston

Robert Quinn

A. O. Ranson
Robert Reynolds
Ward A. Rice
Margaret Ann Riggle
Gwen Robbins
Haddon Robinson
Zelda Jeanne Rouillard

Henry Z. Scheele
Patricia L. Schmidt
Edward Simms
N. M. Small
Charles D. Smith
I. Jay South
Aileen Sundstrom

Robert T. Trammell

Lloyd Van Valkenburgh

David Walker
Mildred Wertz
Gertrude M. West
Kenneth Wilkens
Harry M. Williams
Andrew D. Wolvin

INDEX

A

Accent, 196–197
Acceptance speeches, 564, 565
Acoustics, 189
Action step, 355, 356, 358, 375–376, 482–483, 563, 570, 579
  actuating speech, 550–551
  courtesy speeches, 565
  ending a speech, 421–425
  good-will speech, 585
  persuasive speech, 519, 521, 523
Actuate, speech to, 148, 230, 231, 233, 374, 547–558
  action step, 375–376
  cause-effect sequence, 386
  content, 548
  manner of speaking, 548
  motivated sequence, 358–363
  organization, 548–551
  persuasion, 233
  sample outline, 551–553
  sample speech, 553–558
Adler, Mortimer J., 302
Agenda, for problem solving, 112
Agnew, Spiro T., 411
  A Farewell to the American People, 573–579
Alternation, of speaker-listener roles, 72, 89, 116, 154
Analogy, 301, 304–305, 323
Anecdote, humorous, 474, 479–480, 482
Apologia, 567, 570
  See also Farewell speech
Appeals, *See* Motivational appeals
Appearance, of speaker
  and audience response, 165–166
  televised speech, 604, 605–606
Applicant, for employment, 66–71
  criteria for judging, 63–65
  detrimental behavior, 70
  interview guidelines, 68–70
  questions, for interview, 67–70

Appreciation, in listening, 451–452
Aristotle, 125, 243
Articulation, 186, 189–196, 243, 603
  articulatory mechanism *illus.,* 193
  exercises for, 212–216
Attention, 44–45, 332–350, 410–420
  beginning the speech, 410–420
  broadcast speeches, 608
  definition and conditions affecting, 332–334
  factors of, 336–343
  gaining, 248, 343, 410–420
  and gestures, 171
  holding, 332–343
  listening skills, 38
  nature of, 332–334
  nonverbal behavior, 167, 169, 171
  speaker's movement, 169
Attention step, 355–358, 368, 482
  actuating speech, 549
  charts, illustrating steps, 361, 362, 364, 365, 367
  entertaining speech, 365–368, 481–483
  informative speech, 492
  persuasive speech, 519, 521, 523, 529–533
Attitudes
  for acceptance of message, 248–249
  audience, toward speaker, 243, 245–248
  definition, 249, 264
  effect on voice quality, 186
  ending a speech, 420
  formation/change, 265
  group discussion, 91–92, 93–94, 100, 101
  and identity-formation, 135
  interpersonal transaction, 46–47
  listener, 17–18, 454
  and message reception, 185
  and motivational appeals, 270, 284–285

  nonverbal expression of, 168–170
  related to listening skills, 450, 451
  self-confidence, 127–131
  speaker, 12–14, 246, 455
  and speaker purpose, 236
Audience
  adapting nonverbal behavior to, 177
  analysis of, 148, 242–257
  attention, 332–343
  attitudes, in persuasive speech, 527–528, 529–533
  authority to act, 235
  awareness of communicative purpose, 10
  beliefs and speaker's proposal, 527–528
  choice of specific purpose, 235–236
  choice of subject, 227, 228, 237, 239
  cognitive balance, 18, 249, 269, 354
  cognitive dissonance, 269, 354
  equilibrium and motivational appeal, 266
  expectations, 247
  hostility, and persuasion, 530–531, 532–533
  information, sources concerning, 259–260
  radio and television, 598
  response to *ethos* of speakers, 245–247
  and responsibilities as listeners, 448
  social facilitation, 138
  speaker behavior, 167
  speaker purpose, 236
  and speech occasion, 259
  values and message reception, 249–257
  See also Listener
Audience response

actuating speech, 547
ending a speech, 420
illus., 252–253
motivated sequence, 353–356
to nonverbal delivery, 165–168, 170, 176
as purpose-determinant, 148, 152
speaker's acceptance of, 460
to speaker's purpose, 230–236, 239
See also Listener response
Authority
of group, 232, 235
poking fun at, 476–477
testimony of, 313
Axiom, reasoning from, 525–526

B

Bateman, J. Carroll, 416
Beginning a speech, 409–420, 528
Behavior
defensive, 46–47
of employment-applicant, 68–71
of group discussant, 97, 100, 105–106
interaction of communication elements, 23, 24
in interpersonal communication, 22, 36–37
and motive needs, 264, 265, 266–270
nonverbal; *See* Nonverbal communication
speaker, 8, 10, 12–14, 46, 127–131
speaker-listener relationship, 13
See also Body language; Cues, behavioral; Delivery; Gestures; Movement
Beliefs
analysis, of audience, 243
and audience response, 236
definition, 249, 264
in group membership analysis, 94
and listening skills, 454
and motivational appeals, 270, 284–285
and persuasion, 14, 232–233, 547
securing, 518–524
and speaker's proposal, 527–528
See also Attitudes; Emotions; Motivational appeals; Opinions; Values

Bell, Elliott V., 429
Bingham, Walter Van Dyke, 63
Biography, as speech material, 293
Bjorklund, Jan, *Nice People*, 358–361
Block, Marvin A., 302
Body language, 152–153
as attitudinal index, 169
gestures, 171–177
illus., 174–175
physical delivery, 166–167
See also Behavior; Cues, behavioral; Delivery; Gestures; Movement; Nonverbal communication
Bogaard, Ann E., *You—A Sponge?* 441–443
Breath control, exercises for, 203
Broadcast discussion, 591–592
Broadcast speech, 597–609
microphone techniques, 602–604
organization and content, 607–608
types, 598–599
See also Media; Radio and television
Brown, Charles, 460
Brown, Howard, 551
Burlesque, as humor, 477–478
Bushnell, Louise, 309–310
Business meeting, 36–42, 113–114, 515, 581
Byron, Lord, 204, 207

C

Carrington, Richard, 311–312
Carroll, Lewis, 214
Carson, Rachel L., 217
Causal relation, reasoning from, 526–527
Cause-effect sequence, 386, 389–390, 494
Chairman, *See* Leader, group discussion
Chalkboard, use of, 102, 316
Challenge, at end of speech, 421
Channel of communication, 8, 9
dyadic transaction, 41
ethics, 459
influence on message, 18
interaction of communication elements, 22, 23, 24, 25, 138
speaker-listener spatial relationship, 170

Charts, 72, 116, 147, 154, 195, 227, 361, 362, 364, 365, 367, 377, 588–589
use of, 316, 371, 391
Claims, analysis of, 516–524, 527–528
Classification, of speech materials, 296–297
Closed question, 40, 61, 92
Cognitive balance, 18, 249, 269, 354
Cognitive dissonance, 269, 354
Coleridge, Samuel Taylor, 204
Common ground, 37, 308, 463, 584
beginning a speech, 411, 414
methods of establishing, 246
persuasive speech, 530, 532
and recognition of value-orientations, 254
See also Rapport
Communication
attitude-formation/change, 264–265
chain, 139–141; *illus.*, 139
elements of, 8–29
eye contact, 167
interpersonal, 34–73
nonverbal, 164–180
process, 138–140
public, 123–153
small group, 88–115
verbal, 185–203
See also Speech communication
Comparison, as verbal support, 301, 305, 320–321, 323
Conciseness, 383
Conditioning, cultural, 165–166, 243
Conditioning, social, 36
Confidence, *See* Self-confidence; Trust
Conflict, resolution of, 104
Connective phrases, 440–441, 496, 608
See also Transitions
Consensus
in small group communication, 88–89, 91
and speaker purpose, 462
Consistency theories, 269, 354
Consonant sounds
articulation of, 189, 192
phonetic alphabet (IPA), 194–195
Content, of message, 15, 17, 23
See also Speech content
Contrast
attention factor, 332–333, 339, 340
in visualization step, 374–375
Convention, social, 19, 22, 23, 24, 29, 172

Conversation, 35–48
    establishing rapport, 36–42
    interpersonal transaction, 36, 37, 48
    maintaining interaction, 41–46
    terminating the transaction, 47–48
    See also Interpersonal communication
Convince, speech to, *See* Persuade, speech to
Coordination, of subpoints, 390–391
Courtesy, speeches for, 563–566
Credibility, *See* Ethos
Cues, behavioral, 35, 38
    as attitudinal index, 168–169
    interview feedback, 53, 70
    listener's awareness of speaker's attitudes, 12, 13, 14
    nonverbal aspects of message delivery, 165–167
    and sensitivity to audience response, 257
    See also Behavior; Body language; Delivery; Facial expression; Gestures; Movement; Nonverbal communication
Culture, 244–245, 250–251
Custom, 19, 22, 23, 24, 37, 258–259

D

Darrow, Clarence, 415
Debate, public, 8, 586, 587, 590
Decibel, 188
Decision-making group
    discussion plan, 108–113
    discussion purposes, 90–91
    sample questions for, 114–115
    six-stage agenda *illus.*, 112
Dedication speech, 567, 570
    sample speech, 571–573
Definition, methods of, 497–499
Delivery, 164–180, 185–203
    adaptation to audience, 242, 243, 246
    attention factors, 337
    channel requirements, 18
    definition, 164
    and *ethos* assessment, 245–246
    guidelines for effective, 131, 152–153
    influence on message, 11
    listener's evaluation, 456
    manner of, 39, 151, 152, 153

    and nervous energy, 129–131
    nonverbal, 152–153, 164–180
    presentational methods of, 142–143, 146
    radio speech, 599, 602–604
    speaker's attitude, 13–14
    televised speech, 604, 605–606
    vocal, 185–203
    See also Behavior; Body language; Cues, behavioral; Facial expression; Gestures; Manner of speaking; Movement; Nonverbal communication
Detail, principle of, 437
Dewey, John, 108–113, 354
Diagrams, use of, 316, 320, 321, 371
Dialogical perspective, of ethical judgment, 460
Dictionary usage, 429, 497
Didactic method, of proof, 323, 324–325
Diphthong, 194–196
Discussion, definition of, 88–89
Discussion group, *See* Group discussion
Discussion leader, *See* Leader, group discussion
Disraeli, Benjamin, 185
Dissonance, *See* Cognitive dissonance
Distinctness, of articulation, 189–196
Donne, John, 207
Dudley, Guilford, Jr., 422
Dyadic communication, *See* Interpersonal communication

E

Educational programs, 581
Eiseley, Loren, 433, 434
Eisenhower, Dwight D., 413
Ekman, Paul, 172
Elliott, Harrison, 112
Emerson, Ralph Waldo, 217
Emotional appeals, *See* Motivational appeals
Emotions, 47
    effect on voice quality, 186, 197
    facial expressions, 176
    and tension, 97
    See also Attitudes; Beliefs; Motivational appeals
Emphasis
    gestural, 171–177
    vocal, 198, 199, 202

Employment interview, *See* Job-seeking interview
Encyclopedia, as speech material, 292
Ending a discussion, 104–105, 107–108
Ending a speech, 420–425
Endorsement, 421, 424
Ends of speech, *See* General ends of speech
Enjoyment, of speech activity, 136–137
Entertain, speech to, 148, 230, 231, 472–483
    audience attitude, 247
    content, 473–474
    listener's enjoyment, 451–452
    manner of delivery, 573–574
    motivated sequence, 365–366, 482–483
    occasion, 452–473
    organization, 481–484
    purpose, 472
    sample speeches, 483–486
Enthusiasm, 547, 548, 562, 563, 581
Enunciation, *See* Articulation
Ethical judgment, in speech communication, 458–463
    actuating speech, 548, 550
    perspectives, 458–462
    value-framework of audience, 251
Ethics, *See* Ethical judgment
Ethos, 14, 38, 47, 245–246, 548
    attention factors, 337
    of group discussant, 95–96
    listener's evaluation of speaker, 455, 457
    physical appearance of speaker, 166
    and speaker's effectiveness, 125
    and speaker's persuasive ability, 14
    and use of humor, 417
Etiquette, 37
Etymology, as definition, 498
Eubanks, Ralph, 314
Eulogy, 567, 570
    sample speech, 570–571
Evaluation
    forms, 161, 465, 466
    in listening, 447, 453–463
Evans, Louis Hadley, 304
Evidence, 524–525, 528, 529, 532, 548
    See also Proof; Supporting materials; Visual aids
Exaggeration, as humor, 475–476

Example, 491, 498, 530
    illustrative, 306–308
    persuasive speech, 529
    reasoning from, 525
    specific instance, 309–310
Expectation, and attention, 334, 335
Experience, personal, 171
    message material, 288–289
    speech subject and self-confi-
        dence, 127, 128
    subject choice, 147
Explanation
    single-idea speech, 320, 321
    supporting material, 301, 302–
        303, 371, 491
Extemporaneous speech, 143, 146, 151,
    198
Eye contact
    for awareness of listener feed-
        back, 152
    broadcast speeches, 606
    importance of, 165, 167–168
    in manuscript speech, 178–179
    nonverbal communication skill,
        180
    self-confidence, 127

F

Facial expression, 35, 38, 41, 153, 431
    as attitudinal index, 176
    audience feedback, 168
    informant feedback, 53
    as nonverbal communication,
        166–167, 180
    televised speech, 604
    transaction process, 138
    use in manuscript speech, 179
Fact, claims of, 516–517, 518–520
Fannin, Paul, 424
Farewell speech, 566–567
    sample speech, 573–579
    See also Apologia
Feedback, 9, 29
    facial expression, 176
    group discussion, 89
    information-seeking interview,
        53
    interaction of communication
        elements, 23
    interpersonal transaction, 35
    job-seeking interview, 57
    public communication, 123
    responsibilities of listener, 448
    speaker's analysis of listener, 257

speaker's self-image and deliv-
    ery, 12–13
speaker's sensitivity to audience,
    133
speaker-listener relationship, 168
transaction process, 138
Feelings, See Emotions
Figures of speech, See Imagery
Findley, John, 313–314
Flecker, James Elroy, 216–217
Force, vocal, 199, 202, 219–220, 602–
    603
    See also Loudness
Formality, degree of, 29, 35, 72, 89,
    116, 123, 154
    analysis of occasion, 258–259
    enthusiasm, 562
    group discussion, 89, 91, 97
    guided interview, 52
    public communication, 123
    word choice, 431
Forms, of communication, 8, 26–29
    interpersonal, 34–73
    public, 123–157, 226–227
    small group, 88–116
Forms, of humor, 474–481
Forms, of support, 301–309
Friesen, Wallace V., 172
Frost, Robert, 222
Full-content outline, 395–396

G

Garrison, William Lloyd, 223
General ends of speech, 148, 230–233,
    239
    to actuate, 233
    definition, 231
    to entertain, 231
    to inform, 231–232
    motivated sequence adapted to,
        367
    to persuade, 232–233
    subject and specific purpose,
        233–234
    thought processes of listener,
        354–355
Gestures, 129–131, 152–153, 166–
    167, 171–177, 179–180
    broadcast speeches, 606
    conventional, 172
    descriptive, 172, 173
    of hands and arms, 153, 172–173
    of the head and shoulders, 153,
        173, 176

idea-projection and reinforce-
    ment, 171–177
use in manuscript speech, 177,
    178, 179
use of nervous energy, 130
    See also Behavior; Body language;
        Delivery; Movement; Nonver-
        bal communication
Gilbert, William Schwenk, 215–216,
    221–222
Good will, speech for, 580–585
Gores, Harold B., 417
Gould, Samuel B., 423
Grady, Henry W., 437
Graphs, use of, 316, 491
Greeting, personal, 368, 410, 412
Greve, Donald, 307
Griswold, A. Whitney, 439
Group-centered interaction, See Small
    group communication
Group discussion, 88–116
    definition and characteristics,
        88–90
    discussant-types illus., 119
    effectiveness in problem-solving,
        88–89
    group types and purposes, 90–91
    leadership functions, 100–105
    membership, 94–95
    organizational plans, 106–114
    participant responsibility, 90,
        91–92, 95–100
    preparation for, 93–95
    profile of effective participant,
        105–106
    purposes, 90–91
    requisites, 91–95
    speaker-listener relationship, 27,
        28, 29
    See also Public discussion; Small
        group communication
Group discussion leader, See Leader,
    group discussion
Group dynamics, See Small group
    communication
Group process, See Small group
    communication
Gruner, George, 305
Guided interview, 51, 52

H

Hall, Edward T., Jr., 419
Halprin, Andrew H., 166

Hand, Learned, 439
Haydon, Harold, *The Testimony of Sculpture*, 571–573
Hearing
    communication chain, 140
    listening skills, 447–453
Henry, Patrick, 424
Hepner, Harry Walker, 55, 67
Hesburgh, Theodore M., 412
Hierarchy of values, 250–251
Hopkins, Gerard Manley, 208
Hostile audience, 246, 530–531, 532–533
Humor, use of, 472–481
    attention step, 368
    beginning a speech, 410, 417, 418, 419
    common ground, establishment of, 246
    group discussion, 97
    informative speech, 491
Humphrey, Hubert, 421

I

Idea-reinforcement, 152–153
Ideas, exchange of
    dyadic transaction, 41, 44, 45
    group discussion, 89
    job-seeking interview, 57
    public communication, 123
Ideas, major, *See* Major ideas
Identity-establishment, as speech function, 134–136
Illustration, 320, 323, 376, 474, 532, 569, 584
    actuating speech, 549
    attention step, 368
    beginning a speech, 418–420
    ending a speech, 421, 423–424
    factual, 306, 307–308, 418–419
    hypothetical, 306–307, 418
    informative speech, 492, 493
    need-step elements, 369
    supporting materials, 306–308
Image, produced, and reproduced, 436
Imagery, 548
    informative speech, 491
    types, 431–436
    visualization step, 375
Imagination, in listening, 451–452
Implication, method of, 323–324
Impromptu speech, 142
Incongruity, 474, 478

Inducement, statement of, 376, 421, 424
Inflection, 201–202, 604
Inform, speech to, 148, 230, 231–232, 489–504
    audience attitude, 247
    cause-effect sequence, 386
    concluding, 499
    content, 490–492
    manner of speaking, 490
    motivated sequence, 364–365
    occasion, 490
    organization, 492–499
    purpose, 490
    sample outline, 499–504
    sample speeches, 504–511
    satisfaction step, 370–371
    sequential arrangement, 385
    time limit and specific purpose, 236
    types, 489
Information-learning group, *See* Learning group
Information-seeking interview, 35, 49–55
    conducting, 53–54
    developing a procedure, 51–52
    evaluation of results, 54–55
    selecting the informant, 49–50
Information, speech, locating and classifying, 288–297
Instance, specific, as verbal support, 309–310
Instructions, oral, 489
Integrity, of speaker, 124, 125
    See also Ethos
Intelligibility, as voice component, 186–197
    exercises for, 210–217
Intensity, *See* Loudness
Intention, personal, 376, 421, 424
Interaction, 22–25, 26, 425
    audience's assessment of speaker, 245–246
    group discussion, 91–95
    listening skills, 447
    as multi-dimensional process, 138–141
    speaker's reaction to audience feedback, 257
International Phonetic Alphabet, 194–196
Interpersonal communication, 7, 8, 34–73
    communication chain, 138–140
    establishing rapport, 36–42

    ethical evaluation, 460
    eye contact, 167, 168
    general principles, 35–48
    illus., 27, 42–43
    maintaining interaction, 41–46
    nonverbal components, 164–179
    qualities and characteristics, 34–35
    social facilitation, 22, 34, 138
    speaker-listener relationship, 26, 27, 28, 29
    terminating a conversation, 47–48
    See also Dyadic communication
Interview, 34, 35, 48–73
    information-seeking, 35, 49–55
    job-seeking, 35, 55–73
    message material, 289–290
    methods of conducting, 51–52
    process-phases *illus.*, 60
    types of format, 51–52
Interviewee, employment, *See* Applicant, employment
Interviewer, employment, 62–66
    criteria for judging applicant, 63–65
    profile of, 62–63
    task and abilities, 61–62, 66
Intimacy, 29, 35, 37, 72, 89, 116, 123, 154
Intonation pattern, 200, 202
Intrapersonal communication, 135
Introduction, of speeches, 409–420
Introduction, speech of, 561–563

J

Jaw, 189, 192, 194
Job applicant, *See* Employment applicant
Job-seeking interview, 35, 55–73
    communicative purposes, 56
    persuasion, 515
    process-phases, 56–60
    process-phases *illus.*, 60
    sample transcript, 76–86
    useful questions, 61–62
Johnson, Lyndon, 412
Journals, as speech material, 292

K

Kees, Weldon, 167, 170

Keller, Paul, 460
Ketcham, Victor Alvin, 436
Key, vocal, 200
Key-word outline, 395, 396
Kipling, Rudyard, 205
Kirk, Grayson, 412
Knowledge, speaker's background of, 124, 125–126, 237
Krulak, V. H., 309

L

Lamb, Charles, 433
Language, 303, 548, 550
    appropriateness to subject and occasion, 431
    broadcast speeches, 608
    communication chain, 139, 140
    ethos assessment, 245–246
    imagery, 431–437
    interaction of communication elements, 23
    listener's evaluation, 455–456
    origin and development, 134–137
    phrasing major ideas, 383
    style of message, 15–16
    wording the public speech, 428–441
    See also Meaning, of words; Style, of message; Wording; Words
Leader, group discussion, 95, 100–105, 106, 107, 109, 110, 111, 113, 114
Leading question, 61
Learning, as attention determinant, 334–335
Learning group
    discussion plan, 106–108
    purposes, 90–91
    sample questions for, 114
Lincoln, Abraham, *The Perpetuation of Our Political Institutions*, 533, 534–540
Lindsay, Vachel, 206, 439
Lips, 189, 192, 194
Listener, 8, 9, 44–45
    adapting nonverbal behavior to, 180
    attention, 38, 167, 169, 332–343
    attitude toward speaker and subject, 245–248
    awareness of message, 10

communication chain, 138, 139, 140
feedback and speaker's self-image, 12–13
group discussion participation, 95
interaction of communication elements, 22, 23, 24, 25
interpretation of speaker's physical behavior, 165, 166, 167, 168, 170, 176
motive needs, 270–282
purpose, 451–453
response, to message, 16–18, 19, 22
responsibilities, 447–464
speaker's attitude toward, 13
speaker's sensitivity to, 133
thought processes and motivated sequence, 353–355
vocal delivery and message reception, 185
See also Audience
Listener response, 9
    communicative situation, influence of, 19, 22
    interaction of communication elements, 23, 24
    speaker's self-image, 12–13
    See also Audience response
Listening, 447–453
    for appreciation, 451–452
    and ethical judgment, 447, 457–463
    evaluation, 447, 453–457
    in group discussion, 92–95
    inefficient habits, 448–450
    interpersonal transaction, 38
    message reception, 17
    skills, 44–45, 447–453
    for understanding, 452–453
Loaded words, 438–439
Logic, 525–529, 550
Longfellow, Henry Wadsworth, 205
Loudness, 243
    exercises to develop, 211–212
    speech intelligibility, 186, 187–188
    variation of force for emphasis, 199
    See also Force
Lower, Elmer W., 422
Luft, Joseph, 90, 97
Luker, Neal, 313
Luncheon meetings, 581

Lundborg, Louis B., 421

M

MacArthur, Douglas, 567
Magazines, as speech material, 292
Major ideas
    actuating speech, 548
    arrangement, 385–388
    beginning and ending a speech, 409
    final summary, 422
    listening for understanding, 452, 453
    memorization, 121, 143, 151
    outline preparation, 396, 399
    phrasing for outline, 383–385
    selection, 381–382
    structuring for listener, 353
    supporting materials, 300–317
Manner of speaking, 247
    actuating speech, 548
    affected, 194, 197
    appropriateness of humor, 417
    courtesy speeches, 564
    entertainment speech, 473–474, 481
    good-will speech, 581
    group discussion participation, 97, 100
    informative speech, 490
    introductory speeches, 561–562
    nomination speech, 579
    persuasive speech, 524
    public communicator's effectiveness, 131
    radio broadcast, 599, 602–604
    self-confidence, 127
    television broadcast, 604–605
    tribute speech, 567–568
    voice quality, 186
    See also Delivery, vocal
Manuscript speech, 143
    broadcast speech, 602, 604, 606
    oral punctuation of, 198
    physical delivery, 177–179
    practicing, 151
Maps, as visual support, 316, 320
Maritz Inc., 356–358
Markham, Edwin, 206
Martin, Douglas, *A Case for Optimism*, 483–484
Marvin, Richard, *Man's Other Society*, 24, 540–543

Maslow, Abraham H., 267–269
Mass communication, 8, 9, 154
    See also Broadcast discussion; Broadcast speech; Media; Radio and television
Mast, Linda, 424
Meaning, of words
    accuracy, 428–431
    derived from association, 438
    loaded words, 438–439
Media, 8, 9, 18, 26
    See also Broadcast discussion; Broadcast speech; Radio and television
Mehrabian, Albert, 176
Melody pattern, *See* Intonation pattern
Memorial services, 567
    See also Eulogy
Memorization
    key-word outline, 395
    major ideas, 128, 143, 151
Memorized speech, 143
Message, 8, 9
    beginning a speech, 410–420
    communication chain, 138, 139, 140
    content, structure, and style, 15–16
    defining general and specific purposes, 230–237, 239
    ending a speech, 421–425
    evaluation by listener, 447–448, 452–463
    influence, of channel on, 18
    influence, of communicative situation on, 19, 22
    influence, of delivery, 11
    interaction of communication elements, 22, 23, 24, 25
    interpersonal transaction, 35
    language and phrasing of public speech, 428–441
    listener-response variables, 16, 17, 18
    nonverbal delivery, 164–179
    preparation, and analysis of audience, 242–257
    preparation, and analysis of occasion, 242, 258–259
    and projection of self-image, 135
    public communication characteristics, 123
    reception, and speaker *ethos*, 245–246
    reception, and speaker's appearance, 165–166
    recording of material, 294–295
    sources of material, 288–293
    speaker's self-image, 12–13, 135
    speech and identity-formation, 135
Microphone
    adjusting loudness level to, 187, 188
    articulation, 192
    techniques, 602–603, 604
Miller, Joyce, *Why Ice Floats*, 155–157
Milton, John, 474
Models
    as nonverbal support, 316, 320
    of speech transaction, 9, 25, 27–28
Montgomery, Dick, 414
Moore, Bruce Victor, 63
Motivated sequence, 269, 353–376
    actuating speech, 358–363, 548–551
    adaptation to general ends of speech, 367
    adaptation to audience attitudes, 529–533
    burlesqued, for entertainment, 482–483
    charts, 355, 361, 362, 364, 365, 367, 377
    claim of fact, 519–520
    claim of policy, 517–518
    claim of value, 520–522
    courtesy speeches, 565–566
    definition, 356
    entertainment speech, 365–366
    informative speech, 364–365, 492–499
    introductory speech, 563
    and listener's mental processes, 353–355
    Maritz Inc., *illus.*, 357
    outline preparation, 398–399
    persuasive speech, 529–533
    sample outline, 400–406
    steps, 368–376
    traditional divisions of a speech *illus.*, 377
    See also Structure, of message
Motivation, *See* Motive needs
Motivational appeals, 260, 264–285
    action step, 376
    actuating speech, 548, 549–550
    adaptation to listener, 284–285
    attitude-formation and need-satisfaction, 265
    audience's attitude toward subject, 248
    broadcast speeches, 607
    definition, 266
    ethics of persuasion, 463, 550
    and *ethos* assessment, 245–246
    evaluation by listener, 454
    methods for making, 282–284
    need-motive relationship, 269–270
    persuasive speech, 516, 527, 528, 529
    phrasing major ideas, 383, 384
    types, 270–282
    See also Attitudes; Beliefs; Emotions; Opinions; Values
Motive needs, 16
    attention-determinants, 334–335
    definition and classification, 266–268
    See also Needs
Mount, Anson, 413
Mouth, 189, 192, 193
    illus., 194
Movement, 152–153
    attention factor, 333, 337–338
    broadcast speech, 604, 605, 606
    functions of, 129–130
    manner of, 170
    in manuscript speech, 177, 178, 179
    nonverbal communication, 169–170, 180
    of self-confident speaker, 127, 129, 130
    and spatial relationships, 169–170
    tension reduction, 176
    See also Behavior; Body language; Delivery; Gestures; Nonverbal communication
Movies, 316
Muscle tension, 153
    body language, 166–167
    nervous energy and physical activity, 129–130
    posture, as attitudinal index, 168–169
    and voice quality, 199–200
    See also Nervous tension

N

Needs
    attention factors, 333

attitude-formation/change, 264–265

audience attitude toward subject, 248

interrelationship with motives, 269–270

Maslow's hierarchy of, 267–269

See also Motive needs

Need step, 355, 356, 358, 482

    actuating speech, 549

    courtesy speeches, 565

    good-will speech, 584

    informative speech, 492–493

    introductory speech, 563

    nomination speech, 579

    persuasive speech, 371–373, 519, 521, 523, 530, 531, 532, 533

    structural elements, 368–369

    tribute speeches, 569

Negation, 498

Nervous energy, 130–131

Nervous tension

    "mike" fright, 592

    posture of speaker, 169

    reduction of, 127–131, 169–170, 176

    See also Muscle tension

Newspapers, as speech material, 290

Nichols, Ralph G., 448

Nilsen, Thomas, 459

Noise

    adjusting loudness level to, 187–188

    adjusting syllable duration to, 189

Nomination, speeches of, 579–580

Non-structured interview, 51, 52

Nonverbal communication, 11, 18, 29

    eye contact, importance of, 167

    gestures, 171–177

    group discussion messages, 89

    idea-reinforcement, 152–153

    interpersonal transaction, 35

    physical delivery, 152–153, 164–179

    speaker objectives, 167

    See also Behavior; Body language; Cues, behavioral; Facial expression; Gestures; Movement; Posture

Notecards, 294–296

    illus., 295

Novelty

    attention factor, 333, 339–340

    entertainment factor, 472

Noyes, Alfred, 206

O

Oates, James F., Jr., 303

Oates, Whitney J., 495

Objectivity, 38–39, 46–47

    in discussant's evaluation of speaker, 95–96

    group interaction, 91, 100

    group leader's function, 101

Occasion

    actuating speech, 547, 548–551

    analysis, 148, 242, 258–259

    appropriateness of language, 431

    courtesy speeches, 564, 565, 566

    entertainment speech, 472–473

    good-will speech, 580–581

    introductory speech, 562, 563

    persuasive speech, 515

    physical appearance of speaker, 166

    pronunciation standards, 196–197

    reference to, 368, 410, 412, 419, 482, 584

    speaker's sensitivity to, 133

    specific purpose, choice of, 235, 236

    subject, choice of, 237

    and vividness of language, 383

    See also Physical setting; Situation, communicative; Social context

Oliver, Robert T., 312

    The Influence of Public Speaking in America: Building Blocks in a Free Society, 506–511

Open forum, 586, 587

Open-mindedness, 38–39, 47

    group discussion participation, 100

Open question, 40, 61–62, 92

Opinions

    definition, 249, 264

    group participant's evaluation of, 95–96

    and motivational appeals, 285

    speech and identity-formation, 135–136

    See also Attitudes; Beliefs; Emotions; Motivational appeals; Values

Oral communication, *See* Speech communication

Oral instructions, *See* Instructions, oral

Oral practice, *See* Practice, oral

Oral reports, *See* Reports, oral

Organization, 149–150, 242

    broadcast discussion, 591–592

    broadcast speech, 607–608

    discussion plans, 106–118

    entertainment speech, 481–484

    ethos assessment, 245–246

    to facilitate understanding, 452

    good-will speech, 584–585

    informative speech, 490–499

    nomination speech, 579–580

    outlining, 381–406

    persuasive speech, 518–524, 529–533

    research reports, 496

    as self-confidence factor, 128

    traditional divisions of a speech, 376, 377

    tribute speeches, 568–570

Outline

    for actuative speech, 551–553

    discussion plans, 106–113

    for entertaining speech, 366

    full-content, 395–396

    for informative speech, 503–504

    key-word, 395, 396

    for motivated sequence, 372–373

    for persuasive speech, 519–520, 521–522, 524

    preparation, 149–150, 391–400

    to provide focus, 102–103

    requirements of good form, 392–395

    sequential patterns, 493–495

    skeletal, 372–373, 503–504, 519–520, 521–522, 524

    technical plot applied to, 399–400

Outline, samples

    actuating speech, 400–406, 551–553

    full-content, 400–406

    informative speech, 150, 499–502

    key-word, 395, 396

    motivated sequence, applied, 362–363, 364–365, 366

    sequential combination, 388

    single-idea speech, 320–322

    technical plot applied to, 400–406

Outlining, 381–406

    arranging subpoints, 388–391

    forms of, 392

    motivated sequence applied to, 362–366

    phrasing major ideas, 383–385

selecting major ideas, 381–383
sequential patterns, 385–388
technical plot applied to, 400–406
types of, 395–396
Overstatement, 475–476
Overstreet, H. A., 415, 439

P

Panel discussion, 585, 590
Parallel development
    courtesy speeches, 566
    persuasive speech, 532–533
Parallelism
    outline preparation, 397, 399
    phrasing major ideas, 383, 384–385
Parliamentary procedure
    chart for handling motions, 588–589
    public debate, 587
Parody, as form of humor, 477–478
Participant, group discussion, 95–97, 100, 101
Pause
    for emphasis, 188, 198–199, 202
    radio broadcasts, 603–605
    rate of speaking, 188
    television broadcast, 605
    as thought punctuation, 198–199
Personal reference, 412–414, 419
Personality, 23, 24
Person-to-person communication,
    See Interpersonal communication
Perspectives, of ethical judgment, 458–462
Persuade, speech to, 148, 231, 232–233, 374, 515–533
    audience attitude, 247
    cause-effect sequence, 386
    content, 524–529
    manner of speaking, 524
    motivated sequence, 363
    occasion for, 515
    organization, 518–523, 529–533
    orientation toward audience, 527, 528, 529–533
    parallel development of need and satisfaction step, 371–373
    purpose, 232–233, 516–518
    sample speeches, 533–543
    satisfaction step, 371–374
    supporting materials, 371
    techniques, 527–529

time limit and specific purpose, 236
Persuasion, 515–558
    actuating speech, 233
    as communicative purpose, 10
    and ethos, 125
    evaluation and ethical judgment, 453–463
    good-will speech, 580
    motivated sequence, 353
    purpose of job-seeking interview, 56
    restatement, 314, 324
    speaker's credibility, 14, 125
    and values, 250
Peterson, Jon P., 416
Peterson, Peter G., 304
Philosophical perspective, of ethical judgment, 458–459
Phonetics, 194–196
Phrasing
    connectives, 440–441
    extemporaneous speech, outline, 143
    major ideas for outline, 383–385
    and outline preparation, 397, 399
    of speech introduction, 415
Physical setting
    effects, 259
    interaction of communication elements, 23
    and listener response, 19
    See also Occasion; Situation, communicative; Social context
Piccard, Jacques, 415
Pin-it-down question, 61–62
Pitch, vocal, 199–202
    exercises for varying, 219–220
    loudness level, 199–200
    methods of varying, 200–202
    microphone techniques, 603
Play on words, as form of humor, 476
Poe, Edgar Allan, 439
Pointing, of need, 369, 530, 531
    actuating speech, 549
    good-will speech, 584
    informative speech, 493
    persuasive speech, 519, 521, 530, 531
Point of view, See Attitude
Policy, claims of, 516, 517–518, 523
Political perspective, of ethical judgment, 459–460
Political speeches, 547, 580
Positive reinforcement, 38, 41
Posture, 38

as attention-index, 334
as audience feedback, 168
body language of speaker, 166, 167
and conduct of interview, 53
in delivery of manuscript speech, 179
naturalness of delivery, 152
self-confidence, 127
speaker's attitude toward self and audience, 168–169
televised speech, 606
Practice, oral
    to gain self-confidence, 128
    memorization and key-word outline, 395
    nonverbal communication skills, 179–180
    for radio broadcasts, 604
    speech preparation, 151, 152
Practicing, 141–143, 151–153, 185, 202–223
    achieving vocal skill, 141–142, 202–203
    broadcast presentation, 592
    conversational speaking manner, 131
    effective message delivery, 165
Prentice, Perry, 419
Prepotency, of basic needs
    attention factors, 333
    illus., 268
    Maslow's hierarchy, 267–269
    See also Motivational appeals
Presentation speech, 567
Probe-and-prompt question, 61, 62
Problem-solution sequence, 387, 495
    outline, sample, 495
Problem-solving
    group discussion effectiveness, 88–89
    individual vs. group, 89
    and motivated sequence, 354
    objectivity and group discussion, 100
Problem-solving group
    discussion plans for, 108–114
    questions to stimulate, 102
    six-stage agenda illus., 112
Problem step, See Need step
Process, of speech communication, 8–26, 91–95, 134–141
    phases of job-interview, 56–62
    problem-solving agenda, 108–113
    See also Interaction; Transaction

Pronunciation, 196–197
 exercises for, 216
Proof, 463
 analogy used as, 305
 didactic method, 323, 324–325
 implicative method, 323, 324
 reasoning, 525–527
 subpoints, 390
 supporting material, 301
 testimony, 312, 313
 See also Evidence; Supporting
  materials; Visual aids
Propaganda devices, 463
Propositions, analysis of, *See* Claims,
 analysis of
Propriety, 19, 22, 37
Proximity, as attention factor, 338–
 339
Public address, *See* Public communication
Public-address system, 187, 188
 See also Microphone
Public communication, 7, 8, 26–29,
 123–154, 226–227
 audience assessment of *ethos*,
  245–246
 broadcast speech, 597–609
 choice of subject, 227–228
 communication chain, 138–140
 definition and characteristics, 28,
  123
 discussion-types, used for, 585–
  592
 eye contact, 167–168
 functions of, 134–141
 general ends of speech, 230–233
 illus., 28, 144–145
 nonverbal elements, 164–170
 orientation toward audience, 242
 presentational methods, 142–
  143, 146
 purposes, 230–237
 as source of self-satisfaction, 137
 speaker-listener relationship, 26,
  28, 29
 speaker-types *illus.*, 132
 speech evaluation forms for, 161,
  465, 466
 speech-material sources, 288–293
 verbal support for, 301–315
Public debate, *See* Debate, public
Public discussion
 broadcasting, 591–592
 planning guidelines, 590–591
 types, 585–592
 See also Group discussion; Small

group communication
Public meetings, 515
Public speaking, *See* Public communication
Puns, as form of humor, 476
Purpose, communicative, 10–11, 29,
 56, 148, 226, 230–237
 actuating speech, 547–548, 549
 analysis of occasion, 258
 audience attitude toward, 246–
  247
 beginning a speech, 409, 414
 broadcast speech, 597
 courtesy speeches, 564
 entertainment speech, 473
 evaluation by listener, 453
 factors determining selection,
  148, 234–236, 242
 general, 230–233, 239
 general end and subject, 233–234
 good-will speech, 580, 581
 of group, 89, 90–91, 92
 informative speech, 490
 and interaction of communication elements, 23
 interpersonal transaction, 35, 46
 introductory speeches, 561–562
 job-seeking interview, 56
 message-preparation guide, 237,
  239
 and motivated sequence, 376
 and motivational appeals, 266
 nomination speech, 579
 and outline preparation, 396, 397,
  398
 persuasive speech, 516–518
 public communication, 123
 specific, 233–237, 239, 417
 tribute speech, 567–568
 and values of audience, 250

Q

Quality, of voice, 186
Questionnaires, as speech material,
 290
Questions
 closed, 40, 61, 92
 by employment interviewer, 65–
  66
 formulation of, for interviews, 52
 group discussion, 91, 101–102,
  103, 112, 113–115
 leading, 61
 open, 40, 61–62, 92

rhetorical, 368, 410, 414–415, 419
 types useful to job-seeking interview, 61–62
Quotation, as verbal support
 action step, 376
 attention step, 368
 beginning a speech, 410, 415–
  416, 418, 419
 ending a speech, 421, 422–423
 tribute speeches, 569

R

Radio and television, 151
 adapting speeches to, 597–609
 audience, 598
 manner of delivery, 197, 599–606
 public discussions, 591–592
 as speech-material source, 293
 See also Broadcast speech; Media
Ragan, Dennis, *Backaches*, 504–506
Ramification, 369, 549
Range of voice, 200
Rapport, 36–42, 47, 180, 463, 599
 broadcast speech, 599
 establishment in interpersonal
  transactions, 36–42, 47
 nonverbal communication skills,
  180
 See also Common ground
Rate of speaking, 192, 194
 achieving variety of speech, 198–
  199
 exercises for varying, 218–220
 factors affecting, 188–189
 for radio broadcast, 603–604
 for television broadcast, 605
 varying, for emphasis, 202
Reality, role of speech in ordering of,
 134–136
Reasoning
 actuating speech, 548, 549–550
 forms of, 525–527
 persuasive speech, 525–527, 528,
  529
Reference, as speech material
 to experience, 436–437
 to occasion, 343, 410, 412
 to subject, 343, 410–412
Reinforcement, 493
 See also Forms, of support
Relaxation, 38
 exercises for throat, 204
 interpersonal transaction, 38
 use of movement to achieve, 176

Repetition
    as attention factor, 333
    parallelism of phrasing, 384
    See also Summary
Reports, oral, 489
Reports, research, 496
Reputation, *See* Ethos
Response, *See* Feedback
Response, speeches of, 564, 565
Restatement, 320, 322
    ending a speech, 420
    in summaries, 420, 422, 424
    supporting materials, 301, 314–315, 323, 324
Rokeach, Milton, 250
Roles, 29, 36
    attitudes and speaking behavior, 13
    speaker's adaptation to, 135–136
    speaker-listener alternation of, 72, 89, 116, 154
Roosevelt, Franklin D., 315
Ruch, Floyd L., 332, 338
Ruesch, Jurgen, 167, 170

S

Sampson, Edith S., *Choose One of Five*, 334–350
Sanderson, Ivan T., 432
Sarett, Lew, 207–208
Satisfaction step, 355, 356, 358, 482
    courtesy speeches, 565
    good-will speech, 585
    informative speech, 493–499
    introductory speech, 563
    nomination speech, 579, 580
    persuasive speech, 519, 521, 523, 530, 531, 533
    structural elements, 370–374
    tribute speeches, 569
Schalliol, Charles, 423
Scott, Robert, 459
Self-confidence, achievement of, 127–131, 152
Self-image
    affected by listener's response to message, 17–18
    formation of, by speech, 134–136
    influence on behavior and message, 12–13
    speaker's posture, 168–169
Sensitivity, 133, 257
Sevareid, Eric, *Eulogy for the Astronauts*, 570–571

Sherwood, John J., 354
Simplicity, in word choice, 430–431
Sincerity, 100, 413, 414, 548, 563, 564
Single-idea speech, 420
    entertainment-speech organization, 481–482
    organization and development, 317–322
    sample outlines, 320–322, 324–325
    supporting materials, 320–322
Situation, communicative, 8, 9, 19, 22
    broadcast speech, 598–599, 605, 606
    interaction of communication elements, 22, 23, 24, 25, 138
    and public speech preparation, 258–259
    speaker's sensitivity to, 133
    See also Occasion; Physical setting; Social context
Situational perspective, of ethical judgment, 460–462
Size, novelty of, 333, 339–340
Slang, usage, in speech, 440
Slater, Philip E., 255–256
Slide projections, as nonverbal support, 316
Slides, vocal, 200, 201
Small group communication, 7, 8, 88–115
    communication chain, 138–140
    definition and characteristics, 88–90
    evaluation forms, 118, 121
    eye contact, 167–168
    group-discussant types *illus.*, 132
    illus., 27, 98, 99
    leadership functions, 100–105
    nonverbal elements, 164–179
    orientation toward audience, 242
    participation in, 90, 91–92, 95–100
    preparation for, 93–95
    problem-solving effectiveness, 88–89
    profile of effective discussant, 105–106
    requisites for productive interaction, 91–95
    speaker-listener relationship, 26, 27, 28, 29
    types and purposes, 90–91
    See also Group discussion; Public discussion
Snow, C. P., 432

Social context
    analysis of, 258–259
    influence on message structure, content, and reception, 19, 22
    interaction of communication elements, 23
    interpersonal transaction, 36–37
    speaker's sensitivity to, 133
    tribute speech, 567
    See also Occasion; Physical setting; Situation, communicative
Social facilitation, 22, 138
Solution step, *See* Satisfaction step
Source-credibility, *See* Ethos
Southey, Robert, 214–215
Space sequence, 386, 388
    sample outline, 494
Spatial relationships
    adjusting loudness level to distance, 187–188
    speaker's distance from audience, 170
Speaker, 8, 9, 10–14, 23–29, 123–133, 139–141
    adaptation to audience attitudes, 529–533
    analysis of audience, 249, 252–257
    analysis of occasion, 242, 258–259
    appearance, 165–166
    attitudes, 473, 474, 581
    audience-awareness, 128–129
    audience's attitude toward, 245–247
    communication chain, 138, 139, 140
    delivery, 152–153, 164–179
    ethics of techniques, 462–463
    ethos, 14, 38, 47, 245–247, 548
    facial expression as attitudinal index, 176
    gestures, 171–177
    interaction of communication elements, 22, 23, 24, 25
    knowledge and background, 125–126
    listener's attention, 335
    movement, 152–153, 169–170
    personal characteristics, 124–133
    posture, 168–169
    purpose, 10–11, 148, 230–237, 246–247, 453, 454
    purpose and listener's thought processes, 354–356
    self-reference, 412–414
    sensitivity, 133

sincerity, 413–414
specific purpose, 235–236
types *illus.*, 132
use of pause, 198–199
vocal delivery, 185–203
word choice, 429–431
Speaker-listener relationship, 13
and characteristics of communication forms, 26–29
eye contact, 167–168
group discussion characteristics, 89
job-seeking interview, 56
motivated sequence, 353
in public communication, 123
and transactional attitudes, 17–18
Specific instance, as verbal support, 301, 309–310, 323, 532
Specific purpose, 233–237, 239, 417
Speech
development of, in infants, 134
egocentric nature of, 135
functions, 134–141, 489
process, 8–26, 91–95, 134–141
and reality-ordering, 134–135
socialization factor, 136
source of pleasure, 136–137
Speech communication
basic elements, 8–25
evaluation and ethical judgment, 453–463
facilitation of attitude change, 249
forms, 7, 8, 26–29
forms, charts of, 72, 116, 154
information sources, 291
means to self-satisfaction, 136–137
multi-dimensional process, 22–25, 91–95, 138–141, 245–246, 257, 425, 447
orientation toward listeners, 242
Speech communication transaction, *See* Transaction
Speech content
actuating speech, 548
broadcast speech, 607–608
courtesy speeches, 564–565
entertainment speech, 473–474
good-will speech, 584
informative speech, 490–492
introductory speeches, 562–563
persuasive speech, 524–527
tribute speeches, 568
See also Content, of message

Speech materials
attention-generating, 343
audience attention and focus, 336
beginning a speech, 415
broadcast speeches, 608
classification methods, 296
gathering, 149
good-will speech, 584
organization and outlining, 381–406
recording, methods of, 294–295
sequential organization, 493
sources, 288–293
specific purpose as criterion, 237
Speech organization, *See* Organization
Speech preparation, 146–151
analysis of audience, 148, 242–257
analysis of occasion, 148, 258–259
essential steps *illus.*, 147
full-content outline, 395
gathering material, 149
key-word outline, 396
major ideas, selection and arrangement of, 381–388
organizing material, 149–150
practicing, 151
process, 226
specific purpose, determination of, 148
subject choice, 147
wording, 151, 428–443
Speech purpose, *See* Purpose
Speeches
basic types of, 230–233, 472–558
classroom evaluation, 464
conclusion of, methods for, 420–425
determining effects of, 456–457
ethical evaluation of, 458–463
evaluation forms, 161, 465, 466
introduction to, methods and materials for, 410–420
nonverbal delivery, 164–179
presentational methods, 142–143, 146
special types of, 561–585
titles, 228–230, 239
vocal delivery, 185–203
See also Message
Springen, Phyllis Jones, 411
Stage fright, reduction of, 127–131
Stanmeyer, William A., 418
Statement, 569

actuating speech, 549, 550
informative speech, 493
need-step elements, 369
satisfaction step, 371
Statement, startling, 368, 410, 415, 418, 420, 492
Statistics, as verbal support, 301, 302, 310–312, 313, 315, 369, 491, 532
Status, 13, 36, 94, 95
Steps, vocal, 200, 201
Stevens, Leonard, 448
Stevenson, Adlai, *A Funny Thing Happened to Me on the Way to the White House*, 483, 485–486
Strauss, Jack I., 308
Structure, of message, 15, 18, 29, 232
dependent upon thorough subject-knowledge, 11
interaction of communication elements, 23
motivated sequence applied to, 353–376
supporting material, 317
See also Motivated sequence; Organization
Structured interview, 51, 52
Study group, *See* Learning group
Style, of message, 15–16, 18
group discussion participation, 97
interaction of communication elements, 23
See also Language; Wording; Words
Subject
adapting nonverbal behavior to, 177, 180
adapting, to occasion, 258
appropriateness of language, 431
attention step, 368
and audience attention, 336
beginning a speech, 409, 410, 411–412, 419
categories, 237–239
choice, 147–148, 226–228, 242
complete coverage, 382
humor, 417, 472, 474–481
narrowing, 147–148, 396, 398
reference to, 343, 410–412
and speaker's attitude, 13–14
and specific purpose, 233–234
vividness of language, 383
Subject, knowledge of
and adjustment to audience feedback, 257

audience, 247–248, 451
choice of topic, 228
gathering material, 149
group discussion participation, 92, 93–94
information-seeking interview, 54
information sources, 288–293
interaction of communication elements, 23
and message delivery, 165
and message reception, 17
needed by public discussant, 590
needed by speaker, 11
and speaker's self-confidence, 127–128, 152
Subordination, 490
outline preparation, 393, 396, 397, 399
subpoint categories, 389–390
Subpoints
outline preparation, 396, 397
sequence and coordination, 388, 390–391
supporting materials, 391
Sullivan, Arthur Seymour, 215–216
Summary
action step, 376
ending a speech, 421, 422
final, 420, 422, 424, 440
informative speech, 495, 497
initial, 370, 440, 495–496
satisfaction step, 370, 371
Supporting materials, 300–327
actuating speech, 549–550
attention factors, 338
entertainment speech, 482
informative speech, 491, 492, 493, 495, 496–497
listener's evaluation of, 452–453
motivated sequence, 366
need step, 369
nonverbal, 315–317
outline preparation, 396, 397, 399
persuasive speech, 524–525, 530, 531, 532
satisfaction step, 495, 496–497
selection and arrangement, 242, 381, 388–391
single-idea speech, 317–322
subpoints, 391
tribute speeches, 570
used ethically, in persuasion, 463
used in didactic method, as proof, 323, 324–325
used in implicative method, as

proof, 323, 324
verbal, types and uses, 301–315
See also Evidence; Proof; Visual aids
Syllable duration, 192
exercises to develop, 211–212
as factor of speech intelligibility, 186, 188–189
Symposium, 586, 590
Synonyms, 429–430

T

Tact
in group discussion participation, 96
in group leader's behavior, 101
Technical plot, 399–400
Television, See Radio and television
Tension
reduction, by humor, 97
and speaker's purpose, 462
Tension, nervous, See Nervous tension
Terminating a conversation, 47–48
Testimony, 369, 371, 530, 532
as proof, 323
as supporting material, 301, 312–314
This-or-nothing technique, of persuasion, 528
Thomas, Dylan, 209
Thought process
and intrapersonal communication, 135
and motivated sequence, 353–356
Time limit, 29, 35, 483
broadcast discussion, 591
broadcast speech, 607
and choice of specific purpose, 236
and choice of speech subject, 228
for group discussion, 89
introductory speech, 563
narrowing of subject to fit, 147–148
and outline preparation, 396
public communication, 123
Time sequence, 385, 388
sample outline, 494
Timing
effective gesturing, 177
interview pacing and termination, 53

terminating a conversation, 47–48
in using visual aids, 317
Titles
functions and requirements, 228–229
speech preparation, 239
Tittle, Ernest, 438
Tongue, 189, 192, 194
Topic, speech, See Subject
Topical sequence, special, 387, 388
sample outline, 494
Tradition, 23, 24
Transaction, speech communication, 8–26, 91–95, 134–141
as affected by listener's values and speaker's purpose, 250
basic factors and relationships illus., 9, 25
basic forms illus., 20, 26, 27, 28
communication chain, 138–140
ethics of, 459
in job-seeking interview process, 55–61
interaction of communication elements, 22–25
involving group consensus and individual responsibility, 88–89
Transitions, 491, 496, 608
See also Connective phrases
Tribute, speeches of, 570
content, 568
organization, 568–570
purpose and manner of speaking, 567–568
sample speeches, 570–579
Trick-and-trap question, 61
Triteness, of words, 439–440
Truman, Harry, 463
Trust, 38, 47, 245
See also Ethos
Tuchman, Barbara W., 437

U

Understanding, in listening, 452–453
Unexpected turns, as form of humor, 478–479

V

Value, claims of, 516–517, 520–523
Value-orientations